DATE DUE

THE LAST OF A BREED

ERROL D. SEVERE

First Edition
Copyright © 1997 by:
Errol D. Severe

Printed in the United States of America

Designed and written by: Errol D. Severe

Printed by: Plus Communications, St. Louis, Missouri

Cover illustration by: Errol D. Severe
Photos courtesy of Lockheed Martin, John Goswick, Merle Prestwood, and the National Archives

AT-6's in formation   Terry Love

Published by Lighthouse Productions Inc.
542 CR 2073
Eureka Springs AR 72632
501-253-5008

Library of Congress Catalog Card Number: 96-0943739
ISBN 0-9656957-0-0

Dedication

Through all the years,
hardships and tears.
Through times of peace,
Through times of war,
Our comrades soon will leave this shore, to
Climb ever higher, toward Heaven's door.
Lest we ne'r forget,
These men called "Cadet,"
The "Last of a Breed,"
Volunteers to the need.
The end of a line,
These buddies of mine,
They are "Cadets" to the end,
These men I call "Friend."

Preface

Someone once said....

Psychiatric evaluations have found the majority of fighter pilots to be perfectionists, driven to succeed and determined to control their world. Most are first-born children with an unusually close father-son relationship. They are confident, showed a great desire for challenge and success, were not introspective and tended toward interpersonal and emotional distance. Most studies have found pilots to be mentally healthy with little neurosis or pathology.

Other traits of fighter pilots: dominance, rationality, responsibility, and aggressivesness as well as flamboyance and a tendency to seek thrills. They are also very sociable but also highly self-sufficient. They have tattooed on their foreheads in invisible ink, "I am in control." After all, when you live life at the edge you appreciate it more.

The fighter pilot's ability to focus on solving emergencies depends on a technique known as "compartmentalization"; putting different parts of life in separate boxes. Once inside his plane, the pilot sheds the ordinary concerns of the outside world; flying is too dangerous to allow pilots time to think of wives and children. Nine out of ten separations or divorces are initiated by wives. Are pilots childlike with a zest for life that children have? "Hey, Dad, are you ever afraid when you fly?" "Hell, yeah, that's what makes me such a great pilot."
From Volume 17, Number 5, Edition number 128 of the "FAHS Newsletter."

When one writes a book, it seems there are traditional formats and designs that convention dictates be done. The foreword is one of these. I thought long and hard as to whom I would ask to write it. Since many think the "Foreword By ....," should have the name of some famous person and thereby contribute to the successful sale of a book, I first thought of some well known movie stars who are also pilots. One of them is unable to comply because of health problems, and the other simply ignored me. Then I thought, perhaps some Cadet who made General would be good. But most of them, though famous in certain circles, did not have universal appeal. What was I to do? Suddenly, it became crystal clear! I finally realized that this book does not need to have some "famous" person's endorsement by writing the foreword. There is only one person who knows what this book really is and that person has been involved with me in it from the very beginning—and that is Beth, my wife. Now, she is not a household word yet, but she is an accomplished playwright, and composer, as well as a fine recording artist. But most of all, she is most beloved, both by me and by God. I could not have written this book without her. She deserves all the credit for making this work grammatically correct, and her steadfast faith and encouragement were pivotal in its completion. So it is with overwhelming gratitude, that I chose to honor her, and so it is that the foreward is written by Beth Severe.

Errol D. Severe

Acknowledgments

This book is only a small portion of what there is to be written about this great program, and the men who were skilled and determined enough to complete this most rigorous training. There are literally tens of thousands of wonderful stories, and so many variations to the training that there is no way to cover it all. I only hope that what I have written here will inspire those of you Cadets who read this, to either write down your stories, or put them on tape. Once we are gone, these great events will be lost forever. What we have lived should be preserved at the Aviation Cadet Museum for future generations to learn from. I deeply regret that one group that I contacted refused to cooperate in telling their part in this program. I tried numerous times to get information and interviews, but to no avail, and that is why they are merely mentioned.

There are so many, many people to thank for their help in making this book a reality that there is no way I can remember them all. Here are the most prominent: The fine staff at Air Force history, in particular Mary Lee Jefferson, and Herman Wolk, and from Randolph history department, Bruce Ashcroft. One of my mentors who reviewed this work prior to its completion and who was a great encouragement to me personally, is Herbert M. Mason, a noted and successful author.

Nothing is constructed in a vacuum. I have, as others before me, built on the shoulders of those who came before. One of the most helpful was Colonel Robert F. Schirmer USAF (Ret.) who for the past fifty years has been compiling information and writing stories about the Cadet program.

Lew Johnston was a tremendous help in compiling the master mailing list. I wish to thank Lee Reisthoffer for his great faith in me, even to the point of paying for two books long before they were completed; and my fellow Cadets many of whom sent pictures, money, stories, and verbal support. I owe all of you more than I can ever say.

Thank you all,
Errol

Cadets return the battle flag captured from General Santa Ana at the Battle of San Jacinto, Texas in 1836.

R. Schrawger 50-F

Foreword

I consider it a honor that Errol asked me to write the foreword for his book. I have seen him through all the struggles, and witnessed the intensity of his dedication to this mammoth project. I've had to put many hours into this work, but he has put his life into it.

I believe that for more than any other reason for writing this book, was Errol's overwhelming desire to give recognition to the great men of the Flying/Aviation Cadet Corps. They have made up the majority of our rated officers in every major war from WWI through Vietnam, including, of course, WWII and Korea. The intense training and discipline these men endured, were responsible for making them into a unique breed of men, such as has not been equaled in the field of aviation training. There are many today who aren't even aware of the pilot training program that ended in 1961. This program was responsible for the expert training of the men who represented our nation in the skies.

Over and over again, graduates of this program shared with Errol how the Flying/Aviation Cadet Corps made them into the men they are today. It changed their lives, giving them positive direction and purpose, strengthening them for life, enabling them to be overcomers and leaders. It amazes me to find in conversing with some of the men, the great similarity in their thinking and rationale.

Having been inspired to write, *The Last of a Breed*, Errol had only a glimpse of the magnitude of the project. It would entail countless phone calls, hours of writing, and as many hours of reading and studying the subject of the Flying/Aviation Cadets. Since he was one, and is a typical lifelong pilot, with a great love of flying, he was the ideal person to write the stories, and make them come alive to the reader. This book reads more like a novel than a factual account. Errol conjures up such emotion and realism, that the reader feels he's actually there, experiencing with the men, all the bravery, fear, loneliness, hardships, and total commitment of a combat flyer.

This is your story, Flying/Aviation Cadet graduates—not the story of any one Cadet or group, but a panorama of experiences, events, and history. So, come on fellas, and climb into the cockpit, fasten your seat belts, strap on your parachutes, put on your helmets and goggles, and take a trip back in time. Join your fellow Cadets, and relive the excitement, the glory, the fear, and heartaches, as well as triumph, as you soar the skies once again. You were, and are, and ever will be, *The Last of a Breed*!

Beth Severe

Major Showalter, President of the Aviation Cadet board, swearing in 1,600 Aviation Cadets at Soldiers' Field, Chicago,Illinois, June 26,1942

National Archives

Yes Sir, like a mirror, Sir!

R.G. Anderson 55-N

Table of Contents

WELCOME to the AIR FORCE
THRU THIS RECEPTION CENTER
PASS THE BEST AIRMEN OF THE
WORLD'S BEST AIR FORCE

Lackland AFB Aviation Cadet reception center, 1955   Franklin J. Lane 54-?

Chapter 1
The Last of the Last of a Breed

WILLIAM F. WESSON

March in northern California can many times be wet and blistery, but not on March 29, 1968. It was a record-tying 81 degrees. The last time it was that hot was in 1931. The smog index was twenty-one, well over the eye-irritation level of fifteen. As William F. Wesson arose that morning, he looked out his bedroom window for a morning weather check. Yuck, the sky was a sickening yellow. Still half-asleep, he wandered into the kitchen where his wife, Betty, was fixing breakfast. His four-year-old daughter, Jennifer, was helping mommy get the cereal from the cabinet, while eighteen-month-old Billy, was banging his hands impatiently on the tray of his high-chair. Bill picked up a cup, filling it with freshly-brewed coffee. After taking a few sips, the cobwebs started to clear from his mind. "Betty, I've been thinking; you've been stuck here in this house for weeks. Ever since the kids came down with the chicken-pox, all you've done is take care of them. What do you think about going to a nice restaurant for lunch today?" Betty, delighted with the prospect of finally getting a day out, excitedly replied, "Really? Well where would we go?" Bill suggested, "How about the 'Nut Tree' up in Sacramento?" A little deflated, Betty replied, "But that's too far to drive with two kids." Bill answered smugly, " Who said anything about driving? Tony said I could use his Bonanza, as long as I take the time to check him out in it." Unable to contain her excitement, yet with a hint of concern in her voice, Betty blurted out, "But honey, you only flew it once for an hour; are you sure you're comfortable in it? I mean it's nothing like the engineer's seat on T.W.A., is it?" With a somewhat cocky reply, Bill retorted, "Of course it's OK, airplanes are pretty much alike;

I've just got to get used to the fan being up front—let's call a baby-sitter for Billy, OK?"

By the time the baby-sitter arrived, they were all dressed and ready to go. Betty issued a few short instructions to the sitter, and away they went to the Reid-Hillview Airport, located just four miles south of San Jose. Along the way, Bill was teasing his wife about causing the aircraft to be overweight, because she was eight-months pregnant with their third child.

After arriving at the airport, they parked the car near the flight-line next to one of the taller hangars. Betty and Jennifer went into the air-conditioned terminal while Bill readied the aircraft for the flight. During the preflight, he noticed the left fuel tank was almost full, but the right tank had only a few gallons. Since it was so hot, and the flight was not very long, he thought he would buy fuel when they arrived in Sacramento. He also reasoned that as close as the tanks were to the fuselage, the fuel unbalance was not enough to cause any real control problems.

Completing his walk-around and preflight inspection, Bill went into the terminal for a cool drink of water, a short pit stop, and then joined his wife and daughter. Leaving the comfort of the terminal, Bill and Betty leisurely strolled to the waiting aircraft, as Jennifer, excited about flying to a restaurant for lunch, ran on ahead. He had left the doors open so the cabin would be a little cooler. Picking Jennifer up, Bill set her in the right rear seat, behind her mother. Betty climbed up on the wing and seated herself in the right front seat. He closed the right cabin door, and proceeded to climb into the pilot's seat, leaving his door open for ventilation. He quipped to Betty, "Well, it's not quite the T-38 I used to instruct in, but it will get us there just the same." "OK honey, here's the checklist, you read it and I'll respond." Betty, not at all familiar with aircraft procedures said, "Where do I start?" Somewhat agitated by the heat and his wife's lack of knowledge, Bill responded sharply, "At the beginning. Where it says 'Before Starting'; just read the items with numbers." Feeling a bit chided, Betty replied, "OK, dear, no need to get angry, I'm not a pilot, I'm just a pregnant wife." Without further comment, she started reading the checklist: "Seat Belts and Shoulder Harnesses" .... "**Fasten,**" "Parking Brake".... "**Set,**" "All Avionics"...."**Off,**" "Circuit Breakers"...."**In,**"

valve"...."**Left Main,**" "Shall I go on to the starting part?" "Please. It's hot!".... "Mixture".... "**Rich,**" "Propeller".... **"Full Increase"** "Throttle"...."**Open,**" "Ignition Switch"...."**Both,**" "Auxiliary (wobble) Fuel Pump"...."**Pumping to get 10 P.S.I.,** this sure is a weird way to prime an engine, retorted Bill; I feel like I'm pumping up a foot ball.".... "Starter"...."OK, let's crank her up." Bill pressed the starter button, the propeller turned several blades and the engine roared to life. From the back seat Jennifer squealed, "Wow Daddy, it's really loud." Betty continued with the checklist, "Oil Pressure"...."**Check,**" "All Engine Indicators".... "**Check,**" "Avionics Equipment"...."**They're set,**"

1947 Bonanza of the type the Wessons were flying   Beech Aircraft Co.

"Landing Gear Handle"...."**Down,**" "Flaps".... "**Up,**" "Cowl Flaps"...."**Open,**" "Light Switches"...."**Off,**" "Battery and Generator Switches"...."**On,**" "Ignition Switch"...."**Battery,**" "Fuel Quantity Indicators"...."**Check,**" "Activate fuel selector valve several times by rotating the handle from tank to tank to ensure that the selector valve is free"...."OK, I know, I did that. Just read the numbered items." She meekly replied, "Yes dear.... Fuel selector

"lights"...."It's 1:30 in the afternoon, I think we can see without them." Making sure that there were no other taxiing aircraft approaching, he called ground control, "Hillview Ground, this is Bonanza 8709-Alpha, ready to taxi." "Roger 09-Alpha, taxi to runway 31-left, wind light and variable. Altimeter 30.10." "Roger 09-Alpha, 30.10." Bill advanced the throttle, and as the aircraft started rolling, he tapped the right brake to turn toward the southeast, parallel with the runway. As they taxied along, Bill asked Betty to continue with the checklist so they would be ready to run-up and roll when they reached the departure end of the runway. As they reached the run-up area, he told her, "Honey, there's no need to read the run-up part, I can do it faster than you can read it."..."OK, run-up complete; now let's continue with the rest of the checklist and we'll make sure I didn't miss anything." Betty continued reading on down to the "Take off" part of the checklist. Now ready to launch, Bill called the tower, "Hillview Tower, this is Bonanza 8709-Alpha, ready for take off." "Roger 09-Alpha, cleared for take off, no delay, Cessna on a two-mile final." "Roger 09-Alpha, Rolling."....

William F. Wesson was born on September 9, 1940. In the previous year, 1939, Bill's mother, Nellie Geague, of Mexican descent, was married to William A. Goswick, of Scotch-Irish descent. Nellie was 16 when they were married, and by all accounts, a beautiful young woman. Bill Goswick was working for the Santa Fe Railroad at the time. Their marriage was a stormy event, almost from the start. Bill always enjoyed a good party, and never missed the opportunity of attending one. He would many times come home feeling no pain. Nellie would get on his case about his drinking, which in turn caused him to start making excuses. Before long, another fight ensued, which at times resulted in, at the very least, verbally-abusive treatment of Nellie. Being a mixture of half Mexican and half Scotch-Irish didn't help Nellie cope with the circumstances. It takes two to have a fight, and she did her part. After several years of constant fighting, Bill and Nellie Goswick were divorced. Becoming very remorseful, Bill promised faithfully that he would get his life straightened out, if only Nellie would take him back, and for a time, he did show a great deal of improvement. He was a really nice guy when he wasn't drinking. Both of them were still very much

in love with each other, so after being divorced for a short time, they agreed to try again, and were remarried. Unfortunately, this was not to be the end of the marital strife between these two. They were divorced again in 1949, when young Bill was just nine years old.

In 1951, Nellie married Elijah Wesson. Not

William Goswick, Sr. at primary training WWII
Mary Goswick

wanting Bill to feel like a stepson, Elijah adopted him as his own. Bill, who had been told many derogatory stories about his real father, decided he would like his name changed to Wesson. After the usual court hearing, and paperwork, William F. Goswick officially became William F. Wesson.

When he was seventeen, Bill decided to find out the truth about his father, William Goswick, whom he had heard little from in the past eight years. He went down to Casa Grande', where his father was living with his wife Mary, his half-brother John, and half-sister Katherine, both of whom he had never met. Much to his surprise, he was welcomed with open arms by the Goswicks. As far as young Bill knew, his dad didn't care about him at all. He soon learned that many of the things he had been told about his dad were simply not true. Bill Goswick had tried to maintain a relationship with his son by sending him birthday cards and gifts, which had never been given to him. This was a time of healing, and discovery. He stayed with the Goswicks for the summer, helping out in his father's crop-dusting business as he could. I'm sure that the influence from his father, who had been a pilot in WWII, and the excitement of the crop-dusting business, were largely responsible for Bill's decision to become a pilot.

In December of 1959, William F. Wesson arrived at Lackland AFB, in San Antonio, Texas, as thousands before him had done. He was a brand new Aviation Cadet, in class 61-F—my under class. It would be convenient if I could say I knew him. However, there were so many young men there, and we were all so busy with our own problems, that most of us don't remember too many of the others. I must say though, that his picture stirs a slight memory of one of my "raunches" (a term used to describe a new underclassman). All of us were assigned two men that we were personally responsible for "teaching the ropes." We were called the "raunch-masters." Such were the traditions of the Cadet Corps. But, be that as it may, I never had a chance to see him again after Lackland. Class 61-F was so large (about 400 men) that it was split into three groups for primary (that was normal), but this group was also sent to three bases for Basic. The previous Cadet classes had been sent to two bases, Reese AFB, at Lubbock, Texas, and Vance AFB, in Enid, Oklahoma. 61-F were sent to these as well, but some of class 61-F were sent to Webb AFB, at Big Spring, Texas. Bill Wesson was in that group. These guys had it made. There were no upperclassmen to contend with, because there were no other Cadets in training at Webb. It was strictly a Student-Officer, pilot-training base. In order to try and

instill the discipline that the Cadet Corps is known for, the commander assigned some of his flight instructors, who were recent graduates of the Aviation Cadet program, as training officers for this class. Needless to say, the officers who were assigned to this duty were less than pleased. When the duty day was over, they went to their homes, and left the Cadets of 61-F to their own devices. What a deal.

One bright and sunny day in November of 1960, a formation of two T-33's departed Webb on a routine formation flight. Flying in the cloudless sky, high over Texas, the formation flight leader made a slow, smooth, barrel-roll—too slow, and too smooth, and the end result was that they dished out with the nose too low and the airspeed too high. They were in a rather steep dive and rapidly approaching their maximum limiting airspeed. Pulling about 3 G's, the student who was flying did something we were taught never to do while in trail formation; he said, "Speed-brakes, now." (He deployed his speed-brakes several seconds after the call, so the trail ship would not run up their tail-pipe). As both of the ships in the formation actuated their speed-brake switches, both pairs of aluminum panels popped from beneath their individual aircraft, like silver "Jack-in-the-boxes," just waiting for someone to release the door catch. The instructor in the lead ship, chastised the student for deploying the speed-brakes in trail, and took control of the aircraft. Suddenly the #2 ship fell well behind and below the lead ship. The #2 ship radioed lead, "Jehu Lead, this is Jehu Two, my engine flamed out." (As the speed-brakes deployed, they had severed the fuel line that had worked loose from its retaining clamps, and it was cut by the movement of the speed-brake actuator). A/C Walter W. Westmoreland was the student, and Lt. Frank C. Brasington was the instructor in the lead ship. Lt. Brasington replied to the solo student in the #2 ship, "Wesson, try a relight." "I did, Sir, it won't start." "OK, hold a glide speed of 250 kts., and we'll come down and check you over. We're still plenty high, so don't go getting in a hurry." "Roger, Jehu Two." The lead ship made a tight 360-degree turn and descended after #2. Positioning their aircraft slightly behind, and below him, they could see fuel streaming out of the bottom of the fuselage. Lt. Brasington said, "Wesson, you're losing fuel, you had better punch out of it. We'll slide off to the side and follow you down." A somewhat higher-pitched voice responded, "Roger, Jehu Two, ejecting." The canopy blew clear of the aircraft, up and over the vertical stabilizer, quickly followed by the seat, with Bill Wesson firmly strapped to it. As the crippled aircraft descended toward the Texas prairie, its sole passenger seemed to be in the seat a very long time before he finally separated from the ejection seat, tumbling end over end. With his adrenaline pumped up to maximum, Bill jerked the handle of the ripcord on his parachute, expecting that he would be jerked upright by the billowing canopy at any second. But there was no sudden jerk. He was slowing in his descent, but he was still falling much too fast. Terrified, he looked up to where the canopy of his chute should be, but it had not filled out. It was only partially inflated. He pulled, jerked, and twisted, in an effort to completely fill the parachute; all to no avail. He hit the ground hard. Westmoreland saw dust fly up, and said in a choked voice, "I don't think he made it." Circling low, the men in the lead ship looked for some movement to signal he was still alive, but saw none. The lead ship stayed on the scene until the rescue helicopter arrived, and then silently returned to Webb. After landing, Westmoreland and Lt. Brasington mechanically went through the post flight ritual—filled out forms, debriefed the crew chief, and then went inside the line shack. As they walked through the door, Westmoreland noticed that everyone from Buzzard Flight was there, all seated at their individual tables. For a moment no one said a word. Then, one of the students yelled, "He's alive!" Westmoreland's shocked reply was, "He's *What*?" Spinning around to face the student who had made the announcement, he said, "But he landed so hard. Where is he?" Someone replied, "They're bringing him to the dispensary." Yelling he was going to the dis-

pensary, Westmoreland bolted through the door, and ran the half mile to the dispensary, attired in his flight suit and jump boots. He arrived just in time to see Bill being wheeled in at the far end of the corridor. Bill was semiconscious when he arrived at the base infirmary. He realized that he was numb from the waist down, but thank God, he was alive. The doctor informed him that his back, and hip were broken, and as soon as his condition could be stabilized, he would be airlifted to the hospital at Lackland AFB, in San Antonio, Texas. Some time later when he arrived at Lackland, he was immediately ushered into the operating room where surgeons set his hip, and repaired his back. Bill was

Bill Wesson with full body cast   John Goswick

put in a full body cast.

Cadet Westmoreland later returned to the line shack feeling much better than he had just a short time before. He then had to endure the long debriefing process, filled with endless questions trying to get him to recall every detail of the flight, from the preflight briefing until they blocked in after the flight. Some time passed before things at Webb returned to normal, but they were never quite the same again.

By January, Bill was able to move about mostly on his own, although he was still in the cast. One day the crushing news came that his father, William Goswick, was reported missing on a night flight in his AT-6. He had been coming to San Antonio to deliver his previously-sold aircraft, and had planned on visiting his injured son. Even though Bill was still recuperating from his accident, he convinced the doctors to let him return home and help in the search for his father. It was April before William Goswick was found with the wreckage of his AT-6, high on a mountain near Aqua Prieto, Mexico. Bill Wesson had really only known his father for a little over three years—not much time to create a real father/son relationship. He greatly regretted all the years of his life that he and his real dad had been apart, and how he wished he had spent more time with him. Life is so fragile....

On the same day in May 1961, that William Wesson was to be discharged from the hospital at Lackland, he received a letter from the commander of A.T.C. (Air Training Command), informing him that he was physically unqualified for flight duty, and he would not be allowed to finish his flight training. Totally depressed by his accident, and the loss of his father, and now the crushing news that he was no longer an Aviation Cadet, Bill Wesson sat alone in his hospital room wondering just what would happen next. There was a knock on the door, and in walked Bill's best friend in the Cadet program, Mike Fisher. His entrance was like a ray of sunshine. He had just graduated in April, and was at Randolph for KC-97 training. Bill was so glad to see him that he poured his heart out to him, recounting all the tragedies of the past several months. After listening patiently, Mike jumped up from his chair, grabbed him by the arm and off they went to the commander's office, which happened to be at Randolph. A sergeant greeted the new 2nd. Lt. and his friend, and reaffirmed the letter of his dismissal. Bill asked the sergeant how he could be considered physically unfit for flight duty, when only the previous day the head flight surgeon at Lackland had

given him a complete physical exam, and pronounced him fit to return to flight status. The Air Force now had a dilemma. All of the Aviation Cadets that were still in training would be graduated before Bill could finish his training—(classes 61-G-1, 61-G-2, and the seven-man class at Reese, 62-A). Furthermore, they certainly did not want to continue a program for only one man. However, after a lengthy conference with the head Flight Surgeon, they did. On June 8, 1961, Bill arrived back at Webb. He was the only Cadet on the base. In a typical military manner, he was given a Commander's Award (72 hours on the tour ramp). This was as a result of him going out of the chain-of-command to get himself reinstated. Of course if he hadn't, he would not have continued in the program, and never would have graduated.

Since Bill was unable to graduate with the next class of student officers in 62-B-1, he was assigned his own class designator, 62-B-2. His rank ran the entire spectrum, from group commander, on down to airman. He was all there was in his class, the smallest class ever to exist in the Aviation Cadet Corps.

On Wednesday, October 11, 1961, Aviation Cadet William F. Wesson, became 2nd. Lt. William F. Wesson. Since he was the very last pilot Cadet to graduate in the entire U.S. Air Force, the ceremony was a really big show. Brigadier General John A. Hilger, A.T.C. Chief of Staff, and Wing Commander Colonel Wilson H. Banks shared in pinning on his bars. Deputy Wing Commander Colonel A. F. Taute spoke of Lt. Wesson's long and difficult struggle to complete pilot training. Lt. Colonel Henry G. Mictor, 3560th Pilot Training Group Commander, administered the Oath of Office; Lt. Colonel Benjamin F. Yeargin Jr., Commander of 3561st Pilot Training Squadron, presented the pilot's wings to Nellie Wesson, Bill's mother, who pinned them on him. Colonel Yeargin said Lt. Wesson would join the instructor staff at Webb after he completed the basic instructor course at Randolph.

Brig. Gen. John A. Hilger (L)., and Col. Wilson H. Banks
pin 2ndLt. William F. Wesson's bars on.   W.H. Banks

William F. Wesson with his instructor at Webb AFB 1961   John Goswick

Col. Wilson H. Banks (L) congratulates Aviation Cadet William F. Wesson (C) and 1st Lt. Ross Pike, Wesson's instructor, following their flight at Webb in T-33 number 50-14300. This "T-Bird" had over 6,000 total hours logged after this flight. This was the last flight for this bird. It was retired, and put on display at Webb AFB. (It did remain at Webb until its closing. It is presently at Dyess AFB. It should be at the Aviation Cadet Museum.)

W. H. Banks 39-C

They Have Served Well

These two Webb-based T-33's have both reached the total of 6,000 hours flown. The 6,000th hour on each was flown Thursday. Flying "300" was Aviation Cadet William F. Wesson, last cadet to train at Webb with his instructor 1st Lt. Ross Pike. T-33 Number 302 was flown by Maj. Harris B. Wilhoite, Wing Flying Safety Officer. Maj. Wilhoite matched the aircraft hours in passing through 6,000 hours himself on this flight. Accompanying Maj. Wilhoite on this flight was Capt. Richard Valladares of the Guatemalan Air Force. Capt. Valladares, newly arrived at Webb AFB, will be here for a year as an instructor pilot in the 3560th Pilot Training Group.

Weary Old T-Bird On Last Flight, Gets Honored Site

As Webb T-33 Number 50-14300 lifted off the runway Thursday afternoon, a page in aircraft and flying history at Webb AFB was turned.

This weary old T-bird had just completed 9½ years of Air Force service and was flying its 6,000th hour in the air. Ranking high in point of service and hours flown, "old 300" has been selected as the T-33 to be placed on permanent memorial to the "T-Bird Era" at Webb at a place of honor near Wing Headquarters.

As an added note to this significant last flight, base training officials selected Aviation Cadet William F. Wesson and his instructor, 1st Lt. Ross Pike, both of the 3561st Green Flight, to fly this jet on its last flight. Cadet Wesson will be the last cadet to graduate from flying training at Webb, when he completes his flying training near the end of September. In its flying training history thousands of cadets have trained at Webb.

There is also a strong possibility that Cadet Wesson may gain the distincation of becoming the last pilot training aviation cadet in the Air Force to complete training and receive a commission as a second lieutenant from a pilot training course. USAF navigator training still regularly enters aviation cadets as students.

The only contender for last pilot aviation cadet honors is a cadet still in training at Reese AFB at Lubbock. This cadet is currently scheduled to complete training prior to Wesson.

Col. Wilson H. Banks, in commenting on the proposed T-33 memorial, said that authority has been granted to Webb to retain a T-33 of Webb's choice to be permanently displayed as a memorial to this remarkable jet trainer and the maintenance men and pilots who worked to maintain and train with the "T-Bird."

In the coming months, as the T-38 Talon supersonic jet trainer is phased into Webb's training program, the T-33 will gradually disappear from the local training scene.

Big Spring Daily Herald, Sept 1, 1961

It was lonely, being the last   John Goswick

Wesson's graduation with student officers. He is second from left.   John Goswick

10

Last Aviation Cadet Graduates

Wednesday, October 11, was an historic day for Webb, and great day in the life of Aviation Cadet William F. Wesson.

That day marked the end of Aviation Cadet training in the Air Force's pilot training program. Wesson, the only remaining cadet in the entire USAF, earned his pilot's wings on that day.

The graduation ceremony at Wing Headquarters was grandiose in that the one-man member of Webb's Class 62-B2 had his second lieutenant's bars pinned on him by Brig. Gen. John A. Hilger, ATC Chief of Staff; and by Wing Commander Col. Wilson H. Banks.

Deputy Wing Commander Col. A. F. Taute reviewed the long and courageous struggle of Cadet Wesson in completing pilot training.

Lt. Col. Henry G. Victor, 35-60th Pilot Training Group commander, administered the Oath of Office; Lt. Col. Benjamin F. Yeargin, Jr., commander of 35-61st Pilot Training Squadron, presented the pilot's wings, and the cadet's mother pinned them on him.

Cadet Wesson, who entered basic pilot training at Webb in Sept. 1960, had been in training for less than two months when he was involved in an airplane accident which hospitalized him for several months. Last May he was released from the hospital and reassigned to Webb. On June 8 he was reinstated in the pilot training program.

Unable to graduate with Class 62-B1, he was put into 62-B2.

In his remarks during the special graduation exercise, Col. Taute brought out these other significant facts: Wesson entered Aviation Cadet training at Lackland AFB, San Antonio, in December 1959; he received preflight training at that base; and finished primary training in T-37 jets at Spence Air Base, Ga., on Sept. 3, 1960.

Col. Yeargin said that Wesson will join the instructor staff at Webb after completing the basic instructor course at Randolph AFB, San Antonio.

"The Prairie Pilot' is an unofficial newspaper published weekly by the Big Spring Printing Company, Inc., in the interests of personnel at Webb Air Force Base, Texas. "The Prairie Pilot" receives Air Training Command Press Service, Air Force News Service, and Armed Forces Press Service material. Opinions expressed herein do not necessarily represent those of the Air Force"

VOL. II, NO. 29   BIG SPRING, TEXAS   FRIDAY, OCTOBER 20, 1961

Base Paper Observes Press Week

Starting last Sunday and ending day after tomorrow, Webb has been observing National Newspaper Week.

It has been a week in which no one frowned on newspaper people for blowing their own horn. At the Base Commissary, the Base Exchange and other places, photos of the Prairie Pilot staff were on display.

(The airmen thirds seen with the editor were Larry Lawrence of Schnectady, N. Y., and Don Smith of Wheeling, W. Va.)

A fixture here at Webb (from all appearances) is the editor, who is observing his third "Newspaper Week" at this base. What the trio was doing was simply going over the previous week's issue, checking for errors and critiquing the layout — especially Page 1.

And now for a little horn blowing:

In the past year this House Organ (Prairie Pilot) has been an information and morale tool for the wing commander.

Individual attainments of officers, airmen and civilians have received coverage in proper

Money Tree Slogan Contest Opens; ATC Offers Cash for Janie Saying

Now that the Scottish brogue of Janie Dollar has rubbed itself sustaining factor in the current "Money Tree" campaign. Air

2D LT. WILLIAM F. WESSON

As the Wesson family continued their flight...

Bill pushed the throttle forward. Feeling the surge of power from the engine, little Jennifer could no longer contain her excitement, and shouted, "Daddy, I'm hungry, I wanna eat." Betty, realizing that takeoff roll was not the time for lunch discussions, turned to Jennifer and said, "Honey, Daddy's busy, we'll have lunch in a little while." The Bonanza roared down the runway, lifted off into the air, climbing like a bird. Bill reached over and retracted the landing gear, when suddenly the engine started to backfire; immediately realizing there was a serious problem, he started a left turn back to the runway. At that point, they were only about 300 feet above the ground. The backfiring shook the entire aircraft, and suddenly it stopped; the engine had failed! Bill called the tower, "Hillview tower, 09-Alpha, our engine has quit, coming back to land." He then realized that they were too low to make it back to the runway. He saw a road straight ahead—if only he had enough airspeed and altitude to make it. Rolling back to the right, he leveled out from the turn, dropped the landing gear, while continuing his struggle to maintain control, he frantically tried to somehow keep the aircraft from hitting in the ditch that was located just before the road. With a last desperate effort, he attempted to hold the aircraft in the air for just a few more seconds, but the airspeed was too low, the stall warning horn blared in his ears—it was too late. He screamed, "My God we're not going to make it!" The ground rushed up as the aircraft slammed into the road, bounced back into the air, and crashed through the top of the chain-link fence surrounding the playing field at Clyde Fischer Junior High School. As it hit the fence, the fuel tanks ruptured, and because of the aircraft's rapid deceleration, the fuel flew forward into the still hot exhaust stack, instantly igniting it. The entire aircraft was immediately engulfed in a bright orange ball of fire. The sounds of tearing metal and the roar of the fire, drowned out the screams of those trapped inside. Sliding to rest on the playing field, it continued to burn. Only the crackling sound of the fire, punctuated with an occasional small explosion emanating from the battery, light bulbs, and

tires could be heard. The acrid stench of burning flesh filled the air like the black hand of death. In the distance the eerie wale of sirens seemed to be sounding a song of mourning. All else was still. William F. Wesson, his wife Betty, their four-year-old daughter Jennifer, and their unborn baby, were instantly killed. Very little was left of 09-Alpha; because of the intensity of the fire, even the bodies were burned to ashes. It was several hours before the fire fighters could get close enough to find their remains.

Gone from this earth was the Last, of the Last of a Breed William F. Wesson. He was the final pilot Aviation Cadet to pin on his wings.

Reid-Hillview airport in 1968. Dotted line indicates flight path, X is crash site.   Santa Clara Co.

12

Chapter 2
The Way I Saw It

August in Oklahoma is usually blistering hot. 1994 was no exception. I drove up to Enid to visit Vance AFB where I had graduated from the Aviation Cadet pilot training program, some thirty-three years before. I had never been back, but had always thought of doing so. Nothing was the least bit familiar as I fought the traffic crossing town. Thirty-three years ago there was nowhere near as much traffic as now. Back then I drove this route every weekend that I could manage to obtain a pass and get off of the base.

Eventually I left most of the traffic behind, and the two-lane blacktop road became much more familiar. Some of the small towns I passed through even seemed to be slightly familiar. But still, they could have been a hundred other towns, in a hundred other places. As I drove along, my mind drifted back to the countless times that I had taken my old '57 Plymouth up and down this very same road. I was twenty-years old, a "hot shot" pilot, and had a gorgeous gal waiting in "Oak City," as we called it. Boy, how times change. I was now 54, my car was an '86 Saab 9000, and that "gorgeous gal," has been my wife for thirty-three years, and she is still as gorgeous as ever.

Following the signs to Vance AFB, I drove down the long entrance way to the base. The guard shack was still there, but everything else was completely foreign to me. I inquired of the guard as to the location of the headquarters building. He was quick to give me directions, but I decided to drive around the base a little before going to headquarters and see what I could recognize. To my amazement, almost nothing looked the same. The "new" (in 1960) barracks were still the same, the chapel was familiar, the "chow" hall was the same, except it now had a sign, "NCO Mess," on the outside wall. The officers club

looked pretty much the same on the outside, but inside it was nothing like it had been. Even the water tower with its red and white checkerboard pattern, had been repainted tan and brown.

This couldn't be an air force base. It looked like a college campus. I drove back to HQ which was now a nice, new brick structure. I entered the building, climbed the stairs, and lo-and-behold, there on the wall opposite the dispatch desk, was a photograph of the Vance I knew. I asked when the picture was taken, "Oh, about 1947," was the answer. The base had remained basically the same for so many years, it seemed such a shame "progress", had replaced history. I took some time to visit with some of the student officers, who were congenial, if not patronizing. I must have seemed to them, to be a dinosaur from a bygone age. Of the instructors, even the most senior, was commissioned after my time. How to make a guy feel old. I was very surprised to find out that pilot training classes today consist of only seven or eight students. During my time we trained well over two-hundred in each class. I could see the hand writing on the wall; budget constraints have taken over as the top priority. The safety and preparedness of our country have slipped far down on the list. Looking back at the last seventy-seven years of history, it seems that every time we, as a nation, stop training pilots, we are soon embattled in another war. Every time a war starts, we are caught in the well-known American position; with our pants down. You would think we would learn from history, but since we don't, we are bound to repeat it.

After I had concluded my visit with the instructors and students, I had planned on a visit with the base historian. But as I exited the headquarters building, I was greeted by huge, black clouds coming in from the south, with bright flashes of lightning and loud claps of thunder. Knowing that I still had over eighty miles to drive back to Oklahoma City, I quickly resumed my trek to the parking lot. As I reached in my pocket for the keys to my car, I stopped and looked out at the flight line. The familiar high-pitched whine of jet engines rang in my ears, and the unmistakable odor of burned jet fuel filled my nostrils; my mind drifted back to another time. October, 1959

CADET LIFE NEAR THE END OF THE PROGRAM

It was with mixed emotions that I arrived at the Philadelphia, Pennsylvania airport, at about seven p.m., and met the eight other recruits going to Lackland AFB, in San Antonio, Texas. My parents had come with me to see me enlist, and be sworn into the United States Air Force. They took me to the airport that evening. As the plane departed I could see them waving, and my mother choking back tears, as I left on my great adventure. I was one of only four young men who were Aviation Cadets, the other four were enlisted airmen. Even though the four of us visited on the flight, I never saw the other three again after we arrived at Lackland, and entered into our pilot training class designated 61-E; scheduled to last 64 weeks. During the flight, first to New Orleans, arriving before dawn, then on to San Antonio bright and early the next morning, I had plenty of time to contemplate what I had done. I had agreed to serve in the USAF for two years as an enlisted man if I did not complete my pilot training, and four years after training if I did. I had no concept of what I was really in for.

As a young child, I grew up in the Paterson area of New Jersey, an area called Prospect Park, to be exact. I was still a youngster when we moved to the rural area of the same state. As far back as I can remember, I had always been infatuated with airplanes; building models was a great love of mine. I'm sure that most little boys of the WWII, and post

war era were just as "plane crazy." My first model,

Author at age 2 1/2 with unidentified airplane.

Author 61-E

that I recall, was a solid pine DC-3. My mother helped me build it on the living room floor of our home, in Prospect Park. I was about four-years old. As I grew older, I was given a fifty-cent-a-week allowance, and I almost always spent it on some glider or rubber-powered airplane. The A.J. Hornet was my favorite rubber-powered, (it cost my entire fifty-cent allowance), and Testors glider, the one with the 3/4" long round-steel weight in the nose, was my favorite glider. I think these were ten cents each. As I grew older, my love of airplanes only became stronger. I remember my Uncle Ron, taking me to an air show, probably my first, right after the war. I was in *seventh heaven*. They flew a "Black Widow" that could climb straight up. Boy was I impressed. Anytime there was an airplane sitting anywhere that we drove by, I would shout, "Daddy stop! Let's look at that airplane." I had books on airplanes, pictures of airplanes, models of airplanes, and airplane toys, either hanging or sitting all over my room; I'm sure my mother loved to dust all that stuff.

We had a small farm near Hope, and although my dad was a carpenter by trade, he loved to work in his garden; well, small truck farm was closer to the truth than a "garden". Every spring my dad would buy our year's supply of meat. It consisted of a pair of one-year-old black angus steer, and three piglets. We also raised chickens (eggs, fried chicken, etc.) and we even sold some of the eggs for extra money. Money was something there was never an abundance of, but there was always enough so we could live comfortably. Every fall we would butcher the steer, and pigs. We always had plenty to eat. So much so that one of my infamous statements lives to this day; arriving home after school I asked my mother what was for dinner (kids are always hungry), to which she replied, "Steak." Since there were only the three of us to eat all that meat, we ate steak real often. I replied, "What, steak again?"

One day while I was out flying one of my model airplanes, I heard an airplane overhead, and something I cannot do, even now, is ignore an airplane overhead. This time though, I saw something drop out of the plane. Wow! I had secretly hoped that perhaps one day some bomber or fighter would be forced to land on our place. I didn't think about any one being hurt, I just wanted to have a first-hand look, and maybe even fire one of those neat machine guns they shot in all the war movies. Well, you know how kids dream. Unfortunately, this event was not nearly as exciting as my dreams, for the objects dropping from this plane were only thin strips of some kind of aluminum foil. What a bust. (I didn't know about chaff). As I became older (something that all living people do), my love of airplanes grew into an overwhelming desire that could not be satisfied by mere models; I wanted to fly real airplanes.

I was working as a carpenter with my dad in the summertime, so I had a little spending money of my own. When I was eighteen, I joined an Aero Club at Lake Susquehanna airport, just a few miles from home. It cost $100 to join, and I believe a Piper J-3 Cub rented for $6.00 an hour wet. At that time I only made about $2.00 an hour, so my parents helped with the $100, and that was a lot of money in 1958. But at long last, I was going to become a pilot. As I could afford it, I learned to fly that old Cub. Dual was $10.00 an hour, so I was very happy when I could solo. After all, I did have a great amount of flying experience—a whole six hours. It was about time that I soloed. I still remember that first solo. It was early evening, the weather was clear, the wind was dead calm. My instructor, Don W. Hudgins and I, had previously flown an hour, and after we landed, as we were taxiing in, Don asked me if I thought I could take it around by myself. I guess I said, "Yes," because he got out and said, "Don't be nervous." and walked away. I fishtailed to the end of the grass strip, did my run up, checked for traffic, turned her toward the other end, applied full throttle, and held on. What an experience. Only me and God. But I was the only one *with skin on* in that little yellow bird. Everything seemed to happen so quickly; before I knew it, I was airborne and climbing, at least the airplane and my body were—my mind was still somewhere on the runway. I remember thinking that the only way I was going to get back to earth in one piece, was to fly this thing. So fly it I did. As I flew around the pattern looking down on that little soft, green patch, it seemed so much smaller than it had just a short time ago; funny how fear changes our perspective. Turning a left base, I pulled the carburetor heat knob out, throttle to idle, and down we came. On final, I pushed the throttle up, just a bit to clear the engine, then back to idle; almost before I knew it, the soft sound of rushing wind, much like the sound of a passing bird, greeted my ears, followed by the soft "thunk" of big balloon tires on grass. I had flown! At that moment, all my boyhood dreams were somehow realized. True, this only served to awaken a hunger for more hours, and bigger and faster airplanes, but to a boy who had for years dreamed of becoming a pilot, this moment would always stand out in his book of greatest memories.

The time must come in every young man's life when he has to make a decision as to what he is going to learn to do that someone will be willing to pay him for doing. I knew I wanted to fly and earn a living at it. I had not heard of the Aviation Cadet program as yet. I did, however, hear about the Air Force Academy and managed a congressional appointment to go there. This was my next dream. The Academy was brand new, and I reasoned that anyone getting in on the ground floor, so to speak, would do all right. I never liked algebra in high school, or perhaps it was more to the point that I never liked the algebra instructor. He was the football coach, and since I was a *big* boy, he naturally thought I should give my all for good old Belvidere High. I guess I would have if my parents had been shortsighted, but thank God they were not. They reasoned that I might sustain an injury that would stop me from flying, so they wouldn't sign the permission slip for me to play. I said all that to come up with some excuses for flunking the Academy entrance exam. Yep, lousy in algebra. Well, on to the next dream.

My parents and I decided that I would go to the University of Miami. At that time they, along with Embry Riddle, had a course in Airport Management, which included flight training up through a commercial license. Since I only had 27:45 in the old Cub, I was still not a licensed pilot. Off I went to Florida in my 1950 two-door Ford. Being only eighteen and not exactly sure of anything, let alone, what I wanted to do with the rest of my life, I changed my major to mechanical engineering, when I arrived at school. I also joined the USAF-ROTC program. I was even crazy enough to join the drill team. Little did I know of what was to come. After one semester of less than stunning performance, I quit.

Confused and frustrated, I looked for my niche in the big picture. Someone, I can't remember who, told me that there was a test that one could take, and

if he passed, he would be sent to USAF pilot training. That's for me. I wouldn't have to put up with the four years of schooling; I could take a shortcut to my real purpose; I could be a *jet jockey*! I visited my friendly Air Force recruiter as soon as possible. After filling out the necessary paper work, I was told that I would have to go to the Air Force base at Harrisburg, Pennsylvania, to take a battery of tests. While waiting for the day of the test to arrive, I studied everything I could get my hands on that might be relevant to the test. I wasn't going to flunk this one. The tests ran for three days. And what a physical exam. Those of us who passed were as perfect a physical specimen as could be found. And the written tests were something else. I thought my brain would pop. Before taking the written exam we were told that we could qualify as pilots or navigators depending on how well we did. After what seemed like an eternity, the test results were in. I had qualified as a Pilot trainee. Yahoo! We were told that (if I can remember correctly), out of each 300 applicants who took these tests, only twenty-five would qualify as pilots. At last I felt that now I was on the right track. I was going to Lackland AFB, and learn to fly jets.

A few weeks later a letter arrived from the Air Force verifying that I had been accepted into the Aviation Cadet pilot training program. Enclosed with the letter was an explanation of some of some of the things that I was to expect, and a list of items I was supposed to have during pre-flight. The letter was as follows:

Clothing: Take a minimum amount of civilian clothing since Cadets are not permitted to wear such clothing during the 12 weeks pre-flight training course. (A/C's are not required to send civilian clothing home).

Money: Cadets receive a $100.00 partial payment on the third day after arrival at pre-flight. They receive the first months pay approximately 25-30 days after entry into training. The partial payment is deducted from their pay in two $50.00 increments beginning with the first month's pay. An Aviation

Cadet receives a base pay of $115.00 (unless in pay grade E-6 or E-7) plus $47.88 subsistence. Cadets pay $1.45 per day for meals. Social Security and Income Tax are withheld from the Cadet's pay. Club dues of $4.00 and laundry/dry cleaning of $10.00 per month must be paid. The mandatory base purchased items cost approximately $50.00 and the $100.00 partial pay is intended to cover the cost of these items in addition to paying for their meals until they draw their first subsistence allowance. It is recommended that if possible Cadets have approximately $50.00 when reporting to pre-flight.

RECOMMENDED ITEMS THAT A CADET SHOULD TAKE TO PRE-FLIGHT:

(If not in possession upon arrival these items must be purchased within one week after arrival).

2 pair shoe trees
3 pair athletic socks (white wool)
2 cans of shoe polish (black)
2 shoe shine rags
6 flashlight batteries
1 toothbrush case
1 box cotton balls
1 nail clipper
1 soap dish
1 comb
1 cardboard shoe box (large)
1 pair shower clogs (white rubber)
2 wash cloths
1 box laundry soap
1 bottle bleach
1 pencil (mechanical)
2 athletic supporters
3 white towels
1 shoe brush
1 sponge
1 can shaving cream
1 razor or electric razor
1 pkg. razor blades
2 bars of soap
1 can tooth powder (any brand)
3 handkerchiefs
1 roll adhesive tape 1"

2 collar stays (one piece)
2 collar stays (two piece)
2 pair shoe laces (black)
1 pen
1 pkg. notebook paper (three ring)

ITEMS THAT MUST BE PURCHASED AT BASE EXCHANGE: (To insure uniformity)

2 pair shoulder boards
2 pair Pre-Flight stripes
2 pair P.T. shorts
1 P.T. cap
3 pair white gloves
2 belt buckles
3 pair garters
1 coin purse
1 notebook, large blue, zipper
2 pair blue or red stripes
1 flight cap
1 pair athletic gym shoes
1 flashlight
1 dozen pips
1 sewing kit
3 sets collar brass
1 metal name tag

I checked off all of the "bring from home" items and loaded them in my suitcase. For anyone who thought that in the military the government supplies everything, think again.

PREFLIGHT AT LACKLAND AFB

As the old blue Air Force school bus pulled into Lackland that lovely October day, I remember peering out of the window and seeing men marching in formation everywhere I looked. Some with white gloves, singing as they marched. Pretty neat, I thought. Boy was I wrong. It was OK to be an observer, but a participant was another matter. As we disembarked the bus, a sergeant with a loud voice *greeted?* us. We were told where to put our bags. Then we were put in a "bunch", not really a formation, and *marched?* to the supply warehouse, what a gaggle (a bunch of untrained men trying to march).

Cadets marching at Lackland AFB   R.G. Anderson 55-N

basic necessities—not the least of which was our green fatigues, from which comes the term "Green Men," (as we were referred to during our first six-weeks as underclassmen). The airman issuing the shoes must have thought I was a real "wise guy" when he asked me my size, and I said, "14." But to my amazement, he disappeared for a few moments, only to reappear with a pair of the biggest brogans (Air Force issue high-top shoes) anyone had ever seen. Gee, they must have known I was coming. We were again formed into our gaggle, and this time led to the "barber shop." This was the home of the infamous thirty-second haircut. Man,

There, at the Green-Monster (the supply building) we moved up in a long line, and we were issued our

Green Men formed up at Lackland AFB   Al Nichols 55-Q

they shaved it all off. To make it even worse we had to pay $.75 for the pleasure. Much of what happened after that is a blur. I remember being formed up outside our barracks in our lovely "Green Men" suits, and being verbally chewed up and down: "Hit a brace, Mister," "Reach for Texas, Mister," "Chest out, stomach in," on and on they went, these "de-

Bird-type doggy latrine on the right front, Sir!" (a red fire-hydrant). "Sir, off the left front, Sir! approaching raunchy Bluebird formation, Sir!" (a Cadet navigator formation).

In addition to all the daytime hazing, we went to classes as well. And of course we marched in formation. Our subjects and hours of instruction

Main Academic building at Lackland AFB   Frank Lane 54-?

mons from hell." (They were Cadets from our upper class 61-D). We marched everywhere we went, "Left, right, left, right, get in step, Mister, where are you looking, Mister? Cage those eyeballs, Mister!" It never stopped. "Sing!" We sang. All the old favorites? such as; "Off we go into the wild blue yonder ..," "Hark the preflight angels shout,.....days and we'll be out." "I had a girl in New Orleans, she had... ," well, you get the idea. In preflight we were referred to as "Red Birds," and the navigator Cadets were "Blue Birds"; there was great competition between the groups. Some of the more interesting marching calls when we approached a road intersection went like this: "Road guards out." (the men designated 'road guards' would advance to the intersection); "Sir, off the right front, Sir, a fine Red

were: Leadership:23, Effective expression:22, Applied Math:17, Applied Physics:27, Strategic Intelligence:20, Safeguarding Military Information:2, Operational Intelligence:22, History and Tradition:15, Career and Classification:3, Military Law:8, Supply:4, Administration and Organization:10, Flight Operations:4. In addition to the academic subjects, we had military ones as well: Aviation Cadet Honor Code:9, Aviation Cadet Organization:9, Customs and Courtesies:10, Marksmanship:8, Small Arms:5, Drill and Voice and Command:44, Inspections and Parade:44[1]—and then there was good old physical training—just like in the movies, hundreds of men on a nice, paved, hot, flat field. Oh, the pushups, side-straddle hops, deep-knee bends, sprints, you would have thought we were in training for Notre Dame. We all had to do a timed hundred-yard dash. Wow! How was I going to do that, I didn't have any sneakers; no size fourteens on the base. So as it turned out, I set the record for the dash in a new category—Brogans. Of course I was the only one in the category, so it wasn't too hard to hold the record. Along with all the previous fun, we were always subject to being stopped by an upperclassman, or "TAC" officer (regular Air Force Training Officer) and given an on-the-spot inspection. We were also responsible (after being there for seven days) for knowing our "Cadet Knowledge." The routine generally ran like this: "Halt Rabbit!" We would come to an immediate stop at as stiff an attention as we could muster. "Are you a rabbit, Mister?"—at the top of our lungs— "No Sir!"—"Then why did you stop?" We only had three authorized answers—"Yes, Sir!" "No, Sir!" and "No Excuse, Sir!" This was the "No Excuse, Sir!" one. Then they would start verbally taking us apart piece by piece. "What did you shine those shoes with, Mister, a candy bar?" "Look at that "Gig" line, Mister." (the line your fly, belt buckle, and shirt seam made when all lined up); of course we looked down to see if it was really off—"Cage those eyeballs, Mister!" (look straight ahead); on they went until they had, had enough fun torturing us, and as one last *Coup-De-Grace*, they would scream, "Post me one, Mister!" (slap your left shirt pocket so as to make as loud a pop as you could stand, smartly remove a demerit slip, and present it to

the inspecting officer); at which point he would whirl away to find another victim.

Meals during the first six-weeks as underclassmen, were to say the least, quite interesting. They were not exactly like going to Grandma's for Christmas dinner. We sat at attention, on the front few inches of the chair, eyeballs "caged," and food (if we could get it on the fork without looking at it) was lifted straight up to a point that was level with the mouth, followed by an ensuing ninety-degree turn, and down the hatch. It's amazing how good one could eat a "square meal" after some practice. I think it was the survival instinct, because If you

"Are you a rabbit, Mister?"   "No, Sir!"

Al Nichols 55-Q

20

Dining Hall #24 where the Cadets ate their three "square" meals every day.   Frank Lane 54-?

dropped anything—heaven forbid—the dialog went like this: "Sir, Aviation Cadet Severe requests permission to ask question, Sir!" "Ask question ask" was the reply. "Sir, request permission to go on a rescue mission Sir!" "What type aircraft are you going to use, Mister?" (here it got a little dicey). "An F-102, Sir!" "Mister how will you get an F-102 in with no runway?" "Correction, Sir, I'd use a helicopter, Sir!" "Cleared for rescue mission." Needless to say, none of us had a problem with gaining weight. Trying to eat in this atmosphere was worse for some than for others. A/C Jim Denning made the near fatal mistake of taking the hazing personally. He lost twenty pounds during the first several weeks of training. This would not have been so bad if he had weighed 200 lbs. to begin with, but he was only 120 lbs. soaking wet, when he arrived at Lackland. He was so upset by the upperclassmen that he was going to S.I.E. (Self-Initiated Elimination). He figured it was quit or die. He went to his TAC officer, Lt. Klett, and said he would not sur-

vive if he couldn't eat, so he wanted out. The Lt. listened patiently, and then said, "Mister Denning, you shouldn't make such a decision on an empty stomach." Leading A/C Denning outside, just as A/C McNaught (from 61-D) was marching by, Lt. Klett said, "Halt, Mister!" Of course he screeched to a halt at full attention. The Lieutenant positioned himself in front of McNaught, and ordered him to take Denning to the BX snack bar and get him something to eat. After polishing off three cheeseburgers, two large orders of fries, all washed down with a very large coke, the world seemed to be a better place. A/C Denning rescinded his request to leave the program.

After the evening meal formation, the hazing was on in earnest. We polished the barracks floor with the great big commercial polishers; that is, after we scrubbed the previous coat of wax off on our hands and knees—sometimes twice in one day. Then there were those nasty black scuff marks on the baseboards. Solution—get some toothpaste and

21

A/C MacAfee and several classmates waxing the floor.   Jim MacAfee 61-E

through the takeoff, and climb (complete with engine sounds of course); it's mighty uncomfortable against that wall. then someone would yell, "You're above ten-thousand feet—quick get on oxygen!" You would then be fitted with a "jock" strap over your nose, and an aerosol can of shaving cream squirted under it. Ah, boys and their games.

Each pair of underclassmen were assigned an upperclassman who was to teach us "the ropes," so to speak. Mine was named Webb—only last names were in vogue—he was

cotton balls, a group of thirty or so Green Men, and have them polish them off. Other forms of entertainment such as the "Green Chair," or flying the "Spad" were not used too often—whew! The Green Chair was conducted in the basement, just in case a TAC officer should wander in (orders were, No Hazing). So much for orders. We were told to squat with our backs against the wall. Then we were told we were in some type of aircraft. We would go

better known as "Spider." As "Raunchmasters" go, he was much better than most. Under different circumstances we would have been good friends. (Spider washed-back to our class, and we were good friends, unfortunately sometime later, he washed-out.) He taught us the proper way to enter a room, if an upperclassman was in it: standing outside the room, back against the wall, adjacent to the door, we would pound on the wall and in our best, loud voice yell, "Sir, please pardon me, Sir! Aviation Cadet Severe requests permission to ask question, Sir!" The reply: "Ask question ask." "Request permission to enter room, Sir!' "Permission granted." Boy, did we learn to communicate effectively.

One of the real highlights of our training was the daily white-gloves inspection. Yep, the TAC officer actually wore white gloves to check for dust in such obvious places as the top of baseboards, door trim, and bed rails. Of course every item we had must be in its exact location, the exact distance apart, facing the correct direction, etc. Inspection sure was an easy way to *earn*? enough demerits to get on the "Tour ramp." This was the place where you were privileged to wear out your shoe soles. On the weekend when you might get a few moments to yourself,

Flying the "Spad"   Martin Buckley 61-E

Drawer #1   Martin Buckley 61-E

Drawer #3   Martin Buckley 61-E

Drawers and lockers as they were required to be set up for inspection. There were six drawers and two lockers.

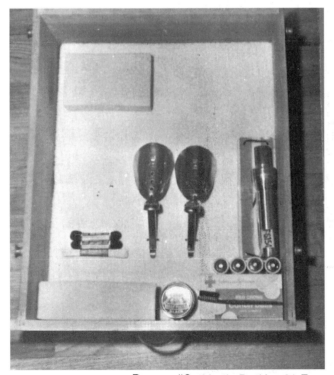

Drawer #2   Martin Buckley 61-E

Locker #1   Martin Buckley 61-E

23

most of us were marching tours. We were in full dress uniform of the day, with white gloves, and *eyeballs caged*. We marched back and forth at the rate of one tour per hour.

to "cock of the walk," overnight. Look out 61-F. All we had to worry about now was the dreaded TAC officers. Well, not quite all, we still had to pass all of our courses. And there were the Cadet

Cadets walking on "Tour Ramp" at Lackland AF Al Nichols 55-Q

Of course in the very beginning, the Green Men were given other things to occupy their free (?) time—like "Pick Pick." We would form a line along the street, facing the barracks, and walk or crawl across the grass toward the building, picking up every piece of trash and every cigarette butt found laying on the ground—sure were a lot of people who smoked back then.

At last the day came when our upper class graduated from preflight, and moved on to primary. We could have cared less where those no good #%..s went, just so long as it was away from us. But the good news, if there could be any at Lackland, was that now we were upper class. It was amazing to see the change. We went from "scum of the earth,"

officers who thought the stripes on their shoulder boards, meant they were tigers. They were as bad

Cadets assigned to "Pick Pick." Martin Buckley 61-E

Inspection of underclassmen at Lackland AFB   R.G. Anderson 55-N

as the TAC's, even to their own classmates.

It was the first part of December when we became upper class. With the prospect of the Christmas season approaching, it was very depressing for most of us. This would be the first Christmas away from home for the majority of us. There would be no gathering of the family, no large turkey, roasted to golden brown and almost bursting with dressing, no presents under the tree; in fact, no tree at all. The weather didn't help either, as it was a very wet December, and for Texas, it was cold. Every morning when reveille would sound at 5:00 a.m., we would do our routine: throw our

Author's flight, L. to R.: J. Prah, Rear, G. Fowler, unknown, Author. In front second from right is R. Fleer. The rest are un-remembered .   Russ Fleer 61-E

25

clothes on (not nearly as carefully as when we were under class) put our blue rain covers on our officers hats, don our raincoats, and launch out into the pre-dawn darkness. As the first sergeant of our squadron, it was my job to make out the morning report—nothing much really, just one paragraph stating that all were present or accounted for. Then I would come out after everyone had formed up, and walk behind the lines, saluting each Cadet officer as I passed, struggling to keep my hat from blowing away, and shielding my face from the sting of the persistent rain. As I marched on to deliver my one sheet of paper to the HQ, the Cadet group commander would shout, "Gro..oup"—each squadron commander would shout, "Squadro..on," followed by a brief pause, and then the command, "Ten Hut!" would echo between the now empty barracks, and the sound of several-hundred men slamming their left heel into their right heal, shot through the darkness like cannon fire.

We were given a three-day leave for Christmas. That was not nearly enough time to go home to New Jersey, nor enough for any of us to go anywhere, unless our homes were nearby. Making the best of a grim situation, the idea was put to my squadron to act as "Santa Claus" for an orphanage that was near the base, and treat them to a Christmas party. Everyone thought it would be a great idea, and we all chipped in to buy presents and refreshments for the kids. We did have one problem to overcome though—the USAF. Nothing, I repeat, nothing, is done without clearance from above. No, not from GOD, but from the head TAC officer—he just *thought* he was divine. Russ Fleer, our squadron commander, suggested that since this party was my idea, I should face the "You Know." I checked my uniform for any possible defect and pressed on to the HQ building. The captain was expecting me, as of course I had presented the idea to our squadron TAC officer first (chain of command, you know). Bright and shiny, full of enthusiasm, into the lion's den I went; I snapped to attention, gave my sharpest salute, and he said, "Get your head on straight, Mis-

ter." I guess my head was listing a degree or so to starboard—Boy, what a grouch! Well anyway, he did allow us to do it.

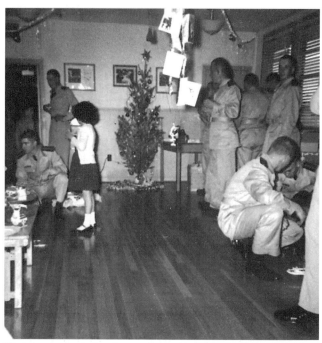
Christmas party for the orphans in the barracks day room. Author standing by the doorway.   Russ Fleer 61-E

More of the Christmas party, the little girl in both pictures is probably a movie star by now. Russ Fleer 61-E

Russ Fleer, Guy Fowler, and I, took the money we had collected and went to the Base Exchange to buy the toys. Man, did we get a bunch. We were each loaded with a large box stuffed with goodies.

It sure was a long walk back to our barracks carrying those boxes of toys. We had also bought paper, ribbon, bows, tape—all the items necessary to get the job done. I guess we looked like the gift wrapping department at Macy's. The next day, the bus arrived with twenty-five or thirty little guys and gals. We had cake and ice cream, soft drinks, and of course, presents. The look on those children's faces helped each of us through this very trying time; we gained much more than we gave. I often wonder if any of the kids, who would now all be grown, remember that time. It doesn't really matter, though, I remember.

In January, it was our turn to leave preflight. "Hark the preflight angels shout, no more days and we'll be **OUT!**" We had all packed our B-4 and duffel bags (Air Force version of "Samsonite"[2]) and waited nervously for the cabs to come and take us to the airport for our flights to our individual homes.

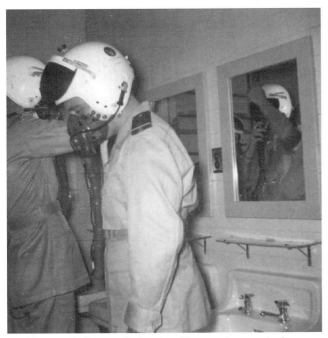

61-E gets their new helmets. Now we're ready for preflight.   Martin Buckley 61-E

We had all been assigned to our primary flight-training bases—mine was Bainbridge, Georgia—the others were at, Graham, Bartow, and Spence. We also had ten-days leave. Boy, did we ever need that leave. It was January 12th, 1960.

It's hard to believe so much had happened in so short a time. Being away from home for this length of time, although a relatively short time to most folks, seemed like an eternity to me. I couldn't wait for that old Braniff 707 to get to Idlewild (JFK). As it turned out, I was on a record-setting-speed run. (The plaque is on my wall to prove it.) It was after dark and snowing when we landed. Looking out the left window, I could see the snow swirling into the air in a huge whirlwind as the 707's engines were put in reverse thrust. The landing lights illuminated each snowflake, making it glisten like crystal. It looked more like a winter wonderland than an airport. As we slowly taxied in, I strained my eyes trying to see into the terminal to find my father and mother, who were to pick me up and take me back home. Home—what a warm-fuzzy word. After the hugs and kisses and the two-hour drive in the snow, we pulled into the heated garage under my parent's house, leaving the cold and snow outside. Oh, it was wonderful to be back, I walked up the stairs into the kitchen, and all was as I remembered—the table next to the window, the rocker by the refrigerator, my father's work shoes under the rocker, with his white socks hanging over the tops. It was all the same; but it was all different. Actually, the house wasn't different, but I was. I had left as a child, but returned as a man. The past three months had accomplished what they were designed to do; I would never be the same again.

My mother couldn't wait to show off her son in his nice new uniform. During the time I was on leave, she invited all my friends over for a party; there was lots of food, lots of laughs—it was great. She took great delight in having me pull up my pants leg, and show everyone my "Zap" rag stuffed in my sock, it was used to touch up our "spit" shine.

My leave went by quickly. All too soon I had to depart for Bainbridge. Several months before I enlisted, I bought a 1957 Plymouth, which had been left at home when I went to preflight. Was I ever glad to have my "wheels" again. I loaded it up with my stuff, along with a huge lunch, a thermos of milk, and launched off toward Georgia. Along the way, I

to say, we never outgrow our need for milk. Hey, don't laugh, it worked. My first and last (I hope), in-flight fire.

I'm happy to say the rest of the trip was uneventful, except that by dawn we were **HUNGRY**! The lunch had long since disappeared. We stopped in a little southern town with, of course, a little cafe. We all ordered a huge breakfast—three eggs, sausage, and—what the heck was this white stuff with butter floating in the middle of it? This was the first time I had ever seen "grits". "How do you eat this stuff?" I asked. The other two "Yankees," didn't have a clue either. Oh well, milk and sugar are good on anything.

PRIMARY AT BAINBRIDGE AB

Author departing for Bainbridge in the '57 "Blue Bomb."   Author 61-E

picked up Jim Stoveken, and I think, Ray Singer, fellow Cadets also assigned to Bainbridge. Being indestructible, steely-eyed Cadets, we drove straight through. Sometime during the night, I stopped and let Jim take over the driving. I crawled into the back seat to get some much needed shuteye. After we had driven a few miles, something made me look out the back window. Sparks, they were coming from under my car. I shouted, "Jim, stop, we're on fire!" We screeched to a stop; sure 'nuf, he had left the emergency brake on. On this car it was on the drive shaft, and it was burning. Here we were in the middle of the night, right smack-dab in the middle of nowhere, the car was on fire, and we had no fire extinguisher; what could we do. Milk—that's wet, I grabbed the thermos, crawled under the car and dowsed the brake with milk. Guess Moms are right

Arriving at Bainbridge Air Base was almost as much of a shock in the positive sense, as Lackland was in the negative. Driving down a long lane lined with large pine trees, we were soon greeted by a "Welcome to Bainbridge Air Base" sign. We pulled onto the paved, shaded parking lot, and gazed out on the nicely-cut lawns, and neat, relatively modern buildings, nestled in a forest of pines. I thought, *This place is a country club.* It had really nice, two-men-to-a-room barracks, golf course, Cadet club, officers club, base exchange; in short, all the things real people, in the real world, were privileged to enjoy. It almost made one "figmo." (so relaxed that one could care less). Because it was run as a civilian contract school (Southern Airways), the entire mood was one of cooperation and teaching. The mission here was to teach us to become aviators—

28

Our day still started at 5:00 a.m., but at least we could get up, shower, shave, etc., and walk, not march, over to the chow hall. There was no one hazing us, no shouting, no Cadet knowledge, not even any lurking TAC officers. A guy could get used to this. The academics were very difficult, as we were taking college-level courses. They consisted of the following: Flight Instruments 16 hrs., Principles of Flight 20 hrs., Aircraft Engineering 37 hrs., Aviation Physiology 12 hrs., Aural and visual code 10 hrs., Navigation 50 hrs., Radio communications 18 hrs., Weather 28 hrs., Flight planning 31 hrs., and Flying safety 3 hrs. It makes one wonder—

Barracks at Bainbridge AB. L. to R: "Spider" Webb, G. Oleander F. Assaf, W. Sitter, Ratcliffe, Thome, and S. Gibbons at right rear.
Jim MacAfee 61-E

not to give us a ration of S....! The instructors were all WWII pilots—most, but not all, were really nice guys. Even the support people were friendly and helpful.

We started out flying the Beechcraft T-34, a really fun airplane. Since I had some flying experience, it was much easier for me than some of the others, like Bob Hasbrouck. He was from the inner city in Chicago. He had never even driven a car, let alone flown an airplane.

The infamous "Track" at Bainbridge AB   Jim MacAfee 61-E

Bainbridge AB, 61-E putting underclassmen in 61-F through "Disneyland."

Jim MacAfee 61-E

Bainbridge AB, 61-E showing the ropes to 61-F. Jim Prah in foreground.

Jim MacAfee 61-E

only *three hours* for flying safety? That must be why we were such "Tigers." And of course, we still had our military courses—Drills, ceremonies and inspections 36 hrs., Leadership responsibilities 10 hrs., Communicative skills 8 hrs., Physical training (supervised sports) 19 hrs., and anyone, who ever served under coach Hardy in his physical *Conditioning*, program, consisting of 37 hrs. of pure physical torture, will, no doubt, have stomach cramps and probably "barf," at the remembrance. I thought physical training was bad back at Lackland on the "Brogan" course. This guy was out to kill us. Ah—but he was such a polite gentleman. In his sweet southern drawl, honey dripping from his lips, he would say, "Now ah know you boys can run the two miles in formation, with no trouble at all. You wouldn't let ol' coach Hardy down, now would ya?"—Ha! let him down—what about us? He found a spot in the shade and watched; we were the ones dragging our bodies around and around that old dirt track. I can't remember just how many guys fell to the ground, and "barfed" their guts out, but it was a bunch. Then there was "Disneyland," at least that's what we called the obstacle course. We had to climb ropes, go hand over hand on the horizontal ladder, run through the

Jim Prah makes history.

Jim MacAfee 61-E

tires, crawl through the pipes, and last, but not least, scale a ten-foot wall. I'll never forget Jim Prah (about 5' 3") trying to get over that thing. He sure spent a lot of time hanging by his arms. He may not have gotten any taller, but I'll bet he could drag his

T-34 landing at the Bainbridge auxiliary field named Donaldson.   Author 61-E

knuckles on the ground without bending over. If Lackland got us ready for college football, Bainbridge had us ready for the starting lineup at Green Bay. But I must confess, I was never in better physical shape in my life.

It was with some apprehension that I, and my fellow Cadets, entered into our "Line Shack," for the first time. At my table there was Jim Stoveken, Darryl Myers (I think) Bruce Holmes (student officer), and myself. We were all seated. The instructors came in, and we snapped to attention, only to be greeted with, "All right fellas, sit down—my name's Henry Evans—everyone calls me "Pop." Well, so much for military formality. He was great. A tall, thin, soft-spoken man, very patient, and a very fine instructor. He passed away many years ago; he is missed.

We did most of our T-34 training over at an auxiliary field called Donaldson. This kept our slower aircraft from messing up the faster T-37 traffic pattern. I remember one day "Pop" and I were out doing the usual pilot things; acrobatics, touch and go's, and practicing forced landings. He would pull the throttle to idle and say, "forced landing"— I would tell him which field I was going to land in, and proceed to fly just as if I were really going to land. This time it seemed like he let us get really close to the ground, perhaps 100' or so, before he said, "OK, let's go." I immediately firewalled the throttle, the engine coughed, then took hold. I said, "What happened?" He said, "Next time don't forget to change fuel tanks." Pop saw we were low on fuel in the tank we were feeding from, so he had his hand on the selector, and as soon as the engine sput-

hit that plane! OK, I've got it." Whew, touchy little pup. OK, we, or should I say, *he* got us to the end of the run way. I called mobile control and said we were ready for takeoff. "Roger Baker 12, cleared for takeoff." I depressed the "power steering" button, and promptly zig-zaged onto the runway, stopped, set the brakes, and ran the before-takeoff checklist: 1. Shoulder harness-**Locked**, 2. Canopy-**Close, Lock, check light out**. 3. Flight controls-**Check free and proper movement**. 4.Wing flaps-**Extended 50%**. 5. Directional indicator (J2)-**SET**. 6. Pitot heat and defroster-**Climatic**. 7.Throttles-**100%rpm**.8.Engine instruments-**Check**.a. Tachometers-**100%rpm**. b.Exhaust gas temperature indicators-**Check**. c.

Pop Evans and Author at Bainbridge AB   Author 61-E

tered, he changed tanks. He figured he would teach me a lesson. He did, I didn't make that mistake again. I made a lot of others, but not that one. We were only given 27 hrs. in the T-34—not much time, but enough to tell if we could be taught to fly the twin jet T-37. Pop once told me that he could teach a chimpanzee to fly, if it could only talk. I wonder if he was trying to tell me something?

I'll never forget the first time we went up in the Cessna T-37, what a little screamer. The nose wheel steering is hydraulic—it's turned on and off by a little button on the stick. Hold in the button and push in the right rudder pedal, and you turned right, push in the left....well, you get the idea. We were just starting to taxi out when Pop said, "You taxi"—hey, no problem. "Look out for that fuel truck! Don't

T-37 Cockpit   Jim MacAfee

32

Fuel flow indicators-**Check**. d.Oil pressure gages-**Check**. e. Loadmeters-**Check**. f. Hydraulic pressure gage-**Check**. 9. One and zero system lanyard-**Check**. I popped off the parking brakes and away we went. The runway started to slide by, slowly at first—the scream of the engines penetrated my helmet—the aircraft shook with the power of two jet engines at maximum thrust, faster and faster we rolled; at about 80 knots, I eased back on the stick, and the nose started to rise— the next thing I knew, we were airborne. We were going like a scalded dog. I was so busy, Pop pulled the gear up as we approached 110 knots. Wow, I was a teenage "jet jockey!" I had never flown a jet before. As we climbed out, I was really impressed by the quiet and smoothness—nothing like the old T-34. Leaving the traffic pattern, we climbed higher and higher— it all seemed so effortless—we were now above 20,000 ft., higher than I had ever flown an aircraft. We did the usual maneuvers, aileron rolls, barrel rolls, loops, etc.. I was then given a spin demonstration. Pop pulled the throttles to idle, held back pressure on the stick to keep us level at our altitude; the nose came up more and more, then "wham!" the right wing dropped violently—the nose pitched up, and the world was spinning. Then he pushed forward on the stick to show me what an inverted spin was like, not enough to enter an inverted spin, just enough to show me I never wanted to do one. Man, that sucker spun even faster. Then he showed me the spin recovery (yes, please recover!)—stick full back, full right rudder, kick left rudder to stop the turning, slam, and I do mean slam, the stick full

Morning "Drive Off" at Bainbridge AB, Cadets form up to march from the barracks to the flight line. J. MacAfee's back, Foreign Cadets Zarpor & Yeroui (with the bandages due to an auto accident).   Jim MacAfee 61-E

forward. Boing! we were out. When we were back at level flight, and my stomach was back in place, he told me he had been doing the same demonstration some months back with a foreign student, except the student wasn't on his first ride, and he was demonstrating it to Pop (part of the training). There must have been a breakdown in communication's, because the student accidentally put them into a full, inverted spin. The T-37 was known to be a "bear" in a spin, which is why we were forbidden to do them solo—it didn't always recover. Pop had not tightened his seat belt and shoulder harness as much as he should have. There was enough slack for him to be lifted from his seat and pressed against the canopy; and he couldn't reach the rudders to effect a recovery. They were descending at a terrific rate; being helpless to do anything else, he ordered, "Bail Out!" They both reached down to the seat ejection handles, pulled them up one notch, and "wham!"—the canopy blew away. One more notch and they were violently propelled out of the aircraft, into the very cold wind. Fortunately, the chutes opened just like they were supposed to. Pop said it would have been a very pleasant experience floating over the countryside, with a billowing canopy of white holding him aloft, except that his hard plastic ear-plug container, attached to a zipper on his flight suit, had been under the parachute harness when he ejected. It had caught just right in between his ribs, and in the shock of the chute opening had separated them, causing excruciating pain. He spent quite some time in the hospital; in fact, we were his first students since returning to work. I now understood why he was so adamant about having our seat belts and harnesses tight.

The flying was really more fun than work. We were split into two groups; one flew mornings, the other afternoons. Later on, we would switch periods. Mornings were best, because most every afternoon, thunderstorms would come up and make us come down early.

Here at Bainbridge, we even had time for social functions, i.e. chasing girls. We were given open post on Saturdays and Sundays. We could come and go as we wished, unless of course we had tours to march. Not a common thing at primary, thank Heaven. I discovered that if I were to join the base glee club, I could have Friday nights off also. Singing was OK—the chance for another night on the town was even better. It wasn't too long before I met a girl named Shirley Foster, who was introduced to me by our dispatcher, Ome

Dillard. Most of my free time from then until I left, was taken up by this gal.

One bright and beautiful early summer day, I took off solo in my "Tweety Bird" (T-37). The traffic pattern happened to go over town that day. I had at least ninety hours of flying time by now; I was the "Ace of the Base," or so I thought. I picked out Shirley's house, lowered the nose, and buzzed the heck out of it. I pulled up and did an aileron roll, which would have been fine, except for one thing. I looked up at the ground as I went through inverted, and said to myself, "What am I doing here?" I was low, really low, and in that moment's hesitation, I allowed the nose to come down; I panicked. I threw the stick to the right as hard as I could, and simultaneously jerked it full back. I blacked out. As I regained consciousness, for a second I thought I had gone blind. My sun visor in my helmet had been up—the "G" forces had pulled it down and locked

Party at the Cadet Club at Bainbridge AB. L. to R.: Jim Stoveken, Pop Evans, Bruce Holmes, and Author.

Author 61-E

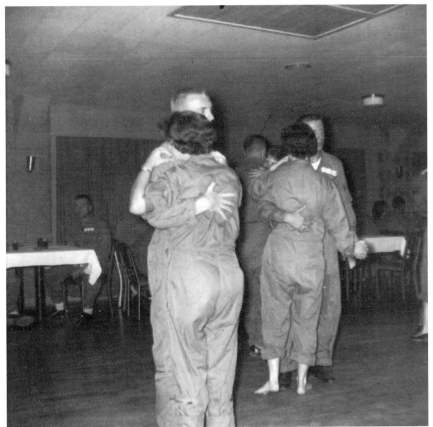

Flight suit dance at the Cadet Club, Bainbridge A.B.   Jim MacAfee 61-E

wasn't even home when I went by. What a bummer.

All during my time in training I wrote letters home. Some of them are in the following pages.

10 June 1960

Dear Dad and Mom,

Would have written sooner but waiting to hear if you are coming down for graduation, whether or not Shirley comes up. Omie (flight dispatcher) said can fly from Atlanta, Georgia. to New York for $33.00, by jet yet. Suggest you look into it, should be same coming the other way. Atlanta is about 150 miles due north of here. You could get on a train or bus (maybe taxi, ha! ha!) and come in someplace around here. Speaking of Omie, she went to the hospital about two weeks ago for a small operation. Came home and got the mumps. Still isn't back to work. She lives on Lee St. and the address is ...

I just came back from the flt. Surgeon. I've got some kind of infection causing something like boils on my legs. Doc gave me some pills and ointment. Said it seems people are more susceptible to skin infections here. Doesn't know why.

I've got my instrument check on Tue. (14 June). Is supposed to be my hardest flight check. Also have my weather final. Going to be a rough day.

Have about 75 hrs. total time so far. Only 25 hrs. to go. Got three excellent's in Link so far. Flying in airplane not as good.

Will be all through with academics next Thursday. if I pass my weather final. (Going to be a tough one).

Poppa's boy is doing good, went fishing last week. Appreciate card very much.

(11 June) I lost question and answer sheet. Sorry. Went to see Doc today about infection on my legs. Said he thought were boils, but doesn't think

it. I raised my visor and looked at the accelerometer. It showed 9.5 "G's." Now I was scared! I had way over stressed the airplane. In fact, the wings had buckles in them that I don't think were there when I took off. If I were caught, I was sure to be kicked out. It's amazing the dumb things we do when we are young (sometimes even when we are older). If God didn't look after young pilots, we never would live to be old ones. What was one to do? I very gingerly flew the rest of the period, and came back to the base making as smooth a landing as possible. After shut-down I got out the old 781 (maintenance log) and proceeded to write the airplane up for one "G" over the maximum limit of six (I think that was max). Hey I was a little crazy, but not stupid. That evening I called my girlfriend to see if she was suitably impressed. Her mother answered the phone and said, in her slow southern drawl, "Errol, don't you evah do that ahgain! Ah just walked in the house when there was this terrible roar—liked to scared me to death." Shirley

so now. Believe more like impetigo. Are large red spots with swelling and puss in center. They are starting to bleed. He gave me some more pills and salve. Hope will cure it. Are quite painful. Tonight is Friday but decided to stay home for a change. Am very tired. Will get my inst. check on Monday morning, Pop tells me. Can't have too rough a weekend.

Love, Errol

The very next weekend the base was having an open house. I was stuck on one of the T-37's to answer all the "interesting" questions asked by the local folk. One young man, about twelve, said to me, "Last week one of these here things like to took the top out of our pear trees!" Oh, boy. Of all the people to tell that to. They were looking for the instructor who did that roll the entire time that I was there.

I guess this event really brought home the idea that I could be killed flying these things. Up until then it was all fun and games (the flying, that is). I must have really been disturbed more than I remember, as my mother, some years later, gave me a drawing I had sent her, that I had drawn during that time. I didn't really remember it, but she did. It's really gross. Very well done (if I do say so) but also very morose. I thought that I was the only one who was thinking I would be killed during that time. Thirty-five years later I mentioned it to Jim Tassie (one of my classmates) and he said he also had such thoughts; perhaps we all did.

One sunny June day, I was out on the flight-line, preflighting an airplane, and I noticed that the T-37

on final looked different. As it got closer, I realized it had no canopy. I had never seen a convertible model before. I later found out that Rick Sack in my under class, 61-F, was doing the "forbidden" maneuver, solo spins. Sure 'nuf, it didn't come out, so in preparation for bailing out, he pulled the ejection seat handles up to the first notch, which blew the canopy. Lo and behold, the change of airflow caused it to come out of the spin. (Maybe they should modify all of them.) I can imagine what that Cadet was thinking: "Hot dog, I saved the airplane! But how am I going to explain the missing canopy?" Discretion being the better part of valor, he brought

T-37 on the ramp at Bainbridge AB   Jim MacAfee 61-E

it back. He was either really brave (the seat was now armed, and a shock, like a hard landing, could have set it off), or more scared of coming down in a parachute; I don't know which. I think he was given the dreaded "CA" (commanders award) it was defi-

36

nitely no honor. It was 72 tours, Yuck!

15 June 1960, 21:30

Dear Dad and Mom,

So how's by you? By me is OK, except for these boils. Have about six, one on my butt. Much painful. Doc is giving me penicillin and I took a blood test today. Still don't know what the trouble is. Sure hope they clear up soon—are really a mess.

Had no trouble on my instrument final. Had a mild case of checkites, went away after got airborne. I haven't got my grade slip on it yet. They are always slow on final slips. Should have gotten a good at least. I think I gave him a good ride. Only trouble I had was when the Omni went 180-degrees out of phase. I'm the Omni expert around here and I thought I had run into a situation I couldn't figure out. Wasn't my fault though, indicator was at fault.

Going to take the "Blue Goose" ('57 Plymouth, as Jack calls it), down to the hobby shop tomorrow, and try to get ready to go home. Have to take out the radiator and solder it, change the left rear tire (have to have it recapped when I come home), grease, oil change, filter change, wash, clean, and polish. Will probably take till time to go home to get it all done. Have either morning or afternoon off now, so will have time.

As I said in my last letter, Atlanta is best place to fly into. Graduation is supposed to be the 15th, still not definite. Shirley and parents would like you to come down on the 10th and stay a few days. Rest would probably do you good. Can have my car when here. Well, all the room and news for now.(Have 81 hrs., only one more check ride; is final check).

Love, Errol

In the following letters you will see that my mother sent me questions to answer; it was the only way she could keep up. I was much too busy to do much writing. I felt obligated to fill out the answers.

Q: How's the instrument checkout? Do OK?

A: Got by it OK. Think I got a good. Will tell you score when I get it.

Q: How's the night flying?

A: All through except for my day-night.

Q: Any honorary rank yet? Maybe Col.?

A: Negative, a private I am and will stay.

Q: How's the weather down your way? Temp?

A: Still very warm. Cold front has passed, so perhaps will cool off some. Today was 94-degrees.

Q: How's the weather course coming?

A: All through. Got 83 on final and 81 course average. All through with academics except for a military class now and then.

Q: How's Shirley doing in school? Senior?

A: Is through with junior year, is senior.

Q: Get the map from GA to Hope from Sunoco yet?

A: Negative on the maps.

The only time that I ever played any golf was during my tenure at Bainbridge. We had a beautiful course, and clubs could be rented for a very small fee. After two or three rounds, I realized I would rather shoot guns than golf balls; besides, I was much better with the guns.

26 June 1960

Dear Dad and Mom,

Have Omie's angel all cut out and put together. She is supposed to take it apart and Woodlife it so that it will be ready to paint. Came our pretty good. Borrowed a Craftsman saber saw from one of our instructors to cut it out. Workshop would have cut time in half. Still can't beat Pop's tools. (My father is a carpenter).

Room is in normal weekend mess. Got my side straightened up pretty well. Jack's (John McNea—washed out at Vance) still trying to dig out from under the wreckage.

Was thinking perhaps you could come down on Friday before graduation. Our graduation dance and banquet are that night. As for time—flight arriving at 09:21 is fine. If I can't get there I know Mrs. Foster or Shirley would be glad to pick you up. I'll leave the day up to you. Let me know whether Fri., Sat., Sun., Mon, etc.

Mr. Foster smokes Marlboro's. By the way, what size dress do you wear?

Think of some ideas on how to pack my stuff. Think we need a house trailer.

Please send, or bring your recipe for spaghetti, iced tea, and pizza pie. Mrs. Foster would like to learn about Yankee cooking.

Shirley says to say Hey! Also Mrs., Omie, Carol, etc..

Guess that's all for now. Oh, by the way, is there anyone who wants any fireworks or watermelons? Can get both here. Only 18 days as of Monday.

Lots of Love, Errol

We were to graduate from primary on July 18, 1960. My mother flew down from Jersey several days before. She said when she arrived at Bainbridge "International", she thought the pilot must have landed at the wrong place. It was a narrow, short runway, surrounded by grass and pine trees—not even a terminal. When they taxied in, it was on the grass; I guess the city couldn't even afford a paved ramp during those years. But when she saw the old blue Plymouth, she knew this must be the place. I had arranged to have her stay at Shirley's house. North meets South. My mother was (and still is) a person who will do almost anything to bring or send some favorite food to anyone who would appreciate it. This time she had brought all the fixin's for an honest-to-goodness northern pizza. I don't know how she kept all that stuff from spoiling. Anyway, she built the pizza, and Shirley's mother, being from the old South, fussed over getting the table set just right, drinks in order, napkins properly folded, etc.. By the time she was through, the pizza was cold. We ate it anyhow. Shirley's mother said, "This pizza is really good"; big mouth me said, "You should try it when it's hot." So much for "Yankee" diplomacy.

Hot dog, graduation day! We all dressed in our tans, officer hats, and of course, white gloves, and proceeded to the flight line for the parade. We marched, saluted, eyed right, etc., all over the place, much to the delight of all the family and friends at this gathering. Then we were called to the reviewing platform, one by one, and given our certificates of completion. Phase two had ended. One more to go. On the back of my ATC form 266 (flying grade sheet) is a typed inscription: ***It is recommended that this student be continued in the Pilot Training Program.*** Signed: Henry R. Evans, Civilian Instructor. I'm mighty proud of that.

After the ceremonies, I picked up my already-packed baggage, then loaded it along with my mother's bags in my old Plymouth. There was another Cadet who needed a ride north and as soon as he loaded up, we all jumped in for the drive home. We drove through the night, switching drivers. After dropping the other Cadet off in Annapolis, Maryland, Mom and I pressed on home. It took a total of twenty-four hours or so to drive the entire distance. We were beat; but it sure was good to be home again—but only for a very short time. I had to be at Vance AFB, in Enid, Oklahoma, by July 26th.

After our class left primary, 61-F became the upper class. Down at another primary base named Bartow AB in Florida, A/C Mike Larkin had been spending much of his time touring the ramp. He finally walked off all of his tours, just in time to go to a dance on Saturday. There was only one small problem—he had exceeded his weekly number of demerits by one half of a demerit, which meant that technically he was restricted to base. To make matters worse, there was a gal he had met from New Hampshire with a nice chest (as he put it) that he really wanted to take to that dance. He reasoned, what the heck, who's gonna know. As he and the young lady were wheeling around the dance floor, who does Mike come face-to-face with but the dreaded Tac Officer; Captain Donald G. Harris. Mike and his girl quickly whirled away; he was hoping against hope that Harris hadn't seen him. Bright and early on Monday morning, a message was sent to A/C Larkin to report immediately to the Tac Officer. Uh-oh, trouble ahead! Not to elaborate unnecessarily, Cadet Larkin was kicked out of the program.

Two weeks later the base commander sent word that he would like to review Larkin's case. A/C Larkin went post-haste to the Colonel's office. He poured his heart out with all the reasons why he should be allowed to come back into the program. The Colonel said, "Mister Larkin, your class did an outstanding job several months ago helping to raise money for projects on this base. I owe your class a favor. Tell you what: I will contact your Cadet class officers and offer them either a three-day pass for your entire class, or they can have you back. You're dismissed." Mike went back to the barracks with a heavy heart. He was liked fairly well by the rest of the guys, but he was far from the fair-haired favorite. He couldn't blame the guys for choosing the pass. Heck, he might do the same thing if the situation were reversed. The next day the Cadet commander and his adjutant came to his room. The Commander said, "Mike, you broke the honor code when you left the base when you were restricted. However, any of us probably would have taken the same chance, not that that, is any excuse; I hope you have learned your lesson. We all voted to bring you back." To say the least, there was one happy camper in that barracks.

I have since told this story to several people. All but one chose to take the three-day-pass. We Cadets as a group, had more character and loyalty than most, we have always been one-for-all and all-for-one. And as I said to one young man to whom I told this story; "This is the kind of men that I trained with, and this is the kind of man you should be when you grow up."

Our class was divided between two basic training bases; Vance AFB, in Enid, Oklahoma, and Reese AFB, in Lubbock, Texas. Not wanting to waste any of my precious travel time, I waited until the 24th to leave. I had been up rather late the night before. (Not my fault, the girls liked the uniform). The next morning I left very early (yawn) and drove alone until I picked up Jim McAfee at Newark, Ohio,

some ten hours away. It was murder. I bounced along the Pennsylvania turnpike doing all I could to stay awake. I sang, turned the radio up loud, even rolled down the window, and stuck my face out into what had now become rain. At times it seemed as though I would never make it. Boy, was I ever glad to see Mac. We just took time to load his gear, and off we went. I was in the back asleep by the time we were on the highway. It's a good thing we do things like this when we are young. At least this trip was uneventful. We didn't even have an on-board fire. Good thing, I didn't have any milk.

BASIC AT VANCE AFB

Vance was as *un*-country club as it could be. It was pure military. We drove to the entrance and were greeted by the usual Air Force style sign, "Welcome to Vance AFB, Headquarters of the 3575th Pilot Training Wing"; But this place had an AP in a guard shack. We had to sign in and get a temporary permit to enter the base—on to the HQ, sign in there, get our barrack's assignment, sticker for the car, etc. Instead of tall, cool, pine trees, we were in an almost treeless, flat, hot prairie. The barrack's were straight out of a WWII movie—long wooden buildings, covered with at least twenty coats of paint. The weather was hotter than the hammers of Hell! We parked the car at the closest parking lot to our barracks, grabbed our "stuff," and climbed the several steps into the building. What a bummer. One long hallway, with rooms on each side, and two bunks to each room. I thought it was time travel back to 1943. The "john" was a real sight. At our last "residence" we had one tile bathroom (complete with shower) between each pair of rooms—four men shared it. This was just like *No Time for Sergeants*. All the "johns" were lined up around the wall, about ten of them, and one large shower for the whole barracks. We have to live here for six months? Yuck! As it turned out, the barracks were the least of our problems. We were back in the regular Air Force. It seemed like we had been at college for the last six-

3576th HQ sign at Vance AFB, Enid, Oklahoma.   Jim MacAfee 61-E

Food is OK, not too bad. Also, can eat anything or any <u>way</u> we please.

Town here looks OK. Just hope I don't get on tour ramp, so I can get into town on weekends. That will make it a little easier to put up with. It's going to be a <u>very rough</u> six months.

Graduation date is 27 January. Sure hope can hold out that long. Heat is really bad. Also for one week have to get up at four o'clock in the morning. Next week is 06:20; we alternate every other week. Four o'clock really is going to come quick.

Address is just one to get stuff to me. Not any box number yet. Will send box number when I can. Going to be very busy here. Well, guess that's all for now.

Love, Errol

months; this place was very much like going back to Lackland. A real bummer.

26 July 1960

Hi folks,

Boy this is some place. Really "Hell!" It's hot, humid, and miserable. The military part of the training is a real pain, or so they say. Haven't done anything yet. Have an S.M.I. on Saturday (Saturday Morning Inspection).

Barracks are lousy. They are basic airmen's barracks with rooms built into them. Really are lousy and <u>hot</u>! Latrine is really bad. Like a pigpen. Nothing here is air-conditioned. Going to be rough in class. Have no refrigerator. Only things that will keep, or can be eaten up quickly.

Upper class don't seem to give us any trouble. Only military.

The upper class (61-D, B and C) were all over us again. We did "pick-pick," endured inspections, marched everywhere, and once again were victims to the dreaded TAC officers. I guess this was all part of the plan. Tear 'um down, build 'um up, tear 'um down. It must have worked, but it wasn't pretty, especially when you were the one being torn.

We were back to marching and singing everywhere we went. Our first time at the flight line we did the usual, formed up, marched the half mile or so in the blazing sun, endured an inspection, in the same hot sun, then were dismissed to go to our line shack. We were now two to a table; the attrition rate was high. Our instructors were all Air Force officers—no civilians. Although military courtesy, saluting, coming to attention, etc., were observed, at least it was not the "me master, you slave" thing. These guys were pilots; their job was to turn out a finished pilot (is there such a thing?) and that's what they proceeded to do. My first instructor was Lt. Jim Kinney. He was transferred out about half way through (were we that bad?), and Lt. George H. Albrecht (Gus) took over the task of teaching Jim Tassie and I to fly the "T-Bird" (T-33). Gus was a real-world sort of guy. He never was upset by anything. He flew F-86's in Korea. I guess teaching a couple of young Cadets was an anticlimax, although we did our best to keep it interesting. He was always going to show me how to split-s down to the traffic pattern; don't recall ever doing it though. Gus was killed in Vietnam.

Old barracks at Vance AFB A/C Jay Brewer shaking out his dust cloth. Author 61-E

Our day started in the predawn darkness (I

Devil Flight, marching to the flight line, at Vance AFB   Larry Pullen 61-E

41

never did get used to getting up so early); we

Vance AFB, Lt. Gus Albrecht standing, Author on the wing, A/C Jim Tassie kneeling.   Russ Fleer 61-E

marched over to the chow hall, downed the grub, went back to the barracks, did the three S's, then marched to class, or to the flight line, depending on which period we were flying. Our academics continued to be difficult. We had the following subjects: Aviation Physiology 9 hrs., T-33 Engineering 22 hrs., Flight Planning 34 hrs., Weather 33 hrs., Flight Operations 35 hrs., USAF Instrument Examination 5 hrs., Survival 26 hrs., Flying Safety 3 hrs., Celestial Navigation 24 hrs., and Nuclear Weapons Delivery Phase 1. 17 hrs. On the military side was the following: Drills, Ceremonies and Inspections 55 hrs., Leadership Responsibilities 14 hrs., Career Development 10 hrs., Communicative Skills 8 hrs., Physical Tng. (conditioning) 17 hrs., and Physical Tng. (Supervised Sports) 40 hrs. The difference between primary physical training and basic was remarkable. In primary it was, "Hell" here it was mostly fun and games. I still really wonder about only 3 hrs. of flying safety; no wonder we were so careless.

On weekends while we were under class, we were pressed into doing the usual Cadet things; polishing floors, cleaning johns, etc. After a month or so, the upper class backed off a bit, and we even got to go to town. Of course the TAC officers didn't back off. We were always getting surprise inspections. The tour ramp was very active these days, not like good old Bainbridge.

In many of the letters that I wrote home, I mentioned how my memory was so bad. It's no wonder, our day started at 4:00 a.m. for one week, and 6:20 a.m. the next, and back to 4:00 a.m. the following week,

T-33 on the ramp at Vance AFB, notice the WWII Aviation Cadet insignia on the hangar.   Author 61-E

and so on. Our days ended at 10:00 p.m.. That meant that our typical work day was from sixteen to eighteen hours long. Along with the daily pressures of all we were learning I'm surprised I could even remember my name.

My first ride (called dollar) in the T-Bird was with our flight commander, Captain James L. Lamar. We often flew with someone other than our assigned instructor. We took off and climbed to the amazing altitude of 35,000'. The training syllabus said we were to be taken to "high" altitude on our first ride. It was kind of neat—I hadn't been that high before. I didn't know then that one day that would be a normal cruising altitude for the airliners I was to fly in the future.

3 August 1960

Hi folks,

Just a line or two to let you know I'm still alive.

Had my first ride in the T-33 today. Nice airplane. Has aileron boost, similar to power steering in a car. Real sensitive. Seems to be only problem, outside of learning all the procedures. Flew with Captain Lamar (Flt. Comm.) today. He said I shouldn't have any trouble. Said I did real good, as was only first time I've flown a '33.

Please send my auto insurance policy, notarized statement from Dad saying I can have the car here, and am allowed to have it. Need it cause car is in his name. Need insurance policy also for registration on base. Really a lot of rigamarole. Also need my college transcript. Please send my auto stuff A.S.A.P.. Need it immediately to register car. Well, all the room for now.

Love, Errol

The first time I made a takeoff in this bird, I couldn't stop from wagging the wings. You could tell who was new to the airplane. They always waved at you. Just as the T-37 had power steering to the nose wheel, the T-Bird, had it to the ailerons. After a few hours we got used to it. This airplane had another strange characteristic; it not only had no

power steering to the nose wheel, it had no nose wheel steering at all. The only way to steer it on the ground was to use the right or left brake to turn the full castoring nose wheel. It worked OK, most of the time; however, too tight a turn, and bingo, cocked nose wheel (wheel at 90-degrees).

4 August 1960

Dear Dad and Mom,

Sure is hot here still. Have to take at least one shower a day, usually two, and could still use more. Have 2:40 total '33 time. It's a nice airplane. Is very complicated, very much like a "Rube Goldberg." Have gotten G on both my rides so far. Instructors seem to think I will be all right. My instructor is an ex-F-86 fighter pilot. He is a very good pilot. Can really fly. His name is 1/Lt. Jack Kenny. Seems like an OK chap, although I haven't really gotten to know him real well.

Have Friday afternoon off; hope we have it to ourselves and don't have to cut grass or some stupid thing like that.

Glad you got a vacuum, bet it is real nice. Hope you have real good luck with it.

Well, all for now. Have another S.M.I. and Open Ranks inspection on Saturday. Good Lord blessed me last week, no demerits. Afraid this week will be worse. Hope not, as I have an aversion to the tour ramp. Oh well, good Lord willing, I'll be OK.

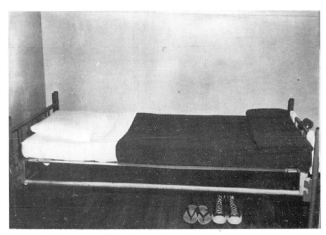

White collar bed required for the Saturday Morning Inspection. (S.M.I.)   Martin Buckley 61-E

Love, Errol

Q: Who is your room mate?

A: McAfee, the one who drove out with me.

Q: Want any food yet? What kind?

A: Only thing could send would be something like chocolate chip cookies.

Q: Receive Jockstraps in time? Receive package yet?

A: Roger on Jockstraps and package.

10 August 1960

Dear Mom and Dad,

So how's by you? By me is rear-end draggin'. Much tired. This is the 04:00 week. Really gets to you after awhile. Glad only two more days to this week. Had Aviation Physiology exam the other day. Got 83. Not as good as I thought I would get. Had Engineering mid-phase today, passed it but don't know for sure what grade is. Should also be about 83 or so.

Have 8:40 T-Bird time. Really a hard aircraft to fly. I can believe them when they say, "If you can fly and land a T-Bird, you can fly anything"—really a dog to land. Oh well, some day maybe will be OK. It's not really as bad as it sounds.

Weather here is much better. High was about 86 today. Gets real cool at night. Good sleeping, only not enough time for it. It's 07:30 now and still have shoes to shine and some studying to do, oh me—not enough time to do anything.

Well all for now.

Love, Errol

Q: Receive all the packages?

A: Roger, all came through OK. Please don't send any more civilian clothes. I know you mean well, but I don't have need for so many.

Q: Been on tour ramp? (we hope not).

A: Not yet, been lucky so far.

Q: Any town passes yet?

A: Yes, so far every Saturday afternoon and night, and all day Sunday.

Q: Need anymore black socks?

A: A few pair wouldn't hurt.

Q: Should I have some iron pills sent to you?

A: Negative, don't think I need them.

Q: Receive policy, etc., OK?

A: Rog', everything, still haven't had a chance to register car yet.

Q: How is you instructor?

A: OK, chews quite a bit. Having some difficulty flying. Should be OK. Expect to solo on Monday afternoon if all goes well.

Q: Want any cookies?

A: Yes, chocolate chip. (Not too many other things please).

17 August 1960

Dear Mom and Dad,

Will try to send a few lines out. Should be reading something, but don't feel like it, so will write a few lines.

Am playing "Oklahoma" on stereo now. One of the guys here has a few stereo records. Sound real good.

Flying going OK, still have some trouble, of course, but am coming along OK I guess. Will be getting my first check ride in about seven more hours. Probably next Tuesday, or Wednesday.

Monday will be one month down, five to go. There is a rumor that we will graduate just before Christmas. Would be nice if true. At any rate will get about fourteen days at Christmas.

Weather here is quite windy. Cloudy and a bit humid and hot right now. I was glad to find out that three weeks restriction-to-base rumor wasn't true. Also we can eat any way we please. Can read mail at table, hit each other, anything at all. Food is quite good. Can wear flight suit anyplace but headquarters or chapel.

I will have to take some pictures after I solo and show you what the well-dressed "Jet Jock" wears. Believe me, everyone here is a real Jock, and a gung-ho group. Have two patches on my flight suit and hat is red with 76 on front and lightning bolts on sides. Real snazzy, also gave us white and red checkered solo scarves. Helmet can also be decorated. Still have my "baby" on mine. Hope I can keep her. (Sexy girl drawn on tape by author at primary and stuck to back of his helmet). Will call on Sunday about two o'clock your time.

Love, Errol

Q: How are your boils?

A: Haven't had any lately, thank God.

Q: How many hours in?

A: 13:05

Q: How much time?

A: Would have soloed in 11:30. As is may solo tomorrow. Instructor said today that I have the ability, only need good weather.

Q: Landings improving?

A: Somewhat.

Q: Mid-Phase engineering grade?

A: 79, got 88 on final.

Q: Did you solo?

A: Supposed to have soloed on Monday, weather is still holding up solo. Clouds and poor visibility, also 30 kt. winds.

Q: Will you have alternating weeks of 4 a.m. rising the whole six months?

A: Roger. Next week is 4 a.m. week.

Q: Have you cut grass in time off?

A: Sometimes.

Q: How's "blue bird?" (also known as "blue goose")

A: Still haven't had muffler fixed nor adjusted valves.

Q: Met any cute "corn flowers" yet?

A: Women situation is much worse than at Bainbridge.

On the day of my first solo in the T-33, Lt. Kinney and I flew half-an-hour or so, came in and made a full-stop landing. We taxied to the ramp,

Tour ramp at Vance AFB   Vance AFB H.O.

45

and he said, "Let's see you take it around one time, And don't cock the nose wheel!" Then he climbed out. There I was, in an aircraft that not too many years ago was a front-line fighter, fixing to go it alone. Hot dog! I held short of the runway as per mobile's instructions. I was in front of a four-ship formation. "Devil 25, cleared for takeoff." (our flight was called "Devil Flight"). I gave it a shot of power, tapped the right brake to turn, damn, I cocked the nose wheel. There I was alone on a very busy runway, holding up a four-ship formation, with my nose wheel pointing at the ramp, and the rest of the plane pointing down the runway. The procedure to rectify this mistake was to run up the power and pump both brakes simultaneously, causing the nose to bounce, which would result in the wheel eventually straightening out. I gave it a large shot of power, pumped the brakes—I was moving. The only problem was I was moving toward the grass. I gave it even more power, hit the left brake, and it started turning; off I went, a nice semicircle turn, and then straight down the runway. Was I ever glad to get in the air. (So were the guys in the formation, as one of them reminded me some years later—he had been in the lead ship).

23 August 1960

Dear Dad and Mom,

Sorry didn't get to talk to you on Sunday. I forgot you were going out. I really don't pay much attention to dates, except 25 December, and 27 January.

Is quite hot here. Hope it's 95-degrees today. If it is then we don't have to go to retreat. Retreat here is a real mess. It's in class-A bush jackets. They are really hot.

Tell Papa I'm sorry I didn't say anything about his letter. I really did appreciate it and also the one

or two I got at primary. I'm very forgetful. Have a few things on my mind here, so please accept my apology.

Have 18:55 total T-Bird time. Will have my transition check ride on Friday, or Tuesday. Will be my first flight check ride here. Don't anticipate any trouble. Will probably be starting formation next week, and they tell me this is very difficult. Oh well, so are a lot of other things.

Have a leadership final tomorrow. Sure hope I can guess well enough to pass it. I really don't know very much about it. I like technical subjects much better, they're not quite so dry. Well, all for now.

Love, Errol

We were learning some new skills—one of them was formation flying. I was with Lt. Kinney

Author after his solo T-33 flight at Vance AFB.   Author 61-E

in a two-ship formation. We were number two, he was flying, tucked in tight on the lead ship's right wing. He said, "You've got it." "OK," I said, then the strangest thing happened; the other ship started going all over the sky. I was pushing, pulling, right rudder, left rudder, more power, less power, whew! The temperature was cool in the cockpit, but I was sweating. After a few minutes of these wild gyrations, the instructor took over again. Amazing, Lead settled right down. Formation was the most difficult thing for me personally to master.

In-flight formation at Vance AFB performing a crossover. Author 61-E

31 August 1960

Dear Mom and Dad,

Have had my final transition check. Had it on Monday. Was supposed to be a normal instruction ride with Major Yates. About half way through the ride, he said he would call it an E-6 (check ride) if my next two landings were as good as previous. So got an 89—Good. Funny thing was that it wasn't supposed to be a check ride. He gave me a choice of an above average score on this ride, or waiting and taking a scheduled check ride with the possibility of overall excellent. Decided may have a bad day next time so one in the hand opposed to two in

the bush, etc.

Have started some instruments—today will possibly fly my first formation ride (such fun?).

Yesterday we had one go in. Student and instructor OK. Airplane was totaled. Happened on takeoff. Really very lucky to be alive, let alone not hurt. Lost power on takeoff and dropped in the dirt off the side of runway. Airplane really a mess.

Am writing on the commode. Continuing yesterday's letter. Flew my first formation ride—good grief! It is really rough. I only flew about two minutes during entire flight. I couldn't hold that thing in position for beans. It is really hard. Right now looks impossible, but I think will be OK after I get used to it.

So far we have lost four men (S.I.E.) and two look like they are going out on flying deficiency. One of them is Jack McNea. Feel really bad for him.

Today I will probably go up on another formation ride. Should be fun. Lt. Kenny got some good laughs yesterday. Enclosed is this month's flying pay. Must close as want to get this out this morning. (Have 22:00 hrs. total).

Love, Errol

The next weekend I was driving into town on a stretch of four lane road, when I got the idea to practice formation on the other cars. They probably thought I was some kind of nut. But it worked. I could finally visualize what I was trying to do. After that, it became fun. Except for a few times, like when I was solo, and the lead ship, in a two-ship formation, and Lt. Wingo was in the number two ship with one of our German students. We broke formation so he could practice his "join-up" on me. I'm up there in a nice gentle right bank, looking back and to my right, and I see this plane coming at me like it's *shot from guns*; at that moment I would like to have been somewhere else. I felt like a target ship. The next thing I know, (things happen fast at almost 300 kts.) I'm looking straight up at the other airplane, which is inverted about three feet above my canopy. Their inertia carried them right on passed me. Boy, was I ever glad to be alive! I joined up on them and we went home. You might think ol' Wingo was dangerous; well, not exactly, but a hot shot, you bet. On another day, I was number four in a four-ship formation, and lead was, that's right, Wingo. We were in a V, and I was on his left. It was a beautiful day, the air was smooth, all was right with the world. That is, until I noticed we were getting lower and lower (wing men just follow where ever "Lead" goes); now we were really low, like about 100' (good thing Oklahoma is mostly flat). Out of the corner of my eye, I saw a building dead ahead. I was a bit nervous. But no need, we probably cleared it by thirty feet or so, or should I say, Lead cleared by that amount; I was stacked down (progressively lower). When we got back to the ready room, Lt. Wingo came up to me and chewed me out for not keeping my eyes on Lead. He could see my eyes glancing at the upcoming obstacle. That's how close a formation we flew.

T-33 formation takeoff at Vance AFB   Author 61-E

20 September 1960

Dear Mom and Dad,

Well here I am again, just had a real wild thunderstorm go through. Made much noise and rain. Wish it had come when it could have gotten us out of something, like around 04:00, it could have let us go back to bed and sleep till around 07:00. No such luck. Was mostly a waste, didn't get us out of anything, darn it.

I was thinking today about how much time we put in every day. This week is around eighteen hours per day. Next week will be sixteen hours per day. Is heap much time to work. Wish could collect overtime. Would make a real pile of money.

Just finished polishing our floor. Looks better than it ever has since we've been here. We are going to move into the new airmen's barracks around the first of October. They are new brick buildings. Much nicer than these old fire traps. Also start eating in the new airmen's dining hall. Will be a bit inconvenient until we actually move to the new barracks, but after that will be fine.

Had my final exam in Flight Planning yesterday. Got an 86. Also got an 86 on my mid-phase so naturally got an 86 average for the course.

Been flying instruments. Had two rides. No foreseeable trouble with them. Always been able to hack them OK.

The weather here will soon be getting colder.

Well, guess that's all from "Vance Tower to Severe Jet—Mom and Pop, over and out, will standby for further transmissions this station.

Love, Errol

Q: When do they usually get snow out your way? Was wondering about sending snow tires.

A: They tell me they don't get too much snow. It's possible I won't need them unless I go where there is a lot of snow.

Q: How far is Oklahoma City from Enid?

A: About 80 miles.

Q: Who is the girl from Chickasha, Oklahoma? How did you meet her? (Nosey Rosy asking).

A: Name is Kay Mason. Met her at the Y.W.C.A.. She is very nice and is going to school twelve miles north of Oklahoma City.

Q: Is that ladder necessary to get into T-33?

A: Heck yes! You could get in the rear seat without it by crawling up on the wing, but you need it to get into the front seat. It's eight or nine feet to the edge of the cockpit.

Q: How many hours? A: 35:00.

Q: How's formation flying coming?

A: Haven't flown any formation in over a week. Been flying instruments. Not doing too bad. Got an excellent on my link lesson today.

Q: How are you doing on you models?

A: Haven't even touched them. No place to work on them, and no place to display them.

Q: Did you get package?

A: Yes, thanks. Slipper-socks arrived fine. Much thanks for them and food. Have heaps and gobs of gum now, and plenty of food.

6 October 1960

Dear Dad and Mom,

Have been grounded all this week with a cold. Is really not too bad, but got an ear block on Monday, and I was grounded. Probably be able to fly tomorrow. Don't really feel bad, just tired as this is the 04:00 week.

Going to O.C. (Oklahoma City) this weekend.

Sure will be glad to see Christmas come this year. Be real nice to get home again.

Supposed to turn second-class on 14 October. Will mark halfway point.

We have class rings available here and cost from $40.00, to over $100. Gram Roberts wanted to get my high school ring, do you think this would do instead? Ask her and see what she says.

Don't have much else to say, and am very tired, so will sign off for now.

Love, Errol

Q: Have boils completely disappeared?

A: Yes, still have scars where they were though.

Q: What would you like for Christmas?

A: Don't know for sure. Been thinking about a 35 mm camera. Would be nice for aerial shots. Also thought a dark suit of the fall variety would be nice. Don't really like heavy winter ones. Saw a real nice "Peter Gunn" style here, was $55.00. Please give me your opinion. I would be willing to help with the cost.

Q: Are you keeping off the tour ramp?

A: So far I have. Don't know how long will keep it up though. Never know about these things.

Q: How many hours? A: 48:55.

Q: Anymore formation now?

A: Not yet. Will get some latter part of next week. Got an 83-G, in B-3 mid-phase formation check.

Q: Which best describes the T-Bird: Beautiful—Graceful—Lovely—Sleek?

Devil Flight at Vance AFB Back row L. to R.: Jim Tassie, Kurt Schreiner(Germany), Unknown, Earl Adams, Hugh Carron, Larry Culp, Jay Brewer, Errol Severe, Pete Hegseth, Bill Sitter, Fred Stone. Front row: Chuck Nettle, Larry Pullen, Blaine Corrick, Jim Wallace, Ken Vondrack, Jay Langhurst, and short and center: Jim Prah. Jim MacAfee 61-E

A: A lead sled, or super hog. Really not such an impressive aircraft, believe me.

Q: Do many have trouble with formation?

A: Yes, quite a few.

Q: How's formation going now?

A: OK, but not really terrific, is quite hard for me, too nervous I guess.

Q: How did you do on the Peer rating?

A: Don't know, haven't been counseled on it yet.

Q: How did you make out on the Flight Operations mid-phase exam?

A: Got an 81, not too good.

1 November 1960

Dear Folks,

Well, I bet you thought I'd skipped town. Not that I don't want to, but they won't let me.

Went to O.C. last weekend. Had a very nice time. Took this girl I had met previously to the Halloween party at Tinker AFB officer's club. Great party, really a nutty bunch. Met some real nice people there.

Have 62:40 hrs. and a new flight instructor—his name is Lt. George H. Albrecht (Gus). He's really very nice, and we can have a lot of fun with him. Biggest gripe I have is he has a habit of riding the controls. I told him about it but he doesn't realize he is doing it. He really loused up a landing on me yesterday. I knew we were way off, but with him riding on the controls I couldn't do anything about it so we hit kind of hard "Boom!"

Formation is coming quite well now. I'm starting to smooth out. Hope to have my final formation check this week if weather and everything else goes OK.

We had some pretty bad weather over the weekend and also last week. It's quite cold here now. Hope we get a good week of weather so I can get formation over with. Will then be ready to go right through instrument. Is much easier if you fly the same type mission every day.

Many thanks for the money for suit. I think it is <u>really</u> <u>nice</u>. Sure you will like it also.

Anything special you would like me to bring from out here? If so, let me know and will see what I can do. Am going to try to get a ride out of Tinker for Christmas as can't afford to pay both ways. Seems like good chance of a flight out of there to some place around home. It will save much money, only trouble is never know when one is going my way, so will have to wait and I never know when I will get there, but shouldn't be too bad.

Well all for now.

Love, Errol

Q: Have we met Bob Carlson?

A: No, he was at Spence AB for primary.

Q: What furniture is in your room?

A: Two desks, two chairs, two easy chairs, two floor lamps, two desk lamps, two beds, two dressers, two closets, one bathroom, etc.

Q: How many boxes of Christmas cards will you want?

A: One of the comic type would be fine.

On the night of November 4, 1960, I was assigned as C.Q. (Charge of Quarters). All I really had to do was answer the phone, and make a bed check after 22:00 to be sure all the good little Cadets were tucked safely in their bunks. At about 21:30, the phone rang; I picked it up and said, "3576th pilot training squadron, Aviation Cadet Severe speaking." The voice on the other end said, "Errol, this is Jim Grubb; Carter and I won't be back by lights out—would you sign us in?" Not wanting to incur the wrath of my upperclassmen (they were in 61-D), I replied, "Sure thing." I hung up the phone and proceeded to sign them in. No big deal, they were to graduate in three weeks; who's to know, I rationalized. The next morning, the whole corps was in an up-roar. I asked one of my classmates what was going on; he replied, "Grubb and Carter were in a car wreck last night, Carter's dead and Grubb broke his back." Oh no, what a shocking tragedy! I knew these two young men very well, and I was greatly saddened by the realization that they would never fulfill their dreams (Jim Grubb is in a wheel chair to this day). Suddenly I realized that I had signed them in. I figured I had, had it. Once they checked the sign in book, they would know I had falsified government records; I was sure to be kicked out. After several days of silently sweating it out, with nothing being said, I figured I was in the clear. Thank God, no one ever questioned how they had signed in while they were off the base.

After reading the newspaper account (on the following page) some thirty-five years later, the only thing I can figure out, is that since they had the accident after midnight, the brass must have thought that they had signed in, and then left for town again. All of these years have passed, and I just now found the article that was in a letter that I had sent my

Aviation Cadet Killed, One Injured In Wreck

This newspaper account, and the one following, were both printed together on the front page of the *Enid Morning News* on Saturday, November 5, 1960.

A one-car accident shortly after midnight Thursday just north of the Enid city limits killed one man and put another in a San Antonio, Texas hospital with a broken back.

Dead is aviation cadet Robert L. Carter, 22, Vance, whose home is Belton, Mo. Carter was pronounced dead of head injuries on arrival at an Enid hospital.

Aviation cadet James D. Grubb, 23, Squire, W. Va., believed to have been the driver of the car, is reported in critical condition. Grubb was first taken to St. Mary's hospital and was flown to Lackland Air Force Base hospital, San Antonio, Texas, shortly before noon Friday.

GRUBB

Oklahoma Highway Patrolman Don Patton said the car, a 1955 Jaguar, traveled out of control 235 feet before coming to a stop after throwing out both occupants.

He said the car was traveling at a high rate of speed and slid sideways 85 feet before hitting the island at Chestnut street.

Patton said the car went another 65 feet before turning over, then came to rest on its top another 85 away, still on the island.

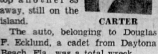

CARTER

The auto, belonging to Douglas F. Ecklund, a cadet from Daytona Beach, Fla., was a total wreck.

Services for Carter are pending at Brown Funeral Home.

ONE MAN LIVED AND ONE MAN DIED when this small English sports car went out of control early Friday morning and rolled over on North Van Buren north of the railroad overpass. The driver of the car was hospitalized with a broken back and the passenger was killed. Both were stationed at Vance AFB.

---

mother, in November, 1960.

As the following story relates, flying is inherently dangerous, and even more so when training is involved.

It was a cool and cloudy day on November 5, 1960. A pair of two-ship formations were scheduled to fly. One of the aircraft had a mechanical problem and had to be scrubbed. Plan "B" was put into effect, and it became one, three-ship formation. The lead aircraft was flown by A/C Francis Dings, in the front, or student seat, and Lt. Allan Lewis who was his instructor, in the back. The number two ship was flown by A/C James D. Howell, and his instructor, Lt. Martin Marquardt. The third ship was flown by A/C David L. Ferguson, and his instructor, Captain Fields. This was during the first part of formation training. The flight was from the 3575th P.T.S., our sister squadron at Vance. Lead taxied into position and held—number two pulled up off the left wing, and number three behind and to the right. "Hustler flight, cleared for takeoff," came the instructions from mobile control. "Rolling". Number one and number two went to full throttle, and in about 2,500 feet they lifted off into

JET TRAINER CRASH KILLS VANCE PILOTS

Inquiry Board Probes Debris For Crash Clues

Instructor, Student Victims Of Accident Friday Afternoon

TRAINER CRASHES—The tail section jutting out of the drainage ditch alongside South Enid Boulevard is almost the only recognizable piece of a Vance AFB T-33 jet trainer that crashed and burned Friday afternoon. Both occupants in the plane were killed.

A Vance Air Force Base T-33 jet trainer on a student formation training flight crashed and burned shortly after take-off yesterday afternoon, killing both pilots.

Dead are the instructor, First Lieutenant Alan P. Lewis, 25, 507 North Norwood street, Arlington, Va., and the student aviation cadet Francis J. Dings, 20, New Hartford, Conn. Both pilots, leading a three ship formation mission, were assigned to the 3575th Pilot Training Squadron at Vance.

Base spokesmen said until the crash occurred, everything about the flight was normal. After the impact in a drainage ditch beside a county road about two miles from the base, the aircraft remained relatively intact, according to base officials.

The base accident investigation board immediately moved the wreckage to the base for study, and began interviewing witnesses to the crash.

The plane, apparently off course, crashed about a quarter-mile northeast of the OG&E sub-station and less than a half-mile from the home of

Ding

Irvin Larkey. It landed just at the edge of a wheat field owned by Joe Traynor. The wreckage set fire to a pasture owned by Ben Blansit on the east side of the road, but the blaze was quickly extinguished.

Larkey's father, Charles Larkey, the only one home at the time of the crash, said he heard the plane come over just west of the farm, and "it was making a lot of rough...

53

the overcast sky. About fifteen seconds later, number three went to full power, and he too lifted off and joined on the right wing of Lead. The flight climbed through the overcast ceiling at 2,000 feet, turning toward the west and into the formation area. They broke out about 3,000 feet. All of the aircraft were full of fuel for the approximate, one-and-one-half-hour mission. Number Three said, "We have an up-lock problem; it will take a few minutes to correct. We have to cycle the gear, we'll break off till we've fixed the problem." "Roger, Hustler One; Roger, Hustler Two," was the reply. Hustler One climbed well above the number three ship, and since Three was slowed down, they started making practice gunnery passes on Hustler Three. Sweeping in from the left and under Three, the number One ship rolled up from the right of Three, and over the top of him. Ferguson, flying the number Three ship, looked up as Lead passed by at about twenty feet overhead inverted, canopy to canopy. He saw Dings sitting with his hands on the canopy rails—Lt. Lewis was obviously flying the aircraft. As number One passed off the left wing, now right side up, Ferguson, with the up-lock problem solved, went after them. He noticed he was having a hard time keeping in position, as the number One ship, now back in the lead position, didn't seem to be flying correctly. Down they went toward the cloud deck below; Ferguson being unable to hold his position on the other aircraft, passed off his right wing. Breaking through the overcast at 2,000 feet, and now near vertical, Ferguson thought, "Oklahoma is coming up too fast!" Hauling back on the stick, he came very, very close to being a part of the Oklahoma dirt. On the accelerometer, he had pulled about seven "G's." Ferguson and his instructor climbed back up above the overcast. None of the other ships were in sight, so they proceeded to the pre-briefed rendezvous spot expecting to rejoin the flight. Before they reached the spot, the radio came alive with mobile control calling all aircraft that were flying, by individual call sign. All checked in but Hustler One. The aircraft had crashed about two miles from the

base, on the edge of a wheat field owned by Joe Traynor. A/C Glenn W. Redmond, who was visiting in mobile control at the time, saw the column of black smoke rising into the air, and knew someone had lost an aircraft. After landing, Ferguson went to the crash scene, and from the shape of the crater, and position of the wreckage, it was evident that the aircraft had been in a flat spin. A flat spin is almost impossible to recover from, especially from such a low altitude. There was no time to eject. Both men were killed instantly. This event caused a new base policy. If your aircraft is out of control below 10,000 feet, eject! I didn't know Lt. Lewis, but Fran was a good friend, and I had known him since Lackland. He is missed by all who knew him.

22 November 1960

Dear Dad and Mom,

Well I made it back from the cross-country OK. Almost got stuck down in Sewart AFB in Tennessee. We had an oxygen leak and a fuel leak, but they fixed them both. Part of our trip back was at 40,000 feet. Had to let down after an hour or so as Tassie got the bends. Was OK after we let down. Reason we were so long before taking off at McGuire was we needed oxygen and their oxygen cart broke down. It took them a heck of a long time to get another one. About one hour and fifteen minutes to be exact.

Hope to have my 60-4 check next week. Sure will need the good Lord's help, as my instrument flying isn't too good. Did they put that I was home in the paper? Got the drawings from Lionel, he really did a very nice job.

Well all for now. Going to O.C. this weekend and check on flight home for Christmas.

Love, Errol

Night flying was another new experience. The first time I taxied out solo at night, I was totally confused by the blue taxi lights. I thought I never would find the runway. Flying at night by yourself over the flat Oklahoma prairie can become a mind game. Looking up at the stars looked just like the lights from the houses scattered below. With no moon, it's possible to not know which way is up. I was mighty glad for the instruments. After several trips around the pattern, and several landings, I started to feel much more comfortable. It seemed I could do no wrong. Every landing was a "grease job." Once in a blue moon everything just seems to go "Serria Hotel.".3 I didn't think anyone noticed my landings; after all, it was pitch black. When I had finished my flight period, as I came into the

Have had all weekend off. I was off from Wednesday night until tonight at 22:00. Nice to be off, but it cost too much to eat out and run around. It's also very boring at times.

What can I get you-all for Christmas? I don't want to hear the "you don't have to" bit; I want some specific items, you know 1.-2.-3., etc. OK?

I really don't know what to get so Mom—you tell on Pop, and Pop—you tell on Mom.

Expect a cold front through here at anytime.

New (in 1960) barracks at Vance AFB. We lived in this building for several months before graduation. Vance AFB H.O.

line shack, and started putting my gear up, the assistant flight commander, Captain John M. Vowell, came in. He asked if I was "Devil 4." I replied, "Yes Sir." (I thought I must have messed up somehow). "Fine landings," was all he said. Wow! A compliment from an instructor. That almost never happened. I fairly floated back to the barracks.

27 November 1960

Dear Mom and Dad,

Just finished eating a pot of soup. Didn't get out to eat, so cooked in. Clever huh?

Ol' thermometer will drop like crazy. It's 70-degrees now, and when front goes through it will drop 10-20-degrees in 5-10 minutes. Really a different place. One minute it's nice and warm, then zowie; you freeze.

Had a very nice Thanksgiving dinner at Lt. Albrecht's house. Had turkey, mashed potatoes, peas, salad, shrimp cocktail, olives, celery, carrots, etc.. Was topped off with pumpkin pie and whipped cream. Mrs. Albrecht is really nice, and an excellent cook.

Have only four rides to go in instruments, the

fifth is my 60-4 check. Need the good Lord's help to pass it, let alone get the excellent I want.

Don't expect to get out of here until the 22nd. I'm taking a gamble in the hop from Tinker. I only hope I'm lucky and get one out on the day I can leave, and don't have to wait.

Well, don't know what else to say so I'll sign off for now and write Aunt Ann. (Temperature is now 68, supposed to go down to 18 tonight).

Love, Errol

*Q: **When returning from your cross-country did you make it by 5:00 p.m.?***

A: Yes, had about 15 minutes to spare.

*Q: **Eat the sandwiches?***

A: Sure thing. Only lost one of them. Had them sitting on the wing when another '33 taxied past and his jet blast blew them about fifty feet. Managed to salvage all but one.

*Q: **Grade on cross-country?***

A: All goods, with a few excellent's. Instructor said I had excellent self-reliance. Means I'm independent I guess.

*Q: **Total hours now?** A: 94:00*

19 December 1960

Dear Mom and Dad,

So you almost had to get the snowshoes out, "eh wot?" Sure hope you have some snow left when I get home. A white Christmas would be real nice.

Have my new Christmas record "Holly and the Ivy" by the Morman Tabernacle Choir playing now. Is really beautiful.

Has warmed up considerably here. Had some snow a week or so ago. Was real pretty, about 1"-2".

My solo nav. to Reese AFB, at Lubbock, Texas, went real good. Got the flu right after I got back. Good thing not during flight.

Hope you like the box of stuff I sent. Sure glad it's not damaged.

Glad the shop is coming along so well. Sounds like Pop is building shops before breakfast between the snow flakes.

Well, all for now. Hope to see you on the 22nd, good Lord willing.

Love, Errol

*Q: **Total hours?** A: 109:45 T-33 time.*

*Q: **Celestial Navigation grade?** A: 83*

*Q: **Do you think you will come into McGuire or another Air Base?***

A: Don't have any idea. I could have gone to Mitchell AFB in NY today if I could have gotten off. It can be anywhere on the east coast.

*Q: **Will you call upon arrival or beforehand?***
A: I'll call on arrival most likely.

*Q: **How was weekend of 16th party, etc.***

A: Really wonderful in spite of the fact I've been sick since Thursday with intestinal flu. She (Beth) is really a fine girl.

*Q: **Receive soldering iron OK?***

A: Yes, thank you very much. I've already soldered the machine's wires (Blue Goose) and it's working fine.

*Q: **Move into new barracks yet?***

A: Yes, but I liked my previous single apartment much better. I still have a single room which is to my liking.

With about one month to go to graduation, we were all required to take another physical. I mean, really, we had a three-day physical before we were even allowed to take the written test for Cadets; then another one at Lackland during preflight, and now still another? In fourteen months, how much could our physical condition deteriorate? Oh well, ours was not to question "why," but only to "do or die." To most all of us, this was more of an inconvenience than anything else—all of us but one, that is. A/C James R. Prah, was very apprehensive. The Air Force said the minimum height was 5'4", and he was really only 5'3" tall. They were not exactly flexible on any rule or qualification. Jim, a very quiet, unassuming type person, with a profoundly dry sense of humor, was not his normal happy-go-lucky self the day of the exam. He had so far managed to escape being caught on the first two exams. On the first one, they had him back up to a wall with an inch scale on it. He crawled up that wall like a snake. He managed to be 5'5". On the next exam, he was wearing shoes, so he scooted up in them to a grand height of 5'4 1/2". This time, though, the flight surgeon had him take off his shoes and socks, and stand on the scale for a weight check. This is the type of scale that has a sliding height gauge on it. There was no way to cheat on this one. With some amazement, the doctor said to the nurse seated at the desk, who was writing down the information, "Hey, this guy's only 5'3"!" Jim's heart sank, the Jig was up—and with only one month to go. The doctor continued, "I'm sorry, but you just don't measure up. The Air Force says you have to be 5'4". There are no exceptions to the regulations; I'll have to recommend you be terminated immediately." The nurse, who obviously had quite a few years on the doctor, barely looked up as she said, "I'll just put down 5'4" and let's get on to the next one." And so they did. Whew, that was too close.

My favorite part of "Basic," was instrument flying. It probably was my favorite because that's what I did best (after a slow start). Lt. Albrecht thought I should really get a top grade on my final instrument check. The night before the check, I sat on my bunk and told myself over and over, "I must do great." I psyched myself up so much, I couldn't sleep. Needless to say, I turned in much less than a sterling performance the next day. Gus just couldn't understand it, neither could I. It was my worst case of "checkitis" ever.

Our instructors were as much a mixed bag as we were. We had Lt. Thomas B. Thompson, who, every Monday morning, would announce the "pro-tip of the week." Some little tidbit for we inexperienced guys, from the master (so he thought). And ol' Lt. Hollarn; he was nicknamed "Hollerin Hollarn," and was probably the most verbally abusive instructor we had—Just ask Russ Fleer. Then there was Captain Alfred C. Daniels. He was our only black instructor—a huge man—but very nice. He was assigned the only black student we had, a student officer from Ethiopia, named 2/Lt. Mengiste M. Tirfe. When he went on his solo cross-country, Captain Daniels said he would tie a ball of string on him so he wouldn't lose him. The English language had for the most part, eluded him, and his flying skills were a bit elusive also.

On the 25th of November 1960, Larry Pullen and I drove down to Oklahoma City (about eighty-miles distance) for the weekend. He was dating a girl there and she had fixed me up with a friend. I never did like blind dates, but as a favor, I went. I guess I'll never know just how "blind" she was, for I arrived at the appointed place, at the appointed hour, but she didn't. Oh well, it's a big town, there must be another girl somewhere in it. I was cruising around and came upon a sign that said, "YWCA Dance Tonight". Since nothing was pressing, and I still had the whole weekend ahead of me, I went on in. Little did I know what was about to happen. There was the normal goings on—a band (it played real music), guys on one side, girls on the other, and the large, "no man's land" in between. My keen steely-eyed gaze locked on the target—a tall, thin, beautiful blonde. She was there with her girl friend. It was time to lead, follow, or get out of the way. I put on my best Cadet smile, and pressed on across the dance floor. To make a long story short, we danced together all evening. When she found out I was a Cadet from Vance, she said her roommate in nurses' training, was married to a Cadet stationed there. "Uh-Oh. Cadets can't be married." "Oh, but they are" was the reply. I said I knew the guy, and she had better not tell anyone else. Bob Davy was in my under class, 61-F. No one ever did find out. (Earlier this year, 1996, I talked with Bob on the phone. He thanked me for not telling on him, and said he never would have graduated if I hadn't kept his secret.)

After the dance I asked if I could take her home, but since she had driven, that was somewhat of a problem—solution: "I'll follow you home. You can drop off your girlfriend, Carol (later to be Glenn Redmond's heart-throb) and we can leave from your house." Seemed like a good plan to her. I met mom and dad, who were somewhat puzzled that their daughter wanted to go out for pizza, with a guy she had just met. Besides, it was about ten o' clock at night. Beth won out. It was on this first "date," that I was to say something that I have not heard the end of to this day. At the restaurant, we ordered our pizza, and talked a great deal. It seemed like we had always known each other. I was really making points. Noticing that she had only eaten two slices of pizza, I said, "A big girl like you should be able

Beth Norton and Author at Downtown Airpark Oklahoma City   Larry Pullen 61-E

to eat more than that." Ouch! I meant "tall"—how to impress your date. We saw each other as much as possible during the next two months. She was the kind of girl you write home about. When we couldn't be together, I called, or wrote. It was love at first sight (or was it bite?).

When Beth and I met she was a student nurse

at O.U. School of Nursing in Oklahoma City. We started writing letters to each other immediately. Sometimes letters will tell of events much better than one can remember them, especially after so many years. They accurately convey events just as they happened. This first letter from Beth to me was written on Wednesday, 30 November. Read on and you will experience one of the fastest courtships on record, and they said it wouldn't last.

Wednesday, 30 November 1960

Hi,

Well, by some miracle, they assigned my working day to Friday. So If you still want to do something Saturday night, I would be able to.

I don't really have anything else to say, since I hardly know you. I feel rather strange writing to you.

I don't know if you remembered my home phone number or not. It's GA-7-9828. I'll probably be home Saturday, if not my phone number at school is GE-9-9397. Here's hoping I see you.

> *Sincerely,*
> *Beth*

After some phone conversations this was my letter to Beth.

5 December 1960, 08:32

Hello Blondie,

They have given us a few minutes off this morning so thought I would devote them to you. Now aren't I sweet? (don't answer that; just agree).

Needless to say, I had a very enjoyable weekend. I certainly hope you did also. I got the feeling Sunday that you thought I didn't want to be with you. Please, Beth, don't think that. I wanted to be with you _very_ much. Now that you have had time to think about the weekend I hope you still feel the same way about me. I realize things happened extremely fast, but I'm very glad they did, are you?

I hope I can see you this coming weekend, as I will be going home soon and won't be able to see you for two weeks. Then I'll be back for three weeks and go again for a month, from there I don't know where I'll go. So as you can see our time together is already extremely limited; so much so that I don't want to waste any time that we can possibly have together; comprendo?

A friend of mine (Cadet) wants to know if you have any more real pretty girlfriends. He would like to come down this weekend and also go to the dance next weekend. His name is Glenn Redmond, and he is from N.Y., twenty years old, 5'11" tall, black wavy hair, good build, and is really a good-looking guy. He also has a terrific personality. I told him I would ask, so the rest is up to you. He would like a date for Saturday night, and would prefer a girl with a car as his is in N.Y. (Carol is OK, but not Glenn's type, he is a real live wire).

I talked to Bob Davy tonight and he is going to try to get a special pass for 16-18 December, so he can come to the dance also. I've already written my letter requesting a pass. I should have it back in a day or two. I told Bob to copy my letter, as they are requesting the same pass.

I want to send your parents a "Thank You" card as soon as I can get someplace to get one. In the meantime please thank them for me as their hospitality was much more than wonderful, and I am very grateful to them.

I hope you will reconsider about this Saturday night. The time that we have together means so much to me. I really can't tell you in words how much. Please, Beth, if there is any way to break that date with John, it would make me very happy if you would. I realize it's not fair of me to ask such a favor, but I guess I'm just selfish. So _please_ _reconsider._

Errol

Beth had made the date with John before we had met. Her mother would not allow her to break the date. It was quite interesting when John came to pick her up. Glenn and I were sitting on the couch in her parents' living room; we were introduced with no explanation. I wonder what John thought? Glenn and I stayed at the Norton's watching TV and then went to Tinker AFB and spent the night in the BOQ. Beth and I had a date for the next day.

7 December 1960, 18:17
Dear Beth,

I was very happy to receive your letter today. Also very glad your parents didn't mind putting up with me.

I passed my 60-4 check yesterday. Didn't get an excellent due to my stupid mistakes. I was just a bit nervous. Check pilot said it would be a good grade but as yet I haven't seen the grade slip, so I don't know what I got.

Hope you don't think badly of me for asking you to break the date with John. I also hope you can see my side.

Unless I hear otherwise, I will be down on Saturday about the same time as before. I will try to make it earlier if possible.

Errol

P.S. Glenn will come with me unless you tell me not to bring him.

12 December 1960, 18:05
Hi Honey.

How are you this fine type day? I hope the weather has cleared up down there. It's fairly well cleared up here, and very cold.

I passed my Celestial Navigation final today. Got an 83. Didn't have nearly enough time. I had to make wild guesses at four or five of the questions. It showed up in the final score. At least that is another milestone on the way to my wings. Only have two more actual courses in academics. We have just started Survival and we will have Nuclear Weapons after we return from Christmas leave.

Tomorrow I'm supposed to make a solo flight to Reese AFB at Lubbock, Texas. It's another Cadet base, and it will be nice to see some of the old gang again. I have to do my flight planning tonight so I can save some time in the morning. There is about one and one half hours of paper work that must be accomplished before I'm ready to take off. Bet you didn't know it was so much trouble just to get a lil-ol bird in the air. It's not necessary for every flight, only when you go to another base. It's a total of 700 miles down and back. Will take about three hours for the round trip. Normally it would only take two hours, but they have us routed on a longer route so we can log more time.

Beth, I want to tell you what a wonderful time I had with you this weekend. I've had a real nice warm feeling since I've been with you. I feel better than I have in a long, long time.

Everything seem OK for this weekend? I want everything just as we have planned. I want it so much that I'm always afraid something will happen to spoil it. But good Lord willing, everything will turn out real well.

Beth, I can't tell you how much I miss you. I only hope I can show you this weekend.

All for now.

Errol

P.S. Say hello to your folks and thank them again. Glenn really likes Carol. I only hope she feels that way towards him, he is a real nice guy.

13 December 1960

Dear Errol,

I should be in bed now— I'm tired and I have to get up bright and early in the morning, but I thought I'd drop a line or two before retiring.

I have requested Sunday night for one of my working days, but they gave me Satur-

day morning for the other working day. I'm going to have to work on changing that because it will never do. If I worked Saturday morning I would have to be back in the dorm Friday night at 12:00 or 1:00—knocking out any "after-dance" party. I'm going to try and straighten it all out tomorrow.

I can't wait for this weekend, I think we'll have lots of fun. I think Dana and Carolyn decided to go after all. If there is anything you can do to encourage Bob Davy to go to the dance, please do.

Love,

Beth

14 December 1960, 19:42

Dear Beth,

Was very happy to receive your letter today. Would have been disappointed if I hadn't received one.

Sure hope you can get off work on Saturday so we can go to the dance. Anyway you can get a friend to replace you? That's what we do; don't know if it's applicable to this case though.

I'm very glad that Dana and Carolyn are going—it will make it even better. Bob will be down, but he has to be back by 10:00 hrs. on Saturday. At

Beth Norton and Author at O.U. School of Nursing annual dance.   Author 61-E

least he will get to spend the night with Mary.

I flew forty-five minutes solo today. Had some weather move in, so they called us back early. I was northwest of here at 500' over the ground and going about 500 mph. It really is pretty as there is a lot of snow out that way. Still haven't gone on my cross-country to Reese. I hope I can go tomorrow and get it out of the way.

I hope everything works out to be absolutely perfect and wonderful this weekend, as it means a lot to quite a few people (especially me). Well for now, see you on Friday, good Lord willing.

Errol

14 December 1960

Dear Errol,

I got your sweet little letter, and I just had to write even though I do have a zillion-and-one things to do. I'm very proud of you for passing your final, and making such a good grade. It's a shame you didn't have more time, so you wouldn't have to guess, but I guess on all my tests. Sounds as if you have an interesting schedule ahead of you. How did your solo flight go?

I got my time all straightened out, so that I work Friday morning and Sunday evening. You better appreciate it, too, because it took a lot of contacts and talking. I did it for you, but I did it for myself also (so I could see you).

I'm very happy you had a wonderful weekend, because I did too.

I'm just like you about this weekend. I can't wait and I'm so anxious for it that I'm scared-to-death something will happen to spoil it. Let's don't let it.

I've really got to get busy, just wanted to drop you a line. Be real sweet and take good care of yourself. Here's hoping I see you real soon.

Beth

Meanwhile, back at the base, it was business as usual. I launched out solo, one cold, clear, December day. Our training was mostly over, and we

were just flying out our time. Flying low, and fast is really fun! I had not done a low altitude roll since I "almost went through the top of them pear trees." I figured it was now or never. I was, at the time, following the river; it bent right, left, right, left. Whoops, on my left and almost directly under me, was a barnyard full of chickens—I was about 200', throttle full forward, right on the barber pole (max airspeed). As I passed, I looked back over my left shoulder. Wow! all the chickens were now in one pile in a corner of the yard. I pulled the nose straight up, full right aileron, and around I went. I leveled off about 5,000'—a victory roll; Serria Hotel! I wonder how many of those "enemy chickens," I had killed? I hoped the farmer didn't get my number. On $115.00 base + $50.00 flight pay, per month, I sure couldn't afford to pay for many chickens.

23 December 1960, 17:35 EST

Hi Honey,

Well obviously, I'm home OK. Hope you picked up the car OK. I wanted to call you before I left, but it was a bit too early. We arrived at Tinker at 05:10 and I was going to call you at 07:30 but as it turned out we got a hop out around 06:10. It took us to Middletown, Pennsylvania, which is about a hundred miles from home. From there we went into Harrisburg, Pennsylvania, and took a train to Newark, New Jersey. The fellow who went with me had his parents meet us at the train station in Newark, they then took me to my friend, Frank Santoloci's house in Prospect Park; about fifty-two miles from home. I spent the night with him, and my parents came down the next day and picked me up.

We have lots and lots of snow; about 8"-10." It's really beautiful, I wish you could be here to see it, and we could take that walk down the snow-covered lane we talked about.

The Christmas decorations really look pretty against the snow background. It's very cold (2-4 degrees) but at least the wind isn't blowing so it's really quite nice. Roads are very slippery in spots; especially the one to our house.

I expect to arrive at Will Roger's Airport on 30 December 1960, at 1:15 p.m. your time. Not sure of the Flight number, but I think it's 819. At any rate it is from Idlewild, New York to St. Louis, to Oak City (Oklahoma City). I would appreciate it if you would meet me at the airport. If it is necessary to contact me here, phone number is GLobe-9-4267, and is a Hope, New Jersey, exchange. Well Beth, guess that's all for now, hope this gets to you in the normal two days.

Errol

3 January 1961, 14:30

Hello Darling.

Hope you will excuse the familiarity but I just can't help myself. I'm laying in bed writing this, and for some strange reason I don't feel too well. Seem to be coming down with a pip of a cold. Where could I ever have contracted such a malady?

Honey, I hope your parents weren't upset when you told them of our engagement, I really hope they didn't try to discourage you.

I told Glenn last night. He almost popped a gasket. I said, "Hey Glenn, guess what?" he said, "What?" obviously I said, "I'm engaged." He looked kind of funny, then said, "To who?" He was afraid it was this girl I had back home. When I told him it was you, he was very happy for us, and said he was jealous. He wished it were he and Carol.

Honey, I can't tell you what a wonderful time I've had this past weekend. I hope every time we are together we can be progressively happier.

I hope you don't mind my telling everyone about our engagement, but honestly darling, I'm so happy and proud, that I just have to tell people.

Lt. White, our TAC Officer just came in. I didn't want him to know I'm back from the line, as he will most often find some stupid thing for us to do when we get any free time. Told him I don't feel too good, so maybe he will leave me alone, I hope.

I've got to try and get that report on Mexico done this afternoon and night. I also am trying to get some more of the Spirit of St. Louis read. I

wanted to write you first however, as no one else is here and it's real nice and quiet. That way I can think about you and us (almost) uninterrupted. I've got my mind on you constantly. I sure do miss you Beth. I sure hope you miss me also. I wanted to write you every day this week, but it's really impossible as I have so much to do that I can hardly believe it. I don't think I've had so much to do in such a short time, since I first got here.

I've got the C.O.D. (Cadet Officer of the Day) typing my overnight request for this weekend. I will try to get a double overnight, from Friday night till Sunday night; on the weekend of the 13th-15th. I know you will be working on Friday, but at least I can see you some Friday night and we can be together all day Saturday and Sunday.

About the graduation dance: It is Thursday, 26 January 1961, and starts about 9:00 p.m. Graduation is on Friday morning at 10:30 a.m. As for dress; they tell me it ranges from a few long formals, to semi-formals, to cocktail dresses. So you can wear almost anything. They don't wear many long formals so semi or cocktail is fine. You will also need a dress for graduation (not a new one, just a nice one). Well darling, guess that's all for now. See you on Saturday, good Lord willing.

I Love you!! Love,
Errol xx

4 January 1961

Dear Mom and Dad,
Just a few lines to tell you of recent events.
Expect to go on my nave check today.

Most important event is (don't faint) I got engaged, on 1 January 1961 to Beth, of course. I know you think this is very sudden and all, but I'm sure, and so is she. Her parents approve and I hope mine do too. Really though, she is a fine woman and I'm sure we will be very happy. Please try not to think it's just a passing thing. I've been down this road before, and I know this is for real.

All for now.

Love, Errol

Q: How was you trip back to Vance?

A: Fine, made good time. I didn't know, but arrival time here was one hour in error. Arrived about 14:15 instead of 13:15. I called Beth and she came and got me. She had called the airport and couldn't find out when I was coming in or on what flight, so she waited until I called.

Q: Any new snow?

A: No, they had some in O.C. shortly before I arrived, but was all gone when I got here.

Q: Go to party New Year's Eve?

A: Yes, went to a party at the Hotel Biltmore. Went with Dana and Carolyn (Beth's brother and his wife) there were about thirty people all together.

Q: All the fellows arrive back at base safely and on time?

A: All but a few. (All safely, but some late).

On my last dual ride, we did all the usual pilot things; takeoff, climb, loops, Immelmanns, Cuban eights, cloverleafs, rolls, etc. Then the instructor said, "I've got it" and proceeded to climb vertically. As the airspeed dropped off, he said, "You've got it"—no big deal, just another vertical recovery. Roll inverted, pull the nose through the horizon, pick up some airspeed, and roll out. All went as planned until I went to roll out. The left wing started to drop—I put in some aileron to level the wings, but there was no response, and the left wing dropped even further (remember we are still inverted) then all hell broke loose. We tumbled end over end, twice I think, ending up in an inverted spin. We were up against the canopy—dirt, checklist, all sorts of stuff, was floating around. We were in the twilight zone of maneuvers. I pulled the throttle to idle, and said, "You've got it." I was busy checking my chute straps, bailout bottle, etc. We had started this fiasco around 15,000'. I didn't take time to try and read the spinning altimeter; our orders were, if we were below 10,000', out of control, eject! I knew we had to be close to that altitude. As I reached for the ejection levers, all of a sudden "pop," out she came. Level flight having been once more established, I

asked the instructor what he had done to effect the recovery. "Nothing," was his reply. The good Lord was still looking after me.

8 January 1961-18:50

Dear Dad and Mom,

Well, still haven't found out where I'm going to be stationed after training. Our assignments have come down and by the time you receive this you will already know what I'm going to be flying after here. We pick our assignments at 10:00, Thursday, 12 January. Will probably call you Thursday night, but may wait till I can talk to Beth before I do. If that is the case, I will call Friday night or Saturday morning. I'm afraid I may get B-47's which is supposed to be the worst assignment. However, it's too late to worry about it now. Will have to take what I can get. They have one RB-50 slot in Japan, I would really love to have it but are most likely lots of guys that feel the same way.

Only have one more flight in the T-33 as a Cadet. Supposed to fly solo mission on Friday, the 13th.

Only have Nuclear Weapons course left. Is quite interesting. I got my officers uniform last Friday, and it fits real good except the pants are a little large. Wanted them a little big, but I'm afraid their a little too much. Oh well, I can have them taken in at a later date.

Hope Beth will come up this Friday night. I only have one double overnight left and I will save that for the last weekend.

Well as I said before, you may hear from me before you get this letter. So until you do, will say so long—not really so long is it?

I was very glad you were both pleased about the engagement, and I'm sure you will love Beth as I do.

Love,

Errol

Q: How did you do on Nav. check?

A: Got an 86, not nearly as good as I expected.

Q: Did you find a hotel for us to stay in?

A: Will go tomorrow night I believe. Mr. and Mrs. Norton, Beth, her brother, Dana, and his wife, Carolyn, may all be here for the dance as well as the graduation, so I will make reservations for all.

Q: Get your graduation ring?

A: No, it hasn't come in yet.

Q: Could you tell us some of your and Beth's plans for the future? Are you getting her a ring?

A: Yes, I plan on getting her a ring when I graduate. I have one on layaway here. It's an evening star design, white gold with a twist instead of straight. Has one stone, three-eights karat. The wedding band is matching and interlocks with the engagement ring. Cost $75.00. I think it's very pretty. I plan to give it to her on the night of 26 January. We expect to be married in September; however, not absolutely sure of date yet.

Q: Does Beth plan on getting her R.N.?

A: Yes, if possible. She can be married and still finish her schooling, but it will depend on where I am sent. It's a very big problem.

(After phone conversation with Beth the evening of the 8th).

Honey,

It was so good to talk to you . Golly, you don't know how happy I am that your parents approve, but I'm especially glad that you do. I miss you terrible honey. Sure looking forward to seeing you on Saturday. I have to do some work now.

Love, Errol

There was a chance that I would be able to choose an RB-50 assignment and be stationed in Japan. I thought this would be a great assignment. I knew it would mean that Beth would have to give up her nursing career, and her parents would be very upset about that, and having their daughter move half way around the world with some stranger. I had to call and present the possibility to her, so she could help me make the choice, if indeed there even was one to make. Youngsters always over exagger-ate and this was one of those situations. Much to do about nothing. As it turned out I didn't get the assignment anyway.

On Friday the 13th, 1961, we were having a dance at the officers club on base. I breifed our frends that I was going to give Beth her ring that night. They were very cooperative, and made themselves scarce. I lured Beth out to the "Blue Goose" and gave her a present. Of course what do all women say, "Is it for me, what is it?" I lied and told her it was a necklace. When she opened the box and saw the ring, she immediately became very upset. She was frightened at the reality of the situation, and upset because I was so pushy. It was not your typical presentation of the engagement ring ceremony. Needless to say, it put a damper on the evening. However, a day or two to think about it and she came around, just like I knew she would.

January 15, 1961, Sunday night.

Hi Sweetie,

I couldn't wait to write you, although I'm dying to go to sleep (you're going to think I'm a sleepyhead).

I'm so happy and excited about it all. It seems so perfect. I hope everything turns out the way we planned it.

I can never tell you how sorry I am for the actions on my part the night you gave me the ring. I could just kick myself. I almost want to turn time back and accept it again the way I've always pictured it. I know you had it all pictured in your mind how it would be with everything perfect. Then when I was so childish, you were disappointed. Honey, I've disappointed you so many times, I know you must love me deeply or you wouldn't have put up with me. I don't know what has made me like that— I've always been known as happy-go-lucky smiling Beth—never moody. I guess there's truth in the song, "You Always Hurt the One You Love." I guess it was just pressure and confusion. I think since we've got it kind of planned and decided, it'll be different. I'll sure try, Honey, it's so silly to be that way.

Oh, my precious, precious ring! Honey, it's the most beautiful ring in the world! I love it—and especially the meaning behind it. You made a wonderful choice of rings—they're exactly what I wanted. Everyone at school just went wild over it. It's so wonderful to be able to tell them I'm getting married in May. But when I think about it, it is quite a while. A little over four months. It's so much better though with everything and everyone considered. I hope I can get the school situation all straightened out—have to, because I want to be with my husband.

Doll face, I would love to write you all night, but I must get my beauty sleep. I've got to build up beauty for my wedding day, so my bridegroom will be proud of me.

I don't know how I'm going to study or sleep or anything. Knowing me, though, I probably won't have any trouble sleeping.

I'm writing this listening to all the songs we heard tonight. I have to not think about being there, because I want you with me right now and always. Waiting is going to be hard, but think of all the many years we'll have together.

Oh, Honey, hurry back to me. Please be extra, extra careful always; and always love me.

I love you,

(Future) Mrs. Errol D. Severe

I flew my last flight as an Aviation Cadet on January 16. I was solo, and it was a clear cold day, with a fresh blanket of snow that covered the flat land as far as the eye could see. The sun sparkled on the vast white landscape; the small houses, farms and roads, were laid out like the patchwork of a quilt below me. But today I was out for just plain fun. I descended to 500' above the ground, pushed the

throttle full forward, and watched the airspeed indicator wrap up to almost 500 kts. This was great, the closeness of the ground gave me the full sensation of speed. Hot dog, this is what flying is all about.

Final approach at Vance AFB for the final time.   Author 61-E

But all too soon it was time to return to base. As I rolled out on final for the last time at Vance, I could not help feel some remorse. So many difficult days, and nights, and now it was all over; never again would I know the heartache, nor the triumph, nor the camaraderie that only those of us who have been Aviation Cadets could know. For a fleeting moment, I wished it would never end, but just for a moment.

16 January 1961, 18:30

My darling Beth,

Oh, how I miss you Honey. I had such an absolutely wonderful weekend. I can't tell you in words just how wonderful our time together is. I wish I could find the words to tell you how much I love you Beth. I've got your picture here in front of me and as usual I talk to it as I would talk to you. Guess I'm crazy; not really, just very, very, much in love. I only hope that you feel as strongly about me and us, as you did last night. I still do, if not more so. Time just can't go by quickly enough until May. Then it will undoubtedly go much too quickly. Whenever I'm with you, time goes by at an unbelievable rate. When I stare at your picture you seem to wrinkle your nose up in the cute way you always do when we're together. Oh, Honey, I need you so much!! I'm really so lonely without you. I have a hard time even concentrating in class. Somehow you always creep into my mind and I start drifting off with you. Even today as I was flying, you were there with me. I could almost see you when I looked back to the empty rear cockpit. The stereo is playing "Ebb Tide," one of my favorites. It just makes me miss you more and more.

Sunday morning there was a big fire in Enid. You have probably already heard about it. It burned out several large stores and damaged several others. One of the stores that was completely burned out was Zales Jewelry. That's the store where I bought your ring. I sure am glad that I picked it up when I did. I had originally planned to wait until closer to graduation, but I guess the good Lord knew more about it than I did, so I picked it up before it was burned up. If it had, I don't know if I could have found another just like it. One of the other stores was Bates Brothers, which is where I had my officers uniform to be altered. Their store was just smoked, not burned. The manager assured me he would have the odor removed and also sell them to us at a reduced price, so it could all turn out in my favor.

I flew my last flight as a Cadet today. It was 1:40 hrs. It was a beautiful day to fly, really enjoyed it. On Friday I have my final in Nuclear Weapons which will complete my training. I now have 280:49 hrs. total flying time. I've got the civilian regulations to study so that I can get my commercial license based on military proficiency. I hope to take the exam on our way back to O.C. after I graduate on the 27th. Then I can take everyone for a ride.

I've submitted my request for a double overnight for this weekend. Lt. White said I didn't have to put a reason in my letter; he already knew what I

wanted it for. Just think, Honey, good Lord willing, this will be my last weekend as a Cadet. I'll be a real "person" again. Even a supposedly gentlemanly type "person" by an act of Congress already. Oh, about announcing our engagement to the papers: If you could wait until I graduate you can put Lt. instead of A/C. Sound better? I would also like to send one to my hometown paper to let my friends back home know I'm getting married a little before it happens so they won't be so shocked.

Please send me Voye's address and telephone number, as Ferguson wants to call her or write her or something.

Well, my Darling, I guess I'll have to close for now.

<u>*I love you Beth!!*</u>

Errol

The remaining days to graduation were filled with duty assignments after graduation; uniform fitting, class rings, and of course, Beth.

On the 18th we had a huge party. It was a catered affair, consisting of 40 pizzas, and $180 worth of booze. Let me tell you that there were some cross-eyed pilots the next morning.

As things wound down, the pressure eased. We were finally being thought of as humans, and soon-to-be officers. Everyone got a little "Figmo". About two weeks before graduation, A/C Anthony Bertucci was caught coming over the fence one night, long after "lights out". He was promptly given the good old "CA"—seventy-two tours to walk off in the next two weeks. It's a good thing most of the training was over. Except for meals, old Tony was always to be found marching on the ramp, up until graduation. But at least, he didn't march alone. A/C Kenneth M. Vondrak had made time with one of the instructor's girlfriends back at Primary. The Lt. was more than a little "hacked." He tried his best to get Vondrak washed out, but the Commander had a better plan. He gave Ken a double "CA"—the only one I have ever heard of—144 hours on the tour ramp. Ken walked every weekend thereafter while

Our graduation party the night before graduation. L. to R. Author's father and mother, Charles and Bette Severe, Author and Beth, Beth's father and mother, Leonard and Rosemary Norton. Author 61-E

in Primary. When he graduated from there, and went to Vance, he thought he was at last through with tours, wrong! When he reported to the Commander at Vance, he was given this greeting: "Mister Vondrak, you will walk off every one of those tours. Even if you have to do it in an officer's uniform." As I said, this was back in the Air Force—no more

country club. As a result, Vondrak never had a weekend off base—not in the entire six months we were at Vance. He sure did have time to study though. He was first in academics in our class. Unfortunately, he was dead-last in Military Aptitude.

On the night before graduation, A/C Vondrak and his roommate A/C James A. Tassie, took a cel-

61-E graduates!   Author 61-E

They had the presentations inside—good thing, it's cold in Oklahoma in January. We were all there, dressed in our new officer's blue uniforms, spit-shined brims on our hats, shoes sparkling like diamonds, ready to be commissioned as second lieutenants in the United States Air Force, and receive those silver pilot wings we had worked so hard for. Everyone except one, that is—Larry Culp, he was the last in our class to graduate. Through every fault of his own, he had overslept. He was spending the night with a "friend" in Enid. He arrived just as the ceremonies ended. The rest of us were assembled outside, and our names called one by one. As newly-commissioned Lt. Kenneth Vondrak shook Major Scott's hand, the Major whispered in his ear, "Lt., you have one hour to get off this base."

I was now officially 2nd Lt. Errol D. Severe.

ebration trip to town in Tassie's dad's new Chrysler. As sometimes happens with pilots, they found themselves in a bar. While they were there, they managed to get loaded. Coming back to base, after hours, the guard at the gate ordered them to halt. Not being in complete control of their faculties at that point, they spun that old Chrysler around, peeled rubber, and sped off. The AP's said they were doing about 80 mph, before they caught them. Don't you know that the Commander was some happy to see these guys, bright and early, on graduation morning. Major Rufus W. Scott was the director of military training. He was ready to throw the book at both of them, when his assistant, Captain David Kahne, intervened. He said, "Major, let's not ruin graduation; besides, we have no way of being sure just how fast they were driving; the AP's didn't have radar." Major Scott reluctantly agreed.

At long last the day arrived. January 27, 1961. We had made it! My mom and dad had driven in from New Jersey, and of course, Beth was there.

2nd. Lt. Errol D. Severe gets his wings.   Author 61-E

68

Beth pinned my bars on, and my mother, my wings. All this occurred as a large flight of T-33's flew overhead, followed by a four-ship formation; one of the planes in that formation pulled up and away, as it passed overhead—the "missing man," flown to honor the two men who had been killed in training.

Was it worth all the work, heartache, tears and sweat? I asked Pop Evans that very same question back in Bainbridge. I think his answer is echoed by the many who had come before, and those few after. "Son, Ah wouldn't take a million dolla's to go through that again, and I wouldn't take a million dolla's to not have gone."

Unable to deal with the realization of more separation from Beth, and basically impatient for the wedding date to materialize, I convinced Beth to elope with me. We drove to Denton, Texas, where we were married on February 4, 1961 at 09:30 by a sweet old one-legged judge. The rest is history.

My duty station after graduation was Westover AFB, at Springfield, Massachusetts, where I was to fly the KC-97 tanker in the 384th ARS.

Boeing KC-97 on the ramp at Vance AFB 1960.   Author 61-E

[1]Aviation Cadet Informational Booklet, January 1955

[2]Trademark of the Samnsonite Corp.

[3]Pilot term, means Sh.. Hot!, Guys, try to explain this one to your wife.

69

Vance AFB, 1947

Vance AFB, 1995

Vance AFB HO

Chapter 3
From The Beginning

The beginning of something as large as the United States Air Force Flying/Aviation Cadet, Training Program, is a little hard to put down as to an exact time and date. To pinpoint the beginning of an idea, such as taking the best young men we had, testing them both mentally and physically, and calling those who passed the extremely-rugged testing, Aviation Cadets, or Flying Cadets; now that is even harder. We did have some help with the original idea for this type of training from our brothers to the north, in Canada. Our system was modeled after theirs, but our pilot training program for Cadets was phased out in 1961, and theirs is still in existence. It's safe to say that the USAF really started when the Wright brothers made their first flight, although the Army didn't realize it at the time. In fact it was many years later, that the Army brass came to the realization that this first, tiny, motorized kite, as it evolved, would change the history of mankind. And when they did finally start to realize its potential, putting it into action in the role of a weapons delivery system, only came about after much kicking and screaming. That is true for all but a few visionaries, such as Lt. Frank P. Lahm, Lt. Benjamin D. Foulois, Major William Mitchell, and later, Lt. Colonel Hap Arnold. Most of the early Army officers saw the airplane as nothing more than a mobile, artillery observation post. They envisioned it only as a means of sending signals back to the ground to inform headquarters of enemy position, strength, and movement—much as the observation balloon had done since the Civil War. Then they would leave it up to the artillery to deliver the ordnance. And if the truth be known, a great many of the generals of the early 1900's, still used tactics that were very similar to those used in the War Between the States. I think it now becomes obvious why the Air Corps was initially put under the Army Signal Corps' direction.

At the beginning of the United States' involvement in WWI, our Air Forces consisted of fifty-two officers and thirteen-hundred enlisted men. Of the officers, only twenty-six were qualified pilots. Our inventory of aircraft totaled fifty-five. General Pershing in commenting on our air strength said, "Fifty-one are obsolete, and the other four obsolescent." We had no aircraft industry, as such, in this country. We only had a dozen factories that were even set up to manufacture aircraft. Those were mostly small proprietorship, certainly not capable of turning out the number of aircraft a war situation called for. The design of the aircraft was antiquated, to say the least; few of them were suitable for combat. In 1916, it took nine aircraft factories to build a total of sixty-four aircraft, with an order for 366. The French and British must have thought that since we were the world leaders in auto production, we could most certainly turn out aircraft at the same rate. Apparently they thought an aircraft was nothing more than a car with wings. When the French Premier, Alexandre Ribot, sent our government a telegram on May 26, 1917, requesting the formation of a flying corps of 4,500 airplanes—including personnel and material—President Woodrow Wilson gave his blessing, and dumped it into the laps of the joint Army and Navy Technical Board. It didn't seem to matter that we couldn't do it. In typical American style, we were determined to give it the "old college try." Of course the French also needed pilots to fly the aircraft, and mechanics to maintain them. They were quite conservative with their request; all they wanted from us in the campaign of 1918, was

5,000 pilots, and a mere 50,000 mechanics. Reflecting the bravado of our country, Howard E. Coffin, the chairman of the newly created Aircraft Production Board, while addressing an aviation luncheon in New York on June 8, 1917 said: "Mere numbers of men count for little in this great struggle; the land may be trenched, and mined, and netted, and the submarine may lurk in the depths, but the highways of the air are free lanes, unconquered as yet by any nation. America's great opportunity lies before her—the road to Berlin lies through the air. The Eagle must end this war!" The members of the press in attendance were quick to capitalize on his words; the headlines of *The New York Times* read:

PRESIDENT TO ASK $600,000,000 FOR GREAT AIR FLEETS. Baker Champions Plans, "A Few Trained Aviators May Spell the Difference Between Victory and Defeat." TEST OF AMERICAN METTLE—Automobile and Typewriter Factories to be Called Upon to Help.

The first plan of the Signal Corps as to the number of air service squadrons for this war, was to organize 48 reserve aero squadrons. This was to be in addition to any regular Army squadrons that were formed. The Aviation school at Mineola, Long Island, was the designated organization point for the 1st Aero Company, New York National Guard. In May of 1917, the school was issued orders placing it on active duty as the 1st Reserve Aero Squadron. Captain P. A. Carroll, a New York attorney, was placed in charge of building the barracks and overseeing the preparation of the site for training. Captain James E. Miller, a banker, was in charge of recruiting in New York City. A small number of reserve officers had received flight training under Army supervision, and had passed the Reserve Military Aviation test. These men received commissions in the Signal Officers Reserve Corps at the beginning of WWI. They were to be the nucleus of the Reserve Aero Squadrons.

THE PIONEERS

Captain Joseph E. Carberry, a veteran from the regular Army 1st Aero Squadron (not to be confused with the Reserve 1st Aero Squadron) was the instructor who taught these first "Guard" pilots. Carberry had flown in the "Punitive Expedition"

Flying Cadets watching the arrival of a New Liberty Caproni CA-5 at Hazelhurst Field, Mineola, LI in June of 1918.
National Archives

against the Mexican bandit, Poncho Villa, which started on March 15, 1916. Some of the men also trained at Mineola were: Major Bolling, Captain Miller, 1st Lieutenants Joseph H. Stevenson, D. Raymond Noyes, Blair Thaw, and Robert M. Oliphant. Additional training was conducted at the aviation school on Governor's Island, N.Y., organized by Captain Carroll, under the direction of Major General Leonard Wood, the commander of the Eastern Department, U.S. Army. The following officers were trained to fly there: Captain Carroll, 1st Lieutenants Frederick T. Blakeman, Seth Low, Hobart A. H. Baker (The "Hobey," a famous athlete from Princeton) Cord Meyer, Edwin M. Post, Jr., Charles Reed, Quentin Roosevelt (the son of "Teddy") and Geoffrey D. Dwyer. While these men were not Cadets, they were typical of the type of men from whose ranks would soon come the start of the Flying/Aviation Cadet pilot training program as we know it.

A true unsung hero of the times, and a man who was responsible in a larger sense, for bringing the Flying Cadets to Europe, was Major Raynal C. Bolling. Not only did he arrive in Europe with full powers to represent the Secretary of War in matters pertaining to the aircraft and engine production program in the United States, he took it upon himself to start the production of trained pilots as well. Since there were very few combat-worthy aircraft in the United States, and the training aircraft that we had were 3,000 miles away, Major Bolling contracted with the French to obtain the necessary planes with which to train our Cadets. Shortly before he arrived in late June, 1917, an Aviation Board had been appointed, and plans were being made for an American pilot training school at Issoudun, in the heart of France. Wanting the American Cadets to have the most up-to-date training in European schools, Major Bolling arranged for several hundred American Cadets to attend several different French flying schools. The original long-range plan was to have ground school and primary training handled in the U.S. The advanced training was to be handled in

Major Raynal C. Bolling *Americas First Eagles*

France, especially the pursuit, as there were practically no combat-ready-pursuit aircraft in the U.S. at that time. The British had also agreed to train a few, and the Italians said they would take about 500 at Foggia. On this basis, Major Bolling cabled the United States and requested that 1,000 Cadets be sent immediately.

The first detachment of forty-seven American Cadets to be trained in France arrived under the command of Captain Miller (one of the original men of the 1st Aero Squadron). These men were specially selected as the most promising candidates to form the vanguard of our air forces[1] and were scheduled to train at Tours. When they arrived in France, on July 23, 1917, their hopes were high. Some of the men in this group were: Cadet Charles Ricter, a former district manager of a large electric company, and Cadet Allen T. Davies, a former State Senator from Arkansas. All of the early Cadets were men of high breeding—most were college graduates, and many were from wealthy families.

Ten of this first group of Cadets in France were assigned to administrative duties in Paris at Air Service Headquarters. The rest were sent to the French flying school at Tours. They were soon all given commissions as ground officers, prior to their entering flight training.

Due to shortages of almost everything, these first Cadets didn't arrive at Tours until August 15, 1917, and commenced their primary flight training there.

On August 1, 1917, Major Lawrence S. Churchill arrived at Issoudun with a force of 200 enlisted men. These men were a construction force with the formidable task of building the barracks and hangars at the still nonexistent school. Major Churchill was accompanied by Captain Thomas L.B. Lyster, the man in charge of actual construction. For a time, they were billeted in barracks that were used by Lafayette while training the French troops to be used to assist the Americans in the Revolution.

On September 2, 1917, the first 53 American Cadets to be trained in Great Britain, arrived at Liv-

Cadets receiving instruction in machine gun operation. The gun is mounted on a "Tourelle." Tours, France.

erpool on the steamship, *Aurania*. They were under the command of Lieutenant Geoffrey J. Dwyer. They were originally scheduled to go to France, but it was found that there was room for them in the British training system. In uncharacteristic style (for the British), they were marched down the Strand, amongst a curious crowd of onlookers, to the Headquarters of the Air Ministry in the Hotel Cecil. They were gathered into one room and given their first briefing on foreign soil. Major M. Freeman, R.F.C., and Captain J.A. Drexel (Colonel Bolling's designated American Aeronautical Officer for the British Isles) conducted the event.

Mr. and Mrs. B.R. Mason
P. O. Drawer # 44
Waco, Texas
U.S.A.
Postmarked: Pas-de Calais, France, October 1918.
  My Dear Father and Mater,
  The past two or three weeks have been more than strenuous, and I have hardly had time to write since my last letter. You should have received a cable during the interval tho', and hereafter I shall cable more frequently instead of waiting for the opportunity of writing a long letter, which is sometimes impossible.

The first American Flying Cadets arrive in England.   *Americas First Eagles*

One of these first Flying Cadets was Herbert M. Mason. The following letter to his mother and father was written in October 1918 some seven months after he graduated from the British flying training program. It gives real insight to the subject of air combat during WWI.

It is possible today because the weather is dud. With the mist, the low clouds and a 60-mile wind at 3000 feet, it is hardly worthwhile leaving the hut.

Lots of things have happened since my last letter-so many I hardly know where to start-I don't mean to myself especially, although I have had some novel experiences and one or two tight moments.

The war news you know yourself, and by the time this reaches you the news of today will be very old and the map itself will be changed. But isn't it wonderful, and aren't the "doughboys" the greatest fellows in the world? If you only knew! They are fighting like tigers, and what they take, they hold—they never surrender.

Little stories that are heard here and there of almost unheard-of courage and valor of those fellows make me feel so very proud of being an American. At first, they didn't quite seem to grasp the idea that we should feel proud of ourselves. They knew we would be able to deliver a "punch", but it was always "tomorrow." But now we are here and are proving ourselves and in such a way that they will not forget. We shall always be able to hold our heads high with pride among other nations.

Everything is going splendidly, everyone is in high spirits over here and working hard to whip the Boche, and I am sure the same spirit prevails over there.

I told you that I have become a "fly-by-night" didn't I? Yes, I like it all right. On moonlight nights it is beautiful, and with a good observer in front one is satisfied with life most of the time. But-oh-some of the nights when the moon has gone and the world is dark and your engine coughs and a cylinder misses

once, then twice! You look below and sit tight. Your observer does the same and shrugs his shoulders. And waits.

Thoughts rush inside you brain.

Are we out of petrol? Is there a break in the fuel lines? Will she hold until we get home? She sounds weaker. W-e-a-k-e-r. Oh, please, good old engine! Keep on ticking for another half-hour until we can get home.

That happened to me once, and that half-hour was an eternity. She kept getting weaker and weaker, and towards the last would barely keep us in the air. But we got back, and after an hour's work on the engine and the bomb racks filled we were off again.

Once my engine cut out completely without a moment's warning and I lost my prop entirely. I signaled for a parachute flare and took one look below-that was enough! There was just one chance and I took it.

Pulling her up in a stall, I howled to the observer to strap himself in and to never mind the flare. He nodded and I switched over to my emergency tank, pumping as fast as I could. I put her nose straight down, and down and down for a straight two thousand feet we dove. The wires shrieked and groaned, and it was Good old bus, don't, for Jimminy's sake, (that's my mascot, a Kewpie doll) don't shed your wings. And, Will she start before we hit the ground?

She did. She kicked on two or three cylinders and then roared. The most beautiful music in the world, and the night didn't seem half so dark. We flattened out and made for home. You don't know how I love my engines-when they save me like that.

It is most interesting to watch your observer. I had a splendid little chap last month named Shorty Gaipa. He was

French Farman FE-2-B night bomber.   Herbert M. Mason Jr.

76

so keen about the work it was a pleasure to work with him. I used to threaten to tie a rope around him, because every time he dropped his bombs he would nearly fall over the side trying to see them hit the target.

It is fascinating. Sometimes I've caught myself sideslipping all over the place trying to keep a lookout for other machines and at the same time watching for the sparks of fire as the things struck. When Shorty got a good hit he would stand straight up while I was in the middle of a turn, his body parallel to the ground, and clap his hands. He was always jumping around looking at the searchlights or for other machines. In a tight spot he always turned around and grinned, just to let me know he was game and trusted fate-and me.

I say that because he was new to the game and I was the first pilot he had worked with at night. Before I left that squadron he told me he would gladly go on any kind of attack with me. He was such a kid and I liked him immensely. I don't suppose I shall ever see him again.

Just one more proof of the luck my Kewpie brings me, and I will stop talking about "I." One night, when it was just getting dark, we took off with a full load of bombs. Right after leaving the airdrome and climbing for altitude, Bang! Crash! Crash! Crash! Bang! What the-why the-how the! Dam it!

My engine tore itself to pieces in the air. A valve jammed first, then the stem broke, the cylinder head blew off. Of course the connecting rods had to go and the pieces were all going back into the prop. I never switched everything off so quickly in my life. Another moment and the engine surely would have jumped out of the mounts.

There were trees below and only one field within gliding distance, and I had my doubts about getting into it. I was afraid she would catch fire and come to pieces before we could get down, and there were these racks full of bombs to consider! Would we crash? Somehow we found ourselves safely in the field in a perfect landing. Thank heav-ens we hadn't gone far. Now do you think I would fly without "Jimminy", or "The Duck." Well, hardly!

Dan Waters isn't with me at present. His fiancee has just come over and is in Paris. I think he is trying to get leave, and yours truly is to be best man at the wedding, if he can get there himself.

Our fellows of the Oxford bunch are going strong. Reed Landis has about fifteen Huns to his credit now. Poor little "Tip" was killed last month. His squadron ran into a Hun circus of about fifty machines and put up a wonderful fight, but were so outnumbered it was useless and not all of them made it back.

K—, who was with me most of the summer, has been missing for some time, and I am afraid he isn't a prisoner. He hasn't been officially reported killed yet, so I must not mention his name. He was flying very low, returning from a trip over the lines and "Archie" got him. Fragments ripped his wing to shreds. He went down and tried to regain control but I don't think he did. He was seen to crash in Hunland.

I felt badly about it for some time because we were such pals, and K—was one of the best. But there have been so many, and they have all been such splendid men. We must not forget.

Now that they are being pushed back the Huns are trying hard for peace. Please! They must not have it. They are not whipped yet. They have not had half the punishment they deserve and are still as treacherous as ever. Last week they left a corpse behind them on a stretcher and when a medical corps detachment went out to give him a decent burial they were blown to atoms as soon as they touched the stretcher. They had mined one of their own dead!

It used to be a common occurrence for them to nail a stray dog of cat to a door in some French village when they retreated, knowing that sympathetic Tommies would try to release the poor things. The animals were wired to a detonation device that below the rescuers to bits. Do such people deserve peace? The chaps fighting over here don't, not yet.

If the weather improves tomorrow I shall get

an early start and should get to X-before lunch, and X-is not far from the lines. Last week I flew over part of France, across the Channel in a ship, over part of England by train, across London on the Underground, then took a taxi to the hotel from Headquarters, and before I turned in was promised a ride in a submarine.

Perhaps the accusation that pilots lead a "fast" life is true. Sometimes we do. But I think we can take care of ourselves. I believe we in the A.E.F. are quite a happy family and are getting nearer Berlin every day.

Lots of Love, Your Son,
H.M. Mason
1st Lt., Air Service
U.S. Army

Curtiss JN-4D

All of the Cadets in England were sent to Oxford to receive instruction in the English flying system. They had been taught practically the same courses in the ground schools in the States, which made it easy to score high grades on the exams—usually 90 % or more.

In late September or early October of 1917, a body of Cadets, which was called the First English Detachment, arrived in England 203 men strong. (They were in reality not the first, they were pre-ceded by 53 men on September 2.)

After almost seven weeks of preflight, the first (in England) "Upper class" moved from Oxford on October 20, to their primary training base at Stamford. Here, they established the No. 1 Training Depot Station. They were equipped with DH6, and Curtiss J.N. aircraft, similar to those used in primary training in the U.S. These Cadets were, unlike those in other times and places, accorded all the amenities given to commissioned personnel. They used the officers' mess, club, and whatever else there was to use.

In the first part of October, another group of about 150 men (the Italian Detachment originally scheduled for Italy, but during transit the plans changed) arrived in England under the command of Major Leslie MacDill. It was quickly learned that there was no room for them in the Royal Air Force schools. They were then sent to France and upon arrival in France, one third of them were sent to Italy for a projected class. The men who were sent to Italy, were replaced in France by members of the American Ambulance Service, who had enlisted in the Aviation Section, as a way to hopefully get into the Cadet program; and in this case, it seemed to have worked. The rest were sent to Tours, but National Archives there was no room for them in that school either. Not only was there no room, but no one seemed to know what they were there for, or what to do with them. (Some things never change.) They then proceeded to Issoudun, after passing through Paris, where they had themselves fitted with the latest new uniforms.

Arriving in Issoudun, about 150 miles south of Paris, in mid-October, they found nothing that was as they had expected. This was known as the worst mud hole in France. That first night they slept on the floor of the quartermasters shed. The next day, the commanding officer informed them that they were not expected there, and there was no room for them. There were not even any barracks for them to live in. The C.O. said they could really help the

Barracks, water tower, hangars, etc. at Issoudun, France.   National Archives

war effort if they would join in the construction of the field—and if they would build their own barracks, they could live in them. What a guy. At any

General Pershing and Major General Duncan at Issoudun, France, 12/12/17.   National Archives

rate, the Cadets had little else to do, so they all pitched in and built the barracks. No sooner had they completed them, than here came a bunch of student officers from the U.S. (They were called R.M.A.'s, Reserve Military Aviators.) They were the first American-trained flyers that were ready for advanced training. So, guess what—the Cadets were forced to give up their barracks to the "Raunchy" student officers. It's no wonder that the Cadets have always resented the S.O.'s. The plight of the Cadets continued to sink lower and lower. They were now doing all the things expected of a private in the regular Army. They dug ditches, pulled K.P., picked up stones; some even volunteered to be crew on the American railroad, the winding "Snakey Valley" line, which ran some twelve miles between the town of Issoudun, and the aviation camp. Of course it was no picnic for anyone at Issoudun. Even the R.M.A.'s had to pick up stones from the field on the first day they arrived, so they could fly their first lesson the following day. The plight of the Cadet was punctuated by a statement made by General Pershing during an official inspection of the Third Aviation Instruction Center at Issoudun. Noticing a large number of Cadets busy at construction, he inquired of the commanding officer, "Who are all these men I see here?"

"Cadets brought here for construction, Sir," was the reply.

"You mean INstruction, don't you, not CONstruction?"

"No, Sir, I mean CONstruction!"

The Third Aviation Instruction Center at Issoudun was, at first, supposed to be the center for all American flight instruction—going from primary to advanced at one location. The men were supposed to receive their pursuit, bombardment, observation and aerial-gunnery training all at Issoudun.

Cadets learning to lead targets by trap shooting. National Archives

and night, finally managing to have three aircraft ready for the official opening of the base on October 15th. One of the planes, being flown by a French Lieutenant, managed to nose over in a ditch; oh well, there were still two more.

On October 24th, the first class of advanced students started their training. They had received primary training at Tours, and were a mixed bag, consisting of Cadets, and Student Officers. Of this group came some of the greatest names in pioneer aviation, including: Lt. Douglas Campbell, Lt. Edward V. Rickenbacker (the first two American Aces), Major James Meissner (a Cadet at this time, he later became an Ace of distinction), Lt. Quentin Roosevelt (Teddy's son), and Lt. Hamilton Coolidge (chief test pilot at Issoudun, and later an

Captain James E. Miller, as previously mentioned, was now the commander of the 26th Aero Squadron. (The 1st Aero Squadron had been disbanded, and the most experienced men were sent to form other squadrons.) Captain Miller was given the monumental task of turning this mud hole into an American training base. Needing experienced help, he enlisted the services of Capitaine Prospere Pelissier, the oldest chase pilot in the French Air Force, and the holder of the Legion of Honor. When Captain Pelissier arrived on October 6, 1917, there were about twelve Nieuports sitting around, unassembled. With a trained force of mechanics, this would not have been too large of a problem; however, there were no American mechanics who had ever even seen a Nieuport, let alone know how to assemble one. Not to worry, Captain Pelissier persuaded five French mechanics to come to the rescue. They worked day

French Nieuport 27 National Archives

Ace in the 94th Squadron). But by mid-December of 1917, it was decided to make Issoudun a 1,200-plane school, devoted entirely to pursuit, or "chase" training.

Lt. Douglas Campbell, America's first Ace. Aircraft is a Nieuport 28. National Archives

Perry, a Master Signal Electrician, and between the two of them, designed, and built, the first airplane mudguard. It was used throughout the war at numerous fields. Due in large to "Yankee" ingenuity, within a year, following this humble beginning, Issoudun became a school with over 6,000 personnel, and went from one flying field, to fifteen. The entire complex spread over several square miles.

Even with all this development, no fully-trained-pursuit pilots were sent to the war from the U.S. One reason was that we had few pursuit aircraft in the States. The supply of this type of aircraft was so limited, that as late as October 1918, the pilots were forced to learn combat and gunnery in Thomas Morse Scouts and Curtiss Jenneys, both totally unsuitable for the mission. Many times pilots had to train in six different types of planes before completing training. But despite all of this, the base at Issoudun, by the end of the war, had a total force of nearly 7,500 including: 794 student pursuit pilots, 141 student observation pilots; and in the month of October 1918, flew 17,113 hours.

Lt. Campbell became Captain Pelissier's secretary, and Lt. Rickenbacker was in charge of the machine shop. One day the school ran out of propellers, due to the mud splattering from the wheels, which caused them to become nicked and cracked. Ex-race-car driver Rickenbacker enlisted the help of Franklin

The main aviation camp at Issoudun, France. National Archives

During the time it was in operation, it had about 8,000 forced landings. The headquarters of the Medical Research Laboratory, the first Aero-Medical unit, was also based here.

As the numbers of Cadets

Planes and hangars on field #2 at Issoudun, France. National Archives

81

Assembling planes at Issoudun, France. National Archives

the end of 1917, there were more than 1,000 Cadets in France with no schools to enter, and no planes to fly. To get a proper perspective on the upcoming events, one must understand what these men were led to believe. While in the U.S., they were told that places were being held for them in the finest flying schools in Europe. They were to be treated to an extraordinary experience; they would become America's finest aviators. Fame and fortune awaited. They would be trained to kill the Hun and save the

Beginning Cadets at Rouler field, Issoudun with a "Grass Cutter" or "Penguin," built by Moraine-Saluier. It had clipped wings so it would not fly over six feet high. National Archives

who had received ground school in America continued to increase in France, they rapidly exceeded the capability of the flight schools available. By

world for democracy. That's not exactly how it happened.

Flying Cadets lined up for inspection at Issoudun.   National Archives

A Cadet's first solo landing.   National Archives

At least he walked away from it!   National Archives

There was still time for some of life's pleasures. The top picture is the first Flying Cadet band at Issoudun.   National Archives

Picture at left is a friendly game of baseball played during some of the limited free time available.   National Archives

Picture at left is the "Rocking Nacelle"
gunnery trainer at Issoudun, field #7
National Archives

Mechanics repairing a damaged
plane at Issoudun, field # 7.
National Archives

Many a brave Cadet never
saw action, nor made it
home.
The "Aviators" graveyard
at Issoudun.
National Archives

Cadets clowning on a beach near Foggia, Italy.   National Archives

lined with a cheering crowd of natives. In October and November, they were augmented by another 250 Cadets.

The school at Foggia was comprised of modern buildings, with the base being divided into two parts; Campo Nord (North Camp) and Campo Sud (South Camp). The Americans were billeted in South Camp. Due to the near proximity of the mountains, considerable windy weather was encountered. How-

The first Cadets in Italy arrived on September 28, 1917, at the Italian training base in Foggia. There were 46 Cadets under the command of Major William Ord Ryan. In typical Italian style, the Cadets were greeted like Roman conquerors returning from a campaign. A squadron of aircraft met the Cadet's train on its way into town, and accompanied it to the station, where an Italian escort, complete with band, took over and led the parade down the narrow streets

Italian SIA 9-B   National Archives

ever, the Cadets took it in stride, and flew their primary trainers, Farmans, and their advanced trainers, SIA's (until they were condemned due to numerous crashes) in whatever weather was on for the day. They also received advanced training in the gigantic (for the day) Caproni bombers. They were even given a course in night flying. At nearby Furbara, about 50 pilots were given aerial gunnery training.

At the beginning of our involvement in WWI, there were very few pilot training schools in this country. In fact,

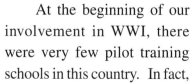

American Cadets basking in the sun at Foggia, Italy.   National Archives

only three primary and no basic or advanced, at least that's what I thought until now—research brought me to ....

Lester J. Maitland from Milwaukee, Wisconsin, was born on February 8, 1898. After the Wright brothers flight, all the young Maitland could think of was piloting a "flying machine." When war broke out in Europe in 1914, he wanted more than ever to fly. On April 19, 1917, at the tender age of nineteen, he enlisted in the Air Service Signal Corps Regular Army. He was, as were many of the men who followed him, sent to Jefferson Barracks, Missouri, for initial training as a ground pounder. After completing his training there, he was sent to Ft. Leavenworth, Kansas, and soon after was transferred to Kelly Field in San Antonio, Texas, on August 1, 1917. He applied for and took the exam for Flying Cadet. *Lo and behold* he passed, and was approved for training on May 15, 1917. Hardly able to contain himself with the thought of really flying, his eager impatience made the five months until he could start flight school, seem to drag on like five years. On October 11, 1917, he was discharged from the regular army, and the next day, October 12, 1917, he enlisted in the S.E.R.C. (Signal Enlisted Reserve Corps). He was now a "Flying Cadet." Lester started in the School of Military Aeronautics on October 13, at the University of Texas in Austin. The curriculum was similar to the other schools of the time. They learned to assemble airplanes, work on the engines (very handy if the ol' engine quit, forcing a landing in a cow pasture), service the different accessories, navigate, make maps, get their bodies in shape, play a little, and work a lot. And of course learn to fly. This was the type of primary school that was prevalent in this country at the start of our involvement in WWI. We had schools at some of the following locations at the start of the war, with others developing throughout the course of the war: Rockwell Field, San Diego, California; Ohio State University at Columbus, Ohio; Ellington Field, Houston, Texas; Eberts Field, Lonoke, Arkansas; Rich Field, Waco, Texas; Hazelhurst Field, Mine-

ola, Long Island; Langley Field, Hampton, Virginia; Post Field, Fort Sill, Oklahoma; Call Field, Wichita Falls, Texas; Camp Dick, Dallas, Texas; Wilbur Wright Aviation Field, Fairfield, Ohio; Carlstrom Aviation Field, Arcadia, Florida; Selfridge Field, Mount Clemens, Michigan; Gerstner Field, Lake Charles, Louisiana; and I'm sure there are others that were used during this time.

Cadet Maitland graduated from primary flight training on December 8, 1917. He then reported for basic flight training to Rich Field, Waco, Texas, on December 10th. Upon passing his RMA (Reserve Military Aviator) exam on May 24, 1918, he was discharged once again, this time to accept his commission as a 2nd lt. in the Air Service, on May 25, 1918. As he awaited his new assignment, Lt. Maitland was utilized as a flight instructor for several weeks, in the school at Waco where he had just been a student. On July 17, 1918, he was assigned as a student officer in the A.O.S. (Aerial Observers School) at Langley Field, Hampton, Virginia. Lt. Maitland completed his observer training on August 24, 1918. (I would like to mention that an observer was held in higher esteem at this time, than a pilot. This was probably a good career move.) He remained at Langley taking a course in Pilot Research Science. He was then sent on temporary duty to Taliaferro Field, Hicks, Texas, for a course in aerial gunnery. After completing this course on October 25, 1918, he was made a graduate Army Corps pilot, with a total flying time of 150 hrs. Next, Lt. Maitland was sent to Wilbur Wright Field, Fairfield, Ohio, to attend Test Pilot School, graduating on April 17, 1919. His permanent duty station was at Luke Field, arriving there on May 15, 1919. He was attached to the 6th Aero Squadron as an instructor pilot.

Lt. Lester J. Maitland flew in the 1922 Pulitzer Races in Detroit, Michigan, and brought back the silver plaque. On June 28, 1927, 1st. Lt. Maitland, and 1st. Lt. Albert F. Hegenberger departed San Francisco, California—destination Hawaii. This was the first nonstop flight ever completed on this route. They arrived there in their Fokker trimotor on June 29th. Both of these men were awarded the Distinguished Flying Cross; for the time, this was a very difficult and dangerous flight, especially since they were utilizing a land plane to fly over 2,400 miles of open ocean.

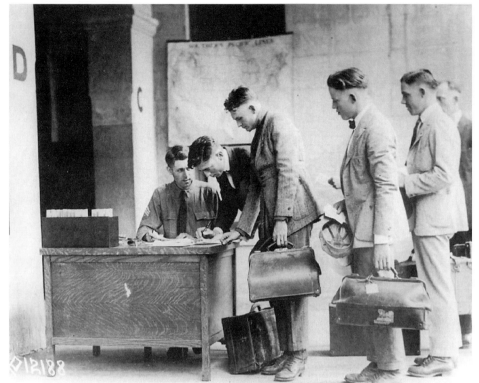

Cadets registering in ground school, Austin, Texas. June of 1918.   National Archives

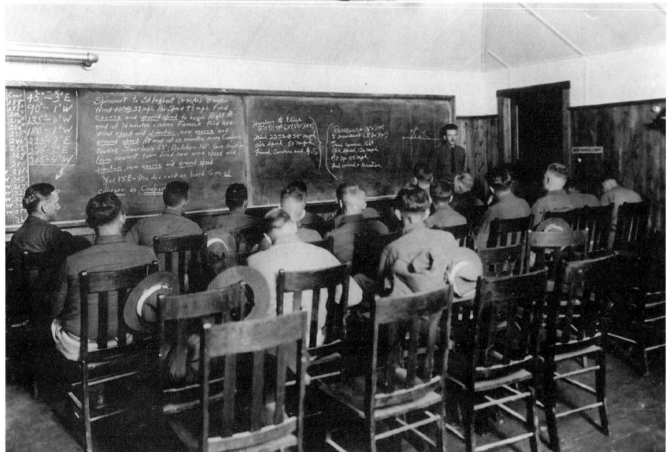

Class in navigation at Eberts field, Lonoke, Arkansas, 12/6/18. Note white hat bands denoting Cadets.
National Archives

Through his long career, Lester J. Maitland flew many different types of aircraft, some of which were various models of the DH, the H2SL, JN6H, SE-5, and Fokkers. Surprisingly, he never did see any combat until December 7, 1941. He was based at Clark Field, Philippines, from 1940 until February of 1942, when he was again sent to Langley Field, and retired with the rank of Lieutenant Colonel. He was one of

British SE-5   National Archives

DeHaviland DH-4   National Archives

those who, despite what has been written in many of the history books, had all of his WWI period flight training in the good ol' U.S.A. It seems every time someone says that's not the way it happened, someone turns up to prove just the opposite. That is especially true in the flight training of our Cadets.

U.S. Huff-Daland TA-2 trainer.   National Archives

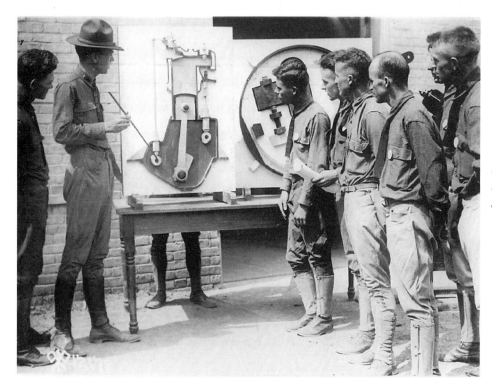

Ground school instruction in engine operation at Austin, Texas, June of 1918.   National Archives

The training of Flying Cadets was difficult and varied. The men in the picture on the right are assembling aerial photos into maps. Rockwell Field, San Diego, Calif. National Archives

In order to completely understand the airplanes they were to fly, the Cadets were taught to actually build them. Rockwell Field, San Diego, California 4/30/18.   National Archives

The Cadets were taught how to maintain every part of the airplane. The man in the picture at right is testing a dynamo. All of this mechanical knowledge was very helpful if they were forced to land in some field far away from any maintenance. Rockwell Field, San Diego, California.   4/30/18 National Archives

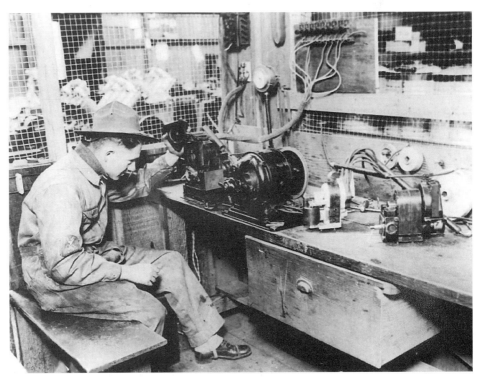

The engine on this Curtiss JN-4, "Jenny" quit after takeoff. Richfield Army Air Service flying school, Waco, Texas.

National Archives

Football game at Call Field, Texas, between the Cadets (Squadron A) and the Cadets (Squadron B) at Post field Oklahoma.

National Archives

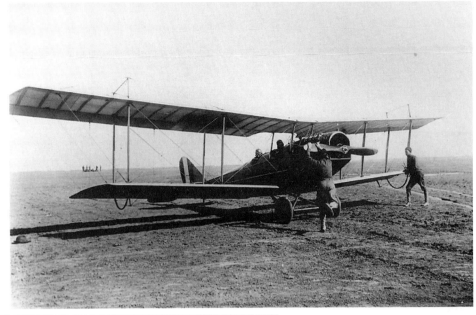

Propping a trainer at the Army Air Corps Signal Corps Aviation school at Ellington Field near Houston, Texas. June of 1918.   National Archives

Standard E-1 Scout. School of Military Aeronautics at Langley Field, Hampton, Virginia. 2/10/18 National Archives

DeHaviland-2 with an English Gnome engine. School of Military Aeronautics, Langley Field, Hampton, Virginia. 1/10/18   National Archives

Aerial navigation and compass work, School of Military Aeronautics, Camp Dick, Dallas, Texas.   National Archives

Map reading, and plane table reading work in the field. U.S. School of Military Aeronautics, Ohio State University, Columbus, Ohio. 7/18/18

National Archives

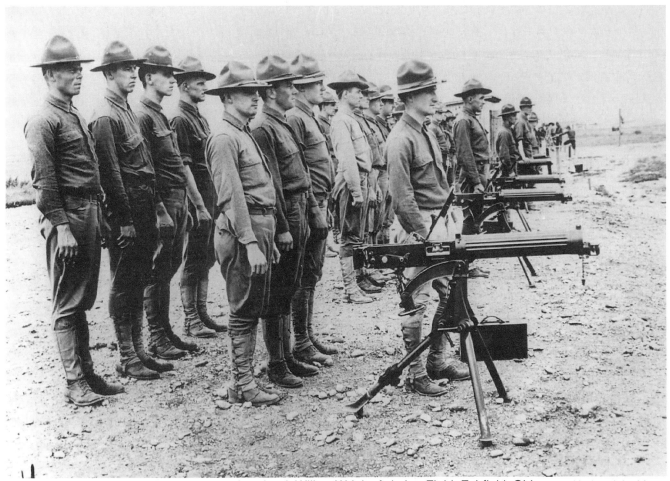

Class in aerial gunnery at the armorer's school, Wilbur Wright Aviation Field, Fairfield, Ohio.   National Archives

Dummy cockpit using two Marlin machine guns to teach firing through the prop, Selfridge Field, Mount Clemens, Michigan..
National Archives

Packard Le Pere-LUSAC-11. This was one of only twenty-seven ever built. They were a fine fighter, but they arrived too late to be of much use in WWI. Only two reached the front before the war ended. This was the only U.S. built fighter to be used in the war, and was designed by Captain G. LePere of the French Air Force mission to the United States. This particular airplane was equiped with a supercharger and variable pitch prop. It was used by Major Shroeder to set a world altitude record of 33,113 ft. on 2/27/20.
National Archives

On December 11, 1917, the 15th and 16th Foreign Detachments arrived at Le Havre, France. They were immediately sent to St. Maixent where there was supposed to be another flying school. Upon their arrival, the Cadets found new concrete barracks, built by the French, but never occupied. Next to them were two much older barracks, one of which had been a Benedictine Monastery, called the Presbyters. It dated back to the Middle Ages. As nice as the barracks were, there was little else. Once again it was up to the Cadets to build their own training base. Many months later, Lt. H.D. Muller of the 12th Aero Squadron (after returning from being a prisoner of the Germans) was asked what kind of treatment he had experienced at the hands of the Boche. He replied, "A damn sight better than I got in France as a Cadet!" Another former Cadet said, "A Cadet is a person, subject to military law, just one grade lower than a German prisoner, but who must remember, that some day he is to be an officer and must conduct himself accord-

Caudron G-3   NASM

ingly." Amen to that!

As the number of Cadets continued to grow, the primary school at Tours was devoted entirely to the instruction of Americans. It was taken over by the Americans on November 1, 1917, and named the Second Aviation Instruction Center. The French instructors were used until American instructors could be trained, thereby replacing the French as soon as possible. Supplies and aircraft were two of the main obstacles to training. There were only 50-60 of the obsolete Caudron G-3's available. Almost every day some were crashed, ground looped, or otherwise damaged. They were all more than one-year old, which in the early days of aviation, was borderline junk. The pilots remarked that their teeth rattled from the rough ride on takeoff and landing roll. By January 1918, there were only about a dozen of the original G-3's left, and they were largely rebuilt from wrecks. During December 1917, plans were started to enlarge the grounds at Tours, and to establish a school for aerial observers there. Due to the fact that the main field at Tours was needed for Cadet primary training, and also due to the scar-

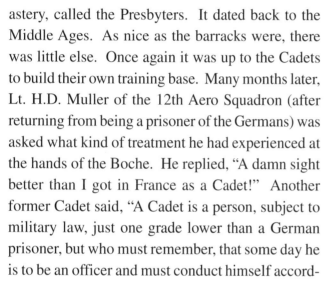
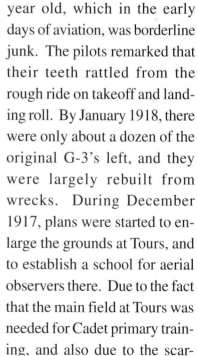

French Breguet 14 with U.S. markings.   National Archives

96

city of observation aircraft, the observer training was delayed long past its original middle-of-January starting date. But, during January, conditions started to change for the better: two new fields were taken over, and by February, they had added a fourth. Barracks and hangars were completed for the observation school. Thirty more of the Caudron G-3's arrived, as well as Sopwith, Breguet, and SIA aircraft for observation training. The Italian SIA was very fast on landing, as well as

English Sopwith "Camel"   National Archives

French Salmson 2A2   National Archives

quite nose heavy. It was so dangerous that it was condemned by the Chief of Air Service—at least they could use the SIA engines on other aircraft. By early spring, more aircraft arrived for observation training; they were: Breguets, Salmsons, and some American DH-4's with Liberty engines. The original capacity of the Tours observation school was about 50 every two months. But, as conditions continued to improve, by mid-summer they were able to turn out a class of seventy observ-

ers every ten days.

There were numerous observer training fields, which of course gave advanced training to the observer pilot as well. A French squadron helped in the training of the first American aerial observers at Le Valdahon. The Air Service took this site over in early 1918, and like several others—Souge, Meucon, Chatillon-sur-Seine, and Coetquidan—converted them into observation schools. At Tours, the men were given theoretical

5th Aerial Artillery Observation School At LeValdahon, Doubs, France. Airplanes are Sopwith, DH-4's, and Brequets.
National Archives

97

instruction. But in these other schools, they were given actual experience in regulating artillery fire from the batteries stationed at those bases, for the sole purpose of training observers.

It should be pointed out that observers were Cadets (who of course would become officers, but during shortages of Cadets, sergeants were occasionally trained as observers). To reiterate, during this time observers were considered as important, or perhaps more important than pilots. The aircraft was looked upon more as a mobile observation post, from which artillery could be directed to fire upon the enemy. The aircraft was thought of as a secondary weapon, with the artillery being the primary weapon used to annihilate the enemy on the ground. The foot soldiers would then run from their trenches, over and through the craters left from the barrage, and attempt to drive the enemy foot soldiers out of their trenches—usually failing to do so. This meant falling back to the trench they had just left, and then waiting for an enemy artillery barrage, followed by the attack of the enemy foot soldiers, who were trying to drive them out of their trench. On and on it went—death and destruction—followed by more death and destruction. Meanwhile, the airmen fought it out in the skies above, and occasionally dropped a few bombs on the already-cratered landscape. These methods and procedures were constantly revised, due to the rapidly changing war. There was a great lack of understanding of the proper use of airpower. Also, there were some rather stubborn jealousies; a lack of cooperation between the ground forces and the air forces was all too common. The observer's job was to take pictures, man the machine guns in the rear cockpit,

and communicate with the ground forces either by radio, carrier pigeons, dropped messages, or flying back to base and calling in the enemy position on the telephone. Of all of these, the radio was the least reliable. The messages were sometimes loaded into a special very-pistol canister which had phosphorous on one end. When fired toward the ground, the propellent in the pistol ignited the phosphorous, causing it to burn for about three minutes with a thick yellow smoke so that it could be located. This method was satisfactory, most of the time. But on one message-delivery occasion, the commander of an artillery battery phoned the 99th squadron headquarters saying they were being bombed by the enemy, and needed assistance.

The problem of preliminary (primary) training had reached such proportions, that in January 1918, a special board was appointed from the Training Section Air Service, to investigate the problem, and make recommendations. There was a total of 1,060 Cadets sitting around at Tours, Issoudun, St. Maixent, and at Headquarters in Paris. It was decided to send them all to St. Maixent, and organize

Observation photo ship at L'Ecole de tir Aerian de Cazaux, Cazaux, France.
French Caudron R-11

National Archives

98

them into a semipermanent force, and then dole them out to other flying schools as openings occurred. The French took in as many men as they could find space for in their schools, and the small Italian school at Foggia did what they could. But try as everyone did, there were just too many Cadets, and too few schools. The men who were unable to start their primary training at Tours, due to there being no space in class for them, were concentrated at the Beaumont Barracks. With nothing to keep them occupied, young men's minds will always come up with something to alleviate the boredom. They organized themselves into the "Beaumont Detachment," and started the first of many Air Service publications, a weekly paper known as the *BEAUMONT BULL*. It was very cleverly written, and although

Cadets working on the base newspaper.   National Archives

small, very professionally done. Here is a characteristic excerpt: "All those who need shoe size six, kindly report to the quartermaster. He has a few size ten." And another—"The captain had just dropped into the kitchen to see how things were going—'Will you please taste this, Captain?' said Devitt, holding up a cupful of doubtful-looking liquid. 'That's pretty good soup,' said the Captain. 'Just what I said, and Butler is trying to pass it off on them for coffee.' "[3]

In February the Beaumont Detachment from Tours arrived at St. Maixent. They immediately took the initiative and organized the whole bunch into

the "Million-Dollar Guard," under the direction of their own Cadet officers. The reason for this name is that this unit (not an official Army unit) was composed entirely of Cadets who, with the rank of private first class, were being paid the grand sum (in 1918) of $100 per month. In comparison, the average ground pounder P.F.C. only received $33 per month.

What a bunch these guys were. They were wild pranksters. In six-months time they had eight different commanding officers. In the first two months alone, they had five different C.O.'s ranging from the rank of major to that of full colonel. On one of numerous such occasions, the malcontent Beaumonts, or the "hard guys" as they called themselves, being quite upset that all this "glorious" war was passing them by, staged an impromptu battle of their own in their barracks. As a captain was strolling by a window, a flying book grazed his stomach. Hitting the ground, he crawled toward the second window, only to be narrowly missed by a canteen whizzing past his face. This proved to be too much; throwing away all composure and dignity, he broke and ran from the area *post haste*!

But despite their varied background, they were a wild, and wooly bunch. Just to give an example of what I'm talking about, here is a true story about some of the Cadets during the early days:

It was London, January 31, 1918. The Great War had been raging on for several years. It was bitter cold. A light fog hung like a soft cloud in the still night air— the kind of fog that makes the street lights stand out like sparkling stars, each crowned with its own halo. Suddenly, the peaceful night was shattered by the high-pitched whine of cold, steely death falling from above. The search lights probed the darkness with bright shafts of light. The engines of the enemy aircraft droned overhead. Flying Cadets, Kelly and Springs, were standing on the street next to the Shaftsbury Theater, watching the show, when suddenly; "Ka-Boom"—the ground shook, and small pieces of buildings fell all around them; the result of a bomb that hit only a block away. Springs said, "Let's get the hell out of here!" With Kelly right behind, Springs ran into the stage entrance of the theater. The show was over, but the cast had been caught in the back, behind the scenery when the bombs started to fall. They were all huddled in one corner of the wings, completely scared to death. Trying to raise their spirits, Kelly managed to get the piano player to come out of the huddle, and play for the group. They started to sing, then to dance. Before long, they had a regular party going. The terrifying sounds of the war were replaced by the refrains of songs such as, "Put All Your Troubles in Your Old Kit Bag," and "It's a Long Way to Tiperary." They partied for several hours before everyone wore out. Springs and Kelly went back to their hotel, and by that time, it was starting to get light. Having made friends with the cast the previous night, Springs invited the entire group to a party at the Court hotel after their matinee. They arrived for tea and an early dinner. The Cadets had arranged for four suites, all on the same floor. Even though "tea" was the headlined drink, liquor and champagne were the beverage of choice. It wasn't too long before everyone was feeling absolutely no pain at all. Flying Cadet, Lawrence Callahan played the piano, while everyone else sang and danced. People were constantly running from room to room, screaming and laughing, falling down, throwing up; in general, having a whale of a party. The next morning Springs, Callahan (Cal), and Grider were much too hung-over to get out of bed before eleven. By the time they had a big champagne breakfast, got cleaned up, and gathered their gear, it was after two p.m. when they arrived back at their squadron. They were supposed to be back no later than nine a.m. When the C.O. heard they were back, he immediately sent for them. With the three Cadets lined up at attention in front of his desk, the C.O. (Captain Horn) said, "Why the bloody 'ell weren't you chaps back here by nine o'clock!" Cadet Grider answered, "To tell you the honest truth Sir, we had such hangovers this morning, we couldn't have gotten out of bed before nine if our lives had depended on it." Captain Horn leaned back in his chair and said, "That's at least original, usually it's a 'bomb raid' or a 'sick aunt.' Where were you last night?" Grider said, "In the Court, Sir." "What suite?" he asked. "Oh, 103,111,115 and some other odd ones," Grider answered. "Well, you certainly made a lot of noise," replied Captain Horn; "I was in 104 myself." Cadet Springs blurted out, "You weren't exactly quiet on your side of the fence; I thought someone was making boilers in there for a while!" At that, the C.O. lost his composure, and started laughing. He said, "I guess I'll 'ave to pardon you blokes this time, as you did tell the truth." As an-after thought he said, "The next time you throw a party, please invite me."[2]

As you can see, they were indeed a wild bunch. Perhaps not wild by today's standards, but certainly by the standards of their day; something that I don't think time, or conditions ever changed. As far as the basic personality of a Cadet, we are all very much alike, truly a different breed. These first Cadets were in most ways, the same as we men of the late forties through the end of the program. One of the main differences between the first Cadets, and those who came later, is that we had much tighter reigns on us. Many of the earlier Cadets drank themselves into oblivion, and it's true, that so did some of the latter men, but that was the exception. In the early days it was the rule. But in the defense of these Cadets, they really were bored. They had come to fly and fight, but all they were given to do initially, was to sit, and get tight. One of the many officers sent to the Cadets to try and lift their spirits was a certain major. After a long and boring speech, he ended his dissertation with the following: "Men you should be ashamed of the childish way you have all been acting. You should be proud to serve your country in any way you can, and if you don't like the conditions here, you can put in your application for discharge." Within two minutes, there was a line of about 700 Cadets at Headquarters. When counted, there were about 800 resignations. Some of the men had put them in twice. Needless to say, the major changed his mind about accepting the resignations.

Due to the long delays in getting into actual flight training, many Cadets, out of desperation, accepted positions in bombardier and observer training, thereby giving up their dream of becoming a pilot. But at least, they reasoned, they were at last able to join the fight.

Putting all of the unoccupied Cadets into one place at St. Maixent, did have some positive aspects; the most noticeable was the forming of a strong bond between the men. There developed a great team spirit, and camaraderie that is shared by all Cadets to this very day.

It was during this time that the experiences learned in the Cadet ground schools, were being used as a basis for the ground schools that were being developed to train officers of the A.E.F. Early in March 1918, in order to keep the Cadets busy, and hopefully out of trouble, schooling began in map-reading, drill, Army paper work, and the theory of modern airplanes and motors. Studies in silhouettes of allied-and-enemy-aircraft recognition had their start here.

As the program expanded, the classes were split into four groups. One each for flying officers, ground officers, engineering officers, and adjutants. The courses for the flying officers were: military discipline, paper work, court martial, A.E.F. orders and bulletins, etc.; and special training in topography, theory of cross-country flying, navigation, instruments and compasses, and types of flying machines. By the time of the Armistice, 1,973 officers had been through the flyer's course and 383 through the ground officer's course.

It is interesting to note, that much of the modern flight-training-ground-school courses had their beginnings in the Flying Cadet training program.

By the summer of 1918, very little primary flight instruction was being given in France. Only a small number of enlisted men, who were already in the war, were selected to become Cadets, and receive primary flight training in the French schools.

Of the 1,060 Cadets that were at St. Maixent in February, by April 1 there were less than 400, and by May, there were only 60. July of 1918, saw the last group of famous Flying Cadets sent away to advanced schools, pitting America's finest against the Hun.

The Cadets in England and Europe rapidly progressed to more advanced flying machines. Half were trained in pursuit aircraft; SE5's, and Sopwith Camels—and the other half in bombers, mostly DH9's. Their training went so well that on March

DeHaviland DH-9   National Archives

16, 1918, the first flight with American pilots was sent overseas to France. Most of them had not been commissioned as yet. A real point of contention, was that the Cadets who had been given primary training in the States had already been commissioned, even though they had not finished their flight training, while the men in England who had started training before these men, and should have been commissioned first, were not. Due to the intervention of Secretary of War Baker, most all of the American Cadets in England had been commissioned by June.

Secretary of State Baker and Major General Black learning about the levers of an aeroplane at the Issoudun Aviation Camp.   National Archives

By August 1, 1918, there were 136 American pilots with the British during the battle of Flanders; thirteen of them were reported dead or missing. By the time the war ended, 284 American flyers had been trained in the British schools, and 71 were still in training.

Aerial gunnery training was a particularly difficult problem; not so much in learning the skill, but in finding a safe place to train. It required a location with decent climatic conditions and with plenty of flying space to provide a free-

shooting area. So far, such a location had been an elusive target. By January 1, 1918, there were only two American officers in the Air Service who had received any practical instruction in aerial gunnery. They had been instructed in the French school at Cazaux, called the Ecole de Tir Aerien. It was located near the south coast of France on a large lake.

It was arranged with Commandant Marzac to send the majority of the American students to this school before sending them to the front. The original pilots of the 94th Aero Squadron, which started operations at the front on April 14, 1918, were the first group of American flyers to go through Cazaux, starting in January of 1918. However, due to the small size of this school, in May of 1918, our forces were compelled to select a new site. This one was near the coastal village of St. Jean-de-Monts in the Vendee. It was a much better choice, as it had accommodations for 300 stu-

Le Chef D'Escadron Marzac, Commandant of the French aerial gunnery school at L'Ecole de tir Aeian De Cazaux, Cazaux, France.   National Archives

The French aerial gunnery school at L'Ecole de tir Aeian de Cazaux, Cazaux, France. National Archives

dents, and had good summer flying conditions, as well as an unlimited shooting area over the ocean. But it wasn't until August 1, 1918, that actual training began. As was the case at most airfields, it was an undeveloped piece

French Farman Avion equipped with rockets. National Archives

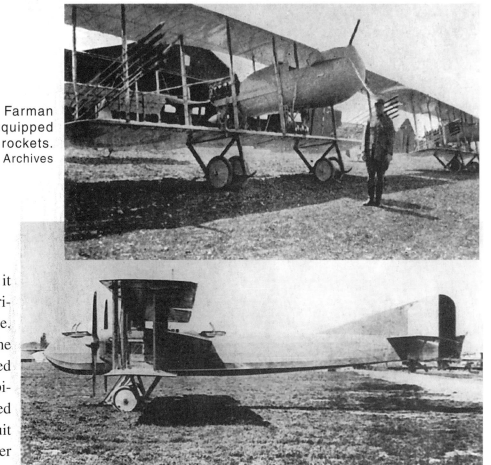

of land when the A.E.F. took it over, thereby requiring American labor to make it useable. Due in part to the ending of the war, this school only produced a total of about 200 trained pilots, where Cazaux had turned out almost 400 trained pursuit pilots, as well as a like number of observers and bombardiers.

French Caudron R-11 bomber. National Archives

Sergeant George Flint, holding the target, is an English instructor assigned to train American Cadets in aerial gunnery. Cazaux, France.
National Archives

Classroom used to teach a course in identification of planes. Paintings by Lt. Chevallier, a French painter and aviator. Cazaux, France.
National Archives

Armament classroom at the aerial gunnery school at Cazaux, France. Captain Paul Delcourt is in the center, and Sergeant Poiret is the instructor on the left.

National Archives

The motorboats in the picture at left have turrets and machine guns mounted on the afterdeck. Cadets were taught deflection shooting by practicing from the moving boats. This was followed by shooting from a hydroplane. They then progressed to the airplane. Cazaux, France.

National Archives

Back in September 1917, the A.E.F. knowing that more advanced bases would soon be needed, sent an officer to Clermont-Ferrand, France, to investigate that sight as a possible base for advanced bombing training. The site, located in the town of Aulnat, was situated in the Puy de Dome mountains—a beautiful place, but not ideally suited to flight training. It was in use by the French, and they were turning out about 40 bombing teams per month. Due to the location of the field, and other problems, this was the maximum number of men that could be reasonably graduated in one month. With the mountains pressing in on all sides, it wasn't safe to have more than 20 aircraft in the air at one time. Formation flying had to be strictly controlled, and night flying was out of the question. However, there were some advantages to this location: the Michelin factory was located there, and they were in the process of building the Breguet bomber. This gave access to French mechanics as well as the opportunity to have our mechanics trained in the maintenance of French aircraft—a skill that was unknown in the ranks of our men.

Lt. Fred T. Blakeman had been placed in charge of setting up the base as an American school, known as the 7th A.I.C. (Aviation Instruction Center). Capitaine Prospere Cholet, a French aviation officer, spent several weeks showing Lt. Blakeman the ropes of planning the courses, and purchasing the equipment needed for the school. On November 15, 1917, the grounds and buildings were transferred to the American Air Service. Two squadrons of men arrived, but there were no aircraft to fly. Due to the persistence of Lt. Blakeman, two old aircraft were delivered. Both aircraft had more than fifty hours on the engines, and were unfit for duty at the front.

Headquarters staff of the 7th Aviation Bombing Instruction School at Clermont, France.   National Archives

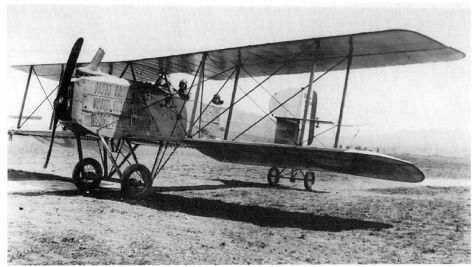

French Breguet BR. 14 B2 at the Clermont bombing school.   National Archives

about 15% of the pilots and bombardiers came from schools in the U.S., with most of them showing up near the end of the war. Those that did arrive in Europe had to be given refresher training at Clermont. They were so poorly trained in the States, that they would constantly get lost on cross-country flights. Colonel W.G. Kilner, who was now the chief of training, started classifying all flyers coming in from the U.S. according to the schools at which they had been taught. By recording their weaknesses, he was able

(Many pursuit pilot's engines were worn out at 14 hours.) Having no French instructors available, Lt. Blakeman, and Captain Cholet had to train an instruction staff. After two months of training the instructors, they were ready for the Cadets; however, they had no more aircraft. It was about a month later, well into the winter of 1918, that the French supplied them with ten more Breguet-Renault aircraft. These were also old and worn out, but they were better than nothing. Supposedly, 40 teams per month would flow from the American school, as it did from the French; but the total output up to November 11, 1918, was only 211 pilots, and 261 bombardiers—somewhat less than 30 teams per month. The students and staff officers, having time on their hands during the winter months, came up with a

New and old bombsights at Clermont, France.   National Archives

distinct improvement on the Michelin bomb sight which was in use at that time. It was named the 7th A.I.C. Bomb Sight, in honor of the school. Most of the bomber training was conducted here; however,

to send officers of field rank, who had experience at the front, back to the U.S., to change the instruction techniques, and improve the overall bomber training program. The pursuit pilots were not a prob-

Loading bombs at the Clermont bombing instruction school.   National Archives

which ended on November 11, 1918 was as follows: 2,550 completely trained flyers—comprised of 1,699 pilots, and 851 observers. In addition to these, there were 172 pilots, and 20 observers serving with other allied air forces. Those still in training were as follows: 2,012 total flyers, with 1,323 pilots, and 689 observers. The total fatalities at all schools was 159; 49% or 78 pilots were killed at Issoudun. The average was 18 flyers graduated for every one killed in training.

After the end of WWI our

lem, as by this time they were receiving adequate training in the U.S.

In January of 1918, a memorandum from the Chief of Air Service Training, stated that another bombing school was needed, as the one at Clermont was not capable of producing more than one-fourth of the expected men required. However, no other school was ever established. They did train some 126 men at Foggia in Italy, with most of them flying Caproni bombers on the Italian front against the Austrian Army.

Lessons in using the "Camera Obscura" which sights the plane and verifies the pilot's view of the target. This was used for practice bombing instruction at Clermont, France.
                                                                    National Archives

By May 22, 1918, of the nearly 2,900 flyers in the A.E.F., less than 500 were in the Zone of Advance (forward area a safe distance from the front), and just a few of the 500 were in service flying at the front. The other 2,400 were still involved in some part of training.

The net result of training during the Great War,

nation had little need for military fliers. After all, this was the war to end all wars. Congress in their infinite wisdom started demobilizing the Air Service as soon as the war ended. There were about 200,000 officers and men in the Air Service, and by the end of the next year there were only 10,000 left. This was a most difficult time for our nation. Our

Italian Caproni Bomber   National Archives

scarce. It was a very difficult time for our fighting men, as is true following all wars.

BETWEEN THE WARS

General Billy Mitchell returned to the United States after spending six months in Germany as chief of the air elements of the Army of Occupation. He was to be the Director of Military Aeronautics. Much to his surprise, the title, and the office had been abolished by the new Chief of Air Service, General Charles Menoher. General Menoher was an infantry officer and knew little of the usefulness of aircraft in war. Mitchell was made the officer in charge of training and operations.

boys who had fought so long and hard were welcomed home by great parades, cheering crowds, thankful friends and relatives; but little else. All of these young men coming home needed a job—some way to make a decent living. But good jobs were

Kelly Field flight line, 6/21/30.   William O. Ash 42-J

General Benjamin Foulois, the father of the Air Force, was reduced in rank to major. Having antagonized most of the General Staff and most other VIP's in Washington, Foulois applied for the post of military attache' and was sent to Berlin in the spring of 1920. Becoming a one-man CIA, Foulois smuggled out a boxcar full of documents and secret blueprints, even sample bombsights and flight instruments much better than anything we possessed at the time. In typical military fashion, petty arguments and dislikes prevailed, and the priceless material was stored in a warehouse and never opened. It was eventually dumped in the trash heap as junk. This was the atmosphere that prevailed in our country at the time.

The Air Service was pushing for a peacetime force of 24,000 men, and wanted to be under an independent command. Unfortunately the Army Reorganization Act of 1920 was passed. The Air Service remained a part of the Army, and was only authorized a force of 1,516 officers and 16,000 enlisted men. The other bad news was, that there was not enough money in the budget, and six years later there were only 919 officers and 8,725 enlisted men on active duty. There were supposed to be 2,500 pilot trainees per year, but by mid-1921, only 190 Cadets had been graduated.

Training resumed after WWI in January 1920, at Carlstrom Field, Arcadia, Florida and March Field, Riverside, California. These were the first primary schools after the war. The designated Advanced schools were located at: Rockwell Field, San Diego, California (Pursuit); Ellington Field, Houston, Texas (Bombardment); and Post Field, Lawton, Oklahoma (Observation). Kelly Field, San Antonio, Texas, had been a training field since 1917. (At first it was named Camp Kelly in honor of Flying Lieutenant George Kelly, who was the first army pilot killed in an airplane crash on 10 May 1911 at Ft. Sam Houston). Kelly Field was made the Air

Headquarters Air Corps Training Center, Kelly Field, 7/27/27.   William O. Ash 42-J

Corps Flying School For Advanced Instruction, on June 28, 1922.

Kelly Field was the only Advanced School until 30 November 1940, when Maxwell Field began Advanced training. Maxwell started Basic training on 5 September, 1940. Basic training was conducted for a very short time while Gunter Field was being prepared as a Basic training base. On 31 December 1940, Brooks Field was designated as a separate station. (Brooks was named after Flying Cadet Sidney J. Brooks who was killed in 1917 on his final solo flight before commissioning).

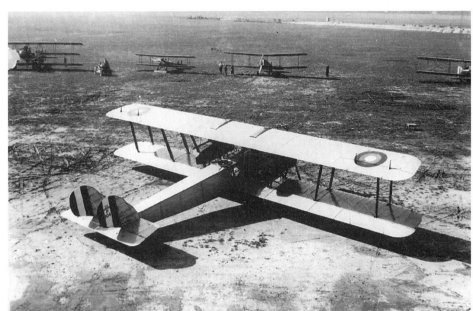

Martin Bomber MB-2   National Archives

The number of men trained under the Brooks-Kelly System (Classes 1-A through 10-A) and the Brooks-March-Kelly System (Classes 1-B through 12-B), was as follows: a total of 477 pilots graduated under the 1-A through 10-A system and 1,050 under the 1-B through 12-B system. Thus, the total pilot production for this eleven-year period was 1,528, or an average of 139 pilots per year (1922-1931). Kelly being the oldest Air Corps Advanced Flying School from which Charles Lindbergh was graduated in Class 4-A on March 14, 1925. In November 1931, basic training began at Randolph for Class 13-B, which had been transferred from March and Brooks.

The equipment that the Air Service possessed in 1921 was 2,881 total aircraft in service and storage. This number consisted of 1,500 Jennies, 1,100 DH-4B's, 179 British SE-5's, and twelve Martin MB-2 bombers. Three years later the total number had fallen to 1,364 and of those only 754 were actually flyable. The equipment was in such a state of disrepair, that within the year ending June 30, 1921, there were 330 crashes and sixty-nine airmen killed. This was nearly one out of every ten of the airmen in the Air Service.

General Mitchell, after successfully demonstrating the mighty destructive power of the aircraft in the sinking of numerous battleships, had aroused such a furor among the general staff and the politicians that he was sent on an

Lt. Lindbergh about to take off at Anglum, Missouri. National Archives

111

intelligence-gathering tour for nine months. His bombing reports were kept from the public by labeling them "Secret." He toured Hawaii, the Marianas, the Philippines, and Japan. He reported that the defenses at Pearl Harbor were almost non-existent. It was his view that we would one day go to war against the yellow race and then we would see which would prevail. As usual, if you were not popular with the powers that be, his reports were thought to be a little short of fantasy, and filed away to be forgotten. Then Assistant Secretary of the Navy, Franklin Delano Roosevelt, shared the opinion of many naval officers that, "It is highly unlikely that an airplane or a fleet of them could ever successfully attack a fleet of Navy vessels under battle conditions." I wonder what he thought on December 7, 1941.

Arriving back in Washington, Mitchell found the Air Service in a horrible state of readiness. Instead of new planes being built and more pilots being trained, the amount of each was greatly reduced. Of the 1,500 planes on inventory, more than half were in dead storage and most all of the others were left over from World War I production. There were only nineteen modern Thomas Morse pursuit aircraft that were flyable. After trying for years to make

our government wake up, General Billy Mitchell was court-martialed in September of 1925; he was found guilty on all eight specifications. He then resigned from the Air Service. It's so tragic that a man with vision and foresight would be treated so by the country he loved. The only highlight is that he was right. How many other fine officers have been destroyed because they had the guts to speak out, and stand against the prevailing opinions of those less qualified.

We were now full swing into the Roaring Twenties. Much like today everyone was seeking a new thrill. Aviation had become a novelty to the American public. What new record could be set; what death-defying act could the flyers perform? The men who had not long before been flying over the Boche lines were now flying from fields, roads, airports; anywhere they could to bring new thrills to the public. There being precious few jobs available, contributed greatly to the "Barnstorming"—after all a man had to eat. And what better way for an airmen to earn a living than flying. Although it was a hard and dangerous time for these men, many of them achieved great goals, and set many records. Lt. John A. Macready flew his supercharged Liberty engine, attached to a LePere fighter to a record altitude of 34,508 feet on September 28, 1921. On September 4, 1922, Lt. James H. Doolittle became the first man to cross the United States in a single day, when he flew his DH-4B from Pablo Beach, Florida, to Rockwell Field in San Diego. He flew the 2,163 miles in 21 hours and 20 minutes.

The most ambitious flight of the 20's was the U.S. Air Service's attempt to circumnavigate the earth. After a successful test flight in October 1923, Donald W. Douglas was

Thomas Morse airplane on winter maneuvers at Camp Skeel, Oscoda, Michigan.
National Archives

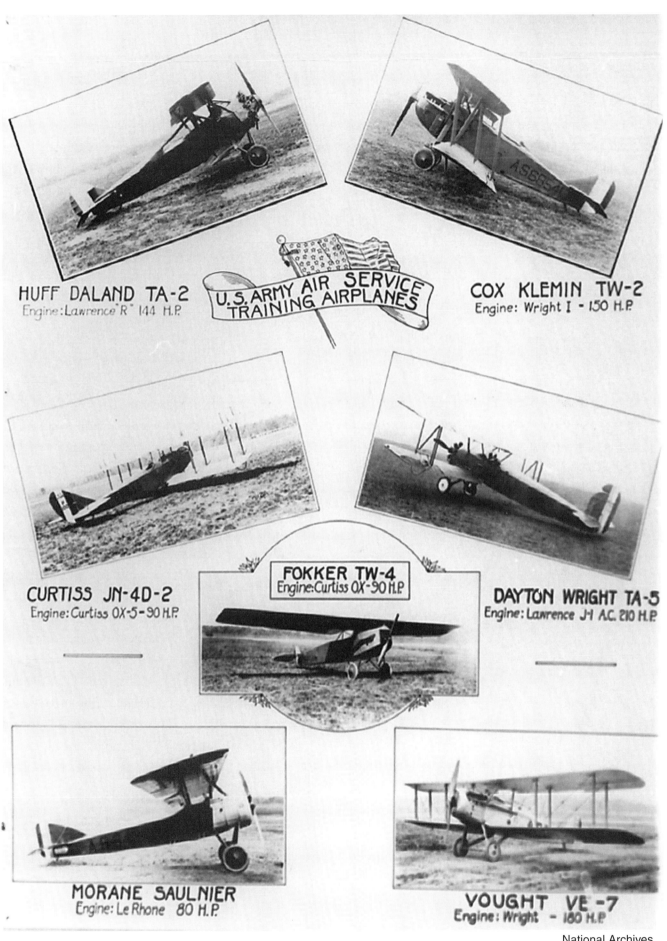

HUFF DALAND TA-2
Engine: Lawrence "R" 144 H.P.

COX KLEMIN TW-2
Engine: Wright I - 150 H.P.

U.S. ARMY AIR SERVICE
TRAINING AIRPLANES

CURTISS JN-4D-2
Engine: Curtiss OX-5 - 90 H.P.

FOKKER TW-4
Engine: Curtiss OX-90 H.P.

DAYTON WRIGHT TA-5
Engine: Lawrence J-I A.C. 210 H.P.

MORANE SAULNIER
Engine: Le Rhone 80 H.P.

VOUGHT VE-7
Engine: Wright - 180 H.P.

Douglas World Cruiser   National Archives

attle lost oil pressure and had to make a forced landing on the water. It was discovered that there was a three-inch hole in the left side of the crankcase, caused by a connecting rod bolt that had worked loose in flight. After spending the night in the cockpit, with the temperature below freezing, the crew was found by a destroyer. After working all night in the freezing wind, a new engine was installed. The other three aircraft proceeded to Dutch Harbor to wait for the *Seattle*. After finally reaching Chignik, the weather held them on the ground four more days as they awaited the passage of yet another storm. The aircraft was chopped from the ice, and after removing more than 400 pounds of ice from the airframe, Martin and Harvey took off to join the others at Dutch Harbor, deciding to take a short cut to save time. The weather worsened, and soon they were on solid instruments. Suddenly a black shape loomed ahead, and seconds later, the *Seattle* crashed into a mountain. The men were not badly injured, but were a long way from any civilization. It took them eleven days to walk out of the wilderness.

On August 3, with the *New Orleans* already in Hornafjord, the *Boston* and *Chicago* departed the Orkneys. An hour and twenty-four minutes after takeoff, out over the open ocean, the oil-pressure gauge on the *Boston* dropped to zero. There was nowhere to go but down. The waves were high and the right pontoon was smashed as they splashed down into the sea. The *Chicago* circled overhead, dipped a wing in salute, then pressed on to Iceland. First, a British trawler came to help, but couldn't get the aircraft in tow. Then the cruiser *Richmond* arrived, taking the airmen aboard, and the *Boston* in tow. At 5:00 a.m. the *Boston* capsized and had to be cut loose eventually sinking to the bottom.

given a contract to build four Cruiser's, a single-engined biplane; they cost $48,000 each. They could be fitted with wheels or pontoons, and had a range of 2,200 miles in the landplane version. They had 400 hp Liberty engines, giving them a service ceiling of 10,000 feet, and a top speed of 103 m.p.h.. It would take some time to fly the entire distance. On April 6, 1924, the cruisers *Seattle*, *Chicago*, and *New Orleans*, took off from Lake Washington near Seattle. The *Boston* was too heavy to lift off of the lake. After shutting down the engine and then throwing out some of their gear, they restarted and soon became airborne following the others toward Prince Rupert, British Columbia. The pilots for this flight were picked by General Patrick. Commanding the mission was Major Frederick L. Martin. Lt. Leslie P. Arnold, LeClaire Schultze, and Erik Nelson. Lt. Lowell H. Smith and Leigh Wade were backup pilots. To complete the two-man crews the pilots picked the mechanics to accompany them. They were: Sgt. Alva Harvey, Tech. Sgt. Arthur Turner, Staff Sgt. Henry Ogden, and Lt. Jack Harding.

The weather for the next several weeks was horrible all along the flight path. The *Seattle* was damaged on landing at Prince Rupert and took several days to repair. On the leg to Chignik, the *Se-*

Wade's and Ogden's spirits were at an all-time low. They would not be able to finish the work they had started so many months before. Lo and behold, General Patrick had arranged for the prototype *Cruiser* to be sent to Nova Scotia so that all of the remaining six flyers could participate in the last leg hom. On September 5, *Boston II*, *Chicago* and *New Orleans* landed at Casco Bay, Maine.

One of the first air to air refuelings with two DH-4B airplanes. They were flown by Lt. Smith and Lt. Richter over Rockwell Field. National Archives

Some of these men were: the pilots of the Air Service who in 1923 flew the first air-to-air refueling when a DH-4B was kept aloft for twenty-four hours and six minutes over San Diego; Major Carl Spaatz, Captain Ira

Douglas World Cruisers over New York.   National Archives

On September 28, 1924, at Clover Field, near Santa Monica, California, the odyssey ended. It had taken these brave men five months and twenty-four days to complete their mission. The total flight time was 363 hours and six minutes.

The twenties was a time for the aviators of our country to perform feats, establish records, and supply our nation with heroes that would inspire many a young man to want to join the ranks of such men.

The crowd at Bolling Field, Washington D.C. waiting for the around the world flyers to land.
National Archives

Eaker, Lieutenants Harry Halverson, Elwood "Pete" Quesada and Sgt. Roy Hooe who, in 1929 flew a trimotor Fokker C-2 named *Question Mark* from January 1 to January 7. They were airborne over 150 hours.

The Air Corps Act

On July 2,1926, Congress passed H.R. 10827, commonly known as the Air Corps Act. (This bill was very similar to the Army Reorganization Act of 1920.) It authorized a five-year program to bring the service up to a strength of 1,518 officers, 2,500 Aviation Cadets, 16,000 enlisted men, and 1,800 first-line aircraft. To those in the service at the time this must have seemed too good to be true; at that time we only had sixty pursuit planes, 169 observation planes, and a few operational bombers. There were less than 120 modern trainers in the inventory. Some Cadets were learning to fly in DH-4's that were left over from the war. Damn, it was too good to be true! The key phrase pertaining to the expansion of personnel, was: "As rapidly as funds are provided by Congress for recruiting, paying, subsisting, clothing, equipping, and otherwise maintaining enlisted men over and above 118,750, not including the Philippine Scouts." The Air Corps was directly tied to the Army. It would get its allotment only as the Army as a whole was increased. So, a year after this legislation was passed, the Air Corps was short 75% of its authorized pilot quota. At the end of the five-year program, instead of having 2,500 new aviators, there were only 1,212. The elimination rate for pilots has always been high, but during these times it was astronomical. In 1926, nearly nine out of ten Cadets were washed out. By the end of 1931, things had improved somewhat, to three out of four being washed out.

| | | | Cadets/ | In Grade | |
Year	Applicants	Qual	Grad.	Grad.	Total
1925	1,057	287	53	78	131
1926	1,550	435	36	78	114
1927	1,640	349	38	73	111
1928	4,010	682	67	89	156
1929	4,095	897	222	55	275
1930	3,738	962	226	80	306
1931	2,081	504	195	60	250
1932	2,609	552	246	53	299

In the years 1926-1935, there were at least a dozen bills introduce into Congress, attempting to make the Air Corps a separate unit from the Army. All failed.

But things were starting to change for the better. General Patrick was replaced as Chief of the Air Corps by Major General John E. Fechet in December, 1927. He chose Benjamin Foulois to be his assistant Chief of the Air Corps. General Fechet really knew little of the aircraft's role in warfare. He tried, as so many others after him, to save money and build an all-purpose aircraft, a feat that has yet to be accomplished successfully. The aircraft he ordered the designers at Wright Field to build, was the Douglas XO-35. It was a twin-engine, gull-wing monoplane with a crew of three, and two light ma-

Douglas XO-35   National Archives

116

chine guns for armament. It proved to be useless as a bomber, and basically showed no improvement over existing observation aircraft which were already obsolete. Realizing his mistake, Fechet ordered a bomber competition fly-off in 1930. There were six manufacturers participating; of the six, two provided outstanding designs. Boeing entered a B-9, a mid-wing, all-metal monoplane, with two 600 hp engines and a top speed of 188 m.p.h.—its ceiling was 21,000 feet. Unfortunately, it only carried a bomb load of 900 lbs. It first flew in 1931, and despite the fact that the WWI Handley Page carried almost twice the bomb load, the B-9 was consid-

Boeing YB-9A and YIP-26   National Archives

ered an aerodynamic triumph. In 1932 Martin flew its B-10. It had a top speed faster than most fighters of the time at 207 m.p.h.. The cockpit was enclosed and the gun turrets were enclosed by bubbles; it had a ceiling of 24,000 feet. Although it also suffered from a very limited bomb load of only 600 lbs., at the time it seemed to be the right tool to assist Army ground operations. The B-10 was ordered into mass production.

The General Staff was still not convinced that the aircraft's role in bombardment could be used to control the sea lanes, defend the American coast, or produce decisive results in any general mission. Such a notion was considered nothing more than purely "visionary."

THE ARMY AIR CORPS

SAN ANTONIO

Late in the summer of 1926, General Frank P. Lahm submitted a report to then Chief of the Army Air Corps, Major General M. M. Patrick, outlining the pressing need to coordinate and concentrate the Army's flying school facilities. Brooks Field, at San Antonio, Texas, was the primary school and was rapidly becoming overcrowded. General Patrick recommended to congress that General Lahms report be acted upon. He also pointed out that San Antonio would be the most likely place to build such a facility, due to the fact that the Advanced Flying School at Kelly was there as was the Air Corps Training Center. The terrain was basically flat, and the climate was excellent (perhaps a little too warm). In February 1926, the House Military Affairs Committee passed a bill authorizing the appropriation of $1,876,000 for a new primary and basic training air field near San Antonio. The Air Corps Training Center was established on July 20, 1926, pursuant to General Order No. 18, War Department, Washington, 16 August 1926. At this time the Army Air Service, became the Army Air Corps.

1. The Air Corps Training Center —1. There will be established and maintained at San Antonio, Texas, an Air Corps Training Center consisting of the following activities:

a. The Air Corps Primary Flying School, Brooks Field, San Antonio, Texas.

b. The Air Corps Advanced Flying School, Kelly Field, San Antonio, Texas.

c. The School of Aviation Medicine, Brooks Field, San Antonio, Texas.

Extract: 1 September 1926.

Pursuant to authorization contained in General Orders No. 18, WD Washington D.C., dated 16

August 1926, Brigadier General Frank P. Lahm established his headquarters at Duncan Field, San Antonio, Texas on 1 September 1926, consisting of the following activities: a. The Air Corps Primary Flying School, Brooks Field, Texas; b. The Air Corps Advanced Flying School, Kelly Field, Texas; and c. The School of Aviation Medicine, Brooks Field, Texas.

Up until June 1926, the School of Aviation Medicine was Located at Mitchel Field, Long Island, New York. On this date (9/1/26) the move was completed to Brooks Field in San Antonio, Texas, along with the Primary Flying School from March Field, Riverside, California. (March Field, was reestablished as a Primary Flying School on 15 June 1927.)

As is so many times the case, the plan was met with great enthusiasm; that is, until someone objects. Then it hit the fan. Congressmen from California and Florida complained that since the government already owned land in both of their states, the bases should be located there. When the bill passed, it did not contain any mention of training bases at San Antonio. However, the Army brass didn't like the idea of separating its training bases all over the country, at least not until thirteen years later.

In April, 1927, fearing a great financial loss to the city, influential citizens and the San Antonio Chamber of Commerce presented a package to the Government that they couldn't refuse—Free land. General Lahm appointed a board of Air Corps officers to locate, and inspect available sites.

By June 1927, Brooks Field had become so crowded that it was decided to re-establish the primary school at March Field, California. The city of San Antonio was having difficulty in obtaining funds to buy land to give to the Government. Many legal problems had to be surmounted. They were under considerable pres-

The Ruggles Orientator was one of the early pilot testing devices used by the School of Aviation Medicine. (1920)   Author 61-E

sure to get the deal finished when they learned that two other cities in Texas were being considered for the site of the new base, and they faced the prospect of losing not only the proposed new training facility, but Brooks and Kelly as well. An ordinance was passed on December 19, 1927, issuing $500,000 in promissory notes to an investment company, with the money to be spent for "general municipal purposes." Payment of the notes was secured by the city's pledge of delinquent taxes, when they were collected, and whatever general revenues were required to pay the interest and principal. The land was officially transferred to the United States on August 4, 1928, when Governor Dan Moody signed a deed of cession for the State of Texas.

THE BEGINNING OF RANDOLPH

Clearing of the ground started on October 11, 1928, and it was officially named Randolph Field on October 17. The field was named after William M. Randolph, from Austin, Texas. He served in WWI as a ground officer, and became a pilot in 1919. He was killed in a plane crash at Gorman, Texas, on February 18, 1928.

When construction started, there were crops still growing in some of the fields, and 180 acres of woodlands had to be cut, and the stumps removed. By October 31, the area was totally devoid of an obstacles to construction. The first buildings were two warehouses and six barracks. The field was officially dedicated on June 20, 1930, with a crowd of about 15,000 people in attendance. It was about half complete at the time.

Advance details came from Brooks and March Fields early in the fall of 1931. The Air Corps Training Center which was headquartered at Duncan Field, moved to Randolph. On October 25, 1931, with a unit strength of 162 officers, and 1,432 enlisted men Randolph Field officially became the

Randolph under construction. Shops and building #128. 2/18/31   William O. Ash 42-J

The south side of Randolph showing school buildings and Cadet Barracks. 12/16/30   William O. Ash 42-J

The main gate at Randolph 2/19/31.   William O. Ash 42-J

Army Air Corps primary-basic flying school. It was one of the largest and finest flying schools in the world, and was called "The West Point of the Air" from the very beginning. Major Frederick L. Martin was the first commander at Randolph. He, as I'm sure you remember, was the leader of the Around-the-World flight, flying the Douglas Cruiser *Seattle*. One of the Cadets in the first class was Cecil Darnell whose stories appear in a later chapter.

The Chief of the Air Corps announced an expansion program for the Air Corps on 10 August, 1937. Under this program, classes entering the Air Corps Primary Flying School during 1938 and 1939 were increased to 344 Flying Cadets. Heretofore, the classes had ranged in size from 70 to 200. Personnel under the then-prevailing program came from four sources: graduates of the U.S. Military Academy, Line Officers, foreign students, and newly-appointed Flying Cadets. Under this new program, Cadet training would be more than doubled. The most readily available source of recruits was the one the Air Corps had always relied on most heavily, namely, the young college graduate. The question which faced the Army was whether such men could be induced in large numbers to join the Air Corps as Flying Cadets. Some in the Air Corps didn't think this could be done unless the prevailing system of recruiting was changed or the standards lowered. The Chief of the Air Corps decided the system of recruiting should be revitalized and modernized; standards were not to be lowered.

A plan was formulated in December 1938 to interest at least 14,400 applicants. Since only 18.5% of the applicants met the physical, educational, and mental standards; a large initial number of applicants was required in order to obtain the 3,600 men required to start training, and end up with the 2,664 graduates needed each year for the 4,500 pilot program. First, applicants had to be examined by Flying Cadet Examining Boards, but before a man could even be examined, his papers had to be filled out and his application checked. To successfully pass the physical examination, candidates had to have normal vision, that is, 20/20 for each eye, without glasses, unimpaired ocular muscle balance, good hearing, a stable and balanced equilibrium, normal color vision, and a stable nervous system.

Successful candidates were placed on a waiting list and assigned to the first class in which they could be accommodated at the primary schools. During the 1939-41 period, students accepted for training were assigned directly to a primary school.

The biggest problem for recruiting was how to get such a large number of men interested in applying to become a Flying Cadet. The answer was, publicity by the Air Corps, rather than the Adjutant General. To avoid friction with the regular army recruiting authorities, publicity was put out in an informal way. The first obstacle that had to be overcome was the venerable Army tradition that the best way to get along with the public was to tell them nothing. Another problem was to get out the publicity without arousing the antipathy of the public toward military training. Both were overcome through the activities of the Public Relations section of the Air Corps.

The publicity program was focused on the colleges and universities primarily to catch the attention of potential candidates. The campaign was based on the idea of glamour. The glamourous life of the Flying Cadet was idealized and romanticized in pictures and stories. The handsome Cadet in flying helmet, goggles on his forehead, his neck wrapped in a flowing white silk scarf, and his face wreathed in a superbly happy smile, became the stock in trade of Air Corps publicity. This glamorous visage was spread upon the pages of every college Annual Magazine in the country in 1939, 1940 and 1941. The photo of every graduate of Kelly Field was sent to his hometown newspaper, along with an attractive write-up of the boy. The message of this publicity was you: too, may become a Flying Cadet and enjoy this glamorous experience. Corn and cheesecake were generously sprinkled with the glamour. The coeds of the University of Texas were brought to Randolph Field for photographing. Flying Cadets judged beauty contests. The soft, symmetrical beauty of Randolph Field's Spanish architecture was spread across the nation in newsreels, magazines, and newspapers. Finally, the slogan: "Randolph Field, West Point of the Air" was evolved and spread across the nation. In 1940, the picture: *I Wanted Wings,* was made at Randolph Field with the cooperation of the Air Corps. With the development of public relations photography and press releases in magazines highlighting the attractions of Cadet life and flying training on a national scale, the picture phase of the publicity was a success. But with the ever-increasing demand for more Cadets before them, the Air Corps publicity men turned to radio to get their story before a wider audience. "The West Point of the Air" series was presented in November and December 1939, in addition to the regular Friday night Army Show. A gratuitous source of radio publicity was the commercially sponsored program: *Wings of Destiny.*

As the training program was increased from 4,500 pilots in two years to 30,000 a year, the burden became increasingly heavy on the publicity officers. The publicity program changed its tone from the glamours of 1939 and early 1940, to one of urgent appeal in 1941. This change was symbolized in the phrase: "Keep 'Em Flying." On 26 June 1941, the War Department sent out "Keep 'Em Flying Requisition No. 1." This requisition ordered the entire Army Recruiting Service to make the procurement of Aviation Cadets its first duty. All previous quotas sent to the Corps Areas were revoked. To obtain the numbers required, it was ordered that every possible approach be utilized, and college and town units pushed. Recruiting Officers were urged to appear before the American Legion, the VFW, and other civic and fraternal organizations and induce them to sponsor Aviation Cadet units. All Reserve Officers were sent a circular letter urging them to assist the Cadet Recruiting Program. The Junior Chamber of Commerce of the U.S. was enlisted in the campaign to procure more Cadets. This was accomplished through the local chapters who were

advised of the Army personnel stationed in their vicinity.

Flying Cadet Examining Boards did a lot of good work. These traveling Cadet examining boards went around hitting the same areas four times each year. They would average 130-135 new recruits per board in signing up applicants. The original three boards in each Corps Area were augmented in the winter of 1939 and 1940 by the establishment of Flying Cadet Examining Boards at each civil elementary Flying school in order to promote the procurement of Flying Cadets. The Boards were required to examine every applicant within five days, rather than delaying them as heretofore for several weeks, and having these applicants end up going to the Navy or Coast Guard to get in quickly for flying training. There was considerable competition between the services to obtain enough Cadets to fill their individual requirements. The reduction of math requirements (trigonometry and spherical trigonometry) made recruiting easier. The name "Aviation Cadet" displaced the name "Flying Cadet" on 20 June, 1941. Class 42-D was the last class to be named Flying Cadets, making class 42-E the first class to be named Aviation Cadets. The Flying Cadets wore blue uniforms, while the Aviation Cadets wore khaki. The classes at Kelly at this time were divided into two flights, A and B. The A flight was known as the "High Pockets," as they were the taller men more suitable to fit into multi-engined airplanes. B flight was known as the "Sand Blowers," consisting of the shorter men, more suitable to fit into fighters.

On 22 October 1941, the OCAC told the recruiters that there was no more backlog of applicants and that future applicants would be assigned to the first class following the processing of papers for application. Good-by Mom and Dad.

Most of the Cadets came straight from civilian life, and the requirements at the time were that he must be at least eighteen but not older than twenty-seven. He may be married or unmarried. He may not be less than five feet four inches nor

Stearman PT-9A   National Archives

flight instruction. The course was eight months long, four in primary and four in basic. The classes arrived in March, July, and October. Advanced was at Kelly where many of our famous pilots received their wings. The new men were called "dodos" after the non-flying bird of the same name. Throughout the years of the program, new men were called many different derogatory names, all part of the training to not take anything personal, and still maintain a sense of mission, regardless of the circumstances. I'm afraid this treatment would end in numerous lawsuits today. Mild hazing was the official word for the "Hell on Wheels" that all of us endured no matter when we went through training. Today I can look back and see the reasons for many of the seemingly non-sensical things we had to do. Here are some of the official reasons for "dodo" hazing straight from the

more than six feet four inches, and his weight must be well-balanced in proportion to his stature—the average Cadet at that time was five feet ten inches in height, and weighed about 160 lbs. He must have "the minimum of a high school education." The pay scale was $75 a month with a $1 a day ration allowance, which provides excellent and plentiful food (so the 1942 book *Randolph Field* says). Some of the other perks were: $10,000 life insurance policy, $150 for regular Air Corps uniforms, paid upon graduation, and a bonus of $500 for each year or part thereof, that he may have served on active duty when he reaches the end of his regular term of enlistment. If, and when, he is commissioned a second lieutenant in the Air Corps Reserve and assigned to active duty, he will draw a basic wage of $205 a month with quarters, or $245 a month without quarters.

Until 1939, Randolph was the only training field to contain both primary and basic

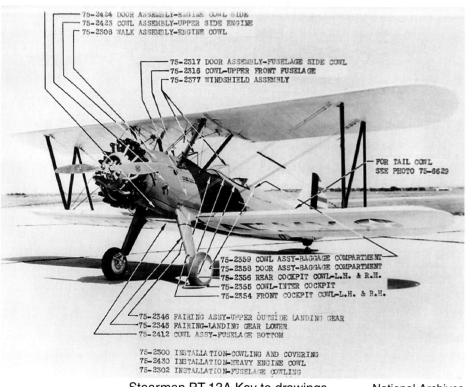

Stearman PT-13A Key to drawings.   National Archives

Cadet's room at Randolph in the early forties.   AETC/HO Randolph AFB

government book about Randolph Field, written in 1942: "The dodo must always move at a dogtrot when outside his area buildings; his muscles and wind were being developed. Making any turn, he must lift his arms and stretch them out with the one on the side toward which he was turning slanting down, the other slanting up; his appearance was amusing to his seniors but also he was automatically learning which way to bank a plane. He must wear his goggles at breakfast, and always carry them hanging from his neck; his breakfast experiences were sometimes mildly embarrassing, but he was becoming familiar with the limitations of visual angles which goggle-wearing flyers must consider. There was an upperclassmen barrack's procedure which required dodos to first, smite their chests smartly, followed by a peculiar squat that was hard on the calves of their legs; that spot on the dodo's chest which he smote at command was the one at which his hand, should he ever have to "bail out" from a plane, would find the ring that released his parachute, and the squat placed his legs and feet in the precise position that promises the least chance of injury in a parachute landing. Of hazing in any more disagreeable sense than these examples there was none." Isn't it amazing how different the official government view is, from reality. No **Hazing,** ha!

The prospect of "washing out" of the program was of course a prime consideration for all Cadets. There were many reasons for a "washout": some men just lacked the necessary muscular coordination to control complicated machinery; others couldn't handle the extremely difficult courses of study; still others couldn't take the pressure of hazing. But no matter what the reason, I have never talked to a single man who "washed out" that did not regret it his entire life. I even had a letter from a man who was a Cadet in the first class after WWII, 48-A, who said he had his private pilot license when he started training, and was determined to graduate. He was washed out in primary at Randolph. His instructor told him that it was not his lack of ability, nor lack of determination, but rather because he was an American Indian. They wanted the *first* class to all look like G.I. Joe. He said this was the most bitter experience of his entire life, and he has never

Instructor and Cadet in a Vultee BT-9 over Randolph 5/1/41 National Archives

gotten over it. There are few other courses of training or schooling that would have such a profound effect on someone's life.

After the Cadet accomplished his first solo flight, he was no longer a dodo; the dodo never flew, but the new aviator had. Most of the washouts were at Randolph; percentage wise, it was higher in pri-

mary, dropping somewhat in basic, and very low in advanced.

Until 1939, the total military and civilian population of Randolph was approximately 3,000. About 250-300 Cadets were sent to advanced training at Kelly each year. On July 1, 1939, with war clouds looming, primary training was no longer conducted at Randolph; it was now being done at numerous civilian contract schools located all across the nation. Randolph was at that time only a basic training facility. The first expansion program began in the summer of 1939, and called for 5,500 pilots to be trained by July 1, 1941. A second program initiated soon after the first, upped the quota to 7,000. The complete training was condensed from four months per phase, to ten weeks per phase. The men still received as much training, but they just did it in less time. It was a hectic pace for instructors as well as Cadets. In the spring of 1941, the quota was raised again to 30,000 a year. By now, the Gulf Coast Air Corps Training Center had been established and it would train approximately 12,000 a year. Randolph was expanded to handle classes of at least 400 men in ten weeks. New classes began every five weeks. It could now turn out about 4,500 Cadets a year.

As of 1942, the civilian primary training consisted of ground school, military training, and each Cadet received about eight hours of dual instruction before solo (some more, some less, depending on individual ability). By the end of the course they had about sixty-five flying hours. Moving on to basic, they were trained in higher performance aircraft such as the BT-9, and BT-14. After approximately five hours of dual, it was time to solo

An active flight line at Randolph 5/1/41   National Archives

were replaced, or modified during the 1920's, and further still into the 1930's. Here is some of the "Slanguage" used at Randolph through the early forties:

Big Dog: The Cadet Battalion Commander.

Bird Dog: A Cadet who cuts in on another Cadet's girl at a dance.

Cadet Widow: A girl who had dated Cadets from several classes.

Gig: Demerits given for misdemeanors. Get enough of them and you earned "tours."

Gig Stick: A rifle, a dirty gun at inspection is sure to earn its owner a gig.

Grab A Brace: Come to a position of very rigid attention.

Gray Ghost: The Stage Commander's airplane, used for final check rides before elimination.

Jeep: The Link trainer.

Kite Flying: Primary training.

Raunchy: Unacceptable, as applied to clothing, equipment, or posture.

Six and Twenty Tootsie: A particularly alluring "date" causing the Cadet to stay out too long on his weekend leave, and thus getting six demerits and twenty "tours."

Star Dust Board: The Cadet bulletin board in Operations which has the list of Cadet names with red stars next to them, indicating an aviation error.

Tour: Punishment duty, walking a designated post on the ramp. One tour=One hour

Washing Machine: The Flight Commander's airplane used for the twenty-hour and forty-hour check rides.

in a new aircraft. By the end of this phase they would have a total time of approximately one hundred thirty-five hours. Moving on to advanced, the Cadets were taught in still higher performance aircraft; the emphasis now being shifted to the use of the aircraft as a weapon, not just transportation. After successfully completing this phase of training, the Cadet was commissioned as a second lieutenant, and pinned on his coveted silver wings.

In addition to the pilot Cadets trained by the Gulf Coast Training Center, they were also responsible for the training of 6,000 men a year to become either aerial artillery officers, called bombardiers (a new term in 1942) aerial navigators, or observers.

It was the policy during the 1920's and early 1930's to place graduates of the Army advanced flying schools on active duty for two years, then place them on the inactive reserve list, thereby making room for later graduates. Many of the Cadets, after being commissioned and serving their two years active duty, went to work for the airlines, and of course were called back to active duty when the war broke out. From the time Randolph Field opened in 1931, until the summer of 1941, more than 6,800 Cadets completed basic training there.

Cadets from all eras had their own language. Many of the expressions in use during the 1918's

The following is comprised of four different interviews; each will give the reader a personal account of the early Randolph days; and great insight into what it was like in the 30's-40's in the Pilot Training section of the Army.

The first is with:

Colonel William M. Brown, Director of Flying, AAF Central Instructor School, Randolph Field, Texas, 1 Nov., 1944 by S/Sgt.. Charles. D. Brown, Hist. Sec., A-2, AAF CTTCmd.(Provided by Colonel Robert F. Schirmer, USAF Ret.)

Q. Colonel Brown, what was your early military training and experience?

A. I was first associated with the Army in May 1931 at March Field where I enlisted. You had to have six months in grade to get priority for a Cadet appointment then without a college degree. I missed the next class and was actually in ten months before my appointment. I was appointed 2 March 1922, and started primary with the first class at Randolph. I took my full training here. There were no streets built here then, and we were in mud up to our ankles half of the time.

Q. Can you describe the Cadet system in use at that time? How was the military training handled?

A. We were divided into two companies: "A" and "B", and had upper and lower classes. There were only two Cadet barracks completed then. They were three-story buildings and the upper class lived on the second floor, surrounded by lower classmen who lived on the first and third floors. We called the upper class the "ham in the sandwich." There were only about thirty-five Cadets in the upper class because the West Pointers who were officers did not live in the Cadet area, but were quartered in the B.O.Q. We never saw them except on the most formal occasions, and then had very little contact with them. Sometimes the West Pointers served as assistant tactical officers. I will say our upper class did a very good job.

Q. Can you describe the first month of training, the so-called "Hell Month"?

A. It was something like a fraternity hell week only it lasted longer. You were in the lower class for four months and there were lower-class customs you had to memorize. You could get demerits and restrictions for breach of lower-class customs. The system was pretty much like it is now with tours being given. I remember one fellow who accumulated 40 tours one weekend, which was more than he could walk off. You could only walk tours at certain times.

Q. How easy was it to accumulate these tours?

A. It was easier to accumulate them than not. Pinky Griffith was the Commandant of Cadets at that time. He was as good as they came. Later, he became the first USAAF officer to be killed in this war; he went to England as an observer. We had Phil Swofford then who was a West Pointer and an A-1 man; he was senior Cadet officer and a good soldier and a good fellow. He had to act as a "Reviewer of Gigs." On Friday morning, or afternoon, you could go before him and make gripes about any unfair gigs you thought you had; he was sitting there with a sheet in front of him and would ask you about your gigs. You could argue about them if you wanted to, but no one ever did. It was your opportunity to

Consolidated PT-1 was a replacement for the JN-4. National Archives

Douglas BT-2B   National Archives

officer. In fact, the organization was called the "Cadet Battalion." We had rifle racks and bayonets in the barracks and we drilled three days a week and reviewed every Saturday. You were always responsible for the condition of your rifle. It was the West Point system as closely as you could follow it in a year's time.

Q. Did you lose a lot of men because of this military system?

A. Not because of the military system. When we lost men it was because of flying. In my class, for instance, we had 201 students and only 95 of them got to basic and there were 89 that graduated from Kelly. It was normal to lose about 50% in primary. At Kelly Field, we never lost anyone except in the most unusual circumstances.

Q. What did they teach at Kelly?

A. The ground school at Kelly was about the same for all students with some neutral subjects, except for the observation boys whose work was different. We were divided into sections and there was a lot of formation flying, all of us except the observation boys had 113 hours of formation, and the pursuit men had sixty hours of six-ship formation. That was what we flew then, an instructor and five students in formation. We used P-12 and P-1 aircraft in the fighter outfits.

Q. What was the normal procedure for assignment after training?

A. At that time you could only get one year of active duty and there were usually a lot more requests than could be filled. Some of the fellows in my class were ordered to foreign duty and then cancelled; about 12-14 were sent to March Field. You might then be assigned to a tactical unit as a junior birdman in a squadron. There was nothing lower than a reserve officer in those days, and the RA of-

"pop-off," but I can't remember anyone who ever did. We had a tradition of taking care of our own in those days too; that is something that is definitely lacking today. If a fellow got a little out of control in town, the other Cadets would look out for him. Cadets learned to take the punishment no matter how much they might hate the guy who gave it to them.

Q. What was the training given at that time, Colonel?

A. In the eight months that I was here, I was on the east side for primary training where we had the PT-3 and the PT-11. In basic, we used the BT-2 and BT-1, the only difference between them was that one had a radial engine and the other an in-line engine. After the four months of primary and four months of basic here, we went to Kelly Field, but before we left, we made a choice of the type of training we would take at Kelly, whether it was to be pursuit, bombardment, attack, or observation.

Q. Did you continue the Cadet system at Kelly?

A. When we were the upper class here, we had been over the lower class. But at Kelly the old formations were wiped out and a minimum of officers from the students were appointed. We were still more or less on the same footing there. At Randolph we had our student Captain, Lieutenants, and so forth, with a battalion Captain as the top student

A flight of Boeing P-12's.   National Archives

all given an indefinite extension; my class became the youngest to fly the mails. Arnold then organized the third Air Mail Zone with officers in Salt Lake City. Eaker had Route 4 from Salt Lake City to San Angelo, Texas.

They had a clever stunt when you went off active duty and were returned. There was always a day in between those time periods which cancelled out all accumulated leave and other privileges, so you started new again. You had to take a physical each time you went back on duty. Any extra leave time was lost; usually you had accumulated some.

ficers never let you forget that you were there only temporarily. General Arnold was at that time the CO of March Field, and they had just booted out a few reserve officers who had gotten into trouble; which meant that they were all set for us when we arrived. We had Tinker there, and Spaatz was a wing commander; Eaker was a Captain on the post. I spent a year flying test missions without any gunnery. We were operating under the "legislative holiday plan" then; they deducted 15% of your pay and you were supposed to have a day and a half a month off, only you worked just the same. The Civilian Conservation Corps opened up about that time and nearly all the Regular Army officers were cleaned out and sent to run camps. This was when the reserve officers began to come into their own. The pursuit squadron was cut from three squadrons to one composite one. Things racked along until February 1934, when the Army flew the air mail due to a civilian strike, and we were

The first exams for regular Army commissions in five years or more were given about July 1934, and about 800 or 900 took the exams for about 51 positions. Practically no one was commissioned but West Pointers. The next year in 1936, exams were opened again and I got mine then; out of about 780 who applied, some 50 were commissioned. I had spent about two years and four months on active

Vultee BT-13   National Archives

130

Flying Cadets standing inspection at Randolph in the early forties.   AETC/HO Randolph AFB

duty at March Field and had specialized in Link Trainer instrument work.

Q. What was your first assignment after being commissioned in the RA?

A. Ten of us were sent to Randolph as an experiment to become flying instructors. That was quite a radical experiment in those days. They had never used newly-commissioned people that way before. I remember Colonel Harms called us up in his office and told us it was an honor that we had been selected and that there

The flight line at Randolph, BT-9's 5/1/41   National Archives

was a long line of applicants for positions as instructors at Randolph. It was considered a swell spot, and we were all very glad to get the assignment. We knew that flyers with years of experience would have given anything for a "shot" at Randolph.

Q. What were conditions like when you first came to Randolph?

A. We flew in the mornings only; there wasn't any flying on Saturdays or Sundays. Randolph had the reputation of being the "Country Club of the Air." We had a ten-day break between classes when you could usually take a plane and go anywhere on a hop. We thought the rough afternoon air was bad for flying, so we flew in the mornings only. I was there for three years; from October 1936 to June 1939, all on the primary side; there we were using PT-3's and PT-13's; on the basic side, they were using BT-8's and BT-9's.

Q. The instructor's experiment you mentioned earlier, Colonel, was it considered a success?

A. Several months after we had come to Randolph, Colonel Harms said it was a success. This was the first time they had used Reserve Officers as instructors. Later, I remember how all of us were horrified when we were told that men just out of Kelly Field would be used as instructors. This was

really a "radical" departure and we were shocked by the idea of using such inexperienced "greenhorns" just out of school. They did try to take only the best men. (Note: This was Class 40-A).

Q. Was the new idea in instructors tied in with the expansion of the Air Corps?

A. It probably was. It was about 1939 when they began using new graduates from Kelly as instructors. In 1938, things had begun to look pretty bad and we decided to build an air force.

Q. That was when the nine little Randolph's were planned, to step up production?

A. Yes, about that time we got excited about flying and even began flying in the mornings and the afternoons. Classes got bigger but we still did not fly on Saturdays. We lacked the money and the schools to meet the situation. It was then decided to open civilian schools. That was one time in the Army when we did have warning in advance sufficient to do something about it.

Q. How were they set up?

A. They selected thirty-five officers and gave us a series of courses in Cadet administration, regulations and problems that would come up in a primary school, and then sent two or three officers to each of the newly-selected civilian schools. I went to Parks Air College as a new 2nd Lieutenant and we took along a few enlisted men for supply, a first sergeant and technical inspectors. The funds were tied up from June on and there was a delay for some time. Suddenly the orders came about the first of July (1939), and came so fast that there wasn't time to get things ready. They roped off space in one of the hangars at Randolph and put up signs for the destination of the group and you took your furniture and things down and set them in the roped-off square and went on to the school. A lot of people ended up with furniture that wasn't theirs.

Q. What did these schools look like when you first arrived?

A. I got to St. Louis about 26 or 27 June and the enlisted men came along a few days later; I had no authority to hire or get equipment. We found a stack of mail pouches in a corner and fortunately one of our officers could type, so we opened this stuff up and that kept us going for a few days with paper work. On 30 June a class of Cadets came in on top of us, and of course we had no airplanes. Some of the first Cadets we had to hold as much as two months after their elimination because there were no procurement allotments for their pay. There was still only one Training Center and Colonel Robins was the commandant. All nine schools sent their graduates to Randolph for their basic, and they went from there to advanced at Kelly, and later to Brooks too, when it became a kind of Kelly No. 2. The original nine schools were scattered all over the country from California to Chicago and on down to Tuscaloosa, Alabama.

Q. What impressed you as being the main problems of the civilian schools?

A. The weakest thing about the civilian primary setup was there couldn't be enough tactical officers and permanent party personnel in control of the Cadets. There were only three officers to do the job for one school and everyone had more duties than he could perform. You were as busy as a one-armed monkey. We had every problem arise that you would have on a post. We never got off the job until six or seven p.m. every night and the discipline and proper supervision of the Cadets was almost impossible. The effects of this showed up later in combat where there was a lack of discipline. The ground school and the flying instruction were both done by civilians. Some of them were military in their attitude, but some were definitely nonmilitary, and that was not good for the Cadets.

Another problem at our school, and I think it applied to all the civilian schools, was that we could not get the instructors to eliminate students at first. The flying instruction was comparable to any Army school, but it was the hardest thing to get the instructors to realize they had to eliminate some of the Cadets. Not a single student was put up for elimination by instructors at our school in the first class (40-A). The Army had to step in and jerk men. We explained the situation to the school staff and after the first few classes they "played ball" pretty well.

Q. Has the curriculum changed much since then?

A. The curriculum has changed through the years, but it has been more as a result in changes in equipment. The use of the low-wing monoplane in basic eliminated a lot of maneuvers in primary. We adapted maneuvers to the aircraft. As an example, the use of flaps brought a lot of changes so there wasn't as much emphasis on approaches. You could go out and drop your flaps and make a field easily. Retractable landing gear changed things, bringing checklists and what we call mnemonic phrases. All radio has been added and all instrument work. When I went through Kelly there was no gyro or radio on the student's ship; and even when I was at March Field only the flight leader had a two-way radio. Constant speed props are also new. We will always be adjusting the training to the new types of equipment. Training can never be static; there will always be some new gadget to hook into.

Q. What was the expansion made beyond the nine little Randolph's?

A. About September 1940, they decided the nine civil primaries could not take the load and each contractor was directed to open one more school for each school he was then operating. In order to staff them they took several key men from each civil school, the best technical men and supply men, and the training center sent new officers. I went to the new school at Jackson, Mississippi, where we opened the Mississippi Institute of Aeronautics. Other schools were opened in that territory and they expanded similarly on the west coast. We took our first class there on 15 October 1940, and in January 1941, the three Training Centers were set up. Due to the split, I ended up in SEACTC because I was about on the geographical boundary line.

Q. Did this introduce any new problems or did training go on about the same?

A. Things had developed to a point where we were forced to go in for instructor's schools and standardization. When all training was under the one Training Center, all our military personnel at the contract schools had come from Randolph and had been through Randolph. Even when the expansion to eighteen schools was planned, all of our key personnel had gone out from Randolph. We had all been through the same system and we saw eye to-eye on training. When the three Training Centers got started, differences in training began to show up right away; they could see the difference at Randolph because all the students were sent back to Randolph for Basic. About this time, they had an idea to try a contract Basic School in each training center and they picked one contractor to open a basic school, but as I remember this didn't work out very well, and the idea was dropped. (Author's note: The idea was only dropped for the moment, it later became a reality). I don't think they ever had one in this training center (SEATC) during that time.

Another thing they did late in 1942 was to start twin-engine advanced training and they got the idea of standardization to be worked through a central school for instructors. Some time after Pearl Harbor when I was at Greenville, Mississippi, I remember talking to General Yount who was telling a bunch of us his idea for a new school. I just listened to the conversation and didn't say

BT-9's lined up at Randolph in 1941.   National Archives

much about it at the time and had no idea I was to be earmarked for it. I recall he said it was to be a "College of the Air" with more rank than anything like it had ever had before. It was to be the finest thing that there ever was in the way of the Instructor's Schools.

Q. So that was in a sense the beginning of the Central Instructor's School (CIS)?

A. That was the way General Yount was talking about it when it was still being planned. In a way that was the beginning of the CIS.

The second is an interview with:

Mrs. Helen L. Gilbert, Chief Clerk, Secretary's office, Central Instructors School, Randolph Field, Texas, conducted 20 October, 1944, by S/Sgt. Brown, Asst. Hist. Sec., CFTC.

Q. Whose idea was it to build Randolph?

A. It was really Major Royce's idea. He was CO of Brooks Field. They used to get so many complaints about the boys at Brooks warming up their engines. People complained that this noise disturbed their sleep. Major Royce said we should get a new field, but he wanted to go down to the flat country around Taft, Texas.

Q. You believe it was definitely Major Royce's idea to build a field away from San Antonio, and that General Lahm got the idea from him?

A. Major Royce first thought up the idea of an airfield like Randolph Field. He really started this thing, but you see he wanted the new field somewhere else. General Lahm was the one who decided he wanted it around San Antonio. I know this because I was Major Royce's secretary at the time he was CO of Brooks Field; his idea was to get it clear away from San Antonio. I remember the government said it would not buy the land, and they said if the City of San Antonio would buy the land, they would put the field there. So the City bought the site that became Randolph Field. Other's were trying to get the field put near their cities: Augustine, Florida; some place in Oklahoma; and a site in Louisiana, all offered land for this new field.

Q. How did you come to Randolph?

A. I came here with a contingent from Brooks Field on 15 October 1931. After coming from Brooks Field where there was nothing but temporary buildings, Randolph looked like quite an Army Post. When we came, all the administration buildings, and homes were completed, and most of the hangars. The first class entered on 2 November, 1931. We brought one class over from Brooks Field to complete their primary training here. This class was called the "July 31 class." We had classes of "July 31," "Nov. 31," and "March 31"; so there would be three classes entering and three graduating in a year.

Q. Did the Air Corps Training Center move into the Administration Building about the same time Randolph Field was activated? Who was the CO?

A. General Lahm was the CG, but when they first decided to establish Randolph Field, they had no idea the Training Center would move. It was located at Duncan Field at the time. There was no provision made in the plans for a headquarters setup. You see, the headquarters was in a little frame shack at Duncan, and when they came over here to Randolph and saw these permanent buildings and the way the field was, they just decided to stay.

Q. Do you recall when the CG moved in?

A. He moved about 31 October, 1931, a few days after we had moved in. They rearranged the space for the Base CO making room to accommodate General Lahm. General Lahm saw how nice it was and just moved into Randolph.

Q. Do you recall what Randolph looked like in those first days of training?

A. Everyone had lots of space. It was just right. When we came they were just planting the shrubbery, and none of the roads had been paved. The contract called for asphalt roads all over the post, but a Captain Parker of the Constructing QM held up all paving until he could persuade them that concrete (white) should be used, at least on all the main arteries. That concrete is still being used. In February 1943, Randolph Field became the Central Instructor's School. The CIS was actually moved over here from Kelly Field where the first two or three classes were held. They had about 400 students there but when they came here, they dumped 1,400 every four and a half weeks on us.

Q. What do you know from personal observation about the Cadet military system that was used at Randolph Field when the Cadet spent eight months of his training here?

A. The Cadet military system they used was worked out between Lt. Sam Ellis of Brooks Field, and Major Royce, and it was patterned as much as possible after West Point. They got the regulations from West Point and adapted the ones they thought best suited for the type of students they wanted. Lt. Ellis was at that time Commandant of Cadets at Brooks. That was how the Cadet system of training got started, and I know the students got good military training. The Honor System was patterned after West Point also, and it really worked here. They had every Saturday night off and one or two Saturdays in a month, they could stay over until 5 p.m. Sunday evening. They wore their uniforms all but one weekend. They figured that a man who couldn't take a year of what he got here wasn't worth commissioning and wasn't worth having. The first month here they used to call "Hell Month" and they were really put through their paces. Students couldn't leave the post during that first month. There were inspections all the time: room, uniform, and equipment were constantly inspected.

Q. What was the general opinion of this system?

A. I think we had a better type of officer then. Of course, our educational standards are higher now. Any student who went through training then deserved what he got.

The third is an interview with:

Mary A. Buell, Chief Clerk, Office of the Director of Flying, Central Instructor's School, Randolph Field, Texas, 17 November 1944 by S/Sgt. Brown, Historical Sec., A-2, CFTC.

Q. Mrs. Buell, when did you first come to Randolph to work?

A. I was one of the first civilians to come to Randolph from Brooks Field.

Q. Who was in command of the field during this construction period?

A. Colonel Richardson of Brooks Field, was temporarily in command; later Major Frederick Martin (of Round the World Fame) was Commanding Officer here. He became first CO of Randolph Field.

Q. Did you stay in the office of the CO., Randolph?

A. Yes, I was in that office until 1936. You see, we were in one corner of the Administration building and the CG, Training Center was in the other corner.

Q. How was training organized at that time?

A. At first we had the primary training on the east side and the basic on the west side of the field. Later, but I don't remember just when it was, they called them the 1st and 2nd Training Groups.

Q. How much authority did the CO of Randolph Field have during the early 1930's.?

A. Colonel Martin was CO of the post and also the Commandant of the school. So he really had two titles. For administration he was CO of the Post; for training he was the Commandant of the school.

Q. When did the ACTC Headquarters move to Randolph?

A. We moved here and opened in October 1931. The TC was under command of General Danforth when the move was made. General Lahm had left the TC before that. He had never intended to move here; he wanted to remain in what he called a neutral zone. His idea was to have a separate post under the Training Center and as far as I know that Headquarters was to remain at Duncan Field. Randolph was to be built as a post and not as a Headquarters for two commands. It was General Danforth who moved out here and brought the Headquarters and it has remained ever since.

The fourth, and final interview is with:

Mrs. Buchman.

Q. About General Lahm, Mrs. Buchman—

Those dancers who swayed around the floor with eyes closed were a menace to traffic, but we can understand their feelings.

Each table was reserved for four couples but after the first hour visiting became the order of the night.

Men of '41-F Dine and Dance

The roof of the Gunter, a starlit night, fine food, an abundance of drinks, highly danceable music, and lovely feminine guests from one-third of the States of the Union all contributed to make the dinner dance tendered Class '41-F, cadet detachment officers, and flight instructors one of the highlights of '41-F's stay at Randolph.

Another contributing factor was the peace of mind enjoyed by all cadets. Past were 40-hour checks, instrument checks, night flying, and other obstacles. The 70 flying hours were practically completed. Each cadet had proved that he was a good pilot, and his wings were two-thirds won.

The strict formality which necessarily, exists between cadets and officers in the regimental area and on the flight line was dispensed with, and every cadet learned once and for all that the officers were as glad as he that he had progressed so far and so well.

There was no doubt that this night was one for gaiety and celebration. Yet no cadet could forget that this, together with the final dress parade the next afternoon, was the culmination of his stay at Randolph, that in just nine days he would leave forever the regimental area which had been his home for ten crowded but happy weeks.

For those who tired of dancing or sitting around the tables (we don't see why they should), the goldfish pool was available for "tete-a-teteing."

Cadets could pick up pointers from the officers on how to spend an enjoyable evening. Recognize Capt. Grubbs and Lts. Haney, Amen, and Mears?

There was no scarcity of ice, "cokes," sparkling water, soda, and other desired drinks.

Sheraton Gunter Hotel

How long did you work in his office? What kind of man was the general?

A. I came in July 1929. General Lahm had flown up to Texas A&M where I was working in the military department and interviewed me for the job as statistician. That was how I came to work for the Training Center. He left about a year later, so I was in the TC during the time General Lahm was there; for about a year. Miss Rick was his secretary; she had come some time before I did, but I knew General Lahm very well and sometimes took letters for him. I would say that General Lahm was a perfect gentleman in every way; considerate and just, and very firm. He had the courage of his convictions and was not afraid of anything; he didn't hesitate to "stick his neck out" if he thought he was right. He was very human, reserved, and quiet. I think he was had a very strong character with very honorable and high ideals. He was very conservative but was a fearless man, meticulous in his dress and I don't remember seeing him smoke. He was very devoted to his wife.

Q. What were his relations with members of his staff?

A. General Lahm was very loyal to his staff. I will always remember when he left, he had a photo made with his staff and one made with his noncommissioned staff and he wanted each one to put his signature on the back of the photo. He was very human. We had poor transportation to Kelly and General Lahm took a personal interest in this to see what he could do to improve it for the civilians working in our office. He said he would personally call Colonel Tuttle, head of the transportation company and do what he could to improve the service. He was always doing something like that.

Q. When was the move to Randolph made?

A. I came over in November 1931. The staff consisted of General Danforth and Lt. Bob Douglas, his Aide. Captain Cannon was Director of Training. General Danforth was a believer in economy of personnel and he had cut the staff down considerably. He used to say he could run the Head-

quarters himself with one left over. He was succeeded by General James E. Chaney, who remained in Washington for eight or nine months before he came here.

Q. How did the OC operate without its CG?

A. Colonel Henry B. Claggett, CO of Kelly Field was the ranking officer here and he commuted back and forth and ran both Kelly Field and ACTC.

Q. How long was General Danforth here and what do you remember about him?

A. I'm sure he stayed here three years at least. He was a very forceful and positive man, and not very socially-minded. I remember he didn't believe in automobiles, but I don't know what the reason was—well, he didn't have one himself and he was against his officers having cars. He was more the rugged type and certainly not the "gentle gentleman" that General Lahm was.

Q. What do you recall about the military training system—the Randolph-Kelly System?

A. I knew Lt. Griffith who was the first Cadet Commandant here, and knew him very well. He later crashed in England where he had gone on some mission before we were in the war. He was a very strict disciplinarian, a very finished man who gave the impression of a fine background. The system they used in the 30's was "out and out" West Point, and as far as I know, it was approved by the CG's. When Major Fred Martin was CO of Randolph Field, General Danforth would walk down to Major Martin's office and perhaps they would talk a while about General Danforth's experiences in the Philippines, and part of the time they might be discussing problems of the post in an informal manner. Many of the problems were handled this way —very informally. Captain Thomas H. Hastey was the first adjutant at Randolph.

Q. When did you transfer from TC to Randolph Field?

A. At the time General Chaney was appointed CG. After he did not come here, there were rumors that there wouldn't be a Training Center here any longer, and on quite good authority we heard the

Headquarters would be transferred to Maxwell Field. Colonel Harms agreed to release me to the post. Then when the expansion came, I went back to Headquarters with the Gulf Coast TC in the Civilian Schools Division, with Colonel Lyon. I was there in August 1939 when Lt. Jake Smart did all the work organizing the elementary schools, and after about four months, I was back with the post in the flying department again.

CIVILIAN CONTRACT SCHOOLS

The following is the basic outline of the Civil Contract schools for pilot training in the Army Air Corps. This was written by **Robert F. Schimer, Colonel, USAF** (Retired); and first published in the *American Aviation Historical Society Journal* from Volume 36, number 1 through the next nine issues, ending with Volume 38, number 1:

General "Hap" Arnold's Great Gamble of 1939 was to introduce Civil Contracting for the first nine replacements for Randolph Field—and the first Class to be so trained was 40-A. General Arnold, then Chief of the Air Corps, decided that the only way to beat the German Luftwaffe at their own game of overwhelming airpower was to design a pilot training program which could keep up with our American industrial production of U.S. war planes—up to 50,000 planes per year. Thus, to keep pace, General Arnold had to develop a pilot training system that would eventually produce over 200,000 combat pilots in five years or less (1939-1944), which he did.

He started with these original nine civil contract primary flight training schools, adding nine more in a year (1940), then leapfrogging upwards to an overall total of more than sixty such civil primary schools, four of which taught not only primary but basic phase of flying as well.

The capacity of these schools absorbed training for over 8,500 British, French, Chinese, Dutch, Turkish, and Brazilian Air Force Cadets, as well as Cadets for eight other Latin American nations.

It was in September of 1938 when Major General Henry H. Arnold was appointed Chief of the Air Corps. It was as though he had been standing offstage waiting for the call to lead the Army Air Corps to greatness. All through his outstanding career, "Hap" Arnold was a doer and he liked to remember people's names. It was said that he once knew the first names of every officer and enlisted man he had ever met in the Air Corps, including the names of their wives and children. And his way to lead was to startle, inspire, and move the complacent to action to meet the objectives he had charted, leaving the details to them.

In 1938 there were approximately 700 qualified candidates available for enlisting as Flying Cadets in the flying training program, per the office of the Chief of the Air Corps letter, dated 21 December 1938.

The Cadet pay in 1938 consisted of: $127.50 per month, which included $75 flying pay, $30 for rations, and $22.50 for rental allowance.

General Arnold found that even though he had to make a great gamble in 1939, it was the only hope our country had to build an air force fast enough, and large enough to win a world war; the clouds of which were already on the horizon. He was faced with the problem of how to expand the pilot production from 500 per year (then the capacity of Randolph Field) to at least fourfold that amount to 2,000 per year. What he really needed was several more "Randolph Fields" to work his plan of expanding the Air Corps pilot training program. But how to get these additional facilities when he had neither the authority nor the funds to do the task? After surveying the assets and capacities of the two sole Basic training bases (Randolph and Kelly Fields), he decided to go outside of the Army and have the primary training done by civil flying schools. He knew most of the outstanding civil flying school owners/operators personally. Interestingly, there was a handful of old-time Army pilots from the World War I days, and a few experienced civilian pilots and flying school operators, who also owned pilot training schools. They were equally concerned that our airpower strength was nonexistent, and they had faith that the answer to meeting the challenge of the German Luftwaffe and the Japanese Air Forces (which had taken these enemy powers over ten years to develop), was to build a superior Air Force of our own. General Arnold had his staff meet several times with the different groups of these civilian operators to find out, first, whether they were interested in performing such training, and second, whether they felt up to the task and had the necessary facilities and trained personnel to do it.

When General Arnold started talking to this handful of older military and civilian pilots about whether they could be depended upon to train Air Corps Flying Cadets, they all agreed that they would do their share and would start a program if called upon. That was what General Arnold was waiting to hear. So he threw them a challenge to start training 40 days from their final meeting in May 1939. They all responded with positive enthusiasm, and instantly set about meeting the 1 July 1939 deadline. He had told them he thought that war was inevitable. He said the Army didn't have time to prepare facilities for the training of flyers and that we were unprepared to cope with all out war. "We've got a job to do and do it fast!" were his parting remarks to them.

This, then, was the genesis of what has been called the greatest single American masterstroke of World War II—the early starting of the training of combat pilots by using civilian flying schools to make up for the lack of expandable production capacity of Randolph Field, whose standard rate of training pilots was only 500 per year.

Years later, in 1942, General Arnold was to say: "The resourcefulness and energy of our people (Americans) would have been of little avail against our enemies if the Army Air Forces had not begun preparations for war long before Pearl Harbor. By December 7, 1941, we were in low gear and were in the process of shifting into second."

The owners of the various civil schools required no prodding, no pressure, no guarantees, no contracts. They were businessmen willing to forget business. They undertook the job, the biggest any of them had ever had, and they took it without any contracts and even without the assurance they would ever be paid (although General Arnold had promised that he would do what he could). They gambled their last dollar and all they could borrow to make good their obligation to General Arnold, to the Army Air Corps, and to their nation. It was their answer to the challenge.

These eight operators knew the nation was heading for a crisis, but they trusted Hap Arnold. Each of them returned to their schools, and based solely on General Arnold's verbal request, they began to make preparations to train the Army Air Corps Flying Cadets at their schools. Thus, the civil elementary school system was born. All of the Air Corp's primary flight training was to be given by civilian contract schools under Army supervision. New schools were added to this system until some sixty-odd schools were in operation by December 1943. This saved some 100,000 Army personnel who otherwise would have been tied up in primary training activities. The wisdom shown in creating this setup (and avoiding the costly construction of nine more little Randolph's) saved the U.S. taxpayer over $283 million dollars a year before and during World War II.

The job that these eight operators did, along with the Air Corps, to get ready for these first Flying Cadets was commendable and truly monumental. In a few short weeks, they, working together, had selected the many flight instructors and put them through the special refresher course at Randolph Field. They had moved over 150 training planes out to these nine locations of the selected contract primary schools. They were busy selecting, modifying, and constructing dormitories and barracks to house the incoming Cadets. All on a desperate, but forthright effort; truly a gamble, to get this program going in the least possible time.

Within 40 days from the afternoon these men had left General Arnold in Washington, D.C., they were receiving Flying Cadet classes assigned by the Army Air Corps—going to work on a tremendous program while a bill to reimburse them was still pending in Congress.

In 1939, when the office, Chief of the Air Corps (OCAC) determined to make contracts with nine civilian flying schools, it was explained to Congress that the use of civilian schools for primary flying training would materially reduce the time required for expansion of the Air Corps. Also, the cost of tuition and other such expenses would be largely offset by a saving in additional airfields, material, personnel, and equipment.

Early in July 1939, the nine civil primary schools had the necessary equipment (planes, etc.) and personnel (both military and civilian) and were ready to start operations.

The expansion of the basic pilot training program presented no serious difficulty for the time being, since the facilities at Randolph Field were more than sufficient to accommodate the graduates of nine civil primary schools. Kelly Field, which conducted advanced flying training, was augmented in the spring of 1939 by the addition of Brooks Field as a sub-post. These two fields proved adequate for the preliminary expansion.

General Arnold had been lacking authority to enlist the help of the civilian schools. He had made that plain to the operators, and that fact alone made it a real gamble for them. But the program, lacking ''official'' sanction, was started anyway. The idea was to build an Air Force pilot potential and there was no time to lose in waiting for "authorization". The immediate goal was 2,400 pilots a year. It was soon raised to 7,000, and then to 12,000; then to 30,000, but it was to go far beyond that figure by the end of the program.

Congress did eventually authorize the program; but authorization was granted by just two votes. The operators knew they had gambled but they hadn't realized that the ice on which they were skating was quite that thin.

General Arnold when interviewed in (1944) said, "At the time of its inception, the idea for the use of civilian contract schools was criticized as being against precedent." Even so the heads of the nine civilian flying schools were called on by the Air Corps to begin the unauthorized and unprecedented program.

Years later (in 1944), Lt. General Barton K. Yount, then CG, AAF Flying Training Command, wrote to Captain Maxwell W. Balfour, Director of the Spartan School of Aeronautics, Tulsa, Oklahoma, (he was one of the original eight contractors): "It seems only yesterday that this command placed its entire future in the hands of a few patriotic men such as yourselves. Without the nucleus of civil contractors, this command could not possibly have expanded from four or five hundred a year to the astounding rate of 100,000 pilots per year."

The story about General Arnold and his eight old-time friends deserves to break out of the dark past, for it was Arnold's answer to the boastful Luftwaffe. It is the story of a full-speed-ahead project unparalleled in military history.

Thus, in 1939, faced with the necessity of expanding the rate of pilot production from 500 to 2,000 per year, the Army had solved the problem by concentrating the limited facilities then available at Randolph and Kelly Fields in basic and advanced flight training, respectively, and turning over all primary (elementary) flight instruction to nine civilian schools.

By 4 May 1939, the original nine civil primary schools had been selected, but the execution of the plan depended upon availability of funds. Although Congress had not yet appropriated the money, the eight contractors (Parks had two schools in the original nine: Parks Air College at East St. Louis, Illinois, and the Alabama Institute of Aeronautics at Tuscaloosa, Alabama) went ahead and secured the facilities needed to meet the training requirements. Indeed, it was not until the very end of June (1939) that Congress made the appropriation for reimbursing the contractors. If the owners had not been willing to go ahead without the guarantee of compensation, the revised 4,500 pilot-program mission would have failed. The revised program called for 2,298 instead of the original 4,500.

Only the cooperation of the contractors made it possible for the expansion program to start on schedule on 1 July 1939. In part, the reason for reducing the original goals of 4,500 to 2,298 pilots was the fact that there would have been a shortage of 230 primary training planes, 96 basic training planes, and 55 advanced training planes.

On 1 July 1939, two and a half years before Pearl Harbor, there were nine civil primary flying schools opening their doors to 390 Flying Cadets of the Army Air Corps, and 17 student officers (West Point graduates). They were located all across the country from California to Nebraska and Illinois, to Texas and Alabama, for a total first class of 407 students.

The majority of the data, and some of the photographs shown in these articles came from the historical files of Flying School Class of 40-A. This was the first class of Flying Cadets and student officers to enter primary pilot training in what was then known as the 4,500 pilot program. This program originally called for sixty-six Cadets/students to be entered into the civil primary schools every six weeks. But this figure was reduced in January 1939 to 396 students every six weeks, due to shortages of planes and instructors at the beginning of the program.

The original nine civil primary schools to be covered in this series are the following:
1. East St. Louis, Illinois—**Parks Air College**, Cahokia, Illinois (Parks Airport I).
2. Glenview, Illinois—**Chicago School of Aeronautics**, Curtiss-Reynolds Airport.
3. San Diego, California—**Ryan School of Aeronautics**, Lindbergh Field.
4. Tuscaloosa, Alabama—**Alabama Institute of Aeronautics**, Hargrove Van de Graff Field.
5. Lincoln, Nebraska—**Lincoln Airplane &**

Flying School, Municipal Airport.
6. Glendale, California—**Grand Central Flying School**, Grand Central Air Terminal.
7. Dallas, Texas—**Dallas Aviation School & Air College**, Love Field.
8. Santa Maria, California—**Hancock College of Aeronautics**, Santa Maria Airport.
9. Tulsa, Oklahoma—**Spartan School of Aeronautics**, Tulsa Municipal Airport.

Note that one operator, Mr. Oliver L. Parks, opened two primary contract schools: East St. Louis, Illinois, and Tuscaloosa, Alabama, in July 1939.

Dates of opening and closing are shown for all nine schools. Five of the schools: Glenview, Illinois; Lincoln, Nebraska; Dallas, Texas; Glendale, California; and San Diego, California, were to be closed within two years. The first of these to close was Lincoln, Nebraska, which had such poor winter flying weather in 1939-40 that it had to be moved to Lakeland, Florida, in August 1940. The next school to be closed was Glenview, Illinois, near Chicago. It was moved to Albany, Georgia, in August 1940 for the same winter weather reasons. The Albany school, which Darr had opened in Georgia in August 1940, had to gradually assume the student load from Glenview. However, the Glenview school did not actually close until March 1941. Then the U. S. Navy took over the field (located near Chicago) which became "U.S. Naval Air Station, Glenview, Illinois." At about the same time in August 1940, Dallas became overcrowded at Love Field and the training program was moved to Ft. Worth. Concurrently, the Glendale, California school was replaced by the Ontario, California school in August 1940 and was renamed Cal-Aero. Over a weekend in July 1942, San Diego's Ryan School of Aeronautics was moved to Tucson, Arizona, to become Ryan's second "branch" school. This was due to the overcrowded aerial traffic on Lindbergh Field. By this time Ryan's first " branch" school had opened at Helmet, California, in August 1940.

Seven of the original nine schools were redesignated from their Air Corps Training Detachment category to AAF Flying Training Detachments (AAFFTD) after the Army Air Forces had replaced the old Army Air Corps designation in June of 1941.

The last column shows the approximate number of pilots entered and graduated by each of these original nine civil schools during their lifetimes of flying training activity. By the mid 40's each of these original nine schools that were run by eight civil contractors was supplemented by nine "branches."

In 1941, yet another nine "branches" were opened to bring the total up to twenty-six (less the three which were then in the throes of preparing to close operations as indicated above). These twenty-three schools (net) as operated by the original civil contractors were to produce almost half of the 240,000 pilots who were trained and graduated from 1939 to 1945, when the last of these schools was closed. Over sixty such civilian-run primary schools (including four basic) were opened from 1939 to 1944 to conduct General Arnold's expansion program.

Scattered through six of the nine contract schools were seventeen West Pointers who were taking Primary Flight Training in officer grade. To us, as Flying Cadets, they were in a class by themselves. Some of them acted like it, while others did not. Eight of them made it through the course and got their wings, while nine did not. This was a 53 percent washout rate—a 47 percent graduation rate.

During the Class 40-A survey made to confirm what type of plane was actually assigned to each Primary School (Civil) for use of the Detachment Tactical officers, one 40-A member, Colonel Bill Johnstone, remembers the following story about the BC-1 being flown at Glendale Primary in July 1939: "To the best of my recall, the powers-to-be had a BC-1. I specifically recall the retractable landing gear, plus a Colonel Smith (Medical Officer) who flew it once at Glendale and then complained to our Commanding Officer, Captain Day, because it was so slow. Captain Day teased him unmercifully because he (Colonel Smith) had left his plane's

gear down all the time (i.e., Colonel Smith was evidently not familiar with the retractable gear feature on the BC-1, confusing it with the old BT-9 he had been checked out on earlier at Randolph)."

The success of the civil elementary training program was immediate, and exceeded the expectations of even the champion of the plan, such as Brigadier General Barton K. Yount, then Assistant Chief of the Air Corps. He had sat on the Board of Officers which had formulated the civil elementary school plan in November 1938. On his return from a visit to all the new civil schools in July 1939 (Class 40-A), he wrote Colonel A.W. Robins, Commandant of the Air Corps Training Center (Randolph Field, Texas): "All in all, I am most agreeably impressed with the setup as a whole, and I feel that the training program at the civil schools is going to be a great success."

In 1943, Colonel John R. Morgan who, as Director of Training at the Air Corps Training Center during this early period, had a great deal to do with the planning, establishment and supervision of the civilian schools, was asked: "If the job were to be done over again, would the solution still be considered the best in the light of subsequent knowledge?" To this, Colonel Morgan, who on his own confession had originally been skeptical, replied: "Yes, the results were very gratifying, and certainly exceeded our expectations at the training center. It was a lifesaver and the only solution."

The time left to prepare for war was rapidly running out. By mid-1940, the Luftwaffe had struck, and German planes and panzer divisions were delivering knockout blows on the unprepared nations of Europe. The German victories mounted, the destruction spread, and there was no apparent way to stem it. The map of the continent was fast being changed as the arms of the swastika cast their widening shadow. Hitler was making good his public boasts. And the United States was still without an air force.

Air Corps recruiting was stepped up and it went fast. The training program couldn't keep abreast.

It took twelve weeks for a Cadet to complete the primary course. One class would be midway through the course when another class came into the school, and the schools were operating at full capacity. It was soon obvious that eight men operating nine schools couldn't possibly do the size job that General Arnold had envisioned.

At the nine primary contract schools, Class 40-B was almost as large in number (396) as Class 40-A (407). This meant that the operators had a second deadline to meet six weeks after the training period had started for Class 40-A, the first class of civilian trained Cadets. By mid-August 1939, the schools had to have double the existent capacity required to train Class 40-A, in order to handle the influx of Class 40-B.

PARKS AIR COLLEGE, INC.

The Primary school located at E. St. Louis was **Parks Air College, Inc.** (Air Corps Training Detachment), at the Parks Airport, East St. Louis, Illinois (Cahokia Illinois), and was established in 1927. The owner/operator was a Mr. Oliver Lafayette Parks (10 June 1899-28 February 1985) and this school was known as the 311th AF Flying Training Detachment (as of August 1941).

Oliver L. Parks, as a youth, enlisted in the Army Signal Corps for training in 1917. He withdrew his enlistment upon the persuasion of his par-

ents, but later joined the Marines with whom he served both in Santo Domingo and in France. After the war, and a year at Washington University in St. Louis, Parks began a spectacular career as a salesman, but eventually gave that up for flying. He owned a secondhand Standard J-1, and had a transport license, so he went into the aviation business, hopping passengers. His own flying ability was uneven and he figured that perhaps the established flying schools weren't giving their students enough flying instruction. That idea prompted him to go into the business of training students himself.

With that in mind, Parks Air College was opened on 1 August 1927, and the original operation had little or no resemblance to the modern institution into which it developed. Parks was not only the proprietor but he was also the school's original staff of instructors. The operation was housed in a rented hangar at Lambert Field, and the school had only two planes. Shortly after the school opened, Parks crashed while flying some passengers. The passengers escaped injury but Parks spent the next five months in a hospital. He was still on crutches when he rented the present site of Parks Air College, near Cahokia, Illinois. Little did he know that years later, in 1938, he would be one of the main civil school operators to be approached by Major General Henry H. Arnold, chief of the Air Corps, to discuss ways of meeting the Air Corps' critically short pilot program. From its humble beginnings it had grown into one of the leaders in training civilians for the aviation industry, as executives, pilots, mechanics, and many other occupations required by modern aviation.

In October 1938, General Arnold telegraphed Parks, to come to Washington, D.C., and to bring with him two other owners of civilian flying schools. The purpose being to discuss the feasibility of civil-

Standard J-1 with a 90hp Curtiss OX-5 engine. National Archives

ian flying schools undertaking the training of Army Air Corps Flying Cadets. Parks then requested Mr. C.C. Moseley of the Curtiss Wright Technical School, Glendale, California, and Mr. Theopolis Lee, of the Boeing School of Aeronautics, Oakland, California, to accompany him to Washington to meet with General Arnold. These four men, in October 1938, laid the groundwork for the development of the present system of primary flight training of Flying Cadets of the Army Air Corps by civilian fly-

Part of the flight line at Parks, with PT-13 and PT-19 airplanes.   Terry Love

ing schools. This meeting resulted in Parks and seven other flying school operators being called to a subsequent conference in April 1939, with General Arnold, at which time plans were agreed upon whereby these private flying schools were to contract with the Army Air Corps to provide primary flight instruction for Army personnel. Although the Congress had not yet approved a bill then pending to appropriate government funds for this purpose, General Arnold, feeling the pressing need for the establishment of these primary flying schools, urged the civilian operators who met with him to immediately make plans, i.e.,to build needed additional facilities and employ the necessary personnel to start the program. Realizing the need for such training to be urgent and having faith in General Arnold, Parks and the other private flying school operators immediately readied themselves and their organizations to take on the job of teaching Army personnel to fly. The first contract between Parks Air College, Inc., and the Army Air Corps was entered into on 28 June 1939. The primary flying training program was approved and financed by congressional action, with the enabling act becoming law on the night of 30 June 1939.

In 1939, twelve years after its establishment,

when the Army was looking for commercial flying schools in which Army Flying Cadets could be taught primary flight training, Parks Air College was among the first nine schools selected. The first officers to report for duty at this station reported by virtue of Para. 26, AGO WD S. O. No. 141, 17 Jun. 1939, and were as follows (the three tactical officers): 1st Lt. Robert B. Davenport, A.C.; 2nd Lt. William M. Brown, A.C.; 2nd Lt. Robert L. Johnston, A.C. ; also, Captain Frank W. Lane, M.C.. In addition to the above-named officers, the first cadre included Captain Leonard H. Rodieck, who reported for duty 4 July 1939. Captain Rodieck was the Central District Supervisor for the A.C. Training Center. The Morning Report for 26 June 1939 included three Flying Cadets and four enlisted men. The Flying Cadets were: Russell M. Church, Jr., George H. Blase, and Harold Garber. The enlisted men were: T/Sgt. Louis W. McKenney, S/Sgts. Henry J. Shaeffer, Arthur E. Soball, and Private Wm. S. Singer (Med. Det.). Lieutenant Davenport assumed command 23 June 1939. Lieutenant Brown was appointed Adjutant, Engineering Officer, Operations Officer, and Summary Courts Officer, in addition to his flying duties. Lieutenant Robert L. Johnson was appointed Commandant of Cadets,

Supply Officer, and QM. Captain Lane was appointed Flight Surgeon. The morning report for 1 July 1939 shows the same officer personnel, 40 Flying Cadets, and six enlisted men. The list of students in Class 40-A, Section "A" was: Coulter, Robert E.; Damon, Harry F., Jr.; Dow, James F.; Fandel, William H.; Gibbons, Robert J.; Johnson, Leland W.; Lambert, Paul M.; MacInnis, Raymond L.; Perry, Arthur C.; Springfield, Berkeley I.; Thyng, Harrison R.; and Turner, Jack W. (1st Lt.). In Section "B" they were: Billings, Robinson; Blase, George H.; Church, Russell M., Jr.; Gay, John E.; Hassemer, David W.; Lippincott, Robert S.;

Boeing PT-17 "Kaydet." National Archives

Field Manager, Henry F. Schnittger. The Ground Course Instructors were: W.V. Brown; G.H. Hamilton; C.H. Karvinen; H.C. Larrick; J.A. Marshall; N.W. Scanlon; C.J. Schwarz; J.W. Terrell; W. H. Thompson; D.H. Weber; and H.J. Zimmer. The Chief Pilot was, George J. Gruen. The flight Instructors were: Frank Aueting; Arthur Edwards; Kenneth Gobel; Harvey J. Glass; Robert J. Hughey; Joe B. Lambert; Fulton Moore; Robert L. Myrick; H.R. Renninger; B.B. Rice; Richard M. Ruble; Howard Trunnell; and E.J. Weisbruch.

During a tornado alert at Parks. Terry Love

The aircraft that were assigned to this detachment when operations began (1939) consisted of twenty-seven Stearman PT-13's. On or about 1 August 1940, these assigned airplanes were replaced by seventy-four Stearman PT-17's. This was at the time when the size of each class of Cadets was increased from about forty to about 110. In November 1940, the PT-17's were replaced by seventy-four PT-19 airplanes. Additional aircraft had gradually been added since November 1940, bringing the ag-

Ljunggren, Ernest N.; Mullen, John J.; Normand, Charles G.Y.; Stoddard, Edward F.; and Walter, Carl P. The total students in both sections was twenty-three. There were twenty others that were eliminated; seventeen in Primary, and three in Basic.

The School President was; Oliver L. Parks; Vice President & General Manager, Walter P. Thorpe; and

gregate that they then had to the following: fifty-nine PT-19's; nine PT-19A's; twenty-nine PT-19B's; with a grand total of ninety-seven planes.

On 1 August 1940, the headquarters of this detachment and all flying activities were moved from the grounds of Parks Air College to another flying field known as Curtiss Field. This latter field is about one mile north of Parks Air College. All aircraft and flying operations were transferred from Parks Airport at that time.

Curtiss Field was laid out and its buildings constructed by Curtiss Flying Service, Inc. (later merged into Curtiss-Wright Corp.), in 1929, at a cost of about $1,800,000. It was originally used by Curtiss as its operating base for an aircraft school, airplane sales, maintenance, aerial photos, and charter trips. The field was also to serve as a base for Transcontinental & Western Airlines, but this plan was never realized. The entire layout covered 569 acres, and was first used as a flying field in February 1930, being operated by the Curtiss Flying Service, Inc., until 1933. The company then leased the field to Charles R. Wessell, who operated it as a commercial airport until 1 July 1940, at which time Curtiss leased the field to Parks Air College for use in the Army flying training program.

Curtiss Field has a rather unique history and played a prominent part in aeronautical history in this country up until the time it was taken over for use in the Army training program. The site was originally chosen by Charles A. Lindbergh, who was then in the employ of Transcontinental & Western Airlines. The first man to land on the field was the late Smith Reynolds, president of the Reynolds Tobacco Company, makers of Camel cigarettes. Among the prominent figures in aviation history who flew from the field are James H. Doolittle, Charles A. Lindbergh, Amelia Earhart, Art Goebel, Wallace Beery, Wiley Post, Wilbur Shaw, Clarence Chamberlain, Louise Thadden, Patrick J. Hurley (at that time Secretary of War, now Brig. General), W.K. Vanderbilt, Colonel Horace Hickam, Jim Haizlip, and Bellante and Costes (the two Frenchmen who were the first

to fly the western route over the Atlantic Ocean). During 1937, 1938, and 1939, the U.S. Navy used Curtiss Field for dive-bombing practice—the planes being stationed at Lambert Field, Robertson, Missouri. Ten-pound bombs were used—this practice usually being carried out on Sundays and attracting large crowds from St. Louis and the surrounding area. It is of interest to note that James H. Doolittle (later General), while testing a racer over the field in 1932, was forced to parachute onto the field due to an engine failure.

Climatic and weather conditions were not always the best for training, poor visibility being the chief cause of the cancellation of flights from Curtiss Field. During the average January, the visibility at Curtiss Field (airport later named Curtiss-Steinberg Field) is two miles or less during 40 percent of the daylight hours. The three concrete runways at Curtiss-Steinberg Field (Parks Airport at this time not being used by the detachment) are 1,000 feet in length—the field affording additional runway space of about 2,500 feet for each of the said three runways. Barracks A, B, and C were of concrete and masonry construction while barracks D and E were of wooden construction. The ground school buildings were of concrete and masonry. The mess hall was of masonry, wood and concrete, while the dispensary was located in a building of masonry and concrete. The four hangars on Curtiss Field were of masonry, concrete and steel, and the pilot house was of wood. On 5 August 1942, the first Link Trainers were received at this detachment and Link Training instruction began shortly thereafter. These Link Trainers were Type C-3. The first shipment consisted of three machines and on 1 September 1943, two more trainers were received and installed.

An auxiliary landing field known as Aux. Field No. 1 was established and put into use on 3 July 1940. This field was located about three miles SE of Belleville, Illinois. Another auxiliary landing field, known as Aux. Field No. 2, was established and put into use in August 1942, and was located about four miles northeast of Millstadt, Illinois. Both

Beech Travel-Air used as an instrument trainer at Parks.   Terry Love

craft.

The first class, 40-A, was given a course of flying instruction that covered a period of twelve weeks and included sixty-five hours of flying time, in addition to ground school and other instruction. This same course of instruction continued until Class 41-C on 17 September 1940. At that time the course of flight instruction was changed from sixty-five to sixty hours and the duration of the course from twelve to nine weeks.

of these fields were under lease.

The original Parks Air College facilities remained open at Parks Airport I, to continue its original and basic programs which consisted of providing all branches of commercial aviation with properly trained graduates.

A total of 5,090 Cadets had reported for duty at this detachment; of this number 1,949 were eliminated from further flight training for an elimination rate over the entire program of 41.0 percent. Of the number eliminated, 1,733 were eliminated for flying deficiencies while the other eighty-four were eliminated for medical or other reasons. Therefore, a total of 3,141 Flying and Aviation Cadets have successfully completed their primary flying instruction at this detachment.

Over the course of this instruction, five Aviation Cadets met their deaths while engaged in routine training flights. All these deaths were instantaneous upon the crash of the air-

On 15 December 1939, General H.H. Arnold, chief of the Air Corps, and his staff, made an inspection visit. The men flew there in a B-18 aircraft. On 24 July 1942, Major General F.B. Wilby, commanding general of the U.S. Military Academy, visited the field with his staff. Brig. General Hubert R. Harmon, C.G., AAF Gulf Coast Training Center, visited this detachment in May 1942.

On 7 June 1941, the observance of Flying Ca-

Whoops! An unfortunate Cadet hit the brakes too hard.   Terry Love

Boeing B-18 at Parks.   Terry Love

safety belt fastened and, with the canopy being partially open, he was thrown out of the plane, and did a complete somersault in the air and landed on his back at the rear of the aircraft, facing the rear, with one leg on each side of the vertical fin. Woodrich then grabbed the horizontal stabilizer at each side of the fin and hung on while Mattis landed the plane. They were flying at an altitude of about 500 feet at the time the Cadet was thrown out of the cockpit. Woodrich suffered nothing but a torn sock. This unusual event received national publicity and Cadet Woodrich was invited to relate his experience and did so, on, *We, the People*, a nationwide network radio show.

The Honorable Calvin Johnson, congressman from the 22nd District of Illinois, presented the Aviation Cadet detachment a flag of the United States that had flown over the national Capitol; and this flag was raised in an Army Day ceremony, 6 April 1943. Oliver L. Parks made the presentation with

det Week involved a detachment of approximately 200 Aviation Cadets from Parks Air College participating in a parade held in St. Louis, Missouri. Over 7,000 soldiers took part in that parade, most of the men being from Jefferson Barracks, Missouri, and Scott Field, Illinois. Fifty-two of the Army training planes assigned to this detachment participated in the program by flying in formation in groups of three over downtown St. Louis.

On 10 July 1941, a very unusual occurrence took place in the course of a routine training flight from Curtiss Field. Flying Cadet Victor H. Woodrich of Three Oaks, Michigan, and a civilian instructor, David J. Mattis, were approaching Auxiliary Field No. 1 in a PT-19A Fairchild trainer, equipped with a canopy, for a practice landing. Woodrich began climbing the plane so sharply that Mattis feared it would go into a stall and used his controls to thrust its nose down sharply. Woodrich did not have his

PT-19 at Parks.   Terry Love

the Cadet detachment and certain of the officers present.

The first detachment commander, Major Davenport, later became a full colonel and was heading the Frederick Army Air Field, Advanced Flying School, Frederick, Oklahoma, in 1944. Later, as Colonel, AF-Ret., he died on 24 February 1979.

Gruen stayed on as Director of Flying until 22 March 1943, when he resigned his position. Weisbruch took this job until December 1943 and was succeeded by David J. Mattis.

As the number of Cadets per class increased, so did the instructors, until in 1944, there were sixty-two on duty at Parks Air College.

Fred Mueller was in charge of all maintenance mechanics. On 1 July he had seven mechanics under him. In 1944 there were twenty-seven more; in 1943 he had forty-three.

Ground school instructors were under Frederick Roever and included: Harry Larick (engines); George Hamilton (airplane structures); Kenneth Williard (meteorology); and Fulton Moore (navigation).

During the course of flight training instruction, two civilian flight instructors had been killed while engaged in their duties; these were: S.L. Harris (Harris Field was named in his honor at Cape Girardeau Primary), killed on 4 February 1941; and Edward O Koch, killed 14 September 1943, both of whom were flying routine training flights.

On 1 February 1944, Captain John F. Davis, then C.O., 311th, received official notice that the Cadet training program for Parks Air College would cease with the graduation of Class 44-G on 12 March 1944. Two classes were in the process of training when the inactivation order was received: Class 44-F and 44-G. With the graduation of Class 44-F on 7 February 1944, there was a surplus of civilian and military pilots, mechanics, and planes. The problem of placing the civilian personnel in employment where they would best benefit the war effort was solved by the contractor, Oliver L. Parks. The Air Transport Command (ATC), represented by Major

Harold M. Skeels from Dallas, Texas, accepted nineteen of the civilian pilots and seventeen of this number joined the ATC during the second week of February. Ten other civilian pilots were absorbed by other primary training schools. One pilot went to work for Parks Air College. Of the thirty-two flight instructors remaining, it was believed six or seven would join the ATC and the remainder would go to primary training centers. Likewise, the civilian mechanics who were no longer required at Parks all found employment with the major airlines, principally American Export Lines of New York and United Airlines of California. It was felt that the remainder of the mechanics would be absorbed by these two lines. Although the news that the training program would cease was received with disappointment, the fact that all civilians found employment elsewhere without delay was met with a note of relief and satisfaction by the entire training complement.

In summarizing the history of this detachment, it occurs to the writer that the most appropriate comment that could be made—a point that should be most forcefully emphasized— is that the arrangement of the combination civilian-military instructional program functioned smoothly and successfully at this detachment. The great majority of the men who had been assigned to this detachment for flight training had no previous pilot experience and almost none had any prior contact with aircraft or aeronautics; yet in the short space of time in which they were stationed there, the majority of those boys progressed most rapidly. Not only does this speak well for the mentality and adaptability of the American boy, but it also substantiates and serves to ratify the judgment of the Chief of the Army Air Forces (General Arnold) in deciding to use civilian schools and civilian instructors as the first step in converting the raw recruit into a combat pilot.

Between 1940-1944, Oliver L. Parks, ran a total of five civil primary schools. These schools entered a total of 22,848 student pilot trainees and graduated 15,005 from primary training, including

4,000 British RAF Cadets; also several hundred French and Dutch Air Force Cadets, along with thousands of aircraft mechanics. For this contribution, he was honored by both Great Britain and the United States. Later, in 1984, he was elected to the Illinois Aviation Honor Roll for that year.

A total of 3,141 Flying/Aviation Cadets and student officers, trained under Army supervision, were graduated from Parks Air College primary into basic and advanced between July 1939 and March 1944, when the combat pilot training program at that school was discontinued.

In 1977, Parks Air College, now known as Parks College of St. Louis University at Cahokia, Illinois, was deeded to the university by Mr. Oliver L. Parks.

During World War II, Parks, starting out with two of the original nine contract pilot schools, opened three others at the following locations: Missouri Institute of Aeronautics, Sikeston, Mo.;. Mississippi Institute of Aeronautics, Jackson, Mississippi; and Cape Institute of Aeronautics, Cape Girardeau, Missouri. This does not include the moving of his school contract operations from Parks Airport I to Curtiss Field, Illinois, in August 1940.

The following are comments from some of the graduates of Parks:

Dave Hassemer — "My most memorable and happy days were getting my first flight in a PT-13 at Parks and feeling like a real Flying Cadet at last. My first solo flight, took me until I had twelve and one-half hours of dual before I was let loose. The only other two guys who took longer to solo didn't wash out in primary but they did wash out in basic at Randolph (Bretell and Rickenbaugh). Incidentally, my first solo landing was as smooth as any I ever made."

Colonel Carl P. Walter—"How did I get to be an Army Air Corps Cadet? Well, in 1937, the 'old Air Corps' sent a Cadet recruiting and medical examining team to the University of Wisconsin where I was laboring on my engineering degree. Most of the school jocks plus the whole ROTC battalion, including me, took their tests for the hell of it. To mass mortification, almost everyone flunked the physical, including me. Most flunked on eyes. I was different. I flunked on a busted nose, souvenir of freshman boxing. Might interfere with my 02 intake at a high (12,000 feet) altitude, they said. So I forgot it, though I did get my nose reamed out, graduated, and became an impoverished junior design engineer, commuting three hours a day in the rat race to New York City, poring all day over lens-lighting layouts for industrial plants, schools, stores, and hospitals, with lots of unpaid mandatory overtime, etc. By 1939, the winds of war were blowing across the Atlantic. President Roosevelt proclaimed his goal of 25,000 aircraft, and the pilots to fly 'em. The hard-pressed Air Corps dug through its old records, picked up all the old rejects, and sent each of us a personal letter asking if we would like a free second physical. Free? I needed one anyway, so sure. This time I passed (the Army doc seemed to

A PT-13 at Parks, with a *real* Flying Cadet   Terry Love

151

know I would) and they immediately offered to enlist me as a Flying Cadet, with $75 per month, free medical, free food, clothing and tent, all the airplanes I could handle, and if I survived for thirty years, a fat pension (hah!). I thought the deal over long and carefully for about thirty milliseconds, then went back to my office and told my bosses to take this job and shove it, then went down to Newark to enlist. The fat, friendly sergeant swore me in, gave me travel orders, and a voucher for train fare to East St. Louis; looked at me, shook his head sadly, and sent me off with one piece of memorable advice: 'Son, in the Army keep your mouth shut, your bowels open, and never volunteer.' I squandered the travel fare, heeled around until the day before I had to report, drove nonstop from New Jersey to St. Louis, stopped for an Army 'skin' haircut, then drove into the newly opened Parks Air College Air Corps compound. A supply sergeant took my papers, shoved a set of fatigues and a pair of boots at me, and pointed me toward the contract barbershop. 'But, Sarge, I just got one this morning.... 'Mister, I said go get a haircut. NOW! ON THE DOUBLE!' I had started my new career."

Second Lieutenant James Frederick Dow— Upon graduation from the University of Maine in 1938, with a degree in mechanical engineering and a commission (ROTC) as a 2nd Lieutenant, Infantry Reserve, he served a year at Ft. Williams, Portland, Maine, under the Thomason Act, receiving the grade of 1st Lt., Inf. Res., First Corps Area. Later he took the physical exam and applied for enlistment in the Air Corps as a Flying Cadet. He was accepted and in June 1939 and he went to Parks Air College in East St. Louis, Illinois., for primary training as a member of Class 40-A. Three months later he moved on to Randolph Field, Texas, for basic flight training. By January 1940, he had been sent on to Kelly Field, Texas, for his advanced flight training where he graduated 23 March 1940 as a pilot and was commissioned a Second Lieutenant, Air Corps Reserve. He spent April on field maneuvers with the Third Army in Georgia. In May he was assigned to Mitchel Field, where he joined the 5th Bomb Squadron, 9th Bomb Group. He was being indoctrinated in B-18A medium bombers when he met his death.

In 1940, Bangor Airport, Maine, was designated as the primary site in Maine for Aerial Defense of the Northeast Coast. Construction began on facilities for the 43rd Bomb Group which arrived in April 1941. In January 1942, the base was named Dow Field in honor of Second Lieutenant James Frederick Dow of Houlton, Maine, who was killed while on a training flight in a formation of four B-18A's over Long Island, near Mitchel Field, New York. That flight took place on 17 June 1940, and Lt. Dow, and three other 40-A classmates were among the eleven military persons killed when two B-18A bombers collided in midair, causing them to crash separately only moments later. By the end of World War II, over 100,000 combat aircrew members and their aircraft had passed through Dow Field on their way to and from Europe as an aerial port. Dow Field later became Dow Air Force Base and alternately was under the control of the Strategic Air Command and Tactical Air Command for a number of years. Dow AF Base was deactivated officially in July 1968 due to cutbacks in defense spending. Dow AFB is now Bangor International Airport.

After Dow was deactivated, the University of Maine bought some of this large installation and expanded the university, calling it the South Campus of the University of Maine at Orono. The trustees of the university decided to perpetuate the name and memory of Lt. James F. Dow by designating the most impressive and important building on their South Campus—the library/chapel—as the "Lieutenant James F. Dow Hall" (1978).

CHICAGO SCHOOL OF AERONAUTICS

The **Chicago School of Aeronautics** (Air Corps Training Detachment) Curtiss Reynolds Airport, Glenview, Illinois was established in 1928. The owner/operator was Mr. Harold D. (Hal) Darr (1893-1955). As of August 1941 it was named the 52nd AAF Flying Detachment.

In the spring of 1939, the Army decided it would have to greatly expand its pilot training program. After due consideration, it was concluded that the most satisfactory system for rapid expansion would be the use of the large number of civilian instructors in this country. An invitation for bids was offered among an approved list of proposed operators. Harold S. Darr submitted a bid which was accepted on 28 June 1939. At that time he was renting the Curtiss Reynolds Airport at Glenview, Illinois. The North Suburban Flying Corporation changed its name to the Chicago School of Aeronautics when It secured its government contract for training Flying Cadets for the Army Air Corps.

Darr was a native of Iowa and had enlisted in the Army Air Service in June 1917. After receiving his commission, he was assigned to the Army training base at Kelly Field, Texas, as an instructor. He also served at Brooks Field, San Antonio, and at Carlstrom, near Arcadia, Florida, where he attended the aerial gunnery school. He remained at Carlstrom as an aerial gunnery instructor until his discharge from the Army in 1919. After the war, Darr formed the Curtiss-Iowa Corporation and opened flight training schools in Iowa. He was a distributor of Curtiss planes and helped to introduce the Curtiss Oriole, one of the first commercial models used after World War I. Later, in 1930, Darr was employed by the Curtiss Company in various capacities until 1932, when he joined American Airlines. In 1935, he entered business for himself and started a flying school at Curtiss Field, Glenview, Illinois, which he rented from the Curtiss Company. Shortly afterwards, Darr opened a CPT (CAA) flight School at Palwaukee Airport, which was also located near Chicago.

The Air Corps Training Detachment of the Chicago School of Aeronautics, Curtiss Reynolds Airport, Glenview, Illinois, was opened 1 July 1939. This field consisting of 360 acres near the village of Glenview, was located about 20 miles northeast of Chicago, in Cook County. The flying equipment used at this detachment was loaned to this school by the U.S. Army, and started with five PT-13A airplanes and one BC-1 for the use of officers of this detachment. This equipment was stored in a very large hangar that was 650 feet long. The airport consisted of a medium-sized flying field on which were located three runways, and a single hangar, which contained an office and classrooms on the second and third floors. The U.S. Navy had permission to use the field and to occupy three-fifths of the hangar. Darr serviced and stored privately owned airplanes and had two instructors, Mr. Savage and Dwight Morrow, who gave flying lessons. Darr also operated a CPT (Civilian Pilot Training) school at the Palwaukee Airport which was located about five miles from the Curtiss Airport.

On 24 June 1939, the first steps were taken to prepare for the 1 July opening when Captain Clinton F. McIlney, Medical Corps, arrived and joined as per par. 25 ,WD SO 141, 17 June 1939. First Lieutenant A. J. McVea, A. C., joined 25 June as per par. 26, WD SO 141, 17 June 1939, and assumed command under authority contained in AR 353500, par. 7a(1). First Lieutenant Noel F. Parrish, A.C., arrived and joined this detachment on 25 June 1939, as per par. 26, WD SO 141, 17 June 1939.

This school was originally established at Curtiss-Reynolds Airport near Chicago. Darr had become associated with Air Corps Major R.W. (Shorty) Schroeder in the establishment of Curtiss Field in 1928. He organized the Chicago Aviation Corporation in 1934, which leased and operated Curtiss-Reynolds Field at Glenview. The school at Glenview was one of the original nine civil schools to participate in the Army flight training program. Army Flying Cadets (Class 40-A) first started to receive primary flight training there under civilian auspices on 1 July 1939. It was in operation almost two years as a contract school without a single fatality, and was moved to Albany, Georgia, in August 1940. When the Glenview school closed on

March 12, 1941, the Albany school took over the existing student load.

The Chicago School of Aeronautics started operations with nine instructors, including Mr. Savage, who was the chief instructor. Prior to the opening of the school, the instructors were sent to Randolph Field, Texas, for a two-week course in Army flying. They went in three groups, with 50 percent of the first group of four being eliminated. In the second group of six, all graduated. Two-thirds of the third group of three were eliminated. Savage stated that the primary difference between Army flying and civilian as he had then been instructed, was that precision was not just limited to actual flight, but was applied to every phase of handling of the plane, i.e., taxiing, mode of donning your parachute, etc.

The Flight Instructors were Florian K. Savage, director; Dwight Morrow, chief pilot; Warren Malrick, "Sandy" McCorkle, Rudolph Reprecht (former Luftwaffe officer who married an American girl and emigrated to the U.S. a few months before the school opened) and four others.

The Ground School Instructors were the Director, Casey Jones, Mr. Parrish (Maintenance), and Fracares and Taufort.

The first class (40-A) was compelled to use the Administration Building at Palwaukee Airport for their barracks, pending the completion of the new barracks. The students were transported back and forth by a bus chartered by Darr. The Army's Detachment Office was temporarily located in Darr's office in the hangar at the Curtiss Airport. The Administration Building was completed on 28 August 1939, and the students and the detachment office were moved into this new building, which housed students and also provided space for the offices.

On the date of opening, 1 July 1939, Darr had completed the construction of a two-story-frame barracks and mess hall building, which housed all the operation of the detachment, except the parachute room, the academic rooms, and the maintenance department. These were all installed in the large hangar.

In the summer of 1940, a one-story building which contained the administrative offices, on one side and the academic rooms on the other, was built at the insistence of the Army.

Class 40-A began 1 July 1939, and was composed of four officers and twenty-one Flying Cadets, of which two officers and seven Cadets were eliminated; sixteen students were sent to Randolph Field for Basic on 30 September 1939. Class 40-B began on 19 August 1939, and was composed of twenty-three Flying Cadets of which seven were eliminated and sixteen were sent to Randolph Field for further training on 18 November 1939. Class 40-C began on 30 November 1939, and was composed of twenty-four Second Lieutenants, of which six were eliminated and eighteen were sent to Randolph Field for further training on 30 December 1939. This class also had four Flying Cadets of which one was eliminated and three were sent to Randolph Field, making a total of twenty-one students who graduated the primary course of instruction. Class 40-D began on 15 November 1939, and consisted of thirty-two Flying Cadets of which eighteen were eliminated and fourteen were sent to Randolph Field for further training on 17 February 1940. Class 40-E began on 30 December 1939, and consisted of twenty-one Flying Cadets, of which nine were eliminated, and twelve were sent to Randolph Field for further training on 30 March 1940.

There were only a few accidents in 1939—on 26 July 1939, a Flying Cadet landed on top of a civilian airplane. The tail of the Army plane was hit by the propeller of the civilian plane on the ground, damaging the tail wheel of the Army plane, and the propeller of the civilian plane. No injury was suffered by personnel. On 6 September 1939, a civilian mechanic nosed a PT-13 over on its nose while taxiing from the hangar to the flight line, damaging the propeller and engine, but no one was injured. One Flying Cadet was injured in line of duty but not while flying. He fell off a haystack while engaged in recreation? and fractured his left arm at the elbow. This happened on 25 September 1939 (Class 40-B).

With the establishment of SEACTC (South East Air Corps Training Command) at Maxwell Field, July 1940, the Army's students at Glenview, Illinois, were gradually received at Albany, where a new contract school was organized 9 July 1940. The students from Illinois, who were sent to Albany, were referred to for sometime there after as the guys from the "Glenview School." However, the Glenview School did not actually close until March 1941 (to make room for the U.S. Navy takeover of Curtiss-Reynolds Airport at Glenview for Navy Flight training which had been pending for over two years), and continued training regular pilot classes through Class 41-F which entered training there on 4 January 1941 and graduated 18 March 1941. The Chicago School of Aeronautics had graduated 240 pilots since starting AC elementary civil training on 1 July 1939.

Chicago Aero Tech, Inc., is shown listed on the roster of civil elementary schools in SEACTC as of 15 July 1941. It was the original name of the school at Albany, Georgia, when the move was first made from Glenview, Illinois.

Captain McVea, the first commanding officer of this detachment at Glenview, Illinois, was relieved to take command of the new training detachment opened by Darr in Albany, Georgia, and Captain Parrish replaced him at Glenview. Parrish retained command until the Chicago school was closed. Then Captain Parrish was assigned as C.O. at Tuskegee Primary, Alabama, the Negro pilot training school. Originally this training of Negro pilots was to have been done at Chicago School of Aeronautics, Glenview, Illinois. Why it was changed is not stated in the historical notes.

By 1940, there were about 30 PT-13's assigned to Glenview for training classes of about forty-five Cadets. The instructors having been qualified by the previously mentioned course at Randolph Field. The original instructors were permitted to qualify other instructors. All instructors of flying had to have 1,000 hours minimum flying time. The mechanics were required to acquaint themselves with the tech Orders, but had to have an A&M license from C.A.A..

In the fall of 1940 and spring of 1941, Cadets wore their civilian clothes off post; flying was five days a week; there was rifle drill three afternoons a week; ground school had been reduced from 204 to 140 hours; and the Cadets were inspected each Saturday morning.

The continuing evolvement in the balance of operational necessity, versus the quality of training, called for constant changes in the program. The "stall series" was very much less complete in 1939 and the technique used in doing the maneuvers varied slightly. At that time (1939) the aerobatics were not done both ways as was later the practice. During those early days of operations at the Chicago School, they were done only to the left (to take advantage of the engine torque). Some difficulties were encountered from adverse weather, but all classes were graduated on schedule. Regulations required that flying in the open cockpit planes should be postponed when the temperature dropped below 10°F; but flying was sometimes done when it was 10 below.

One of the major reasons for moving this school to a more southerly climate was the hard winter weather at this latitude. The same thing happened to the Lincoln School of Aero at Lincoln, Nebraska, which was also moved to a southern climate, Lakeland, Florida.

At the Glenview, Illinois Primary School, from 1 July 1939 to 18 March 1941, 483 students (both Flying Cadets and student officers) were entered and 240 were graduated for an overall graduation rate of 49.6 percent. This included Classes 40-A through 41-F.

Hal S. Darr was given the Order of the British Empire (OBE) by the British Air Ministry in 1947 for his part in training British RAF Cadets at his primary/advanced school (No. 5 British RAF Training School, Ponca City, Oklahoma) at which RAF

Cadets were trained.

When asked, "What circumstances led to your applying for Flying Cadet Training in the Army Air Corps?" the following "Glenview guys" answered:

Captain Raynold A. Berg (Pan Am)— " It certainly was not for love of the 'Beer Barrel Polka' which every night to the wee hours reverberated through our barracks that were directly above the Glenview Airport honky-tonk bar. Nor was it for love of bananas, which to this day I detest, after having eaten socksfull of them and was still barely able to make my weight limit for my physical to enter the Air Corps as a Flying Cadet. I was at Yale Graduate School on a scholarship, having achieved an M.A.. I was poor as a church mouse, waiting tables, bell-hopping, operating elevators, and being frankly, tired. My intention to pursue a Ph.D. required more money, acquired with less effort. What better way than to have one year's Air Corps training and be paid to fly my own plane weekends in the Connecticut National Guard, while pursuing my studies at leisure? Evidently prescience as to upcoming political events were not my forte. I do recall while at Glenview, General Arnold came to inspect midway through our training. The Army had not supplied us with proper uniforms and our excited TAC officers suggested very strongly that we purchase the necessary items such as khaki belts, shirts and the peaked cap. I was the only one to refuse and appeared at inspection bareheaded. Arnold stopped before me and questioned my appearance. When I explained I would not buy what the Army was obligated to supply, he said I was correct and the situation of supply would be redressed."

Colonel John J.B. Calderbank— "I had always been interested in a military career since early high school days, primarily the U.S. Military Academy. A close friend of mine from home was a Flying Cadet, graduating in the class of 39-A. As graduation from Purdue neared, a flying career had much more appeal than an engineering job in industry; so when the Air Corps team came to Purdue in April/ May 1939, I applied. I was appointed a Flying Ca-

det, being sworn in, and received orders to go to Chicago School of Aeronautics, Glenview, Illinois, in June 1939."

Colonel Joseph A.L. Greco— "Between 1935 and 1938 I was enlisted in the Connecticut National Guard as a buck private, infantry. I wasn't impressed with the duty or their training, but I stuck it out for three years. Those were Depression years and one took any job one could find. After graduation from college in 1937, I was assistant buyer of the toy department in a large department store in Hartford, Connecticut, with the enormous salary of $12 per week. Boring as hell! I was thinking of going down to the oil fields of Venezuela to seek my fortune. Even considered joining the French Foreign Legion. Good thing I didn't as most of them got shot up in World War II. I think it was in March of 1939 that Life magazine came out with a cover story about the West Point of the Air with lots of photos that excited my imagination. I had never flown except for about one-half hour as a passenger in a light plane sometime in 1936. I applied, went to Boston Army Depot for the physical, and to meet the Board. I don't know how many applied but it was at least twenty, and Johnny Knox and I were the only ones to make it. As a matter of fact, when it came time to board the train for Chicago from Springfield, Massachusetts, Knox was on the same train. One humorous thing that happened—after my physical exam in Boston I boarded a bus to go home to Hartford, and grabbed a magazine to read on the trip home. They had shot my eyes with belladonna and my vision was blurred. I couldn't make out much in the magazine, but after a couple of hours my vision cleared. I never had that experience before and I was sure worried. Anyway, I got my orders for Chicago about the end of April or first of May . . . and so . . . off we go!"

RYAN SCHOOL OF AERONAUTICS

Ryan School of Aeronautics, Inc., a California corporation, was incorporated 5 June 1931, succeeding to the pilot training, airplane sales and service, airline operation, and airplane manufacturing business, which had originally been established by T. Claude Ryan (1898-1982) in San Diego in September 1922. The name of the corporation was changed to the Ryan Aeronautical Company in January 1935, and at the same time Ryan School of Aeronautics was organized as a wholly-owned subsidiary. Since that date the Ryan Aeronautics Company's principal activity was the manufacture of military and civilian airplanes and aeronautical accessories, while the Ryan School of Aeronautics was engaged in the training of civilian and military pilots, airplane and engine mechanics, aeronautical designers and engineers, and other aviation technicians requiring specialized training. On 8 May 1939, the War Department announced from Washington that Ryan was among the nine schools selected for contract pilot training. The first class (40-A) of thirty-five Flying Cadets began flight training on 1 July 1939. New classes arrived each six weeks for the three-month training program which consisted of 65 hours of flying and 225 hours of technical instruction.

T. Claude Ryan soloed in the American School of Aviation at Venice, California, in 1917. After less

solo flight ended in a crash-landing, wiping out the plane, but with no injury to him. The company soon "folded." Shortly thereafter, he was accepted by the Army for flight training, but then the Armistice came along (11 November 1918) and he was notified that his services were not needed. He then attended Oregon State College studying engineering for a year. By the fall of 1919 he was back for flight training. This time for some real training with the new Flying Cadet class at March Field, California. Out of a group of 75 Cadets, only 30 graduated from the 50-hour primary stage. Ryan was one of three completing the course of pursuit pilot rating. Rather than go to Kelly Field for advanced training, Ryan volunteered to go on aerial forest fire patrol over Northern California and Oregon in late spring of 1921. Ryan landed in San Diego (1922) fresh from forest patrol work as an Army flying officer in Oregon and Northern California. He hoped to get into commercial aviation but found no immediate opportunity. So he went to work for an automobile supply company. Meanwhile he took advantage of his reserve Army commission and began to fly at Rockwell Field. Then came his chance. He heard of an airport on the San Diego waterfront, controlled by the San Diego Harbor Authority, that was available for private development. The former operator, it seemed, was wanted by the authorities on a smuggling charge. Ryan went to look at the airport and found it consisted of one runway, set among some electric wires, poles, and a couple of smokestacks. Where others might have been discouraged, Ryan saw his opportunity in this hopeless-looking establishment and decided to take it. He made an arrangement through the Commanding Officer, Rockwell Field, for the purchase of a discarded Army plane (a JN-4D). The officer was General (then Colonel) H.H. Arnold,

Curtis Biplanes of the Army Signal Corps, Aviation Section, San Diego, California in February of 1913.
National Archives

than 400 minutes of instruction at a cost of $500, which consisted mainly of taxiing a Curtiss pusher-type airplane about the area, Ryan soloed and his

157

subsequently CG of the AAF. The plane cost $400, and Ryan didn't have enough money. He drew out what he had in the bank and made up the difference through the sale of his Model T Ford.

Rental of the airport was $50 a month. His office was a piano box. The location proved to be so bad that Ryan soon transferred his operations to a salt flat further up the bay. That field was to be known as Ryan Airport, and it was here that the first test flight of the Spirit of St. Louis was made by

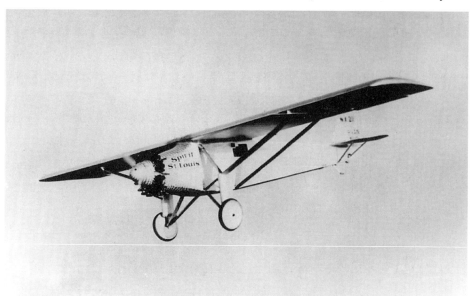

The *Spirit of St. Louis* built by Ryan Aircraft Co.   National Archives

Lindbergh in 1927. Ryan engaged in flight instruction, accepted barnstorming engagements, provided sight-seeing flights and hopped passengers. He bought a half-dozen dilapidated biplanes and rebuilt them with the help of four mechanics he had hired.

Two years later, he inaugurated the San Diego-Los Angeles Airline (1926), the first year-round-passenger-scheduled flight in the country. Later, he had established the Ryan Aircraft Company at San Diego, struggled along for several years, and had set up a training school by 1922. Then in 1927, just prior to Lindbergh's famous flight, Ryan dissolved his partnership and left the firm; however, he still maintained the flying school.

Earl D. Prudden, vice president and general manager of the Ryan schools, and vice president of the Ryan Aeronautical Company, got his first job with Ryan in the late '20s, selling courses for the school. Prudden enlisted in the French Army in World War I. After the U.S. entered the war in 1917, he was given a commission in the American Army, but continued to serve with the French. After the war he entered the real estate business in Detroit. Prudden was in San Diego on a visit when he decided to go into aviation. He took a selling job with Ryan. Then he began spending his Sundays at the airport "as a sort of barker," persuading people to take rides in Ryan's planes. Soon he was selling airplanes as well as signing up students. He was elevated to the vice presidency of the company in 1931.

Prudden was the active manager of Ryan School of Aeronautics and participated in the preliminary planning conferences and meetings called by General Arnold and others of Arnold's staff from 1938. In 1939, he represented Ryan at a Washington, D.C. conference with General Arnold. Prudden also helped set up the new schools for Ryan at Hemet and later at Tucson, Arizona. Prudden had been born in Duluth, Minnesota, in 1895. He died in 1958.

On 19 June 1939, Ryan's first contract with the U.S. Government on the training of Flying Cadets, to start on 1 July 1939, was signed. This provided for forty-five students to enter training; fifteen PT-13 training planes were to be furnished by the Air Corps. This first contract was No. 535-ac-12873, dated 19 June 1939.

Construction was immediately begun on barracks and messing facilities adjacent to Lindbergh Field.

Plans were complete so that on 1 July 1939, 35 Flying Cadets were receiving flight instruction. This was part of Class 40-A. These Cadets were housed in the Brown Military Academy facilities located about six miles from Lindbergh Field. Bus transportation was provided to and from the field and a garrison organization was established with reveille, duty hours, and other functions being performed in conjunction with the military academy. By mid-August the Cadet area was ready, complete with mess hall, assembly area, and bungalow-type barracks on the hill directly across Highway 101 from the Ryan School. Cadets walked to class after this improvement.

The Ryan Aeronautical Company factory building was pressed into use for maintenance and storage, shops, classrooms, lecture halls, rooms for demonstration groups, and the AC Training Detachment headquarters was also maintained in this building.

Hospital facilities were provided by the station hospital at Fort Rosecrans nearby. Major Porter, M.C., handled the medical program for this detachment in 1939. On 17 June 1939, the War Department at Washington, D.C. had issued Special Order No. 141, directing Captain Wynn C. Horton, A.C., and 2nd Lt. Lloyd P. Hopwood, A.C., to the Ryan School of Aeronautics, Inc., effective on or about 23 June 1939. Upon arrival at his new station, Captain Horton had issued General Order No. 1, organizing the Air Corps Training Detachment. The assigned mission of the Air Corps Training Detachment, Lindbergh Field, was to carry on all necessary supply, administrative, and supervisory functions required for:

1. The proper accomplishment of student flying training.

2. The proper administration of assigned military and civil service personnel; and

3. The complete compliance by the contractor of the terms of the contract, assisting when necessary in the proper execution thereof.

The burden of the administrative work rested on the shoulders of Captain Horton and Lieutenant Hopwood, as they were the only officers assigned to the detachment at that time. One Civil Service Jr. Clerk-Steno, and six enlisted men, shared the duties as administrative and personnel clerks as well as being Technical Inspectors, Engineering and Supply, and Operations clerks. A personnel roster of 9 December 1939 shows that Captain Horton was Commander, Supervisor, Member of the Flying Cadet Examining Board, and Academic Board. Lieutenant Hopwood was Adjutant, Operations Officer, Engineering and Supply Officer, Summary Court, Assistant Supervisor, and Recorder of the Flying Cadet Examining Board and the Academic Board. All flight training was under Paul Wilcox, Director of Flying for the Ryan School. Technical

Ryan PT-16 6/22/39   National Archives

training and maintenance of aircraft came under the direction of Walter K. Balch, Chief Technical Instructor of the Ryan School.

The initial flying equipment consisted of PT-13's (five each) and Ryan YPT-16's (four each).

The Flight Instructors were; Chase, Murdock, Kerlinger, Blauvelt, Ben Hazelton, Bill Howe, Ben Johnson, Pete "Swede" Larson, William P. (Doc) Sloan and Bill Howe, an ex-barnstorming pilot.

Personnel policies during this initial period were slightly different from those observed later (say in 1943), in that up to Pearl Harbor time, eliminees, instead of reverting to enlisted status as in later years (1943, etc.), were given an honorable discharge from the U.S. Army. After the war started in 1941, eliminees were given the opportunity to apply for navigation or bombardier training. In 1939, Lt. Hopwood, Personnel Officer, contacted all leading airlines and aircraft manufacturers in the country and was very successful in placing eliminated Cadets in good paying ground jobs, as well as putting to good use, the training the Cadets had received prior to elimination.

When the expanded Air Corps training program first got under way, officials of Ryan School called back from positions in commercial aviation, many of the best graduates of recent years in their commercial flying school. As a result, the Ryan staff was an unusually close-knit organization, functioning under the able direction of Paul Wilcox.

"Doc" Sloan, Instructor at Ryan School of Aeronautics, in 1939, commented: "I started flying at the Ryan School of Aeronautics in 1937 as a student, and got my commercial in April of '38. Finally got on the payroll there in 1939, after spending a year building up my time and teaching ground school part time at 40 cents an hour. I ferried a Ryan STM to Honduras for the Honduran government in 1938, and got on full time (at $125 per month) as an instructor—enlisted in the Army Air Corps Enlisted Reserve in 1938, and was finally commissioned a 2nd Looie in July 1940, after flunking the physical several times because of a color deficiency—memorized all the color charts I could beg, borrow, or steal, and finally beat the color-vision ray. My log book shows that my first students (40-A) were Avery, Wheeler, Sullivan, and Swanson, which started on 5 July 1939. All four graduated from Primary. I met Avery in Washington, D.C., in 1960 when he was a full colonel. Bill Large, 40-C, was the only student that I had who made BG, and that was with SAC. CO of the Ryan contingent was Captain John Horton and number two man was Lt. Lloyd Hopwood. Both of them made general officer before the war was over. As far as I know,

Horton is still alive, but Hoppy died about four years ago in Florida. Hoppy went on to be our first CO at Hemet and left there as a lieutenant colonel in less than two years. He was responsible for a helluva lot of changes in the AAC, including the later Service Pilot ratings for non-school grads. (Note: Horton made BG; Hopwood was a Lt. Gen.)

Our original classes were really prototypes—they arrived by bus or train—no uniforms, no military background, no nuthin' but a desire to fly. Later, when they established the Stanine Ratings at Santa Ana, and were able to categorize applicants more carefully for pilot, navigator, or bombardiers, our elimination rate dropped to less than five percent. But in '39 the standard washout rate was about 30 percent; a crying shame, really, since most of those eligible for training at that time were the cream of the crop. I salvaged one potential washout who was previously employed as the driver of a mucking machine in a mine, by holding my hands down behind me on the rudder pedals to cure him of slamming the airplane through the air—told him if he pinched my fingers he was finished! He ended up with a very fine feel for the plane, and my bruised hands were worth the effort. From Ryan they all went to Randolph for Basic and then to Kelly for Advanced. All told, Ryan trained almost 14,000 pilots at the three Ryan schools.

Another group of instructors was sent down to Randolph following our first group, and Rozzy Blauvelt might have been in that group. We had one elimination in that group and I think the balance of instructors were trained locally. I ended up several months later checking instructors into the program, and I think we had about 200 of them between San Diego, Hemet, and Tucson, when we expanded to three schools, and at the last count, I think there were more than 65 schools involved in the program. (Ed. note: sixty-six schools involved).

I got called to active duty in '42, changed uniforms, took a $200 cut in pay as a 2nd Lt., and went on checking students 'til '44. Then, went to Visalia as CO of the primary there, down to Thunderbird as

CO there, and then to China with the 14th AF in B-24's. Hoppy had me lined up for a P-51 squadron in England, but someone must have stepped on my IBM card with a pair of golf shoes. They gave me 13 hours in a B-24 in Pueblo, and I led 37 of them to China. Talk about the blind leading the blind, but that's another story. Made L.C. before getting out of active service in '47, but stayed Reserve 'til '62.

Consolidated B-24   National Archives

Then went back to Ryan in aircraft sales (Navion), production test piloting, engineering, finally manager of international marketing, before spending two years in Iran as managing director for Teledyne, Inc., where I retired in January 1976."

The Army had its own criterion for flight instructors. So did each contract school. Here is the background on some of the civil school's screening actions to select instructors for the refresher course (1939). Earl D. Prudden, General Manager of the Ryan School of Aeronautics, said, "We combed the files for the names of graduates of our commercial schools for possible instructors. We selected fifteen names for the first group. We were looking for men with the greatest amount of log-time, men whom we felt were adaptable on the basis of their flying and personality record. Of the fifteen selected, thirteen passed the Randolph Field Army refresher course. Later, Randolph graduates were used by the Ryan Schools to give refresher courses to new instructors and to standardize them in accordance with Army requirements. Ten of the fourteen total instructors received their training at the Ryan School. All fourteen were graduates of the Instructors' School at Randolph Field, Texas, and the average logged flying time of this group was 2,000 hours.

Paul Wilcox, Robert Kerlinger, Verner Murdock, and William P. ("Doc") Sloan were already employed on the commercial staff at the Ryan School. William Howe had been instructing military pilots for the Honduran Air Force and flying commercially in Central America for TACA. Ben Hazelton was operating his own flight service in Toledo, Ohio, as was Joseph Duncan in Sacramento, California. Rosmond Blauvelt was instructing students in New York, while Ben Johnson was similarly occupied in Los Angeles, and Dick Huffman in Cincinnati, Ohio, and William Evans in San Diego. Clarence Prescott and Lee Garner jointly operated and Prescott owned, the Linda Vista Airport near San Diego. Peter "Swede" Larson had long been active in commercial flying in Detroit before joining the Ryan School instructional staff.

Small classes, intensive study, and detailed training aids were keynotes of the original ground school program as initiated by Ryan School of Aero. Walter K. Balch, Director of Technical Training, went to Randolph Field in the spring of 1939 to assimilate the ground school curriculum set up by the Army Air Corps. The transition from civilian ground school courses to those required by the Army was not too great since the already established Ryan program included the same data. The mechanics course offered by Ryan School furnished innumerable mock-ups, models, working diagrams, and test stand equipment to supplement that which was furnished.

In the early 1920's, Ryan School policies were firmly established to provide flight training on a scientific, conservatively operated basis. Recognition of this was given in 1929, when the U.S. Department of Commerce set up high standards of qualification for commercial training schools. At that time, Ryan became one of the first schools in the country to receive the Approved Transport Flying and Ground School Certificate, the highest then issued by the U.S. Government (CAA).

Flight courses covered the complete range of aviation training from student pilot grades through master pilot training, with supplementary courses in instrument flying and qualification of flight instructors. High standards for flight instructor personnel were always demanded and the school's commercial pilot training program established an outstanding safety record. Under CAA and the Civilian Pilot Training (CPT) programs, the Ryan school was selected for the standardized training and qualification of flight instructors. The CAA also granted the Ryan School the rating of Approved Airplane and Engine Mechanics' School. In June 1940, when the Air Corps training program was further enlarged, the Ryan School got its proportionate share of additional Cadets to be trained. Facilities were not adequate either for housing or administration or medical needs. Construction was started on barracks that would house 72 men at the corner of India and Sassafras streets in San Diego. Soon an addition was built on Lindbergh Field for flight operations, as well as for administration and ground school. Also, an adequate dispensary was set up in order that minor surgery and all physical exams could be given by the flight surgeon assigned

to the detachment. Recreation and mess halls were constructed at the barracks and Cadets were fed "family style," space being provided for the whole school to eat at the same time.

The original ground school staff consisted of seven instructors. The courses consisted of Electricity and Mechanics; Mathematics & Structures; Radial Engines and Propellers; "V" Engines; Navigation; Meteorology; Engine Theory, and parachutes. Additional training aids such as, engine cutaways that would move, and engine boards for use in the lab classes, were included in the original ground school curriculum. There were no training films, film strips, or identification equipment used in ground school at that time. The successful performance in the early days can be attributed to the excellent organization of the Ryan School as well as the fact that for the first time in Air Corps history, primary training was given in low-wing monoplanes, the Ryan YPT-16 and PT-20 trainers. This move marked a departure from a thirty-year Army precedent of biplane primary trainers.

Following extensive flight testing at Wright Field, the Army adopted the Ryan PT-20A. This low-wing monoplane was found to be superior to the previous biplane-type trainer for two reasons: First, the Ryan has a higher performance than the

Ryan PT-20A with a Kinner R-440-1 engine. 10/28/40   National Archives

older type training planes. It was more responsive to controls and so tended to more nearly approximate the higher performance planes used in advanced training. (It was very underpowered, however) Second, the low-wing monoplane produced pilots who adapted themselves more readily to low-wing monoplane types, practically standard for all classes of military combat planes. Stearman PT-13 and PT-17 biplanes were used at West Coast ACTC Primary Schools along with Ryan PT-16 and twenty-one monoplanes. The Stearman planes, equipped with the sturdy Lycoming or Continental engines, gave very little difficulty in maintenance. The Ryan PT-16 planes, however, were underpowered with the Menasco C-4 125-hp engine, and were a constant source of trouble, both in maintenance and operation.

When Brigadier General Davenport Johnson visited the Ryan School at San Diego at the end of May 1941, he found only three planes in commission, out of 40 planes assigned to the school. He was told by Ryan officials that 22 planes was the most they had ever had in commission at one time. As a result of this very unsatisfactory condition, the San Diego school had difficulty in graduating students on time. Although the PT-21's had been in use several months in San Diego, they proved to be inadequate for operation at the Hemet Detachment, which was 1,500 feet above sea level. Excessive takeoff runs and poor performance at higher altitudes indicated a shortage of horsepower, but despite these deficiencies, the PT-21's were retained at the school and operated simultaneously with the Stearman PT-13's. The difficulties of operating two different types of airplanes were numerous. From a maintenance standpoint, increased personnel were required, and confusion in the hangars was kept to a mini-

mum only through the capable supervisors on hand. Traffic conditions were hazardous because of the differences in speed of the two planes, and a constant revision in traffic patterns was necessary.

Lindbergh Field which was located in the southwest skirt of San Diego, on Highway 101, consisted of land that was filled in and built up from San Diego Bay. The surrounding terrain was rough and hilly, and unsuitable for practicing forced landings, pylon eights, and other low-flying maneuvers. Flying conditions at this field could be considered year round with exception of the winter fog conditions that prevailed on many days until the middle of the morning. Afternoon flying weather was considered ideal. The field had a trapezoid shape with two paved runways, 900 x 1,150-plus and 800 x 1,000 feet. Surface finish was oil on decomposed granite.

William P. "Doc" Sloan, a former civilian instructor at Ryan's Lindbergh Field, 1939, remembers ferrying PT-13's from Randolph: "Eight of us were sent to Randolph, arriving there about 1 June for a two-week indoctrination course. Paul Wilcox, then currently the top instructor at Ryan, was our lead man. Paul (or Pablo, or Stinky) probably had two-or three- thousand hours at the time, and been with Ryan for several years—a truly great pilot and mother hen for the rest of us. Claude (Ryan)

Ryan PT-21 with a Kinner R-440-3 engine. 4/17/41   National Archives screened former Ryan students for prospective instructors, and came up with Ben Hazelton, Dick Huffman, Bill Evans, Pete Larson, Ben Johnson, and Joe Duncan (I'm fairly certain that Joe was a former student), and myself. We went from San Diego to Randolph on a train, and the first two weeks at Randolph were hectic. They ended with a spot-landing contest between the civilian and Army instructors, which they won when Captain Russ Spicer (later a Major General) stalled in from 30 feet up and split the landing line with his collapsed PT-13 landing gear—Foul Play! But we paid for the beer later.

According to my log book, it took us four days to ferry nine Stearmans from Randolph to San Diego, with stops at Dryden, Marfa, El Paso, Lordsburg, Tucson, and Yuma. Captain W.E. (Wee) Todd was the Army type who made sure we wouldn't get lost, and I don't think we were ever a hundred feet off the ground on the whole trip, except to approach an airport. We flew three elements of three planes each, with Todd down the middle of the highway, Wilcox on the right with his two wingmen, and me on the left—most of the time peeking under the phone wires to hold formation. We chased horses, cows, coyotes, rabbits, antelope, and, in Juarez, even a few stray senoritas (that must have been Larson or Duncan). Approaching airports along the way, Todd drilled us in the Lufbery circle, nine of us, tail on tail in a tight circle—to peel off individually for landings. Lousy formation, but a helluva lot of fun, and with no FAA or CAA to bug us. It was free flying, the likes of which neither you nor I will ever see again."

In late 1939, one deficiency of Lindbergh Field was the crowded conditions. This field was used by Consolidated Aircraft Company, American Airlines, Western Airlines, the Coast Guard Station, Ryan Aeronautical Company, a reserve squadron, as well as many transient aircraft. However, the CAA had always given the primary training aircraft from the school the "light" from the tower and all other aircraft tower radio service. At that time (around December 1939 and early 1940), the Flying Cadets were flying entirely from the main airdrome at Lindbergh Field and plans were being laid for two new auxiliary fields: Gibbs Field and Mission Field. But when these two auxiliary fields became a reality, the main airdrome had become more congested than ever, so buses were provided to carry the Cadets to the auxiliary fields. Only the instructors flew the aircraft back and forth to Lindbergh Field for first echelon maintenance and servicing.

The military training program in 1939 was not of the caliber it was in primary later during 1943. However, there were letters in the file of the Detachment from the Commanding Officer of the Basic School at Randolph Field attesting to the good appearance, military bearing, and soldierly qualities of the Cadets sent to his command from Ryan for basic flying training.

Upon arrival in San Diego, all new Cadets were immediately put into classification as a "dodo" (an extinct bird that could not fly). As the incoming Cadet was issued his coveralls and goggles, he subjected himself to the whims and often to the direction of the upper-class hazing. Quaint customs such as when grapefruit was served at breakfast, the "dodo" must put his goggles over his eyes, or when an upperclassman spoke to a Cadet, he must rise, stand at attention and give the names of those Cadets who soloed or were "washed out" that day. If this attempt failed, he was forced to eat a "square" meal. This phase of the curriculum actually did have some definite purpose when so many of the Flying Cadets came from various colleges where they had assumed some importance in the curriculum or perhaps from civilian life where they had been in business long enough to get rather definite ideas concerning their own capabilities and worth. The mental training and military discipline rapidly and rigidly brought most of them to a more unified type, making them more receptive to air and ground discipline. As time went on and "raw material" changed, many amendments were made in this type of thinking.

Cadet inspections were held weekly and a

group of Cadets stood retreat each day at the barracks. Excerpts from the Cadet Regulations show that they had more actual "housemaid's work" to do than they did in the later (1943) barracks arrangement. They were required to polish brass doorknobs, dust curtains and dressers, wash bathtubs, and beat out rugs in earlier organizations.

No Cadet funds, mess funds, or funds for recreational purposes were authorized during this period, but Cadet social activity during the early program was not a major problem, since the Cadets were housed at the bus line near the center of activity in San Diego. However, a "dodo" dance for the lower class, and a graduation dance for the upper class were classics. These dances were sponsored by the Cadet Detachment as a whole. "Dates" were furnished from a list maintained by the school's civilian athletic and recreation officer.

The training of Flying Cadets in primary flying at the Ryan School during this initial period of history (1939) can be summed up as having been "very successful" only being accompanied by a few "growing pains," such as the need for additional buildings and auxiliary fields which were soon constructed. There was a lack of service facilities, i.e., quartermaster, finance, etc., due to the small size of the original detachment; however, these facilities/services were available and used at Camp Callan, California, as well as Fort Rosecrans located across the bay.

The original class (40-A) of Flying Cadets to be graduated from the Air Corps Training Detachment consisted of 23 Flying Cadets who were transferred to Randolph Field, Texas, for basic flying training on 22 September 1939. By the time Class 40-C arrived, there were 57 Flying Cadets and six student officers under training at Ryan.

In the summer of 1939, when Ryan began military pilot training, its commercial school had a record-breaking enrollment of commercial flight students from all over the U.S. and many foreign countries. At that time, when Ryan became one of the original nine commercial schools to conduct primary

training of Army Flying Cadets, it was the oldest aviation school in the U.S. under its original management.

One of the former Flying Cadets of 40-A, Colonel John F. Carp (Ret.), had this to say about flying conditions for the first class of 40-A at Ryan Primary from July to September 1939: "During the period of time that we were Cadets at Lindbergh Field while attending Ryan School of Aeronautics, the field itself was not crowded and the traffic pattern was never crowded. Other planes were there using Lindbergh Field but we just avoided each other without any special effort. Class 40-A did all its flying from Lindbergh Field. There was one small auxiliary field named Rosedale that we also used. It was a dry, dusty square of dirt, hardly any grass or vegetation, and it was miles from the nearest town. Rosedale Auxiliary was used for stages and for spot-landing practice. We always returned to Lindbergh Field whether solo or dual. I don't recall ever using or hearing about Gibbs or Mission Fields (later auxiliary fields for Ryan Primary in late 1939 or early 1940). Rosedale might have been at Hemet, California, where Ryan moved later on. The only vivid memory about landing at Lindbergh Field that I have today was the final approach which led directly over the 'Chicken of the Sea' tuna plant. The sudden aroma caused plane and pilot alike to shudder. We were still flying our Stearman PT-13A's. At that time, the control tower at Lindbergh used the 'light' to signal us an OK to land. I cannot recall ever being delayed or waved off. Most of the traffic was our own PT-13's and if it was congested (as I understand it was later at Ryan) we evidently learned to handle it right."

On 24 July 1940, a second contract (W535-ac-15367) was signed by Ryan and provided that 150 students (as a maximum) would be sent to San Diego and Hemet schools. Later, Ryan's school contract was amended to provide training for a maximum of 192 students/class at the two Ryan schools.

In July 1940, the Army pilot training program, in order to produce 7,000 pilots per year, called for the continuation of the nine commercial schools on a greatly expanded basis. A total of 1,292 students were entered into these schools every five weeks. About two-thirds of them were graduated and sent on for basic, advanced, and specialized training, to one or more of the three Army training centers at Randolph Field, Texas; Moffett Field, California; or Maxwell Field, Alabama. The overall pilot training program was done in four phases:

1. Ten weeks of elementary (primary) training.
2. Ten weeks of basic training.
3. Ten weeks of advanced training.
4. Five weeks of specialized training in combat-type planes.

Thereafter, the officer pilot was assigned to a service squadron and there he received additional flight and military training as a part of his regular Army duties.

Meanwhile, the original Air Corps Training Detachment at San Diego (Lindbergh Field) was doubled in size and the training program speeded up from the former twelve-week course to the new ten-week course. After this ten-week elementary training, the next class of Cadets was transferred, upon graduation, to the newly organized West Coast Training Center's Moffett Field, California, for their basic training. Originally the A.C. Training Detachment instructed classes of thirty-five students every six weeks for the twelve-week course, but it soon increased to sixty-five Cadets per class by July 1940. This enlarged student load placed a strain not only on the available instructor personnel, who could qualify to the standards set up by the flying school, but also on the plant facilities as well. This necessitated the purchase of additional land and supplemental buildings to be added to the barracks, mess hall, and other support facilities.

The twelve-week Flying Training Program was shortened to ten weeks, and then, a short time later, to nine weeks. The morning fog at San Diego in winter really slowed down Cadet flying training schedules. As the length of primary training shortened in duration, the courses were intensified to meet the growing demands and the ground school instructors spent a majority of their time with the Cadets and less time in the civilian school. The ground school staff remained more or less static until the Air Corps Training Detachment at Hemet, California, was activated on 25 August 1940. At that time, some new instructors were added and some of the more experienced men went to the new school at Hemet, California.

In 1941, the training increased fivefold. The barracks erected in 1939 were enlarged to house 128 men, and fourteen additional bungalow-type units each housing four men were built. (This eventually became the Best Rest Motel after WWII.)

Early in 1941, a civil service employee was hired to establish an athletic training program on Lindbergh Field. Drills were held on the ramp each day, and Cadets received gas-mask instruction and marched at times with their gas-masks on. A parade and graduation review were held for each class and were surprisingly good in spite of the fact that a majority of the men had never marched before.

The high federal government (CAA) ratings granted Ryan in 1929 were maintained for the entire twelve years right up to the outbreak of World War II, at which time all commercial training was discontinued in the coastal areas (Pacific), and all Ryan facilities were devoted exclusively to military requirements. Training continued on an increased basis at San Diego for over three years until August 1942 when operations were transferred to Tucson, Arizona. The entire school was moved there over one weekend.

During the five and one half-year period, July 1939 to December 1944, Ryan operated three schools for primary training of flying/Aviation Cadets. These were the original school at San Diego, California; the 5th AAF Flying Training Detachment at Hemet, California; and the 11th AAF FTD at Tucson, Arizona. More than 14,000 pilots were trained at these three schools. During peak periods, the Hemet and Tucson schools had more than 1,200 Cadets in training at one time. Flight instructional staffs, technical training, and operations and maintenance facilities, also kept pace. The organization employed more than 300 flight instructors and a maintenance department consisting of over 300 employees to service the more than 300 training planes in daily use.

The training at Hemet reached a peak in September 1943 with 19,324 student flying hours; and in December 1943 at Tucson with 18,910 student flying hours logged for that month.

Being eliminated from the Army's pilot training program was not the "end of the world" for a student who failed in the flying course. Many of these learned to adapt and find outlets for their youthful energies. As in the case of James H. Macia, Jr., of Tucson, Arizona, a student of Class 41-A; he was eliminated because of flying deficiencies and, as was the policy of the day, required to remain at the school for several months while awaiting orders to another school for further training. During this period of inactivity, Mr. Macia applied himself in ground school to the extensive navigation course, and also took meteorology in preparation for becoming a student navigator-bombardier. The ground school course certainly paid off for him, as he became chief navigator for General (then Lt. Colonel) Doolittle in the historic Tokyo raid of April 1942. Using Ryan

PT-16 and PT-20 military primary training planes, made by the parent Ryan Aeronautical Company, the Ryan School of San Diego was the first training organization in the U.S. to give initial flight instruction of military pilots in low-wing monoplanes.

The Ryan School of Aeronautics, San Diego, California, closed its operation contract with the Army Air Forces in August 1942 having produced a total of 794 pilots from July 1939 (Classes 40-A through 42-E).

In recognition of the wartime contributions of the Ryan organization in training military pilots, T. Claude Ryan, received the Presidential Certificate of Merit signed by President Harry S. Truman in December 1948.

When asked the question, why did you join the Air Corps? Several of the Ryan graduates responded as follows:

Lt. Colonel E.H. Berkenkamp— "I had graduated from the University of California at Berkeley and was seasonally employed by the U.S. Forest Service as a timber cruiser and surveyor for land acquisition. For some reason, yet to be determined, I considered it mandatory to become an aviator. I went through the preliminaries at Oakland Airport (Naval Res.) in the spring of 1938 for naval aviation training. Then I departed into the backwoods as chief of party on a survey team. About two months later a letter from the Navy arrived with instructions to report to the Naval Reserve Unit in August. I graciously thanked them (by letter) and advised them that the USFS needed my services and that I would be in touch at a later date for aviation training. The later date was in early 1939, and I learned that the Navy took a very dim view of my failure to accept the earlier August date. I then went across the bay to

North American B-25, the type used on the Doolittle Raid. National Archives

167

Hamilton Field, and went through the pre-selection preliminaries with the Army Air Corps. Then back to the timber country job while waiting for results. A letter came from the War Department with instructions to report to Hamilton Field on 27 June 1939. This time I left the woods as soon as possible and was inducted on the June date along with LeBailly and Barlow."

Colonel James G. Barlow— "I had wanted to fly as a young high school lad. My uncle, Leon D. Cuddebuck, was the first airmail pilot who flew between Boise, Idaho, to Portland, Oregon, in an old Swallow aircraft. He was chief pilot for Varney Airlines (Los Angeles to San Francisco). Later, he was Director of Operations, Western Division, United Air Lines; and still later, Director of CAB, Western Division, Oakland, California. He told us kids (my brother and me) the thrilling stories of his adventures. So it was no wonder we wanted to have a go-at-it. My brother, Stan, learned to fly the hard way—he paid for it—then flew as a test pilot in B-17's for Boeing during the war. He had started flying in 1936, so I just had to do it, too. In 1935 I enrolled at Santa Clara University on an athletic scholarship (football)—certainly not for academics. A friend of mine owned a Taylorcraft Cub; he flew it out of Alum Rock Airport, just east of San Jose. There I got about 12 hours of time over a two-year period. I was hooked.

One day, while at a bar in Oakland, with the lady of my loving care (at the time), we were sipping the nectar of spirits. We were watching and listening to a major in full attire of the Air Corps singing and playing, and eyeing my lovely lady. Needless to say, I lost her to him, and then and there, I said to myself, 'Barlow, you gotta go Air Corps. Look how easy that guy got the girl.'

In 1936, there came to the campus of SCU a team of Air Corps officers, enlisting Cadets. So I applied, and received the discouraging statement, 'Come back when you're a senior'. Again in my junior year, I met another team and got the same statement. So, in 1939, after graduation, I visited the offices of the Air Corps at Moffett Field, and a wonderful lieutenant colonel told me, 'Come on into the real world'. After I had my nose and other parts of my body fixed up from their scars of football (two Sugar Bowl games), the flight surgeon said, 'You're fit!' I almost didn't make it. There had been another Santa Claran, Hal Bundy, who flew a P-12 into a football field during a game and scared all the people there. I thought to myself. 'If he can do it,' well, so could I. So I just flew the Cub all around the school on a Sunday. And the

Boeing XB-15 a forerunner of the B-17 with a P-26.   National Archives

school fathers asked if I were the one, being all George Washington-like, I could not lie. I was proud and said. 'Yes.' I was told to cease and desist. On 23 June 1939, a government letter told me to report for a physical and then I was told to report to San Diego and Ryan Primary, where my whole dream came to fulfillment."

Colonel John F.Sharp—"As long as I can remember, I was always intrigued by airplanes. At age 11, I saw Charles Lindbergh when he made his famous flight around America after his solo flight to Paris. At age 13, I rode my bike 20 miles to see and shake hands with French flyers, Captains Coste and Bellante, who flew a giant biplane from Paris to New York. In the meantime, I would go to see any air show the Army Air Corps would put on in or near Salt Lake City, Utah. At age 15, I took my first airplane ride. I had saved my lunch money and finally had enough for a short ride—a Curtiss Pusher, no less. I remember the pilot climbed into the front in a business suit and felt hat. Where were the helmet and goggles? The white scarf? Boots, gloves and all that macho stuff that gave a pilot his image? I was mortified. My first great adventure had already turned sour. The wind didn't even ripple the guy's hat. Well, I continued to save my lunch money and took flying lessons at $5 a crack for 20 minutes each. It took several years at 25 cents a day but I finally soloed in a Waco F on 27 May 1937. I remember the date because a news event overshadowed my accomplishment that day—the opening of the Golden Gate Bridge in San Francisco.

I continued to fly the Waco when I could afford it, but in the meantime I was flying a neighbor's homemade airplane, a Corben Jr. Ace, Egad! I also took up with some bum who had an unlicensed Eagle Rock with a cracked engine block. We barnstormed and buzzed around staying one step ahead of the law until we finally wrecked the plane. My father finally said, 'Stop this nonsense! If you're going to fly, join the Army Air Corps.' So I applied, was accepted, and was sent to March Field for a physical; passed that and was told to wait. I waited.

Then in early 1939, a contingent of Army pilots and doctors came to the University of Utah and gave physicals to a whole bunch of potential Cadets. I lined up but was told I didn't need to take it, because I had already passed. Bingo! In a couple of weeks everybody was called but me. Panic! I started contacting everybody from the President on down. Finally, someone in the War Department sent word for me to get another flight physical and send it to them immediately. The one civilian flight surgeon in town and I got together, and I told him my sad tale. He took pity and ran me through a complete physical. I airmailed it (special delivery) back to the War Department. After a week of sitting on pins and needles, I got my call to join the troops of Class 40-A at Ryan in San Diego."

ALABAMA INSTITUTE OF AERONAUTICS

The Alabama Institute of Aeronautics, 51st AAF Flying Training Detachment (as of July 1942) was located at Hargrove Van de Graff Field at Tuscaloosa Alabama (Established 1939). Mr. Oliver Lafayette Parks, (10 June 1899-28 February 1985) was the owner/Operator.

This school, which was approved by the CAA on 1 March 1939, became the first contract school in the Southeastern states. On 1 July 1939, it became one of the original nine contract primary flying schools of the U.S. Army Air Corps—one of two schools operated by Oliver L. Parks.

The parkways, tall trees, a brick administration building, and barracks spaced along a curved roadway, gave this contract school (on the site of the old municipal airport about three miles from Tuscaloosa) the appearance of a college campus.

It was here, starting 1 July 1939, that the first class of Flying Cadets (Air Corps) known as 40-A, commenced training in primary flight school. This school was given a quota of 40 students. There were eight officers training in-grade and 35 Cadets. By the end of the Primary phase (twelve weeks) on

26 September 1939, four officers and ten Cadets had been eliminated, leaving four officers and 23 Cadets to go on to Basic Flight Training at Randolph Field, Texas. At Randolph, one officer and five Cadets were washed out; one more Cadet was eliminated at Advanced Training at Kelly Field, Texas. This left three officers and 17 Cadets to eventually graduate at Kelly Field on 23 March 1940.

The Institute of Aero at Tuscaloosa, Alabama, was opened by Oliver L. Parks, founder of several other AAF Primary civil flying schools located at East St. Louis, Illinois; Sikeston, Missouri; Jackson, Mississippi; and Cape Ginardeau, Missouri. Both Parks and Walter P. Thorpe, the vice president and general manager, served in the U.S. Marines in World War I. Thorpe became associated with Parks in the establishment of Parks Air College at East St. Louis, Illinois, in 1932. The School manager was Walter P. Thorpe. The Ground School manager was Mr. Sierra. The Director of Flying was John Marcotte. The Flight Instructors were: Chief Pilot Art Woodbury; Walt Kulzer; Larson; Art Nelson; Wiley Riehl; J.M. Sierra; Art Wintheiser; and Ben L. Gigstad.

In August 1939, Tuscaloosa was not considered entirely satisfactory by Headquarters, Air Corps Training Center, at Randolph Field, Texas. A party of officers from Washington, D.C., was sent to Tuscaloosa to "clean house" for Parks. Colonel Robins, CO, Air Corps Training Center, Randolph Field, in a letter to Captain Rodieck, the Central District Supervisor at Parks, stated that, "It was a great surprise to us when we arrived at Tuscaloosa to find that the barracks had been enlarged, extra toilets and showers installed; there was a brand-new building for the cafeteria, and the auxiliary field is now in good shape. The water supply has been fixed and it is now chlorinated. Parks has been down here continually for the past two weeks and has been personally supervising all these things." Thus was Tuscaloosa made satisfactory to the Air Corps.

From the summer of 1939 until July 1942, American Flying Cadets (who were known as Aviation Cadets after June 1941) were trained in Primary flight. Then for several months, British Cadets were trained here for the Royal Air Force. After that the Institute became an "All-American" Primary flight training base. However, that wasn't to last for long as there was another shift in plans, and beginning in July 1943, the Institute gave flight and ground school training to French Aviation Cadets. During the training period of the French Cadets, they had four women interpreters on the flight line to translate instructions from English into French for these students.

Despite its earlier problems, the training detachment at Tuscaloosa appeared to SEACTC (Southeast AC Training Center) inspectors to be an "excellent" organization by 31 October 1941. A total of 252 students were being trained. All were U.K. trainees. Difficulty was experienced in getting enough training planes. Seventy were desirable, but only sixty-two were available at the time. The No. 1 British School at Terrell, Texas, William F. Long Branch, opened in August 1941, as the Terrell Aviation School. It started training 7 June 1941 at Dallas. The No. 2 British School at Lancaster, California, was at War Eagle Field; it was a Moseley School. It opened 20 August 1941, and started training 4 June 1941 at Glendale. Then RAF Cadets moved to the Polaris Flight Academy at Lancaster in August. The No. 3 British School located at Miami, Oklahoma, was a Maxwell W. Balfour School from the Spartan School of Aeronautics, and it opened 13 July 1941. It started training at Tulsa, Oklahoma, on 16 June 1941, upon arrival of it's first British students (forty-six each). The Cadets were moved to the Miami, Oklahoma site in July to continue their training. The No. 4 British School was Falcon Field, at Mesa, Arizona; it was a Southwest Airways School, and was run by Hayward & Connelly, opening in the summer, 1941. The No. 5 British School was at Clewiston, Florida, part of the Riddle-McKay Aero College. It opened 25 September 1941. This was the last to open of the six British Flying Schools in the U.S. The No. 6

British School located at Ponca City, Oklahoma, was a Darr School of Aeronautics unit. It opened 7 August 1941.

The other schools that taught British Cadets were: Tuscaloosa, Alabama (Alabama Institute of Aeronautics), a Parks school; Lakeland, Florida (Lodwick School of Aeronautics), a Lodwick school; Americus, Georgia (Graham Aviation School); Camden, South Carolina (Southern Aviation School); Albany, Georgia (Darr Aero-Tech), a Darr school; and Arcadia, Florida (Carlstrom Field), an Embry-Riddle school. These six schools in the SEACTC region started training RAF students with class 42-A, 7 June 1941.

Under the 7,000-Pilot Training Program as set up by OCAC (Office, Chief of the Air Corps), the detachment at Tuscaloosa, Alabama, was scheduled to start training 3 August 1940 with a per-class quota of 54 students (and estimated student capacity of 87). The training planes allotted were 56 PT-17's and one PT-17A.

Tuscaloosa entered 1,335 Cadets during the period 1 July 1939 to 6 November 1941, producing 828 graduates (based on a 62 percent graduation rate). Classes 40-A through 40-H entered 323 Cadets; Classes 41-A through 41-I entered 567; and Classes 42-A through 42-E (UK) entered 445. The Pilot production from Class 42-F through 44-G (which graduated on 12 March 1944 and was the last class at Tuscaloosa Primary) is unknown. An estimate based on the then-current entry rate of 120 Cadets per class would total 2,880 for the last 24 classes; a graduate rate of 60 percent would produce the figure of 1,728 graduates for this last period for the Tuscaloosa Primary. This would give an overall total of 4,215 Cadets entered and 2,556 pilot graduates at Tuscaloosa for the five years of its operation at a 60.6 percent graduation rate.

When asked the question, "What circumstances led to your applying for Flying Cadet training in the Army Air Corps?" this was one of the answers:

Major Horace E. Dimond—"This will be known as 'My Back Door Entry into Flying School.'

Scene: Street corner with an Army poster which mocked me: 'Use your two years of college and learn to fly.' I remember standing there musing about taking makeup courses in high school subjects just to be able to graduate, and thinking of how many miles I was currently from even thinking about college. There was, however, only one ever-present driving force in my being, and an ever-present influence that never let me move from my objective and that was to go to flying school. Enlistment, I was told, was the only possible step for one who had neither the capital nor grades to get into college, but that perhaps, just perhaps, I could fall into the category of soldier-student, on my own time, of course, that might afford me an opportunity.

Persistence and threats by my parents persuaded me that graduation from high school was a real necessity, and so, with effort, this was accomplished, and in 1937 I enlisted at Mitchel Field, Hempstead, New York, much to the chagrin of my folks. Reporting to Mitchel, my recruit days lacked any glamor whatsoever, since I spent a great deal of time shoveling coal into the basements of some senior officers like Major Sam Connell and Lt. Colonel Tom Hanley. I only came close to an airplane when I was free to wander the flight line on a Wednesday afternoon or on weekends. There, I pictured myself flying the B-10's and B-18's including some O-47's of the 97th Observation Squadron. I spent a lot of time at the post library studying all I could get hold of in the way of subjects required for a G.I. appointment to flight training. I had subsequently found out that this was an area where one did not have to have college training. While I was thus engaged, I was appointed an observer and student forecaster in the 2nd Weather Squadron in Base Headquarters. This was after I had finished my apprenticeship on the coal piles and then on guard duty for a time. Progress was at least nominal when tragedy struck. While swimming in the enlisted men's pool, I dislocated my right shoulder. There went my aviation career.

Arriving at the hospital, I was attended to by

North American 0-47, 5/11/38.   National Archives

then Major Mike Healy and Captain Ty Morehouse of the medical staff. Thanks to them, I was given 'line of duty' and shipped off to Walter Reed Hospital in Washington, D. C. The library at Walter Reed was of inestimable value in covering the subjects necessary for the test, and after an operation called a nicola, I was, according to Doctors Sloat and Peterson, as good as new.

Returning to duty at Mitchel in April of 1938, I again hit the books, and fortunately for me, there were a couple of friendly pilots available to me who were glad to give me an occasional hand up and a point of view as to my progress. Perhaps you may recall a couple of them. I was able to accost Captains Rosy O'Donnell and Elwood Quesada and John Doyle, but I really received my greatest assist from a young 1st Lieutenant named Lauris Norstad, who at that time was Base Adjutant.

Finally, the day arrived. Up to the top floor of Headquarters I was sent to take my examinations which ultimately lasted two days, and close to eight hours at a sitting. After the ordeal, I felt washed out and somewhat dejected, realizing that there were several things I could have answered differently, but that was over now. I had just come from the graveyard shift in the Weather Office and had settled down in bed in the barracks of the 2nd Air Base when I was rudely awakened by the 1st Sergeant. I remember he wiggled my shoulder and growled: 'Wake

up!' Out of one eye I protested that I had just put in eight hours on duty and please go away. 'OK,' his voice came back, 'If you don't care that you've been appointed to flying school, I certainly don't give a damn!' I don't know how I did it, but I left the cot almost without touching the blankets, wide awake. From then on and until I left for Primary Flight Training at the Alabama Institute of Aeronautics at Northport, just outside of Tuscaloosa, I wasn't much good to the weather outfit or to anyone else. The realization of having attained the only thing I really cared about was too much to take quietly. By the way, Walt Kulzer was my instructor and the one who soloed me."

LINCOLN, NEBRASKA

The Lincoln, Nebraska (Air Corps Training Detachment) also known as the Lincoln Airplane & Flying School, was located at the Municipal Airport and established in 1925, as the Lincoln Standard Aircraft Corp. Later it became the Lincoln Aeronautical Institute (the corporate name for both the flying and mechanics schools—1938). The owner/operator was Mr. Ernest J. Sias (1877-1955). The school Mgr./Supt. was, C.P. Bowers; Ground Course Instructors were: Charles A. Pierce, Dickson J. Hazelrigg, and Eugene D. Freeman. The Chief Mechanic was Mr. King. The Flight Dispatchers were, Schmidt and Westcott. The Flight Instructors were: Clem Whittenbeck (Director), Captain Wm. J. Chapman, Myron N. Larkin, Richard G. Beeler, Roy Lanning, James L. Hurst, William Kimsey, W.L. Amos, and M.D.Holman. Holman became Director of Flying as Class 40-A left for Randolph Field. He had been a barnstormer, airline pilot, flying instructor, and member of the Army Air Corps.

The Lincoln Aeronautical Institute, under the direction of the pioneer, Nebraska Aviation School owner, Ernest J. Sias, contracted with the Army in 1939 to train Cadets in primary flying. Flying Cadets learned to fly here in Stearman PT-13A's. Twenty-three Cadets arrived in Lincoln as the first group of trainees in June 1939. Two classes, 40-A and 40-B, passed through Sias' school from 1 July to 4 November 1939.

First Lieutenant Roy T. Wright, A.C., was the first Commanding Officer. Later, as a Colonel, he was CO of the Advanced Flying School, Malden, Missouri. Wright had one other officer, 2nd Lt. Oliver E. Ford, A.C.(K.I.A. 7/44 in a P-38 over Bucharest, Rumania). The Medical Officer, Captain Scott M. Smith, M.C., and five enlisted men completed his Lincoln staff in 1939.

Only ten of the twelve PT-13A's that were used to train the first class of twenty-five students were on hand at the start of training. During July, two more PT-13's were flown in, bringing the total to twelve. Later several more were delivered in preparation for training two classes at once: 40-A and 40-B.

Political pressure was exerted to get a school at Lincoln, Nebraska. The head of the school, Ernest J. Sias, was an ex-preacher, and (it was understood) had never been up in an airplane. He was not a desirable man to head a school, yet because his school, had the oldest continuous flying history of any in the country; it was hard to turn him down. It was felt that weather made the selection of this school inadvisable. The Lincoln, Nebraska site was disapproved by all the Air Corps inspectors prior to the opening of any of these contract schools; however, it was approved at the last minute due to political pressure from Washington, D.C.

Part of the information regarding the early history of this school is shown in official historical records as having been furnished by (then) Captain Roy T. Wright, A.C., first Commanding Officer at the Lincoln A.C. Detachment (1939-40); and from Marion D. Holman, former flight instructor at the original contract school at Lincoln, Nebraska, in July 1939 (when both were assigned to Lakeland, Florida, in 1940-42).

On 1 July 1939, it was one of the nine original civilian contract schools selected by the Army Air Corps to give primary flying to Army Flying Cadets under training supervision. The operator, while he maintained a flying school for a period of some 14 years, knew little about running an Army Flying School or selecting the personnel to do so. In order to improve the quality of instruction and instructors at the civil schools, the idea of having the instructors come to Randolph Field was conceived. This was one method of ensuring that the flight instruction to be given Flying Cadets in the first classes of the new civil school program, would measure up to the standards set up by the system of check-rides with the AC Tactical Officers stationed at each civil school. This eventually worked out fairly well. The schools and instructors were afraid of not being good enough for the high standards demanded by the military, and only the best pilots came at first. This accounts for the high rate of elimination of the third and last class. The schools were scraping the barrel for instructors at that time.

In February 1939, it was decided that approximately 125 students would be sent to Randolph for the special flying instructor course. The contractors were informed that it would be at their own expense except in cases where the students were reserve officers. A curriculum for this instructors' school was approved, which called for 21 hours (exclusive of cross-country) of refresher training in every phase of flying which was to be taught to the military students in the civil schools.

These classes at Randolph were abandoned after the graduation of the Third Group on 20 July 1939. It had been planned to train approximately 125 instructors, and 138 had already completed the course and received their Certificates of Proficiency. Moreover, the quality of the last class was extremely poor. Therefore, the CG, AC Training Center advised the Office, Chief of the Air Corps, that further schools would be a waste of time and money. Because of lack of experience in selecting personnel, the first two men picked to operate the flying department of the school were considered unsatisfactory by the Air Corps supervisor (Lt. Wright). Upon request by the civilian contractor, these men were permitted to make an attempt to supervise the flying schedules. After many failures, these two pilots were relieved and M.D. Holman was recommended for the position. His duties began as Director of Flying on 5 November 1940. As a result of his fine record, he was given the position of Director of Flying when the school was moved to Lakeland, Florida.

At the opening of the school on 1 July 1939 at Lincoln, the contractor first housed the students in the local YMCA dormitory. A week later, the Cadets of 40-A were transferred to a converted fraternity house near Nebraska Wesleyan College at 5007 Huntington Avenue. These housing facilities were not adequate, since the Cadets were crowded into a very small place. Travel between University Place and the flying school near the present-day city airport was by a 40-seat bus with LINCOLN AIRPLANE & FLYING SCHOOL lettered on its sides. The Cadet housing was rapidly improved; by September 1939 Air Corps inspectors found the Cadets now comfortably housed in town, with no complaints. Sias even put in a request for cockpit covers for the PT-13A's as a protection for the pilots against the cold weather common during Nebraska winters.

E.J. Sias started and financed the original flying school in Lincoln, Nebraska, about 1925, picking up the old Lincoln Standard Aircraft Corp. (originally it had been the Nebraska Aircraft Corp). The building for its factory was located at 2409 "O" Street, Lincoln, Nebraska. Ray Page was the former president of this firm, with O.W. Timm as the chief engineer. The old Lincoln Standard Aircraft Corp. had been started in 1920. This was where Lindbergh started flight training in 1922.

From 1920 to 1937, the Lincoln School and its two predecessors, Nebraska Aircraft Corporation

and Lincoln Standard Aircraft Corporation, turned out over 5,000 pilots and mechanics. And the Lincoln School also trained a large variety of foreign pilots from Cuba, West Indies, Central and South America, Philippines, and Canada.

In 1929, Lincoln Standard Aircraft Corporation School was one of the first schools in the U.S. to receive Approved Transport Flying and Ground School Certificates. CAA also granted Lincoln School the rating of Approved Airplane and Engine Mechanic School.

The Lincoln School, together with the airplane factory which was originally located in the same building, was headquarters for those men whose names are written indelibly into the pages of aviation history. Such names as Charles A. Lindbergh, Ray Page, Ira Biffle, Tuck Gardner, Vincent Burnelli, Otto Timm, Cliff Currier, Errol G. Bahl, Ira Slonniger, Bob Cochran, Hodge Smith, Myron Larkin, Shorty Lynch, E.V. Thomas, Bill Brooks, Dick Hazelrigg, August Pedler, Hart Bowman, and Captain Harding, to mention a few, were men who had made important contributions to aviation progress. To old-timers in aviation, this roster of veteran pilots who at one time or another made Lincoln their headquarters, will call to mind some of the earliest episodes in aviation's development.

Charles A. Lindbergh, who started his flight training at the Lincoln School, will be remembered, of course, for his epochal solo flight over the Atlantic. Ray Page, widely known aviation executive, will be remembered not only as a successful builder of airplanes, but also as the promoter of Page's Aerial Pageant which presented what was probably the greatest array of talented barnstormers, parachute jumpers, wing walkers, and air circus performers known to those early times. It is estimated their exhibitions were witnessed by some 20 million persons throughout the United States.

Major Bill Brooks with the Military Air Service of Honduras gained national prominence by being the first to land an airplane in Yellowstone National Park. August Pedler first startled citizens of Lincoln when he flew a Lincoln Sport Plane out of Farnam Street in downtown Omaha. He is probably best remembered as one of the participants in the Dole Race to Hawaii in which he lost his life in the Pacific. E.V. Thomas, onetime factory representative for Nebraska Aircraft Corporation, established a record by being the first pilot in America to land an airplane in the Grand Canyon of Arizona. Ira Biffle and Turk Gardner brought further notoriety to Lincoln when they were engaged to fly the airmail on its original scheduled flight from New York to Chicago.

No fatal accidents occurred in training at Lincoln Primary though Cadet Schirmer made a forced landing in September northwest of Lincoln, wrecking the plane but suffering only minor injuries. He remembers attending the auto races there, and enjoying the excitement.

The State Capitol Tower, served as a landmark for us Cadets while flying around Lincoln in our training planes (PT-13A's). We didn't do more than barely notice it when we were still flying dual with our instructors. But after soloing and when we started practicing aerial maneuvers by ourselves, we really appreciated seeing that tower in the distance to orient ourselves and find our base field again.

Captain Chapman, AC Res., who was my instructor while at Lincoln, worked hard to teach me the rudiments of maneuvering our PT-13 and how to anticipate stalls so as to avoid spins. He also taught me how to keep everything under control and in a predetermined sequence in the event we encountered a stalling condition while doing other maneuvers. This was very fortunate for me, because when my plane's engine quit on the third consecutive slow roll I was practicing by myself, his quiet, firm training penetrated my momentary panic (it was so quiet up there without the engine and prop going, and so lonely, too); I immediately dropped the nose, after completing the slow roll to an upright position, to prevent a stall. Then I started looking for a suitable place to land. By that time I had lost so much altitude (I estimate I had started from 3,000', but the three slow rolls had brought me down to about 1,500 feet above those hills) that I was hard-pressed to decide on a landing spot. When I did, I pancaked the plane on top of a small rise of land, with ditches and gullies on all sides. I was afraid of going over on my back if my landing gear hit a downslope gully. I did remember to turn off the main switch to prevent a fire, just before I hit the ground. The last thing I remember seeing were the landing gear wheels coming up through the lower wing. I understood from my classmates that Mr. Sias was very irked with me after my forced landing because I had "washed out" the PT-13, even though I had walked away from the wreck. Some classmate there told me later that Mr. Sias couldn't understand why I had to wreck one of "his" Army trainers like that! Of course, with a gash over my right eye from not removing my goggles in my excitement to make a good landing, and with three ribs cracked and big bruises on my legs from the stick wobbling back and forth and side to side on impact, I was not as worried about the condition of "his" plane as he apparently was.

Lieutenant Ford gave me three separate check rides on three separate days after my forced landing. I breezed through them all for I had made up my mind not to let that forced landing bother me. Captain Chapman, my instructor, worked with me constantly on each of our rides together after that crash landing of mine. He would patiently explain how to find a suitable landing spot, note the direction of the wind so as to land into the wind, slow the landing roll, and reduce the risk. We flew over the site of my forced landing and Chapman would point out several places I might have landed without pancaking the plane as I did. It was all good training and I appreciated his dedication to my welfare as a pilot. I've never forgotten his advice and later, when flying, I found myself subconsciously picking out good places to land. He was the most patient instructor I had during my entire flight training in the Air Corps. I'm sure it was his dedication to my learning some basic good habits of flying that put me through the rest of the course as a Flying Cadet. He told me (and so did Lt. Ford) that my forced landing experience put me way ahead of all the others in the class, since it would make me more aware of the nature of the emergency and force me to think ahead and be prepared for the next one.

In our class of twenty-three Flying Cadets at Lincoln Primary in 1939 was one, Ted Pfleuger, a native of Lincoln, who later washed out at Randolph. Ted and I roomed together at Randolph Field during our Basic Flight Training. Ted was having problems with his stall maneuvers, as I recall. I know those thirty-two different kinds of stalls in our BT-

North American BT-9   National Archives

9's were difficult to comprehend, much less remember. I almost washed out myself, because I wasn't kicking the rudder hard enough to start recovery procedures after the stall had occurred. But I finally made it on one check ride with Lt. George F. Schlatter, check pilot. It was his encouragement and constant urging (almost rawhiding) that got my attention, and I responded with the correct force and made all my stall recoveries like he wanted them. But Ted didn't make it and he was very disappointed to be washed out. And I was sorry to see him go. I thought he had it made at Randolph. But if he couldn't learn stall recoveries, it was best that he wasn't kept in the course. I read somewhere that

stalls killed more Cadets than any other maneuver in training in World War I, and that's why our Army flight training emphasized them so much.

Several of the members of Class 40-A recall their primary flying experiences and Cadet life as follows: Pat Trees' logbook shows that he had his first flight on 7-3-39 with M.D. Holman as his instructor. Pat also remembers one dance with many ladies from the Wesleyan College. Bud Sands says: "On my second check ride with Clem Whittenbeck (School Director of Flying), he decided to do some aerobatics, which were taboo. It didn't take long before I was blacked out, with my head lying on the side of the cockpit. Nobody ever said a word.... Then, on my first solo flight, Holman told me to land as near as possible. Well, I did too well and almost landed on him. I was so preoccupied with seeing him running with his parachute . . . that I must have bounced fifty feet into the air."

It would seem that Class 40-A was on the interface between the old most-anything-goes way of learning to fly and the intensive schooling and practice as taught by the Army Air Corps to its Flying Cadets. It was a class that was the transition marker between the old barnstormers and cropduster pilots and the precision flying required by the military in modern warfare.

Of the twenty-three Flying Cadets in Class 40-A, the first class in the contract primary program at Lincoln, eight were eliminated, leaving fifteen to be transferred to Randolph Field, Texas, for Basic Flying phase. At Randolph, one Cadet washed out in Basic; but none at Kelly in Advanced. Thus, fourteen were successful in graduating and receiving their wings at Kelly. The overall elimination rate from Primary, through Basic and Advanced training was 39.2 percent. The overall graduating rate was, therefore, 60.8 percent.

Since this school was the place where Charles A. Lindbergh took his first flying lessons, it is considered appropriate to include the following excerpt from a letter to Colonel Schirmer from Bud Gurney who retired as an airline captain years later. (Bud first knew "Slim" Lindbergh here at this school in 1922. He was the one who gave Lindbergh the nickname of "Slim.") "Lindbergh arrived at Nebraska Aircraft Company's hangars on 1 April 1922. He paid . . . the $500 for his lessons. Ira Biffle was his

German Fokker DVII biplane, still in WWI paint.   National Archives

instructor. Lindbergh got eight hours in the air but they wouldn't let him solo. They had already sold the airplane (a Fokker biplane) in which he had learned to fly. Errol Bahl, the barnstormer, showed up and took delivery on his plane. Lindbergh talked Bahl into letting him join the barnstorming tour as an unpaid helper. It wasn't until the spring of 1923 when Lindbergh borrowed $900 from his Little Falls, Minnesota bank and bought himself a plane; a Curtiss Jenny (JN-4)) with a 90-hp engine, top speed of 70 mph, and then soloed himself in the strange plane. It took him all day and many "almost" crashes and hefty bounces, but he had finally soloed. This after a year of wingwalking, parachute leaps, etc., to gain experience in the air; plus picking up enough mechanical knowledge in the Lincoln factory to be

able to take care of the average aircraft engine of the time."

The school did have some problems. On 2 January 1940, Captain Rodieck (the District Supervisor of Lincoln, E.St. Louis, and Chicago Primaries—his office was at Parks) wrote a letter to Colonel Robins about the situation at Lincoln Primary: "Inasmuch as I consider this to be a personal letter to you, I do not hesitate to state that the heads of the school appear only interested in getting their checks on time. At my other schools, the civil heads run the schools, supervised by the Air Corps personnel. At this school, Lt. Wright and Lt. Ford and the enlisted men run practically everything. The only time the heads of this school appear interested is when you or some of the inspecting party comes through. I fear a gradual letdown, particularly among the civil instructor personnel, due to the fact that, in addition to working in very severe weather, they have no time to call their own, but have to stand around too much, as well as work on weekends. I am afraid that results will eventually show up in the product they send to Randolph. However, it is only fair to state that Lt. Wright does not thoroughly agree with me on this. If the school continues to operate satisfactorily as far as their students are concerned, Lt. Wright and Lt. Ford and all the enlisted men deserve exceptional credit for being able to make a go of it with the handicap they have. Temperature here today is 8° F. below zero, with deep snow."

Three of the original nine primary schools were not recommended mostly because of weather conditions; and also, in the case of Lincoln, the unsatisfactory ground school facilities. Subsequent developments were to prove that the fears of the Air Corps Training Center were fully justified, and it became necessary to move both the Glenview and Lincoln schools. A graphic account of the difficulties at Lincoln has been given in a letter from the Commanding Officer of the Lincoln Detachment: "I cannot see how we can finish Class 40-B early. In my letter of a few days ago, I explained about our wind troubles of September. Well, October is starting out worse. We have only flown two half days. Yesterday we called flying off at noon when the wind hit 29 mph. A few hours later, it was 37 on the surface. It is now 8 a.m. and Class 40-C is flying. The wind is all right now, but up at 5,000 feet, it is over 50 mph. So by noon, it will probably be down on the ground. Class 40-B is only a few hours behind, due to continued weekend flying; but their progress and performance is poor due to the many interruptions, rough air and lack of weekends for relaxing. Seven out of the last eleven check rides have been failing. From this I feel that I will have to give all of them at least an extra five hours' flying time at the end of the course." 5 October 1939, 1st Lt. Wright.

Many difficulties were encountered the first winter of operations at Lincoln. Canopies could not be obtained for the training planes, and 12 degrees F. was almost the minimum temperature in which they were able to operate. During the winter of 1939, the temperature reached -20 degrees F. on three different occasions. Runways were cut in the snow, and the students soloed under these conditions without accidents. However, there was one stretch of weather which lasted thirty days, during which no flying was performed due to cold and snow. This necessitated the holding-over of one entire class. With its training program thus hampered by such unfortunate weather conditions, the government found it necessary to recommend a transfer of the school. Sias was informed of this decision and plans were made immediately to move the school at a future date to the Army approved site in Florida.

Sias outlined the possibilities to the Lakeland, Florida Chamber of Commerce. They, in turn, made arrangements for him to meet the City Commission. Then Sias, President of the Lincoln School of Aeronautics, discussed the possible location of an Army Flying School in Lakeland. He told them what would be required of the city to secure the school. President Sias explained that he was on a scouting trip for a location in the south and was interested in knowing if Lakeland wanted the school and how badly they wanted it. The Commission withheld action and their decision, pending further conferences between the City Manager and Sias. Further negotiations between these two were continued on 20 and 29 May 1940. A tentative proposal was embodied in a letter addressed to Sias and mailed to him on 29 May 1940. All original contacts with the city of Lakeland were made by Sias himself. However, he was not quite definite in any of his arrangements in transferring the school. It appeared that he presumed the Lakeland School would only be temporary; therefore, all negotiations were made on that basis.

Meanwhile, H.S. Darr (operator of the Chicago School of Aeronautics at Glenview, Illinois) and Albert I. Lodwick, a veteran of the aviation world and the President of Stinson Aircraft Company, negotiated with Sias for the purchase of his contract with the Air Corps. Through many interviews, they discovered that Sias was trying to sell all his holdings in the flying school at Lincoln. Therefore, he was quite interested in receiving their offer. With a contract price of $36,000 agreed to by all parties, Sias transferred his contract to the Darr-Lodwick partnership as of 20 July 1940. Negotiations at Lakeland were then captured by Darr, who was the operating partner. Lodwick, for the most part, was the silent partner throughout these negotiations.

The new school was opened August 1940 at Lakeland, Florida, 32 miles east of Tampa. It represented an investment of $500,000. This school as relocated carried on for one of the first nine civilian-operated Army, primary flight schools.

Sias was so attached to his Lincoln School that when the Air Corps decided to move the school south, he preferred to sell rather than move.

The transfer of operations from Lincoln, Nebraska, to Lakeland, Florida, occurred in the latter part of August 1940. Captain Wright, Lt. Lemon and several NCO's moved from the Lincoln School and organized the new detachment at Lakeland, Florida.

With the movement of operations to Florida, half of the civilian personnel transferred to Lakeland, and the remaining portion stayed in Lincoln to finish the class that was then in training there (Class 41-B). The transfer of training began at Lakeland with Class 41-C (18 September 1940).

From 1 July 1939 to 14 October 1940, approximately 305 Cadets were entered in the Lincoln Primary and 209 were graduated. This gave an elimination rate of 31.2 percent and a graduation rate of 68.8 percent. This period covered Classes 40-A through 41-B. For Classes 40-A through 40-H, there were 174 Cadets entered and 111 graduated, with a graduation rate of 63.7 percent, in spite of poor flying weather during the winter of 1939. The final period of training covered Classes 41-A and 41-B, which trained during the summer months of 1940. In these two classes, 131 Cadets entered and 98 graduated. The Cadets in Class 41-C who had been sent to Lincoln for training were diverted to Lakeland, Florida, for training.

Replies to the question, "What circumstances led to your applying for Flying Cadet training in the Army Air Corps?" were as follows:

Colonel Robert B. Coen—"My desire to fly started a long time ago, almost it seems from the time I was in the seventh grade. Given an assignment to write an essay about my plans for a career, I wrote about Aeronautical Engineering and Flying. By the time I went to high school, the flying bug had infected me hard. Next door to our house lived a young man who already was a pilot. His name was Glen Doolittle. He had a Waco airplane, using it primarily for barnstorming and advertising purposes. He was also the lead pilot among a small group of people engaged in developing an experimental flying-wing type of plane. This was being done in the garage back of the house across the street from where I lived. This airplane was called ARUP and it actually flew many times. Even today a friend, Roland Goheen, has the original drawings and the 16mm film of the flights that the ARUP made then. Well, in such a neighborhood as a young impressionable teenager, I just went along with the tide. I washed cowlings and sold tickets for rides in the Waco, always with the hope that I would be selected to go along when it came time to throw out the advertising flyers.

This was an interesting period of my life (in South Bend, Indiana). My family was not able to enter me into a college program that summer after I finished high school. I stayed out a full year and worked as an apprentice engineer in the Bantam Ball Bearing Company. We went to classes in engineering conducted by the owner of the company, after working a full shift at 40 cents an hour. This was my first real opportunity to enter the capitalist society and I bought stock in the company on a onesy and twosy basis. By the time the company sold out to the Torrington Corporation the following spring, I had acquired a substantial number of shares. Then I had enough money to attend Purdue University.

The first year I supplemented my income by working for my room and board. The Purdue Glider Club was an outlet for whatever spare time I had for the next three years. The club was flying a four-place Gross F-5, a primary glider and a soaring glider. Looking back, I find it hard to believe that 21 mph on the airspeed indicator was an acceptable cruising speed.

Then, at the end of my junior year, I decided to go to Flying Cadet training after the ROTC summer camp. Finally my time came to go to Chanute Field to enlist and take the physical exam. But once there they talked me into finishing my senior year at Purdue and to return to Chanute after I had graduated. That was good advice. So I did. During my senior year a powered flight program was launched and Purdue was one of the schools selected to participate in this pilot training program. We flew Piper Cubs. Following graduation in June of 1939, I entered the Flying Cadet program of the U.S. Army Air Corps and was assigned to begin my training at the Lincoln Airplane and Flying School at Lincoln, Nebraska. My flying career had begun."

Major General Harry J. Sands, Jr.—"The idea of becoming an Air Corps pilot started with me along about high school age when I used to go to Norton Field, Columbus, Ohio, with my dad to see the fighter planes come down on a barnstorming tour from Selfridge Field. They were from the First Pursuit Group and flew P-6E's and P-12's amid a hell of a lot of noise, dust, etc. I remember they wore leather jackets, leather helmets, white scarfs, high

Curtiss P-6E's in formation 1/10/39.　　National Archives

boots, etc.... the works. Even Sam Brown belts, I believe. Anyway, I thought they were right next to God in their flying machines and decided I should be the same.

Along about that time a Barling bomber went down in a field close to where I lived east of Columbus and no one was injured, but there was a lot of commotion and I crawled all over the infernal machine. It even had machine guns on it or I thought so anyway, and a place for bombs, too.

Well, I went to Ohio State University and took ROTC and applied for an appointment to West Point. Thought that would be the best way to go. War clouds were already all over Europe and I was sure

we would be involved very soon. At the end of my junior year I received notification of the possible appointment to West Point. With only one more year of ROTC to be a second lieutenant, I couldn't see the sense to going back to square one on the Hudson. So, I passed it up and applied for Army Air Corps pilot training. Took my physical at WPAFB and didn't pass. Had a deviated septum (nose broken a few times). Major Schwicktenburg was the flight surgeon (later to be the flight surgeon for the astronauts), and he promised that if I would have the nose operated on, he would pass me.

It was OSU graduation time by now (December 1938), so I skipped graduation and had my diploma mailed to me and took off for Tampa, Florida, for a date with the surgeon at Tampa General Hospital. After the submucous resection operation, I highballed to Akron, Ohio, by way of the flight surgeon at Wright Field, who approved my physical, and went on to the Goodyear Tire & Rubber Company, where I had a job with the Goodyear Flying Squadron (had nothing to do with flying but was a training squadron for engineering and other graduate trainees). There I worked until the following June 1939, when I got the appointment to the Lincoln Airplane & Flying School where I joined the finest bunch of guys I have ever been associated with. You know the rest."

Colonel Robert F. (Frank) Schirmer—"I can remember what I was doing in 1927 when Lindbergh made his famous solo flight across the Atlantic on 20-21 May: I was sitting on the steps of our front porch at 859 Marion Road, Bucyrus, Ohio, listening to the radio. From boyhood on I built model planes, first those with rubber band motors and scale models of all the Cleveland Air Races planes, etc. In 1930, I visited Wright Field and saw the original

Air Corps Museum's collection of scale models of all the planes of the old Engineering Division. Later, in 1932, I had my first airplane ride from the old Dayton Airport in a Keystone transport plane; the pilot looked like he was only sixteen or seventeen years old. I attended Wittenberg College for two years (1932-34) on a scholarship; then transferred to the Ohio State University at Columbus, Ohio, for my Mechanical Engineering degree, graduating in September 1936. I used to watch Jesse Owens, the great Olympic sprinter, practicing in the Ohio State Stadium track. After graduation, I got a job with the Production Engineering Department of the In-

Engineering Division M-1 Messenger. The assembly on the top is for Dirigible attachment.
National Archives

ternational Harvester Truck Plant in Springfield, Ohio. I made 'shearing charts' for the punch press operators whose machines stamped out parts for the trucks.

One day, in 1938, I was sitting at my desk working on the charts when an acquaintance came by and dropped a copy of the pamphlet: 'Flying Cadets of the Army Air Corps' on my desk. I picked it up, read it through and almost immediately applied to Wright Field for the Flying Cadet physical exam. I had just soloed in an Aeronca light plane at the local Springfield Airport after eight hours of dual

instruction there. I passed the physical at Wright Field; I was one of eleven applicants who were then applying. I was the only one who passed the physical. Several months later I was ordered to Ft. Hayes, Columbus, Ohio, to be sworn in and to receive my orders assigning me to Lincoln Airplane and Flying School, Lincoln, Nebraska. George Prentice and I were sworn in together at Ft. Hayes during this processing. We met again when we started our flight training at Lincoln in July 1939."

GLENDALE CALIFORNIA

The Glendale California (Air Corps Training Detachment) or the Grand Central Flying School, was located at the Grand Central Air Terminal. It was established in 1932. The owner/operator was Major C.C. (Mose) Moseley (1894-1974). It became the 2nd AAF Flying Training Detachment (as of August 1941).

The head of the Faculty was Captain Harry C. Claiborne, ACR. The head of the Ground School was Lewis Holmes, and the Director of Flying was Art Strunk, Lt. ACR with the Chief Instructor being Ralph Thome. The Flying Instructors were: Captain L.S. Heral, ACR, Lts. George S. Sanford, W.H. Clark, W.S. Eliot, Arthur Strunk, John E. Nunn, Henry G. Reynolds, all ACR; Lts. Wm. Stansbury, R.S. Garrison, A.N. Kelly, and W.F. Hausman (all Navy Reserve), and Floyd E. Barlow. The Ground Course Instructors were: Dr. Irving Krick, I. Gringerton, C.S. Williams, Charles A. Zweng, Merlin H. Gale, J.R. Roth Anton Lygum, Rex Finney, L.L. Loomis, F.M. Cole, and Ralph Thorne.

The Detachment Commander was Captain Edwin (Bunky) M. Day, A.C., the Adjutant was 1st

Lt. W.B. Offutt, A.C., The Commandant of Cadets was 1st Lt. Leslie Raybold, A.C., and the Medical Officer was Lt. Colonel Andrew W. Smith, M.C.. Also, making his headquarters here was Captain Kenneth D. McNaughton, who was Western District Supervisor for the Army and who, in addition to general supervision of the Air Corps Detachment at Grant Central, supervised the other two A.C. detachments at San Diego (Ryan) and Santa Maria (Hancock). He reported to Randolph Field, then the Air Corps' only training center. The Flying Equipment consisted of twelve Stearman PT-13's.

"Ground School Instruction at Grand Central Flying School" (Article from the *Glendale Newspaper,* dated September 12, 1939. George E. Brown Collection). "Someday he may pilot a heavy bomber through antiaircraft fire. Or, he may be playing around in a dogfight where much more is at stake than his life. So, he must have special preparation—plus. Sixty-four fledgling Army Air Corps pilots are finding this out today as they pursue their intensive training at the Grand Central Air School. Not only must they learn how to operate a plane, but they must know how the engine is built, how to read maps for cross-country flying, how to wear parachutes scientifically without being conscious of their presence, and how to do logarithms and operate a slide rule. The novelty of the adventure has worn off. Today they swing into the 6 a.m. to 8:30 p.m. routine hardened physically, alert mentally, and with a serious realization that they are face-to-face with an unusual opportunity. An hour and a half a day they fly in the dual-controlled planes. Half of the faculty of 25 experts teaches flying. But 45 minutes each half day in the air is a small part of the strenuous program. An intensive system of thorough instruction is given by the other half of the faculty in classrooms of the Curtiss Technical Institute on the other side of the Grand Central Air Terminal from the barracks. Courses are being given in airplane engines, maps, and air navigation; meteorology, airplane construction, federal aids to air navigation, personal hygiene, theory of flight, math-

ematics, and parachute instruction.

Major C.C. Moseley, head of the Grand Central School, has assembled in addition to the expert teachers of flying, a group of equally proficient instructors for the ground school courses. Meteorology: Dr. Irving Krick of the California Institute of Technology; and Irving Gringorton, graduate of Mass. Institute of Tech. Navigation: Clarence S. Williams, who plotted many of Amelia Earhart's flights; also, flights for Art Goebel and Roscoe Turner. He's a LCdr., USNR. Theory of Flight: Charles A. Zweng of Grand Central Air Terminal; author of a book on aerodynamics. Algebra, Trig and Math: Merlin H. Gale, graduate of University of Cincinnati; John R. Roth, of Curtiss Technical Institute. Military Hygiene: Dr. Reynolds Smith, Captain, California National Guard Reserve. Federal Aids to Flying: Anton Lygum, Grand Central Air Terminal certified by the Civil Aeronautics Authority, who directs all air traffic for the student instruction at the airport. Parachute Rigging: Rex Finney, who has made more than 120 parachute jumps since 1930. Airplane Construction: Lester L. Lollis, former Army instructor in airplane maintenance. Airplane Engines: F.M. Cole, eight years with the Curtiss Technical Institute. Chief Instructor: Ralph Thorne of the Curtiss Technical Institute; formerly with Ryan Corp. of San Diego before and after the flight of Lindbergh. Head of Ground School: Lewis Holmes, ten years with the Curtiss Institute."

When Major Moseley opened his first Army primary school at Glendale, the original instructors were Reserve officers in the Army or Navy. But, with the coming of war, that was completely changed. Overage pilots who could pass the Army refresher course were recruited to teach the Aviation Cadets. Many overage pilots tried without success to get into the AAF to fight in the air in World War II. They were told time and again that their experience would be far more valuable training younger men to fly. In every section of the country old veterans accepted jobs as flight instructors in the civilian contract schools. Some did it gladly, others with resignation. The idea of being 'on the shelf' hurt, and was a natural feeling. Yet in reality the vets were not on the shelf at all. Their work as instructors surpassed in importance the flying job of any one individual combat pilot. They were contributing not to the skill of just one pilot but the combined skills of many.

Moseley supervised the Curtiss-Wright Technical Institute at the Grand Central Air Terminal, Glendale, California, in 1939, and had been the supervisor since 1929 when it was started. But Moseley did not have a flying school at the time and could not be an Army contractor for the expanded pilot training program until he had one. Students desiring to fly who came to Curtiss-Wright Tech Institute were sent across the field (Grand Central Air Terminal) to Joe Plosser whose Grand Central Flying School had exclusive rights to conduct any flight training at Glendale. Plosser had formed his school in 1932. The upshot of this situation was that Moseley worked out a joint venture with Plosser. The Air Corps contract was secured using Plosser's Grand Central Flying School as the base of operations.

The partnership never functioned as such. The school was to be staffed with Air Corps reservists for one thing, and Plosser was not willing to let his nonmilitary instructors go. They finally went their separate ways and Moseley ended up with the Grand Central Flying School. It was a takeover in name only. Plosser retained his staff, facilities, and equipment and simply changed the name of the business to the Joe Plosser Air College. (Ed. note: I am indebted to John Underwoods book for the above explanation).

Grand Central Air Terminal which had been leased from Curtiss-Wright since 1934, was purchased outright by Major Moseley in June 1944. At that time, the "Air Terminal" was dropped in favor of "Airport." It had ceased to function as a terminal when Mexicana moved out some months earlier. Curtiss-Wright Technical Institute, having completed the training of the last class of Air Corps mechanics, became Cal-Aero Technical Institute. The name changing was largely administrative and did not involve the contract flying schools. Pilot training had been greatly curtailed and was soon to be phased out altogether at the Grand Central Airport. Also, war production was winding down by the fall of 1944. The terminal had opened in 1923 and was used extensively for aviation scenes in early Hollywood films. In 1929, Charles Lindbergh piloted the first transcontinental flight from there, a trip to New York. On board that day were movie stars Mary Pickford and Douglas Fairbanks, Sr., among other celebrities. Amelia Earhart used the airport frequently. And Howard Hughes built his first plane, then the world's fastest, in Glendale in the early 1930's. The airport was busy then, but began to lose business later in the 1930's with the opening of Mines Field (now Los Angeles International Airport) and Union Air Terminal (now Burbank Airport). The Glendale airfield was a training-site for thousands of Air Corps Cadets and civilian recruits from Britain's Royal Air Force during World War II. By 1955, "Mose" was a very rich man, having sold the Grand Central Air Terminal for $16 million. Later in the 1970's, the terminal became an industrial center. But efforts were made to convert the old buildings of the terminal into an aviation museum to revive the memory of Grand Central which served as the main airport for the Los Angeles area during the '20's and '30's. John Underwood, the writer, says that Grand Central was the cradle of the airline industry.

The original contract between the Army Air Force and Grand Central Flying School at Glendale was dated 19 June 1939 (W535-ac-12875), which called for not more than 45 students and using no more than 15 PT-13's for flight training. The second contract was awarded on 15 July 1940, and called for a maximum of 325 students for all three Moseley schools at Glendale, Ontario, and Oxnard, California.

This school was one of the original nine civil

contract primary schools in the Army's expansion program for pilots. The first class of 40-A had its start here with thirty-seven students (all Flying Cadets) reporting for training on 1 July 1939. Major Corliss C. Moseley, known as "Mose" to his friends, the civil operator of Grand Central Flying School in 1939, was the first airman to win the International Pulitzer Race trophy. That was in 1920, when he flew a plane sponsored by the late General Billy Mitchell and established a speed record of 176 mph. Major Moseley had served in France during World

As of 10/18/18 these were the remaining members of the 94th Aero Sq. which along with the 27th, 147th, and 95th, were all under the 1st Pursuit Group. L.to R. Lt. Rickenbacker; Capt. James A. Messiner; 1st Lt. Reed Chambers; 1st Lt. Thorne C. Taylor; Joseph H. Eastman. Photo taken near Rembercourt, Meuthe-et Moselle, France.   National Archives

War I with the U.S. Air Service; he was a member of the 27th Pursuit Squadron, of the first Pursuit Group, along with Rickenbacker, Luke, Quentin Roosevelt, and other top pilots. After the war and until his resignation from the Army in 1925, Moseley was in charge of all Air Service schools. He also served as a test pilot for all new types of Army planes developed and built at the Engineering Division, Wright Field, Dayton, Ohio. He organized the original Western Air Express Corporation, one of the first commercial carriers of mail in the U.S.. He was responsible for organizing the California Air Na-

tional Guard. John Underwood says in his *Madcaps, Millionaires, and Mose* : "General Arnold and Major Moseley, having served together in the immediate post-World War I years, were the best of friends. Moseley's participation in the proposed civilian primary flight training program was not only desired, it was expected. Arnold needed administrators he could trust and count on to perform. The program was an experiment in the fullest sense. The contractors were being asked to throw in with Arnold, knowing full well that appropriations had yet to be voted on. There was no guarantee they would even recover their own not inconsequential investments."

The new Air Corps Pilot Training Program was initially designed to graduate 2,134 pilots by 1 January 1941, and provided for new classes to be constituted at intervals of six weeks, starting 1 July 1939. Students who washed out would be given a second chance to qualify for flying as navigators and bombardiers. It was understood then that the contract program would last only as long as it took to bring the Air Corps up to strength. No one dreamed that it would not end until 240,000 pilots had been trained.

There were other programs running concurrently with the Air Force Aviation Cadet pilot training and many instructors and combat pilots were trained under these programs. The Civilian Pilot Training Program (CPTP) was established on 27 June 1939. The idea was to create a pool of college-trained pilots, male and female, which could be drawn upon in a national emergency. (This was to be accomplished without incurring the wrath of those involved in the great pacifist movement of the late 30's and early 40's. These people came from all walks of life, many were in congress and the news media. But they all had one thing in common; they wanted nothing to do with any war anywhere, and this mindset even carried over into pilot trainingwhich they considered training for war). The Air Corps and the Navy, of course, would have first call on their services. Thirteen colleges and universities were initially recruited to participate in the training of some 300 handpicked students. (This number grew to over 1,000 during the next several years.) The next step was to train 10,000 pilots and $4 million was budgeted by the CAA for that purpose. Glendale Junior College was among the 300 schools picked to administer the program. Approximately 50,000 pilots were eventually trained under this CPTP program, 10 percent of which were non-college. On 13 December 1941, the President signed Executive Order number 897 turning control of all CPTP training centers over to the War Department. Thus changing the name of the program to the War Training Service (WTS) after that date. To save the Air Force money training men who were not likely pilot material, the College Training Detachment was formed from January 1943 until August 1944. Here potential pilots were screened at various colleges all across the country, and only the best were sent on to the Aviation Cadet program.

Braniff Captain Ernest Hummel, 40-A— "I recall the day, July 1, 1939, that the bus picked up the Cadets at the casino (where we lived) and hauled us across the field to the long row of training planes. The Stearman PT-13A's, with Lycoming R-680-7 radial engines, were lined up with mathematical precision in the old Army Air Corps style. There couldn't have been less than fifteen. (Author's note: Actually there were twelve.) The aircraft appeared to be new, and the sight of all identical ships with the blue and orange paint in spotless condition was enough to boggle the mind of any, truly airplane-worshipful twenty-year-old. Grand Central Air Terminal and its long concrete runway was our home field, but only the first takeoff and last landing of the training days were made there. The field was an airline airport and American Airways (now Airlines) and Compania Mexicana de Aviacion used it as a terminus.

Each instructor took one Cadet and each pair was assigned to a primary trainer. All the planes would be cranked up at one time and the long line would taxi out and take off at close intervals. In tandem, the line would thread a route out through the San Fernando Valley, avoiding another airline airport at Burbank, also at Van Nuys, and end up at the auxiliary field known as Chatsworth. This was about a mile square of thickly dust-covered earth, with high trees on three sides. All the flight training was done at Chatsworth with precisely drawn boundaries for the various zones. At the end of the day, with all Cadets and instructors covered with dust, the twenty-one-mile trek back to Grand Central would begin. Most of the instructors were ex-military pilots and would let off steam by flying formation and doing acrobatics on the trip home.

Our Cadet housing was a large building which had functioned as a gambling casino for many years. The main room which contained all the bunk beds for the Cadets had a ceiling which we will all remember. It was covered with very artistic paintings of voluptuous and nude females, gamboling around the scenery. All the upper bunk occupants had an unobstructed view of these babes and as a result the last thought before sleep at night and the first one in the morning were of a very carnal nature. The food at Glendale was excellent, far above anything we had subsequently at Randolph or Kelly. Our flying commandant was a Captain Edwin Day, a short and round individual and very-well liked by the Cadets. He obviously liked to eat and he was often seen checking the kitchen at noon and ascertaining that everyone was getting all the food they could handle. The casino was across the runway from the airline terminal. It was at the foot of the Hollywood Hills and a few yards from the present Golden State Freeway. There was a swimming pool and all the blandishments of Southern California just around the corner. It was a sort of idyllic summer.

Captain Day flew with all the Cadets at one time or another. A check ride with him was something else. After determining whether or not the Cadet was up to standard at that point, he would pat his head in the old 'I've got it' sign and give the Cadet a real demonstration of what could be done with a Stearman by an expert. It was a linked series of maneuvers done so damn smoothly and without hardly any loss of altitude, you couldn't help but be impressed to the utmost. And all the while he would have a big grin on his face. Captain Day's assistant in the flying department at Glendale was a dour, misanthropic loner by the name of Lieutenant Raybold. He would often buzz into Chatsworth in the detachment's BC-1 and give a number of check rides. It always seemed that the washout rides fell to this individual. When he would depart Chatsworth, he managed to churn up enough dust with the BC-1 to blot out the sun for a long time. The instructors used to cuss this guy loudly and longly.

The prime contractor at Glendale was C.C. Moseley, and thereby hangs another tale. Major 'Mose' as he was popurarly known was a famous aviation figure in his own right. He had been a well-known Army Air Service test pilot at McCook Field (presently Wright-Patterson AFB). Subsequently he, along with four other pilots, pioneered the Air Mail operation between Los Angeles and Salt Lake City. They flew the big Douglas M-2 biplanes with open cockpits and liquid-cooled Liberty engines, through fair weather and foul, winter and summer, Major Moseley was a great guy. He was sincerely interested in the welfare and flying progress of all the Cadets. It was tough to get him to talk about his own exploits, but we tried. Southern California was, and is now, the focal point for more aviation interest than all the other states combined. Our every move at Glendale made all the newspapers, and Major Moseley was a hero there to the day he died."

Frank B. Howe, an official of Grand Central Flying School, tells a story about civilian complaints concerning noise generated by the primary training planes in southern California in 1939: ". . . We had established an auxiliary field near Northridge in the San Fernando Valley. In short order, a movie director started yelling to heaven that the 'deafening noise' of the training airplanes (actually the putt-putt of Boeing Kaydets) was distracting his blooded horses. He attracted quite a following among the small ranchers who said their hens were being so frightened that they ceased to lay eggs. So we moved the auxiliary field to an isolated place south of Reseda. Again the howls came. We were making it impossible for a certain movie outfit to take pictures at its 'ranch.' We were scaring chickens. We were a menace to civilization. (This was before the days when it was patriotic or fashionable to support the Air Corps.) Despite a courageous pair of valley editors, Jimmy Lintner of Canoga Park, who dared the wrath of the critics by running a banner line across the entire front page saying: "Better the Star in the Circle Over San Fernando Valley than the Swastika"; and John Hungerford of Reseda, a World War I veteran, who really took his neighbors to pieces editorially; "We were hailed before the Los Angeles City Planning Commission. After a dozen hearings, the August commission passed the buck to the City Council which conducted an elaborate 'hearing' which was packed to the guards. We were supported in ringing speeches by numerous prominent American Legion commanders and others; the opposition—from a high-priced movie lawyer. We never had a chance. The City Council voted 12 to 3 to oust the Air Corps training from San Fernando Valley."

Here in part is the editorial from the *Reseda News* (California) of October 6, 1939, in which editor and publisher John Hungerford "took his neighbors to pieces." It read: "All that hollering about the Army planes being a nuisance was enough to make the ordinary citizen who has any respect for his country get hot under the collar. These complaints about the chickens being so scared they wouldn't lay, and those stories about pure-blooded horses shivering from fright were too much to swallow. However, they were sufficient to make the Army hunt up another site rather than permit the squawks to go on. It's hard to see what difference it makes where the Army field happens to be. People might as well make up their minds that the Army is going to train pilots in some place and regardless of where that place happens to be, someone is going to be inconvenienced...."

Such inconvenience, happily, was accepted without complaint by the great majority near whose localities the new airports were built. Sites for the training bases were selected for the most part in the isolated sections, in the desert, on the plains, and away from towns.

In August 1940, the training of American Cadets was shifted to the Ontario field, and Major Moseley began training volunteers for the American Eagle Squadron in November 1940 at Glendale (Grand Central Air Terminal). On 4 June 1941, the first British RAF Cadets began training at Glendale, which became No. 2 British Flying Training School. On 20 August 1941, the first British RAF Cadets were sent to War Eagle Field at Lancaster, California, and then that school site was designated Polaris Flight Academy. In December 1941, the refresher training of recruits for the American Eagle Squadron was also moved from Glendale to War Eagle Field at Lancaster, California. Grand Central Flying School, Grand Central Air Terminal, Glendale, California, produced a total of 467 pilots from 1939 to 1941, when it was discontinued.

Following Pearl Harbor, Major Moseley, at the request of the Headquarters Western Flying Training Command, started Basic Training of Cadets at Ontario (Cal-Aero Academy) along with the Elementary Cadet Training on 22 March 1941. And the first American Cadets began arriving at Polaris Flight Academy, Lancaster, California, on 8 August 1942, for their Basic Flight Training, along with elementary training. On 27 July 1944, the basic flight training program at Polaris Flight Academy was stopped and Polaris Flight Academy was closed. Then Mira Loma Flight Academy moved from Ox-nard to Lancaster to provide primary flight training in the better facilities of War Eagle Field.

In October 1944, Cal-Aero Flight Academy at Ontario was closed, leaving only Mira Loma at War Eagle Field operating. On 4 August 1945, Mira Loma Flight Academy closed its doors, ending five years of flight training at War Eagle Field.

Of the thirty-seven students who showed up for the first class at Grand Central, eleven Flying Cadets were eliminated and twenty-six Cadets went on to Randolph Field for Basic Flying. None were eliminated in Basic, but one more Cadet was lost in Advanced at Kelly, leaving twenty-five to graduate. The overall elimination rate for the entire nine months of training was 32.5 percent, or a graduation rate 67.5 percent.

For the training of RAF Cadets during 1941-1944, the British Air Ministry awarded Major C.C. Moseley, THE MOST EXCELLENT ORDER OF THE BRITISH EMPIRE— OFFICER GRADE.

A total of 401 RAF Cadets and 81 Eagle Squadron pilots were graduated from the two Moseley schools at Lancaster and Ontario, California.

Replies to the question: "What Circumstances Led to Your Applying for Flying Cadet Training in the Army Air Corps?"

Airline **Captain Ernest B. Hummel**, Panagra/Braniff—"I graduated from South Dakota School of Mines and Technology in 1935. Since the Great Depression was hardly over and times were still tough, positions in the profession were scarce as hell; however, one did open up in a West Coast lead smelter. The plant and its associated chemistry laboratory were just about the unhealthiest places to work in all creation. OSHA would have shut them down in nothing flat. After four years and the contemplation of foreshortened longevity, a long-term interest in aviation began to erupt. The low overflight of formations of Martin B-9's from nearby Hamilton Field provided me with a continuous stimulus to do something, however wrong it might be.

Changing professions at that point was a pretty heavy matter. The long line of prospective inductees entering the physical and psychological examining rooms at Hamilton looked ominous until it was noted that almost all of these healthy-looking individuals were leaving via a side door after having been busted for one reason or another. There was no choice of training school location offered, but Grand Central at Glendale turned out to be one of the best."

Colonel Charles W. Johnstone—"I was graduated from the University of Nevada, May 1939, as the ROTC Honor Graduate, which stipulated a granting of a regular commission in the U.S. Army, Infantry. This program included being called to active duty, at the Presidio, San Francisco, late in the summer of 1939. During the latter part of May, a friend of mine indicated he was going to Hamilton Field to take the physical exam for Flying Cadet, and I agreed to help him drive there. At Hamilton Field, the friend reported to the hospital for his physical. I went to the hospital waiting room and there, during the waiting period, I was approached by a Colonel Smith, U.S. Army Medical Corps. Colonel Smith asked me what I was doing there, and after my explanation, asked why I didn't take the physical too? He informed me if I passed the physical, I would be signed up for Flying Cadets; and when called to active duty, I would be transferred from Flying Cadet status to 2nd Lt., Infantry, USA; and then would be placed on flying training status. That seemed to be a great idea and I enthusiastically agreed. In summary: 1. My friend failed his physical. I passed mine. 2. Colonel Smith didn't have the slightest concept about Army administration (or the regulations about going through training in grade). 3. I remained a Cadet throughout my flying training. 4. After a competitive examination in 1942, I received a Regular Commission in the Army Air Corps."

Colonel Wilson T. Jones—"George E. Brown and I were attending the University of Utah when a team of Army Air Corps Flying Cadet recruiters flew in and over in two sexy looking O-47's. It touched an adventuresome chord in both of us, and I drove 500 miles on an old beat-up Harley-Davidson motorcycle from Salt Lake City to Denver, Colorado, for my physical. I sent my application to Washington, D.C., and took private lessons in a puddle-jumper airplane. Then I switched to mathematics as my college major. And then I left school before graduation to head for Glendale, California, and primary training at Grand Central Flying School."

Mr. Robert T. Lamson—"In 1937-1938, I was attending the Boeing School of Aeronautics in Oakland, California. During a class in aerodynamics a visitor, Eddie Allen, a noted experimental test pilot, told of his experiences as a military aviator and test pilot. He was in Oakland at that time to do the initial tests on Alan Lockheed's Alcor. I got to know Eddie and dreamed of getting into test flying myself. It was he who suggested that I apply to the Army Air Corps for military flight training and point towards getting into the flight testing program at Wright Field. I first applied in the spring of 1938, but finally received orders to report to the Grand Central Flying School at Glendale, California, in July of 1939."

Lt. General Eugene B. LeBailly—"My interest in flying began in about 1922, when a World War I Jenny biplane landed on our baseball field at Shoshone, Idaho, a small town located on the Snake River plains of southern Idaho. The population was only about 2,000 people. This is where I was born and spent my early youth. This Jenny was the first aircraft I had ever seen, and I still dearly remember how the young pilot wore a leather jacket and a leather helmet with a squirrel tail fastened to the top of it. What an impression that pilot and that airplane made on me. My desire to fly began there.

During the next few years, although my interest in flying remained, I just did not have the opportunity to see airplanes or any flying people. The next time my interest was aroused was at the Southern Branch of the University of Idaho at Pocatello. In 1935, two of my classmates tried to talk me into going to the Navy Flying School at Pensacola. A person only needed two years of college to enter.

But I decided to complete my work toward a degree first, especially after talking to Pan American personnel people. Pan American Airways was just beginning to receive considerable publicity with their proposed worldwide operations. In 1935, I had visited the Pan Am office at Treasure Island in San Francisco Bay. The advice I received from them in answer to my question, 'What background would be best for a young man to have in order to fly for Pan Am and then enter their management offices?' was: 'If a young man capable of passing a rigorous physical exam was to graduate from, for example, the University of California here at Berkeley, with a degree in Foreign Trade, then attended the Army or Navy flying school and received his wings, he would be just the kind of a man Pan Am prefers to hire.'

That summer of '36 I transferred from Idaho to the University of California, changed my major from Geology to Foreign Trade, and in 1939 I graduated from California with a B.S. in Foreign Trade, and enrolled in the U.S. Army Flying School with the Class of 40-A. Thirty-four years later I retired from the U.S. Air Force with over 8,000 pilot hours in 62 different types of aircraft after having lived in nine foreign countries. I have never regretted my decision to make flying my career and for staying in Military Aviation. I decided to stay in the Air Force because of three commanders I had during the World War II period. They were: General Stuart P. Wright, who as a major was my first squadron commander; General John K. Gerhart, who was my immediate commander in World War II; and finally, General Curtis LeMay, who was my 3rd Air Division Commander in the 8th Air Force in England. He personally led us on some of the toughest missions we flew. Until the final year of World War II, I still planned to fly with Pan Am when the war ended. It wasn't until World War II that I became interested in making my career in the U.S. Air Force. I have never regretted this decision—and am happy that I was lucky enough to join the Class of 40-A on that June day in 1939."

Colonel Robert M. McLeod—" About Eas-

ter of 1939, a Flying Cadet examining team which was making the rounds of many universities visited the University of Nevada campus for a week. I had heard of the team being there, but had no interest in applying. That is, until one day —a Friday and the last day of the team's visit in Reno—when a few of us were sitting around the fraternity house and the subject of Flying Cadet came up. One guy said something to the effect that there was no use in anyone taking the physical exam for Cadets because no one could pass it. I thought I could and said so. Thus, on somewhat of a dare, I went for the exam. I was lucky because the team was almost packed up and nearly ready to go when I appeared. But they unpacked and examined me. I passed the exam. Early in June '39, I was invited to report to McClellan Field in Sacramento, which I did. I was assigned to Grand Central Flying School for primary training. And you know the rest of the story.

When in school I did not like the military. In fact, I took three years of ROTC in high school in order to be exempt from ROTC at the University of Nevada. It must seem unfair to some who had planned for years to fly and/or get into the Flying Cadet program and couldn't make it or if they did, to later wash out. And then have some yard bum like me to literally fall into the program. It turned out to be a blessing for me because I liked every part of the Air Corps and Air Force. I have often told people when asked if I liked the service, 'I never had a bad day in the service.' And I really and truly enjoyed flying. I was fortunate in that respect, too, because I was able to stay on flight status right up until I retired."

DALLAS, TEXAS

The Dallas, Texas (Air Corps Training Detachment) or Dallas Aviation School & Air College, located at Love Field was established in 1926. It became the AAF Flying Training Detachment (as of July '42). (See Brady Primary). The operator was Major William F. (Bill) Long (1895-1976).

The school at Dallas was also one of the first nine contract schools. Army Flying Cadets of Class 40-A began their primary flight training there on 1 July 1939 under Major Bill Long and his staff.

Major Bill Long was fondly known as "Mr. Dallas Love Field." He was the founder of the Dallas Aviation School and Air College. He led a very interesting life. He was a WWI airman, barnstormer, adventurer, pioneer, fixed base operator, civilian and military training school owner, airline executive, financier, rancher, horseman, marksman, raconteur, historian, and scholar. He was awarded the Order of the British Empire for WWII RAF pilot training. As of 1971 he was dynamically active as bizjet consultant and cattleman, with offices at Southwest Airmotive. Long was well-known to Cadets while they were at Dallas Aviation School and Air College absorbing Primary Flight and Ground Training under Bill's excellent staff of experts. Class 40-A was the first of the classes in the expanded Army Air Corps pilot production programs. Since the Dallas Aviation School & Air College's Air Corps Training Detachment was inactivated prior to the establishment of the Historical Program (started in 1943), no history of the school was prepared during the life of the organization. Therefore, this part of the school's history was prepared by the Historical Section at Hqs., Central Flying Training Command, at Randolph Field, Texas.

The history of the Dallas Aviation School and Air College was divided into two parts. The first extended from sometime in 1926 when the school was organized, until 16 March 1941 when it was moved from Love Field, Dallas, Texas, to Curtis Field, Brady, Texas. The second period extended from 16 March 1941 through the war period.

The President was Major Wm. F. Long; the Secretary and Treasurer was C.E. Harmon; and the Superintendent was, H.H. Bowman. In the Ground School department, the Head Instructor was G.A. Douglas; the chief engine Instructor was Mr. Lievre; the other instructors were: Gray, Lambert, Phillips, Russell Norwin, and Hart H. Bowan. The Flight

Instructors were: C.E. Shankle (Director), Cates Eppright, Hal F. Folkers, Carl W. "Stormy" Roderick, "Stumpy" Walton, R.H. Weisner, Richard Griffin, Horace C. Heising, and John Threadgill.

This Air Corps Training Detachment had the following officers assigned: Captain Emmet F. Yost, A.C., Commanding Officer; 1st Lt. James Price, A.C., Adjutant; 1st Lt. Daniel Hook, A.C., Commandant of Cadets. Medical officer: Captain Myers, M.C. Captain Yost also commanded the Mechanics Training School at Dallas Aviation School, Love Field, from 2 October 1940 to 21 March 1941.

The Station History of Curtis Field, Brady, Texas, recorded the story of the Dallas Aviation School's activities from its transfer to Brady. Thus the history of the school during intervals from 1 July 1939 to 15 March 1941 was not written even though the transfer from Love Field to Curtis Field did not entail any changes in the relationship between the contractor and the U.S. Government. This history traces the story of the Dallas School of Aviation's contribution to the Air Corps' training program while the school was located at Love Field. The Dallas Aviation School was established in 1926. It was certified by the United States Department of Commerce (Civil Aviation Authority-CAA) for both flying and mechanics' training in 1929. It was recognized by the aviation industry and was located in a state whose climate is favorable for flying the year around. This school was the cradle of aviation industry in Texas.

The Dallas School of Aviation and Air College was incorporated in 1938 by retired Air Corps Major William F. Long, and W.B. Click. Major Long was president of the school; Click became the director of the school. They were first approached in December 1938 on the possibility of becoming a training school for Flying Cadets in a contemplated expansion of the training of pilots by the Air Corps. The school was interested and later became one of the original nine elementary flying schools. This school, which at the time, was located at Love Field, became a part of the first expansion program on 19

June 1939, with contract W535ac12872 drawn up between the U.S. Government and Major W.F. Long, president of the school. The "Air College" portion of the original title of the school was dropped at that time. The school operated under this contract from date of activation 1 July 1939, until 17 July 1940, when a new contract, W535ac-15369, was drawn up between the school and the U.S. Government. During 1940, an amendment to the contract was put through. This increased the financial allotment to the school so it could better handle the larger student flow during its second year of expansion.

Prior to the activation of the Dallas Primary Air Corps Detachment, the president, Major Long, was instructed to send the men he thought would qualify as flying instructors to Randolph Field, Texas, for training. He had a large instructor group and was asked to send one half in one class and the remainder in a later group. Many of these men made a very poor showing and failed to pass the flying requirements for instructor ratings. These men were, for the most part, good fliers but the Army requirements for primary instructors were very high. The men who did qualify were given a certificate of approval and were qualified to instruct students at all civil contract elementary schools. Mr. Shankle, one of the men who washed out of the Instructors' School, favorably impressed the officers at Randolph Field, and he was recommended to Major Long of the Dallas school to be hired as Director of Training. This advice was welcomed and the school was more than repaid by Shankle's work. Major Long said, "Our original bunch of instructors were veteran barnstormers and cotton dusters. It takes a real honest-to-God pilot to be a cotton duster. Cotton dusting is dangerous flying. The pilot flies as low as three feet over a cotton field, dodging shrubs and trees, while he sprays calcium arsenate over the field to kill the boll weevil. Some of these dusters naturally had a little trouble with the young Army men who were putting them through the refresher course. A 'duster' would resent a young squirt trying to teach him to fly an airplane." When these pilots, with thousands of flying hours of barnstorming and crop dusting, were being checked out by "young" Army instructor pilots at Randolph Field, before the primary schools opened, they had a difficult time accepting the "precision" flying of the Army which was demanded of them.

The instruction of young army fliers had to be standardized in order to prepare them in primary for precision flying, which included formation flying and aerobatics against skilled veteran pilots of the enemy air forces. Nevertheless, these old pilots rebelled at the thought of having to change from their "free-swinging" ways of flying to the more disciplined methods of standardization required of them so they would be qualified to teach the "Army way." Some of these old pilots had never flown with a "T" to refer to when landing on an airfield. They had become accustomed to watching the trees bending in the wind or the normal single wind sock. They soon found out that they had been unaware of the fine points of precision flying which no one had told them about. Most civilian instructors who had never had any Army pilot training were unaware of these methods of flying until they were being checked out at Randolph Field under the highly specialized refresher course that was designed to ensure the same precise habits of flying that made Army flying a little more safe and much more efficient.

By late 1940 a plan was in operation that sent supervisors and assistants, with a supply of planes, from training center headquarters to the schools to train instructors, and also maintenance men, who would in turn train others. In 1942, regional instructor schools gave training to civilian instructors for primary schools and in 1943-1944 such instruction was given at the Central Instructors' School at Randolph Field. Refresher training for the civil instructors for Dallas Aviation's new civil school at Terrell, Texas, was given at Spartan (Tulsa). Meanwhile, the Dallas and Tulsa schools continued giving training to the British (UK) Cadets until the new civil schools were ready to operate and receive the UK Cadets from Dallas and Tulsa.

The instruction given under the original contract (from 19 June 1939 to 17 June 1940) consisted of 65 hours of flying and 225 hours of Ground School, with 24 hours of Military Training. The flying instruction was divided between dual and solo instruction. Dual received 30 hours and solo was 35. This instruction was given in PT-3 type aircraft which were built in 1928 by the Consolidated Aircraft Corporation. They had no flaps, or instruments. The determination of the Cadet was about the only thing that kept the plane in the air. (Ed. note: Although these obsolete primary planes might have seemed impossible to fly to the historian who penned this part of the history of Dallas Primary School, these PT-3's were still good, rugged trainers for primary students. They did have the few basic instruments mounted not inside, but outside the cockpits, such as the oil pressure gauge mounted on a wing strut, etc. There were five instruments: Oil Pressure, Oil Temp., Altimeter, Magnetic Compass, and Gas Gauge.)

Cadet Bumgarner, 40-A, stated: "The first four of these were mounted on stems to the outside of the fuselage, and were located forward and to either side of the front windshield. The fuel level indicator protruded from the underside of the top wing. This gas gauge was a graduated, glass tube in which a free-floating cork revealed the amount of fuel on board. A convex mirror was attached to a wing strut, and an altimeter was on the left side of the fuselage forward of the front cockpit. It indicated the altitude in feet above the ground (not above sea level). All the altimeters in the PT-3 were set to read zero on the ground. The mirror was used to allow the instructor in the front cockpit to observe the Cadet pilot without getting a "crick" in his neck. No tachometer was furnished for the PT-3. The propeller was not adjustable in pitch so the only control over the engine rpm was with the throttle and the elevators."

Cadet Gould, 40-A, another trainee at Dallas adds: "The PT-3 had no wheel brakes and, as a result, wing-walkers got plenty of exercise while parking the 'bird' on a windy day. It had no tail wheel either, but the tail skid, with an extra heavy iron section welded to it, did improve ground-handling characteristics. The landing gear did not have hydraulic shock struts, although the 'bungee cords' assisted in 'hangar-high' bounces by errant Cadets."

The PT-llD's used at Tuscaloosa Primary had the same number of instruments for the pilots, but by 1932 these had been placed inside the cockpits for easier reference.

Under the original contract it was proposed that a training program would be for 12 weeks. At no time would the number of military students matriculated be more than 70 per class, nor would more than two classes be in training at any one time. A maximum of five students per airplane would be in training at any one time. The second contract called for a ten-week program, a maximum of 100 students per class and no more than two classes in training at any one time. Military students would be limited to five students per plane. The first contract called for using the PT-3 type airplanes. The later contract called for a new PT-19 type (Fairchild) aircraft which

Consolidated Aircraft PT-3   National Archives

was of completely new design, being a low-wing monoplane.

Love Field was a well-equipped airport and was

Fairchild PT-19   National Archives

used continually by the commercial air transport lines. There were facilities for all phases of flying, including night flying. The Dallas school itself had hangar space to handle numerous planes. Maintenance and tool repair shops were at their disposal at all times. The terrain surrounding the field was level and ideal for emergency landing fields.

The housing at Dallas was inadequate prior to the activation date of this Air Corps Detachment but two special dormitories of wood, steel and concrete were built to house 120 students. Each dorm had 20 rooms, with the capability of housing three men in each. The rooms contained single steel beds, mattresses, coil springs, a study table with an individual lamp for each student, three shelves, and a closet (four feet by 20 inches) for each student. Gas heaters were in each room; these supplied hot water for showers with hand lavatories in each room.

Mess facilities were in the local cafeteria. This was not capable of feeding the additional men brought to the Dallas school. Through the efforts of Captain Myers, the senior flight surgeon, the cafeteria was enlarged and the kitchen made more sanitary. After these improvements, the cafeteria proved satisfactory.

The medical facilities at Dallas barely covered the immediate necessities. The field only had a first aid station, but the Dallas school had agreements with local doctors and the hospital to care for major illnesses and to supply an ambulance when needed.

There were no drill fields within walking distance so all reviews were held on the ramp at the airport. There were also no physical training facilities at the Dallas Aviation School. The city of Dallas ultimately supplied them. The YMCA's accommodations were made available and the public parks were always open to the students.

There was no chaplain or any church at the school, but transportation was supplied to the local churches and the men attended services in town. Recreation was furnished by the city of Dallas.

During the early period of training, the Army Air Corps had very high educational requirements which the applicants for pilot training needed for acceptance. After the expansion program was put into effect it was found that there were not enough applicants with these qualifications. As the requirements were lowered, however, it was found that the students were doing just as well as the previous Cadets who had the college training. Some of the higher Army officers decided that perhaps a man did not really need a college education to fly an airplane efficiently. The largest number of washouts was always attributable primarily to flying deficiencies rather than to physical or academic failures.

In 1939, for Class 40-A, there were twenty-nine PT-3's and PT-3A's being flown.

From 11 December 1939 to 17 June 1940, there were seventeen accidents at Dallas; twelve of these were with no damage to the PT-3 aircraft (loose throttle, engine failure, broken propeller, engine smoking, lost bearings, broken crankshaft, oil line broken, cylinder studs broke, exhaust valve stem broken, etc.). The other accidents were more serious and usually damaged the aircraft beyond repair. (Ed. note: While it is understandable why the newer PT-19's were brought in for the second contract period, it was made plain in historical notes on both Dallas and Tulsa that there were not enough PT-13's available on 1 July 1939 to furnish all nine contract primary schools; so these obsolete PT-3's had to be used for this initial period to get training started).

The original contract gave the Dallas school an estimated sum of $535,000, which was payable as follows: For each student graduated and approved by the government (C.O. of Air Corps Det.), $1,170 was to be paid the contractor; for each eliminated student, the contractor was to be paid $18 for each hour of aerial instruction. This way of paying was used from 1 July 1939 until 17 July 1940, when the second contract was signed. After 17 July 1940, the second contract called for 10 weeks of training instead of 12 as specified originally; sixty hours of flying and 140 hours of ground instruction; military training was not given a definite amount of time. The new contract awarded Dallas school amounted to $757,922.40. This was to be paid under two different classes:

1. For each student graduated in a government-overhauled plane $1,050 was to be paid the contractor—for each eliminated student, the contractor was to be paid $17.50 per hour of aerial instruction.

2. For each student graduated in a contractor-overhauled plane, $1,386 was to be paid. Each Cadet that washed out was to be paid for at the rate of $23.10 per hour of aerial instruction.

The majority of men washed out of the Dallas Aviation School because of flying deficiencies. From the time of the school's activation to its move to Brady, Texas, only 10 men washed out for reasons other than flying deficiency. During this time seven students were killed in training.

Some of the fatalities were as follows: 13 Nov. 1939—While making a practice forced landing (both instructor and student were killed); 24 April 1940—One instructor and two students killed in midair collision; 14 August 1940—A Cadet was killed while making a 360 degree overhead approach. He had completed four practice landings but while making the fifth, his engine died, and he spun to earth from about 500 feet; 2 October 1940—A Cadet was killed while making a practice approach from a 180-degree overhead landing from 600 feet. During the base leg of his approach, he made a flat turn into the field and fell into a right spin. He hit the ground just west of the runway.

During the complete training program, it was surprising that more midair collisions did not occur. The traffic at Love Field was very heavy and congested at all times of the day. The air lanes had large transports arriving and leaving the field continuously. With this to cope with, the operations officer had his hands full and did a wonderful job. The instructors must also be given credit for the great work they accomplished with the Cadets under such trying conditions.

Although this school at Love Field was transferred during March 1941 to Brady, Texas (Brady Aviation School), thus closing the school at Love Field, Love Field was opened again for primary training under contract with the British Government on 6 June 1941, to accommodate 50 British Cadets (RAF) for several weeks, so their training would not be delayed. The new school for the British (No. 1 School) at Terrell, Texas (Texas Aviation School), eventually opened in August 1941, and the British Cadets at Love Field were then transferred over to Terrell for the rest of their training.

During the early months of the Primary Flying Training Detachment, the training of the Cadets along with all the extra duties that developed, was handled very capably. Everyone associated with the Dallas organization proved more than willing to do his share. The first few months were trying and bumpy, yet with everyone's help the training of Air Corps pilots by Civil Contract Schools proved a huge success.

Replies to the question, "What circumstances led you to apply for training in the Army Air Corps as a Flying Cadet?"

Major General Grover C. Brown—"I had always wanted to fly. While attending Texas University, I visited Randolph Field and Kelly Field several times in 1934-1935. During the dull days of the Great Depression this exciting world of Flying Cadets and second lieutenants with their sporty convertibles, adoring girls, and P-12's roaring overhead, looked like the life for me. After that, there was the prospect of a bright future with the pioneering airlines. During this period I used my lunch money to take several flying lessons and consulted a doctor about my physical qualifications. Alas, my eyes did not meet then current Air Corps standards. Now I skip to 1938. I met a retired Army doctor who said a few eye exercises would fix my problem. Hooray! So I made application for the exam at Barksdale and I passed. Again, hooray! Then I burned all my bridges: resigned my job in Jackson, Mississippi, cashed in my insurance, bought a new Chevy, told my girlfriend good-bye, and reported to Love Field, Dallas Primary. My new way of life had begun."

Lt. Colonel W.C. Bumgarner—"I was born in a sawmill camp on Brown Mountain in North Carolina, where my father operated the mill and my mother cooked for the hands. My only affordable higher education was at Appalachian State Teachers College in Boone, North Carolina. Having no political connections, I enlisted in the Army in 1937 to attend the competitive West Point Preparatory School at Fort McPherson, Georgia. Being not among the chosen few, I served the remainder of my enlistment as a buck private in the horse cavalry at Fort Oglethorpe, Georgia, where a redheaded West Pointer who had participated in running the school advised me of the possibility of a reserve commission in the Army Air Corps. Back at Fort McPherson, I received the undivided attention of a bird colonel flight surgeon for half a day and was found fit. In summary, I went to teachers' college to get away from the sawmill and joined the Army to avoid teaching school."

Colonel Lyman H. Eddy—"I graduated from the Citadel in 1938 and several of my classmates went directly into Flying Cadet Training. However, my father had other plans for me. But during the course of the following year, these plans did not work out. I had always had a great interest in aviation since having been a member of a model airplane club at the age of ten. Since my dad's plans hadn't worked out, I made application for Flying Cadet training and passed the physical exam at Fort Bragg. That was it. This was the culmination of a desire that I had, notwithstanding my father's plans for me. I received orders to go to Dallas for primary training."

SANTA MARIA, CALIFORNIA

The **Santa Maria, California** (Air Corps Training Detachment) was located at the Hancock college of Aeronautics, Santa Maria Airport which was established in 1928. It became the 1st AAF Flying Training Detachment in July 1942. The owner/operator was Captain G. Allan Hancock (1895-1965).

This school was also one of the original nine civil contract schools in the Air Corps' primary flight training program of 1939. The first class of Army Flying Cadets began training here on 5 July 1939.

The Army officers in charge of the Detachment were: C.O., Captain E.H. Alexander, A.C.; Adjutant, 2nd Lt. John R. Kilgore, A.C.; Commandant of Cadets, 1st Lt. Otho R. Deering, A.C.; Medical Officer, Captain Tobe, M.C., along with several enlisted personnel.

The school officials were: President/Operator, Captain G.A. Hancock; the Vice-President was E.A. Olson. The Director of Training was Captain R.L. Jones and the Dispatcher was James A. Booth. The Ground School Instructors were: Professor McKellar (Math/Aero), of California Tech; John J. Harrington; Delbert G. Van Ornum; and Mr. Mertz (engines). The Chief of Maintenance was James B. Stone.

The flying equipment consisted of seven Stearman PT-13's.

The Chief Pilot was Joseph B. Potter and the Instructors were: J.B. Bennett; Andrew J. Burke; Fielden A Creech; Captain Elmer G. Da Rosa; Herman G. Denner; Captain Frank Durfee; Lowell P. Lamareux; Horace S. Mazet; Walter D. Olson; George D. Omer; Augustus R. Parrish; Argyle L. Smith; Ira D. Snyder; Foster C. Townsend; James F. Whisenand (later a Major General, USAF, now deceased, per Larry Cole; he was Cole's instructor in Primary); Don R. Woods. Hancock College of Aeronautics was established on 21 October 1928 and has graduated thousands of pilots. Its graduates went into commercial and military flying; many became aircraft engineers, designers and factory executives; others became flight instructors and many became airline pilots. The first class started 1 May 1929 with thirty-six civilian Flying Cadets.

The college pioneered the teaching of instrument flying. It offered its facilities to the late Colonel William C. Ocker, A.C., to carry out his experiments which were to convince the Army and Navy of the value of instrument flying training.

Santa Maria was chosen by Captain Hancock as an ideal spot for aviation training because of its climate. The air school is located twelve miles from the Pacific Ocean in a valley approximately twelve miles wide and thirty miles long, bordered by low coastal foothills. It is in a thermal zone which accounts for prevailing westerly winds of moderate intensity. The claim has been made, but is often disputed, that Santa Maria has more year-'round flying weather than any other spot in the United States. Annual average temperatures are 54 to 74 degrees Fahrenheit.

The college has been an Approved Flying and Ground training School (Department of Commerce and Civil Aeronautics Authority) since 1 May 1930. The college is also an approved Repair Station. All classes were taught in hangars and modern classrooms at Santa Maria Airport, one of the largest and best equipped private airports in the country, located away from the traffic of commercial airways. By a special arrangement with Santa Maria Junior College, these ground school courses and preparatory work were available to resident students without tuition. Thus, these young men were enabled to earn college credits while learning to fly.

Allan Hancock College of Aeronautics was rededicated on Sunday, 17 September 1939, to the "future security of the United States of America." President Hancock gave voice to the idea that the school was training airmen who may someday be called upon to defend the nation. He pledged 100 percent cooperation with the Primary Training Program of the United States Army Air Corps. Dedication of the new administration building, dormitories and the cafeteria took place that Sunday morning in order to accommodate high-ranking officers of the Air Corps, National Guard, and Naval forces, who had to return to their posts in the afternoon. Over the weekend the officers and guests had been entertained by the Santa Maria Valley Chamber of Commerce. A barbecue at the Santa Maria Club was a high spot of the occasion. Among the high-ranking officers at the dedication were: Adjutant General J. Patrick Farrell of the California National Guard; Colonel Rush B. Lincoln, Commanding, March Field; and Colonel Henry W. Harms, Air Corps officer of the Ninth Corps Area from the Presidio at San Francisco: Lt. Colonel Ernest Harrison, Captain K.P. McNaughton; Captain Edwin M. Day; and Captain John C. Horton represented the Air Corps Training Detachments of Glendale and San Diego, respectively. Major Ralph W. Coane, Captain Henry Coles, Lt. Colonel L.W. Hasslock, Captain Harry Bullock, and Lt. Thomas G. Wallace represented the other branches of the service. The program was outstandingly patriotic.

The initial contract for Flying Cadet primary training was entered into between Hancock College of Aeronautics and the United States of America, effective 1 July 1939. It was Contract No. W535 ac 12871 (2902) dated June 19, 1939, and it contained the following information: The school was to furnish Primary Flying Training and Ground Training to Army personnel to matriculate before January 1,

1941; classes were not to exceed sixty per class; the duration of the course was for twelve weeks, with two classes in training at one time; the school was to train five students per airplane loaned by the government; the job of furnishing and maintaining equipment, flying fields, supplies, and facilities (except airplanes and parts) needed for the instruction was assigned the school. Also it was to furnish competent flying and ground school instructors as needed and approved. Flying regulations were to be complied with to maintain safety under CAA standards. Transportation to and from places of lodging and sites of instruction if the distance was over one mile was also the school's responsibility. Records of flying time were to be kept by the school and open to government investigation with actual time from take-off to landing counted. Payments were to be made by Finance Officer, U. S. Army, Wright Field, Dayton, Ohio.

The 2nd Contract, w535-ac-15362, 18 July 1940—provided for Santa Maria Primary to receive a maximum of 132 Cadets per class. Hancock started with seven PT-13's for Class 40-A in July 1939; this was increased to twenty-four by the time Class 40-B arrived (August '39). This went to forty PT-13's by 1940; and to sixty-eight by 30 June '41; and to eighty by 1 December 1941.

The Hancock College of Aeronautics was one of the most elaborate schools in the training program. It was almost a city in itself. The Cadet barracks were permanent type buildings and the school maintained a Cadet club near the airport with trained hostesses in charge. Activities included dancing, games, and movies. Ground school facilities included very adequate classrooms in Santa Maria Junior College located on the field. There were eight hangars, a machine shop, mess hall, and dormitories, all covering 178 irregular acres. It had oiled, level surfaces with natural drainage for flight operation; and one paved runway (N-S) 100 feet wide and 3,000 feet long suitable for all-weather flying. It could accommodate all sizes of planes and was equipped for night flying.

Of the first forty-nine students assigned to this school in 1939 (Class 40-A) nineteen were eliminated—sixteen in Primary, two in Basic, plus one in Advanced, and one was held over to 40-C because of a broken shoulder. This left twenty-nine students to graduate (or 60.4 percent) and receive their wings on 23 March 1940 at Kelly Field, Texas. This was Hancock's contribution to the class of 40-A. (Elimination rate: 31.2 percent in Primary).

At Santa Maria Primary, the pilots entered in Classes 40-A through 40-H, totaled 405. This included the period from 5 July 1939 to 17 May 1940. With a 60 percent graduation rate, there were 243 graduates. From 3 August 1940 (Class 41-B) through 7 June 1941 (Class 42-A), 1,064 students entered in Primary training at Hancock, and 617 graduated (graduation rate of 57.9 percent).

A.R. (Gus) Parrish was one of the instructors for Class 40-A at Hancock. Parrish was selling Fords in 1928 when he had his first brush with aviation. He went up for a ride in a plane in Tacoma, Washington, and he was sold. Parrish had been admitted into the Club of the Incorrigibles. He made his solo flight after four and a half hours of instruction. He flew an F-17 International, "an old plywood ship," with an OX-5 engine. He had started to fly as a hobby, but by the time he had 35 hours, he decided to take aviation seriously. He took a flying course of fourteen months with the Standard Flying School in Los Angeles. Standard was part of the old Aero Corporation of California, headed by Jack Frye, who later was president of TWA.

Parrish got a limited commercial license and paid for part of his training by hopping passengers and ferrying ships. He was still selling Fords, too, besides pumping gas at the field. In those days he charged $2.50 per hour for hopping passengers. When the Graf Zeppelin came to California and was moored at Mines Field, Inglewood, Parrish had a field day. The money flowed in from passengers who wanted to see the Zeppelin from the air. He was soon flying a four-passenger cabin job for a fleet owner and the charge was $40 per hour. Then he went into business in Palm Springs and operated a winter resort from October to May. He trained students and catered to private flyers who owned their own planes. Soon Hollywood celebrities began to use the airport. Then he had 1,500 planes on the field, all privately owned. He started some Hollywood people flying, including Amos 'n' Andy.

In 1939, after operating the Palm Springs Airport for seven years, Parrish sold his lease and went to Randolph Field to take the instructor refresher course. He completed the course in two weeks and was assigned to the Hancock school. The Army gave him a training plane—a PT- 13—with instructions that he was to ferry the ship to the school. Parrish said: "You got your diploma when and if you delivered the training ship to its destination." He arrived at Santa Maria in time to be one of the seventeen instructors assigned to the first group of forty-eight Army Flying Cadets to be trained under the then untried civil primary training program. These veteran pilots were known collectively as the Incorrigibles—*those who would rather fly than eat.* So they accepted their "role" as instructors just to be able to keep flying. This was how they expressed their sincere love of flying—they trained the youth of our country to fight in the skies of the world.

One of the instructors, who had learned to fly at seventeen, and was thirty-seven when he went to Hancock College of Aeronautics to join the staff as a flight instructor, learned how the Army system worked. When he took the Army refresher course at Randolph, which he had to pass in order to qualify for the job at Hancock Primary, he found out the difference between just flying and flying the Army way. He took the flight check with an Army Captain Elmer Da Rosa and on that flight he decided then and there that for all the years he'd been a pilot he'd been flying in a daze. Precision flying was something he had never learned. "But, by God, I know it now," he said. "While flying with Captain Da Rosa I was ashamed to think I didn't know what I was doing. I had 1,000 hours when Captain Da Rosa was still learning to fly. All I can say is, I'm glad I took that flight check course, and I'm glad I stayed at Hancock."

Bob Smith relates: "Part of us were housed at the barracks for the school which was located at Hancock's chicken farm; others were at the Hotel Betteravia." The following is reported by Ray Soper (in 1967): "Elmer Gould's pungent descriptive language on 'flying': 'You push on the GO LEVER, pull on the up LEVER, and steer by the EYEBALL GAUGE—and by golly, it works!'"

Captain Hancock, founder of this school was one of the country's outstanding nonmilitary flyers. He was taught to fly in 1924 by Sir Charles Kingsford-Smith, the man who pioneered transpacific flying by his memorable flight with Captain Charles P.T. Ulm, from the North American continent to Australia in 1928. Captain Hancock sponsored that flight. Actually, the flight of the *Southern Cross*, a Fokker trimotor, was the major reason why Captain Hancock decided to start his school in 1928. Sir Charles Kingsford-Smith and his associate, Captain Ulm, were stranded in Los Angeles with their great trimotored Fokker monoplane when they met Captain Hancock. He flew with them over Los Angeles. They let him get the feel of the pilot's controls as they were looking for a backer. But the skipper was reticent. They were his guests aboard the *Oaxaca* (Hancock's boat) to Mazatlan, Mexico. While the skipper studied the doughty Australians, they gave him details of their flight plan. Their plane was heavily encumbered with debt. The sheriff had attached it, but the skipper stepped in and assumed all obligations, taking title to the plane. The *Southern Cross* was made over into an airworthy craft, equipped with every safety device known in that day. Besides the equipment, and knowing the Tropics as he did, Captain Hancock insisted that the aircrew learn to fly by instrument or "blind-flying," before they started their daring exploit. They had to learn to trust implicitly the dials on their instrument panels. They had to learn the use of radio as a navigational aid. He flew with them and worked with them. When he was satisfied they were all equipped and ready, he gave the "Go" signal and they were off for the Antipodes. When "Smitty" had completed the epochal 8,000-mile trailblazing flight across the vast Pacific, he received a cable making him a gift of the *Southern Cross*. Afterwards he flew around the world and ended his globe girdling tour on Hancock Field in Santa Maria, whence he had started. On the flight to Australia they had flown 3,138 miles to Suva in the Fiji Islands for their first stop; then two more hops to Brisbane, Australia, in the summer of 1928.

Out of the flying enthusiasm engendered by the flight of the *Southern Cross* grew the Hancock College of Aeronautics (initially the Hancock Foundation College of Aeronautics). For within three months of that epochal crossing of the Pacific, the Santa Maria Airport was dedicated and a school was established to train young men in aviation. The school's most earnest student of flying was its founder, Captain Hancock himself.

Sir Charles presented to Captain Hancock the historic compass from the *Southern Cross* which had guided the plane across the turbulent Pacific from Oakland, California, to Australia that summer of '28. This happened after the round-the-world flight was completed at Hancock Field, Santa Maria.

Captain Hancock was a man of wide interests. He was a banker, a scientist and explorer, in addition to being a flyer and aviation enthusiast.

The fleet of aircraft owned by Captain Hancock included an American Transport plane, a Bach trimotor transport, a Lockheed 12, and a Lockheed 14 (both twin-engined transports). Captain Hancock had over 2,000 flying hours, mostly in these planes.

General H.H. Arnold, 1944, commented regarding the value of the Civil Primary Flying Schools: "The Army Air Forces appreciate the vital part the contract flying schools have played in accomplishing a job which we were told couldn't be done, but which we are doing."

Lt. General Barton K. Yount had this to say in 1944: "I can remember back in 1939 when we had only nine contract schools and we worried about what would happen to our safety program in the huge expansion we were called upon to undertake. I can tell you today that the accident rate per thousand hours of flying is lower now than it was in 1939, despite the tremendous increase in total number of hours flown. This record has been achieved without any sacrifice in the efficiency of the training program. You have played a vital part in this effort and I am very proud of the primary schools. Your contributions to flying safety have been superb. It is your solemn obligation to the nation to maintain the efficiency of your flying schools. Your record has been truly remarkable. You are doing a splendid job. Keep it up . . . and better it if you can."

In 1948, President Truman gave Captain Hancock the President's Certificate of Merit for Hancock's meritorious service in aiding the United States during World War II.

In 1960, the Secretary of the Air Force awarded Captain Hancock a Gold Medal and an Illuminated Citation in recognition of his distinguished patriotic service from 1928 to 1960. This was presented to Captain Hancock at Vandenberg AF Base, California, by the Commander of SAC's 1st Missile Wing, Major General D.W. Wade, USAF.

The school produced 8,000 pilots during its contract life with the Army Air Corps and the Army Air Forces (1939 - 1944).

Hancock College of Aeronautics closed out its contract operation in the production of pilots through primary flight training on 27 June 1944 (Class 44-J).

During the peak of Air Corps training period (1944) there were more than 300 Aviation Cadets in a class and occasionally the school had more than 600 enrolled at one time. Hancock College of Aeronautics trained 8,000 Aviation Cadets and student officers for the Army Air Corps/Air Forces from 1939 to 1944, and in 1950-1951 trained more than 1,000 airmen as Aircraft & Engine Mechanics for the Korean conflict.

The following are replies to the question: "What circumstances led to your applying for Flying Cadet Training in the Army Air Corps?"

Colonel Paul S. Bechtel (WWII Ace)— "In April of 1939 I was advised by a sergeant in the PMS&T's office at the University of Wyoming that all of us seniors in ROTC would take the Flying Cadet physical exams when a special examining board visited the university in the next couple of weeks. I told him that I wasn't interested because I was already wearing glasses and I had hopes for a good job after my graduation in the Panama Canal Zone. He said that was interesting but the 'Old Man' had said ALL seniors in ROTC would take the exam. So . . . I took the exam and was quite surprised when I passed. But it all did not really excite me because after four years of working my way through college, that job as a junior engineer in the Canal Zone (at $2,000 per year) looked mighty good to me. As graduation neared, the offer for the junior engineer came through and I accepted. I was scheduled to board a ship at New Orleans on 1 July 1939, en route to the Panama Canal. Meanwhile I had applied for and had been called to two-weeks active duty with the Infantry at Fort Warren, Wyoming, immediately following graduation from the university.

I was about halfway through my two weeks at Fort Warren when my appointment as a Flying Cadet arrived. Everyone was congratulating me and telling me how lucky I was, but I answered that I wasn't about to pass up that $2,000/year job in Panama just to learn how to fly an airplane. But a week later, after many drinks and bull sessions with my second looey peers, I changed my mind, canceled out on my junior engineer job, went to Denver, and enlisted as a Flying Cadet. After enlistment I was sent, along with two college classmates, Larry Cole and Tom Waddleton, to Santa Maria. When we three got to Randolph Field we found Larry Birleffi, another college classmate who was in Class 40-A also. All four of us graduated from Kelly but I never did get to the Panama Canal."

Major Kenneth Bushnell—"I was going to college at Texas A&M at College Station, near Bryan, Texas, and went over to San Antonio and Randolph Field just for the purpose of seeing what it was and how one would go about getting in. I liked what I saw and took an application and the information as to how to apply. I was in ROTC Cadet uniform and was allowed to go anywhere I wanted. I talked to a lot of Flying Cadets. My father had some financial reverses in the depths of the Depression and I was having a tough time getting a college education with *never any money* to spare. I conceived the idea of applying for the Flying Cadet training, getting active duty for two or three years and finishing the remaining two years straight through on money I could save as a second lieutenant on flight pay. I also applied for and was accepted by the Naval Flying Cadet training program at Pensacola. But their orders to report came after I had accepted the Air Corps enlistment and was already in Santa Maria and had started flying.

I didn't get back to get that last two years in engineering school until twelve years later in 1950. There was one professor there at A&M that I had taken classes under twelve years before. I was back in the States from the Pacific and heard that they were closing Santa Maria. Read it in the L.A. newspaper, I guess. It was almost five years exactly from the time it was opened by Hancock for Cadet Training for the Air Corps. I took a B-24 from Muroc (now Edwards AFB) and buzzed the hell out of it on the closing day."

Lt. Colonel Louis R. Kittel—"I was a college student at North Dakota State College at Fargo, North Dakota (1936-1939), when I became a charter member of the 'Carl Ben Eielson' Flying Club (named after the famous Arctic explorer). We were exposed to the wonders of flying in a Curtiss Pusher (with three-cylinder motor) and a Curtiss Robin. In 1937, after my sophomore year, I figured that the quickest way to pursue the adventures of flying was to join the Air Corps. So, I applied, took the physical at Minneapolis, Minnesota, and passed. When I wasn't called up in many months later, I inquired of a friend in Washington, D.C., to find out what the holdup was. Seems as if the Army was waiting for me to finish college. In 1938, I again went to Minneapolis and passed my physical again. In the spring of 1939, I finally received my call and two of us North Dakota boys and two from Minnesota departed for Santa Maria Primary (Hancock College of Aeronautics). If I remember right, Harry Caldwell from Minnesota and I from North Dakota survived the training with the others washing out."

Colonel Kenneth E. Marts—"In July of 1938, I was attending ROTC summer camp at Fort Leavenworth, Kansas. One evening at sundown we saw three Air Corps airplanes in formation come over low and land at the Leavenworth Air Corps Field. A few of us were fascinated and received permission to hike over to the field and get a better look. When we arrived the planes were locked up in a hangar. An Air Corps officer wearing wings saw us and offered to let us in for a short look. He said they were B-10 bombers—the 'latest' thing. He also gave us a sales talk on applying for the Air Corps flying school and fly with them, rather than walking with the Infantry. When I returned to the University of Wichita that fall, I remembered this, and that I had a classmate already in Flying School. His name was Bob Mueller. Bob had dropped out of college after his junior year and had joined the Air Corps as a Cadet for flight training. I wrote to him at Randolph and we corresponded for a while—long enough for him to convince me to apply. I did and was accepted for the class beginning right after graduating from college in June 1939. Bob graduated from flying school in the Class of 39-A, and after one year of active duty, left the Army to fly for TWA. He stayed with TWA through the war and on into retirement. I never saw him again."

Lt. Colonel Robert E. Smith—"In 1936, I observed a blurb in a newspaper, I think it was, that the Marines were looking for prospective pilots. I answered and was told to report to Randolph Field for a physical examination. I did but failed the exam. Not for the 1,001 usual things, but because I couldn't look cross-eyed. How did I know that you had to be able to look cross-eyed to be a pilot? Anyway, I returned to Texas A&M and *durn near* drove the

profs *crazy* as I would practice looking cross-eyed during classes. Finally, I got so that I could look cross-eyed at will. Then I joined the National Guard as I always had had the desire for the military.

I applied for the Army Air Corps in 1938. I was ordered to Randolph again for a physical in February 1939. With two National Guard buddies, I headed for Randolph. One had already passed his physical but knowing that our eyes were to be dilated, thus incapacitating us for driving, he volunteered to drive. En route, we found out that the other buddy could not look cross-eyed either, so we put him in the back seat and ordered him to start practicing. He did. Long story made short: fourteen went in for physicals; two came out. You guessed it. 'Twas me and my N.G. buddy. He almost lost on account of his teeth, but he thought fast when the doctor asked him if he was trying for the next class. He answered yes, although he had no idea which class he would be lucky to enter. The doctor replied: 'In that case, I will pass you and you can get them fixed when you report for flying. There we were, three happy fellows. You might have known them: Howard Cook and Donald Hall of Class 40-B."

Lt. Colonel John H. Traylor stated in *The Aerie*, the Cadet paper at Santa Maria Primary in 1939, that he had attended Allen Military Academy in Bryan, Texas, where he graduated in 1934. He put in another year there in 1937. Then he attended Millard's Preparatory for West Point in Washington, D.C., in 1938. He then joined the 9th Infantry at Fort Sam Houston, San Antonio, Texas, where he attended the West Point preparatory school operated by the government. Then deciding that the Army Air Corps was where he belonged, he took the entrance examinations in April of 1939, passed successfully, and arrived in Santa Maria 1 July, to be Cadet captain of the first class to attend this school under the new Air Corps training arrangement with a civilian flying school to produce combat Army pilots; he passed away in 1968.

Colonel Thomas R. Waddleton—"I had decided several years before that I wanted to try a military life. I fell in love with flying following my solo in 1936. I flew with Fred Wahl and Clyde Pangborn, both early barnstormers. I washed airplanes and cleaned up hangars for time-credit in a 40 hp Aeronca and a Standard Eaglerock. (It had wings and should have flown, but commonly flew like a rock. Aptly named). In 1938, I took my Flying Cadet physical, passed it, and with three years college credit, applied for Cadet training. I was told to go back to school and get my degree to improve my chances. I did, it did. Simply put, I applied for Cadet training because I have been hooked on flying since I saw my first airplane. From the leverage point of actual experience, having been an enlisted man in the horse cavalry, and a second lieutenant, Infantry Reserve, flying, in place of walking or taking care of a horse seemed like a hell of an improvement. 'Twas!"

Major Carl E. Wuertele—"I was in my senior year at Wichita University (Kansas) in 1939. When not in school I worked as a city fireman. I couldn't see being a fireman the rest of my life. I liked the idea of the Air Corps so I applied. I don't know how many of us applied at Leavenworth, Kansas, but three of us passed: Ken Marts, Stephen M. Smith, and myself. We were sent to Santa Maria, California (Hancock College of Aeronautics). Frank Allen and I almost didn't graduate from Primary there . . . we were caught dogfighting out over the Pacific Ocean one day."

TULSA, OKLAHOMA

The **Tulsa, Oklahoma** (Air Corps Training Detachment) Spartan School of aeronautics, was located at the Tulsa Airport, Tulsa, Oklahoma. It became the 314th AAF Flying Training Detachment (as of July 1942). On 1 May 1944 it became the 2565th AAF Base Unit (AAF Contract Pilot School, Primary).

It was established in 1928 by W.G. Skelly (1878-1957), who was the President of Skelly Oil

Corporation and Spartan Aircraft Co.(1928-1942). He was followed by J. Paul Getty, who was the President of Spartan Aircraft Corp. & Spartan School of Aeronautics from 1942-1968. The operator was Captain Maxwell W. Balfour (1895 - 1957), who was also the Vice President, of Spartan Aircraft Co. and the Spartan School of Aeronautics, Inc. (1939-1968). The first Manager was Jess Green (1936-1939).

The Tulsa airport was established in 1928 to accommodate the Ford Reliability Tour. On 3 July 1928, the field was 400 acres of waving wheat, but on 4 July 1928, the next day, when the pilots of the Ford Tour had landed their ships in the wheat stubble, raising a cloud of dust which almost obscured the scene, Tulsa's airport became a reality. Just 18 months later, the airport was officially recognized as the world's busiest in the point of paid passenger volume. For nearly a year this position was maintained against such great airports as Tempelhof of Berlin, Le Bourget of Paris, and Croydon of London, all being forced to yield the spotlight to a new landing field in a southwest American town. By 1939, the Tulsa Municipal Airport had an A-1-A rating, and had become known as one of the largest and finest airports in the U.S.. A modern administration building of concrete and steel dominated the property. Hard surfaced runways and four steel and concrete hangars provided for shelter of more than 100 planes; there was also a complete system of lights and beacons, with radio beam equipment and a government radio station.

In 1929 the first class entered the Spartan School of Aeronautics consisting of five students who went through a six-month training course. This class was composed of World War I flyers who needed the flying hours to keep their pilot's license (which required only 10 hours per year at that time). In that year Spartan was given the highest rating possible by the Department of Commerce (CAA), with Certified Training for Pilots & Mechanics. By 1930, there were thirty students in training. And by 1932, the student population had increased to thirty-five. This led to the formation of the "Dawn Patrol," an organization of student pilots to provide them with flight time as well as cross-country experience.

In the fall of 1938 General Arnold directed Major H.C. Davidson (later Major General) and Lt. E.M. Day (later Colonel) and other officers to visit the Spartan School of Aeronautics at Tulsa, Oklahoma. It appeared that observations in Europe indicated that extensive training was being done by both the Germans and the British on small fields operated by civilian contractors. This roving committee was interested in locating established facilities and personnel for the schools to expand existing facilities sufficiently to provide training for small groups of Flying Cadets as a source of primary training of 12 weeks' duration. Personnel from Spartan visited Randolph Field on two occasions during the late winter and early spring of 1939 to obtain a general idea of methods of operation of both flight line and ground schools. The decisive conference was held in Washington, D.C., on 17 May 1939 at which time General Arnold talked to the eight prospective contractors and gave them the enthusiasm to undertake what then appeared to be a very difficult task. Spartan was represented by Captain Maxwell W. Balfour.

In the spring of 1939, Jess Green, then director of the Spartan School, was sent to Washington, D.C., to try to interest the Air Corps in establishing a pilot training school (A.C. Pilot Training Detachment). Spartan had been chosen to make a presentation to General Arnold, along with fifteen other schools throughout the country. The Air Corps was looking for nine potential facilities that could easily be converted to training detachments, and along with Spartan, had been considering schools that were in operation at Lincoln, Nebraska; Long Island, New York.; East St. Louis, Illinois.; and Oakland, California.

A few weeks later, Jess Green was sent to Randolph Field to gather information on dormitories needed, cafeteria space, and field space for flight training on a much larger scale than the school at Spartan was then operating privately. Green decided that he was not qualified militarily to operate such a massive setup as would be required by the Air Corps officials. He told Skelly that he would run the civilian side of Spartan School, but recommended that Skelly find some more qualified person to undertake the directorship of the Air Corps training detachment. Skelly needed to find the right man to operate both Spartan Aircraft and Spartan School. The first man Skelly found was Captain Maxwell W. Balfour, former Air Corps pilot, who was hired to be a Director of Spartan Aircraft Co., and Sales Department head. He was later made the director of the Spartan School, retaining his position as Director of the Spartan Aircraft Co. Eventually, he was made vice president of the Aircraft Co., which carried with it the directorship of the school. Captain Balfour then obtained an Air Corps contract for the training of Flying Cadets at Tulsa in 1939.

The Spartan Aircraft Company and the Spartan School of Aeronautics were both dreams of Tulsa oilman, William Grove Skelly. After 1942, under the tenure of J. Paul Getty, the School of Aeronautics and the Spartan Aircraft Co. both prospered. Getty was a major innovator in the field of aviation education. The Spartan School of Aeronautics, founded in 1928 during the Lindbergh era when flight was still considered somewhat of a novelty, grew through the evolution of the airplane in the 1930's to its greatest prominence during the Second World War. The war totally engulfed the spirit of Spartan under the direction of J. Paul Getty, and he eventually set the pace and time for Spartan's postwar future in the area of production and education.

The personalities of the men who controlled Spartan were deeply embedded in the roots of the organization. This included not only Skelly and Getty, but Balfour as well. Skelly became intrigued with the fledgling aviation industry in the mid-1920's. Looking for a way to diversify his corporate interests, Skelly purchased the Mid-Continent

Aircraft Company of Tulsa, which he incorporated 17 January 1928 as the Spartan Aircraft Company. From its inception in 1928, through 1939, the fate of Spartan Aircraft was tied directly to the fortunes of W.G. Skelly and his oil business throughout the Depression era. He was instrumental in selecting the site and raising the funds for the Municipal Airport for Tulsa in 1928. He then organized the Spartan Aircraft Co. (by buying Mid-Continent); and later set up the Spartan School of Aeronautics. The Spartan School of Aeronautics, founded in 1928, developed into an institution comprising sixty-two modern buildings (including its branches at Muskogee and Miami, Oklahoma), a student body of over 1,700 and an alumni numbering in the tens of thousands.

J. Paul Getty was born in Minneapolis, Minnesota, in 1892, and was taken by his lawyer father to the Oklahoma Territory for the first time in 1904, when the elder Getty had become interested in the oil rush. The young Paul Getty attended both the University of Southern California and University of California at Berkeley. But in 1912, Paul went to Oxford University in England and got his degree. In May 1916, Paul and his father incorporated the Getty Oil Company of Oklahoma. By age twenty-three, J. Paul Getty had made a million dollars. In 1930, due to his father's ill health, he succeeded him as president of Getty Oil. During the Depression, J. Paul Getty began to build up his company.

The Tulsa school was one of the original nine in the program of the Air Corps (later to be under the AAF Flying Training Command). It, as well as the other Spartan schools, was under the direction of Captain Maxwell W. Balfour, vice president of the Spartan Aircraft Company. Captain Balfour came to Spartan inquiring about buying a Spartan Executive aircraft in 1939, and was hired as a director by W.G. Skelly, president of Spartan Aircraft Company. Thus, Balfour first became associated with the Spartan Aircraft Company as a sales manager. He had been in Tulsa only a short time when he heard that General Arnold was proposing that

civilian commercial schools undertake the training of Army Flying Cadets. The idea appealed to Balfour, and the Spartan School of Aeronautics at Tulsa became one of the original nine schools in the program.

Captain Balfour was a native of Iowa, where he earned a Bachelor's degree at Northwestern University. He went to France and became involved in World War I. He learned to fly there with the Third Pursuit Group, A.E.F. He remained in France after the war, serving as a military attache until 1925, when he returned to the United States. He was then assigned to Mitchel Field, Long Island, New York. In June 1929, while carrying out a field test of a new type plane, his aircraft caught fire at an altitude of about 600 feet. He had a passenger in the plane and they were too low to bail out, so Balfour brought his flaming ship safely to earth. His passenger was unhurt, but Balfour was badly burned and for the next two and one-half years was a patient at Walter Reed Hospital. In all, he required four and one-half years to recuperate completely. Balfour gained his first experience in an aviation school in New York as Assistant Director of Roosevelt Aviation School (1938). His first major job at Spartan was to gear up for handling the primary flight training for many classes of U.S. Army Air Corps Flying Cadets. Balfour recruited his instructors from all over the United States, and they ranged in age from twenty-three to forty. Some had learned to fly with the Army Air Corps, some with the Navy, some had been taught in civilian schools, some by individuals, and some had been graduates of the Spartan school itself. However, all were required to take the Army refresher course at Randolph Field, Texas, before they were accepted as instructors. Due largely to this system of careful selection and training, Spartan started off with an original staff of thirty expert flight instructors. Since the civil school contracts provided that certificates of proficiency should be a condition of employment of any instructor of military students, it was obvious that flying instructors needed to be trained continuously to provide replacements. To meet that need, the Training Center announced on 28 July 1939 a plan whereby the schools themselves would be permitted to train additional instructors who would be used primarily for training military personnel. A continuous training program for the production of qualified civil flying instructors was thus initiated.

Consequently, in the summer and fall of 1940, when nine additional schools were established by the nine original schools, it was possible to staff all of them without resorting to a special instructor course because of the steady increase of flying instructors from the civil schools.

Captain Balfour was assisted by Herrel K. Powell, assistant director. The Commanding Officer/Supervisor assigned to the Spartan Air Corps Detachment was Captain C.A. Harrington, assisted by 1st Lt. Bob Arnold, Lt. Charles B. Root, Lt. H.A. Schmid, and Captain W.R. Weaver, M.C., the Flight Surgeon. Maintenance work was under the direction of Walter L. Starling from the 99th Bomb Squadron of Mitchel Field. Former Flying Cadet Lt. Jay L. Gentry (the second class at Randolph) was Chief of Flight Instruction.

Mr. Jay L. Gentry, tells of his list of flight instructors he was in charge of then. In his letter of 8 August 1977, he says: "My records are not complete as to personnel, but I trusted my memory and came up with the following list. It seems to be complete except for one man who I'm unable to remember: Lee Needham; Sam G. Gribi (deceased); Robert Unban; W.B. Perry; Jim Otzen (deceased); B.L. Stanton (deceased); J.B. Sodowsky; Sam B. Wiper; Glenn Brae; Jim Clarke (deceased); C. R. K. Johnson; R.R. Golemboski; J. K. Stepp; Ray Cullman (deceased); Monty Creamer; Joe Mason; and Frank Brady. Joe Mason was a civilian instructor. He graduated in the Class of '38; and went to Mitchel Field for one year. He taught me to fly a PT-3 at Tulsa. He later rejoined the Air Corps in pursuit at Langley. He retired as a Colonel after Korea."

Gentry had just resigned from active duty with the Army Air Corps just before he came to Spartan at the start of the flying training program. With years of experience as a flying instructor at Randolph Field behind him, he knew what the Army wanted in the way of training for its Flying Cadets, and he set out to model the contract school at Spartan on the Randolph Field System.

The Ground School training was also patterned after the Randolph Field schools. George Hudson was sent to live at Randolph Field for two weeks to observe and note how and what the Cadets were taught there. Upon his return to Spartan he organized the same "hangar" system of instruction. The Cadets found it so valuable that they came for special volunteer classes on Sunday.

New equipment was purchased or borrowed from the Air Corps, and hundreds of persons were drawn from the ranks of civilian aviation to participate in the program as flight instructors, ground school instructors, mechanics, dispatchers, and for administrative and miscellaneous duties. So efficient was its operation that the Tulsa school graduated every class assigned to it on schedule over a five-year period. On 16 June 1939, thirteen Army airplanes (Consolidated PT-3's and 3A's) were flown in from Kelly and Randolph Fields in Texas, to be used for primary flight training. The first class, 40-A, was composed of eighty-five Cadets and one second lieutenant taking training in grade. By October, there were 200 Cadets enrolled in the school, making use of thirty-four Army PT-3's and 3A's.

Under Balfour's direction, Skelly had invested enough capital to build three new dormitories, double the size of the school cafeteria, and add two new training auxiliary fields on the outskirts of Tulsa. In May and December 1940, two new 200-man barracks were constructed, one for Cadets and the other for enlisted mechanic students. In 1942, a full-size gym building was erected to provide for all the athletic program activities for both schools at Spartan. At the main campus in Tulsa, Balfour had increased the number of flight instructors to 101, and the school now had 93 training planes, including the first of the Fairchild PT-19's (low-wing monoplanes).

The daily schedule for the Cadets called for flight training at 8 a.m. and at 1 p.m., lectures in aviation subjects, squad drill practice, and periodic inspections. The first class (40-A) was quartered in two of the new barracks buildings just completed, and had its own mess hall in an extension of the Spartan Cafe. Thirty-four PT-3 and -3A Consolidated primary trainers were assigned to Spartan for the flight training; 13 had already been transferred on 16 June 1939, from storage at Kelly Field.

Flying training was given in twenty-six PT-3A's for the first class by seventeen civilian instructors. By the middle of November 1939, these figures had

Consolidated PT-3's on the ramp at Spartan, 1940.   Richard Johnson

increased to fifty-four PT-3A's and twenty-nine instructors. Gradually, other types of primary trainers were received: PT-13's, PT-17's, PT-23's and by 15 May 1940, the first PT-19's made their appearance. As soon as possible, the latter became the only type, thus standardizing maintenance and supply.

The PT-3 trainers were rugged, even though practically obsolete, but they were pressed into service for Classes 40-A and 40-B at both Dallas and Tulsa due to the shortage of PT-13's to equip all nine of the civil primary schools; in fact, at Tuscaloosa, the PT-llD's were flown, there being only enough to keep that primary school flying.

Reminiscing about the old days:

Cameron W. Lane (40-A) says: "There were

five instruments: Oil Temperature, Oil Pressure, Altimeter, Magnetic Compass, and Gas Gauge. All of these were mounted outside on the fuselage on "stems" fastened to the wing struts. The gas gauge was a glass tube protruding from the bottom of the top wing just ahead of the front cockpit windshield. A cork indicated the level of fuel aboard. There was no airspeed indicator, we flew by sound and feel (the seat of our pants). There was no mixture control (wired-in, full rich). Communications between the instructor and Cadet student were made with speaking tube and hand signals from the instructor who rode in front. On our last flight in September 1939, we were told to do what we pleased. I chose to see how much altitude I could attain. With lots of black smoke (mixture full rich), I got to 12,000 feet. I then kicked it into a spin and was amazed at how fast I lost a lot of altitude. It scared the hell out of me!"

Charles W. Himes, (40-A), tells a story about Albert J. Moye, (40-A): "When Al Moye spun in from 200 feet in a PT-3 at Tulsa and didn't get a scratch, he got out of the wreck and said something like: 'Gimme another airplane.'"

In 1939, Spartan had on hand most of the buildings needed to carry out the first contract with the Army (starting 1 July 1939), including hangars, classrooms, and barracks. For additional hangar and office space, the school took over the second of the two large stucco and steel frame hangars which Southern Airways Fast Express had just abandoned to the fledgling flyers, many traces of whose former occupancy had to be removed. The "S.A.F.E. WAY" signs over the doors of Hangars 1 and 2 still caused visitors endless confusion as to Spartan's relationship with the SAFEWAY chain of grocery stores in Tulsa.

The Cadets bunked in forty-eight-man, one-story frame barracks that had been occupied by civilian students. They ate in a larger frame structure that had been turned into a cafeteria. Most of their flying was from auxiliary fields that the contractor maintained close by. In July 1939, there were three of these fields all equipped with a "T" (wind tee, a modern windsock). In April and November 1941, two more fields were added.

The first contract was not effective until 1 July 1939, but the permanent party personnel began to arrive 20 June and the first four Flying Cadets were assigned and joined 27 June 1939. They were not yet known as such, but these were the original members of Class 40-A. At the time they were simply designated as "Class 1." As they looked around they found themselves in a sort of bowl formed by low hills surrounding the section of the Arkansas River Valley in which Tulsa is located. They were eight miles from the heart of the city in a flat, treeless countryside that offered many landing fields for forced landings. As their instructors took them up for their initial flight in the PT-3's, they noticed that the chief landmarks were the surrounding hills (said by the Indians to protect them from tornadoes), the Arkansas River, innumerable small ponds, woody Mohawk Park to the north, and the ugly furrows of the abandoned strip mines to the west of the municipal airport. They were to learn also that they would lose few days of flying because of unsafe weather conditions, for they were in a land where the sun shines not always wisely but invariably well. When rains did come, they fell in torrents and floods resulted.

At Tulsa, flying was handicapped because of restrictions on the use of the home field, a municipal airport. In some cases, such as later in 1940, it was taking 45 minutes to get all the ships off the ground at noon. The weaknesses in flying training, which started in 1939, included a tendency for the instructors to hold on to doubtful students. This tendency was not restricted to Tulsa; several of the other original nine primary schools exhibited the same fault. Balfour and Gentry set out to find more adequate facilities for pilot training, since the flying

space on the Tulsa Airport was being overcrowded. They located a site just outside Muskogee, Oklahoma (Hatbox Field).

Class 40-A straggled in from 27 June to 13 July 1939, when the 85th (and last) Cadet James C. Latham put in his appearance. By 28 July, three of the Cadets were discharged for flying deficiency. The majority of these Cadets came direct from civil life, but some were still enlisted men, and these latter had to be "appointed" Flying Cadets upon arrival at this station. The first Special Order of the new organization, Spec. Order No.1, on 29 June 1939, appointed twelve enlisted men to be Flying Cadets. Class 40-B began to arrive on 12 August and began their training exactly a week later. Finally, 24 September 1939, Class 40-A, with a strength of forty-nine, was graduated and transferred to Basic Flight Training at the Air Corps Primary Flying School, Randolph Field, Texas. Seven more Cadets were eliminated at Randolph, and one at Kelly, leaving forty-two to graduate on 23 March 1940 at Kelly Field, receiving their wings and commissions as second lieutenants in the Air Corps Reserve. The total for Class 40-A to be graduated at Kelly Field was 220. The elimination rate for Spartan graduates in primary was 47.7 percent, meaning the graduation rate to Basic was 52.3 percent.

Captain Harrington retained command until he was transferred 1 April 1940. He was succeeded by Captain M.M. Day, on 17 April, with 1st Lt. Arnold having command in the interim. Both Captain Day (17 Apr. '40-29 July '41) and his successor, Captain John B. Cornett (2 Aug. '41-1O June '42), were responsible for the joint flying and mechanic training programs under the Gulf Coast AC Training Center and the A.C. Tech. Trng. Command, respectively. Finally, a Captain F.A. Lundell, A.C., arrived on 19 September 1940, to take over command of the Mechanics Training Program. The Mechanics School was known as the 45th AAF Tech. Trng. Det., Tulsa, Okla. The junior project, mechanic training for the Air Corps, had gotten under way with the arrival on 4 August of the first enlisted mechanic students. They were under the direct supervision of Tech. Sgt. W.B. Taylor and two privates, but the entire program was directed by the A.C. Supervisor, Captain Harrington, A.C. In September 1940, the Spartan School began the training of A.C. enlisted men as mechanics, which doubled the strength of the command at this station. This necessitated the construction of additional barracks and eventually in December 1940 the erection of a large new cafeteria building which also housed a barber shop, lounge, soda bar, and a school-operated Post Exchange or store.

At the outset (1939-December-1941), the administrative setup consisted of a Commander, Adjutant, Operations/Engineering Officer, and a Supply Officer (besides the Medical Staff). These were their primary duties. All the A.C. officers were flying officers and for the Operations/Engineering and the Supply Officers, they also acted as check pilots. They rode with all the Cadets to ascertain that they were progressing to standard and well enough to be retained in the program. They also passed final judgment on a Cadet put up for elimination by the school. An additional duty usually performed by the Operations/Engineering officer was Station Technical Inspector. But this apparently heavy burden of duties was considerably lightened by the permanent party of enlisted men which included a fairly competent Sergeant Major, an experienced Operations Clerk and excellent technical inspector.

An obvious need was the designation of a commissioned officer to guide, advise, and discipline the Cadets. For some reason a Commandant of Cadets was not appointed at once; however, there was a 2nd Lt. of Field Artillery, John C. Pitchford, taking flying training in grade whom Captain Harrington (CO) knew from West Point days. Pitchford was in 40-A and he was appointed Commandant of Cadets. But Captain Harrington, shortly afterward, needed an instructor in Ground School Aerodynamics; and he had been the instructor at West Point in this subject when Pitchford was a West Point Cadet. So Harrington selected Pitchford to teach this subject to Class 40-A. Cadet (Henry J. Amen) was chosen to be Commandant of Cadets until a detachment officer could be made available. The lack of a full-time Commandant of Cadets was felt, but could not be remedied until the addition of more officer personnel during summer 1941.

The Dispensary for the Station opened 22 June 1939, with one medical officer and two enlisted men. It was located in Hangar No. 2. The Medical Officer was an Aviation Medical Examiner, specially trained in the examination, care, and treatment of flying personnel. The dispensary was later equipped with the Flight Surgeon's Examining Unit and A.C. Infirmary combined.

The total military strength of the command was ninety-nine at the time of opening. The strength of the command was increased to 211 military by August 1940.

Fifty British U/K students were entered at Tulsa (Spartan School of Aero) on 7 June 1941, so as to get the British training program started. There were three new civil schools (Terrell, Texas; Miami, and Ponca City, Oklahoma) awaiting CAA approval for use by the British, but these approvals were taking too long, so this action was taken on 7 June.

Refresher training for instructors (civil) was to be given at Tulsa (Spartan); and the Spartan and Dallas Aviation Schools were to continue training the British at their respective schools until these new civil schools could be established and opened for training. Approximately 300 men were trained at Spartan through the United Kingdom Refresher Course between 1939 and 1942. Many of these involved in the program were American volunteers (Eagle Squadron) as well as British nationals. Most of the graduates entered the RAF upon their return to England, and many of them served with distinction in the Battle of Britain.

In March 1941, the Women's National Aero Assn. made arrangements with Spartan for the use of planes and hours of instruction to train twenty-five women to become ferry pilots, flight instructors, and airline copilots in case of emergency. There was also the War Training Service (WTS) training conducted by the CAA, in March 1941. In the summer of 1941, Douglas Aircraft Company, Incorporated, opened a huge bomber assembly plant next to the Spartan facility on Tulsa Municipal Airport.

On 22 April 1942, Link Trainer training was started at Spartan. Each Cadet was scheduled for five hours of instrument training before graduation.

On 1 July 1942, the 314th AAF FTD was activated per letter of 25 June 1942, subject: Constitution and Activation of AAF Flying Training Detachment (& C.O. No. 34, 6 July 1942). The designation of the FTD was changed 11 July 1942, to 314th AAF FTD pursuant to the above authority (Hqs. AAF Flying Training Command).

The Technical Training Program at Spartan was separated from the Flying Training Program on 15 September 1942, and a training detachment was activated under the 3rd District of the Technical Training Command, whose headquarters was at Tulsa, Oklahoma.

Major Cornett was transferred 10 June 1942, and was succeeded by Major (then Captain) Paul P. George, 16 June 1942. First Lt. W.H. Stephens commanded the detachment in the interim.

In August 1942, the Mechanics Detachment was increased so the Aviation Cadet and Mechanic Programs reached a total military strength of 927.

In February 1943, the 75th College Training Detachment (Aircrew), University of Tulsa, Oklahoma, was activated and more medical personnel were assigned to the station to cover this increase. By March 1943, all WDAGO Forms 64; physical exams for flying; were assigned to Station Dispensary at Spartan from the Tulsa office.

The 45th AAF Technical Training Detachment (Mechanics Training) at Spartan School of Aero was inactivated 15 November 1943. Training completed.

As of 1 July 1943, the Aviation Cadet Detachment was set up as a training group comprised of two squadrons, each composed of four training flights. Barracks Nos. 10, 4, and 5 were assigned to the Cadet Detachment, and because of their physical separation, the military organization suffered from over-decentralization. The headquarters of the Detachment was set up in Barracks 10 with Office of the Commandant of Cadets located therein, adjacent to the Cadet Officer of the Day, and each new class was quartered in Barracks 10, which made it necessary to divide and move a class into the smaller barracks 4 and 5, where the Cadets were quartered as upperclassmen. A Junior Cadet Officer of the Day maintained an office in Barracks 4. Cadet officers were selected from each class and the ranking Cadet officer in each training flight acted as the Flight Marcher. No effective personnel accountability system was used. Civilian ground school absentee reports were relied upon for this purpose.

Although the Cadet Honor System was in operation, the detachment had not been thoroughly indoctrinated in its function and Cadet officer responsibility was not sufficiently accented. The natural result followed, to wit: loose accountability and a general carelessness regarding observance of post limits. The lack of coordination between the Military Detachment, the Flight Line, and the Academic Department was in part responsible for a fairly high elimination rate, and an equally high percentage of holdovers. Action was taken to move the entire detachment into Barracks 11, since it could handle and quarter all the detachment in one place. More coordination was effected between the three departments, but the officer who was Commandant of Cadets was called to Randolph Field to take the Central Instructor's Course there. With the advent of Class 44-C at this station, the new program was put into effect and remained in effect until the closing of the school in August 1944 (Class 44-K).

At this later date, the flight lieutenants were permanently assigned and were charged with accountability of the training flight personnel at all training formations. Written absentee reports were submitted to the Cadet Officer of the Day who consolidated them into the daily absentee report. Uniformity of dress, military bearing, promptness, and military courtesy were all stressed at all training formations. Ground discipline was accented as the most important correlation of air discipline. The application of the foregoing program with proper supervision was largely responsible for the reduction of the elimination rate and the necessity of academic holdovers dropped to an absolute minimum, due to the fact that study hall for deficient ground school grades was a military formation and supervised by academic instructors.

The Director of Training, Jay L. Gentry, was consulted on all schedules and was responsible for coordination between Flight Line, Physical Training, Academic, and Military Departments. It was firmly believed that sharp military training and procedure is a prerequisite of good flight line performance and satisfactory academic grades.

As of March 1944 the Army Detachment Officer staff consisted of 21 as follows: one major (CO), five captains, eight first lieutenants, and seven second lieutenants. Enlisted personnel included seventeen NCO's: seven corporals, seven PFC's, two privates, and two T/5's. The Medical Attachment consisted of four officers, two NCOs, seven others, and two civilians.

Major Paul P. George was transferred and relieved of command as of 17 March 1944. He was succeeded by Major Robert W. Stewart, who arrived and assumed command on 22 March 1944. Captain Erroll W. Bechtold commanded in the interim. Major Stewart had been a Cadet at this detachment in Class 40-D.

The Contract of 26 July 1943—(w535 ac40875) between Spartan and the government called for accepting 145 students entered every four and one-half weeks for training. The date of graduation was to be 30 July 1943 and every four and one-half weeks thereafter, with the last class to be graduated on or before 30 June 1944. The amount of the contract was $1,034,000, figured at $11.75 per flying hour. Aircraft bodily injury liability insurance, including passenger Cadets, had limits of $50,000/ $200,000 personnel, and property damage with limits of $50,000.

The designation of the 314th AAF FTD, AAF Contract Pilot School (primary), Tulsa, Oklahoma, was changed on 1 May 1944 to: 2565th AAF Bale Unit (AAF Contract Pilot School, primary) per G.O. No. 24, AAF Central Flying Training Command, Randolph Field, Texas, dated 18 April 1944.

A ten-week schedule went into effect commencing with the entry of Class 44-I on 14 April 1944. Class 44-I had not yet graduated but the ten-week schedule was already demonstrating its superiority over the old nine-week schedule. The ability of students to absorb training efficiently as given in Primary flying school was noticeably diminished when the length of the course was reduced from twelve weeks to ten weeks. The further decrease from ten weeks to nine weeks was a decided handicap which made the elimination rate rise. On 14 March 1944, the course for Primary was again set at ten weeks from nine weeks. All instructors of Ground School subjects were convinced that students could not learn as much in the nine-week course schedule as compared with the ten- or twelve-week schedules. The Ground School courses could only be improved to give better instruction by being lengthened. Ground School instructors were almost all professional teachers before they were assigned to Spartan School of Aero. The ratio of ground school instructors to students was 1:40. The total number of instructors was six for 240 students.

Class 44-H entered primary training at this detachment on 9 February 1944. The number of Cadets in the class entering training was 143; ninety-nine graduated and twenty-seven were eliminated for flying deficiency; three were eliminated for physical defects and two for other reasons. Twelve Cadets were held over. One Cadet was injured in a crash.

The program at Spartan was in operation for nearly a year before the first fatal airplane accident occurred 17 June 1940. Then a year and a day passed before there was another fatal crash on 18 June 1941. There was a total of nine fatalities between June 1940 and February 1944. A Flying Cadet was in the first fatality at this station. He was killed while flying solo in a midair collision with a civilian plane. The two occupants of the civilian plane were also killed. On 18 June 1941, a Flying Cadet was killed while flying solo when the training plane he was flying spun in and crashed. A civilian instructor was killed and an Aviation Cadet parachuted to safety on 17 May 1943 when their training plane lost its right wing during a snaproll and crashed. A civilian instructor and an Aviation Cadet were both killed when performing a simulated forced landing on 19 July 1943. Witnesses said the plane apparently spun in when they attempted to stretch the glide too much to make the field selected. An Aviation Cadet was killed 21 October 1943 when his plane failed to recover from a spin while flying solo. A second lieutenant student officer was killed on 14 February 1944 while flying solo when he tried to parachute to safety at a low altitude after failing to recover from a spin. On 10 April 1944 an aviation student and civilian instructor in a simulated forced landing, stalled, and spun in from a low altitude. The aviation student received compound fractures of both legs, while the instructor received a broken left hand.

The last fatal accident was an Aviation Cadet in Class 44-K who spun in and was killed while flying solo on 4 July 1944. The crash occurred in a pasture fourteen miles south of Auxiliary Field N. 6, which was located fourteen miles north of the Municipal Airport at Tulsa, and four miles NW of Collinsville, Oklahoma. The Cadet was making his final gliding turn from the base leg into the approach in process of executing a practice landing while on a routine training flight at the time of the crash. Witnesses stated that the plane went into a flat spin of approximately two turns out of its final gliding turn, which was made in a nosehigh attitude. This Cadet had 24 hours and 57 minutes of flying instruction at the time of the accident.

With Class 44-I, Ground School was back on the ten-week schedule and a five-day week. Twenty-nine instructors were released upon graduation of Class 44-J on 27 June 1944 since their services were no longer required. No new class was transferred to the unit to replace it. Class 44-K remained as the last class to receive its primary training at Tulsa. The west wing of Barracks 11 was closed. Permanent Party personnel for the Detachment were nineteen officers and thirty-seven enlisted men. Headquarters AAF Training Command, Fort Worth, Texas, issued G.O. No. 35, dated 4 July 1944, indicating that the contract at Tulsa Primary would end on 4 August 1944, with the graduation of Class 44-K. They were the last class of Flying Cadets to be graduated from the oldest AAF Contract Pilot School (Primary) in the Central Flying Training Command.

Spartan's army pilot training program started 1 July 1939, and through March of 1944 had helped to train over 12,000 pilots and they had given them more than 300,00 hours of flying. During an average period, each of Spartan's primary schools at Tulsa and Muskogee had 275 Cadets in training either at the base airport or at practice fields scattered over the general Tulsa and Muskogee areas. The last flight to be graduated at Muskogee was in June 1944. A total of 6,564 entered training, and 4,231 were graduated while 2,333 were eliminated during the period from July 1939 and 4 August 1944 when Class 44-K graduated. They also trained over 5,000 mechanics. A similar program for the British Royal Air Force provided primary and advanced training for 2,200 pilots.

The job done by the contract schools is a great tribute to the American system of private enterprise. These businessmen risked their capital and their business reputations to do a patriotic job for the Army Air Corps (later the AAF) of this nation . . . a job which many persons in high places said couldn't be done. These contract schools, among other organizations, came to the rescue of a nation pitifully unprepared for total war. In all probability, the total story will not be told for many years, but every man and woman in the United States can now be proud of this country's Air Force. The contract schools are particularly proud of the USAAF because they have played such a vital part in training many of these pilots and mechanics.

Winston Churchill has said: "We must beware of trying to build a society in which nobody counts for anything except a politician or an official, a society where enterprise gains no reward, and thrift no privilege."

Jay L. Gentry wrote on 8 January 1944: "On 1 July 1939, Class 40A received its first flight training at Spartan School of Aero, Tulsa, Oklahoma. It has been my pleasure from that date to the present (1944) to direct flight operations and see this detachment grow from infancy to maturity. During the early months of this new experimental system of training Flying Cadets little encouragement was received by the contractor (Captain Maxwell W. Balfour), and he was advised almost daily that the program could never succeed at the hands of civilians. In the face of this, he struggled on with failure and bankruptcy looking him in the face. Thanks to General H.H. Arnold and Lt. General B. K. Yount for their assistance and assurance that the program would succeed. It has been our intention to operate this school in as near a military manner as possible for the benefit of the student and his training as a potential officer.

The instructors have been constantly reminded that Spartan was more interested in pilot training than monetary gain. Every Spartan graduate eliminated from Basic training was a surprise to us. Never have we graduated a student that we considered a hopeless case. The weakest point in the whole program is one that could be so easily strengthened and at no expense to the Air Forces or to the contractor. The Civilian Instructor has never been recognized in a public way for the service he is rendering and as a result has been in many instances called a slacker or a draft dodger. He does not want praise, only recognition in the eyes of the public that only the Air Forces can give him. One contented instructor is worth three discontented ones. Even so, it is my opinion that the Aviation Cadets trained in Civilian Contract Schools receive the same quality of training that they would have received by Army instructors. Without the excellent cooperation and assistance of the Air Force Supervisory personnel, we could never have succeeded to the extent we have. Spartan has only the highest respect and admiration for the fine officers and students of the Army Air Forces and as long as this school exists, the brightest spot in its history will be the Aviation Cadet mission."

On the 1st of September 1944, a Certificate of Service Award signed by Major General Walter F. Kraus and Lt. General Barton K. Yount was given to Captain Balfour and the Spartan School of Aeronautics for WWII service to the nation.

On 27 November 1945, General Clinton D. Vincent, USAAF, presented an Award of Merit to Captain Balfour and the Spartan School of Aero in a ceremony in Washington, D.C., on behalf of the AAF Training Command and the RAF Training Program. Vincent cited the achievements of Spartan in terms of the number of Cadets that had received training: Twenty-two hundred British Cadets (at Miami, Oklahoma Primary; branch of Spartan), and over 12,000 Cadets and 5,000 mechanics trained at Tulsa and the Muskogee schools combined.

On 16 December 1948, at a luncheon in Washington, D.C., the Secretary of the Air Force, W. Stuart Symington, presented a "Presidential Certificate of Merit" from President Truman (signed by him) to Captain Balfour and William G. Skelly in recognition of "Outstanding fidelity and meritorious conduct in the aid of the war effort against the common enemies of the United States and its Allies in World War II."

For training of RAF Cadets during 1941-1945, the British Air Ministry awarded Captain Balfour "The Most Excellent Order of the British Empire—Officer Grade." Number 3 British RAF Training School at Miami, Oklahoma, graduated 1,152 United Kingdom, and 114 U.S. pilots during this period.

Balfour remained Director of the School until 1968 when Automotive Industries purchased all

Spartan interests from J. Paul Getty. Captain Balfour died 8 August 1977.

The Spartan School of Aeronautics, Tulsa, Oklahoma, is presently (1987) owned and operated by the National Education Center.

In reply to the question, "What circumstances led you to apply for Flying Cadet Training with the Army Air Corps?" The following are the answers:

Colonel Edward F. Carey, Jr.— "Bob Calhoun and I had enlisted in the summer of 1937 to attend the Army West Point Prep School at Ft. Monroe, Virginia, in hopes of getting a shot at the few Presidential Appointments each year. I was a *service brat* and had known since childhood I wanted to follow my dad into the Air Corps. Until I went to flying school, I had no formal flight training but had ridden as passenger in a number of old military birds. Also, I had listened to a jillion flying stories. We were assigned to Hq. Battery, 52nd Coast Artillery, and did regular as well as school duties. In early '39, it was evident we were not going to make it to the Academy. However, we didn't have the required two years' college to apply for Flying School, so we ended up taking an equivalency exam and physical at Langley (close by), and I guess because of the two years' prep school, we made the grade and one day were surprised by a set of orders sending us to Spartan. I've always had the feeling the Air Corps expansion of the times played a role here or the lack of college would have kept us out of the money."

Lt. Colonel George C. (Bud) Deaton—"From the time of my birth in a small sawmill town in 1915, I grew up with a dream of becoming a military pilot. I loved to play soldier—seeing only a few lone airplanes a year. I kept the dream of being a flying soldier. Lacking a college degree for entrance to Randolph Field, the 'West Point of the Air' in those days, I thought it helpful to enlist as a private. This was not easy in 1934, but my football experience helped me to enlist into an Air Corps that was already at 'full strength.' It was not my good fortune to gain entrance to Randolph Field as a Flying Cadet . . . so after serving a three-year hitch, I returned

to college for my degree. The first offer for the exam came in early 1939 at Barksdale Field, Louisiana. Then the great news by telegram to report to Spartan for Primary Flight Training on 4 July 1939. Thus, my dream world expanded to permit me to meet and have fellowship with the world's greatest guys. Beginning with my beloved flying classmates of 40-A, I have been privileged to meet and know thousands of military folks since those lonely sawmill dream days!"

Lt. Colonel R.E. (Gene) Keyes—"Real simple: I wanted to fly and after testing the water trying to teach school at $1,050 for the school year, teaching chemistry, physics, math, and coaching, I found I had been working my tail off for practically nothing. I think I had about $10 left after room/board and other necessities. I took that drill three months and saw an ad in a magazine for Flying Cadets, cut it out filled it in, and sent it to the Adjutant General (Army). Just before Christmas the paperwork came back and was quickly sent on to Washington, D.C. In January 1939, I received the notice to report to Selfridge Field for the exams. On 17 March, I was passed except for being underweight five pounds. That was quickly corrected. Then I received orders in late April to report to Camp Custer, Michigan, 26 June '39, for duty, and from there to Tulsa for Primary. I drew 'Red' Mason for my instructor. 'Nuff said. He taught me to pull up for fences and to go between barns and silos without clipping the wings."

Lt. Colonel James C. Latham—"My story at first glance may sound contradictory. But not really. I attended The Citadel, a military college. I liked military life and had always been fascinated with aviation. In 1937 an Army Air Corps Screening Team visited The Citadel. I applied for flight training and in spring of 1937 went before the Board in Atlanta, following the exams and the physical. Everything looked 'Go' and the President of the Board (a Lt. Colonel) said that I was very promising Cadet material. I hit Cloud Nine. And then he threw me a curve ball that I missed. He stated my academic and military rating at The Citadel were fine and then he asked: 'Cadet Latham, if I did not approve your attending flying school this year, what would you do?' I answered without any hesitation that I would return to The Citadel and get my degree and apply again for flight training. Without a smile the Colonel said, 'I want you to go back to college and get your degree. Your name will remain on the deferred Cadet Roster. You are to take the annual flight physical and upon graduation notify the Board and request a class assignment.' I had fallen into the trap with no way out.

My senior year in college came and I sent out resumes all over the country. But nothing of worth turned up. A McCrory Dime Store offer came in of about $60 per month. An IBM offer came to go to school for a year and earn about $70 per month. I didn't care for either of those. I took the month of June 1939 off, and decided that I wanted flight school after all. I drove to Atlanta the last part of June. They said a class was starting in July but it would probably be November before I would be considered. The die was cast. I returned home for a summer of leisure.

On 4 July a telegram from the War Department arrived ordering me to report to Fort Benning, Georgia, immediately, for enlistment and that I was assigned to Class 40-A. I was sworn in and was told I was to go to Tulsa, Oklahoma. I had never heard of the civilian primary training program. They put me on a train that same night. My orders said that since they could not provide me with rations in kind, I was authorized $1.00 per day for rations en route. That night on the train, lying in my upper bunk bed, I thought to myself: 'Holy S———, Latham, what in hell have you got yourself in for now?' Upon arriving to join 40-A nine days late, Captain Balfour (the head of the school) told me I had to catch up and solo with the rest of the class or wash out. I soloed with the fewest number of dual hours in my class at Spartan: Five hours, I think it was."

TRAINING CENTERS DURING WWII

The following is a synopsis of the three training centers in use during WWII:

On 1 July 1940, the **West Coast Air Corps Training Center** (WCACTC) was to open at Moffett Field, California. Its operational area was defined 17 December 1940, as all the area from the 108th Meridian west to the Pacific Coast.

On 8 July 1940, the General Order No. 1, Gulf Coast ACTC, announced the establishment of the West Coast AC Training Center at Moffett Field station and Colonel Harms as its commander, both effective as of that date. (Colonel Harms was promoted to Brigadier General on 1 October 1940).

On 1 November 1940, these six civil schools (elementary) were to be passed from Randolph's Gulf Coast ACTC to the new West Coast AC Training Center. (The actual transfers occurred in early 1941):

Ryan School of Aeronautics, Lindbergh Field, San Diego, California

Ryan School of Aeronautics, Hemet, California

Cal-Aero Training Corp., Grand Central Air Terminal, **Glendale**, California

Cal-Aero Training Corp., Oxnard, California

Cal-Aero Training Corp., Ontario, California

Allan Hancock College of Aero., Santa Maria, California

Three of the six new civil schools were just being established and they were: Cal-Aero Corporation at Glendale, California—opened branch schools at Oxnard and Ontario, California; Ryan School of Aeronautics at San Diego, California—opened a branch school at Hemet, California. The Oxnard school was activated 28 June 1940, and on the following day began the training of Cadets of Class 41-A. Ontario was activated 23 July 1940, and started training of Class 41-B on 1 August 1940.

The official establishment of the school at

Hemet took place on 25 August 1940, and training began 9 September 1940, when fifteen students of Class 41-B were transferred from Ryan School at San Diego for completion of their last five weeks of instruction.

The Western District Supervisor was Captain Kenneth P. McNaughton, A.C., whose office was at Glendale, California.

On 1 January 1941, full authority was finally delegated to West Coast AC Training Center from Gulf Coast ACTC (Randolph Field, Texas).

Tentative pilot production programs were as follows: 2,400 in July 1939; 7,000 in May 1940; 12,000 in August 1940; 30,000 in December 1940; and 50,000 in July 1941.

The Civil Elementary schools in operation in June 1941, were as follows:

Ryan School of Aeronautics, Lindbergh Field, San Diego, California.

Ryan School of Aeronautics, **Helmet**, California.

Cal-Aero Corp., **Grand Central** Air Terminal, Glendale, California.

Cal-Aero Corp., **Oxnard**, California.

Cal-Aero Corp., **Ontario**, California; Allan Hancock College of Aeronautics, Santa Maria, California.

Rankin Aero Academy, Tulare, California; Palo Alto Airport, Inc.,King City, California.

Southwest Airways, Inc., Phoenix, Arizona.

Command of the WCACTC was changed on 16 July 1941, when Brigadier General Lynn succeeded Brigadier General Harms. Almost immediately after taking command, General Lynn was shipped out to the Panama Canal Department on 31 July. He was replaced by Major General Barton K.

Flying Cadets at Rankin Aero Academy. L. to R. Cadet Harold Buttles, Instructor Mr. Kuhn, and Cadet Pyle. December 1941.   Harold Buttles

Yount on the same day.

Geographical factors had a great influence on the sites that were selected for training bases.

The sunshine belt was at the start confined to southern California and southern Arizona. On 25 June 1941, the extension of the territory to everything west of the 103rd meridian gave the West Coast ACTC all of New Mexico and a small part of west Texas. Assigned to make the initial site selections was Captain Kenneth P. McNaughton who had been one of two training district supervisors. When asked about the process, he stated: "I had the final selection of the fields and those were busy days. We traveled continually looking for sites... It was at that time (i. e., the fall of 1940) that I got the famous architect, Millard Sheets, to help me design the flying schools, and sent to Germany and got me their latest book on airdrome development..."

Captain McNaughton was later appointed to be the Liaison Officer between Gulf Coast and West Coast Centers while the elementary schools remained under the former headquarters, and was eventually transferred to the staff of the West Coast

(1 April 1941) ACTC.

The West Coast Training Center became interested in the Phoenix, Arizona, region as a possible site for an advanced flying school for the 12,000 pilot program and sent a survey officer there 9 October 1940. Eventually Southwest Airways, Inc., a firm backed by Hollywood Theatrical Agent Leland Hayward and John H. Connelly was contacted. A site which was four miles north of Glendale, Arizona, was selected (Site A) eventually becoming Thunderbird Field. Site B, eleven miles west of Glendale eventually became Luke Field, Arizona.

Up until 15 March 1941, the West Coast ACTC had examined twenty-seven sites of which six were deemed suitable for civil elementary schools.

A Cadet Reception Center was planned for Moffett Field similar to the one at Maxwell Field, used by SEACTC. Originally this replacement center and Headquarters WCACTC were considered to be moved to Santa Ana, California. But by February 1941, Headquarters COAC decided to keep the Headquarters West Coast ACTC at Moffett Field along with a new Cadet Replacement Center. This vacillation between Santa Ana and Moffett Field was caused by the U.S. Navy's plans to take over Moffett Field again; but this never occurred.

Three new schools in West Coast ACTC opened on 22 March 1941, with students of Class 41-H.

As of 4 February 1941 these were the nine original civil elementary schools in operation, their locations, and the dates of their opening:

Glendale, California—nine miles north of Los Angeles 1 July 1939.

Hemet, California—twenty miles south east of March Field, 9 September 1940.

Ontario, California—twenty miles west of March Field, 3 August 1940.

Oxnard, California—Between Los Angles and Santa Barbara, 29 June 1940.

San Diego, California—Lindbergh Field, 1 July 1939.

Santa Maria, California—north of Santa Barbara, 1 July 1939.

King City, California—Salinas Valley, 22 March 41.

Phoenix, Arizona—twelve miles north-northwest of Phoenix, 22 March 41.

Tulare, California—between Fresno and Bakersfield, 22 March 41.

The total number of students in training at this time was: 1,400 Primary, 930 Basic, and 830 Advanced. These consisted of: 75 Navigators, 330 Bombardiers, 800 Flexible Gunners, with the grand total of all students in the WCACTC at 4,365.

The civilian contractors for these schools were as follows: (Air Corps Training Detachment)

ACTD, **Thunderbird I** Airport, Phoenix, Arizona, Activated—5 February 1941.

ACTD, **Tulare**, California, activated—5 February 1941, Rankin Aeronautics Academy, Inc.

ACTD, **San Diego**, California, activated—1 July 1939, Ryan School of Aeronautics, Lindbergh Field.

ACTD, **Hemet**, California, activated—28 August 1940, Ryan School of Aeronautics.

ACTD, **King City**, California, activated—5 February 1941, Palo Alto Airport, Inc.

ACTD, **Ontario**, California, activated—23 July 1940, Cal-Aero Academy.

ACTD, **Oxnard**, California, activated—28 June 1940, Mira Loma Flight Academy.

ACTD, **Santa Maria**, California, activated—1925?, Santa Maria Municipal Airport, California.

ACTD, **Visalia**, California, activated—1 August 1941, Visalia-Dinuba School of Aeronautics (Replaced the Glendale school), training began—3 October 1941.

The first Civil Basic Flying School (at the elementary school grounds), was Ontario, California, where training began on 22 March 1941.

No preflight was given at West Coast AC Training Center until early in 1942, when a reception center for Cadets was established.

With the expansion of the training program in July 1940, from an annual production of 2,000 to

7,000 pilots per year, the schedule was reduced from twelve to ten weeks each for primary, basic, and advanced. This 10-10-10 plan was adopted at the time the West Coast ACTC was established and remained in effect until early in 1942, when our entrance into the war forced a further reduction to nine weeks for each phase.

Under the 10-10-10 plan, a total of 200 flying hours was required of each Cadet before graduation from advanced school. This was broken down into 60 hours flying training in primary, 70 hours in basic, and 70 hours in advanced.

Ground School training required 140 hours of instruction in primary; 98 in basic, and 118 in advanced Single-Engine. The total hours of ground school instruction remained fairly constant at 350 hours for all three phases of training.

The acceleration of the pilot training program can most clearly and simply be demonstrated by noting that, during the eight years from the opening of the primary school at Randolph Field in 1931, until primary training was shifted to the civil schools on 1 July 1939, there were 4,797 admitted to primary schools of whom 2,569 graduated; this is to be contrasted with the 24,395 admitted to primary schools (civil) and the 15,796 primary school graduates for the two and one half year period from 1 July 1939 through 13 December 1941.

Thus a more accurate comparison would be that of the basic stage of performance of all Randolph Field Primary stage graduates with all Civil Elementary Flying School graduates prior to the outbreak of war. The statistics which follow make that comparison:

All Randolph Field Primary Grad.—l July 1931-l July 1939.
Reported for Basic Training—2,590.
Completed Basic Training—2,296.
Percent that graduated from Basic 83.7%.*
All Civil Primary School Graduates—1 July 1939-31 December 1941.
Reported for Basic Training—12,619.
Completed Basic Training—11,269.

Percent that graduated from Basic—89.3% (* Percent based on number to begin Basic Training). In order to figure the number of men that must be selected for training, the estimated elimination rates must be applied in order to come up with the total number of men needed, i.e., for the 50,000 program: the rates for Elementary pilot training were 37%, for Basic 5%, and for Advanced 1%. The rates for Navigators were 20%, for Bombardiers 20%, and for Gunners 0%. (In other words, if 50,000 graduated pilots were needed, over 80,000 Cadets were necessary to start training).

Under the new system, basic flying training was simply contracted from 109 to 75 hours while an entirely new basic schedule calling for 100 hours of ground school instruction and 102 hours of military training had to be set up. This 277 hours of all types of basic training given to the first class, Class 40-A, at Randolph Field, provided the fundamentals for basic training which were to be used with various changes during the pre-Pearl Harbor expansion period and beyond.

During the period before September 1940, all Air Corps Basic Training continued to be carried out exclusively at Randolph Field. Not until 5 September 1940, did the Southeast-Training Center's basic school at Maxwell Field, Alabama, initiate basic training.

In the Gulf Coast TC, two schools other than Randolph Field gave Basic Training prior to Pearl Harbor. The first of these was Goodfellow Field at San Angelo, Texas, where training began with Class 41-E on 15 February 1941. The other was at Curtis Field, Brady, Texas, where on 3 May 1941, class 41-G began training. Training at this latter field was in the nature of an experiment, for Brady was a Civil Contract School previously giving primary training only. Later, two other Air Corps Fields (Sherman, Texas, and Enid, Oklahoma) were to begin Basic training on 20 December 1941.

The first Board of Officers for selection of sites for pilot schools in the **Gulf Coast Air Corps Training Center**, was headed by Lt. Colonel Charles T.

Myers, and it consisted of nine members, including; Majors Jacob E. Smart, Dean C. Strother, and Edwin M. Day. They looked at eight sites that were all located in Texas.

General Harmon noted the difficulty in finding sites for new schools and recommended that here after the already existing contractors be chosen as the operators for all future schools.

There was still the possibility of the Marine Corps taking over Hicks Field, Fort Worth, Texas. The contractor for the Denton School was to be W. F. Long of Texas Aviation Schools, who was then operating the school at Hicks Field. At this time it was planned to have the 75,000 program effective 1 January 1943.

The Training Center's attention was called to the fact that although Brady had become an elementary school, it would be necessary for it to carry its basic student load in the present elementary school program also.

During September 1942, plans for a 102,000 program began in earnest. This tremendous goal had apparently been in the minds of planners ever since Pearl Harbor, if not before. Lack of physical facilities, instructional staff, as well as other factors served as successful deterrents for planning in tenure of higher goals. Colonel Charles T. Myers summarized the program at GCACTC: "On the basis of what the training command gave us, it figures out at; primary class of 5,284; basic at 3,434; advanced at 3,022. They asked us to plan arriving at this program in a series of equal jumps, entering 15% above the normal 55,000 program in the October Primary class and the same number in November, after which each class would enter a sufficient number of students to produce seventy-one more graduates than the preceding class." To take care of this expansion Colonel Myers estimated two new elementary schools, possibly one basic school and no more advanced schools would be needed.

One new elementary school at Avenger Army Air Field, Sweetwater, Texas, was started. There were six new basic schools at the following loca-

tions: Coffeeville, Kansas (All Military); Garden City, Kansas; Majors Army Air Field, Greenville, Texas; Independence Army Air Field, Independence, Kansas; Strother Army Air Field, Winfield, Kansas; and Liberal Army Air Field, Liberal, Kansas.

There were eight new schools for advanced training (All Military):

Aloe Army Air Field, Victoria, Texas.
Altus Army Air Field, Altus, Oklahoma.
Blackland Army Air Field, Waco, Texas.
Eagle Pass Army Air Field, Eagle Pass, Texas.
Frederick Army Air Field, Frederick, Oklahoma.
Pampa Army Air Field, Pampa, Texas.
Bryan Army Air Field, Bryan, Texas.
Dodge City Army Air Field, Dodge City, Kansas.

Thus, it was that during the thirteen months following Pearl Harbor, three new goals were successively planned in order to meet the ever increasing demands of totalitarian war. To raise an annual production rate from 2,250 to 102,000 in four years was a stupendous task. Yet that was exactly what was contemplated before the end of 1942. The following is a partial list of the location of the Civil Elementary schools of the Gulf Coast Air Force Training Center (GCAFTC) in operation in December 1942:

Ballinger, Texas.
Bonham, Texas.
Brady, Texas, (Basic).
Coleman, Texas.
Corsicana, Texas.
Cuero, Texas.
East St. Louis, Illinois.
Fort Worth, Texas.
Muskogee, Oklahoma.
Sikeston, Missouri.
Stamford, Texas.
Sweetwater, Texas.
Tulsa, Oklahoma.
Uvalde, Texas.
Vernon, Texas.

In the twelve months of 1943, the Central Flying Training Command commissioned 20,425 pilots after graduation from advanced schools. This number of graduates was below the figure of the 75,000 pilot training program. Under a 60,000 pilot training program, 20,417 pilots would be graduated each year. Therefore, the average rate of production of pilots during the year 1943 was at the level of a 60,000 pilot training program.

During the first quarter of 1942, the GCAFTC was directed by Headquarters AAFFTC to step-up the pilot training program to attain a new all time high production of 102,000 per year. It was felt that the program might be placed into operation during 1944. But for some unknown reason, the 102,000 plan of 30 November 1942, was soon discarded. It was to have been inaugurated with the entrance of Class 44-K, with the following quotas of students distributed among the three Training Centers: WCAAFTC-2275; GCAAFTC-3730; SEAAFTC-3095.

About two weeks after being notified to gear up for the 102,000 pilot program, the AAF Flying Training Command notified the CG, GCTC, that according to information just received from Headquarters USAAF, a new directive calling for only 79,000 instead of 102,000 would be confirmed as a downward goal. Since the Headquarters GCTC was already approaching the old 75,000 pilot training program, this 79,000 seemed like a dream come true.

By mid-February 1943, construction had finally been completed on the new San Antonio Aviation Cadet Center. The Aviation Cadets, while in preflight at the SAACC, were given a series of classification tests consisting of physical, mental and psychological tests to determine suitability for aircrew training. On the basis of test scores, students were placed in one of the Standard Nine Groups (from which the term "STANINE" was derived). Group Nine is the best score and Group One is the lowest. A student in Group Nine had the physical coordination and strength, the mental skill, and social adaptability necessary to be exceptional rated-officer material. The experience in flying training phases have shown that Stanine Scores are a reasonably reliable guide to a Cadet's future success. The Stanine score was compiled by a grouping of the various test scores. Each student was then rated for his potential ability to complete each phase of aircrew training, and enter that phase of training for which testing showed his greatest aptitude.

When Class 43-A had entered preflight at SAACC, the school had a capacity of only 2,400 students due to delayed construction. Only 2,425 Cadets entered instead of the 3,001 planned to enter preflight for 43-A. This cut down the total number of graduates of Class 43-A on 14 January 1943 to 1,313, or 352 fewer than had been planned. The 4,145 students authorized to enter preflight in Class 43-J on 18 February 1943, compared very favorably with the 2,425 entering the same phase of training in Class 43-A, about a year earlier. Similar improvement was noted all along the line, through primary, basic, and advanced.

The credit to the success of this great training effort, and the eventual huge numbers of Cadets that were trained and sent into combat must go to General Hap Arnold. He "tugged" and "pulled" first at the Air Corps, which then became the AAF, years before WWII, and continued during the war to get this fantastic pilot program started and to keep it going with enthusiasm from all "hands." He had a unique style of management. First, he would announce a great increase to the AAF, and then a short time later, would announce a smaller increase (to make the first increase seem more attainable), but the greater total would be forthcoming as sure as rain a short time later.

Typical of the pressure exerted by higher headquarters for the expanded training activities in 1942, was the letter of 17 August 1942 to the GCTC calling for the immediate increase of production of all categories of trainees to the extent of maximum utilization of personnel, equipment, and facilities. All former considerations governing the output of pilots, such as ratio of students to instructors, and students to airplanes, were to be disregarded. This "All-Out" effort of June 1943, surpassed all previous campaigns to enroll trainees in pilot training even though the air forces themselves had to be scoured for recruits during the campaign; the reason for this was very simple. By the middle of 1943, the Training Command had at hand the facilities to do the job, and the "All-Out" effort came directly from General Arnold. In preparation for it, he ordered on 15 May that the proper steps be taken to complete mental screening tests and final type physical exams on all Air Force officer's and enlisted men between the ages of eighteen and twenty-six inclusive, who would volunteer for flying training. It appeared that the 102,000 program had not been forgotten, and that a production figure of 75,000 per year was not considered sufficient by the War Dept.

General Arnold said there was an "urgent need" for greater numbers of every potential candidate. To make the enlistment in this program easier, the superior officers of the applicants, enlisted or otherwise, were instructed by the CG, not to disapprove the application for Cadet training, or their transfer into Aviation Cadet status. If the applicant could not reach an examining board, the board would come to him. Within a few weeks, on 23 June 1943, this directive was followed up by more specific orders to make the "All-Out" effort effective at once.

The following plan was furnished AAF Gulf Coast Training Center as a directive:

1. All categories are to be increased by the same percentage so that the production is coordinated.

2. Increase the next civil contract school class to the absolute maximum.

3. Report the number of pilots to be entered in the next and succeeding classes consistent with existing basic and advanced facilities.

4. Report the number of navigator, bombardier, and gunner trainees that can be entered in the next and succeeding classes.

5. Do not assign to elementary training students who have not completed four and one-half weeks of preflight training.

The CG, GCTC, General Brant, rendered a report that was not optimistic. After a hurried twenty four-hour survey, it was returned to AAF Flying Training Command. It disclosed the maximum number of students that could be entered into elementary schools, including foreign students, was 4,545 in Class 44-A on 28 June 1943. This figure compared with an entrance figure in elementary schools of 4,189 planned for Class 43-J, under the full 75,000 program. The ultimate entrance figure for elementary was set at 4,785, which General Brant said was contingent upon the ability of civil school operators to secure and qualify locally the necessary instructors. In other words, General Brant felt that increased production could only begin after the entrance of Class 44-A on 28 June 1943, and at a figure that would fall below the once suggested 102,000 program. The one bright spot was the production of instructors which the Training Center believed to be satisfactory for the expansion it could make. The normal production of CFS was felt satisfactory.

While the entrance rate for trainees of Class 44-A would produce graduated pilots in excess of the 79,000 program of late 1942, an even higher figure was in view at the middle of 1943. A compromise might be reached between the 102,000 figure which had been minutely planned in November 1942, but not carried out, and the full 75,000 program which by late 1942 was an accepted measuring stick. In retrospect it appears that in all probability, the 102,000 program had been premature.

No definite change was made as a result of the "All-Out" June campaign until AAFCFTC (Randolph) was directed on 25 August 1942 to train pilots at the rate of 93,600 per year, "with the increase to be effected with the least possible delay." The maximum production of graduated pilots to be reached was 2,800 pilots per class with Class 44-D entering elementary training on 3 October 1943. It was felt that the plan could be met insofar as instructors and airplanes were concerned, although additional instructors would be required. Sufficient airplanes were on hand or had been allocated for this student load, and it was thought that some stations from Technical Training Command might be made available to the Flying Training Command to relieve the student overload in the basic schools. However, General Brant firmly believed: "The number of students proposed for Basic Schools under the plan is considered excessive for existing facilities."

The AAF Gulf Coast Training Center was redesignated **"Central Flying Training Command"** on 23 August 1943, during which time there were 23 contract pilot schools (Primary) in CFTC. All Primary schools were under 2nd Wing and all Basic Schools were under 3rd Wing.

After considering this new directive for ten days, the AAF Central Flying Training Command decided that the increased production could definitely not be met as directed by higher headquarters. They presented the following reason for this view in a letter to CG, AAF Training Command: "The pilot program (93,600 plan of 15 August) ...taxes beyond reasonable limits the facilities in the basic schools of this training command and increases the training load on elementary schools to a point believed too high for the best training efficiency. This information is submitted with a strong recommendation that a reduced program be authorized in time to lower the number entering class 44-D to 4,545 students entering into the elementary schools of this training command, instead of the 5,000 directed by your above mentioned letter."

The AAF Central Flying Training Command's request for the reduction from an entrance figure of 5,000 to 4,545 was granted, and a new flow chart based on that figure was requested by AAFTC on 20 September 1943. In its reply, the AAF Central FTC indicated the following entrance rates beginning 3 October 1943, and continuing through succeeding classes, to be considered as the maximum rate of pilot production.

This plan to produce 2,600 graduated pilots per class to become effective with Class 44-D entering elementary 3 October 1943, remained in effect until the entrance rates were again revised slightly upward by letter from AAF Training Command to AAF Central FTC on 13 November 1943.

It had been determined in conference between Training Commands, that in order to produce an average of 2,800 pilot graduates per class, it would be necessary to enter into each preflight class 4,675 trainees. This figure became effective with Class 44-H entering on 7 December 1943, and the rate of entrance into preflight training was to remain at that maximal figure.

In the final quarter of 1943, planning reached its apex. It soon became clear that, although the need for pilots and trained crew members remained nearly constant and at a high level, the training job was leveling off and that future plans might call for a downward revision.

The AAF Central FTC questioned the pilot-preflight entrance rate of 4,675 in Class 44-H and mentioned, "present plans are for a reduction in the pilot training program" which it understood unofficially was being considered. Ten days later, the AAF Training Command authorized a reduction in the preflight entrance rate bringing it more in line with the ideas of the AAF Central FTC.

In the closing days of 1943, the first official plans for the reduction of pilot training in nearly six years of unprecedented activity were announced. On 29 December 1943, the AAF Central FTC was given a new directive based on an annual program of 85,000 per year, to become effective with Class 44-G entering elementary training on 9 January 1944. Subsequent rapid reductions were as follows: Class 44-G under the 85,000 plan—28,900; Class 44-H under the 75,000 plan—25,500; Class 44-I under the 60,000 plan—20,400. This reduction affected pilot training only. No other changes in training were planned in existing bombardier, navigator, and flexible gunnery quotas. Their production had still not reached the zenith. This command had graduated 8,804 navigators, 8,107 bombardiers, and

28,800 gunners, during calendar year 1943.

Planning pilot production was a highly speculative and complicated procedure. A good number of compromises had to be made. Elimination rates varied from class to class and from one phase of training to another. It should be averaged at the rate of the 60,000 program, although the principal program of the year was the 75,000 program under which many of the later schools had been authorized. The AAF Central FTC graduated 30,832 potential pilots from 20 different civil elementary contract schools in 1943. These trainees were members of Class 43-E graduated on 15 January 1943, through Class 44-D, which graduated 5 December 1943. The major factor in the elimination of Cadets in Primary continued to be flying deficiencies at 28.6%, with resignations at 1.5%, physical disqualification at 1.2%, fatalities at .1% and all other factors at .6% for a total in 1943 of 32% washouts in Primary.

During 1943, 23,060 pilots were graduated from Basic, an average of 85% of the entering classes. In all, eleven stations taught Basic as follows: Brady, Texas,—January to December; Randolph, Texas,—January, to March; the remaining nine stations taught all year. The total number of pilots that graduated from Advanced training in 1943 was 20,416.

By the end of 1943, installations under the jurisdiction of CG, CFTC were located in 20 states, all east of the 103rd meridian. This wide distribution was a product of the establishment of College Training and War Service Detachments in 1943. The schools where flying was actually taught were concentrated in Texas and Oklahoma with a few others in six additional states.

In August 1940 with the expansion of the SEACTC (**South East Air Corps Training Center**) gaining momentum, detailed specifications were drawn up to be followed in the selection of civilian training schools to be used in the elementary flight training of Army students.

Under the 12,000 pilot program plans were ten-

tatively made in December 1940 to operate seven elementary flying schools in the SEACTC; these were located at:

Tuscaloosa, Alabama.
Lakeland, Florida.
Albany, Georgia.
Camden, South Carolina.
Jackson, Mississippi.
Arcadia, Florida.
Americus, Georgia.

Contracts with the last three had not yet been negotiated by 11 December 1940. By 15 January 1941, three elementary civilian schools were placed under the jurisdiction of the SEACTC. These were: Embry-Riddle Company of Arcadia, Florida; Southern Airways Sales Company of Camden, South Carolina; and Graham Aviation Company of Americus, Georgia.

By the end of January 1941, definite plans had been prepared by OCAC to initiate basic training in a civilian school in the SEACTC by 7 June. Headquarters SEACTC opposed this move, pointing out that there was a current shortage of instructors in the civil elementary schools. General Weaver also opposed this move and wondered why it was necessary to do this in SEACTC simply because a slowdown in construction on the West Coast had necessitated such a school being established there. They wanted Army instructors at Basic schools in order that the Cadets might receive more military supervision which, it was felt, they greatly needed. Nevertheless, Headquarters SEACTC surveyed facilities in accordance with existing instructions and on 27 February, both Darr Aero Tech at Albany, Georgia, and the school operated by Embry-Riddle at Arcadia, Florida, were recommended by General Weaver to OCAC as satisfactory for conversion to basic schools. By 8 March, General Weaver had issued instructions to S-3, SEACTC, to determine whether Darr could open such a school by 3 April 1941. The school, however, was not to be located at Albany; but Avon Park was to be considered instead. If Darr couldn't build such a school, Riddle was to be given a contract.

On 18 March, General Weaver recommended that Darr be allowed to establish a basic flying school at Augusta, Georgia, 12 miles south east of the municipal airport. The school was to have a capacity of 100 students per class and was to be available on 3 May. Augusta was finally chosen as a site but training did not begin there until 7 June 1941, as was originally scheduled by OCAC.

The OCAC set up a special site selection board to review sites for additional flying schools to provide a minimum of 1,215 students and a maximum of 1,765 students by 4 October 1941. The minimum estimate was based on the availability of training aircraft; the maximum represented the goal of the 30,000 pilot program.

Sites for elementary civil schools were not to be approved if they were within four miles of the center of a radio range, on-course signal tone, which would present a danger to the students as well as to any other aircraft that was making a range approach. On 24 May 1941, seven additional elementary schools had been approved by OCAC; they were as follows:

Raymond Aviation School, Macon, Georgia.
Hawthorne Flying School, Orangeburg, South Carolina.
Lakeland School of Aeronautics, Lakeland, Florida.
Southern Aviation School, Camden, South Carolina.
Embry-Riddle School, Miami, Florida (Coral Gables, Navigators only).
Georgia Air Service, Atlanta, Georgia.
Akron Airways, Akron, Ohio.

After the addition of the training detachment at Tuscaloosa, it appeared to the SEACTC inspectors to be an "excellent" facility by 31 October 1941. A total of 252 students were being trained at Tuscaloosa during that time and all were UK trainees. Difficulty was being experienced in getting enough primary training planes for this new base— seventy were desirable, but only sixty-two were

available at the time.

The number of civil contract elementary schools in operation at the time of Pearl Harbor, had risen from four schools in December 1940, to seventeen such schools by December 1941.

The seventeen elementary Civil Flying Schools in operation under SEAFTC by December 1941 were:

Chicago Aero Tech, Glenview, Illinois.
Graham Aviation Company, Americus, Georgia.
Darr Aero-Tech, Albany, Georgia.
Southern Aviation School, Camden, South Carolina.
Embry-Riddle Company, Carlstrom Field, Arcadia, Florida.
Lakeland School of Aeronautics, Lakeland, Florida.
Mississippi Institute of Aeronautics, Jackson, Mississippi.
Alabama Institute of Aeronautics, Tuscaloosa, Alabama.
Lodwick Aviation Military Academy, Avon Park, Florida.
Raymond-Brinckerhoff Aviation Company, Douglas, Georgia.
Georgia Aviation Service, Bennettsville, South Carolina.
Hawthorne School of Aeronautics, Greenburg, South Carolina.
Helena Aero Tech, Helena, Arkansas.
Embry-Riddle Company, Dorr Field, Arcadia, Florida.
Greenville Aviation School, Ocala, Florida.
Southern Aviation Training School, Decatur, Alabama.
Tuskegee Institute, Tuskegee, Alabama.

There were also eight civilian training detachments which were located at:

Lakeland, Florida.
Jackson, Mississippi.
Camden, South Carolina.
Arcadia, Florida.

Americus, Georgia.

Albany, Georgia.

Coral Gables, Florida (navigators).

Tuscaloosa, Alabama.

There were three Basic schools in the SEAFTC at this time. They were:

Gunter Field, Montogomery Alabama.

Cochran Field, Macon, Georgia.

Bush Field, Augusta, Georgia.

By 30 June 1941 the SEAFTC had four Advanced schools under its control. They were as follows:

Maxwell Field, Montgomery, Alabama.

Barksdale Field, Shreveport, Louisiana.

Craig Field, Selma, Alabama.

Turner Field, Albany, Georgia.

On 17 July 1941 SEAFTC added two more Advanced schools—one at **Columbus** Army Air Field, Columbus, Mississippi, and the other at **Tuskegee** Army Air Field, Tuskegee, Alabama.

The new directive called for facilities to graduate 3,138 whites and twenty Negro students per class. Tuskegee Army Airfield, under civil contract with the Tuskegee Institute, was used solely for the training of Negro pilots. Only thirty-three Cadets were selected to enter this training in the first class, assuming that thirteen would wash out. It was planned to train black mechanics to maintain the training planes for the twenty Negroes entering per class. In February 1941, Major James A. Ellison, from Headquarters SEACTC, was made project officer for the Tuskegee program for training Negro pilots. Not until 30 April was a site approved for this program. Some 459 Negro enlisted personnel were selected for duty at this station. The Tuskegee Detachment was opened on 19 July 1941, with its first C. O., being Captain Noel F. Parrish, A.C., a white officer who was originally in the Glenview detachment at the Chicago School of Aeronautics. He remained there until 3 December 1941, when he was transferred to a Pursuit Squadron that had been established on 8 November 1941.

RAF pilot training started in SEACTC on 2 April 1941. The RAF took over the 12,000 pilot program on 7 June 1941, when 550 Cadets entered six SEACTC primary schools. When American contracts under the 30,000 program caught up, our training would resume. It was expected the British would occupy the north east sector of the territorial Wing. By 15 November a letter from OCAF stated that 4,000 British students would eventually be assigned to SEAFTC, about one-half of the entire RAF contingent scheduled for training in the U.S.. Six elementary schools in SEAFTC were to receive 539 RAF Students on 7 June 1941. The first to be trained were at the Lakeland school in Florida.

Under the 7,000 pilot training program, 2,181 pilot Cadets were due to be admitted to training so as to graduate before 6 December 1941. Classes 41-A and 41-B had completed Primary and went on into Basic.

Under the 12,000 program, 3,427 pilot Cadets were expected to begin pilot training in time to finish by 13 December 1941.

The 30,000 pilot training program provided for 1,800 students entering every 5 weeks. But Class 42-E, the last quota to enter before the declaration of war, contained 1,386 Cadets, consisting of American and UK trainees.

The approximate total numbers of students who entered SEAFTC schools in time to finish about the day of Pearl Harbor (Classes 41-A through 41-I) was 3,859, well above the 12,000 rate, but far below the 30,000 rate. Of that number 2,412 pilots won their wings. The overall elimination rate for pilot trainees was 35.5% as compared with the 40-50% anticipated by Washington.

By 1942 six more primary schools had been added to the SEAFTC. They were: Riddle-McKay Company, Union City, Tennessee; Georgia Air Service, Atlanta, Georgia; Clarksdale School of Aviation, Clarksdale, Mississippi; Lafayette School of Aeronautics, Lafayette, Louisiana; Wiggins-Marden Aeronautics Corporation, Camden, Arkansas; and the Cape Institute of Aeronautics, Inc., Cape Girardeau, Missouri.

As of 31 December 1942, 3,435 trainees had entered the 22 primary schools in SEACTC.

To increase from the 30,000 program to the 50,000 program would require an increase in total pilot production of 66.7%; or in each class at Primary an increase of 929 men, Basic—590; Advanced Single Engine—227; and Advanced Twin Engine—317. To go to the next level above the 50,000 program it would require an increase of 50%; or in each class at Primary an increase of 1,390 men; Basic—811; Advanced Single Engine—245; and Advanced Twin Engine—500. To figure the number of men required to start Primary and still give the needed numbers graduating from Advanced, the Primary entrance rates were based on 59% graduating from Advanced, with 30% eliminated at the Primary stage, and 9% from the Basic stage. When it was later decided to increase training from the 50,000 program to the 70,000 program, then to the 75,000 program, it was found that the number of entrants into Primary training would have to be increased by still another 48%.

In the fall of 1944, pools of surplus pilots had been accumulating in the Training Command because more of them were being trained than were currently needed for combat. In order to get rid of these pools, Headquarters AAF ordered two five-week training freezes. Normally, the period of training at a given type of school was ten weeks. After preflight, there were three levels of flying training before the student got his wings. These were elementary, basic and advanced, making a total of thirty weeks. At any one time, there were two classes in the schools at each level. While the upper class received its last five weeks of training, the lower class was receiving the first five weeks of training. At the end of each five-week period, the upper class graduated, the lower class became the upper class and a new lower class entered. The first five-week training freeze began in the middle of October 1944. Instead of graduating, the upper class students in elementary, basic and advanced schools were held over for an additional five weeks of training. This

was the first training freeze. While the upper class students were receiving the additional training, the lower class students were receiving the normal upper class training. At the end of the first five-week freeze period, the held-over upper class was graduated and the normal upper class was frozen for five weeks. This was the second training freeze, and put the two classes back into phase.

During the freezes, the quotas for transition schools were filled by using pilots who had accumulated in surplus pools, in place of the students who would have graduated. This tended to get rid of the pools; it also meant that instead of the normal ten weeks of training, students received fifteen weeks of training in whatever phase they happened to be in at the time. Some students received an additional five-weeks training in elementary, others in basic, and still others in advanced training. The first freeze occurred on 14 October 1944 with the second freeze occurring 18 November 1944.

Through the WWII years, from December 7, 1941-August 14, 1945, there were a total of 192,676 pilots and 93,123 bombardiers, and navigators graduated from the many training bases used during the war. The number of training stations for all types of training, ground as well as flight, was at a zenith in July 1943 with a total of 457. This number continued to decline until by the end of 1945 there were only thirty-four still in operation. It appears that the last pilot training class at the end of WWII was 45-H. There were some Cadets who elected to become flight engineers, and of those sixty-eight men in class 925 graduated from Hondo AB on 6 November 1945. They were also commissioned as 2/Lts, there may have been others at different bases.

V-J DAY, TO THE END OF THE PROGRAM

After V-J Day, effective 19 October 1945, the flight-training-course length was increased from the previous ten weeks in each of the three phases (primary, basic, and advanced) to fifteen weeks in each phase. The aircraft used were: PT-13, AT-6, AT-6 and the B-25 for multi-enginc. On 15 October 1946, the training was again lengthened to a total of 52

North American AT-6D, 12/2/44.   National Archives

weeks. This started with Class 47-B. The preflight training had been dropped in October 1945. In October 1947, primary training was abolished and an eight-month integrated basic/advanced course was initiated. On 15 October 1948 a new course was implemented in advanced which consisted of twenty-one hours in the T-6, and seventy-nine hours in the F-80. The P-51 was also used at some bases as an advanced trainer. In June 1949 a one-month preflight training was again established, with the entrance of class 50-D on 11 July 1949. The total course length was now about thirteen months long depending on the weather. By August 1950 the T-28 was beginning to be used in advanced, as well as the T-6, F-80, F-51 and the B-25. In October 1950 the T-33 was brought on the scene. Due to engine problems, all T-28's were grounded in July 1951, which forced the return of the

T-6. The T-6/B-25 courses continued until December 1951. Effective 1 March 1952, the USAF basic pilot training schools were redesignated to primary pilot training schools. The USAF advanced SE and ME schools were redesignated to basic SE and ME schools. Effective 18 March 1952 basic pilot training was redesignated as primary pilot training. On 1 July 1952, due to lingering problems with the T-28, the T-6/B-25 course was again in use. Class 52-F had already been involved in this course since 4 April 1952, before the new course outline had even been published. In February 1953, a new plan was established whereby the course would consist of three months for preflight, six months for primary, and six months for basic. Commissions and wings would be awarded at the completion of basic. The first class to graduate under this course was 54-ABC (renamed from 53-H); they began preflight on 3 November 1952 and primary on 16 February 1953. In May 1954 the PA-18/AT-6 and T-34/T-28 programs were implemented concurrently.

North American XT-28, 4/13/50.   National Archives

The T-34/T-28 began at Marana in May—September at Spence; January 1955 at Moore; March at Bainbridge; and August at Malden. Some training was still being given in the T-6 as well. The PA-18/AT-6 program was in use at Graham, in July—August 1954; in September it was the PA-18/T-34/AT-6; in October—November it was the T-34/AT-6; and the T-34/AT-6/T-28 in December 1955. Hondo employed the T-34/T-6 program for all of 1955. Stallings and Bartow conducted a PA-18/T-6 program throughout 1955. By 11 October 1954 the required flight time was 40 hours in the T-28 and 80 hours in the T-33 or B-25. By the end of June 1956 all of the basic training bases had phased out the T-28 and were either all T-33 or all B-25, with between 110-120 hours required in type. With the entry of class 59-B at Bainbridge came the first jet primary trainer, the T-37. The T-28's were gradually phased out and replaced with T-37's at all primary bases with the last ones being at Spence, which were phased out on 20 July 1960 (class 61-E). The B-25 was phased out on 28 January 1959 with the graduation of class 59-E.

In fiscal year 1954, the production of Aviation Cadets reached a post-war high of over eleven thousand Cadets entering flight training. With the AFROTC program contributing over seven thousand pilot trainees per year, the Air Force now had two major sources of potential flying officers. Cuts had to be made, and the long standing goal of the service was to have a completely college trained officer corps. This goal combined with the large numbers of college trained ROTC officers available made the Aviation Cadet trained officer less desirable. The number of Cadets entering training had dwindled to approximately thirty-five hundred annually by 1957. Further cuts in flight training reduced it to about eleven hundred per annum. By 1959, Aviation Cadets accounted for about twelve percent of all new rated officers, quite a decline from the seventy percent of a few years earlier.

A major change in flight training occurred in 1959 when the USAF shifted from specialized to generalized training. There would no longer be single-engine and multi-engine training; all pilots would recieve the same training. Civilian contract training was ended, and all future training would be with military instructors. The pilot production was lowered from 2,200 to 1,500 per year by the end of 1959.

One of the finest training programs in the world was about to come to an end. Since the time that our young men first boarded the airplanes that took them to fight in the skies over Europe in 1917, until the graduation of the last Aviation Cadet, there has never been, as a whole, a finer more unified group of men in the world. From 1917 up until the mid 1950's, almost all rated officers (those with wings) came from the proud ranks of the Flying/Aviation Cadet Corps.

The last pilot Cadet to graduate in Class 62-B-2 on 11 October 1961 was William F. Wesson. The last navigator Cadet to graduate in class 65-15, on 3 March 1965 was Stephen V. Harper, the last of the Aviation Cadets.

1. Captain Miller later became the commanding officer at Issoudun, and eventually was given command of the 95th Aero Squadron, which was one of the first pursuit outfits on the front. He was the first American flyer to be a casualty of WWI, when on March 9, 1918, he was killed while flying with a practice patrol over the German lines.

2. *War Birds, Diary Of An Unknown Aviator*, by John MacGavock Grider, Ed. By Elliott White Springs.

3. Taken from *America's First Eagles*; by Lt. Lucien H. Thayer. Used with permission.

U.S.Army Air Corps, U.S.Army Air Forces, and U.S.A.F. training bases and their locations. P=Primary, B=Basic, A=Advanced, and TC=Training Command—E=SEACTC, C=CEACTC, and W=WEACTC. X=Othcr. This information is supplied by Lew Johnston, 43-G and used with his permission.

Com. Name	Base: City & State	P	B	A	TC	Comments:
#12 (RCAF)	Brandon, Manitoba, Canada				X	#12 Service Flying Training School. Brandon, Manitoba.
#18 (RCAF)	Boundry Bay, BC, Canada	P			X	#18 Elementary Flying Training School. Boundry Bay, BC.
29 Palms	Condor Field, 29 Palms, CA	P			W	Contract School, 1/1/42 to 4/19/44. 29 Palms Air Academy. Glider training 6/42 to 2/43. Cadets 3/43 to 3/44 F. R. Whers. 12th AAF FTD.
AIA	Van de Graaff Fld., Tuscaloosa, Al				E	Contract School, 9/1/40 to 9/8/44. Alabama Institute of Aeronautics (Parks). US, British & French Cadets.
Albany	Tech Field, Albany, GA	P			E	Contract Primary. Darr Aero Tech. Formerly Chicago. UK & American. #6BFTS started here. Moved to Ponca City, OK.
Albany	Turner AAF, Albany, GA			A	E	AAF Advanced, 8/12/40 to 8/15/46. Also called Turner.
Aloe	Aloe AAF, Victoria, TX			A	C	AAF Advanced, 10/27/42 to 10/31/45. Also known as Victoria. Please Note: Aloe and Foster were both at Victoria.
Altus	Altus AAF, Altus, OK			A	C	AAF Advanced, 6/17/42 to 5/15/45. Designated Altus AFB 1/8/53.
Americus	Souther Field, Americus, GA	P			E	Contract Primary, 3/21/41 to 10/16/44. Also called Souther. UK & US Cadets. William J. Graham.
Anderson Air Activities	Chester Field, McBride, MO	P			C	Contract Primary, 1/28/42 to 3/24/44. Also known as McBride. Graham Aviation, Inc. Emory M. Andersom, William Graham. 56th AAF FTD.
Anderson Air Activities	Malden AFB, Malden, MO	P				Contract Primary for U.S. Air Force flight students 50's and 60's. Also known as Malden. T-34 and T-28 aircraft in 61B.
Arcadia C	Carlstrom Field, Arcadia, FL	P			E	Contract Primary, 3/22/41 to 6/30/45. Also known as Embry-Riddle. Some British training here. WW I Primary
Arcadia D	Dorr Field, Arcadia, FL	P			E	Contract Primary, 10/4/41 to 10/16/44. Also known as Dorr. Embry Riddle Co. 54th AAF FTD. #5BFTS started here. Mvd. to Clewiston FL.
Arledge	Arledge Field, Stamford, TX	P			C	Contract Primary, 4/1/41 to 9/8/44. Also known as Stamford. Lou Foote Flying Service.
Augusta	Bush Field, Augusta, GA	P	B		E	Contract Primary & Basic, 8/25/41 to 9/8/44. Also known as Bush. Georgia Aero Tech. Hal S. Darr.

Name	Field / Location	P	B	A	Reg	Notes
Avenger	Avenger Field, Sweetwater, TX				C	Also known as Sweetwater. #7BFTS started here. First class (43-W-1) of 32 WASPS began at Houston Mun. Airport (now Hobby) on 11/42. Then here on 4/43.
Avon Park	Avon Park Airport, Avon Park, FL	P			E	Contract Primary, 10/4/41 to 10/16/44. Lodwick Aviation Military Academy. Albert I. Lodwick.
Bainbridge	Bainbridge AAF, Bainbridge, GA		B		E	AAF Basic 8/7/42 to 12/15/45. Designate Bainbridge AB 7/11/51. Conducted flying training to 3/31/61
Bakersfield	Minter AAF, Bakersfield, CA		B		W	AAF Basic, 6/5/41 to 1/31/46. Also known as Minter.
Ballinger	Bruce Field, Ballinger, TX	P			C	Contract Primary, 10/4/41 to 10/16/44. Also called Bruce Harmon Training Center. Fred Harmon.
Barksdale	Barksdale AAF, Shreveport, LA			A	W	Barksdale Field 11/18/30. AAF Advanced, 10/15/40. First navigator school. Also known as Shreveport. Became Barksdale AFB 1/13/48.
Bartow	Winter Haven Field, Winter Haven, FL	P				Primary training for U.S. Air Force pilots 5/1/51 to 5/19/61. T-34 and T-28 in 61B. Also called Winter Haven.
Bennettsville	Palmer Field, Bennettsville, SC	P			E	Contract Primary, 10/6/41 to 10/16/44. Also known as Palmer. Southeastern Air Services. Cody Laird & R. G. Lockwood. 55th AAF FTD.
Big Spring	Big Spring AAF, Big Spring, TX			A	C	AAF Advanced. Activated as Big Spring AAF 6/26/42 to 11/30/45. Activated as Webb AFB 5/18/52.
Big Spring	Webb AFB, Big Spring, TX		B	A		Activated as Webb AFB 5/18/52. Deactivate 9/33/77. Basic/Advanced Training for U.S. Air Force pilots.
Blackland	Blackland AAF, Waco, TX			A	C	AAF Advanced, 7/2/42 to 2/4/45. Also known as Waco. Subpost to Waco AAF until deactivated 10/31/45
Blythe	Morton Field, Blyth, CA	P			W	Contract Primary, 6/29/42 — 7/4/94. Morton Air Services & Academy. Ted Morton. 10th AAF FTD.
Blytheville	Blytheville AAF, Blytheville, AR			A	E	AAF Advanced, 1/10/42 to 6/16/45. Designated Blytheville AFB 6/10/53
Bonham	Jones Field, Bonham, TX	P			C	Contract Primary, 10/4/41 to 10/16/44. Also referred to as Jones. 302nd AAF FTD.
Brady	Curtis Field, Brady, TX	P	B		C	Contract Primary & Basic, 12/15/42 to 9/30/45. Also referred to as Curtis. Moved from Dallas. Maj. William F. Long.

Brooks	Brooks AAF, San Antonio, TX			A	C	AAF Advanced, 2/16/18 to 11/ 30/45. Then to Continental Air Forces. Redesignated Brooks AFB 6/28/48. ATC 10/1/59. AF Systems Command 11/1/61.
Bruce	Bruce Field, Ballinger, TX	P			C	Contract Primary, 10/4/41 to 10/16/44. Also known as Ballinger. Bruce Harmon Training Center. Fred Harmon.
Bryan	Bryan AAF, Bryan, TX		B		C	AAF Basic, 6/26/42 to 2/19/47. Activated as Bryan AFB 7/1/51
Bush	Bush AAF, Augusta, GA	P	B		E	Contract Primary & Basic, 8/25/41 to 9/8/44. Also known as Augusta. Georgia Aero Tech. Hal S. Darr.
Cal Aero	Ontario, CA	P	B		W	Contract School. Cal Aero Flight Academy. Had Primary and Basic at various times. Moved from Glendale CA. Maj. C. C. Mosley.
Camden (AR)	Harrell Field, Camden, AR	P			C	Contract Primary, 8/7/42 to 4/15/44. Wiggins-Marden Aero. Corp. 71st AAF FTD.
Camden (SC)	Woodward Field, Camden, SC	P			E	Contract Primary, 3/22/41 to 8/4/44. Also called Southern (SC). British & American. Southern Aviation School. 64th AAF FTD. Frank W. Hulse & Ike F Jones.
Camp Borden	Canada					RCAF
Cape Girardeau	Harris Field, Cape Girardeau, MO	P			C	Contract Primary, 12/25/42 to 5/24/44 Also known as Harris Cape Institute. of Aeronautics. Oliver Parks.
Carlstrom	Arcadia C, Arcadia, FL	P			E	Contract Primary, 3/22/41 to 6/30/45. Also known as Embry-Riddle. Some British training here. Primary training base in WW I.
Chandler	Williams AAF, Chandler, AZ			A	W	AAF Advanced, Mesa Military Airport 6/19/41. Higley Field 10/41. Williams AAF 2/24/42. Williams AFB 1/13/48. Also called Williams.
Chandler	Williams AFB, Chandler, AZ		B			Designated Williams AFB 1/13/48. Basic training for USAF pilots. T-38's in 61B. Also known as Williams.
Chicago	Curtiss-Reynolds Apt., Glenview, IL	P			X	Contract Primary. Chicago School of Aero. Moved to Albany, GA 1941.
Chickasha	Wilson-Bonfils Fld., Chickasha, OK	P			C	Contract Primary, 10/4/41 to 5/1/45. Wilson-Bonfils Flying School. Ray W. Wilson & F. W. Bonfils.
Chico	Chico AAF, Chico, CA		B		W	AAF Basic, 1/6/41 to 4/25/44. Transferred to 4th AF 3/25/44.
Cimarron	Cimarron Field, Yukon, OK.	P			C	Contract Primary, 4/1/41 to 6/27/44. Oklahoma Air College. Clarence Page & Ted Colbert. Also referred to as Oklahoma City.
Clairborne	Wickenburg Field, Wickenburg, AZ	P			W	Contract Primary. Also known as Wickenburg. Harry C. Clairborne & William R. Kent. Glider program 6/42 to 2/43. Cadets 3/43 to 4/44.

Claresholm	Claresholm Fld., Claresholm, Alberta				RCAF Advanced twin-engine school
Clarksdale	Fletcher Field, Clarksdale, MS	P		E	Contract Primary, 7/5/42 to 10/16/44. Sometimes referred to as Fletcher.
Clewiston	Riddle Field, Clewiston, FL	P	A	E	Contract School, 11/12/42 to 12/31/45. Riddle-McKay Aero College. #5BFTS (British Flight Taining School). Moved here from Arcadia D.
Cochran	Cochran AAF, Macon, GA		B	E	AAF Basic, 8/5/41 to 3/45. Also known as Macon.
Coffeyville	Coffeyville AAF, Coffeyville, KS		B	C	AAF Basic, 11/11/42 to 5/31/44.
Coleman	Coleman Field, Coleman, TX	P		C	Contract Primary, 10/41 to 10/44. Austin Flying Service.
Columbus	Columbus AAF, Columbus, MS		A	E	AAF Advanced, 7/23/41 to 6/6/45. Columbus AFB 6/24/48. Contract flying training from 12/20/50 to 4/1/55. Also 7/1/69 to present.
Condor	Condor Field 29, Palms, CA	P		W	Contract School, 1/1/42 to 4/19/44. Also known as 29 Palms (Air Academy). Glider training 6/42 to 2/43. Cadets 3/43 to 3/44 F. R. Whers. 12th AAF FTD.
Connally	James Connally AFB, Waco, TX	B		C	Originally Waco AAF Basic, 9/16/41 to 12/15/45. Designated Waco AFB 7/1/48. Designated James Connally AFB 6/10/49. Also known as Waco.
Corsicana	Corsicana, TX	P		C	AAF Basic, 4/1/41 to 10/16/44. Air Activities of TX. Brazilian Cadets. Wooley, Wooley, Criddle & Booth. 301st AAF FTD.
Courtland	Courtland AAF, Courtland, AL		B	E	AAF Basic, 10/19/42 to 6/30/45.
Craig	Craig AAF, Selma, AL		A	E	AAF Advanced, 7/27/40 to 12/31/45. Craig AFB 9/1/50. Also called Selma.
Craig	Craig AFB, Selma, AL		B	E	Basic training of USAF pilots. T-33 in 61B. Also referred to as Selma
Cuero	Brayton Field, Cuero, TX	P		C	Contract Primary, 4/1/41 to 8/4/44. Brayton Flying Service. C.E. Brayton.
Curtis	Curtis Field, Brady, TX			C	Contract Primary & Basic, 12/15/42 to 9/30/45. Also called Brady. Moved from Dallas. Maj. William F. Long.
Dallas	Love Field, Dallas, TX	P		C	Contract Primary, 7/39 to 12/44. Dallas Aviation Sch. & Air College. Moved to Brady. WW I flying training base. See Love Field. #1BFTS started here. Moved to Terrell, TX.
Darr Aero Tech	Tech Field, Albany, GA	P		E	Contract Primary. Formerly Chicago School of Aeronautics. Moved to Albany, GA 1941. Hal S. Darr.

231

Decatur	Pryor Field, Decatur, AL	P		E	Contract Primary, 10/5/41 to 12/28/44. Also known as Southern Aviation Training School. F. W. Hulse & Partners. 65th AAF FTD.
Del Rio	Laughlin Fld., Del Rio, TX			C	Also refers to Laughlin AAF and Laughlin AFB, same installation in Del Rio, TX. See Laughlin.
Denton	Denton Airport, Denton, TX				Liaison pilot training, 6/10/42 to 12/3/43
Dorr	Arcadia Field, Arcadia, FL	P		E	Contract Primary, 10/4/41 to 10/16/44. Also known as Arcadia D. Embry-Riddle Co. 54th AAF FTD. #5BFTS started here. Moved to Clewiston, FL.
Dos Palos	Eagle Field, Dos Palos, CA	P		W	Also called Eagle Field. Contract Primary, 6/24/43 to 12/28/44. Coast Aviation Corp. Harry S. White & Alexis L. Ehrman, Jr. 15th AAF FTD.
Dothan	Napier AAF, Dothan, AL		A	E	AAF Advanced, 12/20/41 to 11/1/45. Also known as Napier.
Douglas, AZ	Douglas AAF, Douglas, AZ		A	W	AAF Advanced, 11/2/42 to 10/31/45.
Douglas, GA	S. Ga. College Apt., Douglas, GA	P		E	Contract Primary, 10/4/41 to 12/28/44. Wesley N. Raymond & Robt. Richardson. 63rd AAF FTD.
E. St Louis	Parks Airport, E. St. Louis, IL	P		C	Contract Primary, 8/1/39 to 3/12/44. Also known as Parks, IL. Parks Air College. One of several Parks.
Eagle	Eagle Field, Dos Palos, CA	P		W	Also called Dos Palos. Contract Primary, 6/24/43 to 12/28/44. Coast Aviation Corp. Harry S.White & Alexis L. Ehrman Jr. 15th AAF FTD.
Eagle Pass	Eagle Pass AAF, Laredo, TX		A	C	AAF Advanced, 6/42 to 5/1/45. Also known as Laredo. Some say this base was in Eagle Pass, TX.
Echeverria	Echeverria Field, Wickenburg, AZ	P		W	Contract Primary, 6/3/42 to 4/19/44. Also known as Wickenburg. Harry C. Clairborne & William R.Kent. Gliders 6/42 to 2/43. Cadets 3/43 to 4/44.
El Reno	Mustang Field, El Reno, OK	P		C	Contract Primary, 1/16/43 to 12/31/45. Also known as El Reno. Also known as Mustang. Midwest Air School. Clarence Page & Associates.
Ellington	Ellington AAF, Houston, TX		A	C	AAF Advanced, 8/17/40 to 4/15/46. Sometimes referred to as Houston. Designated Ellington AFB 3/31/49
Embry-Riddle	Union City Apt., Union City, TN	P		E	Contract Primary, 7/5/42 to 4/15/44. Also called Union City. Riddle-McKay Institute. 67th AAF FTD.

Enid	Enid AAF, Enid, OK		B		C	AAF Basic, 9/20/41 to 1/31/47. Enid AFB 8/1/48. Vance AFB 7/9/49. Later used for Adv. Vance AFB
Falcon	Falcon Field, Mesa, AZ				W	Contract school, 11/12/42 to 8/45. Southwest Airways. #4BFTS (British Flight Taining School).
Fletcher	Fletcher Field, Clarksdale, MS	P			E	Contract Primary, 7/5/42 to 10/16/44. Also called Clarksdale.
Foster	Foster AAF, Victoria, TX			A	C	AAF Advanced, 5/15/41 to 10/31/45. Also referred to as Victoria. Foster AFB 9/1/52. Please note: Foster and Aloe were both at Victoria.
Frederick	Frederick AAF, Frederick, OK			A	C	AAF Advanced, 9/23/42 to 10/31/45.
Freeman	Freeman AAF, Seymour, IN			A	E	AAF Adv., 12/1/42 to 4/30/44. Also called Seymour.
French Cl.	Tuscaloosa/Orangeburg				E	See Tuscaloosa & Orangeburg.
Ft. Stockton	Gibbs Field Ft. Stockton, TX	P			C	Contract Primary. 6/1/42 to 3/12/44. Also called Gibbs. Pacific Air School Ltd. J. M. Webster. 9th AAF FTD.
Ft. Sumner	Ft. Sumner AAF, Ft. Sumner, NM				W	AAF Advanced, 6/6/42 to 7/16/44.
Ft. Worth	Hicks Field, Ft. Worth, TX	P	B		C	Contract Primary & Basic, 8/16/40 to 6/27/44. Also known as Hicks. Texas Aviation Co. Maj. William F. Long.
Garden City	Garden City AAF, Garden City, KS		B		C	AAF Basic 2/6/43 to 12/15/44.
Gardner	Gardner AAF, Taft, CA		B		W	AAF Basic, 6/2/41 to 6/30/45. Also known as Taft.
Garner	Garner Field, Uvalde, TX	P			C	Contract Primary, 10/4/41 to 6/30/45. Also called Uvalde. Hangar 6, Inc. Latin Amer. Cadets. Some US.
George	George AAF, Lawrenceville, IL			A	E	AAF Advanced, 8/10/42 to 8/15/44. Also known as Lawrenceville. This is not to be confused with George AFB in Victorville, TX.
Gibbs	Gibbs Field, Ft. Stockton, TX	P			W	Contract Primary. 6/1/42 to 3/12/44. Also known as Ft. Stockton. Pacific Air School Ltd. J. M. Webster. 9th AAF FTD.
Glendale (AZ)	Thunderbird Field, Glendale, AZ	P			W	Contract Primary, 7/12/41 to 6/30/45. Also called Thunderbird I or Phoenix. SW Airways, Inc. Some Chinese. Hayward & Connelly. 6th AAF FTD.
Glendale (CA)	Gr. Central Air Term., Glendale, CA	P			W	Contract Primary. Also known as Grand Central Flying School. Moved to Ontario, CA. #2BFTS started here. Moved to Lancaster, then closed. Maj. C. C. Mosley.
Glenview	Curtiss-Reynolds Apt., Glenview, IL	P			X	Contract Primary for very short time. Chicago School of Aeronautics. Replaced by Albany. Hal S. Darr.

Goderich	Canada				X	RCAF
Goodfellow	Goodfellow AAF, San Angelo, TX		B		C	AAF Basic, 8/17/40 to 5/1/47. Also known as San Angelo.
Goodfellow	Goodfellow AFB, San Angelo, TX			A		Reactivated 12/1/47. Designated Goodfellow AFB 1/13/48 to 10/1/58. Conducted flying training until 7/1/78. Then technical training.
Graham	Graham AB, Marianna, FL			A	E	AAF Advanced, 8/8/42 to 10/12/44. Also known as Marianna. Reactivated for flying training as Graham AB 1/27/53 to 8/31/61
Grand Central	Gr.C. Air Terminal, Glendale, CA	P			W	Contract Primary, 7/39 to 9/40. Also known as Glendale. Gr. Central Flying Sch.. Moved to Ontario as Cal-Aero.
Greenville (MS)	Greenville AAF, Greenville, MS		B		E	AAF Contract Basic, 6/23/41 to 3/45. Reactivated, Greenville AFB 12/1/50.
Greenville (MS)	Greenville AFB, Greenville, MS			A		Reactivated 12/1/50 as Greenville AFB. Conducted flying training until 10/60. Technical training from 11/60 until deactivated 10/27/66.
Greenville (TX)	Majors AAF, Greenville, TX		B		C	AAF Basic, 6/26/42 to 11/30/44. Also known as Greenville (TX).
Greenwood (MS)	Greenwood AAF, Greenwood, MS		B		E	AAF Basic, 10/1/42 to 1/18/45. Turned over to Air Transport Comd.
Grider	Grider Field, Pine Bluff, AR	P			C	Contract Primary, 4/1/41 to 10/16/44. Also referred to as Pine Bluff. Pine Bluff School of Aeronautics. William R. Kent & B. Cohan.
Gunter	Gunter AAF, Montgomery, AL		B		E	AAF Basic, 7/40 to 12/13/45. Also referred to as Montgomery. Designated Maxwell AFB, Gunter Annex 3/19/92.
Hancock	Hancock Fld., Santa Maria, CA	P			W	Contract Primary, Sept. 9/14/40 to 6/27/44. Also called Santa Maria and Capt.Allan Hancock College of Aero.
Harrell	Harrell Field, Camden, AR	P			C	Contract Primary, 8/7/42 to 4/15/44. Wiggins-Marden Aero. 71st AAF FTD
Harris	Harris Field, Cape Girardeau, MO	P			C	Contract Primary 12/25/42-3/25/44. Also known as Cape Girardeau. Cape Institute of Aeronautics. Oliver Parks.
Hatbox	Spartan Field, Muskogee, OK	P			C	Contract Primary, 9/16/40 to 6/27/44. Also known as Muskogee and/or Spartan. Also called Hatbox Field.
Hawthorne	Hawthorne Field, Hawthorne, CA	P			W	Contract Primary, 9/16/40 to 6/27/44. Hawthorne School of Aeronautics. Beverly E. Howard.
Hazelhurst	Mineola, NY				X	Early base, 1918, Mineola, Long Island.

HCA	Santa Maria Apt., Santa Maria, CA	P			W	Contract Primary, 9/14/40 to 6/27/44. Also known as Hancock. Allan Hancock College of Aeronautics. Capt Allan N. Hancock.
Helena	Thompson-Robbins Fld., Helena, AR	P			C	Contract Primary, 10/4/41 to 8/4/44. Helena Aero Tech. Rudolph A. VanDevere. 59th AAF FTD.
Hemet	Ryan Field, Hemet, CA	P			W	Contract Primary, 9/14/40 to 12/28/44. Also known as Ryan. Ryan School of Aero.. Moved to Hemet from San Diego. T. Claude Ryan.
Hicks	Hicks Field, Ft. Worth, TX	P	B		C	Contract Primary & Basic, 8/16/40 to 6/27/44. Also known as Hicks. Texas Aviation Co. Maj. William F. Long.
Hondo	Hondo AAF, Hondo, TX		B		C	Activated 7/4/42. Conducted Navigator, Flying, and Contract flying until 12/31/45. Designated Hondo AB 6/5/51. Contract flying training until 10/31/58. Now civil.
Houston	Houston Mun. Apt., Houston, TX				C	Later Hobby. First class of 32 WASP's began here in 11/42 for Class-W-1. Program moved to Sweetwater, TX in 4/43. Jacquelin Cochran headed school.
Houston	Ellington AAF/AFB, Houston, TX			A		AAF Advanced, 8/17/40 to 4/15/4646. Sometimes referred to as Houston. Designated Ellington AFB 3/31/49.
Independence	Independence AAF, Ind., KS		B		C	AAF Basic, 10/12/42 to 11/1/45.
Jackson, (MS)	Robbins Field, Jackson, MS	P			E	Contract Primary, 9/14/40 to 4/15/44. Parks Inst. of Aero. There are reports of some Dutch cadets.
Jackson, (MS)	Jackson AAB, Jackson, MS				E	Activated 5/1/42. Specialized training for Netherlands East Indies to 7/1/44.
Jackson, (TN)	Jackson Airport, Jackson, TN	P			E	Contract Primary, 7/5/42 to 1/27/44. Southern Air Services. Cody Laird & Ben Smith. 68th AAF FTD
Jones	Jones Field, Bonham, TX	P			C	Contract Primary, 10/4/41 to 10/16/44. Also called Bonham. 302nd AAF FTD.
Kaufman	Kaufman Airport, Terrell, TX	P		A	C	Contract School, 11/12/42 to 9/30/45. 321st AAF FTD. Maj William E. Long. #1BFTS here from Love Field. Also called Terrell.
Kelly	Kelly AAF, San Antonio, TX			A	C	Early AAC (1916) . Now Kelly AFB
King City	King City Airport, King City, CA	P			W	Contract Primary, 3/22/41 to 10/16/44. Palo Alto Airport, Inc. H. S. Whitre & A. L. Ehrman, Jr. 3rd AAF FTD.
Kinston	Kinston AB, Kinston, NC				E	US Navy during WW II. Activated as Kinston Air Field 10/17/51. Designated Stallings AB 6/28/53. Contract flying training until 11/7/57.

La Junta	La Junta AAF, La Junta, CO			A	W	AAF Advanced, 11/2/42 to 7/30/45.
Lackland	Lackland AFB, San Antonio, TX				E	Originated as San Antonio Aviation Cadet Center. Became military training center 2/1/46 as Lackland AB. Lackland AFB 1/13/48 to date for military & technical training.
Lafayette	Lafayette Airport, Lafayette, LA	P			E	Contract Primary, 7/3/42 to 3/24/44. Lafayette School of Aeronautics. Wilmot & Hylan. 70th AAF FTD.
Lake Charles	Lake Charles AAF, Lake Chas., LA			A	E	AAF Advanced.
Lakeland	Lodwick Field, Lakeland, FL	P			E	Contract Primary, 9/14/40 to 10/1/45. Started with some personnel from Lincoln, Nebr. Albert I. Lodwick. Early RAF (Arnold Plan). Then US.
LaMesa	La Mesa Airport, La Mesa, TX				C	Contract Liaison & basic glider training, 6/10/42 to 2/26/44
Lancaster	War Eagle Field, Lancaster, CA		B	A	W	Contract Basic & Advanced, 7/28/42 to 10/1/45. Also referred to as Polaris Flight Academy. #2BFTS and American Eagle Squadron and 43-44 Basic classes.
Lancaster	Lancaster Airport, Lancaster, CA		B		W	Contract Basic, 7/28/42 to 6/27/44. Replaced by Oxnard's Primary School 6/27/44. Deactivated 11/1/45.
Langley	Langley AAF, Langley, VA				X	Some very early training here. AAC Training. Command 9/15/44. Langly AFB sometime after Dec. 1, 1945.
Laredo	Eagle Pass AAF, Laredo, TX			A	C	AAF Advanced, 6/30/42 to 5/1/45. Also referred to as Eagle Pass. Claim has been made that this station was in Eagle Pass, TX.
Laredo	Laredo AFB, Laredo, TX		B			Activated Laredo AAF, 5/1/42. Flexible gunnery and Basic training of USAF pilots, 6/2/52 to 9/30/73.
Las Vegas	Las Vegas AAF, Las Vegas, NV			A	W	AAF Advanced 12/31/46. to 12/20/41. Subbase of Mather 8/30/47. Subbase of Williams AAF 4/1/48 to provide advanced fighter training. Later called Nellis AFB.
Laughlin	Laughlin Fld., Del Rio, TX	P			C	Contract Primary. Dallas Aviation School & Air College. Moved to Brady 7/39- to 2/44. WW I flying training base. See Dallas. #1BFTS started here. Moved to Terrell, TX.
Laughlin	Laughlin AFB, Del Rio, TX					Laughlin AFB 5/1/52. Flying training until 4/1/57. SAC 4/1/62. Flying training to present.
Lemoore	Lemoore AAF, Lemoore, CA		B		W	AAF Basic, 12/20/41 to 6/1/44.
Lincoln	Union Apt., Lincoln, NE	P			X	Contract Primary. Lincoln Flying School. Sias School of Aeronautics. Closed very soon; bad climate for flight training. Some staff moved to Lodwick Field, Lakeland, FL.

Lindbergh	Lindbergh Field, San Diego, CA	P			W	Contract Primary. Replaced by Hemet.
Love	Love Field, Ft. Worth, TX	P			C	Contract Primary. Dallas Av. School & Air College. Moved to Brady 7/39-12/44. WW I flying training base. See Dallas. #1BFTS started here. Moved to Terrell, TX.
Lubbock	Lubbock AAF, Lubbock, TX			A	C	AAF Advanced. Lubbock Field 6/26/41. Lubbock AAF 4/26/43. Lubbock AFB 1/13/48. Reactivated 11/19/49 as Reese AFB.
Luke	Luke AAF/AFB, Phoenix, AZ			A	W	AAF Advanced, 2/15/41 to 10/31/46. Designated Luke AFB 6/10/49. Sometimes called Phoenix. #4BFTS started in Phoenix. Moved to Mesa.
Macon	Cochran Field, Macon, GA		B		E	AAF Basic, 8/5/41 to 3/45. Also known as Cochran.
Majors	Majors AAF, Greenville, TX		B		C	AAF Basic, 6/26/42 to 11/30/44. Also known as Greenville (TX).
Malden	Malden AAF, Malden, MO		B		E	AAF Basic, 1/6/43 to 1/15/44. Troop Carrier 6/15/44. Malden AB 7/11/51. Contract flying training to 9/1/60.
Malden	Malden AFB, Malden, MO	P				Primary training of USAF pilots.
Marana	Marana AAF, Marana, AZ		B		W	AAF Basic, 8/29/42 to 9/12/45. Marana AB 9/1/51 to 10/22/57.
March	March Field, CA	P				WW I, and on. Primary training base.
Marfa	Marfa AAF, Marfa, TX			A	W	AAF Advanced, Dec. 5, 1942 to Aug.1, 1945.
Marianna	Marianna AAF, Marianna, FL			A	E	AAF Advanced, 8/8/42 to 10/12/44. Also known as Graham AB 1/27/53 to 8/31/61.
Mather	Mather AAF, Sacramento, CA	P	B	A	W	Also known as Sacramento. Various special flying training classes.
Maxwell	Maxwell AAF, Montgomery, AL	P	B	A	E	At different times, used for Pre Flight, Primary, Basic & Adv. Various subbases have been attached. Now Maxwell AFB.
Mc Bride	Chester Field, Mc Bride, MO	P			C	Contract Primary, 1/28/42 to 3/24/44. E. M. Anderson. 43-J cadet reports a flood, and a move to Vichy, MO—perhaps temporary. 79th AAF FTD.
McAllen	Moore AAF, Mission, TX			A	C	AAF Advanced, 9/20/41 to 10/31/45. Moore AB 11/1/55 to 7/15/61. Between Mission & McAllen, TX. Also called Mission and/or Moore.
McCoy	McCoy AFB, Orlando, FL					Was Pinecastle AFB. Renamed sometime after 1/1/54.
Merced	Merced AAF, Merced, CA		B	A	W	AAF Basic, 9/20/41 to 7/1/45 Flying training and Advanced training for WASP's. Redesignated Castle AFB 1/13/48.
Mesa	Williams AFB, Chandler, AZ					Originally activated as Mesa Military Airport, 6/19/41. Desig. Higley Fld.10/41 & Williams Fld. 2/24/42. Williams AFB 1/13/48.

Mesa Military	Falcon Field, Mesa, AZ	P		A	W	Contract school, 11/12/42 to 8/45. Southwest Airways. #4BFTS (British Flight Training School).
Miami	Miami Airport, Miami, OK	P		A	C	Contract School, 11/12/42 to 8/20/44. Also known as Spartan (MiOK). #3BFTS (British Flight Taining School) started Tulsa, to Phoenix, to Miami. 322 AAF FTD.
Minter	Minter AAF, Bakersfield, CA		B		W	AAF Basic, 6/5/41 to 1/31/46. Also known as Bakersfield.
Mira Loma	Ventura Field, Oxnard, CA	P			W	Contract Primary, 9/12/40 to 6/27/44. Classes 44-I - 45-I. Also known as Oxnard. Mira Loma Flight Academy. Maj. C. C. Mosley.
Mission	Moore AAF, Mission, TX			A	C	AAF Advanced, 9/20/41 to 10/31/45. Moore AB 11/1/55 to 7/15/61. Between Mission & McAllen, TX. Also referred to as Moore or McAllen.
Mitchel	Mitchel Field, LI, NY				X	USMA graduates for students. In 1920, was used for preliminary enlisted pilot training.
Moffett	Moffett Field, Sunnyvale, CA		B		W	AAF Basic. Classes 42-I and 42-J only.
Montgomery	Maxwell/Gunter, Montgomery, AL	P	B	A	E	See Maxwell & Gunter.
Moody	Moody AAF, Valdosta, GA			A	E	AAF Advanced, 6/26/41 to 5/1/45. Moody AFB 1/13/48. Also known as Valdosta. Twin eng. AT-9 and AT-10.
Moore	Moore AAF/AB, Mission, TX			A	C	AAF Advanced, 9/20/41 to 10/31/45. Moore AB 11/1/55 to 7/15/61. Between Mission & McAllen, TX. Also called Mission and/or McAllen.
Morton	Morton Field, Blyth, CA	P			W	Contract Primary, 6/29/42 to 8/4/44. Morton Air Services & Academy. Ted Morton. 10th AAF FTD.
Moultrie	Spence AAF, Moultrie, GA			A	E	AAF Advanced, 7/12/41 to 12/15/45. Also known as Spence. Spence AB 5/15/51. Conducted flying training until deactivated 3/31/61
Muskogee	Hatbox Field, Muskogee, OK	P			C	Contract Primary, 9/16/40 to 6/27/44.. Also known as Muskogee and/or Spartan Field
Mustang	Mustang Field, El Reno, OK	P			C	Contract Primary, 1/16/43 to 12/31/45. Also known as El Reno.
Napier	Napier AAF, Dothan, AL			A	E	AAF Advanced, 12/20/41 to 11/1/45. Also known as Dothan.
Nellis	Nellis AFB, Las Vegas, NV			A	W	Activated 4/30/50. To provide flying and combat crew training. Tactical Air command 7/1/58. Formerly called Las Vegas AAF
Newport	Newport AAF, Newport, AR		B		C	AAF Basic, 11/1/42 to 8/19/44. Transferred to Navy.
North Island	North Island, San Diego, CA					Established by Glen Curtiss in 1911. Many early Army Aviators receive their flight instruction here.

Ocala	Taylor Field, Ocala, FL	P			E	Contract Primary, 11/41 to 9/8/44. Hanley & Spurgeon. Greenville Aviation School. 57th AAF FTD.
Oklahoma City	Cimarron Field, Yukon, OK	P			C	Contract Primary, 4/1/41 to 6/27/44. Oklahoma Air College. Clarence Page & Ted Colbert. Also referred to as Cimarron and Oklahoma City.
Ontario	Ontario Airport, Ontario, CA	P	B		W	Contract School, 9/14/40 to 12/43. Reactivated 6/44 to 10/44. Cal-Aero Flight Academy. Primary and Basic at various times. Maj C. C. Mosley.
Orangeburg	Hawthorne Field, Orangeburg, SC	P			E	Contract Primary, 10/4/41 to 9/1/45. Also called Hawthorne. Some French cadets. Hawthorne School of Aero. Beverly E. Howard., 58th AAF FTD.
Orlando	McCoy AFB, Orlando, FL					Formerly Pinecastle
Oxnard	Ventura Co. Fld., Oxnard, CA	P			W	Contract Primary, 9/12/40 to 6/27/44. Also known as Mira Loma. Mira Loma Flight Academy.
Palmer	Palmer Field, Bennettsville, SC	P			E	Contract Primary, 10/6/41 to 10/16/44. Also called Bennettsville. Southeastern Air Services. Cody Laird & R. G. Lockwood. 55th AAF FTD.
Pampa	Pampa AAF, Pampa, TX			A	C	AAF Advanced, 8/3/42 to 12/28/44.
Parks (AL)	Van de Graaff Fld., Tuscaloosa, AL	P			E	Contract Primary. Parks. Tuscaloosa Institute of Aeronautics. FieldAir. US & British & French. Classes 43-44. One of several Parks.
Parks (CGMO)	Harris Field, Cape Girardeau, MO	P			C	Contract Primary. Parks Air College. One of several Parks.
Parks (IL)	Parks Airport, E. St Louis, IL	P			C	Contract Primary, 7/1/39 to 3/12/44. Parks Air College. One of several.
Parks (MS)	Robins Field, Jackson, MS	P			E	Contract Primary, 9/14/40 to 4/15/44. Parks Institute of Aeronautics. There are reports of some Dutch cadets.
Parks (SMO)	Harvey Parks Apt., Sikeston, MO	P			C	Contract Primary, 9/14/40 to 10/16/44. Mission Institute of Aeronautics. Also referred to as Parks (SMO). Oliver L. Parks. One of several Parks.
Pecos	Pecos AAF, Pecos, TX		B	A	W	AAF Basic and Advanced, 8/28/42 to 5/31/45.
Perrin	Perrin AAF, Sherman, TX		B		C	AAF Basic, 9/20/41 to 10/31/46. Also known as Sherman. Perrin AFB 4/1/48. Flying training until 7/1/62.
Phoenix	Luke AAF, Phoenix, AZ			A	W	AAF Advanced, 2/15/41 to 10/31/46. Designated Luke AFB 6/10/49. Also referred to as Phoenix. #4BFTS started in Phoenix. Moved to Mesa.
Phoenix	Thunderbird I & II, Phoenix, AZ	P				Both Thunderbird I and Thunderbird II often referred to as Phoenix.

Pine Bluff	Grider Field, Pine Bluff, AR	P			C	Contract Primary, 4/1/41 to 10/16/44. Also known as Grider. Pine Bluff School of Aeronautics. William R. Kent & B. Cohan.
Pinecastle	Pinecastle AFB, Orlando, FL				X	Renamed McCoy AFB after 1/1/54.
Pittsburg	Atkinson Mun. Apt., Pittsburg, KS	P			C	Contract Liaison pilot training, 5/25/42 to 10/20/44. McFarland Flying Service. E. H. McFarland. L4's and Glider Pilots.
Polaris	War Eagle Field, Lancaster, CA		B	A	W	Contract Basic & Advanced. Also referred to as Lancaster. Polaris Flight Academy. Maj. C. C. Mosley. #2BFTS and American Eagle Squadron and 43-44 Basic classes.
Ponca City	Ponca City, OK	P		A	C	Darr School of Aero, 11/12/42 to 4/15/45. #6BFTS (British Flight Training School) moved here from Albany. 323rd AAF FTD.
Prince Edward Island	Canada				X	RCAF
Pryor	Pryor Field, Decatur, AL	P			E	Contract Primary, 10/5/41 to 12/28/44. Also known as Southern Aviation Training School. F. W. Hulse & Partners. 65th AAF FTD.
RAF		P	B	A	X	Various bases and programs in the US.
Randolph	Randolph AAF, San Antonio, TX	P	B	A	C	October 1931 to present. Randolph AFB 1/13/48. Historical training site. Various Activities continued. Still active as Randolph AFB. Some cadet history is maintained here.
Rankin	Rankin Field, Tulare, CA	P			W	Contract Primary, 3/22/41 to 8/1/45. Also referred to as Tulare. Tex Rankin & R. S. Norswing. Briefly at Tulsa International Airport. 4th AAF FTD.
RCAF		P	B	A	X	Some Americans trained in Canada. Many transferred to the US services.
Reese	Reese AFB, Lubbock, TX		B			Reactivated 11/19/49 as Reese. Basic training of US Air Force pilots. Formerly Lubbock AAF.
Regina	Regina, Saskatchewan				X	RCAF Initial Training School (ITS). Similar to US Preflight
Reno	Stead AFB, Reno, NV					Helicopter and Liason flying training, 9/54 to 11/6/66. Also called Stead.
Rich	Rich Field, Waco, TX					WW I flying training base. Closed soon after the war, and all aircraft flown to Love Field.
Riddle	Riddle Field, Clewiston, FL	P		A		Contract School. Riddle-McKay Aero College. #5BFTS (British Fl.t. Taining School). Moved here from Arcadia .
Robbins	Robbins Field, Jackson, MS	P			E	Contract Primary, 9/14/40 to 4/15/44. Parks Institute of Aeronautics. There are reports of some Dutch cadets.
Rockcliffe	Rockliffe Air Station, Ontario					Conversion & Training Squadron provided indoctrination and aircraft familiarization training to civilian pilots entering the service.

Rolla	Rolla Airport, Rolla, MO	P				Contract Primary. Existed for a very short time.
Roswell	Roswell AAF, Roswell, NM			A	W	AAF Advanced, 9/20/41 to 11/1/45. Later Designated Walker AFB.
Ryan	Ryan Field, Tucson, AZ	P			W	Contract Primary. Also referred to as Tucson. Ryan School of Aeronautics T. Claude Ryan.
Ryan	Ryan Field, Hemet, CA	P			W	Contract Primary, 9/14/40 to 12/28/44. Also called Hemet. Ryan School of Aeronautics. Moved to Hemet from San Diego. T. C. Ryan.
Ryan	Lindbergh Field, San Diego, CA	P			W	Contract Primary, 7/39 to 8/42. Also referred to as San Diego. Ryan School of Aeronautics. Moved to Hemet. T. Claude Ryan.
Sacramento	Mather AAF, Sacramento, CA	P	B	A	W	Also referred to as Mather. Various special flying training classes.
San Angelo	Goodfellow AAF, San Angelo, TX		B		C	AAF Basic, 6/1/42 to 11/30/45. Also known as Goodfellow.
San Antonio	Kelly / Brooks, San Antonio, TX	P	B	A	C	Early historic training bases. See individual listings.
San Diego	Lindbergh Field, San Diego, CA	P			W	Contract Primary, 7/39 to 8/42. Also known as Ryan. Ryan School of Aeronautics. Moved to Hemet. T. Claude Ryan.
Santa Maria	Hancock Fld., Santa Maria, CA	P			W	Contract Primary, 9/14/40 to 6/27/44. Also known as Hancock. Allan Hancock College of Aeronautics. Capt. Allan N. Hancock.
Scottsdale	Thunderbird II, Scottsdale, AZ	P			W	Contract Primary, 6/26/42 to 10/16/44. Also called Thunderbird II or Phoenix. Southwest Airways, Inc. Hayward & Connelly. 9th AAF FTD.
Sea Island	Sea Island, Vancouver, BC					Basic flying training, similar to U S Primary.
Selma	Craig AAF, Selma, AL			A	E	AAF Advanced, 8/27/40 to 12/31/45. Craig AFB 9/1/50. Also called Craig.
Sequoia	Sequoia Field, Visalia, CA	P			E	Contract Primary, 10/4/41 to 10/44. Also known as Visalia-Dinuba School of Aeronautics. Randall M. Scott & J. L. O'Donnel & John B. Quin. 8th AAF FTD.
Seymour	Freeman AAF, Seymour, IN			A	E	AAF Advanced, 12/1/42 to 4/30/44. Also known as Freeman.
Shaw	Shaw AAF, Sumpter, SC		B		E	AAF Basic, 8/14/41 to 4/1/45. Also known as Sumpter. Designated Shaw AFB 1/13/48.
Sherman	Perrin AAF, Sherman, TX		B		C	AAF Basic, 9/20/41 to 10/31/46. Also known as Perrin. Perrin AFB April 1, 1948. Flying training until 7/1/62.
Shreveport	Barksdale AAF, Shreveport, LA		B	A	E	Barksdale Field, 11/18/30. AAF Advanced, 10/15/40. First navigator school. Also known as Barksdale. Barksdale AFB Jan 13, 1948.

Signal Corps	Aviation School, San Diego, CA	P				1914 US Army base—authorized to train up to 12 enlisted pilots.
Sikeston	Harvey Parks Apt., Sikeston, MO	P				Contract Primary, 9/14/40 to 10/16/44. Mission Institute of Aeronautics. Also known as Parks SMO. Oliver L Parks. One of several.
Souther	Souther Field, Americus, GA	P			E	Contract Primary, 3/21/41 to 10/16/44. Also called Americus. UK & US cadets. William J Graham.
Southern (AL)	Pryor Field, Decatur, AL	P			E	Contract Primary, 10/5/41 to 12/28/44. Also referred to as Decatur. Southern Av. Training School. F. W. Hulse & Partners. 65th AAF FTD.
Southern (SC)	Woodward Field, Camden, SC	P			E	Contract Primary, 3/22/41 to 8/4/44. Also called Camden (SC). UK and US Cadets. Southern Av. Sch.. 64th AAF FTD. Frank W. Hulse & Ike F. Jones.
Spartan (Miami, OK)	Miami, OK	P		A	C	Contract School, 11/12/42 to 8/20/44. Also known as Miami #3BFTS (British Flight Taining School) started Tulsa, to Phoenix, to Miami. 322 AAF FTD.
Spartan (Musk. OK)	Spartan Field, Muskogee, OK	P			C	Contract Primary, 9/16/40 to 6/27/44. Also referred to as Muskogee and/or Spartan. Also called Hatbox Field.
Spartan (Tulsa, OK)	Tulsa Intl. Apt., Tulsa, OK	P			C	Contract Primary, 7/39 to12/44. Also referred to as Tulsa. Spartan School of Aeronautics. #3BFTS started here. Moved to Miami, OK. Capt. Maxwell W. Balfour.
Spence	Spence AAF, Moultrie, GA			A	E	AAF Advanced, 7/12/41 to 12/15/45. Also referred to as Moultrie. Spence AB 5/15/51. Conducted flying training until deactivated 3/31/61.
Stallings	Stallings AB, Kinston, NC					US Navy during WW II. Activated as Kinston Air Field 10/17/51. Stallings AB 6/28/53. Conducted contract flying training until 11/7/57.
Stamford	Arledge Field, Stamford, TX	P			C	Contract Primary, 4/1/41 to 9/8/44. Also known as Arledge. Lou Foote Flying Service.
Stead	Stead AFB, Reno, NV					Helicopter and Liaison flying training, 9/54 to 11/6/66. Also called Reno.
Stewart	Stewart AAF, Newburg, NY	P	B	A		All phases, 5/22/42 to 7/1/46. Primarily West Point cadets—but some few others.
Stockton	Stockton AAF, Stockton, CA		B	A	W	AAF Basic, 1/4/41 to 11/1/45. AAF Advanced. Classes 44-I, 44-J, 44-K and 45-A only.
Strother	Strother AAF, Winfield, KS		B		C	AAF Basic, 11/12/42 to 5/31/44. Also known as Winfield.
Stuttgart	Stuttgart AAF, Stuttgart, AR			A	E	AAF Advanced, 8/15/42 to 1/31/45.
Sumpter	Shaw AAF, Sumpter, SC		B		E	AAF Basic, 7/14/41 to 4/1/45. Also known as Shaw. Shaw AFB 1/13/48.

		P	B	A		
Sweetwater	Avenger Field, Sweetwater, TX	P			C	Also referred to as Avenger. #7BFTS started here. First class (43-W-1) of 32 WASP's began at Houston Mun. Arpt. (now Hobby) on 11/42. Then to Sweetwater on 4/43.
Taft	Gardner Field, Taft, CA		B		W	AAF Basic, 6/2/41 to J6/30/45. Also known as Gardner.
Terrell	Kaufman Apt., Terrell, TX	P		A	C	Contract School, 11/12/42 to 9/30/45. Terrell Aviation School. 321st AAF FTD. Maj. William E. Long. #1BFTS here from Love Field. Also called Kaufman.
Thunderbird I	Thunderbird I, Glendale, AZ	P			W	Contract Primary, 7/12/41 to 6/30/45. Also Known as Glendale and/or Phoenix. SW Airways, Inc. Hayward & Connelly. 6th AAF FTD.
Thunderbird II	Thunderbird II, Scottsdale, AZ	P			W	Contract Primary, 6/26/42 to 10/16/44. Also called Scottsdale and/or Phoenix. Southwest Airways, Inc. Hayward & Connelly. 9th AAF FTD.
Trenton	Trenton, Ontario					RCAF Flying Instructors School.
Tucson	Ryan Field, Tucson, AZ	P			W	Contract Primary, 6/25/42 to 9/44. Also known as Ryan. Classes 42-F - 44-E. T. Claude Ryan.
Tulare	Rankin Field, Tulare, CA	P			W	Contract Primary, 3/22/41 to 8/1/45. Also known as Rankin Air Academy. Tex Rankin & R. S. Norswing. Briefly at Tulsa International. Airport. 4th AAF FTD
Tulsa	Tulsa Int. Apt., Tulsa, OK	P			C	Contract Primary, 7/39 to 12/44 Also referred to as Spartan (Tul. OK). Spartan School of Aeronautics. #3BFTS started here. Moved to Miami, OK. Capt. Max W Balfour.
Turner	Turner AAF, Albany, GA			A	E	AAF Advanced, 8/12/40 to 8/15/46. Also known as Albany.
Tuscaloosa	Van De Graaff Fld., Tuscaloosa, AL	P			E	Contract Primary, 9/1/40 to 9/8/44. Also known as Van De Graaff. Alabama Institute of Aeronautics (Parks). US, British, French cadets. Classes 43-44.
Tuskegee	Tuskegee AAF, Tuskegee, AL	P	B	A	E	Experimental segregated all black school. Activated 8/23/41 to 12/31/45. All phases at this one base. Capt. Parish, AC. 66th AAF FTD. Perhaps once Moton Field.
Union City	Union City Apt., Union City, TN	P			E	Contract Primary, 7/5/42 to 4/15/44. Embry-Riddle.
Uvalde	Garner Field, Uvalde, TX	P			C	Contract Primary. Hang. 6, Inc. Latin Amer. Cadets. Some Amer. Now Garner. L/C J. N. Lapham & Clinton J.Thompson.
Valdosta	Valdosta, GA			A	E	AAF Advanced, 6/26/41 to 5/1/45. Moody AFB 1/13/48. Also called Moody. 2 engine AT-9 and AT-10.
Van De Graaff	Van De Graaff Field, Tuscaloosa, AL	P			E	Contract Primary, 9/1/40 to 9/8/44. Also known as Tuscaloosa. Alabama Inst. of Aero (Parks). US & British & French cadets. Classes 43-44.
Vance	Vance AFB, Enid, OK			A	C	AF Advanced, 9/20/41 to 1/31/47. Formerly Enid AAF Basic, Enid AFB, 8/1/48. Vance AFB 7/9/49.

Vernon	Victory Field, Vernon, TX	P		C	Contract Primary, 9/23/42 to 3/31/45. Col. Dan F. Hunter. Also Victory.
Vichy	Vichy, MO	P		C	Contract Primary. Ex 43-J Cadet reports flood at McBride, then Cadets to Vichy. 79th AAF FTD.
Victoria	Aloe AAF, Victoria, TX		A	C	AAF Advanced, 10/27/42 to 10/31/45. Also called Aloe. Aloe and Foster were both at Victoria..
Victoria	Foster AAF, Victoria, TX		A	C	AAF Advanced, 5/15/41 to 10/31/45. Also called Foster. Foster AFB 9/1/52. Foster and Aloe both Victoria..
Victorville	Victorville AAF, Victorville, CA		A	W	AAF Advanced, 6/26/41 to 11/1/45. Designated George AFB 8/4/50. This isn't George Fld. in Lawrenceville, IL.
Victory	Victory Field, Vernon, TX	P		C	Contract Primary, 9/23/42 to 3/31/45. Col. Dan F. Hunter. Also called Vernon.
Visalia	Sequoia Field, Visalia, CA	P		W	Contract Primary, 10/4/41 to 10/44. Also known as Sequoia. Randall M. Scott & J. L. O'Donnel & John B. Quin. 8th AAF FTD.
Waco	Waco AAF, Waco, TX	B		C	Waco AAF Basic, 9/16/41 to 12/15/45. Waco AFB 8/1/48. James Connally AFB 6/10/49. Also referred to as Connally.
Waco	Blackland AAF, Waco, TX		A	C	AAF Advanced, 7/2/42 to 2/4/45. Also known as Blackland. Became subpost to Waco AAF until deactivated Oct. 31, 1945.
Walnut Ridge	Walnut Ridge AAF, Walnut Ridge, AR	B		C	AAF Basic, 8/15/42 to 7/20/44. Transferred to Navy.
War Eagle	War Eagle AAF, Lancaster, CA	B		W	Contract Basic & Advanced, 7/2842 to 10/1/45. Also known as Lancaster & Polaris Flight Academy. #2BFTS and American Eagle Squadron and 43-44 Basic classes.
Webb	Webb AFB, Big Spring, TX		A	C	Activated as Big Spring AAF 6/26/42 to 11/33/45. Activated as Webb AFB 5/18/52. Deactivate 9/30/77. Basic Training US Air Force pilots.
Wickenburg	Echeverra Fld., Wickenburg, AZ	P		W	Contract Primary, 6/3/4242 to 4/19/44. Also known as Echeverra. Harry C. Clairborne & William R. Kent. Glider program 6/42 to 2/43. Cadets 3/43 to 4/44.
Williams	Williams AAF, Chandler, AZ		A	W	AAF Advanced, Mesa Military Arpt. 6/19/41. Higley Field 10/41. Williams AAF 2/24/42. Williams AFB 1/13/48. Also known as Chandler.
Williams	Williams AFB, Chandler, AZ	B			Designated Williams AFB 1/13/48. Basic training for US Air Force pilots. T-38's in 62-B. Also known as Chandler. See Mesa/Williams.
Windsor Mills	Windsor Mills			X	RCAF
Winfield	Strother AAF, Winfield, KS	B		C	AAF Basic, 11/12/42 to 4/31/44. Also known as Strother.

Winter Haven	Winter Haven Field, Winter Haven, FL	P			Primary training for US Air Force pilots 5/1/51 to 5/19/61. T-34, T-28, and T-37 in 61B. Also known as Bartow.
Woodward	Woodward Field, Camden, SC	P		E	Contract Primary, 3/22/41 to 7/4/44. British & American. Southern Aviation School. 64th AAF FTD.
Yukon	Cimarron Field, Yukon, OK	P		C	Contract Primary, 4/1/41 to 6/27/44. Oklahoma Air College. Clarence Page & Ted Colbert. Some cadets say Cimarron. Also referred to as Oklahoma City.
Yuma	Yuma AAF, Yuma, AZ		A	W	AAF Advanced, 12/15/42 to 11/1/45. Flying training, flexible gunnery, and radar observer training for last few months, until deactivated 11/1/45.

ARMY AIR SERVICE. TWO PLACE PURSUIT and OBSERVATION AIRPLANES

DH-4B OBSERVATION

LE PERE PURSUIT EQUIPPED WITH SUPERCHARGER. Holder of World's Altitude Record of 34 509.5 ft.

National Archives

LOENING PURSUIT

ENG. DIV. XB-IA OBSERVATION

245

Norghrop XB-49 and
the Boeing B-47.
National Archives

Northrop XP-79
National Archives

North American P-82
National Archives

Chapter 4
As They Saw It

In the beginning there was wonder. As man gazed skyward, he was amazed by the many flying creatures that God had created. If only he could accomplish this great feat. If only man could fly....

Primary Flight Training by: William H. Hawkins, primary flight instructor, WWII.

To teach a student to fly, he must first be put at ease around airplanes. How? By showing respect for the airplane—and especially for the propeller. Point out all the parts, such as the wings. Explain the leading edge and trailing edge. Explain lift and the part played by the wing. Explain both positive and negative lift. Explain the ailerons, and what they do. Talk about the fuselage, the cockpits, the instruments and controls. Examine the safety belts and show the student how they should be fastened. Explain their importance. Explain the tail structure, the parts, and their purpose. Show and touch the vertical stabilizer and rudder. Explain the trim tabs and their purpose. Explain torque and how it affects the control surfaces. Explain the elevators and the individual parts. Show the student the tail wheel and emphasize its importance when taxiing. Show the student how to get into the airplane, and help him get seated properly. See that the safety belt is fastened and adjusted properly, and the seat adjusted so the student's feet rest comfortably on the rudder pedals. Show the student how to adjust his feet to use the brakes. Explain the use of the stick (or steering yoke or wheel). Explain pressure on the stick and its importance while flying. (Forget movement). Explain the effects of the controls, throttle, etc.

1st Day: The student is now ready for his first ride. Explain the importance of proper taxiing, the importance of looking around for other airplanes, and other hazards. Demonstrate how to use the rudder pedals to "S" turn the airplane on the ground.

Show the student how to check the magnetos, and explain the importance of doing this prior to takeoff.

The student lightly follows through on the controls. Taxi out on the runway, head into the wind, slowly advance your throttle to maximum power as the airplane rolls forward and gains speed. Use the necessary pressure on the controls to keep the airplane in the center of the runway, and as it lifts off, retard the throttle about 1/3 to climbing RPMs. Check your track over the ground to check drift. Check instruments and angle of attack. Turn out of the pattern and continue your climb to the desired altitude for the first day's maneuvers (about 2,000 feet AGL). The first maneuver is to fly straight and level. After showing the student the effects of the controls, allow him to pick out a point on the horizon and fly to it. Correct the altitude of the airplane with hand signals, such as; level your wings, nose up, watch your altimeter, correct for torque, watch your heading, relax, etc.

The next maneuver is to make some simple turns—90-degrees, 180-degrees, etc. Show the effects of the controls. Have the student follow you, the instructor, through several turns. Then let him try a 90-degree turn. Explain the importance of slight back pressure while in the turn. The release of back pressure when rolling out is important. Check your altimeter to see that you have held your altitude. When the 90-degree turn is perfected, advance to 180-degree turns and 360-degree turns. By this time the student should be tired. Take over and fly the airplane back to the airport, allowing him to follow through. Upon parking, help the student out of the airplane. Allow him to ask any questions he might have. Answer him, but don't over-teach. Save something for the next ride.

2nd Day: While on the ground, explain "S" turns across a road (or straight line marked on the ground). Also tell him we are going to practice straight and level flying, plus turns. See that the student is properly seated in the airplane and his safety belt fastened. Have the student follow through as you taxi to the takeoff position. Check the mags. See that all is clear before takeoff. Turn out of traffic and turn the airplane over to the student to climb to 2,000 ft. Have the student level off and adjust the throttle to cruising RPMs. Have the student fly straight and level. Have the student practice turns. Point out his discrepancies, such as anticipating roll-out, back pressure on the stick to maintain a level turn, proper use of rudder on entering and rolling out of a turn, etc. When level turns have been perfected, demonstrate gliding turns (throttle off) to lower altitude. When reaching 500 ft., select a straight road over some level ground and demonstrate "S" turns. Let the student try some. Remind him to divide his attention between the track over the ground; altitude, turns, other aircraft, etc. After a short practice, have the student do climbing turns to 1,000 feet. Level the airplane and fly straight and level towards the airport. Upon nearing the airport, take over the airplane and demonstrate entering traffic at 500 ft. Fly the pattern. Close the throttle and glide down. By means of a gliding turn and a straight glide, line the airplane up with the runway, and land the airplane. Keep the airplane straight on the runway by use of the rudder pedals. Taxi to the parking area. Park the airplane. Cut off the engine and exit the airplane.

Answer the student's questions. Tell him the next ride will introduce him to power-on and power-off stalls. Do not over-teach. Review what the student has learned, and explain the third day maneuvers. Advise him about eating so that he will not become sick in the airplane. And if he does, he has to wash the airplane. Ha!

3rd Day: While on the ground, explain power-on and power-off stalls. Answer all his questions about the first two flights. Review techniques and procedures.

Go to the airplane. Have the student do a visual inspection of the aircraft and check the control surfaces. Have the student climb into the cockpit, seat himself, and prepare for the flight. The instructor checks the student's seating and proper fastening of the safety belt. The instructor seats himself and allows the student to taxi out of the parking area towards the end of the airport for takeoff. As the student nears the end of the runway, tell him to apply his brakes slowly and very carefully to bring the airplane to a stop. Have him check the magnetos (Brakes on, stick back). Remember, he is taxiing downwind, and if he applies his brakes too hard, the wind could get under the tail surface and stand the airplane on its nose! After checking the magnetos, the instructor takes over and checks landing traffic. If all is clear, he taxis onto the runway for takeoff. Have the student check the attitude of the airplane as it sits on the runway. The horizon, and altitude of the nose is important.

The instructor takes off by advancing the throttle slowly, and beginning his roll along the runway—then advancing his throttle to wide open. As the airplane gains speed over the ground, exert a slight back pressure on the stick for takeoff. When the airplane is airborne, assume a climbing attitude, and retard the throttle to the climbing position (2/3 open). Check the track over the ground (drift). Climb straight out to 300 ft. Level off and make a 90-degree level turn to the left. (Check drift). Resume the climb to 500 feet. Level off and make a 45-degree turn out of traffic and continue the climb to 2,000 ft. Level off and practice straight and level flight; 90-degree, 180-degree, and 360-degree turns. Pick out a straight road and have the student glide down to 500 ft. and practice "S" turns across the road. If the student is proficient, have him climb back to 3,000 ft. At this altitude, check for other aircraft around and underneath by doing "S" turns.

The instructor takes over, flies straight and level, with the throttle at cruising altitude. The first demonstration is a power stall. Use back pressure on the stick, pulling the nose up about 45-degrees until the airspeed drops, and the airplane stalls and the nose drops down. (Keep it straight with the rudder pedals). Advance the throttle and resume cruising speed. Check your altitude and climb back to 3,000 ft.

Now it is the student's turn to stall the airplane. Have him assume the stall angle of attack, (45-degrees nose high) hold the airplane in that attitude until the nose drops. Recover and assume level flight. Now for power-off stalls. Close the throttle and assume a normal glide. First demonstrate a 45-degree stall. When the nose drops, advance the throttle and assume straight and level flight. The next stall will be a 15-degree stall, or one similar to the attitude of the airplane on the ground. Check for other aircraft. Assume glide, gradually break the glide and pull the nose up to the ground attitude. When the airplane stalls, advance the throttle, and assume level flight. Allow the student to do several of these stalls.

By now the student will be tired, the instructor takes over and flies the airplane back to the airport. He enters the traffic pattern, lines the airplane up with the runway, and demonstrates how the power-off stall is used in landing the airplane. The instructor allows the student to taxi to the parking area. After parking the airplane, the engine is cut off and they exit the airplane. The instructor compliments the student for a good flight and answers questions. He explains airspeed, ground speed, drift, tailwind, etc.

4th Day: Tell the student that today we are going to review what he has learned, and practice take-offs and landings. The instructor answers the students questions about flying the airplane. The instructor goes over the procedures and techniques of takeoffs and landings. He explains the traffic patterns.

After the student is seated in the airplane properly, and has been OK'd by the instructor, the student taxies out for takeoff. He goes through all the

procedures of proper taxiing, throttle control, "S" turns, checking magnetos, proper entry onto the runway, lining the airplane straight on the runway, and following takeoff instructions. First he advances the throttle slowly, starting the takeoff roll, continuing, , he advances the throttle wide open to gain flying speed. The tail will rise off the ground. Keep the airplane level until the airplane gains flying speed. The student applies a slight back pressure on the stick, and the airplane leaves the ground. The airplane assumes the climbing attitude. The student retards the throttle to the climbing position. He checks his track over the ground. He corrects for drift with his rudder, nosing the aircraft into the wind just enough to keep his track straight.

The student reviews his instructions from previous flights. He makes a level turn at 300 ft., climbs to 500 ft. while making level or climbing 45-degree turns out of traffic. He continues to climb to 3,000 ft. to practice stalls. The instructor demonstrates 45-degree power-on stalls, 45-degree power-off stalls, and landing attitude stalls. When they have been perfected, they practice gliding turns back to the airport and enter the airport traffic pattern at 500 ft. resuming straight and level flight on the downwind leg of the traffic pattern. Check instruments. When the airplanes wing is lined up with the end of the airport runway, make a level 90-degree turn (checking for drift) and fly along the base leg of the pattern until you are 45-degrees from the position on the runway that you want to land on. Close the throttle and lower the nose into a straight glide. Make a gliding turn lining up with the center of the runway. Continue the straight glide until the airplane is about 20 ft. off the ground. Break the glide, and as the airplane slows and settles down, assume the power-off landing stall. As the airplane loses flying speed, it stalls out and makes a 3-point landing on the runway. Taxi back to the end of the runway and have the student follow all takeoff procedures. Have him check traffic, proceed to the end of the runway, and takeoff again coming right back for a second landing.

The student climbs to 300 ft., makes a level 90-degree turn, and checks for drift. He then climbs to 500 ft. and makes a 90-degree turn onto the down wind leg. He flies straight and level to the end of the runway. Then he makes a 90-degree turn onto the base leg of the traffic pattern at 45-degrees to his desired landing spot. The student throttles back and the airplane assumes a glide. He makes a gliding turn lining up with the runway, and at about 20 ft. off the runway, he begins to level the airplane off and land the as instructed. If he makes a good landing and controls the aircraft properly in its landing roll, he is congratulated, and told to taxi down for another takeoff, and fly around the pattern one more time. After the third landing, he is told to taxi back to the parking area, park the airplane, cut the engine, and relax.

After the flight, if he has questions, the instructor answers them, and congratulates the student. The instructor goes over the day's flight with the student.

5th Day: At all times while flying, the student must keep in mind what he would do in case of an engine failure. He must constantly check his path over the ground for possible landing sites in case of an emergency. He must keep track of the wind direction. This is done by observing the wind lines over water, smoke on the ground, smoke out of smoke stacks, wind blowing through the trees, and other indications. The first thing a student does in the case of an emergency, or a simulated forced landing, is lower the nose of the airplane, and establish a glide. He looks around below for a possible emergency landing site, and maneuvers the airplane by means of glides and gliding turns, down to a safe approach to the site selected. If the student's performance is acceptable, the instructor gives the student an OK signal. He advances the throttle, or has the student advance the throttle, and climbs back to the cruising altitude. These simulated forced landings should be practiced during every flight in the future.

6th Day: This is a day for relaxation and fun

flying. The student seats himself in the airplane. The instructor checks his seating. The student taxies to the end of the runway. He checks his Magnetos. At this time, if the instructor has any advice, he informs the student and gives him instructions to takeoff, turn out of traffic, climb to 2,000 ft., and fly straight and level.

The student is to pick out a road, glide down to 500 ft., and do some "S" turns across the road. After 10 to 15 minutes of "S" turns, the student is told to climb to 3,000 feet. The instructor will demonstrate a spin. First he checks for other aircraft, then he pulls the nose up to 45-degrees in a power-off stall. Third, as the airplane stalls, he kicks full left rudder. The stick is all the way back. As the airplane falls into the spin, he looks ahead of the spin to begin his recovery. At 90-degrees from the direction he wants to pull out of the spin, he kicks full right rudder. As the airplane begins to cease rotation, he eases the stick forward nosing down on the recovery point. He neutralizes the rudder, pulls the nose up, advances the throttle, and climbs back up to 3,000 ft. He then turns the airplane over to the student. The student follows the procedure as demonstrated by the instructor. If the student enters and recovers from the spin properly, he is congratulated. He then climbs back to 3,000 ft. and does another spin. After the second spin by the student, he climbs back to 3,000 ft. and practices his power-off landing stall. Then he glides down to 1,500 ft., flies back to the airport, enters the traffic pattern at 500 ft., and proceeds to land. After landing, he advances his throttle wide open to make a running takeoff. He climbs the airplane to 300 ft., makes a level left turn, climbs to 500 ft., makes another level left turn on the downwind leg. He then flies the pattern, turning onto the base leg, and lands the airplane as instructed. The student taxis to the parking area, parks the airplane, cuts off the engine, sets the brakes, and climbs out of the airplane. This is a good time for questions and answers, and general review of the student's flight progress. He is to be encouraged and praised for his progress, and for giving the instructor a good flight.

7th Day: The student should be getting used to checking the airplane, seating himself properly, and fastening his safety belt. The instructor checks his safety belt. Then the student taxis out for takeoff. He goes through the routine of proper taxiing, checking his magnetos, and preparing for takeoff.

If the instructor approves, the student is then told to taxi onto the runway and takeoff. He is also told to turn out of traffic and do some "S" turns across a road. After 10-15 minutes of "S" turns, he is told to go back to the field, enter traffic, and land the airplane. The student then goes back for a second takeoff. He flies the pattern and again lands the airplane. If this is a good landing, the instructor tells him to make a running takeoff for a third flight around the pattern, and to make a third good landing. If the student flies three good takeoffs, flies a good pattern, checks for drift, thinks ahead of the airplane, and makes a good landing, he is showing good progress.

This is a good time after the student parks the airplane and cuts off the engine, to answer questions and talk flying. Tell the student he is almost ready to solo. Check the student's number of hours of flight time. He should have close to 8 hours.

8th Day: The instructor should be thinking about soloing the student. He should ask the student to taxi out for takeoff. If his progress is acceptable, have the student takeoff and fly around the pattern and land the airplane. After landing, the student taxis back for a second takeoff and landing. If after completing the same procedure for a third time, all three landings are acceptable, have the student park the airplane for a briefing.

The instructor gets out of the airplane and secures his safety belt. He tells the student he will have to adjust his trim tabs to compensate for the loss of the instructor's weight. He tells the student to taxi out for takeoff, fly around the pattern, make a good three— point landing, and then taxi back to where the instructor is waiting. If the solo flight is good, the instructor congratulates him and has him

make two more solo flights. The student parks the airplane and celebrates.

9th Day: By this time the student should be at ease in the airplane. He should be competent in taxiing, checking his mags, and preparing for takeoff. He is instructed to takeoff and climb to 3,000 ft. At 3,000 feet, he flies straight and level and practices 90-degree, 180-degree and 360-degree turns. He is also told to do a power stall and a power-off stall. If these are satisfactory, he is told to do a two-turn spin. If his spin is satisfactory, he is then told to go back to the field, enter traffic and land the airplane. He then makes a running takeoff and flies around the pattern. He makes a second landing and another running takeoff and flies around for a third landing. If all three landings are good and his flying technique is acceptable, he is told to taxi to the parking area.

The instructor gets out of the airplane, and allows him to make his second solo flight around the field. He should check with his instructor after each landing. After the third takeoff and landing, he parks the airplane, cuts the engine, and exits. He asks any questions he has on his mind. He is congratulated by the instructor.

10th Day: This is the day the student will be taught a new maneuver—pylon eights. The student seats himself in the airplane. He checks to see if the seat is properly adjusted and his safety belt is properly fastened and tightened. He then taxis out with his instructor who tells him to follow all the procedures, and to takeoff, turn out of traffic, and climb to 1,000 ft. After he levels off, the instructor takes over. The instructor picks out two points or objects on the ground, so that a straight line between them is 90-degrees to the wind direction. The instructor glides down to 600 ft. and resumes cruising speed. He approaches one of the points (or objects) and banks the airplane so that the wing tip points at the object or point. He pivots around the point. He rolls out of the turn and flies toward the second point. When the other wing approaches the second point, he enters a bank and allows the plane to pivot around.

He again rolls out and flies toward the first point, and continues the turns with level flight between the objects. The student takes over and assumes the flight around the pylons. If he is proficient, he is congratulated.

After the pylon eight maneuver, the student is told to go back to the airport and make three landings. He can make running takeoffs. After three acceptable landings, he is allowed to fly solo around the field, taxi back to the instructor, for critique, and make two more takeoffs and landings. If they are acceptable, the instructor gets back into the airplane. The student taxis to the parking area, parks the airplane, and cuts the engine off. The instructor goes over the day's flight with the student. He reviews his progress. If it is satisfactory, the student is told he will be able to take the airplane up by himself to practice maneuvers.

11th Day: The student is allowed his first solo flight away from the home field. He is instructed to takeoff and climb to 3,000 ft. He is to practice straight and level flight, power turns of 90-degrees, 180-degrees, and 360-degrees. He is told to practice power-off stalls, then drop down to 500 ft. and practice "S" turns across a road. After one hour, he is to return to the airport and report to his instructor, how he made out. He has been looking forward to this day. He should be happy.

12th Day: Today the student will learn about Crosswind takeoffs and landings. The instructor again rides with the student and checks his proficiency, as he performs the maneuvers and techniques he has been taught. If they are satisfactory, he then demonstrates a crosswind landing. The instructor selects a runway 45-degrees to 90-degrees to the wind direction. How is the wind direction determined? It is determined by checking the wind sock on the airport, wind streaks over a body of water, smoke from a smoke stack or fire, and the way trees look when the wind blows, etc.

After the runway is selected and the airplane has been lined up with the airport runway, drift is corrected by lowering a wing into the wind, and holding the nose straight by means of applying pressure on the opposite rudder. This glide will be faster and the student will have to compensate. As he approaches landing, at the last moment, he levels his wings and releases opposite pressures on the rudders. The airplane lands and rolls to a stop. The student taxis to the end of the runway for takeoff. He flies around the pattern, and following the demonstration, lands the airplane. He should make three landings.

13th Day: Today the student will learn how to do Wheel landings. The student takes off and flies the pattern. The instructor takes over on the downwind leg, and sets the base leg farther back from the end of the runway. He closes the throttle, and as the airplane loses altitude, he cracks the throttle to land on a selected spot on the runway. As the airplane settles down, and the wheels touch, the pressure on the stick is held slightly forward in order to hold the airplane on the ground. The fuselage is in the level flight position. As the throttle is closed the landing roll slows, and the tail will settle onto the runway.

After the demonstration, the student takes over, taxis back to the end of the runway, takes off, flies the pattern, and follows the procedure. If his technique is satisfactory, he should make at least 3 wheel landings. The purpose of wheel landings are to clear long runways quicker, and to teach throttle coordination, and control of the airplane.

This completes the first part of primary flight training. The student is now ready for more advanced maneuvers, such as dragging the airplane in to clear the end of the field, slips, etc.

It is very difficult to write down exactly how to fly an airplane. It's even harder to read how to do it and then attempt to fly it. The preceding is however, a good representation of the method that was used by most of the instructors in the early days of flying.

BREEZY WIND

One particularly interesting true story of the

very early days took place during 1932 at Kelly Field. It was told to the author by Jay Gentry, second class at Randolph, several months before he died.

Kelly field in 1932 consisted of new barracks, and large fields on the east and west sides, that were used as runways. However in its day it was a hubbub of activity, training the scores of aviation Cadets to be pilots, and officers, of the Army Air Corps. The A-3 Falcon was the advanced training aircraft in use at that time at Kelly. It was a bright cloudless day, with aircraft buzzing around everywhere. Suddenly one of the migrant workers, working in a cabbage field bordering the airfield, pointed to the sky and excitedly yelled something in Spanish! The other workers got the message. They ran in all directions, falling over their tools, tripping on the cabbage heads, doing anything to get away from that area. Suddenly there it was, an aircraft heading directly toward the cabbage patch, trailing a long plume of white smoke. Over at Kelly the crash crews had been alerted. Sirens wailing, horns blowing, engines roaring, here came the fire truck, followed by the "meat wagon" both in a huge cloud of dust. The disabled aircraft made a fine, "3 points fer 'em all" landing; bouncing along among the cabbages, it quickly came to a halt. A short time later, as the entourage from Kelly arrived, they saw that the cowling of the aircraft had been removed, and the fire appeared to be out. Running up to the stalwart Cadet, the fire chief asked if he was all right. "Yes Sir" was the reply. The chief reached into his shirt pocket, took out a pencil and paper and asked the Cadet his name, "Breezy Wind, Sir," was the reply. (No kidding that was really his name). "Come on son, let's get you to the hospital and see if you're really OK."

Curtiss A-3 Falcon   National Archives

After a brief visit with the flight surgeon, Breezy was notified that the base commander wanted to see him immediately. Uh oh! Breezy arrived at the commanders office somewhat out of breath from the long run from sick bay. He was quickly ushered into Colonel Clagget's office. Inside were the Commander, the chief instructor and a woman stenographer. The colonel congratulated him on making such a fine landing, and was quite happy he had not damaged the aircraft. Then he said, "Mr. Wind, since you didn't have a fire extinguisher, how on earth did you put the fire out?" His face turning red from embarrassment, he glanced at the stenographer, and replied, "Excuse me ma'am, but, well Sir, I pissed on it." The commander, quite taken back by this explanation, could only reply, "Well son, It's a good thing you had a full tank."

MY DIARY AND RECORD OF FLIGHT

To have an actual account of flight training on a day by day bases is a very rare thing. Most of us were two busy keeping up with the program to keep any personal records. But thankfully there are a few of us, who did. Robert F. Schirmer (class 40-A) was one of those who recognized the historical sig-

253

nificance of maintaining a daily diary of Cadet flight training. The following is his **Record Of Flying:**

Friday June 2, 1939: 5:00-5:30 p.m. Made one fairly good takeoff and four poor ones. Still like to land. Gosh—that sinking—settling feeling—boy. Think I'll lay off a day and see if I can settle down.

Saturday June 3, 1939: Tail Skid broken—no flying.

Sunday June 4, 1939: 12:15-12:45 p.m. Took off beautifully—and also made better landing. Made best takeoff I ever made. Landing fast—had to slide slip to lose extra altitude. Wind from NE—for a change. Made several rotten takeoffs and a couple of fair landings.

Monday June 5, 1939: No flying—Tail Skid broken.

Tuesday June 6, 1939: Little wind—took off not bad—but still not so good yet. Circled and landed pretty fair. Made one more takeoff and landing, and on last landing, leveled off about ten feet too high. Next takeoff was better. But on the next landing after actually landed and taxiing—broke bolt holding tail wheel and had to leave plane, and found wheel after about a ten minute hunt, assisted by Harry Britten and others at airport. Took off from directly in front of hangars and circled and landed again. Still not so good but enjoyed side slipping. Am being taught to land faster than usual to get use to my higher speed landings. Next takeoff was better—in fact best yet—due to a lot of coaching from Elden. Came in and landed pretty well. Felt fine—love to fly.

Thursday June 8, 1939: Went out to airport—met Elden—opened hangar doors and added oil—rolled Aeronca out and started it—warmed up for 5 minutes. Elden announced he was going to give me stalls and vertical banks. Boy did I take it calmly—If I had only known what was coming. Took off nicely into stiff west wind about 15-20 mph. Climbed into sunset sky to about 2,100 feet. Then after turning east again, Elden gave me my first experience with stalls—with engine throttled. Cut engine—pull back on stick and wait til nose is stuck

in sky. When flying speed was lost and nose dropped, ailerons had "useless feel" and didn't take effect until nose had dropped enough to regain flying speed. If left wing dropped, right rudder was applied to straighten out and vice versa—otherwise had start of spin. Practiced several of these—my stomach jumping almost out of my mouth—since we lost about 200 feet with each stall. Then Elden showed me a real thrill—a whip stall where with full throttle pulling back on stick, sticking nose straight up in air, and then waiting for nose to drop all of a sudden—and I do mean sudden—and feeling the snap or whip when the nose went down and there we were, straining against the safety belt and looking out through the windshield at the earth directly below. Gosh, did my stomach do loops trying to keep up with my body. No wonder a test pilot gets big money. When we had tried about three of these, I practiced a few more ordinary stalls but by that time I was feeling pretty shaky, rather airsick and my body was perspiring and the cold breeze from the window that didn't help any. Then we did some vertical banks, where after dipping a wing (with full throttle) the rudder became elevator—elevator became rudder, and the ailerons merely served to keep plane in vertical plane. Well, what the snap stalls didn't do, the vertical banks did—boy was I dizzy. My stomach actually groaned (I believe under that punishment) but I swallowed hard and grit my teeth and tried to look halfway happy—but what a battle. After practicing following through a few more vertical banks in both directions, we headed back towards field and did some more side stepping from 1,500 feet to 900. I learned how much aileron to apply to get various amounts of angle and drop speed in the slip. Then we climbed to 1,000 feet again and made a 360-degree turn, sight field, with throttle cut and fighting a crosswind. At about 200 feet, Elden side slipped—it seemed almost into the ground, but at fifty feet we leveled off, and I made a perfect landing—at any rate Elden said I'd never made a better one than that. So to the hangar—what a lesson—what an instructor—what an occupation. I think they are all grand.

P.S. Spent a wobbly two minutes getting back to the student lounge and getting a drink of water and then a half hour relaxing in the studio couch—boy what a day! No more flying until after the Air Force.

Tuesday June 13, 1939: Went up and began practicing takeoffs and landings. Made pretty good approach but bumpy landing. Next time took off pretty good and then made better landing but poorer takeoff—started over controlling rudder and trying to get off too quick. On next landing tried to pull nose up too quickly and didn't wait long enough for that sinking feeling. Am going to get more rest so am better tomorrow.

Wednesday June 14, 1939: This being my birthday (am 26). Made takeoff and circled and landed pretty well. Took off again and then made attempt to land but was too high—so circled and landed pretty well. Took off and climbed to 800 feet. Came back over field, cut gun at 800 and circled and landed OK—took off again and hit old bumpy stump and careened into air but circled and landed across wind at Miller's request and taxied onto hangar ramp.

Thursday June 15, 1939: 5:00-5:30—Helped gas and oil plane. Started and taxied to end of field-wind from southwest. Took off well and circled—came in OK. Took off again—not bad and came in better. Took off better and came in slightly high—side slipped and came in OK. In fact, all my landings and takeoffs were pretty good and I had pretty good luck with my turns, even in a 15 or 20 mile SW wind. No skidding or slipping in turns. Feel pretty good about it all right.

Friday June 16, 1939: 6:00-6:30—Helped roll plane out with Elwood Jensen who is just starting. Made the best takeoffs and landings in my entire career as a "dodo"—that bird without wings. Am going to get solo permit tomorrow from Anginger. Took exam from 4-5 today but need affidavit and two pictures to corroborate. Think I'll be in shape to solo next time.

Saturday June 17, 1939: Couldn't get out to airport today—had too much shopping to do and car was at Potts Body Works getting all dings out of fenders. Got solo permit at 3:30 from Anginger.

Sunday June 18, 1939: No flying—not good enough weather for even parachute jump. Large crowd at field.

Tuesday June 20, 1939: Made several good and pretty good takeoffs and landings, but could notice effect of not flying for several (four) days. Better tomorrow.

Wednesday June 21, 1939: Made a good takeoff but poor landing. After several good landings and a couple of fair takeoffs, called it a day. Still no solo.

Saturday June 24, 1939: Called airport for Elden—went after Jim Kauffman and took him with me to airport to watch my flying lesson. Took off very well. Had good control of plane at all times. Felt good and calm—nerves in fine shape. Made perfect landing, another perfect takeoff and then another fine landing; suddenly Elden turned to me and asked, "Think you can handle her now?" "Sure," I said. So then he said, " Well, taxi her back to the starting place and I'll get out." He then went on to explain that ship would be a lot lighter and easier to takeoff but harder to land since the weight of his body had been eliminated. Then he got out of the plane—I sat there feeling not a bit excited—trying to remember all those final instructions and not caring particularly about anything at the moment.

Then I "gunned" her up and we took off—the plane and I— on my first solo hop. Good easy take-off—circled—while circling felt no particular desire to yell. I believe the thought of that first solo landing kept me busy—so busy I almost forgot about being alone. Came in OK. The wind was a bit rough but handled her okay and made a nice 3-point, soft landing. I began to feel better—more confident and really enjoyed next takeoff—solo again—after seeing Elden nod okay after that first solo hop. Made another circle and than another landing, although wind tried to play tricks with my left wing, but made it okay. Started to taxi in but saw Elden looking at his watch and motioning me to take one more hop, so I turned, taxied and took off. Got more thrill this time and made larger circle to come into field so I could enjoy being alone up there with that engine purring along. Updrafts kept lifting me, so soon I had 650 feet and had to throttle engine and nose down. Afraid to try a bonafide side slip but had to side slip a little to come into landing after it became apparent that I was approaching about 50 feet too high. Made another good landing and taxied over to hangar. Had Elden make out my solo license, and later that afternoon, along with books, magazines, and picture, went to airport and also passed around a box of San Felice cigars in celebration of my solo.

Will leave for Army Monday so my commercial days are over for a while.

Sunday June 25, 1939: Went out to airport and took short hop with Elden. Took off nicely at about 5:15 p.m. and it was just getting dark. Watched airline beacons flashing—could see beams at West Jefferson and South Vienna and also down West near Infirmary.

Someone wrecked the Aeronca today—boys feel pretty tough about it. Tomorrow will see me at Fort Hayes at 8:00 a.m.

Begin Primary -Monday June 26, 1939: Arrived at Ft. Hayes, Columbus, Ohio at 7:45. Dad drove me over. Met George Prentice who had also taken exam at Wright Field. There were eight other candidates present who had to take another physical exam. One candidate had an eye defect and was sent home. Dad left about 4:00 p.m. Rest of us took our oaths and laid around all day until 4:30 waiting for our maintenance pay which amounted to $1.00. But we are to receive three cents per mile for driving. Started out and made Springfield by 5:15—ate supper, cleaned up a bit and then were on our way. Made our night stay at a tourist camp eight miles east of Indianapolis, Indiana. Took shower and wrote a few letters and then to bed.

Tuesday June 27, 1939: Got up at 6:00 a.m.

and were on our way. Drove 430 miles today.

Wednesday June 28, 1939: Visited Municipal Airport—didn't learn much. Arrived at Lincoln, Nebraska at 1:30 p.m. Went up on top of Capitol Building Tower. Registered in at Cornhusker Hotel—$5.00 got an air-conditioned room—even had to use a blanket. Boy were we tired. Drove 320 miles today.

Thursday June 29, 1939: Reported in at Union Airport to Lt. Wright, our flight commander. Still living at the YMCA. Visited Union Airport. Got first glimpse of our Stearmans—PT 13 A's. Sure looked good.

Friday June 30, 1939: Lined up and were assigned by size to different instructors. Our instructor is Captain W.J. Chapman, Air Corps Reserve (Civilian). He immediately called us "Blowers"—being short and had us roll out a plane, and spent the morning showing us how to start and stop the engine properly. Had our first class instruction in math. Got our first shot in arm for Typhoid and inoculation for Smallpox.

Saturday July 1, 1939: Received our first instruction in taxiing—were not allowed to use wheel brakes yet. Moved over to new Frat house. Had class in parachutes—how to use rip cord, how packing is done, etc—from Mr. Hazelrigg the ground school instructor. Finished moving in our new house.

Monday July 3, 1939: Today we had our first flight—our group consisted of: Flying Cadet Caven, Mt. Washington, Ohio, Flying Cadet Jordan, Huntington, West Virginia, Flying Cadet Schirmer, Springfield, Ohio, Flying Cadet Strauss, Evansville, Indiana, and Flying Cadet Westcott, Washington, D.C.

Checked out our flying helmets and goggles. Taxied out to runway, took off and climbed to 2,500 feet. Practiced banks—gentle and medium.

Tuesday July 4, 1939: No flying today. Went swimming in salt water at Capital Beach.

Wednesday July 5, 1939: Had pretty good lesson in climbing turns but need lots of practice coordinating the controls.

Thursday July 6, 1939: Made a rotten showing—no coordination. Slips in banks—poor visibility.

Friday July 7, 1939: Captain Chapman allowed us to do anything we wanted to for first fifteen minutes. Tried a few side slips and other banks and maneuvers. Had first spin today in PT-13A. Just held on and looked around—not so bad. Got second shot in arm for typhoid. Smallpox scar showed me to be immune.

Saturday July 8, 1939: Felt pretty rotten due to typhoid shot. Made a pretty terrible exhibition of how not to fly—no coordination. Had second spin today. Went to bed right after lunch and slept until 5:30.

Sunday July 9, 1939: Recuperated from typhoid shot. Frat brothers Carl Olenberger, Grant ???, came over to see us and we went out pledge rushing.

Monday July 10, 1939: Had a good day. Made good maneuvers and good stalls—made eight out of ten of them—then Captain Chapman had me go into a spin at 3,500 feet. Made a wrong move while pulling out of a spin. I had just kicked left rudder to stop spin, and the plane was nosed down straight at ground, and I shoved stick forward and boy we started to do an outside loop— I yanked back on the stick plenty fast. I noticed that Captain Chapman's shoulders were thrown above the cockpit—not so good—tried another spin and got it okay.

Tuesday July 11, 1939: Made first takeoff by myself and tried to fly a rectangular course around field. The other planes bothered me. I either looked too much for planes and didn't pay enough attention to flying wing low, nose up and down, etc., or I flew the ship and forgot to take time to look for other planes. I did make a good takeoff. Captain said so at least, and a good landing. But the rectangular course was a toughie to get on to.

Wednesday July 12, 1939: Flew a few minutes today (fourteen minutes). Hardly enough to do any good. Up and around rectangular course once

and one landing and taxi back to line.

Thursday July 13, 1939: Got 25 minutes instruction. Had only enough time to do a few landings and about four turns about rectangular course.

Friday July 14, 1939: Got third and last shot in arm. Finally got in a long lesson today. Not bad but too poor on coordination and not looking enough. Made first S turns over road and a couple of landings.

Saturday July 15, 1939: Drilled two hours in a hot sun—105-degrees. Felt pretty poor all day.

Sunday July 16, 1939: Felt tough all day due to shot in arm and upset stomach.

Monday July 17, 1939: Made flight with Captain Chapman. Had trouble keeping throttle and tach together properly. Made first two chandelles. 57 minutes.

Gave ten cc blood from right arm for Wasserman Test.

Had check flight with Lt. Ford. Poor throttle use, too low, banks too steep, S-turns (medium) not 180-degrees couldn't hold altitude, gliding angle too steep, climbing turns too steep with banks too steep, landings poor, coordination poor. 49 minutes.

Tuesday July 18, 1939: Foggy all morning. Had classes in Maps & Math. Saw Army transport DC-V. Was standing around waiting for my turn, when Mr. Wittenbeck called me over and asked me to go flying with him. Got me Lt. Ford's personal parachute—took off and had a swell time. Mr. Wittenbeck was first instructor since I've been here who actually talked to me in such a pleasant manner that I was always trying to do my best for him.

Did banks, stalls, glides, S-turns over road, Three landings and learned how to adjust throttle. 58 min.

Wednesday July 19, 1939: Made a pretty good flight with Captain Chapman. Did more coordinating exercises and more climbing and banking and more S-turns over road. The vertical turns should not be used at low altitude. My throttle control is not as coordinated as it might be. Didn't solo today, but was informed that Lt. Ford requested another check flight with me before I solo.

Thursday July 20, 1939: Went up today and made three pretty good takeoffs and landings. Came in to line and Captain Chapman told me to wait in plane. I watched him walk over to hangar where he saluted and talked with Lt. Ford. Presently Captain Chapman returned and announced that I was going to solo. I was surprised but very willing.

Solo: Tested both mags—taxied and took off. Made all turns but cut gun too soon and had to gun her twice to make safe landing. Then made two takeoffs and landings—each one better than the last. 8:50 total.

Friday July 21, 1939: Had swell time. Had about 19 minutes dual and then Chapman turned me loose by myself again. Made four or five landings and am gradually getting the feel of the ship.

Monday July 24, 1939: Went up for 10 minutes dual. Then made three landings and spent 28 minutes. Then Chapman got back in and we went up to practice coordination exercises and climbing turns. Made about ten chandelles and several power on and power off stalls. Pretty stiff wind today.

Tuesday July 25, 1939: Had another check flight with Lt. Ford. Better than the last time but still have plenty to improve such as:

1. Takeoffs still too steep climb.
2. Climbing turns too steep.
3. Hold stick too tightly.
4. Spins no good.
5. Stalls just fair.
6. Approaches for forced landing not so good.
7. Med. banks not as good as might be.

Next had first solo stage check. Eight of us went up all at once and practiced landing & takeoffs—following a rectangular course—graded by Wettenbeck and Lt. Wright. I got a "D" but still passing. Jordan hit fence, undershot, and washed out left wing slightly.

Wednesday July 26, 1939: Had only 2nd solo stage "A" check flight. Went up with seven others and made takeoff and landings—made first landing in adjacent field off airport perfect. However, for all rest of six landings got an average of "D" but still passing.

Today marks 1st month anniversary in Army.

Thursday July 27, 1939: Went up with Captain Chapman—spent time (49 minutes) reviewing airwork, climbing turns, medium, gentle & steep banks, chandelles, stalls & spins, S-turns over road, glides, forced landings, and landings.

Went up for 1/2 hour by myself. Did climbing turns—two each—gentle, medium, steep banks. Did chandelles, coordination, glides.

Friday July 28, 1939: Had 18 minutes dual—review work. Then went up for 1/2 hour solo to review coordination etc, at 1,000 feet but ceiling too low so practiced S-turns over road at 400 feet instead.

Monday July 31, 1939: Went up and practiced coordination exercises, stalls and spins. Not too bad—glides and climbing turns—landings not so bad.

Went up with Chapman and did coordination and S-turns over road— must learn to hold altitude— did first of 8's over X in road.

Tuesday August 1, 1939: Went up for over 45 minutes—practiced stalls, spins, 8's, S-turns over road and chandelles with Chapman. No solo today.

Wednesday August 2, 1939: Finally got a ship for 32 minutes solo. Made five landings—hit circle three times and overshot once and undershot once— both by 25-30 feet. Then went out and practiced stalls, spins, chandelles and climbing turns and coordination exercises—made another poor spot. Then went up for 58 minutes more and practiced chandelles, stalls, spins, and elementary eights. Made a couple of landings OK—also two forced landings. (Had first encounter with horse at riding stables—one hour)

Thursday August 3, 1939: Went up for 1/2 hour solo. Practiced landings, chandelles— smoothed out banks, turns and climbing turns. Right arm got sore from baseball and coordination exercises. Did a spin and came down.

Went up for 90-degree approach spot landings—made two undershoots, three exact hits, one overshot and another close undershoot—got a "C". Went up and did some more chandelles, spins, and banks.

Friday August 4, 1939: Went up for 54 minutes solo. Did chandelles, coordination, climbing turns, gentle, medium, and steep banks. Also stalls and spins. Tried to smooth out my recovery from spins. Practiced smoothness of controls. Made an extra practice landing and overshot field once. Air very calm.

On solo stage spot landing made 90-degree approach and overshot three times about 30 feet—hit next two on line exactly, but on next one made turn too close to ground—Red flag in. Made good landing on line next time but got a "D".

Monday August 7, 1939: No flying—rain all day.

Tuesday August 8, 1939: Flew—practicing coordination exercises, chandelles, spins, stalls, banks, glides, S-turns, figures 8's, and 90-degree approaches.

Went up with Chapman and did about twelve chandelles, stalls, and spins. (Not so good—put on throttle before straightened out).

Wednesday August 9, 1939: Had 1 hour and 12 minutes up dual with Chapman. Practiced coordination exercises, stalls, and chandelles. Did chandelles until I got idea how to make them smooth. Then did eight or ten spins until I figured out what I'd been doing wrong. Holding rudder too long and wings not kept level with ailerons, made a poor (wheel) landing.

Went up solo and practiced chandelles—fair, then spins. Tried only one turn and then out. Made fair progress but still not smooth enough.

Thursday August 10, 1939: Had 52 minutes dual with Chapman—reviewed spins, chandelles, and then figure 8's and S-turns over road and forced landing. Solo—practiced chandelles and spins.

Friday August 11, 1939: Solo all morning. Practiced 180-degree approach. Went out cross-country and did chandelles, coordination exercises, lazy eights, and spins—S-turns over road.

Then stage 180- degree approach and made fair landings near linc, but still got a "D" grade. Too much overshooting.

Saturday August 12, 1939: Went up and got in two practice landings before stage. 180-degree approach again—Made several overshoots and then two spots. Made a "D" again. Got white flag. Went out cross-country over East Hills Country Club and practiced coordination, S-turns, lazy 8's, stalls, spins, and chandelles.

Monday August 14, 1939: Practiced solo work—not bad but still need plenty of improvement. On dual with Captain, got my first three rolls—one slow roll and two snap rolls. More practice on pylon 8's, forced landings, spins, lazy 8's, and 180-degree overhead approaches.

Tuesday August 15, 1939: Had exactly one hour dual instruction from Captain this morning. Practiced pylon 8's and 180-degree approaches. Spent solo time smoothing out spins, chandelles, and lazy 8's.

Wednesday August 16, 1939: Went up at 7:45 with Lt. Ford for check flight—but was I poor. Whew! Couldn't seem to coordinate exercises. My maneuvers were all jerky and disjointed. I couldn't seem to settle down. My stalls were not so well coordinated. My chandelles were not "flown around"—I merely jerked them around. My lazy 8's were not even remotely resembling a good maneuver. Felt pretty rotten about it and so did Lt. Ford. Said he would ride with me tomorrow (but he didn't).

Thursday August 17, 1939: Wondered if Lt. Ford would check me again today but Schmidty didn't have any check flight scheduled for me so I went up solo for one hour and 47 minutes. Practiced coordination and chandelles and lazy 8's. Practiced a few stalls, spins, and more coordination. Felt pretty tough about everything—don't know if I will ever be a flyer. Am determined to find out whether Chapman has been teaching me correct way to make maneuvers or not.

Friday August 18, 1939: Went up with Chapman dual and discovered that he wouldn't let me practice maneuvers as Lt. Ford had shown me he wanted them done. Talked to Wittenbeck—asked him to ride with me and check all my maneuvers and show me correct methods. Also want him to go over my coordination and strengthen and smooth that out. Feel a little better about it all today. I'm glad Lt. Ford woke me up before I got into too deep a rut in my flying.

Monday August 21, 1939: Had dual with Chapman. Tried me out on chandelles, lazy 8's, pylons 8's, and forced landings. No acrobatics yet though. Got first 360-degree overhead approach. On solo time practiced 360-degree overhead and then a few pylon 8's and chandelles. Feel a little better about flying.

Tuesday August 22, 1939: Made a few more 360-degree overheads and also chandelles and lazy 8's while solo. Practiced coordination too. On dual, Chapman gave me four or five forced landings. Got mixed up and tried to land downwind—was stupid on several others too. Got no acrobatics today and won't until my other airwork improves.

Wednesday August 23, 1939: Had first loop today, was some sensation. Since, my forced landings were better, but could still stand plenty of improvement. Also did pylon 8's, chandelles, lazy 8's, and banks. On solo time, practiced stalls, spins, chandelles and loops—which were all pretty rotten—and lazy 8's, pylon 8's, gliding turns, and approaches, and a 90-degree approach back at field.

August 23, 1939

Dear Mom and Dad,

Received your letter, Mom, and I am wondering if you will please send me that old, cream jacket and yellow sweater, and one other light sweater. It has been a little chilly here in the mornings—about 60-degrees—and at night we sleep with blankets. Funny weather for Nebraska, or so I hear from the natives.

Enclosed is a copy of our Cadet program—both

flying and ground school. When you are through with it, could you please take it out to Elden Miller at the airport—they may like to see it out there.

Another Cadet was washed out yesterday. Couldn't fly far enough, I guess.

Am keeping in good health and in fair spirits, although at times I get discouraged—or fed up— they are really pushing us pretty hard. After flying for an hour and a half each day, I feel like I have done a real day's work—trying to keep the ship level in a stiff wind, full of up and down drafts, and still get precision on all banks, turns, and maneuvers. My last check flight was not a roaring success, but I surely am trying to overcome all my many faults, as is everyone else, because they won't send us to Randolph unless they are pretty sure we could learn to handle a larger and faster ship.

Have a second hand Argus "C" camera which I bought for $13.00 from one of the Cadets here who wanted a different model. Have taken quite a few pictures—sure like the range finder on it. Will send you a few shots when I get the pictures developed.

Well, have to scram to lunch. We are flying in the afternoon now this week, while the new dodos fly in the morning. Got a letter from Aunt Rica which I am enclosing also.

Lovingly your son, Franklin

August 24, 1939: Made good flight with Chapman. Made perfect loop, good chandelles, good lazy 8's, and a perfect one-turn spin—coming out exactly on dot. Chapman was so pleased he showed me vertical reverses and also snap rolls. On my solo time, practiced more loops, vertical reverses and spins, stalls, forced landing, gliding and coordination exercises. Feel a lot better about it all now.

Friday August 25, 1939: On solo time, practiced loops, stalls, spins, chandelles, lazy 8's, and went up to 5,600 feet—highest so far. Temperature dropped about 20 degrees and I was actually getting cold. Motor started to cough, so I advanced carburetor heat control. Did spins and lazy 8's. Sky is some sight at this height.

On dual, Chapman and I practiced more loops, chandelles, snaprolls, and vertical reverses. Showed me a half-roll—I about "blacked out"—all the blood left my head and I was pretty dizzy for a moment at the end of the dive.

Monday August 28, 1939: Had dual with Chapman. Practiced several chandelles, vertical reverses, and a slow roll. On solo, practiced chandelles—tried a slow roll and lost 1,300 feet so fast, I thought I had better get more instruction before I tried again. Not sure about the controls yet.

Tuesday August 29, 1939: Had a check flight with Lt. Wright. Was not very well versed in coordination. Used too much rudder and not stick and rudder together. Lt. Wright said I appeared too nervous and urged me to relax more. On solo time, tried to put into practice suggestions of Lt. Wright. He sure is one swell guy. He is trying his best to help me. I know I must conquer my tenseness and cultivate a more deliberate bearing and a much more relaxed attitude—unhurried, safe-making decisions calmly without jerk or hurry.

Wednesday August 30, 1939: Went up with Chapman who showed me half rolls and slow rolls. Tried vertical reverse again and did about fifteen slow rolls—know what the score is about them now. On solo, succeeded in making three fair half rolls and also several slow rolls. Feel a lot better about my flying. Tried to relax even more today than yesterday.

Thursday August 31, 1939: Had 360-degree overhead stage today, and I managed to hit line two or three times, but due to turning too steeply too low over ground, received a high "D" grade instead of a "C". Then went out and practiced slow rolls—tried relaxing—loops, vertical reverses, half rolls, and spins. Motor started acting up-sputtering. After only one slow roll my tach cut out. Went back to field and made landing okay.

Friday September 1, 1939: Had another check flight with Lt. Wright. Was so poor on coordination and over control on rudder, that Lt. Wright had me land at field while he talked to me about what was wrong with my fundamentals. Went up again—pylon 8's still pretty bad. I have to conquer my nervousness and overcontrolling and tenseness, which are all handicapping my flying. Lt. Wright told me to plan ahead more, look more, and to think more for myself.

Tuesday September 5, 1939: Captain Chapman took me up dual. I took off. Had a 25 mph wind from south and I neglected to crab about 20 degrees into wind—pattern pretty poor. Practiced slow rolls, snap rolls, half rolls and Immelmanns then made error of coming too close to traffic area near field when gliding down for 400' traffic land. Came in for a good approach and landing.

Afterwards in the office, Chapman gave me "hail Columbia" because of my poor mental process, and poor judgement in traffic although my acrobatics were pretty good.

Friday September 8, 1939: Was in fair condition today, but will try to improve more tomorrow. All of us in "tither" because they washed out Caven on Tuesday and Jordan and Blum on Thursday (yesterday) leaving only fifteen of us. None of us were feeling very well about it. No flying last Wednesday or Thursday due to high winds from south and southwest about 30-40 mph.

Saturday September 9, 1939: Lt. Wright gave us more encouragement by telling us that there were going to be no more washouts unless someone "pulled a boner". We would be checked about 60-62 hours by Lt. Ford, and then use last few hours to smooth out our faults. We all immediately felt a hell of a lot better. Consequently, felt more relaxed and flew our acrobatics better for today. Had solo only today.

Sunday September 10, 1939: Went up with Chapman for a little dual. Work showed a lot more improvement and I felt better about it too. Had solo time for a while too. Did my very first inverted flying. Starting at 3,000 feet and after flying inverted for about 30 seconds had lost about 1,000 feet. Missed saluting Lt. Ford today when he greeted me.

September 10, 1939

Dear Mom and Dad,

Hope you are both well and happy. We got some good news the other day. After they washed out two more Cadets leaving only fifteen of us, the Lieutenant (our Commanding Officer) told us that we were the ones to go to Randolph and would have only one more check flight at the end of next week. So if we all pass that one, in full review of all our work and our aerobatics, will be starting for Randolph on September 24 and are to report there on the 27th.

I am studying both ground school and aerobatics so I can pass all the finals.

I am in good health. I sent the scrapbook last Friday so it ought to reach you by Monday.

Well there goes the dinner gong—am hungry! Just finished reading Ben Franklin's Autobiography.

Lovingly your son, Franklin

Wednesday September 13, 1939: No flying Monday, Tuesday or Wednesday due to high wind from south and southwest about 30-35 mph. Gee, are we getting stale??

Thursday September 14, 1939: Went up in high wind (30 mph) today dual with instructor Kinsey. All instructors are each taking up one or more students all dual—no solo. Worked on slow rolls, snap rolls, half rolls, and lazy 8's. Lazy 8's went very good—not enough rudder on recovery. My chandelles also lacked enough rudder on last part of the maneuver. I guess Lt. Wright's lecture about not using too much rudder has soaked in. Have to get used to using my head and judgement more.

Friday September 15, 1939: Had almost one hour dual time with Chapman today. Wind still very stiff and we took off rapidly. Climbed to 3,000 feet and did chandelles. After about four or five, had gained almost 1,000 feet. Did good slow rolls, half rolls, and practiced lazy 8's until I got the idea. Did a good Immelmanns recovery after several attempts. Snap rolls pretty good too. Had a snap roll and a half and a lot of inverted flying.

Saturday September 16, 1939: Went up solo at about 9:25 a.m. and practiced pylon 8's for 15 minutes. Then climbed and did chandelles. Then tried about 10 or 15 minutes of lazy 8's trying to analyze the motions and make them smooth. Then did a slow roll and made a loop with Immelmann on top—OK—then tried another slow roll—OK. Just as I decided to call it a day, the engine stopped. I surely was surprised. I tried to get it to start again but no luck. Was at about 2,800 feet and after losing 1,000 feet, looked for a field, and as I tried to make up my mind, I finally selected one which I thought looked pretty good (although later I was told I had missed several better ones) and started to plan my approach. At the time of my first noticing engine failure, I had completed three 180-degree turns now and heading east. I selected a spot on top of hill to land but realized I couldn't stretch glide so cut in and hit slope (about 15-degrees), and slid along ground. After breaking off both landing gear and washing out lower wing and tearing engine almost off nose, I remember seeing right landing gear tear up through lower right wing and cutting the switch. Then I blacked out and when I came to I was mumbling, "It can't be true—this isn't me, it's a dream." I was shaking my head to clear my brain—fighting off the mist in front of my eyes. Then when it all dawned on me that I had come through alive, and all I could see while I sat there was the dust settling about the plane with one landing gear at left and other strewn on right side of fuselage. The first thought that struck me was, "Gosh, there goes Randolph Field" and then I noticed that my nose was bleeding and raising my goggles (I had forgotten to take them off before crashing) and then thinking, "Gosh, what a mess to make of a beautiful plane." I managed to unhook my safety belt and climb out and everything wasn't so clear yet. I hung on to the side of the fuselage and reached for my handkerchief to wipe off my nose which was still bleeding. Just then I noticed a farmer coming up the hill to see what he could do and when he looked at me, I guess he wondered why I just stared at him—not even saying hello. He said, " Well, I thought you were going to come down because I heard your engine stop way up there." He rushed forward to nose of plane where he shouted, "Say, your gas is leaking out up here." So I immediately went forward and saw what he was pointing at and came back to cockpit and turned off the gas switch. I shook my head a couple more times and then asked the farmer where I could get a telephone. He told me he didn't have one at this farm but that he would take me to a neighbor of his who had one. "Telephones are scarce out here," he said grinning. So, I unfastened my parachute and rolled it up—fastening it into a neat bundle and taking off my helmet and goggles. I followed him over to the barn and house which were about 200 yards away, down through a small gully and up to the house.

I stopped at the well and asked for a drink, washed my face and hands, and began noticing the effect of the shock. Just then the farmer took me over to his car—a 1925 Dodge—and off we went to use the phone.

At the farm (1 1/2 miles away) the farmer's wife called Union Airport and I talked to our dispatcher, Mr. Schmidt, who asked me what happened. I said I was reporting a forced landing and a crash—wiping out landing gear and wing and that I was cut and bruised a little. He said he'd send Captain Smith—our flight surgeon—over, and asked me for directions on how to get there. I told him ten miles north and 1 1/2 miles west of Lincoln.

Then we returned to farm and waited. Another farmer came in and we sent him out along the road in his car to look for Captain Smith and direct him to the farm. Presently, two planes came over and one made an attempt to land. I waved at it and discovered it was Lt. Ford and Sgt. Morris. Next time around he made a landing on top of hill where I had intended to make my original landing.

I went back to ship and met Lt. Ford halfway up hill from the ship. Saluting, I reported— "Sir, Flying Cadet Schirmer reporting a forced landing." He grinned and asked me how I felt and that I'd

better sit down and wait for Captain Smith since I didn't know whether I had any broken bones or not. He and Sgt. Morris started a routine inspection of the plane and asked me questions what happened and when. I filled out form #1 and made necessary entries in remarks column about forced landing.

Presently, Captain Smith arrived followed by a private carrying medical kit. At about the same time, Mr. King—chief mechanic—arrived from field with an assistant who started inspection of plane also. Captain Smith felt my back and neck. He looked at the cuts and bruises and said I wasn't in too bad of shape. I asked Lt. Ford if I could be excused to return to town with Captain Smith—he said okay—I saluted and we went back to Cadet Barracks in Smith's car. He was driving like mad as usual but I was pretty relaxed for I was glad to get back on terra firma again.

That afternoon I had a meeting with Lt. Wright and Lt. Ford in office along with King and Hogchrigg, over whether I had looked at form #1 and seen remarks about magnetos both being bad. I replied that Paul Whittenbeck, a mechanic, and I had both checked ship just right before I took off and that everything was OK and that I had done about an hours worth of flying before any sign of trouble had developed.

I went in and got patched up by Captain Smith and lay down a while—in fact all afternoon. Got a rub down for my shoulder muscles and neck. They were very stiff from wrenching inside the cockpit and also the front of my lower ribs were very sore from the safety belt's pressure.

Sunday September 17, 1939: First Check Flight after crash—went up with Lt. Ford today and he gave me instructions in chandelles, lazy 8's, and pylon 8's. Did chandelles OK and also lazy 8's. While doing pylon 8's had a forced landing (with engine OK) and made a south approach instead of north, although we had taken off toward the south. Had another forced landing from 3,000 feet but had picked a good field and he said "OK"—came back to field and on final leg, I came out of bank too soon—before nose was on point in line with line you want to keep in landing.

Must learn to plan ahead on forced landings more and to "S" around and jockey into best possible position for landing safely.

Monday September 18, 1939: Second Check Flight after crash—went up again with Lt. Ford and didn't feel as well as I did the day before—my coordination was poorer and although my chandelles were OK, my lazy 8's were not as good as yesterdays. I was stalling ship too much. My pylon 8's were not as well flown either—I neglected taking wind into account more. My forced landings had too much S'ing around in them although they were better than yesterday. On my landing, I neglected to take into account the drift caused by a crosswind. I also had to take off again and even then I didn't make enough correction for the wind, for I came in too fast, and when Lt. Ford jerked the controls, I didn't get them again so he landed the ship.

However, I learned one very valuable lesson today. I must learn to:

1. Think first with my head and keep feet and hands still and steady.

2. Be deliberate and make motions only after thinking out a plan.

3. Use a presence of mind method—don't just sit there like a "bump on a log".

4. Be reasonable and think more—Don't be so impulsive.

Tuesday September 19, 1939: Third Check Flight after crash—31 minutes—went up again with Lt. Ford and did better. Made a slow roll OK and chandelles and lazy 8's OK. Then tried Immelmanns. Couldn't get the roll out very well. Lt. Ford gave me some instruction and I began to get the idea. Had one forced landing—OK. After landing again at airport, Lt. Ford told me that I was to go back to Captain Chapman for any further instruction he might care to give me and to solo me, if he wished to. I told Chapman and he had me go up solo. I did, and ironed out Immelmanns and came home again.

Wednesday September 20, 1939: Went up with Captain Chapman and did chandelles, lazy 8's, and slow rolls, then went over to municipal airport and landed. Got drink of water and we took off. Chapman tried a 360-degree overhead but just when landing, another PT got in the way, and so he gunned it and we went around again. Made a pretty good landing second time and returned to field. Went up solo and did chandelles, loops, Immelmanns, and then a few vertical reverses and took a 15 minute trip around the outskirts of Lincoln. Got cold and tired, so after a few more slow rolls and another Immelmann went in and landed. Total time 63:30.

Thursday September 21, 1939: Have to get 1:30 yet. Went up solo for about 58 minutes practicing all primary and fundamental maneuvers, including gentle: turns, medium, and steep turns etc., with a few acrobatics, trying to get precision and accuracy. Chapman took me up and did most of flying. We wandered around and found hill on which I had my forced landing, and starting at same altitude; showed me several fields I could land in and actually made a good approach to one of the best fields. I got a sense of shame for not having done better on my forced landing.

My apparent errors were:

A. Not choosing field when first had trouble with engine, and making a planned approach and successful and safe landing with no damage.

B. By practicing forced landings over rough terrain.

C. Not using my head and thinking and reasoning the situation out calmly, and then acting only after I had thought clearly.

Basic Flying at Randolph Field, Texas.

September 27, 1939

Dear Folks,

Finally arrived at Randolph Field—registered in and was taught how to salute Commandant. Got supper, an army haircut, was issued rifle and bayonet, and clothes. Was assigned a swell room. Have a lot of regulations to learn and there are about four

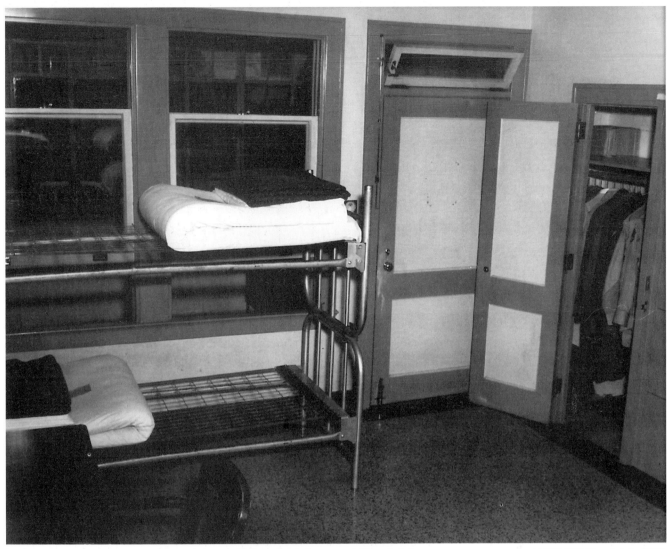

Flying Cadet room at Randolph.   AETC/HO Randolph AFB

hours of drill per day. Boy what a full schedule. Won't get a weekend off until a week from this coming Saturday. Start flying next Monday. We get demerits for dust in the wastebasket or for not making our bed correctly—but it's going to be a great training. I am feeling fine.

Lovingly your son, Franklin

September 28, 1939

Dear Mom and Dad,

Well, I just finished a full day here at Randolph. Boy, do they keep us busy—Up at 5:45 and breakfast at 6:20; make beds, clean room, dust, mop, and shine brass. We drill for three hours in the morning with and without rifles and bayonets. Then it is time for lunch which is excellent (they make sure we get

plenty of milk). Then some more drill and calisthenics.

We are gradually getting our equipment which includes the following: two flight caps, two pair of coveralls, eight pair of silk black socks, one pair of wool socks, one pair of black shoes, four large bath towels, one pair of new gym shoes, one sweat-shirt and regular socks.

Our rooms have swell closets and drawers, and boy are they particular where they want you to put everything and just how to fold it. We just had a formal inspection—am finally getting used to saluting all the officers, and we have to run double-time between any two formations. After I got the army haircut—and believe me it is plenty short—we had our pictures taken. I have only had about ten min-

utes to myself all day. We even have to wipe the dust out of out wastebaskets.

My room is in one of the two new barracks. I am enclosing a pamphlet showing the arrangement of the field or "post" as they call it here. Please return it as soon as you have read it as I need it back.

As I mentioned in my card, I probably won't get a town leave until a week from this Saturday and I will probably have more time off on Sunday than on Saturday, but you all will probably like to see us drill on Saturday, so just let me know when you plan to arrive.

The weather has been rather warm here and I have a sun tan from all the drilling that we have done in the sun.

We start flying next Monday and I suppose ground school will start about the same time. We surely know we are in the Army now, boy—there are demerits for the things you do wrong.

Well, drop me a line when you can and I will try to answer as quickly as I can.

Lovingly your son, Franklin

Monday October 2, 1939: Introduced to Lt. Coleman, J. B. instructor. He explained to us how to start engine on BT-9, showed us flap control, stabilizer setting, prop. control, and how to energize starter, etc. Had 30 minutes flight. Wore goggles while taxiing then after takeoff, closed canopy and was surprised at visibility. Removed goggles—sensation like that of being suspended in midair in a glass bubble—no noise. Heard instructor giving orders over earphones. Did climbing, level flight, gentle and medium banks. It was very surprising the amount of rudder movement required to make decent maneuver. Showed me boundaries of flying space and told me to look around more. On the whole, day was very successful and inspiring. Was up 3rd today and there are four in our class. Sat down at practice field and then took off again—instructor doing all the flying here.

Tuesday October 3, 1939: Went up 2nd today

and handled takeoff but rather wobbly. Did some more turns but still not enough rudder. Practiced glides and gliding turns and learned use of prop control and flaps. Came into traffic with coaching and made a rather rough landing. Took off again and made another turn in traffic all way around and another landing—about same degree of roughness as at first. Came in and stopped motor, made out time and left ship.

Wednesday October 4, 1939: Went up first. (Changed Tee setting first). Made good takeoff but missed rolling up flaps soon enough, and went to 600 feet before I turned out of traffic. Was watching four other planes nearby and so forgot. Made climbing turns but still not enough rudder. Got up near clouds. At 4,000 feet, Lt. Coleman took charge and climbed up to almost 7,500 and finally 8,000 feet. Did three stalls—power off 1-2-3— and three with power on—right, left and straight, then more banks and turns and finally spins. Tried one, but gave it gun before I had started pull up. Came down with gliding turns and then Lt. Coleman took over near traffic and suddenly told me to take it. I changed prop pitch too late and tried to roll down flaps too soon on turn and came in too slow, almost stalling, but landed OK. Signed up for link trainer for Friday at 18:30.

Thursday October 5, 1939: Went up last. Good takeoff but still too rough on controls. Not using enough right rudder. Stalls: Characteristic—power off (prop control forward), front (use rudder) let go. Left and right (no rudder) let go. Power on stall (prop control back) front (don't use rudder) only stick—way back with palm of hand. Right and left (stick back only). Power off stall (prop control forward). Front—recover immediately—right and left—recover immediately. Forced landings—throttle back (prop pitch forward) and stabilizer back. Gliding—immediately get stabilizer back and pitch forward.

Friday October 6, 1939: Went up 3rd. Reviewed stalls—did new stabilizer stall. Gliding turns—90-degrees—not enough rudder. Traffic pattern poor. Not using prop control and flaps correctly. Landings too rough—not enough gun soon enough, not landing in middle of field, making last leg too far away from field.

Weekend—admiration from Lt. Coleman:

"Go out and get relaxed, drunk, or anything, because next Monday maybe I'll let you kill yourself." (Meaning solo either Monday or Tuesday).

Tuesday October 10, 1939: Took off and climbed to 3,000 feet with climbing turns—better today. Then gliding down with gliding turns. Forced landings practiced—poor—missed three entirely. Couldn't seem to pick good field. Went down into traffic level (500') and changed pitch. Forgot to make final turn into traffic—leg too far south. Came and made passable landing. Took off again and made better pattern and landing better. Still troubled with rudder. Did another takeoff and another landing, then Lt. Coleman taxied over to west fence—got out and gave me final instructions to solo. Took off and landed three times. All good landings—pattern could have been better though.

Wednesday October 11, 1939: Went up and did climbing turns to 3,000 feet then cut gun and glided down to 1,000 feet with gliding turns. Lt. Coleman gave me several forced landings but I only made one fair attempt. Seemed to not maneuver or use prop control correctly (low pitch). Came in and landed—WOW—without allowing for drift almost rolled up in a ball. Went around again—Lt. Coleman taking ship and showing me how to make allowance for crosswind when landing. Then I made another landing and did OK so I went up solo, leaving Lt. at edge of field. Made three landings OK then went back to line. Lt. Coleman then told me to take up #556 for 1/2 hour solo and practice stalls. I was surprised and a trifle excited, but up I went. I started engine and taxied out to middle of field. Just as I turned and headed into wind, my right wheel dropped into a hole about six inches deep and eight inches in diameter. I got out and inspected situation. Saw right wing tip was only four or five inches above ground. Got back in cockpit and wondered

what to do. Sat there waving at mechanics—no answer. Finally Lt. Coleman came out and taxied up to my ship in another BT-9. He saw my predicament and told me to let him up in cockpit, and for me to lift and push forward on wings. We did and got out OK. I took off and climbed to 3,000 feet and practiced stalls. Finishing, I glided down in gliding turns and came into traffic, landed, and taxied up to line.

Thursday October 12, 1939: Went up with Lt. Coleman. Approached and overshot Davenport Field (air field) and went around again and made landing OK. Then I took it around with Lt. in rear cockpit and landed OK. Lt. Coleman got out and waited at field house while I went around solo. Made a pretty good landing, then overshot next two. First one due to too much speed and next due to another plane being under and too close, having cut me out on turn. Then made another circuit and came in OK, landing crosswind just before hitting ground, having glided down into wind. Came back to Randolph and Lt. Coleman landed with full flaps. Boy did we glide almost straight down and it was rather tricky landing that way.

Friday October 13, 1939: Took solo ship #514 and went up and practiced stalls, turns, and banks. Came into traffic and found I was headed wrong since they had changed tee setting from northeast to southeast. I went out of traffic and came in again and saw someone changing tee again. Finally got squared away and came in OK. Went up dual with Lt. Coleman. Did climbing turns to 5,000 feet (too steep bank), stalls-characteristic (power-off). Didn't look around correctly before maneuver. Partial stalls not steep enough—not enough rudder. Spins-power on (prop control back). Looking around improperly—lead more into direction of spin. Stick back and rudder full in direction of spin. Hold one turn only, cut engine then opposite rudder full on for 1/2 turn. Follow immediately with a definite forward thrust of stick to stop spin, then advance gun and pull up to partial stall. Had full flaps landing—better use 90 mph and start leveling off at 30 feet and use stick back.

Forced landings—from 3,000 feet set stabilizer and "S" around and look beneath ship and both sides for good field. Pick field and angle around so you make all turns above 500 feet, and then can add or take off flaps to hit field correctly.

Monday October 16, 1939: Went over to hangar F and took first "jeep" ride in link trainer—some fun. Had parents along. They got some thrill watching planes take off and land. I tried to explain everything. Introduced them to my friend Cadets then said good-by and ran to ship to go up with Lt. Coleman. Had pretty good lesson. Went to Davenport Field. Made several overshoots and then good landing. Then went around once solo and made good landing. Went back to Randolph. Lt. Coleman showed me another full flap landing. Then I got same ship and went up solo. Practiced climbing turns and stalls and a spin and came in—felt better.

Tuesday October 17, 1939: Went up to Davenport Field with Lt. Coleman and made a lot of blunders. Traffic—entered wrong so he showed me, landed poor, and then proceeded to overshoot two times. Couldn't seem to hold altitude in traffic (300'-700') and throttle control poor (1,500'-2,100'). Made one fair landing and one which almost ground-looped due to my coming too close to another plane and using brakes too suddenly so that they grabbed. Then got in other ship which A.C. Leverette, another student in our group, had been soloing in, and took off for about 50 minutes solo. Went up to 5,000' and practiced stalls—not kicking enough rudder and changing over with prop pitch control not set correctly. Came down doing gliding turns and into traffic and made landing OK.

Wednesday October 18, 1939: Dual—Not using enough rudder. Stalls—characteristic—fair, stick back—poor, complete—power off—fair, complete—power on—fair, Spin—power on—OK, gliding—OK. Approach to traffic—mistook position of tee. Approach too close to traffic. Should lose altitude farther away. Solo—Went up and practiced climbing turns. Stalls—look around more.

Stick back stalls—hold more left rudder. Better—complete stalls. Glides—OK.

Did spin with stabilizer at T-II and it flattened out too much. Came out OK but vowed to never forget. Came down and landed—good with eight turns flaps.

Thursday October 19, 1939: Solo—Went up and practiced stalls and spins. Climbing turns too much skidding and slipping. Forgot to get cushion and had difficulty in reaching pedals. Still can't look around correctly. Did spin OK but almost "blacked out." Came into traffic and landed with nine turns flaps too far away from hangar parking space.

Dual—Went up to 5,000'—climbing turns—banking too steeply. Not using enough rudder—skidding and slipping. Did characteristic stalls—skidded too much, looking around. Did stick back stalls—should be same attitude as partial stalls. Hold more rudder—get stick back. When nose passes horizon—forward and throttle too. Should practice stalls and turns. Banking without skidding and slipping due to not using enough rudder. Watch prop position on forced landings.

Friday October 20, 1939: Lt. Coleman notified me about check flight.

Dual-check flight with Lt. Mace. Had talk in office before flight. He wanted to know what I thought was wrong with my flying. I told him skidding and slipping in turns, not stalling correctly and forced landings. So I went out and started engine. Made out turn #1 and then Lt. Mace got in and told me "takeoff and climb to 5,000 feet."

Took off—throttle too low (had throttled back after takeoff). Climbing turns too steep and too much bank. Leveled off at 5,000 feet—set cruising prop pitch—set stabilizer. Looked around and skidded and slipped. Did power off—characteristic stall—OK. No throttle forward on partial stalls. Stick back stalls—low rpm. Get nose up to stall position and hold there, gradually bringing back stick to stomach and hold there, keeping nose from swinging with rudder until nose hits horizon, then stick forward and throttle forward. Made banks and turns—90-degree turn left stop, 90-degree turn right—gliding turns, forced landing and back into traffic. Landed with eight turns flaps. Keep 85 mph. Nose down on turns.

Solo—Went up and practiced turns, banks, checking against ball and turn indicator. Got feel of good bank and turn now. Did spirals down to traffic 1,000 feet to look at tee, then glided down to 500 feet. Came into traffic after changing prop pitch control and landed. With eight turns flaps—good landing. Was assigned new instructor.

Monday October 23, 1939: Met my new instructor—Lt. Disosway. Went up and headed for Marion Field on other side of Randolph about fifteen miles. Took us about ten minutes to takeoff, circle, and climb to 1,000 feet, and get over to Marion Field. Spent about 1/2 hour practicing landings—some good and some bad. Main trouble seemed to be that my last traffic leg was too far away from field for accuracy work and my turns lacked enough rudder but were much better. Took off and started back to Randolph when Lt. Disosway decided to call Randolph by radio and tell other students to go on and solo while he spent rest of period with me, since we had a late start due to bad weather. New pointers:

1. Yell "stand clear" just before engaging engine starter.

2. Make last leg of traffic closer to field. Cut engine sooner and less speed. Make last turn at 400 feet and keep glide—don't let nose drop and plane pick up speed after turn.

3. Hold glide to twenty-five feet off ground. Level off slowly to fifteen feet, then hold nose—don't pull up too fast or it will balloon up and cause poor landing.

4. Check for Form #1 in ship.

Tuesday October 24, 1939: Went up dual with Lt. Disosway again and climbed up to low ceiling at 1,200 feet where Lt. took over, and climbed up through clouds and into sun and blue sky above. Went to 4,000 feet and all the miles of billowy clouds below looked like piles of snow—so white and beautiful. Did stalls—learned to hold more right rudder and opposite stick on climbing due to high speed (rpm) and when recovering from right turn or left turn, to just relieve pressure on right foot slightly. Also on stick back or power on complete stalls—to hold rudder more and to make bank steeper on right and left stalls. On partial stalls to hold stalling position with right rudder until just before stalling moment, then nose down and pick up speed. On partial stalls to right or left—use rather steep bank and hold until stall is near then push nose down and straighten out and recover. On glides—use plenty of rudder on entry and recover and very little stick. On forced landings—Prop pitch forward, stabilizer back, look around meanwhile for field. Make all turns above 300 feet. On traffic patterns—Make last leg near field and then after cutting gun, glide along slowing down speed to 80 mph then make last turn towards first and then flaps required. Don't let nose drop on turns. If you keep glide constant (at 80) and pattern smooth and accurate, you can plan landing spot anywhere. Be exact and precise in all your flying.

On landings—establish glide at 80 mph. Start leveling off at 25 feet off ground—keep same attitude. Hold stick there, then as ship settles, bring stick back slowly, not ballooning up—due to rapid back movement of stick—but a gradual nose lifting to coincide with loss of flying speed and lift. Keep good glide and good turns in forced landings. Be smooth but keep those feet on rudders with definite pressure on both rudders and releasing pressure only (not entire foot). Never take off again with stabilizer in T.H. position—too dangerous. Check magnetos and switch both left and right also in off position to see if functioning.

Came back down through clouds. Lt. Disosway flying blind, and windshield getting wet when suddenly after two minutes or so flying blind, we came out of mist and saw good ole terra firma again. It was surely an eerie feeling.

Feel better today about everything. Have my confidence back again and now feel that it is impossible to fail.

Wednesday October 25, 1939: Went up with Disosway and went over to Davenport Field. Had to stay low under clouds (300' under) at 800 feet. Circled and tried to land but overshot so tried once again. Lt. then took over and tried to show me what traffic pattern to use. Then I got downwind leg farther from field so I could cut gun on last leg, and have time to slow down glide, before final turn into field using flaps.

Made two or three better landings so got to go up solo. On first attempt, made good pattern but came in too low over hump of ground and had lost so much gliding speed, that I was almost stalling on edge of field at 60 mph; so nosed down and hit wheels—kerplunk! Bounced about fifteen feet and took off again. Went around again. Made better approach but a sloppy landing—too bouncy and skiddy. Went up solo in other ship (forgot to ask permission to go up to practice airwork by radio) and flew around for about 50 minutes just learning how to make good turns and banks without skidding and slipping-

1. Learned how to use more rudder in glides.
2. How to use rudder (and very little stick) in all turns.
3. More right rudder is required for all turns and how to feel slip and skid.
4. Learned more about how to hold altitude—stabilizer and throttle settings.

Thursday October 26, 1939: Took off for Marion field, up to 1,100 feet but soon went down to 800 feet due to low ceiling—overcast 90%. Approached Marion and made first error. Was only 500 feet and went over corner of field. Then made traffic pattern approach too wide and missed field, so I went around and made better approach and landed. Out of five more landings, I made only about two fairly decent ones—including approaches. Used radio to ask permission to take off solo. Granted and took off. Made good landing according to control radio then made another landing. They changed tee so went around (not using enough stick for a

change). On next landing was pretty bouncy but safe. Last leg was too far back from field and I continually undershot. Then went up solo in #500 (had been in #490) and practiced turns—banks (had radioed and asked for and received permission to take off and practice airwork and returned to Randolph).

Friday October 27, 1939: Went up for check ride with Lt. Schlatter. Took off—OK. Climbed out of traffic and went to 1,000 feet, but later, due to clouds, had to go to 700 feet. Suddenly, Lt. Schlatter said we were going above the clouds, so he told me to increase carburetor heat and turn on Pitot tube heater. Went from 1,000 feet to almost 2,500 feet before sun broke through and we were on top of wonderful white billowy clouds. Did stalls and learned more about how rudder controlled ships movement. Had a little trouble with making complete stall to left (had already done stalls to right and front OK but couldn't seem to kick enough right rudder and tried to use too much stick). Did two spins and recovered OK and was doing partial stall to left and then recovered OK. Lt. Schlatter seemed pleased. Went down through fog again and came out near Kelly Field having drifted about twenty miles. Did 8's over a road at 200 feet and a forced landing, and then entered traffic and landed, but due to poor traffic pattern, had to go around again.

Details to remember:
1. Use rudder instead of stick.
2. Use common sense.
3. Check magnetos at higher rpm. (about 1,500).
4. "S" around a lot when taxiing.
5. Fly with precision. Try to be perfect .
6. Coordination consists of flying airplane and not with any special combination of controls. Timing of movements and controls is more important to achieve results.
7. Dominate the plane—Don't let it dominate you.
8. Look ahead and plan traffic pattern. Choose landing spot then select spot to cut gun on prop-

erly placed 3rd leg.

9. Keep glide—after slowing down to 80 mph

10. Keep nose on point (especially when gliding in for a landing).

11. Look around—especially for fields to land in and for other planes.

12. Be smooth going into and coming out of turns.

13. Ailerons bank—rudder turns.

14. When changing prop pitch throttle engine way back.

15. Roll down flaps rapidly—but roll up slowly.

16. Power—Firecracker vs. Steam Engine—Which?

Monday October 30, 1939: Had another ride with Lt. Schlatter who took me up and showed me how a partial stall to right or left can develop into a chandelle. Practiced these and made lots of errors—not enough rudder, not looking around enough, watching turn and bank, or tach or speed indicator and not watching position of ship in sky. Finally did a few pretty good chandelles then did gliding turns. Learned to watch air speed here too but also feel reactions of ship. Then had a forced landing for practice and chose a field which looked pretty good, but which when we went down to look at it didn't look as inviting, due to having ruts and little drainage channels running across it. Should have picked field to left and used flaps to get in OK.

Came into traffic—made approach (wind about 25 mph) so made last leg closer. Cut gun and made rather rough landing. Faults: Not dominating plane; flying sloppily; not knowing what is required or wanted and then getting results out of plane.

Tuesday October 31, 1939: Today had a new instructor temporarily—Lt. Edwinson—who took off and flew to Davenport Field, and mistook direction of tee position and landed just 90-degrees to traffic pattern and wind. Did another approach, and as we landed, the Lt. in charge changed tee again. I took off solo after asking permission by radio and made two pretty poor landings having cut gun too

soon on base leg in both cases—although second attempt was better.

Went up solo and returned to Randolph. Got another ship and went up solo and practiced turns—climbing and chandelles—until I could do them rather decently. Almost fell into a spin in one of my partial stalls. Also did complete stalls better, recovering with lots of rudder. Then did gliding turns and went in and made two more landings and called it a day. Still not precise enough on traffic pattern—not picking exact spot to land on.

Wednesday November 1, 1939: Went up with Lt. Hawes—a new instructor who showed me a lot of new pointers in the art of flying—about climbing turns, stalls and chandelles, and also demonstrated correct 180-degree approach for a forced landing; stressing smoothness of controls, and also showing what happens when you cross controls and stall ship—snap roll, and inverted position.

Went up solo and practiced climbing turns. Smoothed out turns and banks—gentle and medium turns and practiced all stalls—power off and power on, quick recovery stalls and also partial stalls. Concentrated on using rudder and coordinating with stick. Did chandelles but didn't do those to left as smoothly as to right. Came down with gliding turns and entered traffic OK. Made four pretty good landings, although one was rather bumpy.

Thursday November 2, 1939: Went to Davenport Field with Lt. Hawes (all enter field traffic at 1,000'). Enter traffic only after make sure of tee setting. Learned how to establish base leg and how important it is to establish an 80 mph glide to make a good approach and landing. Had to use lots of flaps, but after five landings dual, got idea and did two solo—not bad, although I did overshoot one pretty badly.

Went up solo and did landings at Davenport and then up to do airwork; chandelles, climbing turns, gliding turns, and a fair landing at Randolph.

Tonight we went back to barracks at 4:30 to eat an early supper. Returned at six and watched first phase of night flying. Students went to different zones with instructor—dual and then after being rolled in, landed three different times, and then soloed several times. Mine is tomorrow night.

Friday November 3, 1939: Went up for an hours instruction in instrument flying to 7,500 feet. Did level flying and banks and turns. Took rest (in rear cockpit) and Lt. Hawes played around by doing snap rolls, slow rolls, and other (chandelles) maneuvers, spins and then a series of slow rolls and three snap rolls. Then after half an hour of instruction, we came in and landed. Then went up solo and practiced turns, banks, stalls, chandelles—OK.

That night went up dual with Lt. Hawes and it was rather cold and pitch dark—although I was surprised how much you could see at night and how smooth flying it was. Made four landings dual and then went up solo. Made three landings and came in and changed clothes and Lt. Hawes took me to barracks in his car. All in all, the radio is a great thing for night flying and all of our control system hinged on it. I didn't have time to notice the bar lights on hangar—although they were on.

Monday November 6, 1939: Went up for two hours solo (got 1:45). Practiced climbing turns—experimenting on correct amount of rudder and stick. Did turns—tried to stay out of clouds. Made some progress on chandelles but too dangerous—too cloudy and overcast—so did banks and turns, gliding turns, and a landing to ramp. Rested for ten minutes and took off again. Practiced more turns and stalls and was about to do chandelles, when I looked out toward left and saw six BC-1's from Kelly Field headed straight at me. I climbed and turned and they sure seemed to be in a hurry. Then later, Lt. Schlatter zoomed overhead and signalled for me to go home and land, or to go down in the underclouds. So I glided down, entered traffic, and practiced landings making seven, out of which four weren't bad.

Tuesday November 7, 1939: Had dual flight with Lt. Hawes. Went up to 5000 feet and practiced chandelles. Procedures: Level flight—then dive plane to 129 mph. Start medium bank and turn at

140 mph. Pull back—not getting too high at 1/4 to 1/2 way around take off stick, pull up higher and then start recovery at 80 mph at roll out at 180 degrees. Note—if too much speed there, keep nose high and then back down to level. If speed is too low-lower nose.

Then did some lazy 8's. Had a lot of trouble in not rolling smoothly from one to another and also in not going through point. Finally after much coaxing and yelling on part of my instructor, (I admired his great patience), I got the idea and kept it from diving and did actually roll in and out of turn better.

Then did slow and snap rolls and a spin. Then went up solo (40 min) and practiced chandelles, lazy 8's and medium turns and also changing gas tanks.

Wednesday November 8, 1939: Went up solo for 1:40 and practiced chandelles, lazy 8's and steep turns. Steep turns—can't seem to keep altitude without making turn too tight. Chandelles—not bad but not making ship react correctly at 1/4 turn—to stay straight and not to wing over.

Lazy 8's—better but still not coordinating enough with stick and rudder to make smooth maneuver.

1. Make climbing turn and at 1/2 (45 degrees) point and drop nose through point with stick and bottom rudder.

2. Then start pulling back on stick to break dive.

3. Stick to level wings.

4. Rudder to start next climbing turn.

Thursday November 9, 1939: Went up for an hour of instrument flying. Did OK at first but due to difference in readings on needle in front and back cockpits, I couldn't get correct amount of needle width for turns. Got too tight on controls and overcontrolled badly toward end of period.

1. When going into turn, go slowly.

2. When correcting, don't wait too long and don't overcorrect or correct too fast.

3. Be smooth—coordinate.

4. Get needle centered and hold there, then get ball back.

5. Don't let ship dive and climb.

6. Watch clock-timing of turns.

7. Watch instruments.

Went up solo and had to stay at 2,500 to be 300 feet below clouds. Had to practice banks and turns and a few steep turns and coordination exercises.

Friday November 10, 1939: Took solo ship and went up through holes in clouds to 5,500 feet. Very beautiful up there. Practiced chandelles, lazy 8's and turns. Kept and eye on field through clouds. Spiralled back into 3,000 feet altitude and glided down to 1000 feet and came in at an angle to traffic at 500 feet. Another plane came in over converse and cut in ahead of me and went over inside traffic pattern on my right and slightly above me. I glanced at my altimeter and noted that I was at 500 feet level exactly, then waited until other plane started turn before I made my turn on base leg. Cut engine and landed OK.

Moved to Basic (east) side of Randolph today.

Monday November 13, 1939: Went up with Lt. Hawes and he showed me the various boundaries of Marion area in which we were to fly and the flying triangle traffic area for traffic from Randolph to the three auxiliary fields. No flying under 2,000-2,500 feet in this area unless landing in one of these fields. Studied traffic-tee pattern.

Went up solo and practiced various maneuvers including—medium and step turns, chandelles and a forced landing—picking my field and making an approach. Had to stay under 4,000 feet due to storm approaching and overhanging. Saw rain storm coming in distance and a few advance drops hit my windshield, so went back to Randolph. Shot two landings. Didn't watch myself close enough on taxiing into ramp after a landing. Almost didn't see a plane taking off directly in front of me.

Tuesday November 14, 1939: Had another hour of instrument flying again today. I went up to 5,000-6,000 feet—was pretty cold. Had trouble being too tense and overcontrolling. Instruments lagged and gave me incorrect reading and conse-

quently I didn't anticipate and coordinate controls quickly enough. Results—rough and dangerous flying. Have to keep needle on point with rudder, center ball with stick and keep altimeter under control with pressure only—not definite movements.

Went up solo and practiced chandelles, steep banks, and lazy 8's. Also was low on gas so had to keep changing tanks. Came in and rested five minutes and then went up again for another twenty-five minutes—total 1:10. One instructor told his students while giving orders for today's maneuvers to climb to 3,000 feet and do some chandelles and then climb back to 3,000 feet and do some lazy 8's-some stuff.

Wednesday November 15,1939: Had ship #260 for an hours worth of solo work. Did chandelles, lazy 8's and turns. Did work in Marion territory when I should have been in Krueger. Came down and met Lt. Wright and Sgt. Aunro who were visiting from Lincoln, Nebraska. Was glad to see them. Said they still had only fourteen planes and looked at me—I got it!

The new Cadets have been coming in (Class 40-B) and were getting squads organized to take care of them.

Went up for night flying. Got a little mixed up on first landing. Using my wing landing lights instead of just flood light in field. Next landing I overshot and had to go around again. Met two other planes, so after calling in went back to my zone and circled (came in for a wing landing light landing and flew into ground—bounced but landed OK).

Thursday November 16, 1939: Went up dual with Lt. Hawes and practiced chandelles and lazy 8's. Got idea a little better I believe to get and hold height in chandelle and to get height and then drop nose through point with forward stick and bottom rudder in lazy 8's.

Went to Zuehl Field and practiced two 180-degree side approach landings—did OK. Then went to Krueger Field and made another good landing, OK. Then went up solo and practiced chandelles and lazy 8's some more. Am in charge of quarters tonight and tomorrow until noon.

Monday November 20, 1939: No flying last Friday—bad weather. Went up solo and practiced chandelles and lazy 8's and gliding turns. Came in and landed. Then went up for check ride with Lt. Mace. Did the following:

1. Takeoff—turned too soon.

2. Climbing with throttle too low (1,800) should be 2,000.

3. Levelled off too high—at 2,750 feet instead of 2,500 feet. (Using cruising pitch)

4. Chandelles—too much speed (150), looked around too much. Didn't keep speed below 140. Bring nose up and left it there—should pull back on stick and get more altitude at 1/2 or 3/4 then start coming out.

5. Lazy 8's—pick point farther away, not too steep a bank, nose up, keep wing from going too high, forward pressure (only) or stick-rotation movement. Get nose through point.

6. Gliding Turns—Don't pull nose up on turns, stick pressed forward and turn, then pull back on stick in turn.

7. Forced landing—Prop control forward, stabilizer back, look on both sides of ship for field, select field, make approach, no turn under 400 feet.

8. Traffic pattern 500 feet.

Tuesday November 21, 1939: Went up dual with Lt. Hawes and practiced the following:

1. Chandelles—dive, start bank at 125 mph, 180-degrees—pull straight up, then pull back more and start recovery with nose high.

2. Lazy 8's—pull up—turn and bank—hold nose high and immediately after neutralizing stick for bank, start using bottom rudder to bring nose through point (releasing pressure on stick if necessary).

3. Gliding Turns—don't pull nose up, keep same gliding speed on all turns, clear engine.

4. Forced Landings—Prop control, stabilizer, look on both sides, check wind direction, be calm, plan 90-degree or 180-degree side approach according to altitude you have

5. Make all steep turns—180-degrees—pylon 8's—do not make steep turns.

Wednesday November 22, 1939: Had an hours worth on instrument flying under hood today. Learned to use airspeed indicator instead of rate of climb indicator. Found I was overcontrolling on turns—rolling into turns too fast and then having to correct for too much trim, etc. On stalls—recovery—and when pulling back—as soon as airspeed starts decreasing push stick forward and keep rate of climb from going past level flight position.

Went up solo and practiced chandelles and lazy 8's. Found I had to use plenty of throttle and lots of stick and opposite rudder to recover each time. Then on lazy 8's found I had to start using bottom rudder as soon as I had gotten enough altitude with stick to make nose go through point.

Monday November 27, 1939: After our five day vacation over Thanksgiving, went up solo and practiced chandelles and lazy 8's. Had mostly overcast sky, poor visibility at 5,000 feet, but managed to keep eyes on good check point on ground and not get lost.

Went up dual and did more chandelles. Dive, 128 mph turn—hold until 140 mph, pull up straight (but with ship banked enough) and slow at first. Exercising climb until when on starting recovery, push stick forward and come out with nose above horizon. Lazy 8's—don't start recovery through point with bottom rudder too soon. Don't let ship dive over 130 mph. On forced landings, watch for windmills for wind direction, but still do not make turns under 300-400 feet. Gliding turns—keep 90 mph, go into turns leading with rudder, come out with stick leading.

Tuesday November 28, 1939: Went up solo and practiced chandelles and lazy 8's. Low ceiling. Could get 4,500 in places but had to keep eye on ground so as not to get lost. Went up and did chandelles:

1. Dive slowly—130 mph start bank—definitely .

2. At 140 mph pull straight back on stick. Take off aileron at 70-degrees and keep pulling back on stick.

3. When at 70-60, push stick forward and also bring wing up and then recover with rudder. On chandelles to right, use no left rudder on recovery only release pressure on right pedal. Lazy 8's—pick point far enough away, get moderate amount of altitude and then follow through with bottom rudder—enough to make nose go through point. Don't allow plane to dive over 125-130 mph. Keep wings from getting too near vertical, by taking off aileron each time.

Wednesday November 29, 1939: No flying. Cloudy and overcast.

Thursday November 30, 1939: Went up for check ride with Lt. Olsen and did chandelles, lazy 8's, forced landings, steep turns and 90-degree turns. Did OK on everything but chandelles and lazy 8's. He said I didn't have feel of ship and said he would have a talk with my instructor. Don't know whether I passed or not. Went up solo and practiced chandelles and lazy 8's some more.

Friday December 1, 1939: Went up for instrument ride. Did fairly well but still am—
1. Overcontrolling.
2. Pulling up nose slightly in turns.
3. Not keeping needle in center.
4. Not keeping ball in center.
5. Rolling into turns too fast and past correct amount of turn.
6. Turns too steep.
7. On stalls—not getting stick forward enough to get back normal cruising speed.
8. On spins—too jerky.
9. On gliding turns—not keeping constant speed and not using shallower turns.

Went up solo—a glorious day. Had swell time doing chandelles (can really do them now) and lazy 8's-not so bad either.

Monday December 4, 1939: Went up dual for instrument ride. Did pretty well but still continued to overcontrol at times and tried to keep needle in center by using too much pressure for to long and not releasing it after each correction.

Went up solo and practiced chandelles, climbing turns, lazy 8's, steep turns and then gliding turns. Landing—10 turn flaps—to close on back (base) leg to field and rolled past operations office.

Tuesday December 5, 1939: Went up for instrument check ride with Lt. Olsen. Did OK except for a trifle overcontrolling and not recovering smooth and soon enough.

Went up solo for an hour. Did acrobatics and did some snap rolls and slow rolls. Did snap rolls to the right OK but couldn't get around to left—fell off upside down and did almost 200 mph before I pulled out. Same with slow roll to the right.

Went up solo again and made two traffic trips around field and two landings with 10-12 turns flaps (45 degrees).

Wednesday December 6, 1939: Went up with Lt. Dalton today since Lt. Hawes was absent. Did 180-degree overhead approach at Marion Field. Did two dual and then two more solos. Faults:
1. Glide too steep.
2. Turn too shallow and too slow.
3. Landings—poor
   a. Breaking the glide at 20 feet.
   b. Having a glide to break.
   c. Pulling nose up, tail down and land three point.

Thursday December 7, 1939: Had two periods solo. Up first period for practicing chandelles and lazy 8's. Am improving at last. Made a landing and rolled down almost to hangar "R" (but didn't use brakes).

Went up solo for acrobatics and practiced slow rolls and snap rolls at 6,000 feet and ended up at 3,500 feet. Did snap rolls to left and did 1 1/2 and pulled on top of inverted position and came out at 200 mph. Tried it again and finally made it. Did slow rolls to right also but still couldn't hold nose on point.

Friday December 8, 1939: Went up with Lt.

Hawes (who has been away for past few days on hunting trip for deer) and went to Marion Field for 360-degree overhead approaches. Did two dual and two more solo. Came back dual and landed.

Went up for 45 minutes solo acrobatics and practiced slow rolls. Getting better on my slow rolls to right and also snap rolls but couldn't make smooth recovery from a left snap roll. Falling off into a half roll past the recovery position each time and pulling out of a steep vertical dive at 190-200 mph.

Monday December 11, 1939: Had two solo periods today—only have to get 3 1/2 hours more to have my 75 hours. Practiced chandelles and lazy 8's and steep turns and practiced looking for landing fields. Went up to over 10,000 feet and did chandelles. Was ten degrees Celsius up there, yet not so cold. Was a beautiful day and a haze hung over the earth about 2,500 feet thick which formed a dirty ring on horizon when I had reached 4,000 feet.

Started smoking cigarettes and drinking cocacola bought by our flight by those who had accumulated stars for prize boners—I contributed four stars worth equal to twenty cents.

Tuesday December 12, 1939: Had two more solo periods—1:05—practiced steep turns at 6,000 feet and climbing turns, gliding turns, slow rolls, snap rolls and stalls. Got into a spin on a left snap roll recovery but came out OK. Made a rather bumpy landing due to cross wind on flaps. Went up again and got 40 more minutes finishing me up with 75:05.

All through flying here in Basic at Randolph now. Will turn in parachute and cushions tomorrow.

Air Corps Advanced Flying School at Kelly Field

Tuesday January 2, 1940: Met our new instructor Lt. Schultz and his assistant Lt. Yow today. Our group includes the following: Rux Sand, Satterwhite, Schirmer, and Scott. We went out into hangar and spent afternoon becoming familiar with all the new instruments in the cockpit, such as the hydraulic system for raising and lowering landing gear and flaps, the new air fuel ratio meter, the manifold pressure dial and the new propeller speed controls. We all took our turns in the cockpit showing the instructor we understood all his explanations.

Wednesday January 3, 1940: Went up with Lt. Schultz and for the first hour spent time in rear cockpit getting feel of the plane. Did gentle banks and turns. Landed at Kelly #3 field and then returned to Kelly (after making three landings at Kelly #3). Made change into front cockpit and missed having extra cushions behind me. I could hardly reach the pedals. Consequently, I had a difficult time controlling ship on landings. Almost ground-looped once in ship #171. Spent 2 hours dual in all.

Thursday January 4, 1940: After waiting for 45 minutes for mechanics to service the ship with gas and oil, I finally took off solo and boy it sure is a sweet ship to fly. (Ed. note BC-1) Spent 1:05 and just had a good time. Flew all around on northwest territory and came in and made five landings, each becoming better.

Friday January 5, 1940: Went up again solo and practiced airwork and then made a series of 8 landings at Kelly Field proper. Got used to calling in by radio and today had first close call when landing. I had come into base leg and saw ship below me and to left several hundred feet. So I turned sooner than he did to clear him and when I had established glide and applied flaps, I pushed nose down and holy smoke there was that plane directly below me. He wasn't 25 feet away. I merely did a gently turn to the right praying that no other plane would be behind me and missed landing on the culprit. I didn't get mad until I had landed safely. Surely made me more cautious and resolve never to get sloppy about my looking around more. Other than that, no other incident occurred.

Monday January 8, 1940: Went up again today and took off before sunrise. I decided to do some exploring and cross country. It was cold as the dickens, so after I climbed to 4,500 feet I set stabilizer and let plane fly itself for awhile and I put on my gloves. Followed due west course to Kelly #2 and #3 and saw Castorville and canal for irrigation and went over almost to Lake Medina. Then decided to return to Kelly Proper but found I had to fly almost directly into sun. Flew southeast course and wasn't lost but couldn't see anything but bright sunny haze and smoke. I lost altitude to 1,000 feet and then when I thought I was near Kelly I thought I had better climb up again to 2,000 feet to miss any out coming traffic. So I cruised around to south more and finally located San Antonio on horizon and then Kelly when I had finally gotten sun to my back. I called in and was told to notice changed tee setting which I did and came in only five minutes late.

Tuesday January 9, 1940: Spent all morning in Jeep (Link Trainer) period (got 50 minutes) and rest of time we spent going over maps and discussing cross country trips and also got our instructor, Lt. Schultz, to tell us what he knew about the air corps tactical units. He graduated from Kelly in 1936 and came back here from Moffett Field, California in July 1939 to instruct.

Wednesday January 10, 1940: No flying due to overcast all morning.

Thursday January 11, 1940: Went up after waiting until 11:00 a.m. for overcast and low ceiling to lift. In Ship #184 Lt. Vereen, a young Lt. who made three landings with me in rear cockpit, showing me how landing gear should be retracted and then put down again. I made three landings in front cockpit and was successful in passing check.

Friday January 12, 1940: Had two hours today to practice retracting landing gear, calling in and then putting it down again, calling in and landing. Made twelve landings. Had to go around field once due to traffic tie-up. Had to come in first few times under gun and no flaps. I was too far from field on base leg. Then started hitting field in 1st, 3rd and making 90-degree approaches OK. Came in high from 800-1,000 feet. Spent ten minutes out in northwest territory doing airwork to relax. Made four-five landings with full flaps. Had to jostle with

cross wind at times.

Monday January 15, 1940: Spent 2:15 at Kelly #3 Air Field and practiced twelve landings with 90-degree and 180-degree side approach. Had close shave on one landing with Bud Sands. Passed physical exam today for first time in six months. Made Schneider number of 16. Felt pretty tired after all the landing and taxiing. Made preference choice today.

Pursuit:
1. Selfridge Field—Mt. Clements, Michigan
2. Moffet Field—San Jose, California
3. Langley Field—Hampton, Virginia
Bombardment:
1. Barksdale Field—Shreveport, Louisiana
2. Hamilton Field—San Rafael, California
3. Mitchel Field—Long Island, New York
Observation:
1. Goodman Field—Ft. Knox, Kentucky
2. Pope Field—Ft. Bragg, North Carolina
3. Brooks Field—San Antonio, Texas

Tuesday January 16, 1940: Had cross country practice today for the first time. Went to Floresville and then south again to Kennedy then went to Paumee to the beam tower and rode beam to near west of Floresville again and then returned to Kelly. Shot nine landings at Kelly for accuracy and 90-degree approaches. Had trouble with engine running too hot and leaving smoke screen behind. Also had to hold down push button to bring wheels all the way up. (2:10) Ears are ringing from the engine noise. Am going to wear cotton plugs.

Wednesday January 17, 1940: Had another session with Jeep. Got 1 hour more. Had Lt. Walmsley (instead of Lt. Schultz). Did flying on beam. Had trouble finding cone of silence and crossing to opposite beam and making 45-degree reverse turn and returning.

Thursday January 18, 1940: No flying today due to poor weather conditions. Winds were at 30 mph and cold weather. We were issued our winter flying clothes tonight.

Friday January 19, 1940: Got winter clothes

for flying today. Went up and had an hour and 10 minutes ride in front cockpit under hood (instrument ride) with Lt. Walmsley. Then spent two periods shooting landings at Kelly #3 with Rux and later solo to Lake Moding and a few more landings at Kelly #3. Total time 3:15.

Monday January 22, 1940: Snowing hard today so no flying. Had instructions in formation flying at hangar. Took some pictures in winter flying suits outside. Snow all over. Turns—watch for one wing dip towards direction . Taxiing—throttle forward slowly. Throttle back when off ground to 30 feet and 200 rpm. Wheels up when leader does. Turns—Inside plane has throttles back. Outside plane has throttle forward. Leader banks normally. Landing signal—stick forward and back, wheels down. Two rear planes drop fifteen feet below to come in behind plane leading and to watch for flaps. Leader and two following planes use 25-degree and 30-degree flaps. Turns—towards echelon (crossover turn) (left echelon becomes right echelon and vice versa). Away from echelon—planes make column behind leader and then gradually go back into formation. Takeoff—in echelon but always go into basic three plane formation unless told otherwise. Landing—spread out formation and each plane drop three, five, or ten feet below each preceding plane.

Tuesday January 23, 1940: Had ride together with F/C Scott today. Took off first as pilot in front and Scott as observer. Practiced turns etc., and then went under hood at 3,000 feet. Practiced turns and climbing turns to 5,000 feet then power on glides etc. We came in and changed seats and I became observer for Scott. Same procedure for him as there was for me. Both made good landings and each of us had trouble keeping course under hood. Total time 2:10. (1:05 28-S, 1:05 29-S observer)

Wednesday January 24, 1940: Another day of dual instrument flying with Scott. Took off as pilot first again and spent an hour and 10 minutes (instrument) and came in. Changed pilots and on takeoff took first aerial pictures of Kelly (first ones I have taken from the air). Took some before we took off of Scott and me in winter flying suits. We listened to radio program and also flew beam for a while. Did some chandelles and steep turns. Total time 2:20. (1:10 28-S 1:10 29-S)

Thursday January 25, 1940: Had another session in Link Trainer today and did orientation lessons in finding beam and doing offset turns and then flying beam to cone of silence. 45 Minutes.

Friday January 26, 1940: Had first taste of formation flying today. Went up first hour in rear seat while F/C Stiles flew up front. We were two of three ship "V" formation with Lt. Schultz leading. Did turns in "V" formation and since ceiling was low (3,500 feet) we all climbed up through it, flying blind, to 5,500 feet. I surely wished I had my camera to take those planes in bright sunlight when we broke through the overcast. Flew there for a while. Sands and Rux and I with Lt. Stengleim and Rux, Lt. Schultz and Sands, and F/C Stiles and Schirmer. Then we let down through the clouds and came out at 2,000 feet right over Kelly. Waited an hour while Scott went up in my place. Ships came down very well coated with ice and snow so instrument flights were called off. Then went up with Lt. Schultz and watched again while formations (Sands, Rux as pilots) were practiced. Then went up again with Lt. Stenglein and we pilots found out how to use throttle and only rudder to slide over into position (no banking). It was some day. Three hours of formation.

Monday January 29, 1940: Had first long cross country today (2:15) with Lt. Miran as observer to help find points. Learned to use time to better advantage:

1. Check points every ten miles.

2. Mark out course heavy on map.

3. Mark out course on map—degrees, miles and minutes.

4. Keep constant altitude. After getting altitude over field and also allow only five-ten degrees for drift correction.

5. Compute time and mark exact time of arrival over each check point for future reference.

6. Drag field at 50 feet.

7. Land in first 1/3 of field.

8. Check over courses before taking off.

9. Keep time between check points more accurately.

January 29, 1939

Dear Mom,

I just now finished reading your wonderful letter. It really gave me a vivid picture of what our grand home is and I want to be there again with you so much after hearing you talk about it so sweetly. Glad you like the poem and candy. Someday I hope I can make you a worthy gift.

Our weather here is again sunny and balmy after our ten-day siege of cold weather. It broke a lot of records; I guess, about a thirty-year record of being cold so long. The old record was seven days of below-freezing weather.

Yes, I know you are going to love Martha too, Mom. Really she is so much like you that I couldn't help loving her. I do hope you can all come down here to see me graduate for I may be getting a lot of important things done that day and I want you and Dad here too.

Am anxious to see the pictures he printed of my film and have been trying to get some shots of our planes flying in formation while in the air. We start a 200 mile cross-country trip today. The weather is perfect and it will take us only an hour and a half to fly that. We have been dressing up in heavy flying suits and getting our pictures taken— everyone dashes around getting everyone's picture. We are learning a lot—are happy and are all anxious to know where we will all be stationed after graduation. Sure will be glad to be making more money.

Sure would like to see Dicky again. I wonder if he would recognize me or not. How are all your flowers? Have you got them all over the front room in the windows as per usual during the winter?

Am enclosing some more clippings of Kelly Field Cadet articles—haven't come to my face yet but I am always near the end of the alphabet.

I wrote Dorothy a long letter—hope to hear from her soon. Also sent Frank Jackson a picture of the three years at Randolph. I suppose he will get a kick out of seeing all the Schirmers again.

Yes, Bob Clark wrote about getting my other gun taken care of. Maybe I will fly over Shreveport and possibly close to Aunt Emma's house since we make flights to Barksdale Field which is located at Shreveport, La. What direction from Shreveport do they live? How Far?

Mom, you had better get the glasses and save your eyesight while you can. I know we'll all love you just as much as we do now when we get them.

So, the Usticks have another new Ford? I asked Dad what he wanted to do about our car but haven't heard from him yet. I know he must be busy.

I won't know whether I can get a furlough between graduation at my station or not unless it happens to be on the way to my station—for instance, if I happen to be sent to Selfridge Field which is north of Detroit, I might be able to go that way, but we won't be notified about where we'll be stationed until sometime after graduation. You know how the Army does things—rather at a slow pace—or it sure seems so to us, huh?

Thanks for all your encouragement Mom. You have been really swell and it has helped me a lot knowing you are there right behind me, being confident and fearless in my own courage—to be a credit to the Schirmers and especially to you and Dad. As I approach the time to be married, have a wife and family, I begin to more fully appreciate your wonderful exemplary lives and I really do want to be a success for you both. I at least want to finish everything I attempt.

Again, I want to wish you many more happy birthdays, Mom, and that you will be a grandmother to my children and to Dorothy's some day and maybe that will be sooner than you expect, for I have a wonderful fine girl in Martha and I know she will be a credit to all of us.

Lovingly your son, Franklin

Tuesday January 30, 1940: Went up for instrument ride with Lt. Yow in (in rear seat) while he was in front. Practiced holding altitude constant while making turns and getting different headings but had trouble. Went all over the sky but finally settled down and flew beam in but just missed cone of silence. Lt. Yow took over and lost altitude to 1,500 feet. Gave me forced landing which I hit okay. Picked a field, made a good approach and went down to about fifty feet. He took over and dipped lower and lower over mesquite and trees and just missing ground—two-four feet—scared me stiff. We'd fly along ground and zoom up over mesquite at 160-170 mph and then zoom down to another open space again. It gave me cold chills but was a good experience. Haven't take any chances trying it. It's a washout offense and slightly unsafe.

Went up for 2 hours instrument dual with F/C Scot and sat in rear cockpit. Flew blind awhile then rode beam. Missed cone again but am still trying. Came down and Scott got in behind and I took off and gave him various exercises under hood while I observed from cockpit. Total time in ship # 182 was 3:15.

Wednesday January 31, 1940: Went up again for instrument ride dual with F/C Scott. Had some trouble flying under hood from front seat but finally settled down. Flew okay then followed beam into cone of silence. Hit it for first time in air then landed and changed places with Scott who flew okay. Did well on beam except I had to take over several times to keep us from flying over San Antonio. He missed cone of silence because beam was so wide and signals so non-distinct. Came in and landed. Went up in rear seat with Lt. Schultz and watched while F/C Scott flew # 3 ship solo and Lt. Yow and Satterwhite flew in other ship. Flew all formation for over and hour. Learned signals better; like how to skid over into and out of formation. Anticipation of action important.

Thursday February 1, 1940 through Monday February 5, 1940: No flying due to rain and fog.

Tuesday February 6, 1940: Took off and flew cross country to Corpus Christi in one hour flat. Had to circle field for ten minutes until called in by control ship. Then landed and reported in by radio and was given permission to taxi back out. Got signal to take off and returned into a head wind in 1:20. (This time included landing and taxiing back to ramp). After this, had instrument ride with Lt. Egger. Did double rate turns in rough air. Learned how to keep stick on high side and made turns easier. Also let down (glide power) adjust speed with pitch and throttle to get 400' descent.

Went up as observer for Scott—radio broke.

Wednesday February 7, 1940: Went up as observer for F/C Satterwhite and flew for 1 hour and 10 minutes. Went up again with F/C Rux who acted as observer while I flew up front under hood. My main trouble seemed to be the following:

1. Not enough bank in turns.
2. Not anticipating climb indicator fast enough.
3. Overcontrolling—too tense.

Then came and hour and a quarter of formation flying led by Lt. Egger who had Rux in back seat, F/C Satterwhite on left and right wing of three ship formation. Took off and I got ahead using too much throttle. Did gentle banks and turns. Finally settled down and later made a formation landing at Kelly # 3 just fine.

Came in and landed at Kelly in formation. I feel tired and back is sore and fingers are plenty sore from working throttle incessantly and skidding with rudders. But it sure is fun.

Thursday February 8, 1940: Went up for three ship formation with Lt. Schultz leading. Had low ceiling. Lt. Schultz reported back to MT-5 by radio about ceiling, visibility etc. as we flew around. Had only 800 feet and visibility of three miles for half an hour. Later it began to clear up to a 2,000 foot ceiling with lower scattered clouds.

Then went up with Lt. Egger (I was in rear seat) while Scott and Rux were wing men. Flew for 2 hours, made four landings and learned plenty (even in rear cockpit) .

Later went up on instrument with Scott who acted as observer and flew orientation problem. Flew dual with Lt. Egger who showed me double rate turns and had me flying beam to cone of silence which I missed.

Rested all afternoon and flew N-26-S at night for over 2 hours local night flying. Made three landings with flood light (was in zone 3 at 2,000 feet) with Scott circling there with me too. Two others up at 3,000 feet. Made good landing with floodlights but when I brought it in under wing lights only I kept leveling off too high and dropped each of three landings in from ten feet or so and with a mighty hard thud but managed to hold her under control. Then changed gas tanks and went to upper zone and circled for another hour (smoked several cigarettes) and took it easy. Came in for final landing fine and was tired after seven hours of flying today.

Friday February 9, 1940: Had last lesson in orientation in Jeep from Lt. Schultz. We certainly are sorry to lose him as an instructor. He has been a real grand fellow and has taught us a lot. He has inspired us all with confidence by his quiet manner and his ability.

Monday February 12, 1940: Had another session in Jeep (35 minutes) in orientation with our new instructor Lt. Robinson—a youngish 2nd. Lieutenant.

Tuesday February 13, 1940: Took cross country Kelly to Flatonia to Yoakum to Victoria to Kelly. Total time was 2:10. Learned how to allow for drift of strong 35 mph wind at 3,500-4,500 feet. Made pretty good E.T.A.'s and also turned in on Kelly radio range with radio compass. Made good landing after a good let down. Had trouble with radio. Could not raise an answer from tower before takeoff. Took off anyway and reported after return. Everything okay.

Wednesday February 14, 1940: Went up for practice in six ship formation. Had leader ship of 2nd element with Lt. in rear seat. Learned to keep formation—giving signals before turning or doing anything. Cross over turns only when not preparing to land. Made two landings at Kelly # 3 and one at Kelly itself—1:10. Windshield all oiled up due to prop fluid leaking out of hydraulic cylinder.

Mistakes:

1. Not giving ships behind enough warning when changing speeds or altitudes.
2. Not keeping up with first element and not high enough.
3. Not allowing enough room to left or right of leading element of three.
4. Putting wheels down or flaps too soon thus slowing down and making it hard on following ships (on wings).

February 13, 1940

Dear Dad,

Received the enlargements and was glad to know you liked Martha. My scrapbook is really getting big now. We only have thirty flying days left and about 35 flying hours to get (75 total). I flew for 7 hours last Thursday—three formation, two instruments, and two night flights—that made up a lot of time which we had lost the week previous due to rain and fog.

"Gone with the Wind" is here—I haven't succumbed to going yet. Have budgeted myself on $3.00 for the rest of February. Martha surely is thoughtful. We have a swell time taking walks, playing games, and going on picnics—having cooks here from Kelly prepare bag lunches for us from our mess fund.

The graduation day has been set for March 23 but that could possibly be changed if we have a flock of bad weather days. Did I tell you what pay I'd be getting when I graduate? I am itemizing it so you will understand why I am doing certain things when I graduate:

Base pay per month 2nd Lt.—$125.00
Flying pay per month—$67.50
Subsistence pay per month—$18.00
Room allowance per month—$40.00
Total pay—$250.50 per month.

I would like to have you here for graduation but perhaps you would rather visit afterwards for Martha and I are thinking rather seriously of being married a day or so after I graduate. I will have a week to ten days of laying around waiting for my orders for stationing to come through from Washington which would be perfect for a short honeymoon. And do we love each other? No question about it.

I am going to the Ft. Sam Houston Bank and borrow the money for the car, wedding, and the ring. Incidentally, I have ordered an Air Corps ring—something I have wanted since the first day I've been at Randolph. I think we will be married at Randolph Field Chapel. About eight others are being married there shortly after graduation and it's a beautiful little church. It's someplace where we can always go back later and celebrate our bonds.

You certainly have been doing some great work with those enlargements. Everyone here in the barracks comments so favorably about them.

I only wish and hope that I can be stationed somewhere in the east so I can come home for a day or so before going to my station. We are allowed 250 miles per day to get to our station after notification.

We will be doing some six ship formation work starting this week. I have half of my required time in the Jeep which is 5 of the 10 hours, but I am studying all about it so I can be more than just proficient.

I have been playing handball again lately and find it's a good way to stay in good, physical shape. I surely am glad to be rid of all the running about as I did in Springfield.

I will be looking forward to your next letter, Dad.

Lovingly your son, Franklin

Thursday February 15, 1940: Jeep—another orientation flight—25 minutes.

Friday February 16, 1940: Instrument ride with Lt. Robinson for 1 hour.

1. To many corrections near cone.

2. Should ride on right edge of beam, both in and out beam.

3. Small corrections only.

Monday February 19, 1940: Did formation six ship today with Lt. Robinson leading. 1st with Scott and Seaman 2nd and 3rd. F/C Sands and Lt. Hughes led 2nd element and Schirmer and Satterwhite on wings. Total time 1 hour.

Did night cross country from Kelly to Pawnee to San Marcos in 1 hour and 30 minutes. Beautiful sight to see the lights sparkling like so many gems set on black and grey velvet. Flew in # 71 and had a little trouble with radio but reported to Pawnee and San Marcos several times to make sure. Found out today about the A.C. order about us going to Mississippi to observe Army maneuvers.

Tuesday February 20, 1940: Had another 30 minutes in Jeep while six flights of section three flew cross country to Brownsville via Corpus Christi. Our turn comes next Friday.

Wednesday February 21, 1940 and Thursday February 22, 1940: Vacation.

Friday February 23, 1940: Jeep for half an hour. Flew by beam cross country.

Monday February 26, 1940: Did formation flight five ship. I was in # 87 which was the 3rd ship of the 1st element with Lt. Robinson with F/C Satterwhite sandbagging and F/C Sands in # 2 position. Scott was loading 2nd element with one lieutenant in rear seat and F/C Seaman # 2 man in second element. Had trouble holding position steadily enough. Made a formation landing at Kelly # 3 after buzzing field at 25 feet in formation. Then made another turn about field and came in individual echelon. Then buzzed field again doing 175 mph and then returned to Kelly proper and landed in pretty fair formation.

My faults were the following:

1. Not staying in formation steadily enough. To far behind and at times too wide.

2. Not staying in position during turns.

3. Not staying behind and below on landings.

4. Not getting down when echelon is on my

side.

Tuesday February 27, 1940: Took off (Martha Watching) at 3:15 in # 97 for Mission and Brownsville. It's a beautiful day. Followed course down south and after 1/2 hour I found I couldn't find check points. I buzzed my first town and found it to be Freer, Texas according to the sign on the water tower. Couldn't find it on map so flew toward east and south and buzzed another town and found it was Benarides and then I

North American BC or BT-2. Similar to the BC-1 & AT-6. National Archives

knew where I was. Flew down and hit Falforias and arrived at Mission airport at 5 p.m. Reported and took off again at 5:05 and arrived at Brownsville at 5:35. Saw Rio Grande for the first time. Followed it all the way to Brownsville. Landed in Pan America Airport. Supervised the servicing, reported, took pictures and then ate. Waited around awhile and sent some postcards to Martha and parents and then watched airliners take off (Braniff, EAL, and Pan America). Took of at 7:45. Went to Kingsville, Corpus and Pawnee and arrived at Kelly. Made poor , bouncy landing with wing lights but managed to land safely. Saw Martha and went to barracks.

Wednesday February 28, 1940: No flying today.

Thursday March 1, 1940: Went up for dual instrument ride with Lt. Robinson. Still too mixed up when working on beam. Did better for first half hour but missed cone both times, although I managed to clip edge of cone both times. Wandered around too much. Had to hold hood under my chin with one hand while flying with the other so couldn't fly full instruments while hood was flapping in my face whenever I looked at my card.

Monday March 4, 1940: Cross country to Dallas by day and return by night. Took off at 2:30 (should have left at 2:20) but due to taxiing was late. Had trouble in allowing too much for drift at times

but hit all my numerous check points. Arrived at Hensley at 4:40 (2 hours and 20 minutes) which included leaving ramp at Kelly to gas pits at Hensley. Ate lunch after servicing plane and wandered around post looking at new BC-1-A's in reserve hangar. There were also P-12's and BT-9's.

Warmed up plane at 6:45 after we had our meeting on operations office porch with the Lieutenant in charge of our flight from Kelly. One Cadet, Johnson W.E., was still missing (heard later he landed in Waco and was fine).

Took off at 7:05 and had no trouble (except had to allow as much as 15 degree drift at times) and arrived at Kelly at 9:05 on ramp. Best night landing to date.

Tuesday March 5, 1940: No flying today.

Wednesday March 6, 1940: Night cross country to Fredricksburg to Temple and back to Kelly all solo. Took of in # 53 (after couldn't get radio to transmit in ship # 88) at 8 p.m. and hit Boone and Fredricksburg OK and took up course at 30-45 degrees but soon found myself in rough air and visibility getting poorer all the time. Went east and hit Austin and followed light line up to Temple at 3,000' on right side of airway. Checked in at Temple fine and then dust closed in again so picked out a beacon at south and west down to 2,000' and stayed there til almost to Austin just following lights. One or two ahead was all I could see. Detoured around Austin and followed light line to Kelly, let wheels down and landed OK. Total time was 2:30.

Thursday March 7, 1940: Went to Abilene with Lt. Robinson in rear cockpit. Hit all check points. Saw Scott and Seaman at various distances. Held altitude pretty well but wandered all over my direct course line but had only a mag. compass to fly by. Landed at Abilene and had refueling and coffee and cookies at airport offices. Came back in 1:25.

Friday March 8, 1940: Dual instrument ride with poor instruments. Flight indicator went out. Didn't pass yet. Went up tonight and flew night cross country around San Antonio. Made good landing. Last cross country trip.

Monday March 11, 1940: Dual instruments. Radio went out of order at 7,000 feet. Came down after only 1/2 an hour.

Tuesday March 12, 1940: Went on time and distance problem to, and over to, Geo. West and met Lt. Robinson at 2:20 in formation. Had to buzz town—Karnes City—poor visibility. Got to Beeville and after circling went back to Kelly by radio beam although wind blew me off course to over near Randolph before I found where I was. Rest of the flight was fine but Sands was only one to get there on time.

Wednesday March 13, 1940: Went out to get into # 87 for time and distance problem and found mechanics working on prop—no good. So had to ride rear cockpit (sandbag) and navigate for Lt. Robinson. Took off in formation with F/C Seaman. Left Kelly at 1:13 and flew towards Victoria. On the way did some low flying over mesquite and river beds. Saw Seaman pass us at Victoria. Later picked up Scott, Sands and Satterwhite and went to Kelly # 2 and got into a twelve plane formation. Later picked up six more and then flew over Kelly Field Proper in eighteen plane formation. Later today, went up with Lt. Robinson for instrument ride and did pretty well. Hit cone three times but wandered off beam a little and got hail Columbia from Robinson. Also got heck for changing gas tanks on

both cross country and instrument ride. Don't know whether I passed check or not. Did two or three let downs also.

Thursday March 14, 1940: No flying.

Friday March 15, 1940: Jeep–new orientation—beam spreading—1 hour 25 minutes.

Thursday March 21, 1940: Sandbagged formation practice. 40 minutes.

Friday March 22, 1940: Dry formation dual. 45 minutes.

Saturday March 23, 1940: Graduation flight dual. 50 minutes.

Sunday March 24, 1940: Practice Flight in BC-1 solo. 10 minutes.

The class of 40-A thus graduated from flight school, and passed into history. This is of course just one of thousands of similar stories. Robert F. Schirmer just happened to write his down. He continued to write his Mom and Dad whenever he could, the following two letters are an epilogue to his training:

April 4, 1940

Dear Mom and Dad,

Just heard from my wife, Martha, and she tells me you dropped her a card from Montgomery, Alabama on your way home. Well, we leave here for Fort Benning, Georgia, on April 10 and arrive there sometime on April 11. We'll let you know what my address there will be.

It was mighty swell of you both to be at the graduation and the wedding. I know Martha and I can never thank you both enough for all you have done for us both. I don't know how I'd ever been able to get through the whole thing financially without your aid. I think you are both swell parents and Martha is so happy to know you and she loves you as her own parents.

We have been on several maneuvers one overnight, and walked about eighteen miles. My feet hurt and have collected a blister on my left foot due to new army shoes which I had to buy to save my good ones. Sgt. Chapman, Scotty, and I went to

Charleston last Sunday and saw the town, Ft. Sumnter and a navy destroyer in the bay.

Mr. Seaman and family sent us $5.00 and a fine letter and telegram of congratulations. I am going to write him a thank-you note soon.

Well, supper time is here and you know how poor my appetite is—ha!

I surely do love my wife and am so glad you found her to be to your liking and meeting your approval. She is your new daughter and I want you to love her as much as any of us.

Lovingly your son, Franklin

June 20, 1940 (*written after a midair collision on June 17 in which eleven were killed*)

Dear Mom and Dad,

Received your telegram and I know how much you have been worried but it can happen to anyone. Don't forget, I am just as anxious about your welfare also. Yes, it was a pretty bad accident but it will undoubtedly result in more conservative regulations as usual after the investigation is completed.

We have been going to navigating school steadily and also flying each day and putting into actual practice what we learn in the classroom. So far I have come within 10 or 15 miles in a 120-mile trip but hope to do better next time—which is tomorrow morning.

Received your enlargements okay and many thanks for all your trouble. Hope you both are feeling well. It looks like we will be going to Panama as navigation instructors in September, which is not as far away as it seems. I am going to leave Martha in San Antonio while she has the baby and sells our car, and then that will give me time to get a place for her to stay and to assure proper conditions for an infant as well. Looks like a two-year tour of duty but I am hoping we can start another stamp collection along with our correspondence about photography and keep up with each other.

Wish we could all see more of one another. On my birthday last week we received a cake from the Mouregus in San Antonio—it sure tastes good. We

are still eating it.

Also received the book *American Practical Navigator* today. Thanks again and I sure hope I can find proper use for it. It seems that I never have enough time to do all I have plans for. Guess that's the way with a busy life, brains, and hands, huh?

Well, I will have some new rolls of film for you soon.

Lovingly your son, Franklin

A LETTER TO MY GRANDSON

Twelve year old Joshua Van Auken had been given an assignment at school to write about someone in his family. One day he was looking through his grandfather's scrapbook and came across an old newspaper clipping about his grandfather attacking fifty Japanese aircraft in WWII singlehandedly. He asked him to write down his thoughts about this very important event in his life. The following is his response:

Robert Danforth Van Auken, 22 February 1994

To: My twelve-year-old Grandson, Joshua Danforth Van Auken

Subject: In Harm's Way

Dear Joshua,

Thank you for asking about my feelings when I "fought against fifty Japs." To describe your feelings about something that happened fifty-two years ago is very difficult. For another person to understand your feelings is even more difficult. For example, can you describe clearly your feelings when you receive a good (or "bad') grade in school, and can I ever clearly understand your feelings? Or could the blind beggar whom Jesus cured, describe clearly his feelings when he regained his sight, or could you ever clearly understand his feelings?

For you to understand my feelings on that day of June 13, 1942 (Australian time), you must know something of my life up until that very moment.

As a growing boy, I was blessed by wonderful Christian parents who taught me love, honesty, and responsibility. In December 1937 at age twenty-

two I was a successful student at General Motors Institute of Technology in Flint, Michigan. My mother was a widow with very little money. I was working very hard but not earning quite enough money to pay my college and living expenses. I felt guilty every time I had to ask my mother for help even with a small amount of money.

I had just learned that the Army Air Corps (the name is now Air Force) was looking for young men to apply for flying training. So the next Saturday I went to the Flight Surgeon's office in the hospital at Selfridge Field, Michigan to sign an application and to be given a thorough medical and physical examination, along with seventeen other healthy-looking young men. Of the eighteen applicants, only John Reid and I passed.

Then in February 1938, John and I were off to San Antonio, Texas by railroad (very little commercial air transportation existed back in 1938). We reported to Randolph Field near San Antonio to commence our flying and classroom training on March 1, 1938, along with 356 other young men from all parts of the United States who had also passed the initial examination.

The training was physically rigorous and mentally demanding. We were up at 5:30 a.m. and worked and studied hard five days a week until about 10:00 p.m. Discipline was strict. In the area around the barracks and mess hall, we could never walk, only run unless we were marching in a military formation. Each Cadet's small space in the barracks was inspected by assigned "upperclassmen" each morning. Each article of clothing had to be folded according to regulation and placed in order in the dresser drawers. Beds were made so that the top army blanket, stretched tight, would "ripple" when the upperclassman inspector touched it. The one wash bowl for four Cadets must have the faucets "milked" so that the inspecting upperclassman could not wet his white gloves when he touched it. And much more. By the formation time at 6:15 a.m. Cadets must have showered, shaved, used the toilet, had their rooms inspected, and lined up to march

to breakfast. Any failure to meet the strict standards resulted in "gigs" and the walking of "tours," carrying a rifle Saturday and Sunday instead of liberty, off base.

Flying instruction was even more demanding. We learned takeoffs and landings, emergency procedures, acrobatics, navigation, formation flying, and much more. And we were taught honor, patriotism, military customs, and devotion to duty. Standards of performance in flying and in the classroom were exacting and difficult to meet.

But the Army Air Corps Flying School was the very best. Probably the only other flying school in the world, equally effective and tough, was the United States Navy's flying school at Pennsicola, Florida. Graduation carried much honor and a Commission as Second Lieutenant.

My friend John Reid "washed out" and was sent back to Michigan for failure to learn to fly quickly enough, so I was the only one who graduated of the original eighteen young men who applied that Saturday morning at Selfridge Field, Michigan. Only 158 of our beginning class of 358 made it through the school.

When the Japanese Empire made its sneak attack on Pearl Harbor on December 7, 1941, I was a good Fighter Pilot. In April 1942 I was the Operations Officer of the 49th Fighter Group at Darwin, Australia. Our Group's mission was to stop the Japanese bombing of that remote Northern Australian seaport. Our fighter planes were P-40's, very rugged with good firepower from their six 50-calibre machine guns (when they worked) but slower and less maneuverable than the Jap "Zero" fighters above 10,000 feet.

The Jap bombers with their Zeros as fighter escorts would fly from Kendari Airfield on the island of Timor, about 450 miles northwest of Darwin to bomb the Australian facilities at Darwin. The Japanese had been winning the war much faster than the American and Allied governments both expected. If they had been able to gain air superiority over Darwin, they might possibly have invaded the Con-

tinent of Australia at that location.

The Japs were formidable fighters and cruel winners. American prisoners and prisoners from other countries were starved, beaten, tortured, and murdered. We hated the Japs. And we were glad for our chance to beat them at Darwin. We didn't allow them to gain air superiority. Many of their attacking airplanes were shot down and crashed into the sea or jungle. Yes, we also lost some airplanes and pilots, but not as many as they lost.

On June 13, 1942, Ben, another American pilot, and I were flying a mission about 1,000 feet over Darwin to help train Australian anti-aircraft gunners (they didn't shoot at us, only practiced aiming their guns at us). Suddenly, we heard on our radios that our radar station had detected a formation of Japanese aircraft approaching Darwin at 26,000 feet from the Northwest. Compared with today's radar equipment, radar in 1942 was primitive and inaccurate.

Our group's three fighter squadrons were at dispersed airfields about thirty to forty miles south of Darwin. For some reason, our radar hadn't detected the approaching Japs until they were about forty to fifty miles from Darwin, too late for our squadrons to intercept them before they released their bombs. I thought that Ben and I, already in the air over Darwin, could intercept the formation head on and shoot down the lead airaaft to disrupt the formation and interfere with the aim for their bombs. Our radar now reported twenty-seven bombers escorted by twenty to thirty Zeros.

At 10,000 feet, climbing over Darwin, Ben and I now saw the Jap bomber formation—three beautifully flown V's of nine aircraft each. Many Zeros were protecting them on all sides. At 12,000 feet

Curtiss P-40N-1   National Archives

Ben was falling behind. I slowed my climb so he could keep up. At 17,000 feet Ben radioed that his P-40 had engine trouble and he waved "good-bye." I was alone. Our three squadrons of about sixteen P-40's each were fifteen to twenty miles behind. I pushed the throttle forward and continued to climb.

Above 20,000 feet my P-40's rate of climb began to slow down. Remember, Josh, the P-40's performance at high altitude couldn't match the Zero's. I had held back too long waiting for Ben. The twenty-seven bombers dropped their bombs. Their formation formed and headed back to the Northwest. The Australian anti-aircraft guns hadn't touched them.

I gave chase out over the Pactfic about five miles behind the Japs. I caught them about twenty miles from Darwin over the blue Pacific ocean. Josh, you wanted to know what I was feeling.

First, our orders were to kill Japs. I was twenty-six years old, with a loyal, devoted twenty-one-year-old wife and a ten-month-old son back home. We must not let those cruel and brutal beasts, those Japs, win the war and inflict their cruelty on our American people, including my own family. Second, I was a trained, professional officer in the United States

Army. As a boy, my parents and the American society of that time had taught me honesty, responsibility, and commitment to duty. The Army taught me discipline, toughness, honor, patriotism, devotion to duty and much more. I was a good fighter pilot, but we were at 26,000 feet where the Jap fighter airplanes outpowered our P-40's.

I attacked from the left side of the formation. Two Zeros slid out from their protective position on the formation to intercept me. Before they knew what happened, I went underneath them and came up under the lead V of nine bombers. Just for a fleeting moment my P-40 stalled despite the full power of its motor. But I recovered altitude and airspeed to come back under the last V of nine Jap airplanes and fired into the belly of one of their bombers. My tracer bullets sprayed into the bomber's belly and I saw pieces flying off. One large piece looked like a man.

To escape the Zeros that would soon be after me, I immediately followed our standard tactic of a power dive straight down. Our P-40 was no match for a Zero above 20,000 feet, but the Zero could not hold together in a power dive with a P-40.

Hooray! I had damaged or possibly destroyed a Jap bomber and got away unscathed. Another attack from the opposite side of the Jap formation had to be tried next. But this time I got into trouble. When I dove my P-40 straight down for about 5,000 feet, the Jap formation continued flying Northwest. Therefore to make the second attack it meant I had to regain the 5,000 feet of altitude and to catch up to the Japs. Keep in mind, Joshua, that my P-40 had little speed advantage over those Jap bombers at 26,000 feet altitude. The Japs were now far out over the Pacific Ocean.

When two fighter pilots worked together in a situation such as mine, they could fly almost side by side with the flight leader's aircraft slightly in the lead ahead of the wing man. In that type of loose formation each pilot could "guard the other's tail" to reduce the danger of being surprised from an attack from behind. But I was alone. The only way I could "guard my tail" was to "S" back and forth. But if I did this, how could I catch the Jap bombers for another attack? I "S"ed slightly, but not enough. Suddenly I heard loud gunfire behind my airplane! Jap Zeros were on my tail. Had their aim been good, my mission would have been over. But their 20 mm cannons (they fired explosive bullets about 3\4 inch in diameter) made a large hole in my P-40's right wing, and just behind that hole a twelve inch wide rip in the entire width of the right aileron. As taught, I immediately shoved the stick forward for a power dive, wide open, to escape the Jap Zeros.

With the damaged airplane, obviously I couldn't fight any more, only try to escape. I continued in the dive, past the "red line" (maximum safe speed) on the air speed indicator until I felt sure that the Zeros couldn't follow. Then I cut the throttle back and eased back on the stick to come out of the dive, only to discover that the stick was stuck and the airplane continued to dive straight down toward a crash in the Pacific Ocean. Obviously some damage had been done to other parts of the airplane that I couldn't see, probably the control surfaces on the tail assembly. With help from the "trim tab", the damaged P-40 slowly came out of the dive. At 10,000 feet I headed for the nearest island.

The Japs couldn't keep up with the P-40 in the power dive, but they wanted to complete their kill of the American pilot who got by their fighter screen and shot up their bomber. I saw two Zeros coming from above and behind, but now my P-40's engine was running rough. With the Zeros close behind and shooting my only chance was a low level bailout. (Routinely, they shot at American pilots descending with their parachutes—we didn't do that to them.) Down to water level, headed for an island. At that time and place in the war we had no airsea rescue. A downed pilot, with only his "Mae-West" inflatable life preserver, had little chance in these shark-infested waters. At fifty feet above the sea, headed for an island, with two Zeros shooting at me and my hopelessly damaged P-40, I opened the canopy and unlatched the seat belt. Only one *chance was left. The gasoline in my P-40 was on fire and the heat of it was intense. I started a roll for the aircraft to be on its back at 500 feet so that I could fall out, but part way around in the roll the aircraft went out of control and I passed out. I woke up in the air. The early bailout training, during our "sweat sessions" as Cadets, while part of the hazing we all went through, had its benefit. In an involuntary move my right hand hit my left side at the rip cord handle. I yanked and the parachute opened. Just in time, too! The two Zeros made one pass shooting at me (I'm still here so they must have missed). I landed in the water and played dead while they circled back to check. Then they climbed off to the Northwest to join their formation to brag about killing the foolhardy American who dared to attack the warriors of the rising sun.*

I was in chest-deep water about 200 feet from the narrow beach of an island. My P-40, now a ball of fire had crashed in the jungle just beyond the beach and its remaining ammunition was exploding. I was alone, but alive. My damaged P-40 had been hurtling toward its fiery end at perhaps 240 miles per hour. (60 miles per hour equals 88 feet per second, so 240 miles per hour would equal 4X88 = 352 feet per second.) Close timing, Joshua. Only one second later and I'd have landed in the dense jungle behind the beach; one second earlier and I would have landed in deep water. Five to ten seconds either way and I'd have been a goner. Did God have a good angel watching and taking care of me? Why?

The beach was within wading distance. On the shore I sat down and tried to piece together what had happened, and to thank God for His series of miracles in saving me:

1) I got by the Jap fighter screen to shoot into a bomber.

2) The Jap pilots shot at me but missed a vital spot.

3) My airplane finally came out of the power dive.

4) I didn't burn up with my P-40.

5) I landed within one split second of a safe spot in shallow water.

All the remainder of my life, I now owed to Him. My legs were very badly burned. All the skin was gone in most places. I shuddered from the terrible pain. The endorphins hadn't helped much yet. (Ask your dad what "endorphins" are.)

I started walking along the beach to get help. A long story goes on from here, Joshua, but you wanted to know what I was feeling when I fought those fifty Japs. This is the story of how it was, how I felt, and why I felt that way.

Many other people have fought for their countries—each story would be different. Did you know, for example, that your Dad volunteered to return to Vietnam for a second tour of duty to fight for his country and for what he believed was right? The North Vietnamese whom he fought were just as cruel as the Japs were in 1942 — probably worse. They, too, starved, beat, tortured, and murdered American prisoners.

Many fighters, but also helpless children, women, and the elderly on both sides of a war suffer and die. War is stupid!

An Australian Aborigine found me walking on the beach and took me to his small tribe. Three of their young men took me from their island across forty-five miles of the Pacific Ocean in a small dugout canoe in a long day and a half. Those black people couldn't have been more kind. On the mainland of Australia, they found some Australian soldiers who got me to a hospital. I couldn't walk from the swelling of my burned legs. After nine months in various hospitals, I went back to work, never to recover completely from my injuries and trauma.

Love, Papa

P.S. About a month after my rescue, Colonel Paul Wurtsmith, our Group Commander, visited me in a hospital tent in the jungle near Darwin and formally presented me with a medal called the "Silver Star" for "Gallantry in Action." I was still very sick and nervous, but honored. Some time later I was awarded "The Purple Heart" for being wounded in combat.

Would I do the same things again if I could? Would you, Josh?

CLASS 42-X

After the start of WWII many things changed in this country. The need for military personal of all types was paramount. The Aviation Cadet program also underwent great change, in order to accommodate the vast number of pilots that were needed for an all-out war.

In the early summer of 1942, it had become apparent that the Training Center was faced with a very acute shortage of flying instructors for pilot training as well as pilots for navigation, bombardment and gunnery training. As the training missions were to be stepped up from 30,000 to 50,000 and then to the projected 75,000 program, the need became correspondingly greater. The shortage arose from the inability of the CG, AAF, to flow back to this training center, pilots for the regular classes to act as instructors; combat needs for pilots had priority over training needs. The requirements of the expanded training program dictated action of some kind to meet the flying instructor shortage.

On 1 and 2 September 1942, General Stratemeyer visited Randolph Field. At that time he informed the CG orally that General Arnold had just approved a plan under which the training centers would be authorized to requisition Aviation Cadets directly from preflight schools and, at one station selected for this purpose, train them for duty as flight instructors. This training of Cadets as instructors was to be carried on as an overload to the regular training program. The graduates were to be definitely earmarked as flying instructors and were not to be available for assignment to combat units.

At the time of General Stratemeyer's visit, no written information had been received from higher authority, but because of the urgency of the situation, General Stratemeyer authorized Headquarters (GCACTC) (Commanding General Air Corps Training Center) to put the plan into effect at once. Since Cadets were to be taken direct from preflight school, it was necessary to synchronize this program with the graduation dates from preflight. A class was scheduled to graduate from preflight school on 6 September 1942, so Headquarters acted immediately. On 2 September, Colonel M. F. Davis and some staff officers were called to Headquarters for consultation. At this meeting it was decided to select 200 especially qualified Aviation Cadets each 4 1/2 weeks for the special instructor's course. On 3 September Headquarters directed Colonel Davis to implement this plan. This change resulted from a hurried computation of requirements for flying instructors. These calculations indicated there would be a shortage of over 500 by 15 December 1942. If the new training program could be initiated immediately with a special three month course of instruction, the anticipated shortage of 15 December could be offset at least partially. It was assumed there would be a 50% elimination rate in this instructor course due to the accelerated rate of training.

The plan was to enter 400 Aviation Cadets a month until the training program levelled off at 75,000, 102,000 or some larger figure. The course was to be a total of 13 1/2 weeks in length, with from 170 to 200 hours of flying time. With the entrance of the third class there would be at least 800 students in this special instructor's course at all times. Randolph Field was selected as the only station in this training center that could handle this kind of student load. As the program progressed, basic training was tapered off and finally discontinued at Randolph. It was assumed that these Aviation Cadets, upon successful completion of this course of training, would be commissioned second lieutenants, rated as pilots and placed on flying status as instructors; eventually they would be assigned to duty with combat units.

The first class of 400 was selected under the above premises and started training 8 September

1942. It was decided to make no use whatsoever of the primary type of training airplane, but to start training immediately in the BT-13 airplane. There was some doubt at Headquarters as to how this departure from the normal flying procedures might affect the elimination and accident rates. Concern as to elimination rates was based primarily upon the accelerated rate of training contemplated. Nevertheless, it was agreed that the opportunity existed for a most interesting experiment which, if successful, might prove to be the basis for a careful restudy of flying training methods. Both the flying and ground school courses were organized to cover all of the subjects given in primary and basic flying schools.

On 8 September the day training started, written authority and vague instructions, relative to this class, were received. Only Class I, physically qualified Cadets were to be selected as potential instructors. Service personnel who had previous flying experience could be selected.

The first experimental class was designated Class 42-X. Four hundred Aviation Cadets began the training. Those selected were, as a group, better than the average Cadet class sent to primary from preflight. This was brought out by the fact that 77% of those entered were in the top half of the STA-NINE Rating Scale, whereas based on probabilities, only 50% of an average class at that time fell at this point on the rating scale. Class 42-X was studied very closely by A-3, Headquarters, and the psychologists of the Classification Center at SAACC. Accordingly, Class 42-X was superior to an average group. Approximately 15% of those entered were eliminated at the end of six weeks' of instruction. It was evident from the results with Class 42-X that previous flight training was a definite advantage and was not indicated in the STANINE rating scale based on psychological tests aimed at giving an indication of ability to learn to fly. One group had a high elimination rate and upon examination of that particular group, it was found that 70% of those entered were without previous flight training. Forty-five of the forty-eight eliminated, or 94% of those in that group, were without previous flight training. It is apparent that regardless of the rating group a man was in, those with previous flight training fared much better than those without any previous flight training.

Class 42-X completed training on 13 December 1942. The final detailed statistics reveal that 400 entered and 235 or 58.75% graduated. At that time, 56.1% of the classes undergoing normal instruction graduated. One hundred and sixty-nine men in the class had more than thirty hours of previous flying training, two hundred and thirty-one had either none, or less than thirty hours of flight training.

The training record of 42-X is as follows: 235 or 58.75 % graduated from the course; 2 or .5% were killed just prior to graduation; 1 or .25 % were disciplinary eliminees at the end of the class; 3 or .75 % were held over & graduated with Class 43-C; 4 or 1.00 % were eliminated for physical reasons; 8 or 2.00 % resigned from flying status; 147 or 36.75 % were eliminated for Flying Deficiencies. This record is based on a total of 400 men who started with this class.

The following presents comparative data on the students who had more than 30 hours of flying training with those who had less than this or none at all. For the students with more than 30 hours previous time: 144 or 85.1% of the group graduated; 16 or 9.5% of the group were eliminated for flying deficiencies; 3 or 1.8 % of the group resigned; 3 or 1.8% of the group were eliminated for physical defects; 3 or 1.8% of the group were held over for Class 43-C.

For the students with less than 30 hours or no previous time: 94 or 40.6% of group graduated; 131 or 56.7% of group were eliminated for flying defects; 5 or 2.1% of group resigned; 1 or 0.4% of group were eliminated for physical reasons.

Class 42-X was an interesting experiment which was not repeated. Only this one class was entered in the all—through instructor course. Late in September 1942, a series of conferences were held at Headquarters Flying Training Command. At these conferences, the CG, Flying Training Command, was assured by CG, AAF, that the Flying Training Command would be allotted from the normal output of the training centers sufficient pilots to meet the requirements of the expanded training program. On 17 December 1942, a directive was received at Headquarters stating that no more classes would be placed in training under the provisions governing Class 42-X.

An interesting sidelight on Class 42-X is that Headquarters believed the graduates were little better than those who had finished basic training in the normal pilots course. All the training Class 42-X received, except the last lO-15 hours, was on BT-13 airplanes. The last part of their training was on the AT-6. Eleven of the graduates of Class 42-X were assigned to Foster Field, Victoria, Texas. General Carter wrote to the station commander relative to them: "They will be given the advanced course of training at your school on a proficiency basis before being assigned to duty as instructors. At such time as they are considered proficient and equivalent to the normal graduates of your advanced school, they may be assigned; after sufficient instructor training; for duty at your station as instructors." This was the final official evaluation of the members of Class 42-X. (The preceding 42-X information was supplied by R. F. Schirmer).

CADET LIFE IN 1943

The following is but one of the many perceptions of Aviation Cadet training during WWII. It was told to the author by **William G. Sherret, class of 43-B:**

William G. Sherret, much like the rest of the Aviation Cadets, really didn't have a clue as to what he had done, when he volunteered for the Aviation Cadet Pilot Training program. He was in college at the University of Colorado. It was early in 1943. Like most young men of the time, as well as young men of all but the latest times, he dreamed of becoming a pilot. With the advent of WWII, it seemed like a perfect time to fulfill that dream.

The first stop on the trail to pilot-dum was a classification center. It was really nothing more than "boot" camp. This one was called Jefferson Barracks and was located south of St. Louis. It was midwinter—cold and bleak. They lived in tents, and were not even issued uniforms for the first week or so. He was fortunate that he had come from Colorado, and at least had a suit. Most of the guys had come from much warmer climates, and only had short-sleeved shirts. After the first week of Siberian torture, they were actually issued uniforms. The favorite items in this deep freeze were the hats, gloves, and of course, the long O.D. wool overcoats. Life, such as it was, became almost intolerable there. They had a small stove in each tent designed to keep them from freezing. When heated to red hot it would not even keep them warm, let alone comfortable. Fifteen men were assigned to each tent. The bunks were stacked three high around the perimeter of the tent—the stove in the middle. Many of the wool coats had burned marks on the back near the bottom, where their owners had gotten too close to the red-hot stove in their vain attempts to get warm. Many were the nights they would bundle up in those coats, several pairs of socks, gloves and hat, and crawl into bed under their one thin wool blanket, hoping they would survive the night. The latrines were located four blocks away. The mess hall was about five miles away, and they spent much of their time marching back and forth to chow. The rest of the time was spent doing the usual "grunt" things like peeling potatoes, cleaning latrines, marching, and freezing. Life was so bad, in order to get some time to rest and warm up, many of the men would take a bar of Fels Naphtha soap, (A yellow lye soap, very caustic), and put it under their arms to raise their temperature, so they would be qualify for "Sick Call". At least that would get them out of the weather, as well as the "other" duties. There were about 30,000 men at Jefferson Barracks during this time. Most were not Cadets, but general infantry.

Jefferson Barracks as it looked in 1943.   Museum Col., St. Louis County Dept. Parks and Rec.—Hist. Div.

Conditions were so bad, that when meningitis broke out, it spread like wildfire. Five percent of the men died from this disease alone during that one winter.

Finally the day came, cold and wet of course, when Bill's class was rescued from Jefferson Barracks.

They took the train north to Moorhead, Minnesota, where the state teachers college was part of the CTD. This train was not a nice commuter special however—oh no, it was the train from hell—packed with troops all comfortably(?) seated on wicker seats. There was one potbelly stove at the end of the car, and it was the sole source of heat for the entire car. It's no wonder everyone crowded to that end. It was cold. Real cold. The dining car consisted of a concrete slab in the center of the bag-

gage car, where a wood camp fire was built. Concrete blocks supported a fifty-five gallon drum that was used to cook stew. Nothing was too good for our fighting men. Bill had but five-weeks training in Moorhead. It consisted of some classroom instruction, and three to four hours in a J-3 Cub. This was done to see who could, and who could not, be trained as a pilot—more or less a first cut. All of his group were living in makeshift quarters in the school gym. You can imagine how much fun it was to try and get a good-night's sleep in such an atmosphere. It's a good thing they were young. They were eighteen and nineteen years old for the most part. His class had a mascot, who was a 100 lb. St. Bernard. He loved the Cadets, but he didn't care for the inspecting officers at all. Anytime there was an in-

A typical College Training Detachment. This one is Flt. 12 of the 302 CTD, Knox College Galesburg, Illinois, 1/44.

Cullen R. Thompson 44-B

spection, one of the Cadets had to first corral the dog so the officers could get in. I wish we had such a dog. After having all the fun(?) one could have in such a short time, they were sent by train to Los Angles, and then on a bus from there to Santa Ana in Orange county south of Los Angles. This was somewhat of a waste base. The men were given some ground school, lots of marching and little else in the four or five weeks they were there. They were, however docked each payday a small amount to pay for grass seed and dog food for the base mascot, a great Dane. After the war was over the entire base staff was court-martialed for grafting money from the Cadets.

It seemed the army must have had a deal with the railroads to move as many men on them as possible. After coming all the way from Minnesota to California, this class was now sent to Thunderbird Field near Phoenix, Arizona.

Thunderbird was a civilian primary-training facility. This gave the fledgling birdmen some relief from the rigors of a straight military base. Now at least Bill and his class would finally get to do what they had signed on to do—FLY! Bill's in-

structor was an ex-rice sower. Yes, they really sowed rice by airplane. His name was Bob Mayberry—a real nut. Bob and Bill spent many fruitless hours trying to do an outside loop in the PT-17 Stearman. They never were successful. Another interesting pastime was to fly really low, and buzz the swimming pools in the area. Bob heard that the girls were swimming in the nude, and wanted some first hand information.

If Bill messed up while he was flying with Bob, his punishment was for the instructor to hold the gosport tube out in the slipstream. (A gosport is a rubber speaking-tube, that is attached to the students leather helmet by copper tubes in the helmet, that were located one over each ear. The rubber tubes were then slipped over these. This allows the instructor to talk to the student, but not the other way around). The air from the slipstream would pressurize the students helmet, causing it to blow up like a balloon. Really hard on the ears. The students tried real hard not to mess up.

The next stop on the trail was preceded by yet another long train ride. It was back to sunny California again. To a town north of Los Angles, called

Lancaster. It's not much today, but during the war it was a hubbub of activity. They arrived about midnight. Much to their surprise, everyone was up, and running all over the place. As the bus pulled in, the upperclassmen shouted, "You'll be sorry!" As soon as they were unloaded from the bus, the instructors lined Bill's bunch up, and announced that one of the training aircraft had crashed shortly before they had arrived, and they were to be part of a search, and rescue mission. Out in the desert they went, walking into the home of numerous snakes, scorpions, etc. In due course they found the student. He was dead, with a partially-opened parachute laying over his body. The instructor was found some distance away, in the same condition. What a welcome to Basic.

Here they trained in the really complex, (compared to the PT-17), BT-13, or Vultee Vibrator as it was known. It had a two-position propeller and a radio—wow, the dawn of modern aviation had arrived.

It seemed every base had its own mascot. Lancaster was no exception. The only difference here was that it was a donkey named "Susie" instead of a dog. "Susie" would show up in the chow hall whenever she wished. The doors were left opened so she came and went at will. Bill remembers many times feeling hot breath on his neck during a meal upon turning around he found that he was nose to nose with a donkey. She loved to run ahead of the taxiing aircraft. And one of her favorite sports was to stand in front of an idling aircraft and lean into the breeze from the propeller.

It was here at basic the decision was made as to what the young pilot would be assigned to fly in combat- fighters or bombers. Bill wanted fighters, P-38's to be exact. The only problem was, that no fighter slots were open. So he went in for the photo reconnaissance version of the, P-38 "Lightning".

"All aboard!" Riding the rails again, this time back to Arizona—Williams A.A.B. Here was the really big time. First the AT-6, with lots of power, plenty of speed, and was it ever easy to ground loop. It was also lots of fun, and perhaps the best advanced-training airplane ever built. It even taught the student what the rudders are for—something that has been lost in modern training. From this experience, one could then step to the P-39, or even the P-51 or P-47. To get used to two engines, as on the P-38, the students were given a few hours in the Curtiss AT-9. This design came about around 1940. It had become evident that with the war already raging in Europe, it would not be too long before the United States became involved. Even though we had a national isolationist policy, which had many people against involving our nation in any war, some far thinking men knew we needed training aircraft, and pilots to fly them. The production AT-9's were all metal construction, low-wing cantilever monoplanes. They were powered by two 295 hp Lycoming R-680-9 radial engines. This aircraft cruised at about 175 mph. It was not near as great a performer as the P-

Republic P-47B, 3/9/43   National Archives

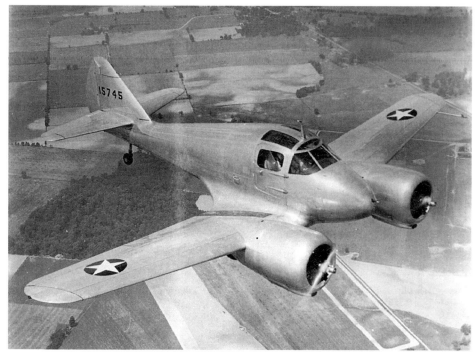

Curtiss AT-9   National Archives

dets, as with all young Cadets, what they had sacrificed, all the hardships they had endured, and all the dangers they had faced, became of little consequence the moment those, coveted, "silver wings," were pinned on their chests. Their dreams had come true.

THE CADET'S WIFE

Meanwhile back at the home front, there were thousands of women who had married into this program. They were a determined, and resourceful lot, as is evidenced by the following story written by: Sidney Daniel, and used with permission from the 43-E *Newsletter*.

Robert E. Daniel and his bride Sidney were married in 1941, a year of great turmoil throughout the world. Robert E., or "Ed" as he was affectionately known, was an Aviation Cadet in class 43-E. His wife Sidney, was also somewhat of a "Cadet." Every nine weeks, her husband was transferred to another base to continue his training. She, a real trouper, and "head over heels in love" with her flyboy, would follow along. The pay for an Aviation Cadet in those days wasn't much, only $75.00 per month. Of course it never really was much pay in any era. There was rent to pay (such as rental quarters were in those days) food to buy and cook (who could afford to eat out); Gas had to be bought for the car (a new dress would have been nice, lots of luck) and for entertainment, a movie once in a blue moon. What a life!

When Ed was sent to basic (Later called preflight) in San Antonio, Sidney was not allowed to join him. At Ballanger, during Christmas time she, and the other wives, would stand outside of the fence and "pray the Cadets up" on their solos; they were only allowed to look, not touch. In those days, ev-

38, but it did serve its purpose in familiarizing the students with the complexities of two engines. The next step was a big one. The United States had contracted with the British to supply their Air Force with the P-38 Lightning. The first three aircraft sent to England were of the Model 322-61's. These had both engines rotating the same way, and were not turbocharged. They also had only 1150 hp. They proved unsatisfactory, and the entire order was canceled. The USAAF confirmed the British tests, and used the approximately 140 airplanes from the first British order as trainers, or for experimental purposes. They were designated RP322's.

This was really what it was all about. At last Bill was to fly his "Dream Machine". Even though it didn't have the power of the combat version, going from the 550 hp of the AT-6 to a total of 2300 hp on this bird was a real kick. To make it even more fun, the first time he flew it, he was solo. There were no two-seat versions at that time. It does indeed take a special breed of man to literally risk everything to fulfill his dream.

Graduating in February of 1944, Bill's class was mighty glad to get out. The training had been mostly, "Hell on wheels." But to these young Ca-

erything these young couples owned would fit in one large beat-up old suitcase. One room was all that they could afford, and many times Sidney could only afford one meal a day. It wasn't hard to keep her figure. Even with all this "hardship," she only remembers those times as "exciting." On their first anniversary, her husband presented her with a wonderful gift: a book entitled *Airplanes of This and Other Nations*, and had the audacity to ask her to memorize it. And she did. Well how else would a young wife be able to converse with a bunch of "flyboy's"?

Thank God that there were many folks who had compassion on the young fighting men and their families. In San Angelo, Gerald Fairbanks and his family opened their home and their hearts to Ed and Sidney. They found a room for her, and his uncle gave her a job at a beauty supply house. She even got to eat two meals a day while they were there. She typed menus in exchange for her meals. Everything was done in the spirit of oneness. Wives shared meals, newspapers, laundry, clothes, tears, you name it, they shared it. Well, not the husbands. The Cadet club was located in the San Angelus Hotel, a favorite meeting place and watering hole. The wives would spend many hours there sharing their dreams, frustrations, and laughs.

Since moving had become such a way of life, the mere mention of the word began to sound like a train ride, "Next stop"; this time it was Eagle Pass. Here come the wives—they were starting to think they were "camp followers." Well, since she and the other wives couldn't live in Eagle Pass, they lived in luxury(?), in the usual, one dingy room, in the nearby metropolis of Carrizo Springs. If there were any advantages to this situation, she didn't see them. The wives had to take a bus from there to Eagle Pass on the weekends; kinda hard on married life. Because of its proximity to Mexico, many of the Cadets would walk in over the bridge. Buy the time the evening was over they usually had so much to drink that they had to have help to get back. Sidney, being a trustworthy person would hold the; "high"

Cadets money, until the next day to preclude some lovely "seniority" from rolling him.

Everyone who has ever been an Aviation Cadet, will testify that it was "Hell". But to Sidney and her peers, we all offer a "hand salute" of eternal gratitude. Many of us would not have made it if it were not for "These."

AT-6 NIGHT ATTACK ON A TRAIN

There are as many different stories about Cadet life as there are Cadets. The following is one of them: The night was crystal clear, the stars sparkled like diamonds. The shadows cast by an almost full moon, gave the landscape, an eerie, unrealistic glow. The whine of starters, drumming of propellers, and roar of numerous Pratt & Whitney R-1340's springing to life, shattered the peace of an otherwise silent night. The location was a basic Air Force pilot training base, somewhere in the southern United States. The Aviation Cadets were off on solo night training. The squeal of brakes, resonated through the darkness as they taxied their AT-6 trainers toward the runway. One by one they are cleared onto the runway, and launched into the night, nothing but dim position lights, and the blue and orange flame from the exhaust, to show their location. One of the Cadets, looking down on the yellow dots of light coming from the homes and buildings scattered over the landscape, noticed a bright stream of white light, it was coming from the headlight on the front of a train, as it made its lonely trek through the night. A sinister plan unfolds in his mind. He flies parallel with the tracks, straight as a string across the flat countryside. Pulling quite some distance in front of the engine, he banks sharply turning to a heading opposite that of the trains, and descends toward the track. Leveling off at 50', he's glad that he is very familiar with the area—no towers, tunnels or other obstacles are in the way. Closing on the train at breakneck speed, he waits until he has about one aircraft length between his prop and the train—on goes his right landing light. The engineer having

Composite of two pictures, by Errol D. Severe.   North Arkansas Line by James R. Fair & AETC/HO

been blinded by the bright light, jerks the emergency brake, hoping against hope, that he can stop his heavily-loaded iron missile before it impacts head on, with what appears to be another train directly in front of him. The wheels of the train lock, sparks fly into the darkness, the bottoms of the wheels turn bright red from the friction. The mighty iron horse screeches to a halt. The aircraft zooms overhead, pulling up sharply into the night sky, never to be seen again.

The next morning back at the base, all personnel are assembled. The commanding officer stands up in front of the men and introduces a rather slight built man in a dark suit. "This is an agent of the F.B.I.; I will let him tell you why you have been assembled here." The agent began to speak, "Last night one of you men flew head on with a freight train, and at the last moment you turned on one landing light, then pulled up. The damage to that train due to the locking of the wheels (which resulted in melting flats on them) is in excess of $100,000.00. We want to know who did it." The Cadets thought— Whoa! This makes a C.A. look like a free trip to Hawaii! For days after that, they were grilled, threatened, coerced; all to no avail. Some forty years later, it still remains a mystery: Who made the night attack on the train?

FIRST CADET TO FLY A JET

The second world war was over. Most people thought it was the "War to end all Wars." However, something was wrong. Not something most individuals could point a finger at, and identify, rather more of a gut feeling. General George Patton was very outspoken on his feelings about our Russian "Allies." He wanted to send captured German troops, with American support, to fight against the Russians. He felt they were very much a threat to the Democratic way of life that we enjoy. As it turns out, the next thirty years proved him to be right. Others must have also felt the impending danger from Communism, and we are very fortunate that

they did. Someone with the "big picture" decided we should again start to build up our number of pilots. After WWII, most were sent back to civilian life. Those who were in training at the war's end were offered the chance to get out, and the few that remained in training were mostly "washed out." You didn't have to do anything wrong, or be an unskilled student. If the instructor didn't like your looks, you were history. As a result, our pilot force was at a very low ebb. This seems to be the usual course of events preceding a war.

At the end of 1946, it was decided to reactivate the Cadet method of flight training. The first class after the war consisted of approximately 83 Cadets. Most of the several hundred men in this class were student officers, men who had been Navigators and Bombardiers in WWII, and now wanted to fulfill their dreams of becoming pilots.

Class 48-A started out at Lackland AFB, in San Antonio, Texas about January of 1947. Preflight training was not in use at this point in time. The men received the same boot camp training that any enlisted man would have received. It was not the usual-upper-class-lower class situation that prevailed both before and after this time. After three months at Lackland, 48-A Cadets were sent across town to Randolph AFB, which had been called the "West Point of the Air." Times were changing rapidly. The men of 48-A were members of the United States Army Air Force. But after seven months of training, they became the first Aviation Cadets in the United States Air Force. On July 26th, 1947, the National Security Act was signed into law. This made the Air Force a separate branch of the service. On September 18, 1947, W. Stuart Symington was sworn in as the first Secretary of the Air Force, and General Carl Spaatz, who had succeeded General Hap Arnold on March 1, 1946, was the first Chief of Staff. As can be expected in an atmosphere of change, new ideas and ways of doing things were bound to occur—such as the experiment in which one-half of 48-A was taught their primary training in the PT-17 Stearman, a standard primary trainer.

Four Aviation Cadets from Class 48-A on the flight line at Randolph.

He had a keen interest in machines and tools, learned from his father who was a machinist. He learned at an early age the exactness and perfection required of machine work. This helped a great deal when he was confronted with one of the more complex machines of his time, an airplane. When he and his classmates arrived at Randolph in March of 1947, it was the culmination of his boyhood dreams and ambitions. At long last he was going to fly. And at the ripe-old-age of eighteen yet. He was in the group that was to fly the vernable PT-17. This fit right in with his dream. Growing up during the prewar era, he had seen many classic flying movies , most all using bi-wing aircraft. Now perhaps, he could be like the movie heroes he had envied as they flashed across the silver screen in their gleaming ships, dogfighting, bombing the Boche—all the neat things that looked to be such fun to a young boy.

The men who were assigned to the AT-6 in pri-

The other half was taught in the AT-6, a heretofore basic, and advanced trainer. It was quite a step from no flying experience to either one of these aircraft, but to the AT-6, it was more like a giant leap. Surprisingly, neither group had any more difficulty than the previous classes that had been trained the old way.

In prior years, the east side of the field at Randolph was the primary training flight-line, and the west was the basic. In the early days, the runways consisted of large grass fields. Takeoffs and landings were always into the wind, as there were no designated or paved runways. In latter days, actual runways were designated and the grass was replaced with pavement.

A/C William B. Kennedy was one of the few Cadets in class 48-A. Born in Minnesota, he was typical of most Cadets. Ever since he was in grammar school, he had wanted to fly.

Boeing-Stearman PT-17 Kaydets at R

mary for three months, had no transition to undergo when it was time for basic. They continued to fly the same aircraft they had been flying, and were even at the same base. The men who had flown the PT-17, however, had a real transition to make. The vernable Boeing/Stearman Model 75, has a long and varied career. Lloyd Stearman formed the "Stearman Aircraft Company" in 1927. In 1939, it became the Wichita Division of the Boeing Airplane Company . In December of 1933, the new Stearman X-70, was first flown. It was designed to compete in the U.S.A.A.C. (United States Army Air Corps) trials for a new training aircraft. The US Navy was somewhat ahead of the AAC in realizing the potential of air power. They bought 61 of the new Stearman Model 70's. They called it the NS-1. It was equipped with a Wright J-5, (R-790-8), 225 hp engine. In the first part of 1936, the USAAC bought 26 of the aircraft and designated it the PT-

13. These were powered by a Lycoming R-680-5 engine, producing 215 hp. They were called the Model 75. In 1937, the U.S.A.A.C. purchased 92 PT-13-A's. The difference between this model and the previous, was improved instruments and a 220 hp, Lycoming R-680-7 engine. The USAAC had received an additional 255 aircraft by the end of 1941—these were PT-13-B models, the only difference was a R-680-11 engine. The C model was built in 1941 with the addition of equipment to make them suitable for night and instrument flying. Only six aircraft were designated C's. In 1940, a new engine was installed in the original PT-13-A airframe. It was the 220 hp Continental R-670-5. This changed the aircraft designation to PT-17, and 3,519 of these were built. Due to engine supply problems, in the 1940 to 1941 period, 150 aircraft were equipped with the 225 hp Jacobs R-755-7 engine, and were designated the PT-18. The USAAC sup-

A class in Nuclear Weapons for 48-A at Randolph in 1947.   William B. Kennedy 48-A

plied 300 aircraft to the RCAF under the Lend-Lease program. These were designated the PT-27. This aircraft was produced in quantity until early 1945. Over 10,000 were built.

The Stearman was a simple aircraft compared to the AT-6. It had fixed landing gear, a fixed pitch propeller, few instruments, two wings, and an open cockpit. Its maximum speed was 124 mph, and it cruised at only 106 mph. Whereas the AT-6 had retractable landing gear, constant speed propeller, enclosed cockpit, and lots of instruments. Its top speed was 205 mph, and it cruised at 170 mph. It also had a 550 hp engine, twice as much raw horse-power as the Stearman, and considerable more torque to contend with. But it was also a challenge, and no Cadet can refuse a challenge.

In the due course of time, basic was behind the men of 48-A, and the Cadets were sent to Advanced training at Williams AFB, in Arizona. Now the real fun began. They were to fly the North American P-51 Mustang. Hot dog! Now here was a real fighter. Talk about the stuff movies are made from, this air-craft was a legend. Every pilot worth his salt has wanted to get his hands on this one, and here was a bunch of nineteen-year-old kids armed with a mere 1,695 hp, P-51-D—Wow!

The P-51 had its start in England. In April of 1940, the British Purchasing Commission contacted North American Aviation, and asked them to design and build, an advanced fighter for the RAF. The contract stipulated that the proto-type must be completed in 120 days. The aircraft was desig-nated the NA-73X. The air-frame was completed in only 117 days; however, the Allison V-1710-39, 1,100 hp engine was not ready in time, so the first flight of the prototype was not until October 26, 1940.

Amazingly, the first production model flew on May 1, 1941. The initial contract called for 320 aircraft. It was quickly learned that the Allison engine's power output fell off quickly with increased alti-tude. None the less it was still a superb flying air-craft. The first models had four .50 cal. and four .30 cal. machine-guns. The first operational mis-sion was flown on July 27, 1942, by #2 Squadron of Army Co-Operation Command. The aircraft was called the "Mustang I". The British were so im-pressed, that an additional 300 aircraft were ordered for the Army Co-Operation Command. North American delivered two of the aircraft to the U.S.A.A.C., which were designated the XP-51. The U.S.A.A.C. had previously contracted with North American to supply an additional 150 aircraft to England, designated P-51, under the Lend-Lease program. These differed from the earlier model by having four wing-mounted 20-mm cannon machine-guns, and self-sealing tanks. The U.S.A.A.C. was quite pleased with the two XP-51's, and decided to order 500 A-36A's. These had dive brakes and un-derwing racks. The armament was comprised of six .50 cal. machine guns mounted in the wings. They were equipped with an Allison V-17110-87,

North American P-51H   National Archives

1,325 hp engine. This was the first model to enter service with the USAAC. A second order for 310 P-51A's was placed at about the same time. These had the Allison V-1710-81 engine putting out 1200 hp. The armament was changed again. This time they had four .50 cal. machine-guns, and underwing racks to hold up to 1,000-lbs of bombs or two drop tanks; however the Mustang was still not up to its full potential, it simply did not have enough power at high altitude with the Allision engines. In light of this problem, four Mustang airframes were equipped with Rolls-Royce Merlin 61 and 65 engines. The test were run at Hucknall, England, by Rolls-Royce. The results were so impressive, that North American took two airframes and installed US-built Packard Merlin V-1650-3, engines rated at 1,430 hp. These were designated the XP-51B. The Packard Merlin engine had a two-speed, two-stage turbocharger with intercooler. In September of 1942, early test showed a top speed of 441 mph, at 29,800 ft. It climbed from takeoff to 20,000 ft. in 5.9 minutes. Needless to say, the U.S.A.A.C. folks were happy campers. They could hardly wait to get contracts written for the huge numbers of this fantastic aircraft that were needed. The number of aircraft ordered necessitated more building space. A second production facility was built at Dallas, Texas. The original plant at Inglewood, California, started producing the P-51B in the summer of 1943. The same version produced in Dallas was designated the P-51C. The differences between these models and the previous P-51A, were: stronger fuselage, new ailerons, and four .50 cal. machine-guns. The total production of B and C models was 1,988. The next model was the P-51D. It had a Merlin V-1650-7 engine that produced 1,450 hp at takeoff, and 1,695 hp at war-emergency power. Two additional machine-guns were added to the wings for a total of six. It also had a bubble canopy, that slid to the rear, in place of the side opening one on previous models. This canopy modification made it possible to see to the rear, an absolute necessity in aerial combat. A total of 7,956 of this model were built.

On December 13, 1943, the US 8th Air Force, based in England, flew their first mission with the P-51B/C's. By early 1944, they were regularly flying bomber escort missions deep into Germany.

Several other models were built, ending with the P-51H. A total of 555 H models were built before VJ-Day ended the war, and the contracts were canceled. The H model (also designated as the M model at the Dallas plant) was considerably lighter than the D model. It also had a water-injected Merlin V-1650-9 engine, producing a war-emergency rating of 2,218 hp. This was, of course, the fastest of all the Mustangs. At 25,000 ft. it could true out at 487 mph—that's moving for a non-jet aircraft. Only one P-51M was completed at the Dallas plant. A total of 14,819 Mustangs were built in the United States, 200 more were built under license by Commonwealth Aircraft Corp. in Australia. However, none of these 200 were completed in time to be used in the war.

It was January 29, 1948—the sky was bright blue; not a cloud was in sight. The temperature was in the low 40's, the wind was light and variable—a perfect day to fly. A/C William B. Kennedy was among six Aviation Cadets at William AFB that had been chosen for a very special experiment. They were to be the first Aviation Cadets to fly the single seat P-80, Shooting Star, jet fighter. Bill was chosen to be the first-of-the-first, on the flip of a coin.

Since there was only one seat in the P-80, dual flight instruction was out of the question. The Army had come up with the "Captivair". (This same idea was used on the P-51). This was a real P-80 put up on blocks, or stands, and chained to the tarmac. The basic idea was not new. It had been done at many other bases, and with many other types of aircraft. This was an early "Simulator". The new pilot could start the engine, raise the gear, operate the flaps, run the check list, and practice emergency procedures. All without ever leaving the ground.

The F-80 was quite a different breed of cat than anything any of the Cadets had flown before. The design was originated in 1943 with a team of engi-

AT-6 Captiveair at Randolph.　　H. Renwick Dunlap 50-A

to 14,500 lb. The B model had the G.E. J33-A-21 with 5,200 lbs of thrust, and 240 were built in the 1946-47 time period. The last model was the C. It ended up with the 5,400 lb thrust-35 engine. In the 1948-'49 time period, 798 were built. This little puppy was somewhat faster than even the P-51. It had a maximum speed (VNE), of 558 mph. It cruised at 410 mph, and could fly as high as 45,000 ft.

Needless to say, It was with some apprehension that A/C Kennedy climbed up the boarding ladder and stepped down into the shining silver bird on that beautiful cold and sunny day. He had several hours in the "Captivair," but this was an entirely different thing. There were no chains to hold him and his eager craft to the earth. This time it was up to him, and him alone to start, taxi, and ultimately fly, this whining, thundering air-machine. Here in front of the crowd, with the newsmen and all his classmates looking on, he knew he had better not mess up. He went through the checklist very slowly, and methodically. He made sure he did his P.D. McCripe oxygen check, (P=Pressure, D=Diaphragm, M=Mask, c=Connection at Mask, C=Connection at regulator, r=Regulator, i=Indicator, p=Pressure Test, e=Emergency Cylinder). As nervous as he was, he knew he would need all the help he could get. The crew chief signaled to him that he was clear to start. He made sure the brakes were set, and hit the starter switch. The thoughts ran through his mind at breakneck speed: "Watch the EGT! (Exhaust gas temperature), don't let it get above 715 degrees. Check the hydraulic pressure, I don't want to cream some bystander. OK, big guy, let's show these folks how it's done." The crew chief showed him the gear pins, and signaled "chocks out." Trying to look as non-

neers headed by Clarence L. Johnson. They were to use the then "new," de Havilland H-1 turbojet engine, developing 3,000 lb of thrust. A minuscule amount of power compared to engines of today, but this was the beginning of the jet age. The first prototypes were designated the XP-80. It was flown by Lockheed test pilot Tony Le Vier. Of the three prototypes, there was only one aircraft to be powered by the H-1 engine. Instead, the G.E. J33, which was rated at 3,750 lbs of thrust was used in the aircraft flown at Muroc Dry Lake test center on June 10, 1944. As development progressed, the gross weights ran from 8,916 lbs to 11,500 lbs for the YP-80, which carried six .50 cal. machine-guns in the nose. The first 13 YP-80's were delivered in October of 1944. Shortly before the end of the war in Europe, two of them were used in Italy for operational trials.

The original plan was for 5,000 aircraft, including 1,000 P-80N's that were to be built by North American at Kansas City. However after VJ-Day, more than 3,000 were cancelled, which included all the "N" models. In December of 1945, 525 A models were delivered. These had tip tanks and underwing bomb racks. The gross weight was increased

chalant as possible, Bill eased in the power and started to roll for the first time in a jet powered aircraft. New thoughts flooded his mind: the instructor said, "Be careful with the brakes; don't cock the nose wheel. Man, this thing won't turn if I don't use brakes. Boy, will I be glad when I get away from this ramp and this audience." Taxiing out to the main runway, he thought about doing his run-up. "This is a jet, dummy, it doesn't get a run-up." In his most professional voice, he called mobile control for takeoff clearance. "Roger, cleared for takeoff, good luck." Lining up with the center line of the runway, he slowly brought up the power. (The P-80 had no automatic fuel control, or automatic anything for that matter, and it was real easy to overtemp the engine, or cause a flameout by heavy handedness on the throttle). At 80% engine rpm, he checked his instruments, and engine gauges—all checked OK. He released the brakes, and slowly pushed the throttle to 100%. He thought, "This thing sure is slow to move, the P-51 would darn near be in the air by now." At about 50 knots, the rudder became effective for directional control; at 85 knots he started to apply a slight back pressure on the stick; at 100 knots he raised the nose wheel slightly off the ground, at somewhere between 110-120 knots, he was airborne. There wasn't time to savor the moment, things happen fast in any aircraft, but especially so in a jet one. His airspeed was passing rapidly through 130 knots—"Quick get the gear up." He thought, "OK, now I need at least 240 knots before I make my turn out of traffic—got it, now let's go for the climb speed of 270 knots. Wow, it sure comes up quick OK, reduce power to 96%. Good grief—I'm sure a long way from the field." Climbing up to 15,000 ft., Bill leveled off and accelerated to 300 knots. He raised the nose about 25

degrees, and pushed the stick hard to the right, simultaneously pushing on the right rudder he was upside down in a yawing roll. He thought, "This thing doesn't need the rudder to roll—a jet doesn't have torque." Before he knew it he was right side up. On the next rolls, he left the rudder neutral, and it sure was smoother. The quietness and lack of vibration seemed almost eerie. The old 51 roared and vibrated like any other high-powered-piston-driven plane. But this jet thing was really different. It took so little effort to get it to do anything. He lowered the nose and let the airspeed build up to 350 knots, and then pulled straight back on the stick. The horizon rapidly sank beneath him, and all he could see was blue sky; he was now vertical. Going over the top, he was inverted, and the blue sky was now mating with the brown horizon. Then as he was approaching vertical, down the backside of the loop, it appeared as though the Arizona desert was rushing up to meet him. Suddenly, as if by magic, he was right side up and the horizon was level again. "Wow, Sierra Hotel!"

After about an hour of pure flying fun, A/C Kennedy reluctantly returned to the field to land this silver bullet. He called mobile for sequencing, and was advised he was number one, followed by a curt, "Don't break it." He entered initial at 240 knots, lined up with the runway, and descended to 300 ft.

Lockheed F-80   National Archives

305

at the approach end of the runway. He then pitched up to traffic-pattern altitude, simultaneously reducing the power to idle. As he climbed and turned 180-degrees to the downwind leg, his speed rapidly fell off to 195 knots. He grabbed the gear handle and pushed it to the down position. Leveling off, he checked his gear-down indicators, and immediately started his turn to final, while putting the flap lever to the full down position. His speed was now 145 knots, and as he rolled out on final, mobile control

main gear was down, "earp," the nose wheel was on. "Whew, I was really beginning to wonder."

It was over—the first time an Aviation Cadet had soloed in a jet aircraft. This was indeed a day to remember. And a day that A/C William B. Kennedy will remember as long as he lives. The other men who made history that day were: A/C Nolan R. Dotz, 19, of Los Angles, CA, A/C James E. Jarvis, 19, of Woodbind, LA, A/C James G. Clayberg, 19, of Cuba, IL, A/C Andrew F McClung,

Aviation Cadet William B. Kennedy after his first solo in the F-80.   William B. Kennedy 48-A

cleared him to land. He reduced power until he had 130 knots, then applied just enough power to hold that speed. Crossing over the end of the runway, he closed the throttle to the idle position, eased back on the stick, and waited, and waited, he thought, "Damn, this thing floats like a boat—the big prop on the 51 would have set me down a long time ago. Where's the anchor?" Finally "squeak, squeak," the

20, of Glen Ferris, WVA, and A/C James C. Bolton, 21, of Minneapolis. The first in the jet age, and still, the Last of a Breed!

Chapter 5:
Cadets in Action, WWII

CADETS IN GRADE

The stars were shining brightly, on the cold, clear night of December 6, 1941, at Hamilton Field located in San Francisco, California. There were sixteen B-17's from the 38th and 88th Recon Squadrons based at Albuquerque, New Mexico, scheduled to deploy to Hickam Field, Hawaii. This was part of the American buildup in the Pacific. There were also two B-24's that were supposed to join the B-17's. They were on a secret mission, but cancelled due to maintenance problems. The crews of this historic flight consisted of numerous enlisted men, a large number of officers, and thirty-one Aviation Cadets. These Cadets were recent graduates of Bombardier, and Navigator training schools. The government didn't have the funds to pay them as officers, even though this is what they were supposed to do; so they kept them in Cadet grade, at a much lower salary, until such time as appropriations caught up with the demand. Quite a number of Cadets in previous classes had their commissions held up for the same reason. No one knew why, but about two hours before they were scheduled to depart, General Ralph Royce administered the oath of office to Aviation Cadet Theodore I. Pascoe, appointing him to the rank of 2nd Lt. Pascoe, thereby reducing the number of Cadets to thirty.

The men gathered in the briefing room, for their standard mission briefing. They were all chatting, some sitting, some standing, when suddenly they heard, "Ten-Hut!" Being spring-loaded to the attention position they all snapped into a brace. They were flabbergasted as the Commander of the Air Force General Hap Arnold came marching down the aisle and up onto the stage. "At ease men." The men sat down, with their total attention focused on the General standing in front of them. "Gentleman," he began, "The relations between our country and the Imperial Japanese Empire are not too good. In fact, I would say they are terrible. You men will most certainly run into some trouble soon. I wish you luck, and Godspeed on your mission." He sat down amongst the men who were murmuring and discussing what he meant by "some trouble." The briefing officer stood up and told the men to quiet down, and continued with the rest of the briefing. Another puzzling event was the presence of General Fickle, a WWI Veteran, the first American in the AEF to fire at an enemy aircraft from his own aircraft in flight. He used a Springfield bolt-action rifle. He was sitting next to General Arnold during the briefing. When the crews were dismissed, Major Truman Landon (later General) accompanied by his crew, which included Aviation Cadet Erwin F. Cihak (41-2B), went over to General Arnold and asked him point blank, just *where* they were supposed to find this "trouble?" Barely smiling, Arnold said, "Oh, I really don't know." It was obvious to the men that he did not want to discuss it any further.

Cadet Cihak and the rest of the crew were discussing the events of the evening as they walked toward their aircraft. In particular they were wondering what they were going to do if they did indeed run into trouble before they reached Hickam. They had no machine guns, or bombs, on board. The eight-hour flight made it necessary to lighten the aircraft, and install extra fuel tanks in the bombbay, and even at that, it would be a hurry-up-and-land-before-you-run-out-of-fuel flight. Their armament was to be installed at Hickam.

As the men started to climb aboard the B-17-E, the crew chief ran excitedly up to the "skipper" and said, "Major, someone has been messing around with the airplane. The elevator trim-tab action was reversed." Major Landon said, "Great work, Sergeant, I'm sure glad you found it now." "Thank you Sir, but this was not the only one. Two other ships have been damaged by sabotage. They won't be on this flight." "OK, Sergeant, keep your eyes open, and let's hurry up and get these birds in the air." With that remark the crew continued to board, the ladder was brought in, the hatch closed, and checklists completed.

gines was deafening. The clear night sky was partially obscured by the smoke belching from these fire-breathing monsters. As they started taxiing toward the runway, number eight called the tower and said he had lost oil pressure on his number three engine, and would be aborting the mission. Soon the night sky was ablaze with the reddish-orange exhaust flames spewing from the mighty engines, as the great birds launched skyward. As number thirteen was starting his takeoff roll, number ten called the tower and reported a runaway propeller on his number two engine. The tower cleared him to land behind the departing aircraft.

Boeing B-17's   National Archives

About 21:15 the order was transmitted from Hamiliton tower for the flight to start engines. Almost simultaneously, sixteen number three engines belching fire and smoke jumped to life. They were soon followed by the number two, four, and one engines, the noise from fifty-six Wright R-1820 en-

The night passed slowly; the constant drone of the engines lulled the men of Major Landon's crew into an almost trancelike state. The air was smooth; the night dark. Perhaps General Arnold was mistaken. At least it was a comfort to the men to think so, as they dreamed of those they left behind. The first rays of dawn approached finding the flight of twelve B-17's (most were C models, Landon had an E model) far from home and far out over the Pacific ocean. About 06:00 the copilot on Landon's crew, eyes red from lack of sleep, nudged the dozing Major, and said, "Isn't that the China Clipper at eleven o'clock low?" Landon, wiping the sleep from his eyes peered out the left front windshield, and seeing a large seaplane that they were overtaking, replied, "Yeah, that's her all right—sure is a slow beast—they took off at least an hour and a half ahead of us. We'll be in our bunks at Hickam long before they even get to the dock." As the B-17 flight came abreast of the Pan American Clipper, Cadet Cihak noticed the Clipper starting a left turn. He said, "Skipper, I thought the Clipper was on the same route as we are; how come he's making a left turn?" Major Landon, somewhat puzzled, remarked, "I really don't know, but the only place in that direction that has a dock is Hilo. That has to be where he's going."

The flight of B-17's pressed on toward Hickam. About 07:53 they could see the islands dead ahead. The navigator said casually, "What are all those planes doing out there?" The rest of the crew jumped up, crowding up to the front windows. One of the crew said, "Look at the smoke over at Pearl—what's going on?" Another said, "If I didn't know better I would say those planes are attacking the base." "Look out! What the Hell is that guy doing; he's coming straight at us. My God, they're Japs!"

Suddenly the realization of what General Arnold had been trying to tell them back at Hamilton sunk in; the Japanese were attacking Pearl Harbor, and these twelve B-17's had inadvertently flown right into the start of WWII. The Jap planes made repeated runs at

the helpless, unarmed B-17's; one of them passed between the number one and two engines on Landon's aircraft so close that, with the canopy slid back, the pilot was clearly recognizable. There are smoke and flames everywhere; Major Landon called Hickam tower and said, "Hickam tower, this is Army 2413, flight of twelve B-17's, what the heck is going on down there?"

Lt. Gordon Blake, the O.D. that morning answered, "Roger Army 2413, Hickam tower, it seems like the entire Jap air force is attacking us—how's your fuel?"

"Hickam, we're mighty low, need landing instructions immediately."

"Roger, Army 2413, the wind is light and variable, altimeter 30.12, pick any runway you like, look out for the Japs, no other traffic."

"Roger Wilco, Army 2413."

The entire scene below, and above, is like a nightmare. It seems as if there are thousands of enemy aircraft—they are everywhere. Strafing, bombing, dropping torpedoes, sowing death and destruction on every side. Suddenly several of our P-40's arrive; they fly right in with the B-17 formation and are successful in driving off the attacking Japanese aircraft long enough for the bombers to make a mad dash for Hickam. There were burning

Mitsubishi A6M8 Reisen (Zero)   National Archives

buildings on the field, the runway was not damaged; nothing else mattered, these twelve aircraft were going to come down soon, one way or the other—they were almost out of fuel.

Zooming down toward the runway flying as close a pattern as they could, ten of the big birds landed safely. One of them had been hit by Japanese tracers in the center section, which set the flare cartridges on fire. They were burning as they landed. They screeched to a halt; with the crew leaping out of every exit, they ran for cover as the B-17 burst into flames, and broke in half on the field. One of the B-17's landed at a pursuit strip, which was at Bellows on the east side of the island; they ran off the end of the runway, and wiped out the landing gear. At least one other B-17 landed on the fairway of the golf course at Kuhuko on the northeast tip of the island.

The other crews that landed at Hickam parked their aircraft as close to the mangrove trees as possible, taking advantage of any cover available. Thinking they were to be invaded at any moment, A/C Cihak ran to the rear of his aircraft, grabbed both his .45 automatic and Major Landon's, and ran for the trees. Looking toward the harbor about a half mile distant, a brilliant shaft of light streamed skyward, followed by a huge ball of fire, and a chest-pounding roar. The Arizona had been hit. In a matter of moments, that great ship along with most of her crew were gone.

The President, Franklin D. Roosevelt in his speech, following the attack at Pearl Harbor said, "December 7, 1941—a date which will live in infamy!" What he didn't say—ever—was that he knew we were going to be attacked, but chose to let it happen. Why? During that time there was a group called "America First." This was one group much like the "Ban the Bomb" and the Vietnam War protesters. They wanted us to stay home and mind our own business. They said they wanted no part of war unless we were attacked. This was the mood of many people in our country at that time. By the pacifist's thinking ingrained in these people, and the

desperation of our government, thousands of lives were needlessly lost. Had we faced our responsibility and taken the initiative, much of this tragedy could have been averted. Perhaps at the time there was no other way to galvanize the people of this country, but what a price to pay for our lack of intestinal fortitude. It will always be necessary for us, as the leading nation of this world, to stop any aggressor who would steal the freedom from any country. And we must stop them before they reach our shores, or we will most certainly pay the price at *our* doors.

Back in the States, our country was outraged by such a devastating attack; millions were glued to their radios anxiously waiting for any update on the tragedy. One of those U.S. Citizens was Cecil Darnell. He was at that time flying for an airline, having completed his two years of active duty in the Army Air Corps Reserves. He knew he would soon be called back to active duty.

A PURPLE HEART

In 1931, Darnell was in the first class to go through Flying Cadet pilot training at Randolph AFB. He was called to active duty after Pearl Harbor, but now it was 1943, and smack dab in the middle of WWII. He was in the South Pacific awaiting orders to assign him as commanding officer of a P-38 photo reconnaissance group. Major Cecil Darnell was taking time to visit with his wing commander, a Bird Colonel, who was also a close personal friend. During a casual conversation the Colonel asked if he had ever flown a B-17. Being a pilot who could, (so he thought), fly anything, he said, "No, but I sure would like to." Not being one to put things off, he found a B-17 crew that was flying that afternoon and persuaded them to let him fly it some. The next morning he and the Colonel arrived at the airstrip—some runway. It was a long pathway cut from the jungle, trees lined both sides, and steel mats had been laid on the ground to provide the "pavement." It was still dark, and a patchy

Boeing B-17-G   National Archives

colonel pushing the wheel forward as hard as he could, but it wouldn't budge. "We're too slow," Major Darnell yelled, as the airspeed, which had only risen to 110 mph, was rapidly bleeding off. "It's gonna stall!" screamed the Colonel. The landing lights were still on, and Major Darnell could see the trees approaching as the left wing contacted the ground with a loud bang, and burst into flame. The screeching sounds of tearing metal, filled the air, and there were pieces of aircraft flying everywhere. Sliding to a halt, the once proud bomber, was now a burning wreck in a jungle swamp. Glancing to his left, Major Darnell saw the Colonel just sitting in his seat, staring in disbelief. Major Darnell thought, "I have to get out of here," and standing up, he put his right foot out of the already open window, and tried to slide to the ground, but he was caught. His left foot was stuck between the seat and the center console. A bright flash caught his eye, a small fire had erupted on the right side, only a few feet from where he was held captive. Looking over his left shoulder, he called to the Colonel for help, but his seat was empty. At that moment, a man appeared from out of nowhere, and he reached into the burning plane, and turned Major Darnell's foot to free him. "Thank God!" he thought, as he limped away. The aircraft was now a flaming mass of twisted metal, and ammunition was exploding everywhere. Fuel was gushing out of the ruptured tanks, and was immediately ignited by the growing flames. Major Darnell saw a large fallen tree, and he and several of the enlisted men took refuge from the flying bullets behind it. Laying there in the first light of dawn, he checked himself over for injuries. Miraculously, he only suffered some minor lacerations. He had no broken bones and no burns. The squadron nearest to the crash arrived in

ground fog hung just about cockpit high. The aircraft had been fueled, preflighted, and since this was a photo recon mission, cameras and support equipment were also on board as well as .50 cal. ammo for the installed machine guns. The crew consisted of the Colonel, Major Darnell, Captain Bill Fairbanks, and seven enlisted men. Major Darnell, being only 5' 4 1/2", tall couldn't enter by the crew hatch in the belly; so he had to go to the rear, where Bill Fairbanks helped him in. By the time he had worked his way to the cockpit, the Colonel said he had already done everything, and all Major Darnell, (in the copilot's position), would have to do, was start the engines. Darnell replied, "Well Sir, I guess I can do that." Since the fog was so thick, and Major Darnell had been flying for an airline before the war, he asked if the Colonel wanted him to make the takeoff. (Airline pilots had lots of bad weather flying experience.) "Oh I can handle it OK." was the reply. Darnell answered, "All right, then I'll open the window so I can see the edge of the runway, and tap on whichever rudder you need to push, in order to keep us straight." The Colonel applied full power to the four 1200 H.P. turbocharged Wright R-1820-97 engines. They started to roll, slowly at first, then faster and faster, and suddenly they were in the air. The control wheel was all the way back; with the

their jeeps. The operations officer, Captain Ben Armstrong, a close friend of Major Darnell, ran up to him, and asked if he was OK. He answered, "I'm fine, but that Sergeant over there is complaining that he is having a hard time breathing." They loaded up the Sergeant and a few others, and took them to the hospital. In what seemed like only five minutes they were back from the hospital, and prepared to load Major Darnell on a stretcher. When they tried to get him on the stretcher. He refused, thinking he was too tough to need assistance. After walking a few steps, his knees buckled. He rode out on the stretcher.

Major Darnell spent the next two days in the hospital. He said, the good Lord must have been looking after him, as he was the only one in the crew that did not have any broken bones or serious injury. His friend, the operation's officer, came to the hospital for a visit. Major Darnell said he had been thinking about what had happened, and wondered if there was anything left of the aircraft? The Ops. officer said, "Why yes, the tail section is still there; the rest is just pieces of metal and ashes." Major Darnell asked if they would check the position of the elevator trim and see if it was about five degrees in the nose—up position. The next day the Ops. officer came by, and sure nuf, it was at four-and-one-half degrees nose up.

After the Colonel was released from the hospital, (some two weeks later, as he had some broken bones), Major Darnell went to his office and asked if he could borrow another B-17. When asked why, he said, " I think I know what happened; the trim was set nose up." The Colonel immediately replied, "No way, we were overloaded." Darnell said, "How could we be overloaded with just a crew of ten, camera equipment, some .50 cal. ammo and no bombs."

The next day they borrowed an aircraft. Leveling off at 3,500,' they reduced power and set four-and-one-half degrees nose-up trim. The Colonel said, "See, that wasn't it." to which Major Darnell replied, " Wait a minute"; and proceeded to push the throttles up to 35" of manifold pressure. Sure

nuf—the wheel came all the way back in their laps. The Colonel never did change his "over-gross" story on the accident report even though he either didn't run the checklist, or forgot to set the trim. Major Darnell, not wanting to hurt someone he admired and cared about, let the matter drop. Major Cecil Darnell was awarded a purple heart. It was not exactly an easy way to earn such an award, but I really don't think there is a pleasant way.

A SLIVER STAR

Shortly thereafter, Major Darnell arrived at his squadron in the South Pacific, and soon learned that there were two things one could always count on in this part of the world; heat and humidity. It wouldn't be too bad if you were laying on the nice white sand getting a tan; however, when you were fighting a war, it was a different matter. The time was: late in 1943, and the location was: one of the many Japanese-held islands. The mission was to take photos for the all out effort, bomb raid, scheduled for the next day. This was the scenario when Major Cecil Darnell, commander of the 6th. photo group, fired up his P-38F-5G. It was just before dawn when he departed his base at Nadzab, New Guinea. He was alone and unarmed, with no escort aircraft, on this approximately 400-mile flight. He flew low over the water to avoid detection by the enemy, salt spray gathered on his windshield. He was sure glad for the external fuel tanks. At this altitude he would burn considerably more fuel than if he were at a more optimum altitude of 25,000'. It seemed a better choice to sacrifice fuel, rather than an aircraft, especially since he was strapped to it. The heat in the cockpit was stifling; he was already soaked through his flight suit. Oh well, just another day full of glory. He pressed on toward his target. About ten minutes from the island, he pushed the prop levers full forward, and the throttles forward until the needles were on the red line painted on the manifold pressure gauge, and he started his climb to above 29,000'. This was as high as the Japanese antiair-

Lockheed RP-38   National Archives

were flashes of light and puffs of smoke dotted all over the landscape below. Through the broken cloud deck he could see that the shells were exploding above the clouds. "Hot dog!" It worked, they had not reset the fuses. "Whew!" Was he ever glad to see the end of that island. Glancing down at the counters on the cameras, he saw that they had not moved. "Damn!" He didn't get the pictures. He had come so far, and he knew how important these photos were to the invasion forces. In his mind, he had no choice but to turn around, and shoot the pictures on manual. He figured the nips would have reset their fuses by now. Sometimes he wished he wouldn't figure so good. It was a sea of flack. "Boom!"—Just below, "Bang!"—Another off the right. Puffy balls of black smoke were all around him. He continued on his course, "Come on Baby. I see the end of the island—Go plane, go!" The flak stopped "Great!" Looking back over his shoulder, he spotted a new danger—two Zeroes. "Oh boy, and me without so much as a spitball." He was

craft guns were effective. He had only been going up a short time when he passed through a broken cloud deck at 7,000'. Popping out at 8,600', he could see that the cloud deck was pretty solid all the way to the island. Damn! Now he would have to come in below the cloud deck to take his pictures. He hoped the enemy would still have their timed fuses set at 29,000', in which case he would flash by before they could reset them to his altitude. Descending back through the cloud deck, he had everything "firewalled," he leveled off just below the base of the clouds, there was the island—right off the nose.

He knew his reconnaissance aircraft would true out about 424 mph, at 25,000', some ten mph faster than the gun ships. Even though he didn't know his exact true airspeed, he was glad for any extra speed he could get. Approaching the island, he turned the camera control switch to automatic, which turned on the four cameras installed in place of the four 50 cal. machine guns in the nose. "Wow!" It seemed like he had switched on the antiaircraft guns at the same time. There

Major Cecil Darnell in the cockpit of his P-38.   Cecil Darnell 31-01

313

passed the island now, and he turned, twisted, rolled, anything to get those zeroes off his tail. Suddenly, he noticed out ahead, over the water lay the cutest little thunderstorm he had ever seen. He made a beeline toward it. Zip, into that black hole he flew. It had to be better in there than it was outside, at least the storm only had lightning, no bullets. He climbed higher and higher; he was bouncing all over the cockpit. The sound of the rain beating on the canopy was deafening, and the lightning was awesome. But every time the clouds would get a little lighter, he would turn toward the darkest part of the storm. On and on, it seemed like an eternity, but in reality it was only a few minutes. Suddenly, there was blue sky. He was at 16,000,' climbing like a rocket, and best of all, no Zeroes. He continued on

for awhile longer, just to make sure he wasn't being followed. Once convinced, he descended to his usual altitude of just off the water for the trip home. Because of his devotion to duty, and the risking of his life by returning for more pictures, he was decorated with the "Silver Star", and soon promoted to the rank of Lt. Colonel.

While the war raged in the Pacific, there was no shortage of action in Europe, but occasionally there was a different mission to fly.

VIP PICKUP

The following story was taken from *The Newsletter*, 43-E, and is used with permission: William E. Shelton entered the armed service in April of 1942 as an Aviation Cadet. He was commissioned as a 2nd Lt. and given his wings in May of 1943—class of 43-E. Bill's squadron, the 107th TAC RCN, moved to airstrip A-46 at Versailles in July, 1944. They were equipped with P-51-A & C models. They also had a few L-4s and a UC-78 Bobcat. It was a hot, dry, August day, little wind, good visibility, just a nice day to fly; that is, if it hadn't been in Europe in the middle of WWII. Bill's Op's officer had assigned him to fly the old Cessna to an airstrip about 125 miles to the southwest, pick up a passenger, and return to Versailles. He says laughingly, he was picked for this mission because of his excellent AT-17 training at Brooks, when he was a Cadet. As he pushed the throttles forward, setting takeoff power, and lifting off into the bright

Lt. Colonel Darnell receiving his medals.   Cecil Darnell 31-01

Cessna AT-17, later modified to the UC-78 Bobcat.   National Archives

a soft thunk he was in. Wheel back, stand on the brakes, whew! "Made it didn't I?" Wiping the sweat from his brow, he gingerly exited the plane and entered the tent. He was greeted by a major who really didn't want to hear his complaints about "his" landing(?) strip. The major informed him that his passenger would be along shortly. It wasn't long before several staff cars pulled up, flags flying. The occupants got out, and after much handshaking and back-slapping, one of them came toward him, wearing G.I. olive drabs, tank jacket, and steel helmet. On his shoulders were two of the nicest stars Lt. Shelton had ever seen. The General said his name, but being somewhat intimidated, Bill didn't understand it. Bill's passenger asked if he could fly from the left seat. " Yes, Sir" seemed the best reply for a new 1st looie. After they were all buckled in, the passenger asked Bill to start the engines for him, which he did post haste. Taxiing to the end of the runway and turning north into the wind, the passenger advanced the throttles very slowly. Realizing the General had no knowledge of this runway, and would have high-

sunshine, his mind started to wander back to thoughts of home, a lazy summer day, a nice cool malt at the old drug store... Just then a jolt from a passing P-51's propwash brought him back to reality. He was not at home, he was in the skies over Europe and that held the ever present danger of an attack by an ME-109 or a FW190. He flew low over the lush countryside, head swiveling left and right praying he would not be noticed. After about an hour of twisting, turning, climbing and descending, he located the airstrip. Well, such as it was. It was grass, and only 800 to 1000 feet long. To make matters even worse, the north end of this tiny green "lawn" dropped off several hundred feet. Great, "This airplane is sure no Piper Cub." Then he noticed an L-5 parked next to a pyramid tent. Being totally fearless (?) (an Aviation Cadet don't you know), his pride swelled up and he thought, "If somebody can put an L-5 in here, by damn I can get this crate in." Coming in from the north, he approached low over the cliff barely above stall, dragging it in with power. As the green velvet patch slid under her belly, he cut the power, eased back on the wheel, and let her sink onto the grass, with

Stinson L-5   National Archives

speed taxied them right off the cliff, Bill abruptly firewalled the throttles. Staggering off the end of the cliff, he snatched the gear up as the General turned them toward home. The sun was almost directly overhead by now, and the warmth coupled with the drone of the engines, was so pleasant that the General asked Bill to take over, and promptly went to sleep. Putting a map up to shade his eyes, Bill marveled at the totally relaxed figure next to him; they were still very much at risk if they enemy should see them. Perhaps the strain of command had taken its toll, and shear exhaustion had set in. He wondered on that lovely August afternoon why was he here? Why not a million other places? It's strange how our minds wander to such thoughts, when are doing something that has become so routine, so effortless, as the flying of an aircraft had become. In his constant scan for enemy aircraft, he finally saw a familiar sight on the horizon—home base. He awakened the General and pointed out the airfield which was then only about five miles away. He promptly asked Bill if he could make the landing. And since this was much more of an airfield, the always safe: "Yes, Sir," was once again initiated. (Always safe when a general asks if he can do something, that is). Calling in to the tower, they were advised they were number one to land, with no other reported traffic. Slowing down to flap-extend speed, he asked for the flaps, shortly followed by the gear. Flying a somewhat larger pattern than normal, the General did a fine job right up to main gear touchdown. Anyone who has flown an AT-17 knows what happened next. He forgot to pop the wheel forward and away they went. After two or three ever higher and higher bounces, Bill put his left hand over the Generals right hand on the throttles and they got the heck out of there. The General, sweat pouring from his brow, suggested Bill make the next landing—a very fine suggestion. Not wanting to embarrass a general, Shelton flew a slightly larger pattern as well. "Flaps", "Gear", "lined up", "airspeed stabilized", "in the slot", nice landing. Taxiing to the ramp, he noticed a couple of staff

cars approaching his parking spot. He advanced the right throttle, tapped the left brake turning smartly into the tiedown—"radios off", "mixtures off", "boost pumps off", "master off"; the drone of the engines was replaced by the whining sound of gyros spooling down. As they were starting to get up, the General asked Bill if he would make a Form #1 for him. "Yes Sir," the standard reply was again in order, even though Bill still didn't know his name. Hoping to avoid the embarrassment of asking a two-star General his name, especially one he had just spent over an hour with in a cramped cockpit, Bill frantically looked for a friendly face. In the staff car crowd was Bill's CO, Lt. Colonel John Atkins. Bill told him the General wanted a copy of the Form #1, and he wondered if the Colonel knew his name? After giving Bill a "You're kidding" look, the CO said, "Boy, that's the commanding General of the 9th AF, Major General Hoyt S. Vandenberg." General Vandenburg went on to become a four-star General and was the second Chief of Staff of the United States Air Force.

When General Vandenberg died, several hundred Aviation Cadets were sent from Pre-Flight at Lackland to march in his funeral procession. The Cadets from West Point, and Annapolis also marched at the same time. The next day the morning paper pointed out just how much better the Aviation Cadets marched than the Cadets of the two military academies.

ESCAPE IN A RICE PADDY

Meanwhile, back in the Pacific the action continues with total disregard for the season.

The sky was a dreary gray, the cloud bases were at 8,000', it looked like it could rain at any moment. The date was December, 25, 1944. War takes no holidays. The 431st. fighter squadron was assigned bomber escort duty for B-24's attacking the Japanese-held Clark Field located near Manila in the Phillipines. 1st. Lt. Floyd Fulkerson, Aviation Cadet class of 42-I, was an element leader in a forma-

Lockheed P-38F   National Archives

tion of fifteen P-38's. Major Richard Bong was also in the group. The element leaders circled the field at Dulag, as their wingmen formed up. Once joined up, the formation departed for their rendezvous with the bombers. Climbing through the overcast skies, they broke into the clear about 12,000'. Flying formation through clouds is a very difficult thing. You must pull in very close to your wingman, so as not to loose sight of him, but not so close as to hit him. After breaking through the clouds, the formation loosened up, allowing a little less tension in the cockpit. They climbed to the briefed altitude of 21,000'. The bombers were dead a head, appearing as small black specks, with long white contrails. Since the bombers were cruising at the briefed, 215 mph true airspeed, it was necessary for the P-38's to increase to their maximum cruise of 414 mph true airspeed. In a short time the specks became larger and larger, until their large boxy forms filled the entire windshield. Taking their position above and to the right of the bombers, the fighter pilots strained their eyes, and swiveled their heads looking for any small specks that would indicate enemy aircraft. Suddenly the radio crackled, "Bandits, eleven thirty, low." In front of, and below the American aircraft, were small specks with flashes of light, caused by the afternoon sunlight reflected off their canopies. Again the radio crackled, "Lead to flight. Lets break em up."

Simultaneously, all fifteen P-38's, props went full forward, throttles to the red line on the manifold pressure gauge, and down they went. In the first pass, several of the enemy fighters began to smoke, a few were in flames. There were aircraft everywhere. The Japanese were fielding about fifty aircraft, to our fifteen. The biggest help to the Americans was that this late in the war, many of the best enemy pilots had been killed. The skill level of those left, was on the average, much lower than ours. The fight raged, Bong accounted for his 38th, Fulkerson nailed one, then heard his wingman call, "Somebody get this ....off my tail!" Glancing to his right, he saw his wingman flash past, with a Zeke close behind, guns blazing. Slamming the wheel to the right, Lt. Fulkerson slid in behind the Zeke, turning, rolling, trying his best to line up the enemy in his sights. "Bingo", he pulled the trigger on the four 50 cal. machine guns, and one 20 mm cannon, all located in the nose of his aircraft. He was so close that he could see the bright stream of tracers leading into the tail, and wings, of the aircraft ahead, cutting out large chunks of metal. Suddenly, the Zeke exploded. It disappeared in a bright flash of fire and smoke, pieces of it zipping past Lt. Fulkersons canopy. In all the excitement of battle, he suddenly found himself alone in the skies over Clark Field. Somehow all of his squadron had disappeared. Well he was not quite alone. Off his left a single "Jack" appeared. Lt. Fulkerson thought, "I might as well get another one." Breaking left to intercept, his concentration was shattered as his aircraft shuddered with numerous bullets slamming into his pylons, destroying both of his radiators. He had been too intent on the "Jack", and had never seen the enemy aircraft come up behind him. He was in serious trouble.

Mitsubishi J2M Raiden (Jack)   NASM

Both engines overheated, and had to be shut down. There was no way he was going to trust his life to a parachute. He rode her in. It's a good thing rice is such a big crop in that part of the world. The paddies it is grown in make a large flat area, with no trees. Not a paved runway, but better than a mountain. "Splat!" hitting the wet surface of the brown and green paddy, muddy water sprayed up and over the wings, engulfing the once proud P-38 in a cloud of mud and rice. Sliding to a halt, he popped the canopy open, and out he jumped. He was determined to be as far away from his battered bird as possible, in the event it should catch on fire. Reaching the edge of the field, Lt. Fulkerson looked back, as a bright flame erupted under the left engine nacelle, rapidly engulfing the entire aircraft. Suddenly from the edge of the jungle, just a few yards away from him, a voice cried, "Amigo?". Quickly recovering from the surprise he shouted, "Amigo!" Boy, was he ever glad to see a group of Filipino guerrillas emerge from the wilderness. Being right in the middle of the Japanese forces, they didn't spend much time talking. With the guerrillas leading, Lt. Fulkerson followed them for days as they made their way some fifty miles to the Sierra Madre mountains.

Two Americans who worked for the O.S.S. were located there, and could help him return to the Allied forces. Since this was less than an ideal vacation spot, they came up with a plan to carve a runway out of the jungle, which would allow a rescue airplane to land. Having to eat rice every day was another strong incentive. It took twenty-six days to build the runway. Water buffalo were the closest thing to a bulldozer that were available. Using the radio supplied by the O.S.S., arrangements were made to pick up Lt. Fulkerson, and a Colonel Atkinson, who had also been shot down. The colonel thought the runway idea was crazy, and said they would walk out. Lt. Fulkerson said, "I didn't join the Air Corps to walk," and continued with the runway plan. On a Sunday morning two cubs landed to take the flyers out. Lt. Fulkerson, who didn't care much for the colonel, said to the Sergeant flying one of the cubs, "The colonel is walking out, he must be at least five miles from here, and the Japs are less than two, let's get out of here." Needless to say, the Sergeant agreed. The truth of the matter was that the colonel had only gone up the mountain to their camp, there were actually no Japanese in the area. They sent a plane in for him somewhat later.

NIGHT SUICIDE ATTACK

On the island of Okinawa, an event occurred that was only known to those that were there. William Sherret was one of them.

It was very late, or perhaps we should say early, that moonlit night, in early 1945. The P-61's had just returned from a mission and landed at their home base in Okinawa. At that time there were thousands

Northrop P-61   National Archives

tling missiles trailing white smoke whizzed past the heads of the defenders. "KaBoom," a large fuel supply blew up! In the light from the moon, and numerous fires, small shapes ran to and fro yelling "Banzai!" This was no air raid. This was an invasion. Our boys lined the running, shouting invaders up in their sights. "Crack!," "Bang!" One down, no two, then three, four, until in the smoke, and light of the burning wrecks, the sound of "Banzai," is heard no more. A few Japanese were captured, and unlike their fellows, they decided it was more honorable to live for themselves, than to die for their country.

As dawn came, the American soldiers and airmen could scarcely believe their eyes. So much damage and desolation, and caused by so few. The same element of surprise that had caused such disaster at Pearl Harbor, had again struck with terrible consequences. How does one cope with attacks like this? It is inconceivable to us to purposely embark on a mission that we have no chance of returning from. But to the oriental mind, brainwashed as it was, dieing for the Emperor was an honor. Living was the dishonor. By morning all of the invading enemy had been killed, or captured. Or so everyone thought. Later in the morning the Adjutant was in his jeep on the way to headquarters, when to his great surprise, a Japanese soldier, one from the previous nights suicide attack, jumped from the jungle right in front of the jeep. Sliding the jeep to a halt, the Adjutant fired one round, and the Jap was dead. The Adjutant hadn't been a very popular person in the 28th photo recon squadron. Now he was considered a hero. What a difference a day makes.

The war was winding down, the Nazis had been beaten and we were sure of eventual victory, but it was no time for letting up on the pressure to force

of Japanese soldiers still on the north end of the Island. They were no real threat. In fact, they were starving. So desperate, were they that they would sneak in to the American camp and steal food. This was during the time of desperate, last ditch efforts by the Imperial Empire. Kamikaze attacks on the American ships were a daily affair. So much so that no American aircraft would go within twenty miles of the ships. Not even the P-38's with their very distinctive profile. On the Japanese submarines, they even carried human controlled torpedoes called "Kittians." On this night another act of a desperate enemy was to unfold. Right behind our P-61 night fighter aircraft, and unknown to anyone, were Japanese in Betsy bombers. Staying close to our planes so that our radar would not pick them up, they crash landed their aircraft on our runway. As their aircraft screeched to a halt, the enemy jumped out, loaded down with hand grenades, and proceeded to blow up many of the American aircraft parked on the field. The alarm sounded, wailing in the night, G.I.'s leaped from their beds. Struggling to get their pants on, the Americans, still half asleep, grabbed their weapons and ran out of their tents, thinking it was an air raid. Some in underwear and others without pants at all. Aircraft were burning everywhere. Ammunition was exploding; "Pop," "Bang," whis-

Japan to surrender.

TARUMIZU

Ie Shima Japan, August 5, 1945. Home base for the 341 st fighter squadron, of the 348th fighter group, of the 5th Air Force.

Lt. Hubert Hendrix (44-G), Lt. Calvin Fortman (44-F), Lt. Joe Ozier, (44-A) (He was later killed during the testing program of the F-104 in 1956), Lt. Duane Kuhlman (44-G), Lt. Don Little (44-G), Lt. J.J. Brady (44-G), Lt. Joe Marshall (44-G), and ten others of the 341 st, slowly walked to the briefing tent on this hot, humid August morning. Once the men were inside, the Colonel entered, and the squadron was called to attention. As the CO stepped up in front of the men, he greeted them with a cursory "at ease." He began, "Intelligence has reported that on the airfield at Tarumizu, are some German jet fighters, along with a huge catapult-like machine, possibly a Buzz-Bomb launcher and some Japanese "robot" planes, that could be German Buzz-Bombs. We're concerned that they could be directed to attack our forces on Okinawa. Men, we are going to make sure that none of that Jap equipment ever gets off the ground. The major will now give you specific targets and brief you on your mission." The

major arose from his seat, and looking over the eager young faces seated in front of him he said, "This will be an all-out effort; we will be coordinating this strike with some of the aircraft from the Seventh Air Force, as well as our own B-25's, B-26's, P-47's and some B-24's. There will be more than 400 aircraft on this strike." (This was the largest air strike in the PTO of the entire war). The men immediately started to chatter. "Quiet down, I'm not finished." "All right, now you P-51 pilots will each carry two Napalm bombs—I want you to come in low, and make sure that you don't miss." "OK, now pay attention to your specific target assignments, then we will brief the weather......"

The men moved out to their aircraft, donned their May West over their sweat soaked flight suits. Their .45 cal. pistols were in their shoulder holsters. As they walked along, the heavy parachutes banged into the back of their legs. Climbing into their individual aircraft, they fastened their shoulder harness and seat belt, pulled on their leather helmets and pushed their goggles up on their heads. The tower called the flight and ordered them to, "Start engines." The relative quiet on the airfield suddenly exploded with noise, as sixteen Rolls Royce engines roared to life. They all taxied out in trail. As they arrived at the runway, and completed their runups, they were cleared onto the runway in groups of four, two in front, and two behind. Once takeoff clearance was given, the first element in the flight roared down the runway, followed a few seconds later by the other, until all sixteen aircraft were in the air. They climbed in a shallow turn, so they could all join up, then they departed on their southerly heading for their target. It was located on the eastern shore of Kagoshima Bay in the southernmost part of Japan. It was

Yokosuka MXY-7 Ohka (BAKA)   NASM

Approaching the beach at Tarumizu as seen through the gun camera of a P-51.   Calvin H. Fortman 44-F

ironic that this was the same area where the Japanese pilots trained for their attack on Pearl Harbor. The flight was to take about one hour and forty minutes. Dropping down right on the deck, they roared along. As they neared Tarumizu, they could see huge columns of thick, black smoke rising into the air. Glancing up, Lt. Hendrix saw a flight of P-47's in a near-vertical dive, unload their bombs on the target which was now dead ahead. Suddenly, he was engulfed in a thick, black cloud; he immediately went on instruments, quite concerned as he was only about 200' above the ground. For what seemed like an eternity, but in reality was only 20-30 seconds, he flew blind; the world obscured by the smoke of battle. As he flashed out of the smoke, he could see his target, but it was already burning. He thought, "Damn, we come all this way and I don't get to blow anything up." His element leader banked sharply to the right, with Hendrix maintaining his trail position—up ahead he could see a building of some sort—he could drop his Napalm on that. All of a sudden, there was a loud, clanking noise. There were .50 cal. empty shells bouncing off his windshield. The lead plane was trying to shake his bombs loose by firing his guns. At the proper moment, Hendrix dropped his bombs, climbed out of the smoke, and rejoined his flight. They looked down on the smoking ruins and knew the airfield, docks, factories, and anything that was even close to them, had been obliterated. Before heading back to Ie Shima, they dropped down and strafed the towns of Kaimondake, and Yamakawa. The next day was August 6, 1945, the day the first Atomic Bomb was dropped. The target—Hiroshima.

THE LAST A-BOMB

The world held its breath—Japan had just experienced a calamity of immeasurable proportions. They would surrender immediately, wouldn't they? Days past, rumors were rampant, but no surrender. The allied command decided that apparently one dose of mass destruction was not enough. It appeared that the Japanese were going to fight on.

Tinian, home of the 509th Composite Group and the 393rd Bomb Squadron. Their specialized mission was to drop the atomic bomb on Japan. Having already accomplished that task once, it looked as if they would have to do it again. Captain Don Albury was the aircraft commander of the B-29 named the "Great Artiste," he and his crew, along with acting aircraft commander, and Squadron Commander Major Charles Sweeny, had accompanied the Enola Gay on the mission over Hiroshima. Their aircraft was equipped with sensors and data-recording equipment to measure the effects of the first bomb. However, there was a problem using his aircraft for this mission; it would take quite some time to remove all of the electronic equipment from the "Great Artiste," so it was decided to use Major Bock's aircraft, "Bock's Car." The crew for this mission consisted of: Major Charles W. Sweeny (41-I), aircraft commander; Captain Charles D. Albury (43-G), co-pilot; Lt. Phillip M. Banes, bomb electronics test officer; Lt. Jacob Beser, radio control officer; Captain Kermit K. Bahan, bombardier; Captain James F. Van Pelt, navigator; Major Frederick Ashworth, bomb commander; five enlisted crew members, and one extra pilot Lt. Fred J. Olivi who had asked to go along for the ride. It was the morning of August 9, 1945. The weather was overcast all the way to the target—Kukora. They started engines, taxied to the end of the runway, and took off toward their rendezvous point where they were to join up with the photo ship, flown by Captain Hopkins. One of the men on board the photo ship was Dave Laurence, a writer from the New York Times. After holding for forty-five minutes, it became apparent that the photo ship was not going to show up. There was no more time to wait; fuel was now a real concern as the transfer pump in the 600-gallon auxiliary fuel tank in the aft fuselage had failed. Major Sweeny realized he would not have enough fuel after having previously flown around a typhoon that had developed, and then continue on to bomb his target, and still return to Tinian. Instead, he would have to land at his alternate, Okinawa, if he could even make it, after the bomb drop. Proceeding to Kukora, they were unable to see the drop point due to the heavy industrial smoke that obliterated the ground. They had been ordered not to drop the bomb, unless they could see the aiming point visually. After making three bomb runs from different directions, and still not seeing the aiming point, Major Sweeny decided they would divert to their secondary target, Nagasaki. As they approached the I.P. (initial point) for their bomb run, it was becoming apparent that they might not be able to drop here either, as the undercast cloud deck had but a few holes in it. This was a matter for great concern. Major Sweeny called Colonel Ashworth, the bomb commander, and asked him what he thought about dropping the bomb by radar, if they couldn't find a hole in the clouds. It was that or in the ocean, as they couldn't land with the bomb on board. Colonel Ashworth went aft to think about what they should do. While he was gone, Sweeny and Albury decided that they would indeed drop the bomb by radar. When Ashworth returned, he said it would be all right with him to drop the bomb by radar. At 30,000 ft., the crew of "Bock's Car" started their radar bomb run, all the while hoping a hole would open up so they could drop visually. Closer and closer they came to the release point, still no visual contact. Fifteen seconds to go—"Major, I've got it!" shouted Captain Bahan the bombardier. The major replied "OK, let her go." "Bomb away." Major Sweeny immediately banked the huge silver B-29 sharply away from the target. Adding all the power the four R-3350's could muster, they sped away from the impending blast. A bright flash of light illuminated the dark-goggled faces of the crew; then suddenly the aircraft pitched and rolled as if caught in a tornado. A huge, white, mushroom cloud loomed high over what was left of the city of Nagasaki, while on the ground only the screams of the wounded and dying echoed through the crackling, flaming, smoking ruins. Hopefully, this dreadful scene would never have to be repeated again. Only time will tell....

(The fuel on board was so low that the crew thought they would have to ditch before reaching Okinawa. Using long-range power settings, they did make Okinawa; however, upon reaching the field, they could not make contact with anyone on the radio. To gain attention, Sweeny ordered all the flares fired. Upon coming out of reverse after landing, the #2 engine quit, due to a lack of fuel. Arriving at the ramp, the ground personnel wanted to know why all the flares had been fired, which indicated dead and wounded. Major Sweeny replied, "The dead and wounded are back at Nagasikia." (As told to the author by Charles D. Albury.)

The crew of "Bock's Car" after their historic mission. They are: L. to R. standing; Major Charles Sweeny, A/C; Captain Donald Albury, Pilot; 2/Lt. Fred J. Olivi, extra crew member; Captain Kermit Behan, Bombardier;Captain James Van Pelt, Navigator; Lt. Jacob Beser, Radar and E.C.M. Front row: Master Sergeant John Kuharek,Flight Engineer; Sergeant Abe Spitzer, Radioman; Sergeant Ray Gallagher, Scanner; Sergeant Ed Buckley, Scanner; Sergeant Albert Dehart, Tail Gunner.
USAF Museum

The tail end of "Bock's Car" taken by Fred J. Olivi immediately after landing.   USAF Museum

IT'S FINALLY OVER.

Back at Ie Shima it was business as usual. The next nine days for the 341st were consumed by the daily missions, escorting unarmed search aircraft, strafing towns, trucks, radio stations, ships, factories; in short, anything that was visible. They even took time to survey the damage from the second Atomic Bomb. The Japanese had virtually no Air Force, so resistance was nil. After the second bomb, the U.S. halted air attacks on Japan for several days, to await their surrender. When they still refused to unconditionally surrender, the war was resumed. On the morning of August 14, 1945, the 341st, was ordered to attack the ships in the bay at Kyushu. The usual sixteen aircraft were launched; however, this time they were told not to bomb any land targets, nor strafe anything inland. The flight took about two hours to reach the target area. The day was clear, with just a few cumulus clouds a few miles out to sea. They were at 11,000'. Lt. Joe Ozier was

the leader, with Lt. Hubert Hendrix on his wing. Lt. J.J. Brady was number three, and Lt. Duane Kuhlman was number four; all were in the first flight. Upon reaching the target, Lt. Ozier peeled off and was followed by the rest of the squadron; all going to an in-trail formation for the bomb run. They each carried one 500 lb. bomb and an auxiliary drop tank. They were to fly on the drop tank until the engine quit, and then change over to the main internal tanks. This would insure maximum utilization of the fuel, as there was no gauge on the drop tank. Screaming down at better than 400 kts., Lt. Ozier found a ship, lined up on it, and then pressed his bomb release. Nothing happened. He was going so fast that he was past the target in a heartbeat. Lt. Hendrix, in trail right behind him, saw Lead pull up, so he lined the target up and pressed his bomb release. He knew his bomb had released as he could feel the aircraft pop up when the 500 lbs. left the wing. Climbing back to altitude, the entire squadron formed up in echelon, which consisted of four flights of four. Lt. Ozier suspected that his bomb had not released, and one of his flight mates confirmed it. He then told the squadron to orbit while he and his flight-of-four aircraft dove down, and he tried to unload his bomb. They peeled off again, but as Lt. Hendrix banked hard left, and pushed the nose over, his engine suddenly quit. He had forgotten to change over from his drop tank. The number three and four men screamed past him as he rapidly decelerated. It took him several seconds to get the tank switched and the engine restarted. Fire-walling the throttle, he dove down to catch the other three aircraft; he was now in the number four position. Flying low over the water, Ozier's bomb finally came off, making a large splash, and I'm sure, killing a lot of fish. He then started to strafe the beach. This was completely

to Calvin Fortman, whom I had the pleasure of talking with, he was the number six man, not the sixteenth. He claims that he is considered to be the last man to drop a bomb in the war, as his bomb also hung on his first pass, and he had to go back again to get it to release. In fact, he said that he was leveled off, at a speed of over 400 kts. when it finally did let go, causing it to strike inland. However, according to Lt. Hendrix, Lt. Ozier was the last man to drop a bomb in WWII when his bomb dropped on his second pass. Lt. Hendrix was probably the last man to fire his guns in WWII, as he was strafing the beach, and was the last man in the first flight. Lt. Don E. Little, sure that he had missed

Lt. Joe Ozier at Ie Shima.   Dan Ozier

against their orders, but since they were all young hot-shots, and it seemed like a good idea at the time, the other three followed suit. Meanwhile, Lt. Calvin Fortman, made his attack. According to the flight-duty roster posted that day, he was supposed to be the number 16, or last man in the squadron. Herein lies a mystery. The official records say that Lt. Fortman, the last man in the formation, was the last man to drop a bomb in WWII. However, according

with his bomb, made another pass and jettisoned his drop tank. He saw it hit square on the deck of a Jap freighter, and bounce into the ocean. He was certainly the last man to bomb a ship with his drop tank. On the way back to Ie Shima, perhaps a half hour or so after the attack, they heard a second squadron from the 348th (enroute to attack another target in Japan) ordered to return to base. The war was over.

"A" Flight of the 341st Fighter Squadron, 348th Fighter Group at Ie Shima, Japan, July-September 1945. Front L. to R.: Hendrix, Carpenter, Hungerpillar, Green. Back: Grazier, Little, Spencer, Watkins, Stangel, Russell, C.L. Brady, Bowers, Buckalew, and Boyer.

Hubert Hendrix 44-G

No one will ever know for sure just who really did drop the last bomb. I personally talked to four of the men who were there, and parts of the story were remembered differently by each man. They all did agree on one thing, that this was indeed the very last attack mission flown by the allies in WWII. Well, almost all agreed—one of the men asked me if I was sure it was really the last.

Lt. Calvin H. Fortman on wing shaking hands with Lt. Colonel William C. O'Dell who was the first American pilot to fly an offensive mission against the Nazi's over Alkwaar Holland, on July 4, 1942.

Calvin Fortman 44-F

As it turned out there were no jet aircraft located at Tarumizu. There were only two prototypes in existence; and they were located at Kisarazu. This model was named Nakajima Kikka (Orange Blos-

Commander Susumu Takaoka was the test pilot.OnAugust 11, 1945, Takaoka attempted another flight; however, due to improper placement of the two RATOG bottles, the take off was aborted with some damage to the aircraft. There was another prototype almost ready for flight testing, and eighteen others in various stages of assembly when the war ended.

Nakajima Kikka   NASM

som). The Japanese Air Attache' in Germany had seen enthusiastic reports on the Me 262 in 1944, and he convinced the Naval Staff to have Nakajima design a single-seat, twin-jet fighter based on the Me 262. It was supposed to have a maximum speed of 432 mph, and a range of only 150 nautical miles, even less if loaded with 1,000 lbs. of bombs. It was to require 1,150' to take off when using a pair of RATOG (Rocket Assisted Take Off) bottles. It was also to have folding wings, making it possible to be hidden in caves or tunnels.

The aircraft was designed by Kazuo Ohno and Kenichi Matsumura. It resembled the Me 262 but was somewhat smaller in size. They started out with the Tsu-11 Campini-type engines, with only 441 lb. of thrust, which were soon replaced by the Ne-12 turbojets with 750 lbs. of thrust. However, the Ne-12 was still too small to power the heavy aircraft which had a maximum takeoff weight of 8,995 lbs. Engineer Eichi Iwaya of the Japanese Navy had obtained photographs of the German BMW 003, which was an axial-flow turbojet engine. Using this information the Japanese were able to design a similar engine. It was designated the Ne-20, and had a thrust of 1,047 lbs. The first, and only flight, was on August 7, 1945, at Kisarazu Naval Air Base. Lt.

Chapter 6
Korea To Vietnam

OVER SEVEN YEARS AS A POW

It was with great anticipation that 2nd Lt. James L. Lamar walked for the first time, into the squadron headquarter's building of the 40th squadron, which was part of the 35th fighter group stationed at Yokota, Japan. Stopping at the First Sergeant's desk, he handed his orders to the sergeant, and introduced himself. "Just a moment Lt., and I'll tell Major Kuykendahl you're here." As the sergeant disappeared behind the cream-colored door, marked C.O., Lt. Lamar started gazing around the orderly room of his new headquarters. There were photographs of different aircraft neatly spaced along three of the walls; the two desks in the room were the standard gray color, each with a large gray typewriter sitting on the slide-out support made for just such a contraption. The walls were the usual cream, and met with a dark-stained wooden floor. On one wall was a large bulletin board, with all sorts of official-looking papers neatly attached to it. In one corner of the room, hanging by a string from the ceiling, and blowing gently in the breeze generated by the slowly turning ceiling fan, was a nicely-done model of a P-51. Lt. Lamar was momentarily transported in his mind, back to his graduation from the Aviation Cadet program in the class of 49-C, at Williams AFB It had only been a short time ago, and now he found himself all the way around the world in Japan—and at a fighter squadron no less. At this very moment, all his dreams seemed fulfilled. I mean what else could a 22-year-old pilot want. He was jolted back to reality by the voice of the sergeant, "Lt., you can go in now." From pure habit, he checked his gig line before opening the door to the squadron commander's office. Stepping smartly in front of the major seated behind another of the large gray desks, he snapped to attention, saluted smartly, and said, "Lt. Lamar reporting for duty, Sir!" "Relax Lt., have a seat; this isn't the Cadet Corps any more." Feeling somewhat relieved, Lt. Lamar relaxed in a brown, cushioned chair off to his right. "Jim, uh, it is Jim, isn't it?" said the C.O. "Yes Sir, it is." The C.O. continued, "We have just turned in most of our F-51's for the F-80, and since that's what you flew in training, it shouldn't be much of a transition for you. But I'm going to give you, and the three other new guys, some time to get the lay of the land, and learn some tricks from the older guys." He continued, "After a couple of months, I'll expect you to do your share of the other duties; but for now, get in as much formation, and gunnery time as you can." Lt. Lamar replied exuberantly, "Thank you, Sir. I'm really looking forward to being a part of this outfit, and I'll do all I can to hold up my end, Sir." The C.O. replied, "Just don't kill yourself; we don't need any hotshots here."

It wasn't many days later that word came down of an impending O.R.I., (Operational Readiness Inspection). Major Kuykendahl called all of the squadron into the briefing room one day to verify the rumors. He reported, "OK, men, it's true, the I.G. (Inspector General) team will be here on Monday—that only gives us six days to get ready. If you guys will work your butts off, and we do well in this inspection, I'll see to it that each of you gets compensatory time off to make up for it. This time won't count against your leave. It will just be free time." All of the men heartily agreed, and did indeed work their "butts" off. To everyone's great delight, the O.R.I. went off without a hitch.

True to his word, Major Kuykendahl gave each of his men the promised time off. Lt. Lamar and his buddy, Lt. Ryan, were given five days off, which started on June 22nd. They called their American girl friends who worked for the US military in Tokyo, and set up a trip for the four of them to a resort some 4-5 hour-drive away from Yakota AFB. Hopping into Lt. Lamar's new '49 Dodge, they raced into Tokyo to pick up the girls. After spending four days at the resort hotel (the girls shared one room, the guys another—I'm happy to say that things were done differently then), and while they were all having dinner in the hotel dinning room, a page came in calling for Lt. Ryan, or Lt. Lamar. Since he was closest to the phone, Lt. Ryan took the call. It was from their squadron commander. He ordered them back to the base immediately, and wouldn't tell them why. They all hurriedly packed, threw their suitcases into the Dodge, and sped off toward Tokyo. Passing through Yokohama, the car had a flat. They quickly installed the spare, and launched off again. Sliding to a stop in front of the girls' hotel in Tokyo, they tossed out the bags (suitcases, that is), kissed the girls, and spun out toward Yokota. Lt. Lamar turned on the radio and listening to the Armed Forces Radio, this is what they heard: "Attention all military personnel, the North Koreans have crossed the 38th parallel and invaded South Korea. All leaves have been canceled; report to your base immediately." They now had the answer to their question. They arrived at the base in only three-hours time, including the flat tire, and dropping the girls off. It must have been some kind of record. And to top it all off, they had not even seen one M.P.

Running into the squadron orderly room, still in civilian clothes, they were greeted by the C.O. "OK you guys, get changed, and get your gear packed; tomorrow we're going to move the squadron to Ashia." It was June 25, 1950.

When the 35th squadron arrived at Ashia AFB, things were in an uproar. Confusion was the order of the day. Lt. Lamar had been recently appointed assistant armament officer. However, he had not yet received any training in this field. Coincidentally, on the very day of the invasion, the armament officer had ruptured a disk in his back, and was in Tokyo to be operated on. It was up to the new "shave tail," to do the job. And it was no easy job. Many

times Lt. Lamar would spend 24hrs. on continuous duty. They were so short of men and equipment, that he had to help load the bombs himself. Because they were so short of staff, it was several days after the start of the war before Lt. Lamar flew his first mission into Korea. The routine was to fill the aircraft with fuel, and load all the armament it could carry. Then they would takeoff and fly 100 miles to the coast of Korea, and then another hour or so inland, strike the designated targets, and then land at the old Japanese airstrip at Taegu, which was designated K-3. Here, they would refuel, rearm, and fly several more missions before returning back to their base in Japan. K-3 was not a nice, long, wide runway set on a nice level plane—quite to the contrary; this was a 5,000 ft. strip of concrete high up on a plateau, situated about 100 ft. above the bay at Pohang. In good weather it was not much of a problem. However, in low ceilings, which were all too common, it was quite another matter to safely land there. One day Lt. Lamar and his element leader were returning from a mission, and found the cloud deck hovering just a few feet above the runway. There was no way to find the field except to stay below the clouds, and of course the runway. Then they would fly down the coast to the intersection of a sharp point of land and the river, make a 90-degree left turn, throw out the gear, lower the flaps, climb up to the runway and land. Ah, the good old days.

After a week or two of flying the F-80 in combat, it became quite apparent that there were simply not enough spare parts to repair the daily battle damage to the relatively new F-80's. Lt. Lamar's squadron, even though they had recently transistioned to the F-80, were now given back the F-51's they had previously flown. At least they had enough spares and equipment to maintain them in flying condition.

Returning one clear starlit night from a mission, Lt. Lamar and his element leader turned initial to K-3. "Pohang tower this is Wolfhound 4 turning initial, flight of two." The reply was immediate. "Wolfhound flight, negative, negative, negative. You are not cleared to land—the base is being overrun—divert to K-2, and await further instructions." Breaking off the approach, they flew about 50 miles to K-2. After arriving at their destination, the two men learned that the North Koreans had launched a heavy attack against the base at K-3. It was not yet known how long they would have to fly out of K-2. After two days of launching from K-2, word came down that K-3 had held against the enemy attack, and the two men could rejoin their squadron.

Most of the pilots in the 35th were WWII veterans. So naturally, they flew as they had in the last war. Initial approach was flown right on the deck, echelon formation, right down the runway at 250 kts. They would then pitch up, and roll left in a tight 180-degree turn, spreading out at traffic-pattern altitude, drop their gear, lower their flaps, and immediately make a tight 180-degree turn to final and a normal landing. The old-timers told Lt. Lamar, "This is the way a real fighter pilot does it." Hey, who's to argue, he was just an inexperienced "Brown Bar"—besides, it was a heck of a lot of fun.

After several days at K-2, Lt. Lamar's flight was sent back to their base at Japan for some R & R. It was a beautiful clear day, Wolfhound flight was a four-ship formation, echeloned right, and tucked in tight, they came screaming in over the mountains, dropping down to the deck, they roaring down the runway, up and around they went. Sierra Hotel! This is flying. After the flight taxied in, parked their planes, and had joined each other on the ramp, a jeep roared up. Out jumped a Lt. Colonel, who was the commander of another squadron, and he said, "Men, that was a great job, very nice approach and landings. But don't do that again. The people who live off the end of the runway prefer to have their roofs right where they are." Rats, so much for the good old ways.

Word came down that a F.A.C. (Forward air controller) was needed by a South Korean unit. Lt. Lamar, being somewhat junior, was sent to handle the job. As he entered the command post, the first person he saw was a U.S. Army Lt. Colonel named Macphail. Upon seeing him, the colonel pulled out his .45 pistol, chambered a round, and abruptly slapped it down on the table in front of him. "Lt., it's a damn good thing you brought a 51 in here. Those damn F-80 jocks strafed one of our truck convoys, damn near killed me!" Lt. Lamar didn't bother to tell him that he had been one of those "F-80 jocks." Of course the colonel didn't know, nor did he care, that it was a real problem for the pilots to identify ground targets with the new jet aircraft. If you started your attack at the normal 250 kts, you would be about 350 kts. by the time you had descended to strafing altitude—much too fast to really identify what you were shooting at.

After flying a total of 100 combat missions in Korea, Lt. Lamar was sent back to the states. In March of 1951, he was sent to Nellis AFB, near Las Vegas where he was an F-80 gunnery instructor. After only a month there, his C.O. called him in and explained, that because they were still flying F-51's in Korea, they needed experienced gunnery instructors in that type of aircraft. Lt. Lamar jumped at the chance. He was single, young, and perhaps somewhat foolish at that stage in his life. At least he knew it would be a lot better for him personally to get away from the "party" life he had been enjoying in Vegas. He figured that he could only burn the candle at both ends for a short time, before he snuffed out in the middle. So, it was off to Luke AFB. After four fun-filled years at Luke, now Captain Lamar, was transferred to Okinawa, Japan, to fly the F-86. He remained there until 1958. The scuttlebutt was that there would be no more need for fighter pilots. All aircraft interception would be handled by surface-to-air missiles, and surface-to-ground missiles could be used to handle the ground targets. It is somewhat amazing how naive, and sometimes downright stupid, our policy-making folks can be. As was soon learned, there is no substitute for a living, breathing, thinking man in the cockpit of an aircraft. A programed rocket just won't cut it—it

North American F-86A National Archives

even talk to them man to man. Wow! That may not seem like much to someone who never experienced the "Class" difference between a commissioned officer and a Cadet, but, believe me, to find a human being in those flight suits was indeed rare.

One thing that I'll always remember of the time that I was training there, was when Captain Vowell would speak to the troops. There was a white "something" that flipped around in his mouth as he talked. I always thought it was a loose piece of skin. I recently

can't adapt to rapidly changing conditions like a man can. It was in this context that Captain Lamar gladly accepted the assignment to Vance AFB, at Enid, OK. At least in the training command he could still fly single engine fighter-type aircraft. Since he was the

senior captain, he was made flight commander of the 3576th PTS, flight IV, Devil flight, in 1958. This was an especially choice assignment, as many of his buddies from the 44th fighter squadron, were given desk jobs.

I first met Captain Lamar in early August of 1960. Captain John Vowell was the assistant flight commander. Captain Lamar was the man who gave me my "Dollar" ride in the T-33. Both of these men were, I thought, much nicer than most of the officers I had been in contact with to date. Here I was a lowly Cadet, and these guys were Captains. And I could

mentioned it to several of my classmates who were also in "Devil" flight, and they remembered the same thing. As I was talking to Jim Lamar recently, recording this story, I mentioned it to him. He laughed and said, "Old John always chewed on a match

Captain Lamar behind his desk in the flight IV line shack. Author 61-E

stick." How about that, 36 years later, and the mystery is solved. It's too bad John isn't still around, he would have had a good laugh over this. He passed away in 1994.

Well, getting back to our story: In 1963, Captain Lamar was transferred from Vance AFB to Williams AFB. Shortly after arriving at Williams, he was promoted to the rank of Major.

Major Lamar's squadron, the 421st, which was part of the 355th group, after completing transition training, was sent to Korat in Thailand. His squadron was flying the F-105 Thunderchief. It was nicknamed the "Thud". There was nothing either in the design nor in the mechanical construction that engendered the aircraft's reputation for crashing. Quite to the contrary, it was really a matter of mission. The F-105 was designed to deliver nuclear weapons at very low altitudes, and very high speeds. It

was not well suited to the same roll as the P-47 used in WWII, which was an excellent aircraft for close ground support. In Victnam the missions required weighting the F-105 down with a huge load of bombs, and launching it into extremely well-fortified targets; it was no wonder many of the men and aircraft never came back. During the Vietnam War, the White House was directing the missions by telling the generals which targets to hit, even which flight path to use for the bomb runs. Who knew less about the day-to-day war than those politicians in Washington? They even gave the North Vietnamese four years to build their defenses around Hanoi. Then our brilliant politicians told our boys to go in and bomb them. It was a slaughter.

By now the Vietnam War was raging in full force. Major Lamar was promoted to the rank of Lt. Colonel in April of 1965. He was the squadron

Republic F-105   AF History

operation's officer and acting commander of the 421st Tactical Fighter squadron. On May 6, 1965, he was leading a flight of four F-105's who had left their base in Thailand on a bombing mission, with the target located about 90 miles northwest of Hanoi in North Vietnam. They were to hit a railroad marshaling yard at Yenbai. The men of his flight had been heavily briefed by Colonel Lamar to maintain radio silence except in an emergency. He made a special point of this as his number four man had very poor radio discipline. The radio was always congested with chatter, and the many varied and distracting sounds coming into the earphones from other aircraft, ground controllers, ELT's (emergency locator transmitters), and aircraft warning systems, all mixed together, were almost overwhelming. Especially so, in the midst of battle.

The normal mission profile was to come in low to avoid detection. As they neared the target, Colonel Lamar pulled up sharply to 12,000 ft., with his flight right behind. He rolled inverted, and pulled the nose down through the horizon, and then rolled right side up to start his bomb run; the flak and smoke were so thick he couldn't even see the target. Diving lower and lower, he was finally able to pick out the target, and pickle off his bombs. Immediately upon releasing the bombs, his aircraft shook from the impact of a flak shell hitting somewhere on the right, in front of the cockpit. A bright orange flame raced from the right side of the cockpit under the instrument panel, clear over to the left side of the cockpit, and in a heartbeat, the cockpit filled with smoke. He still had his speed brakes down from the bomb run, and was going about 450 kts. It seemed the best course of action was to retract the speed breaks, firewall the throttle, and light the afterburner; in other words, get the hell out of there! He climbed to 4,000 ft, jinking all the way (evasive maneuvers), then checking his controls he found they responded correctly. Since the smoke in the cockpit was now clearing out, and he could still control the aircraft, he decided to head west toward the designated bailout area. This way he could be picked up by the

"Jolly Green Giants" rescue helicopters, in the event that he had to leave his ship. He took a moment and radioed his flight, "Oak flight, this is Lead; I've taken a hit..... heading toward the bailout area." Immediately number four replied, "Get out Lead, you've got a big fire going!" Making no reply, Colonel Lamar reasoned that if number four, who was at least four miles behind him, could see a fire on his aircraft, he must be a real torch and would have to eject immediately. Being unable to visually verify a fire, and knowing that a large fire aft would cause his aircraft to explode at any second, he reacted without further thought. As he reached for the ejection handles, he noticed the airspeed indicator was just over 600 kts, and climbing (525 kts was the maximum recommended bailout speed—he was actually right at the speed of sound at his present altitude). Expecting the imminent, and complete destruction of his aircraft, he acted with pure instinct and training. He pulled the handles up, the canopy blew away, and he and the seat followed immediately thereafter. The next thing he remembers is waking up in a clearing, lying on his back. As he sat up, he realized his left arm was broken, and he had numerous cuts and abrasions. Stunned from the force of the ejection, he looked around, and saw his parachute hung up in a tree above him. At about the same time, along came a bunch of black-pajama-clad peasants. They grabbed him and hauled him off, eventually turning him over to a squad of N.V.A. regulars. He was then taken to the infamous Hanoi Hilton.

Sitting on his concrete bunk, Colonel Lamar looked around at his cell. It was very small, being only about 7'X7', and it contained two concrete bunks, one upper and one lower on the same wall. The cell was so narrow that one had to walk sideways to enter. There was a window at the end opposite the door, but it was blocked off. The humidity was high and the smell of mildew permeated the air. Mice, rats, ants, and every type of insect or vermin abounded there. He was overcome by a depression much deeper and more terrifying than any-

Colonel Lamar captured by the North Vietnamese. MIA/Pow

tended to. Colonel Lamar's mind raced back and forth over the events of the last few hours. "What had I done wrong? Why am I here? What could I have done differently to avoid being here?" Suddenly, the sickening realization of what had really happened, hit him like a sledgehammer in the pit of his stomach. The words from his number four man rang loud in his head, "Get out Lead, you've got a big fire going!" "OH NO! My God, that's not what he said!" He said, "Good hit, Lead. You've got a big fire going!" Colonel Lamar had, in the heat of battle, and with the incessant noise from other flights chatter,

thing he had ever felt in his entire life. To make matters even worse, his arm had not yet been at-

The Hanoi Hilton   MIA/POW

335

and the sound of emergency locator transmitters going off in his earphones, misunderstood what was said. He had not been on fire. He shouldn't have ejected! The full realization of what had happened only served to drive him into an ever-deepening depression. He went into shock, and was not even cognizant of events around him. He was totally incoherent for three days.

There were three other American pilots in prison with him at that time. They were Lt. Colonel Sam Johnson (one of Lt. Colonel Lamar's cellmates), Navy Commander Jim Stockdale, and Navy Commander Jerry Denton. The only way they could communicate between the cells, was to lie on their bellies on the floor, and whisper through the small space under the door. One of the men (who ever had the cell nearest to the outside door) would keep a lookout under the door for feet heading toward their cell block and warn the others. Normally, they could only get away with this communication about ten minutes at a time—twice a day—once around noon, and again around five in the afternoon. That was the guards' siesta time. They all tried to communicate with Colonel Lamar, in the hope of bringing him out of his despondency, but it was to no avail—at least not for the three days. Then, slowly at first, he began to hear their voices, very faintly, from across the hall, and of course from his cellmate Sam Johnson. Suddenly, it hit him, these voices were speaking English. Slowly he responded, and bit by bit, he started coming back to reality. He found out their names, where they were from, and how they had gotten into this Hell hole that the prisoners called "Heartbreak Hotel." This cellblock was where all prisoners were held for the first month or two while they were being tortured. It is generally agreed that there is no one tough enough to withstand torture. You either tell them what they want to know, or think they want to know, or you die.

It was about two weeks after Colonel Lamar ejected, that the N.V.A. sent a doctor to set his arm. It had already started to freeze in an unnatural position. To make matters even worse, the doctor left the cast on too long. The combination of no treatment, and improper treatment, caused his arm to become frozen in a 90-degree bend at the elbow. Realizing that he had mistreated Colonel Lamar's arm, the N.V.A. doctor gave him a bucket with water in it, and told him to carry it in the hand of his broken arm, the doctor said this would help to straighten it out. It didn't.

Each cell had leg stocks at the end of the concrete bunks. There were no mattresses. Each man was given two thin cotton blankets. They were not much warmth during winter when temperatures dropped to 35-40 degrees at night. The leg stocks had wood on the bottom, and a metal top piece that had two half circles formed in it. The men were made to lie down on their backs, and extend their legs until their feet were hanging over the wooden stock, then the top portion was lowered over their ankles and passed through a slot in the concrete wall, where it was locked on the outside of the cell. In addition, many times they were handcuffed with their hands behind their backs, and left that way for days or even weeks at a time. There was no way they could lay down with their hands behind their back. During one "special" punishment (incurred because of suspected talking between cells), Colonel Lamar was put in the top bunk, feet in the stocks, hands cuffed behind his back. He had no way to use the old-fashioned chamber pot that they were given. There was no toilet. His cell-mate, Colonel Johnson, had to help him raise up to get the pot under him. During the many times that it became unbearable for Colonel Lamar to hold himself sitting up, Colonel Johnson would get up in the top bunk with him, and put his back against Colonel Lamar's back so that he could rest for awhile. The men literally depended upon each other for everything.

The prisoners were let out of their cells once each day (except on Sunday), and taken outside to a cell that had been converted to a shower. A pipe was run through the wall and a shower head attached. It was cold water both winter and summer. After his shower, and when the guards allowed, Colonel

Lamar would wrap his arm around trees and try to pull it straight. He would pull so hard, that he would almost break it again—all to no avail.

The shock, injury, and depression were enough to drive most anyone over the edge. One day, in desperation, Colonel Lamar got down on his belly, crawled up to the door, and whispered to the man across the hall, who was Navy Commander Jerry Denton. Colonel Lamar said, "Jerry I'm just about at the end of my rope. How do you handle this?" Commander Denton said, "Jim, I've been here six months longer than you have, and this is what I've learned. You must have faith in God, your family, and your country. You must pray every day, and you must take one day at a time. Never mind what happened yesterday, and don't worry about what might happen tomorrow. Just concentrate on getting through today." Colonel Lamar followed that advice.

Several years later, Colonel Lamar was quite surprised to learn that one of the new prisoners was the same pilot who had been his number four man on the day he was captured. This man had completed his tour, gone back to the states for a year or so, and was then sent back to Vietnam. He was subsequently shot down. What goes around comes around.

On February 12, 1973, an aircraft landed at Clark AFB in the Phillipines. As the loading ramp was rolled into position, and the bright lights of the numerous TV cameras turned on, the door swung open and out came the third group, of United States Of America prisoners of war, to land that day. The men were brought out in the order of captivity, with the ones who had been captive longest, being the first to be brought out. Colonel Lamar was the eighty-

third man to be shot down. It had been 2474 days since that fateful day in 1965. But at last, he and his fellow airmen were FREE!

Anxious to talk to his wife after more than six years, Colonel Lamar called her from the Phillipines. She informed him that she was seeing someone else, and wanted a divorce.

Arriving back in the U.S. On February 15th, Colonel Lamar was taken to Wilford Hall hospital at San Antonio, Texas. During the same time period, his wife had undergone surgery at Little Rock, and was in the hospital there. By mutual consent, she was moved to his hospital room in Wilford Hall. His children came to see him there, but they were like strangers. His wife was convinced that it was all his fault that he had gone to Vietnam. She had told the children during all the time that he was a prisoner, that he didn't have to go. She told them he could have gotten out of it if he had really wanted to. They were divorced six months later.

It seems it's not enough to suffer at the hands of a cruel enemy for over seven years; so many of our men were to undergo additional suffering at the hands of those who had been loved ones—causali-

The author and Jim Lamar, reunited after more than thirty-five years at the author's home in 1995.

Author 61-E

ties of war, not once, but twice.

The POW's were treated with honor and respect by their country, and countrymen. But the other men and women who had also fought and died for their country, were many times despised by their countrymen, and seldom, if ever, given a place of honor. Our nation will always be haunted by the shameful rejection of its native sons and daughters who sacrificed all for their un-grateful countrymen.

Colonel Lamar is now living in Austin, Texas, with his second wife, Judy. His arm has lost about 20% of its normal movement. Even after all he has been through, he cheerfully says, "At least it doesn't interfere with my golf game."

Two and one half months later another of my friends was deeply engrossed in the war in Vietnam.

I MADE IT—THE OTHERS DIDN'T

July in most of the United States is a very hot and humid month. At Korat Air Base in Thailand, not only was it hot and humid, there was a war going on right next door in Vietnam. It was the morning of July 27, 1965, at 06:30, when Captain Frank J. Tullo, a classmate of mine from 61-E, was awakened by his squadron commander, Colonel Robert Fair. Since Captain Tullo was the squadron target's and navigation officer, it was his responsibility to prepare the flight plans and refueling needs for the 12th Tactical Fighter squadron. Captain Tullo acknowledged the colonel's call, and slowly sat up on his bunk, putting his bare feet on the wooden floor. As he sat there rubbing the sleep from his eyes, his mind suddenly snapped awake. This was no normal day—today was to be a maximum effort against the SAM (Surface to Air Missile) sites within the 30-mile circle around Hanoi. Not only was this the first mission inside the 30-mile circle (an area that had been allowed to build its defenses unmolested for almost four years), it was to be the first time in history that aircraft would attack SAM sites. Every SAM site was heavily defended by numerous anti-aircraft gun emplacements. To make matters worse,

the most effective attack method, dive bombing, was out of the question, as the SAMs were most effective above 3,000 ft. The only choice was to attack from a very low level with napalm and rockets. The "hootch" (a raised-wooden barrack that housed about eight pilots) that had become home to so many of our men, looked better to him at this moment than it ever had. The plain wooden walls, the louvers covered with screens, where windows should have been, the other pilots' bunks, the pictures of wives and girlfriends; all of these suddenly became very precious to him. He wondered, would he ever see them again? Even the smell of the mildew, and the rapidly scurrying bugs seemed to be almost homelike. Such are the thoughts of men about to face battle, and very possibly, death. He shook his head in an effort to put his mind back on track. Reaching into his locker, he picked up a pair of socks, and slowly slid them on, then pulled on his boots, and stood to his feet. Dressed only in his underwear he went to the washroom and splashed some water on his face. The coolness of the clear water helped him to return to the reality of his situation. He was the number-two man in Dogwood flight. The flight commander was Major Bill Hosmer. He and Frank had been through many tough targets together, and even though they had many times taken hits, Frank felt almost bulletproof on Bill's wing. After all, they had always returned after their missions, and there was no reason to think this would be any different. At least, that's what most men try to make themselves think when faced with eminent danger.

At the briefing that morning, the squadron commander tried to make things as light as possible. He even used most of the jokes in his repertoire. But everyone knew this was not a "normal" mission. The strain and nervousness was on everyone's face. They all had lost friends in the preceding weeks, and those missions were a piece-of-cake, when compared to this one. But be that as it may, the orders were to attack, and that was that.

As he approached his F-105, Frank was once

again cognizant of the awe he had experienced on his first encounter with this huge fighter. It was a fine bird, capable of tremendous speed, but would it be fast enough today? He thought of the four F4C Phantoms who were departing their target area north of the 30-mile circle around Hanoi, just two days ago. They were skirting the circle along the northern border, climbing in tight formation to penetrate a solid cloud deck, when suddenly, a SAM was fired from within the circle; without warning it exploded right below the flight. Two were shot down, and the other two had to make emergency landings away from their base, due to extensive damage to their aircraft. These were the first American aircraft to be lost to a SAM. To say the least, it was a tremendous shock, not only to the pilots, but to the generals and admirals back in the states as well. This event was the basis for this attack. The day before

(July 26th) the missions were reduced to assure as many aircraft as possible would be available for today's mission. The only problem with reducing the missions was, that it tipped off the North Vietnamese that something was up. This gave them time to reposition their SAM's, simultaneously replacing their previous positions with flak traps, and placing wooden dummy SAM's at the traps as well.

Dogwood flight was the last flight of the day to take off from Korat. Their mission was to reconnoiter each of the SAM sites that had been hit by the previous flights, and attack any equipment that had survived. As they screamed into the air, Major Hosmer and Captain Tullo initiated a right bank so the other two aircraft could join on them. Climbing toward their tanker rendezvous, Frank was starting to relax somewhat; the sound of the air flowing passed his sleek fighter, the low roar of the engine,

Republic F-105 climbing toward its target in North Vietnam.   AF History

and the cool air from the air-conditioning, had a way of making everything seem less than real. Why, this could just be a training flight back home in the States. It all looked the same from high in the sky. Suddenly, he was jolted back to reality by Lead's voice in his earphones, "Dogwood flight, Dogwood One, tankers in sight, 12 o'clock level." "Roger, Two"— "Roger, Three"— "Roger, Four." After filling up their fuel tanks, they checked their armament; each had seven pods of rockets, with seventeen 2.75 inch

had anticipated. The radio was alive with distress calls from fighter pilots engaged in the worst combat they had ever encountered. ELT's (Emergency Locator Transmitters) were going off all over the place, indicating pilots ejecting from their damaged aircraft. Racing northward toward the first SAM target, the acrid smell of gun powder filtered into the cockpit as Lead called, "Dogwood flight this is Lead, target in sight." As the flight approached the target, the city of Hanoi was dead ahead, on the ho-

A flight of three Republic F-105's over Thailand.   AF History

rockets in each pod. With all this ordnance they should really do some damage to those SAM sights. The flight from the refueling to the target area was uneventful. As they neared the target area they descended to an altitude of 100 ft. or less. As they switched to the combat frequency for the day, they learned that the defenses were much worse than they

rizon. There was a thick, black smoke-cloud hanging several hundred feet up; the flak was much worse than anyone had seen before. The antiaircraft gunners had the range and altitude figured out, after so many of our planes had come in from the same direction and altitude. The explosions rocked the aircraft; flashes of fire and smoke were everywhere.

The radio crackled with the voice of Lead, "Dog-wood flight, I think they salvoed all their missiles, the smoke and fire from the target is enormous!" Suddenly, as they were almost over the target, Lead realized that the enemy had not salvoed their missiles, but quite to the contrary, there were no missiles located there, only a flak trap. Breaking left they tried to avoid the trap, but to no avail; their momentum carried them right over the guns. As they emerged from the smoke, both aircraft in full afterburner, Frank realized he had a huge red light on his instrument panel that read "Fire!" He frantically scanned the panel for signs to confirm that he actually had a fire, hoping against hope, that it was a false warning. Frank's earphones crackled with the voice of his flight-mate, "Dogwood Two, this is Three, Frank, you're burning." This was immediately followed by, "Two, this is Lead—affirmative, you are on fire." Not wanting to bail out over down-town Hanoi, Frank continued to check the status of his ship, "Lead, this is Two, she seems to be responding OK; I think I can get to the bailout area." Lead responded, "Roger Two, but you had better get rid of the external tanks, and rocket pods." Frank immediately jettisoned his external stores, which lessened the drag, and lightened the aircraft. Someone said, "Dogwood Two, you're really burning, you ought to get out." The flight was now heading toward the west, and a large mountain appeared on the horizon. Remembering his survival training, which stressed the importance of selecting the highest, most inaccessible terrain available, Frank was hoping his aircraft would at least hold together until he reached the mountains, better still, perhaps it would keep flying until he could reach his home base. Flying very low and very fast, the flight pressed on toward the west, but they were still being fired upon by the enemy gunners. Frank began hearing muffled explosions, that were felt in his controls. Approaching the outskirts of Hanoi, he started losing instruments and the aircraft controls became sluggish. "Dogwood Lead, this is Two, everything is turning to crap, I've got to get out."

"Roger Two, I'll call rescue." Frank saw a river just ahead, with what seemed to be a very thick jungle just beyond. As he headed toward this area, the nose of his aircraft dropped slightly; he immediately pulled the stick back, but the aircraft failed to respond. Being at such a low altitude and high speed, he had to eject NOW! He reached down and grasped the ejection seat handles on either side of the seat, and pulled them up sharply. The canopy disappeared with a loud roar. Glancing at the airspeed, he saw the tape was above 500 kts.—Too late, he had to go. He squeezed the ejection handles, "ka-boom!" The events that followed were so violent, that he can't even remember them. The automatic sequence took over as soon as the triggers on the ejection seat handles were pressed. Frank's seat belt and shoulder harness were opened, and another apparatus pushed him out of the seat simultaneously pulling the "D" ring to open his chute. In what seemed like the blinking of an eye, he was dangling in his parachute. Looking up to see if his chute was fully inflated, he realized he could only see out of his right eye. His helmet was torn from his head by the extreme force of the wind, causing the oxygen mask retainer clip to cut a large laceration over his left eye, leaving a loose flap of skin to cover his eye as it filled with blood. He heard his flight disappearing to the west, some antiaircraft fire back toward Hanoi, but all else was relatively quiet, especially when compared to the wind noise of an open cockpit at over 500 kts. As he descended dangling beneath the live-saving canopy of his chute, he could see the city of Hanoi behind, and a small farm house with some cleared fields around it, about a mile away. With no time to digest what he had seen, he hit the ground with a thud. Struggling to his feet, he immediately gathered in his chute and stuffed it under some brush, so the enemy wouldn't see it. He was very fortunate to have landed in "elephant grass" (very thick undergrowth). He figured one would have to be within ten feet in order to see him. Pulling the emergency two-way transmitter from his survival vest, he had no more than turned it on when he heard, "Dogwood Two, this is Dogwood Lead, do you read me?" Even though Lead was safe in his aircraft, and Frank was in imminent danger, just the sound of a familiar voice was reassuring. He immediately responded, "Lead, this is two, I'm OK, just a few cuts and bruises; I'm in a great place to be picked up, whenever the choppers get here." Lead responded, "Frank, I've got a pretty good idea where you are—I'll direct the choppers for as long as I can hang around." Frank could see his flight coming overhead, but every time they came near, the antiaircraft opened up on them. Frank could hear the spent shells hitting in the grass around him. Not wanting to endanger his flight, he called again, "Bill, you guys are getting a lot of flak, you ought to back off some." Lead responded, "Frank, I'm sorry to say we have been ordered back to base, looks like you may be in for the night, hang in there Buddy." As the flight disappeared over the horizon, an immense feeling of loneliness and despair came over him like a dark cloud; suddenly every noise became a threat, every windblown movement of the grass, the enemy. He had to get a hold of himself. He started talking to himself in his mind, "Don't panic, do what needs to be done first. Come on Frank, think!" Regaining his composure, he dressed the cut over his eye, then laid out his emergency equipment to see just what he had; this all helped to keep his mind occupied. He deflated his brightly colored dingy, and hid it as well as any other brightly colored objects. He had one major decision to make; would he try to walk out or wait for the helicopters to rescue him? Staying as still as possible, he pondered the situation, when suddenly he heard the unmistakable sound of more F-105's. Turning on his radio, he called, "Any F-105 over North Vietnam, do you hear me?"—An immediate reply, "Roger, we hear you, you must be Dogwood Two; sorry we can't offer any assistance at this time, but we will relay to the command post that you're still here." All was once again quiet, and very lonely. Frank got back to the business at hand. He moved about trying to get a lay of the land, but it was so

thick and steep, all that his movements accomplished was to completely exhaust him. He snuggled down as far as he could in the grass, and decided to wait until dark to see if a rescue helicopter would show up. It was about 4:00 p.m. He had been on the ground about half-an-hour, when he again heard the sound of engines. These were different, certainly not Thuds, but two propeller-driven aircraft that he recognized as Navy rescue A-1's. Staying as close to the ground, and with as little movement as possible, Frank called again, "Navy A-1, do you read?" "Roger, this is Canasta flight, where are you?" Frank gave them directions until they were directly over his position. "Dogwood Two, Canasta Lead, we see exactly where you are. Be advised, there are busses unloading soldiers south of your position, and they are fanning out towards you." It was very reassuring to know someone could direct the helicopters to rescue him, but he wondered if they would arrive in time. Canasta Lead radioed again, "Dogwood Two, we have to leave the area—we're taking too much ground fire—will return with a chopper." If he could only stay hidden long enough for the enemy to give up trying to find him. Suddenly, several gunshots rang out from below his position, followed by an enormous amount of yelling, and still more gun fire. He could now hear the voices of the North Vietnamese soldiers coming ever closer, hacking at the brush, and firing at anything that moved. He prayed, "Oh God, please help me—don't let them find me." His heart pounding in his chest was so loud that he was sure the enemy would hear. Ever closer they came, then he saw movement about 100 feet away, "Oh, no, it was a soldier." He tried to sink into the very ground he was laying on. But thank God, the terrain was so rugged, and the underbrush so thick that they changed from their northward search to a more westerly one. Frank had laid motionless for about 2 1/2 hours, when he again heard the sound of aircraft engines. It was Canasta flight, and they had a chopper with them. The troops in the valley were firing at the A-1's as they circled over his position. Frank called the helicopter on his radio directing him toward his position. As the chopper approached him, he fired two small rescue flares, but the pilot didn't see them. He then fired two red smoke flares, but still no visual contact from the chopper. Out of desperation, he fired six tracers from his .38 caliber revolver—they saw them! Coming right towards him was the prettiest sight he had ever seen, a huge "Jolly Green" with its sling hanging just above the brush. Shoving his radio back into his vest, Frank grabbed the moving sling, sticking his arms through, and as he hung by his armpits, the crew chief started the hoist raising him six or seven feet, when suddenly it jammed. Frank looked up at the crew chief, and gave him the thumbs-up sign; the crew chief shook his head, and shrugged his shoulders; it was stuck. Barely above the brush, the helicopter pilot, Captain George Martin, decided it was time to get the heck out of there. They were being fired on by the troops in the valley, so with their cargo hanging far below them, the chopper added power and left the pickup point. There was Frank dangling by a cable, and as they turned he was pulled through some bushes and the top of a very large tree. He didn't even care, he was headed home. For about twenty minutes the helicopter circled as they tried in vain to make the winch operate. All the while, he was swinging in the air. Several times he glanced down, only to see some ground troops firing at him. He quit looking down. He then noticed that they had stopped circling, and were now headed toward the farm house he had seen while descending in his parachute. Captain Martin flew low enough to set Frank gently back on the ground, and the instant his feet touched, he slipped out of the sling, and started running toward the descending chopper. Just as he reached the helicopter, he heard automatic weapon fire. He dove through the door of the helicopter, lay flat on the floor, and immediately the chopper pilots went to full power, keeping their heads as low as possible to avoid being hit. Even though the helicopter took several hits, they managed to make a successful departure from the area. It was now starting to get dark, and the chopper was low on fuel. The only sensible thing to do was to land for the night on a hilltop in Laos called Lima Site #36. It was some of the only territory in northern Laos that was held by friendly forces. It was surrounded by the forces of the Viet Cong, North Vietnamese and Pathet Lao. The landing was aided by burning smudge pots arranged in a circle, without which they could not have found this tiny oasis located in this otherwise hostile jungle. A bruised, battered, cut up, and very thankful, Captain Frank Tullo spent that night in a bunker along with the helicopter crew. The following morning they continued their flight back to Frank's home base at Korat.

As a footnote to the story, for the next 28 years, Frank kept asking any Navy or Marine pilot that he ran into, if they had any idea what carrier or squadron Canasta Flight had been with, but no one knew. In late 1993, he was conversing with an ex-Marine helicopter pilot, and mentioned the incident. The Marine eyes lit up, and he said, "They were on the *Midway*, in VA 25 squadron." "Hot dog!" After all these years, perhaps he could find the men who had helped save his life and thank them in person. Someone suggested he put an add in *HOOK* (a magazine). Less than two days after placing the ad, he received a call from someone on the magazine staff, who knew who the men were and how he could locate them. That same day Frank dialed the phone number of Ed Greathouse, Canasta Lead. He was at home, and after an hour or so of comparing notes, they made plans to meet in Houston before the year's end. A few days later, the search was completed with another long phone conversation with Canasta Two, Holt Livesay.

In 1995, on the 30th anniversary of this event; Frank Tullo, George Martin, Ed Greathouse, and Holt Livesay did meet again, all at one place, and all at one time, and thank God no one was shooting at them this time.

On July 27, 1965, five F-105's and a B-66, with three crew members, were shot down. Of the eight men shot down on that day, Captain Frank J. Tullo was the only pilot rescued. Two of the others were captured by the North Vietnamese. The remaining five were killed.

Captain George Martin (L) and Captain Frank Tullo after his rescue. Frank Tullo 61-E

THE BIG PUSH

There is one story to come out of the Vietnam war that is so heroic, and so unbelievable that it must be included in this book, as it exemplifies the spirit of the Aviation Cadet.

Unable to sleep any longer, Captain John R. (Bob) Pardo, (55-N) and his WSO (Weapons Systems Operator), Lt. Steve Wayne, awakened shortly before midnight at their base in Ubon, Thailand. Considering that this was to be the tenth time they were attempting to destroy the Nguygen Steel Mill located twenty five miles north of Hanoi, they were somewhat concerned about flying the same mission again the following morning—March 10, 1967. There was a surreal heaviness and blackness in the night air as they made their way to the briefing room. The dampness of the night seemed to engulf them and weigh on them as a heavy, wet blanket, reflecting the heavy dampening of their spirits. They wondered silently if they would ever see another dawn—many of their friends had not. No matter what the politicians called it, to these men this was war. Even though they had been briefed on this same mission over and over again, they dutifully entered the briefing room and sat down for yet another update by Intelligence. On the first day of this mission, March 1, the men were briefed that the mill was protected by over 200 antiaircraft guns, within five miles of the target. The number of defensive weapons increased daily, and by day nine had reached 1000 guns of all sizes (37mm-120mm) and there were six portable SAM sites, all within a five mile radius of the mill. This meant that almost 25% of the total North Vietnamese antiaircraft weapon strength was concentrated on this one target. As part of the 8th Tac Fighter Wing, 433rd Tac Fighter Squadron, flying F-4 aircraft they were assigned to be Mig Cap—which meant that they had a dual role. They carried iron bombs for use against ground targets, and missiles to be used in the event of enemy Migs attacking the strike force. The strike force that they were a part of consisted of over 100 aircraft from many different bases.

The flight of four F-4's departed Ubon sometime after nine a.m. They climbed uneventfully through the scattered cloud deck to their tanker rendezvous altitude of 18,000 feet. The flights were timed to arrive at their tankers, in the same sequence

McDonnell F-4 Phantom II refueling.   AF Museum

that they were to attack in. The aircraft were flying at this low altitude mainly to help in the avoidance of SAM attacks. If they were up higher, 16,000' to 18,000', it would give the missile too much time to lock onto their aircraft. The F-4's were equipped with a Radar Homing and Warning system, consisting of a small radar screen at both crewmember's stations; this system would indicate the direction of the enemy weapons and the type. The antiaircraft

guns' radar lock-on made a steady buzz in the headsets, and the SAM radar lock-on sounded like a rattlesnake. The standard evasive maneuver, when the SAM warning went off, was to point the nose of the F-4 as straight down as possible, and go as fast as possible, then visually fly right at the missile. When it became so big in the windshield that it looked like you were bound to hit it (the ultimate game of "chicken")—you would then break away, pulling as many G's as possible. This would tend to make the missile start downward, and when the aircraft pulled up again, it would attempt to follow. Because it had such tiny wings it would either break apart or stall, in its attempt to destroy the aircraft.

After a routine refueling, "Cheetah" flight continued on toward the target. Dropping down to 8,000' so as to be below the scattered cloud deck, they sped toward the steel mill. Their headsets were alive with warnings from their on-board radar—numerous antiaircraft batteries opened up trying their best to destroy these sleek flashes of roaring destruction. Unknown to anyone in Cheetah flight except number Four, he had taken a bad hit on the underside of the fuselage, as he neared the I.P. He was still some thirty or forty miles from the target, but he elected to continue on with the bomb run. Nearing the target, Lead called, Cheetah flight, burners now."

Simultaneously all eight engines boomed as raw JP-4 poured into the red-hot exhaust—long, reddish-orange flames shot out of the rear of each aircraft like giant torches as they pointed their noses skyward, zooming to 12,000' to start their "roll-in" on the target. Lead peeled off screaming downward, pressing his bomb release button, he unleashed hundreds of pounds of destruction on the target below; he was immediately followed by Captain Pardo in

McDonnell F-4 headed for its target. AF Museum

caught up with Lead. Training dictates that Cheetah Three, as the element leader, should have stayed with Four. Fear sometime dictates otherwise. Cheetah Lead and Cheetah Three went on to the safety of their tanker rendezvous. Captain Pardo, seeing all of this going on decided that he would drop back and stay with Four. He was just as scared as the others, but he had the character to beat his fear. Lead and Three did not; they allowed their fear to beat them. Cheetah Four and Cheetah Two headed for the east side of Laos about 150 miles distant. Pardo continued to stick close to his flightmates in the severely injured bird. As events progressed, Pardo felt so helpless—there must be something he could do. He began thinking to himself that here was a flyable aircraft—granted, it was soon going to run out of fuel, but it was at least controllable. He was keenly aware that Captain Earl Aman the pilot, and Lt. Bob Houghton, the WSO, would soon have to eject, and given their present position, would most certainly be killed or captured by the North Vietnamese. The question that burned in Bob's mind was: What could he do to help? It was then that an idea started to form. Pardo said, "Cheetah Four, this is Two. Earl, I've got an idea; jettison your drag chute and I'm going to see if I can stick my nose in the hole and push you along." Four replied, "You must be nuts! but what the hell, if you're crazy enough to try, let's go for it." Like a white streak the drag chute passed over the canopy of Cheetah Four who was flying close in trail. Approaching slowly, Pardo attempted to stick the nose of his aircraft into the hole left by the jettisoned drag chute which was located above the horizontal stabilizer. The turbulence was so great that it was virtually impossible to accomplish. Not daunted, Pardo positioned his aircraft under the belly of the other air-

the number two position. As he dropped his bombs, Pardo felt something slam into the underside of his fuselage; immediately numerous warning lights were aglow all over his panel. When they were about 30 seconds off the target, Lead called, "Cheetah flight, fuel check." "Cheetah 2, 5,000 lbs."; "Cheetah 3, 8,000 lbs."; "Cheetah 4, 2,000 lbs.". The "BINGO" or fuel required to get back to the tankers was 7,000 lbs.; it was quite apparent that Four was never going to make it back, and their was some doubt that Two would either. Climbing out over the Red River, Cheetah Four jettisoned all that he could: any remaining bombs, missiles, racks, and external tanks, that by this time were empty. He could not jettison the ECM pod as it was bolted to the aircraft so that in the event of the aircraft crashing, the pod would be destroyed. The flight started climbing to 36,000'. Fearing for his life, Lead kept his aircraft climbing away from the target at 480 kts. Rather than back off on his power so that the second element could catch up, he called Cheetah Three, and Four and told them to go into afterburner to catch up with him. Since Cheetah Four was already 5,000 lbs. short on fuel there was no way he was going to use afterburner. Cheetah three, being inexperienced and on one of his first missions, had the fuel to spare, and seeing his leader heading out of hostile territory as fast as he could go; did use AB and quickly

346

craft and tried to push the top of his fuselage against the belly of the other aircraft. Again the turbulence was so severe as to make this maneuver extremely dangerous to both aircraft. It could also have damaged his canopy to the point that they would not have been able to eject. Sliding back a few yards Pardo continued to study the other aircraft—perhaps he was trying to accomplish the impossible—maybe he was nuts; suddenly he had an idea that just might work…"Earl, how much fuel do you have?" "Just 200 lbs." "OK, tell you what, since you're basically out of fuel anyway, shut her down, and drop your tail-hook; maybe I can push against that." The black exhaust smoke pouring from Cheetah Four abruptly stopped, and the steel tail-hook slowly extended from the aft fuselage. Ever so slowly Pardo inched his aircraft up trying to put the tail-hook in the center of his windshield. With Four's engines shut down, the turbulence was greatly reduced, and suddenly he made contact. The first push only lasted about ten seconds, but it slowed the gliding aircraft's descent from 3,000 ft. per minute, to about 1,500 ft. per minute. If they could only make the contact last longer, they just might make it back to friendly territory and at least be able to eject into some heavy jungle where they could hide until they were rescued. Trying again Pardo said, "Fly smooth, here I come again." For the next twenty minutes, Cheetah Two pushed Cheetah Four—the actual contact only lasting from several seconds to thirty seconds at a time, but it was enough to extend Four's glide to where it looked like they would make it. About ten minutes into the "push", Pardo noticed that the ITT (Internal Turbine Temperature) on his left engine was approaching 1,000 degrees and at that temperature it would soon blow up. He quickly shut down his left engine; however, the resulting loss of thrust caused their vertical velocity to increase to 2,000 ft. per minute, and from their present location, they would not glide far enough to make Laos. With no other alternative, Pardo restarted his left engine—in just a few minutes it caught fire again, so he had to shut it down and continue with just the single engine to power two heavy F-4's. Finally they were over eastern Laos—beneath them lay thick jungle, and by now they had descended to around 6,000'. After backing his aircraft away, Pardo said, "Earl, I think it's time to go, you've got a lot better chance of survival if you guys get out now, before you get too low." "OK, Bob, thanks-a-million, see you later." With that parting statement, the canopy on Cheetah Four blew away, immediately followed by the two men firmly strapped to their seats. After checking to make sure that both chutes opened, Pardo turned his aircraft toward a special forces camp that was about thirty miles away; however, they had only been on that course for several minutes when *their* F-4 ran out of fuel. Being in one of the world's heaviest gliders, Pardo and Wayne were also forced to "punch out."

Of the four men who ejected, only Wayne escaped injury. Both Aman and Houghton had compression fractures of their backs, and Pardo had two fractured vertebrae in his neck after his chute was collapsed by a dead tree, causing him to land very hard on some large rocks. Aman, Houghton, and Wayne were picked up by a "Jolly Green" after coming under heavy, enemy ground-fire, which was suppressed by the "Sandies" (Douglas Skyraiders). Pardo was picked up by another helicopter about thirty minutes later. Aman and Houghton were sent to a hospital in the Phillipines, and Pardo and Wayne were back flying missions within two days. What Captain Pardo and Lt. Wayne did that day exemplifies their great love for their fellow man. They chose to put their own lives on the line to save their flightmates. During the interview for this story, Bob told the author that during combat he had learned that his life was no more valuable than that of any other. He demonstrated that he had the strength of character to carry out an act of genuine heroism, the like of which has seldom been seen throughout history. After this mission, Captain Pardo was severely criticized by higher command for sacrificing his flyable F-4 to save two fellow airman. Twenty-two years later, he was awarded a Silver Star for this great act of heroism.

Chapter 7
Into The 21st Century

FIRST FLIGHT OF THE YF-22

January 8, 1996—0825 hrs. At almost the same instant, two men, in two different parts of the country started on an historic journey. The first man was David L. Ferguson, Director Flight Test, Lockheed Martin, Skunk Works. He was departing his home near Edwards AFB in California. The second man was me. I was departing my home near Eureka Springs, Arkansas. One major difference, other than location, was that we had experienced a 14" snowfall, and I had to walk over a half-mile up a very steep driveway to my four-wheel-drive truck. I had put the truck up on top of the mountain, knowing that I could get out from there. So after dressing in my suit, I donned my insulated coveralls, boots, hat, and heavy coat, picked up my briefcase, cameras, shopping bag full of mail to go out, kissed Beth good-bye, and launched up the mountain. I had taken my suitcase up previously. The temperature was one degree. Meanwhile back in sunny California, temperature in the seventies, Dave was able to get in his car, right in the garage, and drive to the Palmdale Airport. Taking the commuter to LAX consisted of the usual shuffling of baggage, and the long walk to the Delta terminal where he would board his plane to Atlanta. I still had about a three-hour drive to Tulsa where I would board my Delta flight, and proceed to Atlanta. I was driving along listening to a radio station over in Bella-Vista that plays the old-time favorites. The familiar refrains of Frankie Lane singing "Do Not Forsake Me, Oh My Darling", and Elvis singing, "You Ain't Nothin' But A Hound Dawg" on the Ed Sullivan show, brought back so many old memories. It was about this time, January 8, thirty-five years ago in 1961, that my pilot training class, 61-E was receiving our assignments that we would be sent to after graduation. Dave was quite a bit higher in the class

than I was. He landed an F-102 assignment. The best I could do was the old KC-97. So many years had past since those assignments. He has been married to his wife Jan, since 1964; they have two daughters, and one grand son. Dave is now one of the foremost test-pilot's in the world, and was the first man to fly the Advanced Tactical Fighter, the YF-22. I had talked with him many times over the phone, and he seemed to be the old "Fergie" I had always known. But what was he really like after all this time?

I arrived in Atlanta right on schedule, picked up my rental car, and proceeded to drive the thirty-or-so miles to the hotel in Marietta, where Dave and I were

A/C David L. Ferguson at Vance AFB. Author 61-E

to meet for the first time in almost 35 years. (January 27, 1961, was the last time we had seen each other.) As I walked up to the desk to register, a very familiar voice said, "Mister Severe, I presume?" I turned around, and said, "Fergie!" Sure 'nuf, there he was—I couldn't contain myself, and greeted him with a big bear hug. As shy as Dave always was, and still is, he was a little taken aback by the hug. But it was as if it had not been thirty-five years, but rather thirty-five minutes, since we had last been together. We had a dinner date at Paul Metz's house, and since it was already almost 6:00 p.m., I excused myself and went to my room to change. Wearing my new MA-1 flight jacket, with the 35- year-old patches on it, I raced into the lobby where Dave was already waiting. He looked at my Alfred E. Neuman patch with the "What me worry? 61-E" printed underneath, and laughed. He said, " I've still got mine at home." The next question to be settled was who would be the driver, and who would be the navigator. Since I had inadvertently left the keys to my rent-car in my room, we used his car. This left me to be the designated navigator. We launched out into the dark, trying to follow the hand-drawn map that Paul had faxed to Dave. Paul's a great pilot, but as a map maker, he could use some help. After only one or two wrong turns (we were never lost, only temporarily disoriented). We arrived at the Metz homestead—a beautiful home in a lovely subdivision. We were greeted at the door by Paul, his lovely wife Linda, their son, daughter-in-law (9 months pregnant), and Linda's mother—a really neat family. After a scrumptious feast, the men retired to the den for "man" talk, while the women took care of the mess. Being somewhat of a sentimentalist, I was awestruck by the events leading up to this time and the reality of what was going on. Here I was in the home of one of the leading test pilots of our time. Paul has flown the Northrop YF-23 as he was the chief test pilot for Northrop. When they lost the ATF contract to Lockheed, Dave had hired him to replace himself as the chief test pilot for Lockheed. Paul will fly the first F-22, scheduled to fly in May of 1997. He will also be the only man to fly both the YF-23, and the F-22. We

three pilots were sitting there "solving the world's problems," with Paul's son Aaron joining in. (He is about 25 years old.) We were discussing the role models for the young people of today, and how many of the "movie stars" and sport's "heroes" were certainly negative role models. The question was raised as to who could be considered to be proper role models for today. I turned to Aaron and said, "Son, some of the real heroes and role models of today are sitting right here in this room. Your dad and Dave Ferguson are the type of men that you should model your life after." He didn't quite know what to say, after all, this was just "Dad." It was amazing to me that he was so close to greatness and he couldn't even see it. What these men have done, and continue to do, is to make history, and will continue to reward and protect all of us for generations to come due to their efforts. One of the most notable things, was that these men, skilled as they are, have not even a trace of arrogance between them. I have had the privilege of talking with some of our most famous pilots from WWII, and I want to tell you that some of the ones I've talked with, had enough arrogance to fill a hot-air balloon. As the evening drew to a close, we thanked all of the Metz family for their gracious hospitality, and departed back to the hotel, only making one or two wrong turns on the way. Hey, we made it, didn't we?

The next morning I met Dave downstairs for breakfast. We had an appointment with Jeff Rhodes, Lockheed Martin's public relations representative. After some pass foul-ups at the gate, we were greeted by Jeff, who escorted us into the facility. After obtaining passes for my cameras, Jeff drove us around the base explaining the different buildings, and telling us of some of the history. He is quite knowledgeable on not just the history of Dobbins ARB, but also on the Civil War history, much of which took place in the immediate area. Our first stop was the one I had been looking forward to for months—the F-22 simulator (officially called the F-22 Cockpit Concept Demonstrator). We went into the large brick building, up the stairs, through a cream-colored steel door, into a small room with the "box" in the middle of it. As we entered, we were met by the instructor, Charles "Buzz" Buzze, a former F-15 driver. He proceeded to brief me on the missions I was to "fly," using a professionally-laid-out pictorial briefing guide. After about fifteen minutes with the book, he led me to the "machine," and explained how to get into this long, cockpit-like structure. It was not nearly as sophisticated as the simulators I had flown in the airlines, but then again, there was not nearly as much "stuff" in this aircraft. It had no enclosure over the top, only from below the shoulders on down to the floor. Of course the real aircraft has you sitting up on top also, and without the canopy, one would be flopping in the breeze just like the simulator. Here I was at last, sitting on the forefront of technology. A large movie-type screen was in front of me, and the HUD was displayed on it. The lights in the room were now turned off—ah, that's more like it. Now it looked like I was really in the F-22. In the cockpit were six LCD's (Liquid Crystal Displays). The largest one (8"X 8") located in the center, is for the overall situation display and other information that can be called up as needed by pressing one of the small, square buttons (bezel buttons) located around the perimeter of all the LCD's. The one to the right (6"X 6") is the attack display which shows engagements against enemy aircraft. The one to the left (6"X 6") shows the defensive situation with the enemy fighters and surface to air missiles. The one on the bottom located between the pilot's knees, is a store's management display which shows how many air-to-air missiles and/or 1000 lb JDAM (Joint Direct Attack Munition) weapons, are on board. The small (3"X 4") LCD on the upper left shows navigation and communication data, while the one on the upper right, is a backup attitude indicator.

The stick is a side mount on the right, with the throttles for the twin P&W-F119-35,000 lb thrust engines on the left.

The scenario started with me at 40,000 feet and Mach 1.4. The green targets at about forty miles on the SDP (Situation Display Panel) were friendly aircraft. There is a cross-hairs cursor controlled by a small raised circular switch on the right throttle that works much like a mouse on a computer. By positioning it over a target, it will give you information such as aircraft type, altitude, and speed. This is displayed in the lower left corner of the SDP. These were F-16's at 25,000'. Soon four red triangles showed up at a range of 80 miles. I placed the cursor over one of the triangles, and the SDP display showed that there were four Su-27's also at 40,000 feet and we were closing rapidly. By pressing a small bar—type switch on the throttles, the computer formed a "shoot list" with the closest enemy fighter being labeled #1, the next #2, and so on. By moving the cursor to the bottom of the SDP, I changed the radar range from 80 miles to 40 miles. The flight of four also appeared on the other two LCD's. So far, the enemy aircraft had no idea I was even in the air, let alone about to fire my missiles at them. As the first Su-27 crossed the 40-mile-range mark, on the bottom of the HUD, the word "Shoot" suddenly appeared. Buzz told me to press the red button on the top left of the stick. After just a moment's hesitation, the AMRAAM (radar guided) missile zipped past me on its way to the target. Buzz had cautioned me to wait a moment for the missile to appear in my view before I fired again, so I wouldn't inadvertently waste a second missile. The weapons are carried internally, so it takes just a second or so for the weapon's bay to open, extend, launch the missile, and close. This way the stealth capability is not compromised. As soon as I had fired, I hit a button on the throttles that stepped the targeting to the #2 target—the word "Shoot" appeared on the HUD again. I fired again; the next missile zoomed by and I continued the sequence until I had fired at all four targets. Soon the #1 target disappeared, with a boom and flash on the horizon; the attack screen showed the next target about to be hit—boom he was gone. In a matter of moments, all four enemy aircraft were destroyed, and they had no idea I was even in the air. The stealth capability of this aircraft is awesome. The accuracy of the weapons, and the simplicity of the cockpit, make this one formidable weapons system. During one of the scenarios, Buzz had me press a switch that put the F-22 into today's aircraft's radar profile. The enemy radar immediately picked me up, and air-to-air and surface-to-air missiles were fired at me so quickly, that I would have had to do extensive evasive maneuvers, and possibly abort the mission; that is, if I survived. Switching back to the F-22 made me invisible again. A nice warm, fuzzy feeling. After four different missions, with eight enemy aircraft destroyed, and two ground targets blown away, I asked if I could go low level and see how this puppy really flew. In a word, "WOW!" I could even say it backwards. I've flown quite a number of different aircraft, but this one takes the cake. All it takes to fly it is thinking where you want it to go and it goes there (of course having 10,000 hrs of flying time doesn't hurt). After buzzing a simulated aircraft carrier, followed by a victory roll (just to impress the troops on board), I was set up for an ILS approach. Piece of cake. It's as stable as a rock. The flight computer compensates for almost anything. Put it in a 90-degree bank and it just stays there, the nose doesn't even want to fall. Put it straight and level and it will stay there almost like it's on autopilot. They are going to put in a stick shaker, because with the fly-by-wire control system you really can't feel when the aircraft is close to a stall (High Alpha). As a fighter for the 21st Century, I don't think it can be beat. Two of these would be more than a match for sixteen of the enemy. They don't even need a Wild Weasel to suppress the SAM's. With enough of these in our Air Forces, we will maintain air superiority for many years to come. The F-22 is very expensive, but it takes a lot less of them to do the job, and most of our pilots who fly them will come back safely. After all, if you have to launch another mission to destroy a target that should have been hit on the first run, it becomes extremely expensive. This aircraft will be able to get it on the first try. Definitely a better value regardless of price.

Well, I guess all good things must come to an end. After thanking Buzz profusely, we departed the simulator building and Jeff took us over to the hangar where the only intact YF-22 resides. We had to wait a

Lockheed Martin YF-22 with some of the armament it will carry.   Author 61-E

Dave Ferguson and the author in front of the YF-22 with his name on it at Marietta, Georgia.   Author 61-E

few minutes for the guard to arrive. This is a restricted area, and even Lockheed Martin employees must have a guard present. After opening the security lock, we were ushered into a small tool-crib type room where we signed in while the guard turned on the many lights. We walked down a small corridor, and into a hangar, and there it was—the real YF-22. It even has "Dave Ferguson" painted on the left canopy rail. The aircraft is quite large, and sits in the hangar surrounded by the different weapons it is designed to carry. The rest of the hangar is filled with various components of the F-22 structure. The machining of the components was so precise, that they looked more like parts from the Jolly Green Giant's Rolex, than parts for a 21st Century fighter. I was given free access to look at anything I wanted to see; however, I was cautioned not to take pictures of certain areas. I was busily snapping away with my camera, when a guard suddenly appeared

from behind a curtain. He said, "You can't take pictures in here." I quickly replied, "But I have a camera pass." He said, "I'm sure glad you do, because I don't know where I put the bullet." Lighthearted as it was, they are very serious about security.

The next stop was the assembly-line building. It is a huge complex, consisting of the C-130 production line (which takes up the majority of the space) and the still developing F-22 assembly line. The aircraft will be built in three different plants and assembled and test flown at Marietta. Boeing will build the aft fuselage, and wings, and is responsible for the radar, mission software, and the training system. Lockheed Martin Tactical Aircraft Systems in Fort Worth, Texas, will build the mid fuselage, and is responsible for the electronic warfare, communication/navigation, identification, vehicle management system, and support systems. Lockheed Martin Aeronautical Systems will build the forward fuselage, wing edges, and the horizontal and vertical stabilizers. It is also responsible for the weapon system integration, the common integrated processor, and mate and final assembly. After walking our legs off in the plant, we decided it was time for lunch. Jeff knew of a nice restaurant that was located in an old hardware store—great place. He gave us the Civil War history tour on our way into Marietta. After lunch, he asked if we wanted to see anything else, but we couldn't think of a thing except stopping by the company store for a few F-22 items. We gave our thanks to Jeff, and I asked if my wife and I could attend the rolling out of the first F-22 in the spring of 1997; he very graciously said we could. (We can hardly wait.)

Dave and I went back to the hotel, and decided we needed a short rest after the busy day, so we each retired to our rooms. About 5:30 p.m., I called Dave and asked him to come over and we would complete the final part of my mission—the taped interview.

David L. Ferguson was born on October 4, 1938, in Altoona, Pennsylvania. His father was a minister, as are his two older brothers. His dad never did understand what he was doing; whenever someone would ask about his sons, he would reply that he had two sons that were ministers, and his youngest was in the Army. Dave took the Aviation Cadet test when he was just out of high school. He was notified that he had qualified for navigator. Since he had always dreamed of becoming a pilot, he was not about to settle for less. Reasoning that he could take the test again in six weeks, he wrote and told the Air Force that he would like to take the test again, the next time it was given. Much to his surprise, all of his paperwork was returned, and he was informed that he would have to wait a year to re-apply. Bummer! After anxiously waiting for the year to pass, he received a letter requesting him to go to Olmstead AFB, in Middletown, PA for the three-day battery of tests. Although neither of us remembers the other, we should have been there at the same time, since we were in the same class, and both took our test there. This time he qualified for pilot.

After our graduation, Dave went to Perrin AFB near Sherman, Texas for his advanced training in the F-102. After completing his training there, he was assigned to the 4th Fighter Squadron, at Misawa, Japan. He was there from October of 1961, until October of 1963. He was then transferred back to the States and stationed at George AFB, California, in the 355th TAC fighter wing, and the 357th TAC fighter squadron flying the F-105. In May of 1965, he was sent TDY (Temporary Duty) to Korat, Thailand. He remained there until September of 1965, having flown many missions against the North Vietnamese. He was once again sent back to the States and given an F-105 instructor assignment at Nellis AFB, Nevada. In December of 1966, the Air Force offered him a chance to get his college degree under the "Bootstrap" program. After spending two semesters at the University of Omaha, he returned to Nellis in 1967, where he went to the Fighter Weapons School and trained on the Wild Weasel. (They were used for strike force protection, seeking out and destroying the SAM sites). He returned to Korat for his second tour in the summer of 1967, flying combat until April, of 1968 when he was again sent to Nellis, this time to fly the F-111. However, that was during the time the Navy misplaced their boat, the *USS Pueblo*, (it was really captured by North Korea) and Dave was sidetracked to Osan, Korea with his Wild Weasel group, just in case we went to war with the North Koreans again. Once this portion of the Cold War cooled down, he continued his journey back to Nellis, arriving in August of 1968. After checking out in the F-111 (much to his chagrin) his name came out on the AFIT (Air Force Institute of Technology) list. Seeing a graceful way to get out of the F-111, and also to get his master's degree, he lost no time in accepting. He was sent to Arizona State University where he obtained his master's in mathematics. (Dave told me he still has trouble balancing his checkbook). He had previously applied for the Test Pilot School at Edwards AFB, California, and now that he had his master's degree, he was accepted. He started his training in the summer of 1971, and graduated in June of 1972, and he spent the remaining eight years of his Air Force carrier right there at Edwards, flying many different aircraft:

the F-4, U-2, F-16, F-15, and some of the more interesting ones, which unfortunately are still classified. During his last year, Dave became involved with testing for Lockheed, where he met Bill Park, Lockheed's chief test pilot, who had been involved in an early technology demonstrator called "Have Blue." This was a small-scale version of the F-117 type of aircraft used to prove that the idea of true stealth in an aircraft was feasible, and would actually fly. Bill had also done much of the early testing on the "Blackbirds," the A-12, and others. Bill liked what he saw and offered Dave a job with Lockheed when he retired from the Air Force. As soon as he retired, Dave started with Lockheed on the F-117, being the second man to fly the aircraft. The F-117 was such a closely-guarded secret, that no one knew of it flying in 1981. Operational squadrons existed from 1983 on. When the Air Force finally admitted that it existed in 1989, and later on had the official roll out, the aircraft that finally did roll-out was the last one in production. Dave flew about 500 flights in the F-117, completing most of the testing and development of the aircraft. Our country owes him a great deal of thanks for his fine work. He describes its flight characteristics as "unstable". But with the new fly-by-wire systems, it is possible to make almost anything fly, so long as the computer can tell which way the pointed end is pointing.

In 1984, Dave was given his first briefing on the ATF (Advanced Tactical Fighter). It was initially only a paper study, more or less to get input and see if it was possible to produce such an aircraft. In 1986, the Air Force became serious about the program. It asked aircraft manufacturers to submit concepts of what they thought such an aircraft should be like. Seven companies replied, and that was later boiled down to two, Lockheed and Northrop. The Air Force said it wanted each company (who had both teamed with other companies) to build two flying prototypes, as well as GE and P&W to each build engine prototypes. In a most unusual move, the Air Force, suffering under bud-

get constraints, said that each manufacturer would have to put up half of the cost, to be matched by the Air Force. In the Lockheed-led team's case, that was more than one Billion dollars. A great deal was riding on this poker game. Only one aircraft manufacturer and one engine manufacturer would be winners—the others would be losers. There was no in-between ground; it was winner take all.

In late 1986, Dave was assigned to the F-22 program full time. For the next three years, his life was totally consumed by the project. He was deeply involved in cockpit design and layout, systems design and development, and giving his input as to just what he thought an air-superiority fighter should be. He was given a promotion to chief test pilot, and was totally in charge of the F-22 program. The cockpit geometry, control stick, throttles, and layout of the instruments are all of his design. Two other test pilots who worked with him during this time were Jon Beesley, and Tom Morgenfeld. The three of them spent countless hours in the simulator perfecting flying characteristics, control inputs, layouts, and emergency procedures. About three months before the first flight, the Air Force required, in writing, all of the maneuvers that were going to be done in the test program. This consisted of about 200 different profiles. One of the most important, was the aircraft's ability to supercruise; in other words, fly faster than Mach 1 without using the afterburners. They wanted to know how long it could do it, and what speed could be attained, what the range would be, G-load, etc. This is the first aircraft to be able to maintain 9 G's in a level bank. A special G-suit had to be designed to prevent the pilot from blacking out during high G-maneuvers. Dave said, "It works real fine, but 9 G's still hurts like hell!" Hundreds of hours were spent with safety review boards; he had five of them going on at one time. Many hours were spent in the simulator going over flight profiles, emergency procedures, and many more hours were spent in taxi test, engine runs, etc.—all before the first flight. The aircraft was new and untried, and so were the engines. On paper, everything looked like it would work like a charm. But that was only on paper. I doubt if anyone has ever been killed by a piece of paper, but I know many have died on a first flight. NASA Administrator Daniel Goldin said in a recent article, "Every time an experimental test pilot gets into a plane, I think he has a higher risk than we do with the astronauts going into a shuttle."

So it was with David L. Ferguson, a farm boy from Altoona, Pennsylvania, on a cloudy, rainy, morning on the 29th of September 1990. He had planned to fly early that morning, but during the taxi tests, realized that the sun, as it rose in the east, was directly lined up with the runway at Palmdale (Air Force Plant 42). So he scheduled the first flight for 0800 hrs. Arising about 0500 hrs, he showered, had a light breakfast, dressed, and accompanied by his wife, Jan, and their daughter, Teri, along with Jan's sister Judy, drove to the Palmdale Airport. Briefing started at 0600 hrs. The weather, which is normally excellent that time of year, was forecast to be cloudy with numerous showers in the area, not what one would order for a first flight. At 0630 hrs., the lead flight engineer Hap Roshon called from Edwards and said, "Fergie, did you know it's raining out here?" (It's about 25 miles from Palmdale to Edwards) Dave replied, "You're kidding me; it's not raining here yet— well, what the hell, let's just play it by ear." He suited up in just a normal flight suit, as no high-G maneuvers were planned for this flight. He made a pit stop and proceeded to walk slowly to the aircraft, stopping to chat with some of the numerous spectators, including his old friend, Bill Park. It was about 0700 hrs. As he left the crowd and drew nearer to the waiting YF-22, his mind was momentarily flooded with; "What did I forget?—I must have forgotten something." As he arrived at the aircraft, he concluded, "Nope, can't think of a thing." So he climbed up the boarding ladder, and checked the oxygen system, the ejection seat, and made sure the canopy jettison T-handle was secure, and the safety pin removed. Following procedure, he put his right foot

on the seat while holding onto the left canopy rail with his left hand; stepped on the floor with his left foot, and let himself down into the cockpit. It was now 0735 hrs. He then fastened his seat belt and shoulder harness, put on his helmet, and hooked up his oxygen mask, and adjusted the rudder pedals. The APU (Auxiliary Power Unit) was running, and the radio master was on. Through his headsets, he could hear an unusual amount of chatter. He was hooked up to the data room at Edwards, and heard them discussing a telemetry problem. It had nothing to do with the aircraft, except in the sense that the receiver at Edwards was not picking up the data transmitter in the aircraft. This was, however, an abort item. Continuing with the checklist on the left console, he set his position lights, put the LEF (Leading Edge Flaps) switch at normal, Thrust Vector switch off, FLCS Bit (Flight Control Systems Built In) test switch—normal, set the seat angle, Electrical panel switches were already in the proper positions, Alt. Gear handle—in, Parking Brake switch—Anti-skid, Brakes channel switch—Chan. 1, FLCS Test switch—off, CG Control switch—Norm., Throttles—Off, Speed Brake switch—Forward. Now to the left instrument panel—Master Arm switch—Safe, LG handle—DN, IVSC-A, (Inter Vehicle Systems Control) IVSC-B, APU, EPU, (Emergency Power Unit) APAD (Auxiliary Power Access Drive) reset switches—Red guards down. On the right console—Defog knob—In, Wristrest—Adjust, KY-58 (Encoder) Mode switch—as desired, MDP 1 (Mission Data Processor) and 2 switches—Off, Restart 1 and 2 switches—Cold, HUD SRC switch—Normal, INU (Inertial Navigation Unit) Source switch—Off, Interior lighting panel—As desired, COMM-1 backup panel—On, COMM ANT switch—Auto, COMM-1 switch—ON, Tacan switch—Off, COMM—2 switch—Off, IFF switch—Off, TEMP knob—Auto, PRESS switch—Normal, ECS (Environmental Control Systems) switch—Norm., MFD (Multi-Function Display) MODE switch—Auto, MFD power/brightness knobs—Midrange, MSTR MFD knob—Midrange,

DTU (Data Transfer Unit)—Inserted. At 0745 hrs., he ran the BEFORE STARTING ENGINES checklist—Instrumentation—As desired, Nose Boom—Off, MDP-1 and 2 switches—On, RESTART MDP-1 and 2 switches—Warm, L & R GEN switches—Off, MSTR MFD switch—CW, SSD—Selected, Canopy—As desired, Chocks in place, fire guard posted, and intakes and other danger areas clear. He immediately went into the STARTING ENGINES Checklist—Cooling air—Off, RT Eng Start switch—Depress, at 20% RPM, RT throttle IDLE, SSD—Engine at idle—Normal indications, he then repeated the sequence for the left engine. As both engines came to life, he continued the checklist—L GEN switch—Depress, R GEN switch—Depress, External power/air—Disc, NOSE BOOM—ON. He then continued through the AFTER START, and BEFORE TAXI checklists. Calling ground control for clearance, he slowly taxied toward the runway. The telemetry problem had not yet been resolved, but Dave radioed Edwards, suggesting that perhaps a change in aircraft location would solve the problem. He was also in contact with his chase planes over at Edwards; one was an F-15 flown by Tom Morgenfeld and the other a two seat F-16 flown by Jon Beesley, with photographer in the back. Still not sure if there would be a launch, Dave told the two chase planes to hold at the runway. As he taxied along, he could still hear grumbling and chatter about the telemetry problem, while they feverishly worked to re-configure the control room. Now sitting at the end of the runway for what seemed like an eternity, the whine of the two engines at idle had an almost hypnotic, calming effect. Suddenly, he was brought back to reality by someone in the control room shouting, "Damn it, did you change that? Why did you change that? Well, change it back the way it was..... All right, that's better." In just a few seconds, a calm professional voice said, "Uh, Lightning Four, you're cleared for takeoff." Dave then called Lightning Six (Tom Morgenfeld in the F-15) and told him, and Lightning Seven (Jon Beesley in the F-16) to take off. The sky looking toward Edwards was very dark, but Tom said they could navigate around it OK. Dave was still sitting on the end of the runway, lined up for takeoff, and as he looked toward Edwards, he saw Lightning Six coming out of the murk. Now the final checklist before flight. ALT FLAPS switch—Norm, Trim—Center, Speedbrake—Closed, switch forward, Canopy—Close and lock, IFF—Set and check, Seat—15 degrees, EJECTION CONTROL ARMED, SSD—Check engine data, WARNING & CAUTION lights—Check, EPU switch—ARMED. As they had done countless times before on other tests, Lightning Six entered base leg, and when he was about to make his 90-degree turn to final, he said, "Lightning Four, 10 seconds." Having been previously cleared by the tower, this was Dave's signal to start rolling: 08:46 hrs.—Pushing the throttles up to 80%, a final power check, brakes released, power up to MIL; he was rolling. With a quick power check, and seeing the speed was already up to 80 kts., he glanced to his left and saw Tom pulling alongside; at 135 kts., Dave slowly rotated to 8 degrees—at 145 kts., the YF-22 was flying! Raising the nose another 2 degrees, he continued to accelerate; in his mind he was saying, "Please fly, please fly!" A large black cloud directly in front of him cut his savoring of the moment all too short. He said, "Lightning Six, I'm coming left around this cell" (thunderstorm). Making the turn much sooner than the flight plan called for, the now three-ship formation climbed higher into the dark, cloud-covered sky. "Lightning Control, this is Lightning Four." "Roger, Four, go ahead." "Roger, I've got an APU hot light, setting it to low speed.... OK, it's out." "Roger, Four, please advise of any further difficulties." Dave continued the climb with the gear down, at a speed of 240 kts, and on up to an altitude of 12,500', all the while heading toward Edwards. Several calls were made to Lightning Six, to compare the airspeed and altitude readings of the F-15 to those of the un-calibrated F-22. The original plan had been to fly for about an hour, climbing to 20,000', raising the gear and accelerating to Mach .8; however, because of

It flies!   Lockheed Martin

the forty-five-minute delay on the ground, the fuel on board was not sufficient for that long of a flight. Nearing Edwards, Dave could see the runway through the clouds most of the time, but he noticed a large cell over the runway, and after watching it for several minutes, determined that it was moving off of the field. However, there was another even bigger one not too far behind it. Checking his fuel again, he decided to go to the flight cards (like a checklist, but very detailed for each test maneuver) that he would use just prior to landing. They consisted of engine acceleration/deceleration checks, making sure that he had reliable engines for a go-around if the need should arise. He did a series of rapid roll control inputs, as well as rapid pitch in-

puts, all to make sure the aircraft didn't have any tendency toward PIO (Pilot-Induced Oscillations) or in other words, was too sensitive. All of the controls worked extremely well, just as everyone had hoped they would. He now joined on Lightning Six, to see just how the YF-22 would handle in formation flight— again, all was well. Seeing that the one cell had passed off of the runway, Dave thought discretion was the better part of valor, and opted to go on in and land. It was particularly important to keep any new aircraft out of the rain, as the Pitot-static system (airspeed, angle-of-attack, etc.) were not heated, and could conceivably ice over, making the instruments affected, useless. Entering a wide downwind for runway 04, he accomplished the AP-

YF-22 with an F-16 chase plane.

Lockheed Martin

PROACH AND BEFORE LANDING checklist—Altimeter—Check (HUD/SCD), Seat—15 degrees, APU—ON, Left weapons bay door—Closed, LG handle—DN. Turning final, he called the tower, "Edwards tower, Lightning Four, turning final; full stop, gear down & locked." "Roger, Lightning Four, cleared to land; be advised, runway is wet." The approach was flown at about 12-degrees Alpha (angle-of-attack) and a speed of 155 kts-165 kts. Tom was still on his wing encouraging him all the way down—"Lightning Four, looking good, nice angle.... looks real stable.... hang in there, Fergie." At that time, Dave was saying to himself, "Fergie, don't screw it up." On short final for the last fifty feet, Tom continued to call altitude in 10' increments, just to cross-check the YF-22's instruments. The touchdown was smooth—the water cushioning the wheels. He held the nose off until 110 kts, letting it down slowly on the center line of the runway. The controller in the tower said, "Welcome to Edwards, Lightning Four." Dave replied, "Roger, I'm proud to be here." Not wanting to use the brakes anymore than necessary, he let the aircraft roll to the end of the 15,000' runway. Turning off, he taxied back to the ramp, completing the AFTER LANDING checklist, as he rolled along. Turning onto the ramp, he was greeted by a large, cheering crowd. He glided to a stop, set the brakes, shut down both engines, and ran the ENGINE SHUTDOWN checklist. Following established tradition, he was doused with water as he climbed out of the cockpit; after all, it was a first solo. In a mere 22 minutes of flying,

YF-22 turning final at Edwards after its first flight.   Lockheed Martin

history had been made. The very first prototype of the F-22 had successfully flown. There were only two write-ups on the aircraft from the cockpit; one was the APU overheat light, and the other was the angle-of-attack indicator, which was off by 3.6 degrees from actual to the indicated. A relocation of the probes fixed it. On the post-flight-walk-around, the mechanics found that some braces on the gear doors had cracked. Even though the aircraft has a 350 kt gear down limit, and it wasn't flown over 250 kt, the parts were just not built heavily enough to take the air load. A beef-up of the affected parts

cured that problem. In retrospect, it was a good thing that the flight did not go as planned. If it had, and the gear had been raised, it might not have come down again, or at the very least, more damage to the system would have occurred.

Several months later, Dave Ferguson was promoted to the position of Director Flight Test, Lockheed Martin Skunk Works. The man who retired from that position was Hal Farley, the first man to fly the YF-117. Dave has 120 men and women working under him, and his immediate boss is Jack Gordon, the president of Lockheed Martin Skunk

David L. Ferguson after being the first man to fly the Lockheed Martin YF-22. L. to R.: Brig. General James A. Fain, Dave Ferguson, Dan Tellep, and Dick Abrams.
Lockheed Martin

Works. It has been several years since that first flight, and Dave is still working on the forefront of technology. It's great to know that one of the *Last of a Breed*, is still out there, leading our nations airpower into the 21st Century. Hang in there, Fergie!

We few who are left, can be proud that in the relatively short time that the Aviation Cadet program existed, it trained approximately 225,000 boys, who, because of the rigors of the intensive training, in a few short months were turned from boys into some of America's finest fighting men. As the years slip by, and our hair turns gray, we see our bodies becoming older, but in our hearts and minds we are still as we once were; young, strong and daring. We realize that we have more years behind us than there are still ahead of us. Someday when we too are gone from this earth, we will be awarded new silver wings from He who made us all. Let us hope that those who are left behind will read this, and remember who we are, what we have stood for, and what we have accomplished. We were, in our day, the finest young men America had to offer. In our hearts, we will remain Aviation Cadets—forever. **"The Last of a Breed!"**

GOD BLESS THE U.S.A.!

WWI recruiting sign hung in Washington D.C.   National Archives

Greying Wings

Remember we first looked with eager eyes
To God's domain of sun lit skies
And longed that we could earth-free too
Join eagles, clouds in azure blue
And fly.

And we were chosen by fate, why?
To enter God's domain, the sky
And only we, the chosen know
The joy of freedom from earth below
And so,

We took wings of silver then
Topped mountains, storms, looked down on them
Climbed and dived like eagles soared
On silver wings and engines roared
We sang.

With joyous hearts and spirits free
We became as others could never be
God's privileged few who now flew near
O'er rushing wind in flight we hear
His voice.

And only those of us who fly
Could hear Him say His reason why
He gave us more than earthly chore
Then we too join the growing score
Of them,

Whose wings lose silver, turn to grey
With misty eyes come to that day
As faltering leaves in autumn find
A resting place, the sky behind
We stay.

Bound for awhile by earth again
Our wings no longer can sustain
Our spirit, joy, our freedom, flight
'Til God at dawn beyond the night
Will say,

"Take silver wings this time from Me
Once again to fly, be free
Climb, turn, frolic, soar
But now this time forevermore,
Join Me."

By Carl Leming   ©1993 Carl Leming 43-B

Aviation Cadet ad of the late 40's.

BIBLIOGRAPHY

Angelucci, Enzo *The Rand McNally Encyclopedia of Military Aircraft 1914-1980.* New York: The Military Press, 1980.

Army Air Forces Historical Office *The Official Pictorial History of the Army Air Forces.* New York: ARNO, 1979.

Eckels, Mike *The Fayetteville Experience*

Grider, John MacGavock *War Birds* Diary of an Unknown Aviator. Edited by Elliott White Springs. College Station, Texas: Texas A & M University Press, 1988.

Gunston, Bill *World Encyclopaedia of Aircraft Manufacturers.* Annapolis, Maryland: Naval Institute Press, 1993.

Hiscock, Melvyn *Classic Aircraft of World War I.* London, England: Osprey Aerospace, 1994.

Mason, Herbert Molloy, Jr. *The United States Air Force. A Turbulent History.* New York: Mason/Charter, 1976.

Mondey, David *The Concise Guide to American Aircraft of World War II.* Edison, NewJersey: Chartwell Books, Inc.,1944.

Texas Work Projects *Randolph Field* A History and Guide. New York: The Devan-Adair Company, 1942.

Thayer, Lt. Lucien H. *America's First Eagles.* Edited by Donald Joseph McGee and Roger James Bender. San Jose, California: R. James Bender Publishing and Mesa, Arizona: Champlin Fighter Museum Press, 1983.

Office of History and Research, Headquarters Air Education and Training Command. *History of Air Training Command 1943-1993.* Randolph AFB, Texas.

Mitchell, Vance O. *First Generation Personnel Policy and the Air Force Officer Corps 1944-1974.* Air Force History and Museums Program. United States Air Force, Washington, D.C., 1996.

Going Places

AS A U. S. AIR FORCE OFFICER!

Here is a brief picture of one of the greatest opportunities available to young men today . . . a career as an officer in the U. S. Air Force. The finest possible training and experience await you in a field which offers an unlimited future!

N EAGLET! When you complete your course as an Aviation adet, you have received training valued at $35,000 . . . tomatically become a second lieutenant with a rating of lot in the U. S. Air Force! Starting pay is $336 a month . . with even greater opportunities ahead!

WANT TO TRAVEL? If you're assigned to the B-29s, your dreams will more than come true! The U. S. to Japan is just a training flight. Strange countries, new sights, adventure are yours in abundance . . . and with them, flying experience that can't be matched anywhere!

FIGHTERS READY TO SCRAMBLE! If you're assigned to a jet fighter unit, you'll fly sleek F-80 Shooting Stars, F-84 Thunderjets or the new speed record holder, the F-86! You'll be one of the pioneers in a new kind of flying . . . learning the thrill of perfect teamwork in the air!

ATS-EYE! Our airborne night fighters have mechanical es, which see through thickest fog and darkness. And th your own eyes, you'll enjoy sights unknown to earth-gs . . . the breath-taking beauty of the moonlight above e clouds. No other sight quite matches it!

ALL THIS . . . AND A VACATION, TOO! Your work is interesting . . . thrilling . . . but you also get thirty days' leave *with* pay every year! Plenty of time to loll in the sun—take a trip to the mountains—or enjoy a long, leisurely visit with your family or friends. A *real* vacation!

EXPERIENCE with the world's largest air line may be yours. For MATS, the Military Air Transport Service, operates scheduled flights on routes which girdle the globe. Casablanca, Calcutta, Shanghai, Manila are casual names to pilots assigned to this service.

NEQUALLED "AIR FREIGHT" EXPERIENCE may also be yours! ndreds of thousands of tons of air freight are now being ved thousands of miles by big, new cargo planes. New thods are constantly being developed. Another field of ation with great promise for those who learn it now!

A YOUNG MAN'S ORGANIZATION . . . with great opportunities for "going places" fast. The average age of top Air Force commanders is only 47. Two of them are only 41! In the U. S. Air Force able men move up fast! It offers an interesting, worthwhile future to those who can qualify!

Only the best can be Aviation Cadets

If you can qualify, a valuable aviation education, a brilliant flying career, a thrilling future await you. Inquire at your nearest Air Force Base or U. S. Army and U. S. Air Force Recruiting Station about the possibility of becoming an Aviation Cadet!

WIN YOUR WINGS

U. S. AIR FORCE

For single or married men with two years of college (or who can pass an equivalent examination). Between ages of 20 and 26½. U. S. Citizen. High physical and moral qualifications.

. S. ARMY AND U. S. AIR FORCE RECRUITING SERVICE

Aviation Cadet ad from 1949.

Author 61-E